AN HISTORICAL GEOGRAPHY OF EUROPE

An historical geography of Europe

N. J. G. POUNDS
Indiana University

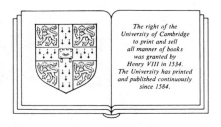

The right of the
University of Cambridge
to print and sell
all manner of books
was granted by
Henry VIII in 1534.
The University has printed
and published continuously
since 1584.

CAMBRIDGE UNIVERSITY PRESS

CAMBRIDGE

NEW YORK   PORT CHESTER   MELBOURNE   SYDNEY

Published by the Press Syndicate of the University of Cambridge
The Pitt Building, Trumpington Street, Cambridge CB2 1RP
40 West 20th Street, New York, NY 10011, USA
10 Stamford Road, Oakleigh, Melbourne 3166, Australia

© Cambridge University Press 1990

First published 1990
Reprinted 1990

Printed in the United States of America

Library of Congress Cataloging-in-Publication Data
Pounds, Norman John Greville.
An historical geography of Europe / N. J. G. Pounds.
p.   cm.
ISBN 0-521-32217-0. – ISBN 0-521-31109-8 (pbk.)
1. Europe – Historical geography.   I. Title.
D21.5.P62   1990
911'.4 – dc20   89-23968
                                                    CIP

British Library Cataloguing in Publication Data
Pounds, Norman J. G. (Norman John Greville)
An historical geography of Europe.
1. Europe. Historical geography
I. Title
911'.4

ISBN 0-521-32217-0 hardback
ISBN 0-521-31109-8 paperback

Contents

List of maps and diagrams   *page* vii
Preface   xiii

Introduction   1
1   The physical basis of European history   9

Part I.   The classical civilizations   23

2   Europe in the classical period   27

Part II.   The Middle Ages   69

3   From the second to the ninth century   74
4   Europe in the age of Charlemagne   92
5   From the ninth to the fourteenth century   113
6   Europe in the early fourteenth century   142
7   The late Middle Ages   187

Part III.   Modern Europe   211

8   Renaissance Europe   214
9   From the sixteenth to the nineteenth century   250

Part IV.   The Industrial Revolution and after   313

10   Europe on the eve of the Industrial Revolution   317
11   The nineteenth century   347
12   Europe on the eve of World War I   440

Index   469

Maps and diagrams

1.1   Landforms of Europe   *page* 13
1.2   Vegetation belts of Europe during historical times   17
1.3   Coastal changes at the mouth of the Tiber   18
1.4   The loess soils of Europe   19
2.1   The Delian League, total membership   29
2.2   Greek settlement in the Mediterranean   30
2.3   Ethnolinguistic map of Europe in the fifth century B.C.   32
2.4   A light Greek plow, as shown on a vase   39
2.5   A Celtic field system in southern Britain   41
2.6   A Greek shoemaker shown measuring for a pair of lady's shoes   42
2.7   A Greek smith, as shown on a vase   43
2.8   The tribal areas of Roman Britain and their capitals, as established by the Romans   49
2.9   The distribution of inscriptions in Roman Pannonia   50
2.10   The distribution of villas in Roman Pannonia   51
2.11   Urban development in Europe under the Roman empire   56
2.12   Rome under the empire   58
2.13   Fragment of the *forma urbis,* showing the *horrea lolliana,* a granary   60
2.14   The water supply of Rome   61
2.15   A relief showing Roman miners, from Linares, Spain   65
3.1   The Roman frontier, as shown in a relief carving on Trajan's Column, Rome   76
3.2   Routes followed by the Germanic and barbarian invaders in the fifth and sixth centuries   79
3.3   Europe at the time of the Emperor Justinian, mid-sixth century   80
3.4   The heavy medieval plow   90
4.1   Political map of Europe in the time of Charlemagne   93
4.2   The Byzantine empire and the Balkans in the ninth century   95
4.3   Ethnolinguistic map of Europe in the ninth century   98
4.4   Plan of Constantinople in the ninth century   100

4.5   Vallhagar, a settlement on the island of Gotland of the age
       of the migrations   102
4.6   Bipartite villas on monastic estates in the ninth century   103
4.7   Trade and trade routes in Europe in the early ninth century   111
5.1   Norse, Arab, Magyar, and other invasions of the ninth
       through eleventh century   114
5.2   A Norse boat, such as was used in the invasions of Britain
       and Iceland   115
5.3   The partitions of the Carolingian empire in the ninth century   117
5.4   The unification of France around the core area of the Paris
       region   118
5.5   Core areas of the states of medieval Europe   120
5.6   Growth of population in relation to growth of the food supply   122
5.7   Growth of the population of England   123
5.8   Town foundation in central Europe   124
5.9   Plan showing the organic (Slav) and planned (German)
       elements in the city of Kraków   127
5.10   Plan showing the discrete elements around which the city
       of Hildesheim developed   128
5.11   The spread of towns in eastern Germany and east-central
       Europe   129
5.12   An example of the extension of a city's walls with the growth
       of urban population: the city of Cologne (Köln)   131
5.13   An open-field system, as it survived into the nineteenth
       century   133
5.14   Cereal cultivation in Flanders in the twelfth century   134
6.1   Political map of Europe in the early fourteenth century   143
6.2   The distribution of population in the province of Rouergue
       (*département* Aveyron), France, 1341   148
6.3   Settlement in Württemberg   155
6.4   Village types in Württemberg   156
6.5   Village types: forest village; nucleated village, or *Haufendorf;*
       round village, or *Rundling;* spindle-shaped village,
       or *Angerdorf*   157
6.6   Prague, showing the "royal" city on the west (left) bank
       of the Vltava and subsequent stages in the growth of the
       commercial city on the right bank   160
6.7   The service area of the small Swiss town of Rheinfelden   162
6.8   Towns in Switzerland in the later Middle Ages   162
6.9   Distribution of the larger cities of medieval Europe   164
6.10   The northwest European cloth-making region in the
       fourteenth and fifteenth centuries   173
6.11   Salt production and the salt trade in late medieval Europe   177
6.12   European fairs in the fourteenth and fifteenth centuries and
       the areas which they served   179

6.13 The *Itinerary of Bruges*, a thirteenth-century roadbook, describing routes from Bruges   181

7.1 Real income of a craftsman, expressed in the volume of consumables that he could buy   188

7.2 The spread of the Black Death   188

7.3 The number of hearths at Volterra and San Gimignano (Italy) before and after the Great Plague   189

7.4 Population of Burgundy in the late Middle Ages, as expressed in the number of hearths (households) per square kilometer   190

7.5 Distribution of population in the Burgundian lands, fifteenth century   192

7.6 The export of wool and cloth from England   196

7.7 The Hanseatic League in the fourteenth century   206

7.8 The Low Countries in the fourteenth century, showing ports and the chief water routes   207

8.1 Political map of Europe, about 1530   217

8.2 Population density in Venezia, mid-sixteenth century   219

8.3 The chief cities of Europe in the first half of the sixteenth century   222

8.4 The ports of Portugal and southwestern Spain in the sixteenth century   226

8.5 Transhumance and drove routes in Europe in the sixteenth century   233

8.6 Ironworking in Europe in the sixteenth century   239

8.7 Nonferrous metal production in Europe in the sixteenth century   241

8.8 Grain-surplus and grain-deficit areas and the grain trade in the sixteenth century   246

8.9 The grain supply of the city of Lyons   247

9.1 The expansion of Russia   255

9.2 The pattern of mortality in a plague year: Brussels, 1668–9   258

9.3 The structure of population in France in the eighteenth century   261

9.4 The population of France (inhabitants per square kilometer) in 1700 and 1745   263

9.5 The population of France, about 1800   263

9.6 Population distribution in Italy, about 1550 and 1600   266

9.7 Population distribution in Italy, 1720 and 1790   267

9.8 The population of Verona   269

9.9 Rome after the planned rebuilding of the sixteenth century   270

9.10 Food supply of Paris, late seventeenth century   273

9.11 Cereal crops in Europe in the eighteenth century   278

9.12 Growth of crops in yield ratios: Great Britain and the Low Countries; France, Spain, and Italy; central Europe and Scandinavia; eastern Europe   279

9.13 The retreat of viticulture and the abandonment of

	marginal vineyards since the end of the Middle Ages	280
9.14	Land reclamation in the Netherlands	283
9.15	Distribution of forest in the Paris region in the sixteenth century	284
9.16	Distribution of forest in the Paris region in the eighteenth century	284
9.17	The cotton industry in Great Britain, about 1800	289
9.18	The woolen industry in Great Britain, about 1800	290
9.19	The iron industry in Great Britain, about 1800	291
9.20	Clothworking in France in the early eighteenth century	295
9.21	The European linen industry in the eighteenth century	296
9.22	Ironworking in the Siegerland and neighboring areas, about 1800	298
9.23	The European iron industry in the later eighteenth century	299
10.1	Political map of Europe after the Napoleonic Wars	318
10.2	Population density in Europe, early nineteenth century	320
10.3	Population density in the British Isles, according to the census of 1821	321
10.4	Urban map of Europe during the first half of the nineteenth century	325
10.5	The growth of the city of Madrid	326
10.6	The cultivation of grain crops in France in the early nineteenth century, by *département*	328
10.7	Generalized agricultural regions in Europe in the nineteenth century	335
10.8	Baltic trade in the early nineteenth century	344
11.1	Gross national product per head, about 1830	351
11.2	Increase in gross national product, 1830–1910	352
11.3	The increase in the gross national product per head in the principal European countries, 1830–1913	353
11.4	The gross national product of Germany, by sector	354
11.5	Growth of population, by employment sector, in Sweden	354
11.6	Growth of population in Europe, by country, 1800–1910	355
11.7	Birthrates by country, 1810–1910	355
11.8	Death rates by country, 1810–1910	356
11.9	The contraction of rural population in France with the growth of towns	358
11.10	Migration from Germany, 1820–60, and the price of rye	358
11.11	Migration within Germany to the industrial provinces of Rhineland and Westphalia, 1880	359
11.12	Migration within Germany to Rhineland and Westphalia	360
11.13	Migration from Italy, 1876–1913	360
11.14	The Jewish Pale of Settlement within Russia, and the migration of the Jewish people into central and southeastern Europe	362

11.15 Distribution of Jewish population in Europe, 1825–1900   363
11.16 Population changes in the United Kingdom in the
       nineteenth century   366
11.17 Population of France, per hectare, 1821 and 1911   367
11.18 Percentage increase in the population of Germany,
       1816–1914   367
11.19 The urban net in Alsace, about 1850   369
11.20 Rank–size graph of the larger towns in Germany in 1801,
       1871, and 1910   370
11.21 The size of the primate city as a percentage of the national
       population, 1800–1910   372
11.22 The occupational structure of Toulouse in 1809, 1851,
       and 1872   372
11.23 The occupational structure of Strasbourg in 1866, 1882,
       and 1895   372
11.24 Migration to Marseilles and Lyons   373
11.25 Migration to Paris: the source of migrants, 1833 and 1891   374
11.26 Changes in a single city block in Łódź, 1827–1914   377
11.27 Distribution of domestic servants in Paris (1872) and of
       working-class population   378
11.28 Haussmann's rebuilding of Paris, 1850–6   379
11.29 The growth of population in greater Berlin   380
11.30 Towns of the Balkan peninsula, about 1910   382
11.31 Cities and towns in Spain and Portugal, about 1855   383
11.32 Cereal production in France   384
11.33 The growth in cereal production in Prussia   385
11.34 Growth in the production of rye and wheat in Sweden,
       1866–1926   385
11.35 Land use and agricultural production in Prussia   386
11.36 Land enclosure in Denmark, 1769, 1805, 1893   393
11.37 Types of plows used during the nineteenth century   394
11.38 Yield ratios and yields in quintals per hectare of wheat
       in France, about 1840   396
11.39 Yield ratios and yields in quintals per hectare of rye
       in France, about 1840   397
11.40 The distribution of weavers in Germany, about 1885   403
11.41 The textile region of Catalonia   405
11.42 The European textile industry in the mid-nineteenth century   407
11.43 The use of charcoal and coke in the iron-smelting industry
       of Great Britain   408
11.44 The industrial region of northwest Europe   414
11.45 The Ruhr coalfield about 1850   415
11.46 Mining concessions along a north–south transect across
       the Ruhr coalfield   416

11.47 The spread of coal mining from Belgium into France with
        the opening up of the "hidden" coalfield   417
11.48 The increase in coal production in northwest Europe   417
11.49 The Ruhr industrial region, 1850–70   419
11.50 Ironworks on the Lorraine–Luxembourg ore field and their
        affiliation with iron and steel companies elsewhere in western
        Europe, about 1910   421
11.51 The movement of ore from the Lorraine–Luxembourg ore field
        and the import of coal, about 1910   422
11.52 The Upper Silesian–Moravian industrial region   423
11.53 The spread of coal mining in Upper Silesia–northern
        Moravia; the distribution of mines about 1860   424
11.54 Zinc mining and smelting in Upper Silesia, about 1860   425
11.55 The increase in coal production from the sectors of the
        Upper Silesian coalfield, 1800–1920   425
11.56 Coal mining in the Upper Silesian–Moravian coalfield,
        in 1912   426
11.57 The Donetz industrial region, Ukraine   427
11.58 Internal transport in France   429
11.59 Internal navigation in France, late nineteenth century   430
11.60 Navigable waterways in the north German plain   432
11.61 Railway development in Europe, 1840   433
11.62 Railway development in Europe, 1850   433
11.63 Railway development in Europe, 1880   434
12.1   Population density in Europe, 1910   441
12.2   Graph showing the clustering of patterns of population
        behavior   443
12.3   The urban population of Europe, about 1910   445
12.4   The distribution of the larger cities in the British Isles, 1911   446
12.5   Population density of European Russia, about 1910   447
12.6   Urban development of European Russia, early twentieth
        century   448
12.7   Wheat growing in Europe, about 1913   449
12.8   Wheat production in Europe, about 1913   450
12.9   Rye growing in Europe, about 1913   451
12.10 Potato growing in Europe, about 1913   452
12.11 Sugar beet production in Europe, about 1913   453
12.12 Dairy cattle in Europe, about 1913   454
12.13 Sheep rearing in Europe, about 1913   455
12.14 Pig rearing in Europe, about 1913   456
12.15 Coal production in Europe, 1912   458
12.16 Iron and steel production in Europe, 1912   458
12.17 Gross national product per head, 1913 (in U.S. dollars)   466
12.18 Gross national product per head by sector for industrialized
        countries and for nonindustrialized countries, 1913   467

Preface

Between 1973 and 1985 Cambridge University Press published the three volumes of *An Historical Geography of Europe*. The present book represents an attempt to condense and streamline these earlier volumes. At the same time its coverage has been extended to include the British Isles and Russia, both omitted from the earlier study. The method, as in the earlier volumes, has been to alternate "horizontal" pictures of Europe at certain critical periods in its history with chapters that trace developments within the intervening periods. The "layer-cake" way of organizing the material has been developed and tested by J. O. M. Broek in his study of the Santa Clara Valley, by H. C. Darby in *A New Historical Geography of England after 1600* (1986), and by others since their publication.

The horizontal chapters, as well as the connecting vertical interludes, have a closely similar organization, dealing in turn with population and urban development, agriculture, manufacturing, and trade. Changes in the physical environment have been touched on only when they seem relevant to human development. It should be possible, by taking the relevant parts of each chapter, to follow the course of, for example, population change or agricultural development through a period of almost two and a half millennia.

I wish to thank the editors of the *Annals of the Association of American Geographers,* the *Journal of Social History,* and the *Revue Belge de Philologie et d'Histoire* for permission to reproduce line drawings that I originally published in their journals; the Librarian of Cambridge University for copies of drawings in his keeping; and my friends and colleagues in the History Department of Indiana University and elsewhere, whose names appear in the earlier volumes, for their continued encouragement and help.

Norman J. G. Pounds

Cambridge, England

Introduction

The central theme of this book is the changing spatial pattern of human activities during the last 2,500 years of Europe's history. Three factors have determined the locations of human beings: the environment itself, the attitudes and forms of social organization of the people who lived there, and, lastly, their levels of technology. These three factors have interacted in a variety of ways. Environments have encouraged, permitted, or restricted human activities and, on the other hand, have been modified to be brought into line with human needs. Human perceptions and attitudes have been an ever present but always unpredictable factor in the equation. The relations of man and the environment have throughout history been modified by the tools which man had at his disposal. Technologies, wherever they originated, have been diffused by human contacts. Sometimes they were welcomed and used; sometimes rejected. These interrelations are immensely complex, and the following model is a gross simplification, but it is this model which is elaborated here:

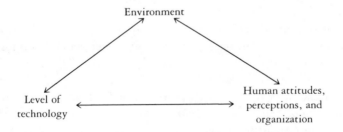

Environment is the total physical setting amid which people live. It includes the terrain: mountain, hill, valley, and plain. These have in many ways influenced settlement, transportation, and communication, not to mention agriculture. One is tempted to think of the influence of landforms as static and unchanging. The "everlasting hills," it might by assumed, were always there, witnessing the coming and development of the human species in the more recent stages of their history. But the physical lineaments of the continents have changed in detail even during the historical period. Changes have, generally speaking, been small and of no human significance, but some have had an impact which no historian can afford to ignore, most notably in changes around the coasts of Europe: the loss of land to the sea and, at the other extreme, the building forward of flat coastlines and the silting of estuaries.

The rocks of which the earth is composed form a vital part of the environment. They provide building materials; they may contain wells of water, pools of oil, and deposits of solid fuel and metalliferous ores. And from the rock, aided by climate and the vegetation cover, soils have been formed and, in their infinite variety, have provided the medium in which crops have grown. Soils which have been cultivated for any great length of time have become modified for good or ill. Soil is "a response to management," and the best soils today are those which have been well managed over the centuries. The impact of man on the structure of soils may not be too readily apparent, but no aspect of his relations with nature is more important.

Lastly, weather and climate are universal and inescapable aspects of the environment, the weather being the day-to-day fluctuations; the climate, the long-term or average conditions. The former could not until recent times be predicted for more than a few hours ahead. The latter was known, and around its procession through the year was built the agricultural calendar and the sequence of festivities and jollifications with which most people measured the passage of time. But the predicted did not always occur; climate was not always what it was expected to be. There were cool, wet summers – sequences of them in fact – and very cold or very wet winters. Each such departure from the normal and expected brought hardship, compensated in some measure by those occasions when the weather was better than expected, the sunshine more prolonged and the rainfall only when it was most needed. Only the most minimal adjustments could be made to weather in the choice of crops, the drainage of soil, and the drying of the harvest. The weather was, and remains, the element of the physical environment least susceptible to human manipulation.

Society itself has inbuilt attitudes to its environment. All societies have been relatively conservative, unwilling to interrupt whatever stable relationships they had been able to establish with their physical surroundings. As a general rule, change in customary practices has been accepted reluctantly, and then as a result of necessity, of the need to cope with shortages of food, of land, of fuel. Stuart Piggott has distinguished between *conserving* and *innovating* societies, the former reluctant to change either their social organization or their ways of exploiting their habitat; the latter accepting change however unwillingly.[1] No particular human activity is ever pursued in isolation; it is part of a system, dependent on and intermeshed with others which are in some measure complementary to it. Any innovation or change must have far-reaching repercussions, and nowhere is this more apparent than in agriculture. Practices such as open-field farming, fallowing, and a three-course husbandry continued long after they had become technically obsolete, because each was intertwined with other practices in a system which

1   Stuart Piggott, *Ancient Europe from the Beginnings of Agriculture to Classical Antiquity* (Edinburgh, 1965), 17–18.

stood or fell as a whole (see Chap. 11). A conserving society was one in which social structure, craft industries, agriculture, and trade were so interlocked that voluntary change became very difficult, if not quite impossible.

The size of the population exerts a continuing influence on environment and technology. Its growth may provoke scarcities and even stimulate invention. It is, within limits, a mobile factor; it can move in search of land or employment. Its size and distribution must be an essential ingredient in the changing spatial pattern of human activities. Behind the pattern and intensity of agriculture, the scale of craft and later of factory industry, and the growth of towns there lies the number of bodies to be fed, clothed, and housed. It is difficult to escape the conclusion that a growing population, even though it may fall well short of truly Malthusian levels, nevertheless sometimes stimulates innovation. The mechanism is simple. Incipient shortages, whether seasonal, irregular, or long-term, lead to small increases in price, and this in turn leads to greater inventiveness to satisfy demand.

The size of the population is a far from autonomous factor in making for scarcity or abundance. It is, in part, governed by social mores, which might, for example, favor early marriage, condone infanticide, or erect large families into a mark of social distinction. It has been subject no less to epidemic and other forms of disease, which are part of the biological environment. Their significance has been increased both by the congestion of densely settled areas and by migration. On the other hand, technological advance has had as one of its consequences the improvement of hygiene and of public health and thus a diminished mortality. How often in the world today do we see that the broad field of innovation, which has had as its objective the reduction of scarcities, has in the end precipitated greater difficulties by increasing population and thus demand.

The third factor is technological innovation. Its purpose has always been to increase or accelerate the productive process, whether in agriculture, the crafts, or in other human activities. Most often an innovation served to remedy scarcities which had themselves arisen through increase in human demand, from an exhaustion of naturally occurring resources, or from a combination of the two. It was an improving technology which allowed the Neolithic farmers to encroach on the forests and the medieval peasants to plow and cultivate the heavy clay soils (see Chap. 6). Technological innovation replaced the simple wind furnace with the high or blast furnace for smelting iron, and other innovations brought about the adoption of coal as an industrial fuel in place of charcoal. In every instance there were those who suffered, but in the long run, accepted wisdom tells us, the change was for the greater good of the greatest number.

Every innovation has had a spatial aspect. It brought about some change or other in materials used, in the labor needed, or the market supplied, and these in their turn necessarily brought about shifts in the location of activities, as those involved in them *perceived* the greater advantages of one place over another. The following pages contain many instances of the geographical shift of one phase of production or another in response to changing factors of production. But no such change has ever been inevitable or automatic. If the relevant data were fed into a computer, it could doubtless be made to calculate the cost-effectiveness of one location in relation to another. Thousands of such calculations are being made today. But earlier peoples were not slaves to the computer. They judged their environment as they *perceived* it, and their perception was always colored in some degree by the values of the society in which they lived.

A PLAN OF CAMPAIGN

How then to organize a study of the shifting spatial pattern of human activity? This activity itself is infinitely varied so that selection and organization become major problems. But in this book a limit has to be set. Only those activities which play a major role in supporting human life are considered: agriculture and manufacturing, the choice of a place to settle and live, and the construction of shelter from the elements. Many other subjects might have been included, each representing in some way the interaction of society and its level of technology with the physical environment. Styles of building construction, patterns of social behavior and custom, even styles of pottery and of decoration all display spatial patterns which change through time and are susceptible to geographical analysis.

Within the broad framework of the interrelationships of environment, society, and technology a restricted number of themes is pursued from the fifth century B.C. to the early twentieth century. They are: settlement and agriculture, the growth of cities, the development of manufacturing, and the role of trade. But underlying each of these themes are two other factors: political organization and population.

The geography of the state might be thought to have little relevance to the study of the themes of this book as they have been outlined above. Indeed, there have been historical geographies from which it had been almost wholly excluded. Yet political organization can never be taken for granted. Boundaries not only set limits to political obligations; they also set bounds to economic regimes. Although the general tendency in this book is to look at the broad spatial patterns of the continent as a whole, one frequently finds abrupt changes at political boundaries, quite unrelated to the physical setting. Their explanation must lie with the contrasted economic and social policies pursued on each side of the line. At the simplest level of late prehistoric Europe, tribal areas were also areas of economic organization. The same goes for the Greek *polis* and the city-region of the Romans. Even during the Middle Ages, when political boundaries might have been thought unimportant, efforts were continually being made to systematize them and to strengthen their devisive influence.

In modern times the state has assumed greater powers and responsibilities than it has ever possessed before, and with increasing demands has come an intensification of the role of political boundaries. They are seen increasingly, and especially in the most recent period, to separate attitudes to land use, to industrial development, to the structures of transportation and communication. One might say that the almost "seamless web" of earlier Europe became broken and fragmented by the political lines drawn across it, so that it became a mosaic rather than a continuum.

The inclusion at every stage of this book of the changing geography of population calls for no explanation or excuse. It is human geography with which we are concerned, and to leave out the population element, as has occasionally been done, is to omit the Prince of Denmark from the drama.

Human settlement is a vital part of human geography. Settlements are where people live, and their size and plan reflect in varying ways both social organization and economic activity. They range in size from the isolated homestead to the metropolitan area. As a general rule they are permanent structures; they cannot, like people and craft industries, migrate, though they may decay and become abandoned. In terms of accommodating people a multitude of small settlements may be no different from a few large, but as responses to human needs for homes and for the opportunity to gain some form of subsistence from the environment they may be worlds apart. The city is commonly thought of as something different and distinct from rural settlement. In fact, it lies at one end of a spectrum which reaches to the isolated farm at the other. The distinction between small towns and large villages is only juridical. Many a large village was as industrialized as a town, and thousands of towns, right up to the nineteenth century, were as agricultural in function as any village. But at the extremes of the spectrum the large city has always been poles apart from the village. Its agricultural functions have disappeared, and it has become a center of manufacturing and service industries and of government and administration.

Urban settlement is given particular emphasis not only because it has, at least during the past century and a half, absorbed a large and increasing proportion of total population, but also because the city has played a role of immense significance in the cultural and material development of western man. A city is a center of specialized production. Frequent reference will be made to the "basic" activity of a city. This is the function whereby it supports itself and pays for the foodstuffs and other materials which it obtains from elsewhere. The basic function of an industrial city is the provision of certain manufactured goods for a national, even for a world, market. That of other cities might be the provision of services, administrative, commercial, educational. Even in the fifth century B.C. such specialized cities were beginning to crystallize from the mass of human settlements, and the process has continued and intensified until the present.

The second theme is land use and agriculture, the utilization of land for the production of food and industrial crops. No aspect of human activity is more closely dependent on the physical constraints set by the environment. Relief, climate, and soil all play a role in determining where people till soil and what they grow. Nevertheless, man has progressively modified his environment and made social, even biological, adaptions to it. It may not be possible to modify climate in any significant fashion, but small steps can be taken to moderate its influence. Windbreaks, contour plowing, basin irrigation, and dry farming are all adaptions to climatic factors. The relief of the land cannot be altered, but slopes can be terraced for cultivation and the choice of crops can be adjusted to slope. Soil is the most susceptible to change. Careless use can, it is true, lead to the deterioration or even loss of the topsoil, but most soils which have been long under cultivation have been so progressively modified and improved by deep drainage, careful plowing, and the use of manure and fertilizer that they bear little resemblance to those first tilled by prehistoric man.

On the quality of the soil, the climate, and the levels of management have depended in the last resort the density of population. Agricultural technology and resulting yields thus assume a fundamental importance, and the very slow changes in agriculture and the levels of agricultural production are an important theme.

Next to agriculture must come the craft industries which have from the earliest times supplied the physical needs of mankind and, through the provision of the tools of cultivation, food production itself. Industries have to be studied from the viewpoints of both the technologies employed and of their structural organization. They thus range from the use of the humble distaff to mechanical spinning, and from the craftsman working alone in his home to the highly structured factory. A feature of manufacturing is the continued existence of the simplest structural forms and the most elementary technologies into the nineteenth century, when they coexisted with the most sophisticated forms of factory organization. The long survival of labor-intensive craft manufactures has in some degree resulted from the surplus of labor in many areas of Europe, but this is not the complete explanation. The inelasticity of social structures has been an important factor in the slowness of change here, as it has been in agriculture.

The last theme in this book is that of the role of trade. Trade is the necessary consequence of specialization of production. From the earliest stages in human social development there have been specializations and trade, if only because such essentials as salt, flint, and obsidian for tools and desirable, if less essential, materials like jet and the precious metals were highly localized in their occurrence. In a sense the specialization of labor was apparent in the Neolithic. What are the flint-workings at Grime's Graves in eastern England and at Spines in Belgium but primitive "factories" from which flints were dispatched to other regions and were, presumably, paid for in other commodities? No doubt most communities, even into the twentieth century, were self-sufficing. Their trade was only of marginal significance. But its volume and variety tended to increase and the routes which it followed to change with supply and demand. Trade is, indeed, a barometer of human progress, and its spatial pattern a theme of extraordinary importance.

The organization of so many discrete themes over so great a period of time presents not inconsiderable difficulties. It would be possible to take each in turn and follow it through the two and a half millennia which this book spans. This method has not been adopted because to do so would be to lose the opportunity to integrate the themes with one another. Instead, a "picture" of Europe is presented as it might have appeared at seven different times in the course of its history. Each of these times was important in its own right in the history of Europe, marking the climax of a period of development. They are the time of Athenian greatness in the fifth century B.C., the culmination of Roman imperial power in the second century A.D., the time of Charlemagne, the early fourteenth century, the Renaissance, the eve of the Industrial Revolution, and, lastly, the first decade of the present century with which the book ends. Between each successive picture has been inserted a kind of continuity, tracing the changes that occurred during the intervening period.

PROCESS

One may ask by what processes these changes were brought about. Change is not quite the same as growth. The latter implies the multiplication of what is already there. Agriculture or an industry may, for example, grow without any change in its internal structure or technology. Change implies some alteration in the factors of production. The heavy plow and the horizontal loom represented change, since they permitted the same labor to produce more efficiently or more abundantly. Of course growth is likely to accompany change, which would otherwise have no sensible purpose, and continued growth may be impossible without change in structure or technology in order to take account of different physical conditions encountered as growth proceeds.

The agents of change appear to be fourfold. First there must be innovation, the discovery and use of a new material or process, or a refinement in an established technology. It is not our purpose to discuss the psychology of change, the human predisposition to experiment or to conserve traditional practices. It is sufficient to say that some people have shown a greater disposition to innovate than others.

The second agent of change is diffusion, the spread of an innovation to other peoples than those who initiated it. This has never been an automatic process. Knowledge of a new "invention" in technology or organization has to be carried by people. Sometimes there has been a desire for secrecy, a reluctance to part with the good news. At other times, there has been resistance to the changes implicit in its adoption. The very great differences in material standards to be found in Europe at any of the periods discussed are, in part, the consequences of resistance to innovative practices.

Specialization is the third agent of change. When a community begins to produce more of a certain article or commodity than it needs for its own consumption, it must part with the surplus. It becomes a specialist. Small-scale surpluses may have little significance, but beyond a certain point specialization must be accompanied by organizational change. It implies innovation. Specialization may be seasonal, like the work of the winter linen weavers of Flanders (see Chap. 11) or part-time, but tends always to become a total occupation. Specialization breeds the expert, so thoroughly versed in his craft or occupation that experiment and innovation come to him naturally. Specialization increases total production, as with Adam Smith's pinmaker, and is thus likely to contribute to change, growth, and human betterment.

Exchange is a necessary consequence of specialization. It is a process whereby the benefits of more efficient production are spread more widely, and, if only by example, encourage further growth. Lastly, migration, which may in a sense be regarded as a form of diffusion, takes people with different technologies and organizational patterns into areas from which they had been absent. Its importance from prehistoric times to the present is too obvious to require elaboration here. It makes no difference that migrants were sometimes refugees and their contribution to change involuntary, or sometimes mere individuals enticed or bribed to carry their skills elsewhere. In these ways were the changes described in the following pages achieved.

I

The physical basis of European history

When the period of written history began in the sixth century B.C., Europe had already been inhabited by members of the human species for a million years or more. During this long span of time they had seen the ice sheets advance from the north and then melt away at least four times. They had been obliged to adjust, both physically and mentally, to this changing environment, and in doing so had gradually raised the level of their own skills and of the control which they were able to exercise over their surroundings. Nevertheless, their levels of cultural development varied from one part of the continent to another. Most of the significant advances in man's material culture, like agriculture and the smelting of metals, had been made in the Middle East and had entered Europe through the Balkan peninsula. From here they had been diffused northwestward to central Europe and then to western. There was always a steep cultural gradient between the more developed regions, like Greece and the Aegean, and the least, such as Scandinavia and the Atlantic periphery of Europe. Such differences, it might be thought, would be bridged in time, as the more advanced cultures spread outward like ripples from their hearth in the Aegean region. But such a leveling up did not, and indeed could not, take place. The receptivity of Europe to new cultures and new techniques itself varied too greatly. There were areas where the Neolithic farmers could establish themselves with the same ease and success that they showed in the riverine plains of the Middle East. There were others where soil and climate combined to repel the agriculturalist, where only the hunter-gatherer could scratch the barest of livings from the land.

It is this variegated pattern of resources which forms the background of this book. Against it are set the changing and slowly evolving patterns of population and settlement, of agriculture, manufacturing, and trade. These were influenced as they developed by the physical environment, but how deeply they were affected has long been a matter for debate. One school of thought, which stems from Greek historical writing of the fifth and fourth centuries B.C., conceives of human society as shaped by its environment. "Soft countries," wrote Herodotus, "invariably breed soft men, and it is impossible for one and the same country to produce splendid crops and good soldiers." And again, "the deficiency of spirit and courage . . . in the human inhabitants of Asia has for its principal cause the low margin of seasonal variability in the temperature," whereas the "inhabitants of mountainous . . .

country . . . will tend to have large-built bodies constitutionally adapted for courage and endurance."[1] From the nature of the environment Greek writers deduced
the probable economy and form of government. Against this can be set the statement of a recent Italian foreign minister, disclaiming any Communist threat to
his country: "Communism is a creed of the plains; my country is mountainous."
The legacy of Greek historical thought is clearly with us still. But such extravagant views cannot be seriously held today. Of course, all human activity is influenced by the physical environment amid which it takes place. Climate, soil, mineral wealth, rivers, and routeways all offer opportunities for man to use, but together
they also set limits to human action. These limits are rarely absolute. Nature never
says, "thus far and no farther may you go, or cultivate the soil, or carry on manufactures." It merely makes these tasks more difficult, so that there comes a time
and place, different for different peoples, where they give up the unequal struggle.
In the last resort it is people who decide whether a given resource or a particular
environment can be used, and how. The harsher the circumstances, the more likely
they are to abandon the effort. One cannot generalize. Peoples' motivation and
resilience are as varied as the physical circumstances amid which they have lived
and worked.

THE HUMAN ENVIRONMENT

The physical environment has not been a fixed, immutable presence throughout
human history. Its alterations within the historical period have been small compared with the giant fluctuations which accompanied the advance and retreat of
the ice sheets, but they have, nonetheless, been of significance in the development
of human societies. Change in the topography of the land has been too slow to
have much importance, though one must not underestimate the ways in which
harbors have silted and the coastline advanced or retreated. But the most important environmental change since the final withdrawal of the ice sheets has been
fluctuations in the climate. The postglacial amelioration has been irregular, broken by phases when cold returned though never on the scale of the Ice Age itself.
Very broadly cool and relatively dry phases alternated with milder and wetter ones.
Change in climate brought about change in the natural vegetation. Broad-leaved
trees spread northward as well as upward on the mountain slopes, only to yield
place at the margin to conifers when the climate again deteriorated. Change in
flora led to change in animal life. The stable relationships established between the
human animal and the environment were shaken, and man was obliged to migrate
or to modify his way of life. Particularly important, in retrospect, was the transition to cooler and damper conditions at the end of the so-called Subatlantic phase.
Peat bog began to form in many areas of central and northern Europe, and to
spread over upland surfaces – the so-called blanket bog – trapping trees and burying
the evidence of human settlement.

1   Hippocrates, as quoted in A. J. Toynbee, *Greek Historical Thought from Homer to the Age of Hera-
clius* (London, 1924), 165–6.

These climatic fluctuations were felt most acutely at higher altitudes and in more northerly latitudes. Here the difference of one or two degrees in temperature or of a few days in the length of the growing season was felt keenly, and led to the abandonment of marginal cultivation. In more southerly latitudes, in Greece for example, they might have been scarcely noticed.

The classical civilization of ancient Greece began in climate which was over much of Europe perceptibly more moist and cool than the average, and this continued for almost a thousand years. It cannot be said that the civilizations of Greece and Rome suffered on the whole, but the Roman soldier on duty along Hadrian's Wall in northern Britain, or in the lower Rhineland experienced a harsher climate on average than that known today. During the Dark Ages which followed the end of the Roman empire in the West there was an improvement in the climate. It appears from both literary and historical evidence to have become a very little warmer and drier in the northern half of Europe. The seas were much less stormy. Celtic missionaries traveled freely in minuscule and insubstantial boats along the Atlantic seaways, and the Norse, in boats which were not much larger, regularly made the voyage from Scandinavia to Iceland, Greenland, and even beyond.

Then, in the later Middle Ages, the climate again began to change. The fluctuation was so gradual that it is extremely difficult to date its beginning, but by the early years of the fourteenth century there can be no doubt that conditions were becoming cooler, wetter, and more stormy. Literary evidence is unanimous on this. The years 1315–17 were marked by cool and very wet conditions, when fields could not be plowed and harvests failed to ripen. This was a period of scarcity and famine – the first of many – and the population of much of western and central Europe was reduced significantly.

The rest of the Middle Ages was wet and stormy. Voyages to Iceland became fewer, and Greenland was cut off and its small settlement perished. Record after record notes the severe storms and crop failures. A tax account of fifteenth-century Burgundy noted of one village that it had been so ravaged by storms that year that neither grain nor wine had been harvested, and in England the *Vision of Piers Plowman* included the dire warning that

> Ere five years be fulfilled such famine shall arise
> Through floods and through foul weather fruits shall fail.

The poet got the periodicity of such famine crises about right. They seemed in the later Middle Ages and early modern times to come on average about every five or six years. Famine was always accompanied by disease, as the weakened body had little resistance to infection.

In the middle years of the sixteenth century another climatic fluctuation ushered in colder conditions over much of Europe, a period known, with a certain exaggeration, as the "Little Ice Age." Much of Europe had always, even during the mildest periods, experienced winters of exceptional severity at irregular intervals. During the Little Ice Age these became more frequent and more extreme. In

Provence wine yields were reduced by the cooler and more cloudy summers. In northern Europe cultivation contracted on the hillsides, and the tree line sank lower in the mountains. The glaciers of the Alps crept lower down their valleys; the snow cover on the passes became deeper and travel more difficult and hazardous. Vineyards and olive groves were killed by the frost, and northern ports and rivers were closed by ice for longer periods of the year. The Little Ice Age seems not to have greatly affected Mediterranean Europe, where, as a general rule, a fall of a degree or two in the temperature might be neither perceptible nor important. North of the Alps it continued far into the nineteenth century. Revolutionary movements both in 1789 and 1848 were preceded by severe shortages of food which were in turn due to bad weather and harvest failure. It should, however, be noted that the severe weather and crop failures of 1816–17, sometimes described as the last great famine crisis in Europe, were in fact due to the violent eruption of Mount Tamboro, a volcano in the East Indies, which spread so thick a blanket of dust through the atmosphere that solar energy was greatly reduced.

The severe winters of the early nineteenth century, so vividly described in the novels of Charles Dickens, gradually became less frequent and less extreme, and by the 1880s it could be said that the Little Ice Age was over. The last century has shown no pronounced climatic trend, though it is sometimes said that meteorological events point to a recrudescence of colder conditions.

These climatic fluctuations have certainly had an impact on human affairs, though, in the absence of precise weather recordings, it is very difficult to analyze it. Their consequences may not be apparent in southern Europe, and perhaps they were not great on the good soils of western and central Europe. It was at the margin of human settlement – in mountainous areas, in Scandinavia and the Baltic region, on the heavy clay soils of England – that their influence was greatest. Here settlement receded during the later Middle Ages and early modern times. And when, in the late nineteenth century, the Little Ice Age ended, settlement crept back into these higher altitudes and latitudes. The advance of agriculture into the vast province of Swedish Norrland (see Chap. 11) at the end of the century was made possible only by this cyclical improvement of the climate.

THE FACE OF EUROPE

The main lineaments of the continent were very much the same in the fifth century B.C. as we see them today. Only in detail has the land changed. Then, as now, it consisted of a great plain which extended eastward from the shores of the Atlantic Ocean until it merged into the much wider plains of Russia (Fig. 1.1). Across it, from south or southeast to north or northwest flowed rivers whose courses time and man have modified only in detail. Toward the north the plain merged gradually, almost imperceptibly beneath its forest cover, into the highlands of Scandinavia and western Britain. To the south the plain was also bounded by hills which lay in compact but irregular masses all the way from central France, through

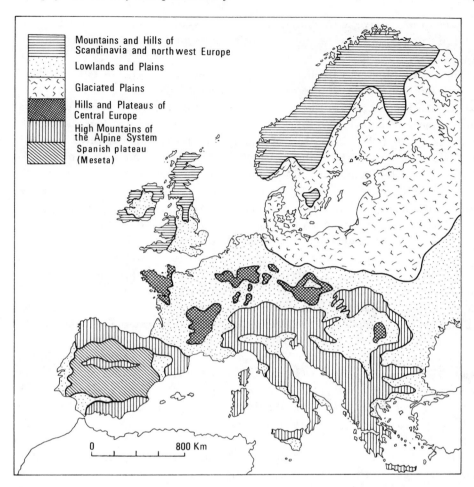

Mountains and Hills of
Scandinavia and north west Europe

Lowlands and Plains

Glaciated Plains

Hills and Plateaus of
Central Europe

High Mountains of
the Alpine System
Spanish plateau
(Meseta)

0   800 Km

1.1. Landforms of Europe

Germany, Bohemia, and Poland to the Ukraine. Between these hills lay gaps and basins, formed by movements of the earth's crust and erosion by rivers. Through them ran the chief routes of human migration and the avenues of what little trade there was at this time. South of these hills and plateaus, mainly forested over their steep slopes and flattened summits, lay the Alpine system, the most formidable barrier to human movement at this or any other time.

These were the principal physiographic provinces of Europe. In each of them terrain, climate, and soil imposed a set of conditions and limitations on human settlement and development. In each the human response had certain common features which distinguished it from the others. Most distinctive was the Scandinavian region where hard rock, a thin and poor soil, and a highly restrictive climate combined to limit human settlement. Until the nineteenth century this area remained the preserve of the hunter and reindeer herder. Its poverty was in some measure compensated by its mineral wealth, though not until the later Middle Ages was this exploited.

The great European plain offered the greatest potential. Its gentle relief nowhere exceeded a thousand feet above sea level. Its surface deposits were, however, more varied. Much of its area in the north and east had been covered by the ice sheets during the glacial period. As they melted they left behind vast spreads of both heavy clay – boulder clay – and of coarse sand and gravel, deposited by flood waters as they escaped from the melting ice. Neither was productive or easy to cultivate, and the sands gave rise to some of the poorest soils in Europe which support the heaths of the Low Countries and northern Germany. The "starveling pines of Brandenburg" were rooted in glacial outwash gravels.

That area of the plain which was not glaciated was very different. It was made up of rocks much younger and softer than those of Scandinavia, but variations in their degrees of softness, as between limestone, chalk, and sandstone on the one hand, and clay on the other, gave rise to a varied relief. The resulting topography consists essentially of ridges, usually asymmetrical with one side very much steeper than the other, separated by clay-floored lowlands. This "scarp-and-vale" characterizes lowland Britain, northern France, and most of the area of Germany, southern Poland, and Russia where it had not been blanketed by glacial deposits. The limestone ridges and uplands yielded a light soil, easily cultivated by prehistoric man. The intervening clays were heavier and damper and yielded less readily to the early plow. Furthermore they were, as a general rule, densely forested. Though early man encroached on these less desirable lands, their clearing and cultivation had to await the coming of more elaborate tools of cultivation in the later Middle Ages.

The central European belt of hills and plateaus rises sometimes steeply, sometimes more gently from the northern plain. It is built of rocks very much older and harder than those which make up the lowlands. Its climate is appreciably wetter and cooler and its soils less productive. These hills were scarcely touched by prehistoric peoples, and it was their wealth in minerals, mainly iron and the nonferrous ores, which was chiefly responsible for their settlement in classical and medieval times.

The Alpine system is made up of a series of ranges, younger, higher, and more rugged than the hills of central Europe. They extend from Spain to the Caucasus, and for much of this distance they present an insuperable barrier to transport and communication. Geologically speaking, they are young topographical features. Insufficient time has elapsed for them to be worn down. Their heights were glaciated during the Ice Age and show today the ruggedness which results from erosion by ice. Yet the Alpine system is interrupted by gaps which have provided low-level routes across them. The broadest is in southern France, between the Pyrenees and the Alps. There is also a wide gateway between the Alps of Austria and their continuation in the Carpathian Mountains. The river Danube flows through this gap between the plain of south Germany and the great, mountain-girt plain of Hungary. It leaves the Hungarian plain by a yet more spectacular route, the succession of gorges which it has cut across the Carpathian ranges. South of the Danube are valley routes through the mountains of the Balkan peninsula to the shores of the Mediterranean Sea.

The Alpine system in its entirety nevertheless constitutes a great divide, not only climatic but also cultural, between northern Europe and the Mediterranean basin. D. H. Lawrence, as he walked from Austria across the Alps to Italy, wrote of the contrast he saw. "North of the Alps," he wrote, "the everlasting winter is interrupted by summers that struggle and soon yield; south of the Alps, the everlasting summer is interrupted by spasmodic and spiteful winters that never get a real hold. . . . North of the Alps, you may have a pure winter's day in June. South of the Alps, you may have a midsummer day in December or January or even February."[2]

When Lawrence crossed the Alps he did not make use of one of the well-trodden gaps which interrupt their continuity. He went by way of a pass. There are countless passes, each reached by a twisting road up a narrow mountain valley, and most lying at heights of over six thousand feet. They were not routes for mass migration, and most were made dangerous and difficult by snow in winter. Some were used by the Roman legions, and Hannibal must have used one of them, possibly the Mont Cenis, in his invasion of Italy in 218 B.C. But the Alpine passes came into more frequent use during the Middle Ages, when they provided the shortest route for merchants between Italy and south Germany.

Few crossings of the Alpine system had more importance than the routes between the head of the Adriatic Sea and the rivers which flow down to the Hungarian plain. Only forty miles separate the Adriatic from the valley of the Sava, and the roads nowhere climb to more than fifteen hundred feet. By this route countless invaders from northern and eastern Europe have entered Italy, and in more recent times both Austria and Hungary extended their political control by this route to the Mediterranean Sea (see Chap. 11).

The Mediterranean Sea is itself almost ringed by the mountains of the Alpine system. Along much of its northern shore they look down onto its waters, separated from them by at most a narrow tract of alluvial land. "Along the shore of the gray sea," wrote Homer, "there are soft water meadows where the vine would never wither; and there is plenty of land level enough for the plow, where they could count on cutting a good crop at every harvest time. . . . Also it has a safe harbor, in which there is no occasion to tie up at all. . . . All your crews have to do is to beach their boats."[3] The Mediterranean region was the most distinctive in Europe. Its dominant feature was its climate, hot and dry in summer, mild but wet in winter. This dictated the nature of its vegetation. Plants grew in winter, flowered in spring, and fruited in early summer, before dying back during the period of heat and drought. Tree crops like the olive and vine grew well, but, Homer to the contrary, grass was not abundant and hay was scarce. The natural

2 *Phoenix: The Posthumous Papers of D. H. Lawrence* (New York, 1936), 49.
3 *Odyssey*, trans. E. V. Rieu (Harmondsworth, 1946), IX, 130–41.

vegetation was adjusted to the dry, hot summer and consisted largely of drought-resistant scrub and conifers. There was little summer feed for animals, which more often than not were moved up into the mountains during the hot season.

The Mediterranean region was always, until modern times, in the forefront of cultural progress. The first great civilization developed in Greece, and it was in the southern Balkan peninsula that crops were first grown in Europe, metals smelted, and towns built. Travel was easy within the Mediterrean basin. The sea was almost tideless, and its storms never had the violence of those experienced in the Atlantic Ocean. It was a nursery of seamanship, and from the earliest times the cultures of the Middle East and of Greece had been carried westward by ship to Italy, the Spanish peninsula, and the shores of the more tempestuous Atlantic.

VEGETATION OF EUROPE

As the climate grew warmer and the ice sheets melted away, coniferous forest invaded the subarctic waste which covered much of Europe, and was followed as it spread northward by broad-leaved trees. By about 5000–2500 B.C., the so-called Atlantic phase, deciduous trees – beech, oak, elm, ash, according to the soil – covered much of Europe (Fig. 1.2). Then the climate became somewhat cooler and drier. The boundary between coniferous and broad-leaved forest retreated, and conifers reasserted themselves on higher ground and on the sandy soils of the northeast. By this time the Neolithic farmers had made significant inroads into the areas of forest, especially where there were good soils for cultivation. The coming of metal tools only hastened the destruction of the forests. The forested soils were cleared for cultivation, but agriculture was only intermittent. Fields were abandoned after a few years, but the natural forest was rarely able to regenerate, and in its place all too often there grew only scrub and heath vegetation.

In the last millennium B.C. the climate became wetter – the Subboreal phase – and these conditions continued through classical times. As has already been noted (see this chap., under "The human environment"), bog began to spread wherever drainage was impeded, imprisoning within it telltale grains of pollen, evidence of the fortunes of the forests, as well as "bog oak," trees preserved in its oxygen-free conditions.

By the fifth century B.C. Europe had already lost much of its forest cover. Woodland remained extensive and unbroken only where the soils were not worth the trouble of cultivating. Throughout the next two thousand years the boundary of the forests continued to recede, until in the most densely settled and intensively cultivated parts of the continent they had been reduced to that irreducible minimum necessary to provide timber, fuel, and forest grazing for local communities.

The Mediterranean region presents a special case. Woodland was never as dense there as it was north of the Alps, and it was even more vulnerable to the depredations of animals and man. Wood was needed for cooking, heating, and even construction, and its growing scarcity, even in classical times, is illustrated in the lines from the poet Menander:

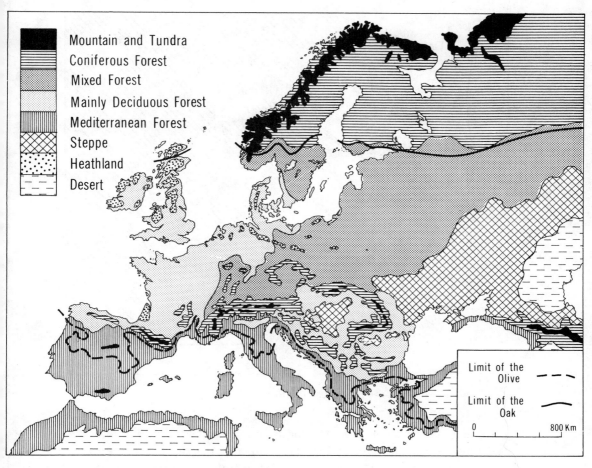

Mountain and Tundra
Coniferous Forest
Mixed Forest
Mainly Deciduous Forest
Mediterranean Forest
Steppe
Heathland
Desert

Limit of the Olive
Limit of the Oak

0   800 Km

1.2. Vegetation belts of Europe during historical times

My flock I was a-herding. . . .
. . . . Came this fellow – he's a charcoal man
Unto this self-same place to saw out tree-stumps there.
Menander, *The Arbitrants,* lines 25–30

There were, however, exceptions. The forests of Dalmatia did not disappear until
the Middle Ages, when they were cut to build ships for the Venetians, and in the
Apennines of central Italy they endured till modern times.

A consequence of deforestation, especially in a Mediterranean setting, was erosion. Without trees to hold the soil in place it was readily washed by the sometimes torrential winter rain into the valleys, where it choked the streams and silted
harbors. Plato, in a well-known passage in the *Critias,* compared the eroded landscape of Greece with "the skeleton of a sick man, all the fat and soft earth having
wasted away, and only the bare framework of the land being left." Sedimentation

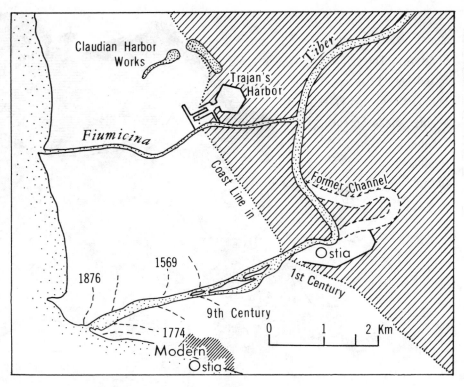

1.3. Coastal changes at the mouth of the Tiber

is the complement of erosion. The soil from the mountains was, in part at least, laid down along the coast and at the mouths of the rivers – hence the water meadows described by Homer. The Tiber has built the coastline forward no less than three miles since the Romans built their port of Ostia at its mouth (Fig. 1.3), and marshes have been gradually forming along many parts of the Mediterranean coastline.

THE SOILS OF EUROPE

The quality of the soil was a factor of profound importance in the human settlement of Europe. It was not the intrinsic fertility of a soil that mattered, but rather the ease with which it could be plowed and sown. It mattered little that the land might have to be abandoned after a few years, provided simple wooden plows, or even hoes, were effective in tilling it. Thus the earliest soils to be cultivated north of the Alps were not the clays, intrinsically rich in nutrients, nor the valley alluvium, which defied man's early attempts to drain it, but the light loamy soils, the gravel terraces, and even the sandy heathlands, than which few soils could have been poorer.

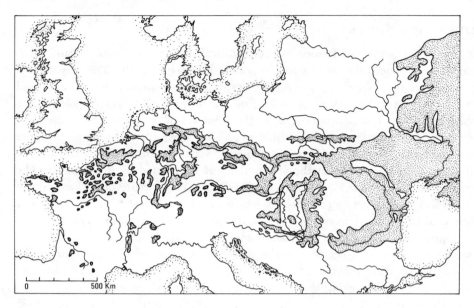

1.4. The loess soils of Europe

Foremost among these lighter soils was the loess. This was a windblown deposit. It derived from the drying clays left by the melting ice and was laid down as a thin deposit over much of the lowland of central and eastern Europe. It combined the chemical qualities of a rich soil with a lightness of texture which made it easy to work (Fig. 1.4). Its importance to early human settlement and agriculture was incalculable. It guided migrations and provided almost the only habitat for the Neolithic farmers of central Europe.

By contrast, the soils developed on the glacial deposits were almost invariably poor; the boulder clay was too heavy and the outwash sands too sterile. Over the ancient rocks of Scandinavia little soil had formed since the ice sheets had melted away, and the best of it was glacial deposits along the valleys and close to the shore.

The soils of the Mediterranean basin had little to recommend them. The whole region was mountainous, and the prevailing rock was limestone. This yielded at best a thin, alkaline soil and, at worst, vast expanses of bare rock on which stunted, drought-resisting bushes strove to gain a foothold. The best soils were formed from the silt brought down from the mountains and deposited in the valleys and along the coast. The richest by far were those of lower Egypt, which were, as Herodotus has told us, the "gift of the Nile." The most extensive fertile regions in the European sphere of the Mediterranean were the valley of the Po in northern Italy and the plains of Macedonia and Thrace. But there were also small patches of fertile lowland, ensconced between the mountains and the sea all around the Mediterranean coast.

RIVERS AND ROUTES

It has been a feature of Europe in the historical period that transport and communication could be developed and maintained relatively easily. The only significant barrier to movement, the Alpine system, was so broken up by gaps and crossed by passes that it was rarely a serious obstacle. Well might Napoleon have remarked, as he looked from Milan to the great arc of the Alps, that these were but "a splendid traitor," so formidable to look at, so easy to cross. Elsewhere, the loess belt and the limestone ridges provided avenues across the continent, dry under foot at most times of the year and rarely obstructed by dense forest. The volume of trade carried on in preclassical Europe was small, but a network of routes had already been developed by which metal goods and tools of obsidian or flint could be carried from one part of the continent to another. The Romans, beginning in the first century A.D., had no difficulty in spreading a close and integrated network of roads over the whole of the continent lying west of the Rhine and south of the Danube. Many of these roads continued to be used and they certainly were not improved on before the nineteenth century.

In the long run, however, it was its rivers which proved to be Europe's most important and enduring asset. Those which flowed to the Mediterranean suffered from the climatic peculiarities of the region. Most dropped steeply to the sea. In winter they were often in spate; in summer many ran dry. These were of little use for navigation. Nevertheless, a few larger rivers were more amenable, deeper and less irregular in their flow. Among them were the Po and the Rhône and, less valuable in terms of their commercial use, the Ebro and Vardar. Even the Tiber was used to bring timber and foodstuffs to the city of Rome.

The rivers which flowed north of the Alps were incomparably more useful than those of the Mediterranean basin. Their flow was more regular; they were deeper, and low water and ice rarely interrupted navigation for more than short periods. Despite their ambitious road-building programs, the Romans made great use of rivers to transport heavy and bulky goods. During the Middle Ages and early modern times long-distance transportation would have been inconceivable without rivers. Rivers radiated from the hills and mountains of central Europe. Those of the northern plain had been profoundly influenced by the glaciation of northern Europe. Their courses had been diverted toward the northwest, so that parts of eastern Europe were put into direct contact with the ports of the North Sea. No insuperable barriers separated the basins of these northern rivers, and in modern times it proved possible to link them to one another by canals (see Chap. 11). By the early nineteenth century it was, in theory at least, possible to navigate a barge from the shores of the Bay of Biscay to the Black Sea, using only internal waterways; it would, however, have been a difficult journey. The vessel would have had to have been very small in order to negotiate all the locks and canals, and the political risks would have been considerable. But such problems were the consequence not of the natural endowment of the continent, but of man's misuse of the opportunities which it offered.

Such were the possibilities and the constraints which the land of Europe offered to its immigrants. Its natural endowment was far from generous. The area of really good soil, capable of cultivation by early man, was small, and the vagaries of weather were such that recurrent crop failures were inevitable. More than a third of the continent was incapable of supporting a settled, agricultural population. By the end of the period covered in this book this area had been increased, in part because the climate had itself improved, but also because a developing technology had extended the cultivable area. The mineral wealth of Europe, by contrast, was not inconsiderable, though much of it did not become known, and in any case could not have been used, before the nineteenth century. Coal was known in Roman times but production was of negligible importance before the eighteenth century. The ferrous metals were of greater importance and these were abundant, widely distributed and easily worked, capable of supporting an iron-using culture before the development of modern technology. The nonferrous metals, particularly those of most use to early man – copper and tin – were, however, highly restricted in their occurrence; tin was found in significant amounts in only two areas, south-western Britain and Saxony-Bohemia. Bronze Age culture was founded on long-distance trade, and the difficulty of procuring bronze and the metals of which it was made must have played a role in the spread of iron-using cultures. The next chapter presents a picture of Europe in the fifth century B.C., near the beginning of the historical period. By this date iron-using cultures had spread across much of Europe south of the North and Baltic seas and had reached lowland England. Bronze cultures survived in northern and western Britain and around the Baltic, but the scanty population of arctic Europe still practiced a late Stone Age culture. The cultural gap between Greece and Lapland was of the order of three thousand years.

SELECT BIBLIOGRAPHY

Bradford, J. S. P. *Ancient Landscapes; Studies in Field Archaeology*. London, 1957.
Bunbury, E. H. *A History of Ancient Geography*. London, 1879; reprint, 1959.
Garnett, A. "The Loess Regions of Central Europe in Prehistoric Times." *Geographical Journal* 106 (1945): 132–41.
Smith, C. T. *An Historical Geography of Western Europe before 1800*. London, 1967.
Thompson, J. O. *History of Ancient Geography*. Cambridge, U.K., 1948.
Wright, J. K. *The Geographical Basis of European History*. New York, 1928.

PART I

The classical civilizations

There is, from the geographical viewpoint, no particular merit in choosing the middle years of the fifth century B.C. for study. A date could have been chosen a century earlier or a century later; the result would have been much the same, for in the material things of life change was remarkably slow. But the middle years of the fifth century B.C. made up for one corner of Europe a period of particular interest and importance. It was the time when classical Greek civilization flourished and bequeathed to posterity a legacy in literature, art and philosophy which has never at any time lost its significance. This gives fifth-century Greece a particular importance, and, though Greek drama may have nothing to do with the distribution of city-states or the cultivation of crops, the latter at least forms part of the background against which the Greek tragedians wrote.

By the mid-fifth century the Greeks had fought their great war against the Persians; they were secure and enjoying the fruits of victory. It was, for the Athenian people in particular, a time for hope and euphoria, such as not infrequently follows a long and exhausting war. A few years later this period of crowded achievement was to be interrupted by jealousies and feuds among the Greeks themselves which were to bring on the Peloponnesian War. This short period is, for the Greeks, one of the best documented in ancient history. Greek historians and dramatists throw an intense light on life and activities in their small corner of Europe. Furthermore, the great interest which posterity has taken in classical Greece has resulted in careful archaeological research throughout the Greek world. The result is that, for the first time in European history, we can look deeply into the lives of a particular people and learn how they lived, even how they thought.

There is, however, an important qualification. If we are looking at Europe as a whole we find that the light which plays on the Greeks at this time does not spread far beyond their limits. The Greek world of Sicily and southern Italy is well known, for it played an important role in the affairs of Greece itself. Archaeology has revealed much about the Greeks' Italian neighbors, the Etruscans, the Carthaginians of western Sicily, and the diminutive settlements which were at this time growing up on the hills beside the Tiber and drawing together to make Rome. But beyond this penumbra we have only preliterate societies of whom our knowledge derives from the confused accounts left by the Greeks and the more positive evidence of recent excavations.

23

Under these circumstances it is difficult to present a balanced picture of Europe. The scene must inevitably be dominated by the civilization of Greece which covered only a small fraction of the area and extended to a small minority of its population. This is unfortunate because the Greeks and their neighbors were only a part of this mosaic of European peoples. Their culture was in material terms part of the late Iron Age culture which had overspread much of the continent. There was no fundamental difference between settlement and agriculture among the Greeks and that to be met with among the La Tène Celts of central Europe or the earlier Iron Age cultures of France and the Iberian peninsula. Crops varied with climate; homes with available building materials; tools with the purposes which they served. But differences tended to be superficial. Material culture among the Greeks, Etruscans, and incipient Romans was basically that of Iron Age Europe.

But superimposed upon this variegated cultural pattern was that of the Greek city-state, that small, independent territory with its urbanized central-place which dominates our perception of the classical world. Most such urban centers remained small and largely agricultural. They were in size and functional terms little more than large villages. But they were distinguished from the latter in two ways: each was the central-place of a distinct territory, and the inhabitants of both the territory and its central-place combined to dignify it with public buildings, to give it a social and aesthetic significance which the simple village could not have possessed.

The Greeks contrasted themselves with the barbarians beyond their cultural borders. In fact, Greek cultural traits were being very slowly disseminated westward through the Mediterranean and northward into central Europe. Here tribal forts were just beginning to take on some of the characteristics of the Greek city, just as Greek artifacts were beginning to be found amid the settlements of the northern barbarians. The cultural divide between the Greek world and the "barbarians" was never as deep as the Greeks themselves – and consequently posterity – have tended to suppose.

The account of the Europe of the fifth century B.C. must give a perhaps disproportionate space to the distribution of the Greek city-state – the *polis*. Through it the Greeks looked at the world, and it shaped their agriculture, crafts, and trade. A great deal is known about the *polis,* but rather less of the agriculture and crafts pursued by the Greeks and the commerce which they carried on among themselves. Nevertheless, each of these fields of human activity is discussed and its spatial distribution and interactions examined. The chapter has not been organized in such a way that it separates the world of the Greeks from the barbarian world. The two were parts of a European culture, and the political and social organization of both *polis* and tribe are considered together. Similarly, agriculture and then the crafts are examined in all parts of Europe for which the evidence is adequate and available, and lastly the commerce of Europe as a whole. The result is to demonstrate a gradient in material culture which declines from its highest point in the Greek world to its lowest in the far northern periphery of the continent. It is not a gradient broken into steps. There is no sharp drop as one passes from the influence of the Greeks to, let us say, that of the Thracians and Celts, and from the latter to the Germanic tribes of northern Europe. In such a journey one is only going backward in time from a highly sophisticated Iron Age culture, through those who practiced more primitive metal cultures, to end with peoples who still flaked stone and fashioned tools from bone.

Six centuries elapsed between the golden age of Greece and that of Rome. The middle years of the second century A.D. have been chosen for a second cross section through the classical world. The period of the Antonines almost selected itself. It saw the climax of the development of the Roman empire. It was marked by peace, less absolute than some of the panegyrists would have us believe, and by a happiness less general than some have claimed. Nevertheless it was a time of relative prosperity when Rome was completing its grip on western and southern Europe, when cities were growing in number and in size, and even the barbarian peoples beyond the Roman frontier were looking to the empire for the supply of pottery, metalware, and other goods which their own craftsmen could not equal.

A jump of six hundred years is made possible by the fact that in the sphere of material civilization there were no changes of deep significance during the intervening period. It was one of growth rather than of change. The classical civilizations were not particularly inventive. Their technologies were those of late Iron Age Europe beyond which they contributed little. Greek genius had been in the direction of literature and the plastic arts. The Romans' energies were directed toward organization and administration. All that they did was on a grand scale, but they did little that other European peoples could not have done had they possessed the vision, the initiative, and the drive.

If there was no great change in the field of technology between the heroic ages of Greece and of Rome, there were profound changes in the political geography of Europe. The city-states were merged first into local leagues and states, and then into the Macedonian empire, which spread its mantle over the whole Aegean and Middle Eastern world. This in turn broke up the Hellenistic monarchies which continued their tumultuous way until they were one by one overwhelmed by the might of Rome.

The growth and splendor of the Roman empire is a drama of epic proportions. Its expansion from an unpretentious city-state to an empire which covered almost half of Europe, not to mention most of the Middle East and North Africa, is a monument to the tenacity and strength of purpose of the Latin tribes of central Italy. It is evidence no less of the feuds and divisions of the Hellenistic world on the one hand and of the tribal weakness of Europe on the other. Part One of this book makes no attempt to trace the shifting political patterns of the Graeco-Roman world. That is a matter for the political historian. It is sufficient to emphasize here that within the limits which the Roman empire set for itself both Greek *polis* and barbarian tribe ceased to be autonomous units and became building blocks in an imperial structure. That intense local feeling which had prompted the Greek *poleis* both to adorn themselves with monumental architecture and to go to war with their neighbors on the slenderest of pretexts was moderated under

Roman control. At the same time its more constructive aspects – its planned construction, monumental building, and attention to the practical needs of daily life – were generalized and bore fruition in every tribal capital of the empire.

In every other sphere of human activity the Roman empire inherited from the Greeks and from the peoples who had inhabited late Iron Age Europe. Differences between the second century A.D. and the fifth century B.C. were matters of intensity or of degree. Agriculture was almost certainly practiced more widely, but the crops, farming methods, and tools were broadly the same. The rural population – and that was by far the larger part – still lived in villages and still regarded the local city or central-place as a governmental and cult center, as a place for the more specialized crafts and for recreation and entertainment. The rich were richer than six centuries earlier; they lived in more ostentatious luxury than the Greeks had done. There had been nothing in the Greek world comparable with the exquisite villa which the emperor Hadrian built as his retreat at Tivoli, or Nero's Golden House, or any of the imperial palaces which crowned the Palatine in Rome. But the Greeks had the skills and technology to have created them had they wished.

Population and urban development, agriculture, food production and crafts, local and long-distance trade in the second century A.D. are surveyed, as those of the Greek world have been. The picture which results is broadly similar, but those qualities which had distinguished the Greek world of the eastern Mediterranean are seen to have diffused westward and northward. The levels of material culture were lifted as the Romans spread their cities and villas to northern Britain, the Rhine, and the Danube. And even beyond its frontier the empire cast its long shadow over the Germanic tribes of the north, developing among them tastes for things Roman and a desire to enter within the empire and to share in these delights.

2

Europe in the classical period

By the mid-fifth century B.C. the long ordeal of the Persian Wars was over, and Athens, triumphant leader of a league of Greek city-states, was building a civilization which has been the envy of posterity. The great Athenian dramatists were writing, and work had begun on Athens's crown and glory, the buildings erected on the steep Acropolis overlooking the city. At the same time colonies established by Greek cities in southern Italy and Sicily were in their different ways following where those of the Aegean had led. At this time Rome was a small town spread over a group of low hills beside the Tiber in central Italy. Only a short distance to the north the Etruscan league of cities had created a civilization similar in some ways to that of the Greeks in the Aegean. Rome had once been part of this loose Etruscan federation, and its independence was at this time far from secure.

Beyond the Alps the La Tène civilization had been spread by the Celts, armed with iron weapons and war chariots, through much of central Europe. They were pressing into western Europe, the Spanish peninsula, and the British Isles. Beyond them to the north and northeast, a Bronze Age culture still survived, and in the Baltic and Scandinavian regions and on the outermost fringes of the British Isles, Stone Age peoples were beginning to learn the rudiments of agriculture. In the far north, against the Arctic, hunters and herders still practiced a culture which had ended ten thousand years earlier in southern Europe. Their tools and weapons of sharpened bone belonged to the upper levels of the Old Stone Age. Never in the span of European history was the cultural gradient between south and north, between Attica and Finland, as steep as it was in the middle years of the fifth century B.C.

THE GREEK WORLD

Political geography

It is difficult to write of a political ordering of Europe at this time, impossible to produce a political map of the continent. Only in the Greek and Italian peninsulas were there states in the sense of territories organized politically, with governments in effective control. Elsewhere there were tribal areas, at best ill-defined and fluctuating.

The Greek world, which embraced the shores and islands of the Aegean Sea with outliers in Italy, Sicily, and beyond, was made up of city-states, *poleis* in Greek. It is difficult to estimate their number. Some were as unstable as tribal units in northern Europe. Others merged with or broke away from their neighbors. No less than 343 belonged at some time or other to the Delian or Athenian League. All claimed to be independent or sovereign, but discovered that independence was tempered by their small size and political weakness. In the Greek view, the city-state was the product of the coming together, or *synoikismos* of a number of neighboring villages. "When several villages," wrote Aristotle, "are united in a single community, large enough to be nearly or quite self-sufficing, the state comes into existence."[1] This is to rationalize a process which was in almost every instance long and slow. A city, in the narrow sense, became the center and focus of the city-state. It usually lay on rising ground for protection. It was commonly walled, and within the fortifications were the closely packed homes of its citizens. Not that all citizens of a *polis* lived within its urban central-place. Many had their homes in the surrounding rural areas where they had their farms. According to Thucydides, the Athenians had once lived in the countryside, in villages, and, though "now united in a single city," many "from old habit generally resided with their households in the country where they had been born."[2] They had to, or the journey from their homes to their fields would have been far too great.

The Athenian *polis* covered about 1,000 square miles, and Sparta almost 3,000. But the vast majority were a great deal smaller than this. Corinth covered only 340 square miles. Most were of less than 100, and the twenty-two city-states of Boeotia, the province lying north of Athens, could on average have had no more than 30 square miles. In such cases, most of the citizens could have lived in their central-place and still have journeyed to the fields each day.

The distribution of *poleis* was in large measure determined by the rugged and broken terrain. Most occupied each a small area of plain close to or on the coast. They were few in the mountainous interior and along the rugged west coast of Greece. The boundary separating each from its neighbor was commonly a barren mountain ridge, as the Kithairon range separated Athens from the city-states of Boeotia. Figure 2.1 shows the distribution of the *poleis* which made up the Delian League. These were only a fraction of the total number. Those of Boeotia and the Peloponnese, for example, were not members and are not shown. In the Peloponnese and western Greece the *polis* was in process of formation. Even Sparta was "not built continuously, and has no splendid temples or other edifices; it rather resembles a group of villages, like the ancient towns of Greece."[3]

The Greek world extended beyond the Aegean to include southern Italy and part of Sicily, as well as the shore of the Black Sea, of Provence, and even of Tripolitania (Fig. 2.2). Here colonists from overpopulous city-states of Greece had migrated and established daughter states. These were fully independent though

1   *Politics*, I.1.8.
2   Thucydides, II.16–17.
3   Thucydides, I.10.

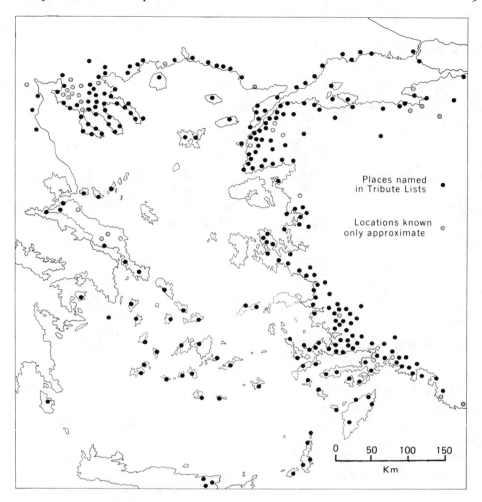

Places named
in Tribute Lists •

Locations known
only approximate ○

2.1. The Delian League, total membership

tied to their parent *poleis* by ties of filial loyalty. How strong these ties could be was demonstrated in the Peloponnesian War. The Greek colonies were much fewer and in general considerably larger than the *poleis* of Greece itself. In Italy and Sicily – *Magna Graecia* as it was called – they clung to the coast, and their political control extended no great distance into their hinterlands. Here the Sicel and Italic tribes continued their traditional way of life in the mountains, influenced, no doubt, but not dominated by the Greeks on the plains below them.

It is not easy to define Greece – Hellas – as that term was understood by the Greeks. It was the area where Greeks lived, but they spoke a number of distinct dialects, and near the borders of the Greek world these passed into the separate languages of the "barbarian" world around them. Despite common cultural elements, the Greeks never knew political unity until this was imposed on them first

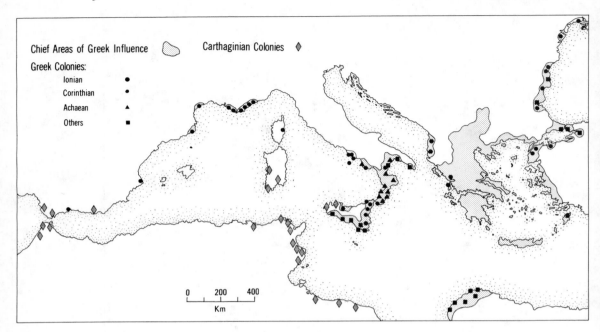

2.2. Greek settlement in the Mediterranean

by Alexander of Macedonia and then by the Romans. At most they formed fluctuating regional leagues for mutual protection. Largest and most powerful was
that created around Athens in order to defeat the Persians. It was turned into an
instrument of Athenian aggrandizement, and frictions within it contributed to the
outbreak of the Peloponnesian War. Other leagues were formed in Achaea, Boeotia, and the three-pronged Peninsula of Chalcidice, which was ringed with *poleis*.
So close was the union of Chalcidic cities that they even minted a common coinage. Whatever their differences, linguistic, cultural, political, Hellas was united
in one thing, its contempt for the *barbaroi* or barbarians, the "lesser breeds without
the law."

One must not think of the Greeks as the only creators of city-states. Closely
similar settlements were made at this time by a very different people, the Phoenicians. They derived from the coastal cities of the Levant. They were seafarers,
who founded their premier colony at Carthage, near the site of the modern Tunis,
in North Africa. From here they established daughter colonies in the western basin
of the Mediterranean. They settled in western Sicily where they founded Motya
and Panormus, the modern Palermo, but were excluded from the rest of the island
by the Greeks. On the other hand, they appear to have been able to keep the
Greeks out of most of the western Mediterranean, and they themselves settled
along the North African coast and in Sardinia and southern Spain. Outwardly the
Carthaginian colonies resembled the Greek, but they were more commercial in

their orientation and some degree of control was maintained over them by their parent city of Carthage.

In addition to the hostility of the Carthaginians, the Greeks of Magna Graecia faced that of the Etruscans and the Italic tribes of Italy. The Etruscans occupied a large area of central Italy, centering in Tuscany. Their language, distinct from Italic, has generally been regarded as of Asiatic origin, and the people themselves as invaders from the east. Doubt has been thrown on this in recent years. Etruscan culture is now thought to have taken shape in Italy itself, and its separateness from that of the Italic tribes is no longer as clearcut as was once supposed. In the mid-fifth century Etruscan culture extended from the Lombardy plain in the north to the vicinity of Naples in the south. It blocked the northward penetration of the Greeks and enveloped that particularly important Italic people, the Romans. The Etruscan cities, notionally twelve in number, formed a loose association, rather like the leagues of Hellas, in which the pride and patriotism of each member prevented any subordination to a broader unity.

It was disunity within the Etruscan league which led to its failure to hold the Naples region. Etruscans were driven from Rome and failed to subdue the Italic tribes of the mountainous interior of Italy. It was their collapse which provided the opportunity for the growth of Rome. Rome in the fifth century was just another small city-state, differing in no significant respect from those of the Etruscans. Its people were Latins drawn from the Italic tribes of the peninsula. They had undergone a kind of synoecism, attributed to Servius Tullius in the sixth century. To him is ascribed the Servian Wall which was built to enclose the original villages of the Roman hills. But this is legend. The so-called Servian Wall was in fact not built until the fourth century. In the mid-fifth century the "city" of Rome led a precarious existence, threatened by both Etruscans and Italic tribes. Its importance lay wholly in the future. At this time the Italic tribes seemed far more powerful. They had checked the expansion of the Greeks in the south and were a continuing threat to Rome itself. They lived in the mountain valleys, where resources were restricted, and their rising population led them to overflow onto the coastal plains. This constant pressure was to lead to the interminable wars waged by the Romans against them, and described in the pages of Livy.

Beyond the sphere of Greeks, Latins, and Etruscans there were no territorial states, and only the most rudimentary political organization existed. Here the Bronze Age was coming to a close, as iron-using cultures were spreading westward and northward. The early Iron Age culture, identified with Hallstatt in upper Austria, had already spread across much of Europe, and a more refined and sophisticated iron culture, known from its type-site in Switzerland as La Tène, was beginning to supplant it. Cultures were diffused in part by the physical migration of people, in part by the movement of individual craftsmen, of whom metalworkers and potters would have been the most important. One must not, however, exaggerate the degree of movement and fusion among the Iron Age peoples of Europe. They formed regional cultures distinguished not by fundamental differ-

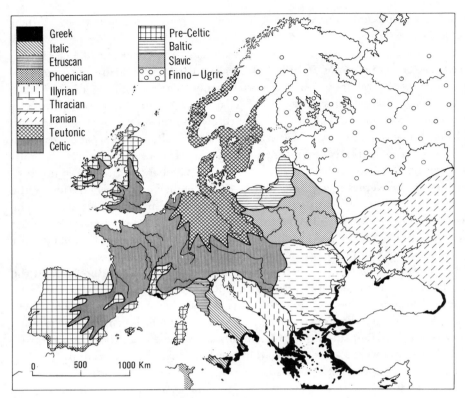

2.3. Ethnolinguistic map of Europe in the fifth century B.C.

ences but rather by stylistic developments in their pottery. Across northern Italy, beyond the Etruscans, were the Comacines, Atestines, and Villanovans. We cannot even assume that their small cultural differences were reflected in political organization. Nor can we say with any degree of certainty what language they spoke, whether they were Italic and thus related to the Latins, or linguistically Celts, or somewhere between the two (Fig. 2.3).

Beyond the Alps lived Celts. Traditionally one speaks of their social organization as tribal. In fact they formed communities perhaps of several hundreds, with some kind of "king" or leader and a central-place for their tribal territory. The latter appears as a general rule to have been a rounded fort, protected by bank, ditch, and palisade. Like the central-place of the *polis,* it probably contained the homes of part of the population and accommodation for the whole in time of emergency. Here the chieftain would live alongside the tribal gods, and here the store of grain would have been kept, possibly, as in southern Britain, in deep, lined pits cut in the ground.

The Celts had for centuries been moving westward and southward from their original homeland in southern Germany. They were helped by their possession of iron weapons and by their use of the most fearsome war machine developed hitherto in Europe, the horse-drawn chariot. Warfare appears to have been endemic among the Celts and between them and the pre-Celtic population. A stratified society was emerging, with a fighting elite which manned the war-chariots, and a mass of tributary peasants. By the fifth century the Celts had progressed partway across Spain where they encountered more primitive Iberian cultures and were checked in the end only by Greeks and Phoenicians from their bases along the coast.

To the north beyond the Celts were Germanic peoples. They inhabited the more southerly parts of the Baltic region, where they had acquired a simple, iron-using culture. They too were spreading broadly in a southerly direction. Was it the Germans who forced the Celts, despite their superior armament, to migrate to the south and west? Or are we dealing with peoples whose agriculture was so unproductive that they were obliged to migrate to find new fields to cultivate, and tended to move where resistance was least? It appears to have been generally the case that both Celts and Germans were pressing in the direction of better soil and less harsh climate.

In the fifth century the Slavs were beginning to appear as a distinct people. Their homeland is likely to have been the plains of what is today southeastern Poland and western Ukraine. From here they were probably advancing very slowly into the steppe and the forest of European Russia. They were, in the main, a settled, agricultural people. They were exposed to invaders from the steppe, of whom the most important and powerful at this time were horse-riding Scythians. These were a pastoral, seminomadic people who dominated and preyed upon settled agricultural peasants. It was against the Scyths that the Slavs built and enclosed their fortified "towns" like Biskupin (see this chap., under "Settlement").

North of the Slavs were related Baltic peoples and beyond them the Finno-Ugric peoples whose hunting grounds reached across European Russia into Siberia. The Balts were simple agriculturalists, who lived still in an age of bronze. It is difficult, if not impossible, to equate material cultures with ethnic and linguistic divisions, but it would be surprising if the Finno-Ugric peoples had yet reached the stage of cultivating the soil or of making weapons and tools of metal. Half a millennium later Tacitus described the Fenni, admittedly on hearsay evidence, as "astonishingly wild and horribly poor."

Population

There is little evidence on which to base estimates of the population of Europe in the fifth century B.C., or, indeed, at any time before the eighteenth century A.D. There was no census, and one can only infer its size from that of armies, grain trade, tribute, and areas inhabited or cultivated. It is evident that many Greeks considered their country to be overpopulated, and Greek colonies were peopled by those for whom there was no room at home. The maximum size of a population is clearly related to its technology and its ability to produce food, and the Greeks made little advance in agricultural science.

We must start with Attica, for it is to Attica that most of the available sources relate: The number of soldiers and warships which were at Athens's disposal suggest from 35,000 to 60,000 fighting men, or a total population of 110,000 to 180,000. To this must be added the "metics" (*metoikoi*) or resident aliens, and slaves, and for these there is no clear evidence. Estimates of the total population of Attica in the era of Athens's greatness range from 200,000 to 334,000. Reality may be about 300,000. This receives some confirmation from estimates of Attica's consumption of grain a century later. It is very difficult indeed to extrapolate from data for Athens to other Greek *poleis* because Athens was exceptional in so many ways. It was able to support a denser population than other city-states because it could import breadgrains from the Black Sea coast and elsewhere. For other *poleis* one can guess at the population from the extent of the built-up area of their central-places, from the probable area of their cultivable land, or from the size of the tribute which they paid to the Delian League. Plato regarded the ideal population of a *polis* as 5,040 men, suggesting with their dependents a total of not less than 15,000. Many, like the microscopic cities of Chalcidice, must have been a great deal less than this.

The only area in Europe that could possibly have equaled the density found in the Aegean lands was Magna Graecia, and Syracuse was the only city that could have rivaled Athens. Yet the size of the towns and the probable extent of their cultivated area suggest that the total population could not have been more than half a million. The total population of Hellas might have been of the order of 1.5 million.

When we turn to the rest of Italy the evidence is found to be even less abundant. On the basis of its cemetery, which has been excavated, the population of one Etruscan city-state, *Caere* (*Cerveteri*), has been put at about 25,000, and that of the urban population of Eturia at 200,000. Neither Rome nor the Carthaginian cities could have been significantly larger.

Estimates of population outside the Mediterranean world must be based, not on the size of inhabited places or the area of cultivated land, for too little at present is known about them, but on the type of economy. Everywhere in Bronze and Iron Age Europe a shifting agriculture was practiced. Yields were low, and the capacity even of the best land to support people was severely restricted. And, furthermore, much of Europe north of the Alpine system was incapable of cultivation at that time. This suggests that good soil would have been unlikely to support more than twenty-five to the square mile and that over much of Europe this total would have fallen to ten or even less. One would be rash indeed, on this basis, to suggest how large Europe's population may have been. It has been suggested that the total near the beginning of the Roman empire was some fifty million. If this is even approximately correct, the number some 450 years earlier was probably a great deal lower.

Settlement

In the fifth century B.C. the "urban revolution," in Childe's phrase, was beginning to spread across Europe. The central-places of the Greek *poleis* were the earliest European cities. Few were large; many were smaller than good-sized villages, but they all had features which distinguished them from purely rural settlements. Most remained, it is true, primarily agricultural, and contained the homes of people who journeyed daily to their work in the fields. But they also contained craftsmen, were the seats of some kind of administration, and provided for the entertainment and recreation of their citizens. The city differed from the village less in its size and the functions it performed than in the facilities which it offered for urbane and civilized living.

The Greek city commonly lay close to, but not on, the coast. The larger of them had a small port on the water's edge, as Athens had in Piraeus, and Corinth in both Kenchreai and Lechaion. Usually the city was built on rising ground which gave it some protection, and it was often dominated, as at Corinth and Argos, by a fortified *acropolis,* seat of a king in the archaic period which preceded the classical. It was usually walled, and in some instances the walls were so long and enclosed so great an area that it is difficult to see how they could possibly have been defended in their entirety. The walls of Athens, for example, were no less than sixteen miles long. To some extent this vast enclosure derived from the need, especially in earlier times, to have space into which to drive animals in time of emergency. As the city grew it commonly spread out over lower and flatter ground, and most of the last cities to be founded were built on flat land beside a river which provided them with water.

The older, hilltop towns were wholly without regular plan. Streets were narrow and twisting, with alleys and courts opening off them. Even in Athens, in words ascribed to a fourth-century writer, Dicaearchus, "the streets are nothing but miserable old lanes, the houses mean, with a few better ones among them."[4] This has been confirmed by excavations carried out near the Areopagus: "a minor street and narrow alleys. . . . built up with lesser houses, commercial establishments, and workshops."[5] The city was "dry and ill-supplied with water," and during winter storms the runoff cut gulleys along the roads. Most homes and workshops were built of mud bricks on footings of stone. Some may have had an upper floor, but most appear to have been single storied. "In private life," said Demosthenes, the Athenians "were severe and simple," and there is no reason to doubt what he wrote or to suppose that other Greek cities were less primitive.

In marked contrast with domestic architecture stood the public buildings. Life in the Greek city was lived in public; it was a "face-to-face" society. Its focus was the *agora,* usually though not wholly correctly translated as "marketplace." Nearby

4   *Geographi Graeci Minores,* ed. C. Müller (Paris, 1882), I, 101.
5   Rodney S. Young, "An Industrial District of Ancient Athens," *Hesperia* XX (1951): 139.

would have been the *prytaneion,* nearest approach to "city hall"; temples, monu-
ments, *stoa* or arcaded walk, and public fountain. Here people passed much of
their leisure time, instead of in their dank and narrow homes. Pausanias, who
went around Greece in the second century A.D. appraising the public buildings in
the manner of a Baedeker, wrote of the city of Panopus in Phocis, "if city it may
be called that has no government offices, no gymnasium, no theater, no marketplace, no water conducted to a fountain," whereas Dicaearchus had no doubt of
the status of Anthedon because "the agora is all planted with trees and flanked by
colonnades."[6]

It was the ambition of every *polis* to erect such structures. They were a matter
of prestige as well as of convenience. They were where people met and talked.
Without them there could have been no Platonic dialogues, though little of such
public discussion could have been as exalted as that conducted by Socrates. Few
cities, however, achieved the success of Athens, but then few had such financial
and material resources. Nevertheless there were not many, as Pausanias demonstrated, which were not dignified with public buildings of some architectural distinction. The tradition of fine building for its own sake was continued by the
Romans. It then disappeared from Europe, not to be revived until modern times.

The cities which the Greeks founded in Magna Graecia were in most respects
similar to those of Greece itself. All had large public buildings, of which a few
monumental fragments have survived at Syracuse, Metapontum, and elsewhere.

Urban development in central Italy was broadly similar to that in the Greek
world. Etruscan cities were large; some were located, like Orvieto and Perugia, on
high ground; all were strongly protected by nature. In these respects Rome con-
formed with the Etruscan urban pattern. All were made up of homes of stone or
mud brick, with temples and public buildings of masonry and some form of defensive perimeter, little different from the humbler *poleis* in the Aegean.

The only other urban people was the Carthaginian. They had come by sea, and
their cities were without exception coastal. They were preoccupied with trade, and
a good harbor was essential to them. A number of their cities, including Motya in
western Sicily, the best known of them, were on small islands, protected from
their often hostile hinterlands. But the few Greek settlements in the western Mediterranean were similar to those in the Aegean, a naturally defended site within
easy reach of good farmland.

Urban civilization was restricted to the Mediterranean basin, and even here was
developed only where Greeks, Etruscans, and Carthaginians had settled. Beyond
its limits were settlements, built by the Iberians or Celts, which were urban in
size but not in the sophistication of their construction and public buildings. Some
may have had few permanent inhabitants and may have served primarily as refuges. Most lay on rising ground and were protected by banks and ditches which
in the most elaborate instances formed a series of concentric lines of defense. Occasionally their defenses were of masonry, as, for example, at Ensérune in Provence

6   Pausanius, X.4.1.; *Geographi Graeci Minores,* I, 99.

and Heuneburg in south Germany. They were very numerous in France where some of them offered a fierce resistance to the Roman conquerors in the first century B.C.; in southern Britain and in much of Spain.

In the plain of northern Europe such protected settlements were fewer. Naturally defended sites were less numerous, and settlements had more often to protect themselves by water and marsh. Among them was Biskupin, built upon an island in a small lake in central Poland. A rising water level forced its abandonment, and it was buried beneath peat and lake deposits. When excavated it proved to be oval in plan, covering almost five acres and protected by, in addition to the water of the lake, a stout palisade. Within were thirteen rows of wooden houses, straight and parallel to one another; in all, more than a hundred houses and a population of more than five hundred. The settlement was primarily agricultural; it had no pretentious buildings, nothing, in fact, to distinguish it from several other such settlements in the northern plain. Yet in size, in its orderly plan, and in its defenses it was clearly approximate to the idea of a city. The urban concept was spreading slowly from the Hellenic world westward and northward into Europe. When, some four to five hundred years later, the Romans brought western and part of central Europe within their empire (see Chap. 3) the ground was already laid for a true urban expansion.

Less is known about rural settlement in the Mediterranean basin, because buildings were less substantial and durable. About half the population of the Athenian *polis* must have lived outside its central city. Most appear to have had their homes in compact villages, though there were also scattered farmsteads and large estate farms like the one described by Xenophon.[7] There were also isolated steadings in the mountains where the shepherds and charcoal burners lived and worked. The settlement pattern must have been broadly similar throughout the Greek world. In their hinterlands, however, were large villages tightly clustered on protective, hilltop sites, such as have survived until today in many parts of Mediterranean Europe. An exception is provided in the *nuraghi* of Sardinia. These were tall, round, masonry structures which dominated clusters of circular, stonebuilt huts. They were probably built for defense, and the tradition of building such towering structures may have derived from archaic Greece and was continued in the *brochs* of northern Britain.

In non-Mediterranean Europe the dominant settlement pattern was one of small villages or hamlets. They varied greatly in site, plan, and style, but data are inadequate for generalization. Many, perhaps most, lay within a short distance of a fortified enclosure which served as their central-place and refuge. Scattered settlements were not uncommon, but they must have been exposed to some danger in this age of internecine warfare. Peasant huts were built mainly of wood, like those excavated at Biskupin. Some were of turf and in some areas, like Dartmoor in southern England and Scandinavia, the rough stone which rose to the surface of the soil was used. Most were probably roofed with branches, occasionally with

7 *Oeconomicus*, IX, XII.

rafters and thatch. Most were rectangular in plan, with a length considerably in excess of their width. Such "long houses" belong to an ancient European tradition which goes back to the Danubian peasants of the Neolithic and was continued until the recent past. The walls were commonly of posts driven into the ground, with the interstices filled with wattle and clay.

Sometimes the huts were aligned on each side of what may have been a road – the origin, perhaps, of the "street-villages" of later times. In marshy areas, such as Frisia, groups of houses were sometimes built on artificial mounds, or *terpen*, which were heightened as the water table rose higher in the damper conditions of the classical period. In Switzerland some settlements were built on *crannogs*, or artificial islands built up from the floor of shallow lakes. The evidence from excavated sites in the Polish and Russian plains is scanty. Here village settlements had to face not only a rising water level, but also the ever present danger from the horsemen of the steppe. Most were protected in some way. A good example is Starzykowe Małe in northern Poland. It consisted of some eight houses with outbuildings, set roughly in a circle and protected by a double rampart of stones. The whole was set on a peninsula of dry land, with lake or marsh on three sides. Hundreds of such villages, once inhabited by peasants, have been found in the belt of broad-leaved forests which stretched eastward across Russia to the Volga and the Ural Mountains.

Farther north, beyond the limits of settled agriculture, were small fishing communities along the shores of the Baltic Sea and the Norwegian fjords. The inhabitants of these communities used tools and weapons made largely of bone. In the interior of Scandinavia and in northern Russia was a scanty population of hunter-herders. They were nomadic, but not without homes to which they returned in the course of their seasonal wanderings. Their economy was Stone Age, but here the Stone Age lasted into times which, farther south, might be called historic.

Agriculture

Most of Europe practiced a subsistence agriculture, and trade in foodstuffs was restricted to a few parts of the Hellenic world. The nature of agriculture in Attica is fairly well known from the Greek writers. Soils were poor and stony, but Athenians made the most of them, terracing hillslopes for cultivation up to heights of one thousand feet. At higher levels, however, there was only rough grazing for sheep, and dry woodland and scrub which provided fuel for cooking. Forest was fast disappearing before the charcoal burner and the goat, and the hillslopes were becoming scarred by erosion.

The crops grown on the lower ground were mainly breadgrains. Barley, which did moderately well on dry, alkaline soils, was the most widespread, but wheat occupied about a seventh of the cultivated area. Vegetables, including beans and lentils, were the chief source of protein. Milk, mainly from goats, was drunk; meat was eaten sparingly; fish was important, but olive oil was the chief source of

2.4. A light Greek plow,
as shown on a vase

fats. It was a sparse diet in which cakes and gruel made from barley provided most
of the substance.

Attica was a land of peasant cultivators who must have been able to provide for
their own sustenance and, over and above, could send some oil, wine, or vegetables
to supply the city. Nevertheless, up to half the grain supply of Athens was imported, chiefly from the coastlands of the Black Sea. Large estates did exist, but
they were rare. That belonging to one, Phainippos, had from seven hundred to a
thousand acres and must have been worked by slave labor. But the family farm
was as a general rule within the range of thirty to fifty acres.

Cultivation was on a two-field system, the fields being cultivated in alternate
years. The fields themselves were almost certainly small and probably square. Field
boundaries were built mainly of stones removed from the soil. Cultivation was by
means of a light plow such as was described by Hesiod and painted on Athenian
vases (Fig. 2.4). The few animals that were kept spent much of their time on the
hills, so that the supply of manure was small.

Attica was not in all respects typical of Greece. Boeotia directly to the north
was moister; its alluvial soils were richer, and its crops evidently heavier. The
well-fed Boeotian was not only the butt of Athenian wit but also the envy of his
neighbor. In Thessaly and amid the mountains to the west grazing was more
extensive and the balance was probably tipped in favor of animal husbandry, the
lowlands providing winter grazing while the highlands were used in summer.

The cities of Magna Graecia were better endowed than those of Greece itself.
Plains were richer and more extensive, and some of the *poleis*, notably Sybaris and
Akragas, were noted for their plenty. As one passed up the Italian peninsula, the
climate became moister and the soils in general richer. Rome and Etruria were far
better suited to crop farming than the Aegean region. The vine became less important, the olive disappeared, and wheat began to replace barley. The lowlands
of Latium and Etruria were settled by peasant farmers, while pastoralism, as is
apparent from the pages of Livy, prevailed in the mountainous interior.

Mediterranean agriculture showed no great advance on that practiced north of
the Alps, where the same kinds of crops were cultivated in much the same way.
But cultivable land was more abundant in northern Europe, and the peasant could

practice a shifting agriculture, tilling a patch for a few years before abandoning it and plowing another. The soils were mostly light and easily plowed. Fields appear, on the evidence of surviving "Celtic" field patterns, to have been small and compact, suited to the light plow, or *ard,* which was generally used. This did not turn the soil, and subsoil striations which have been found suggest that fields were cross-plowed. Breadgrains were more varied than in southern Europe. Barley was still important, but rye was beginning to appear among cultivated crops. The varieties of wheat generally cultivated were emmer and spelt, forms which have since been very largely displaced by others which either yield more heavily or can be milled with greater ease. Even at this early date we find that man, albeit unconsciously, was introducing genetic changes into the crops which he cultivated by his selection of seed for planting.

Throughout Europe, north of the Alps, animal rearing was important. Meat and milk were essential parts of the human diet. Cattle were used for the plow, and horses were bred for war and for drawing the chariots of the Celts. There had been a shift in the balance between different species. Sheep and horses had been comparatively few. Then in the Iron Age the position was reversed. Pigs became fewer, sheep and cattle more numerous, and the number of horses greatly increased. This can only have been due to the destruction of woodland, the natural haunt of the pig, and the increase in cleared land suitable for sheep. Broadly speaking, arable husbandry diminished in importance toward the north as animal rearing increased, and in Scandinavia and the Baltic region the balance was tipped in favor of animals, mainly cattle, in this cool and damp climate.

Only rarely can one gain an insight through excavation into the economy of a rural settlement. This is, however, being achieved at sites in southern England, notably at Danebury and Figheldean, both located on the chalk of Salisbury Plain. The latter held a community of some 275 persons, who cultivated an area of about 370 acres. The tilled land formed compact blocks, separated by unenclosed land which must have provided pasture (Fig. 2.5). This was grazed in summer, while in winter the animals were kept in enclosed fields which thus received a small amount of manure. The cereal could not be sown until spring, and this probably meant that barley was the chief crop. In the vicinity was a hilltop fort which provided refuge, shelter and storage space for the inhabitants of Figheldean.[8] Their actual huts must have been grouped among the fields, but their sites have not been found.

At Figheldean the seasonal movement of farm animals was over only a short distance. But at this time there were also long-distance migrations as farming people learned to use marginal land for only part of the year. In some instances, as in Scandinavia and the Alps, they took their stock higher up the mountainside in summer and brought it back to lower ground for the winter. Such transhumance probably derived from earlier and preagricultural patterns of movement and was

8   Shimon Applebaum, "The Agriculture of the British Early Iron Age," *Proceedings of the Prehistoric Society* (1954): 103–14.

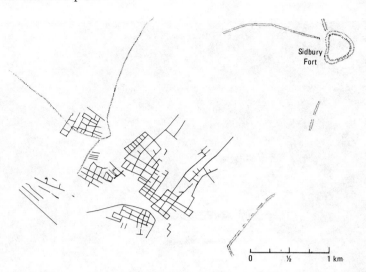

Sidbury
Fort

0   ½   1 km

2.5. A Celtic field system in southern Britain. Small, subrectangular fields were dependent on the hill fort, shown top right

to be found throughout the hilly and mountainous areas of Europe. And there it has in some places continued to be practiced until today.

In the steppe of southern Russia the settled agriculturalists gave way to pastoralists, the seminomadic Scythians, who moved with their herds over the grasslands, lording it over the settled farmers of the forest margin who supplied them with breadgrains. The moister western parts of the steppe were excellent cropland, and were the source of much of the grain imported by Athens and a few other *poleis*.

Manufacturing and mining

In the fifth century manufacturing was little more than a domestic craft, though some historians claim that there were in Athens a few large workshops manned by slaves. Only in mining was the scale of operations significantly larger. For Athens alone does the literary and epigraphical evidence allow one to build up a picture of manufacturing activities. Most were carried on in workshops which opened off the streets and courts of the city. Here lived the masons and bronze workers, tanners and leatherworkers, fullers, dyers, and weavers. The congestion, with its accompanying heat, noise, and smells, is left to our imagination. Some craftsmen, particularly masons, lived outside the city and commuted to their daily work. Some crafts tended to concentrate in particular districts; *Kerameikos* was the home of many of the potters. Indeed, it has given its name to "ceramics." There was also a "Street of the Marble Workers." Spinning and weaving were carried on in the home, and every housewife was, like Penelope in the *Odyssey,* employed con-

2.6. A Greek shoemaker shown measuring for a pair of lady's shoes. [After a Greek vase illustrated in H. Blümner, *Technologie und Terminologie der Gewerbe und Kunste bei Griechen und Römern* (Leipzig, 1912).]

tinuously, but doubtless more effectively, with distaff and loom. The cloth was then dyed and fulled.

Xenophon in the *Cyropaedia* compared the narrow specialization of craftsmen in the larger towns with the breadth of their activities in the small. In the latter, he wrote, "the same workman works chairs and doors and plows and tables, and often . . . houses, and even so he is thankful if he can only find employment enough to support him. . . . In large cities . . . inasmuch as many people have demands to make upon each branch of industry, one trade alone, and very often even less than a whole trade, is enough to support a man: one man, for instance, makes shoes for men, and another for women; and there are places even where one man earns a living by only stitching shoes, another by cutting them out, another by sewing the uppers together, while there is another who performs none of these operations but only assembles the parts."[9] Adam Smith had nothing over Xenophon.

The level of Greek technology was low and showed little advance on that of the age of Homer. It is customary to blame this on the institution of slavery, which kept the cost of labor down. Vase paintings are a prolific source of information on the crafts of ancient Greece (Figs. 2.6 and 2.7). They show weaving being carried on with a narrow vertical loom; iron being smelted to a bloom of soft iron in a low-shaft furnace, and forged to simple shapes on an anvil; and pots being turned on a wheel operated by the potter's foot. Spinning and weaving were found every-

9 *Cyropaedia,* Loeb, ed. (Cambridge, Mass., 1968), I, 333.

2.7. A Greek smith, as shown on a vase. [After H. Blümner, *Technologie und Terminologie der Gewerbe und Kunste bei Griechen und Römern* (Leipzig, 1912).]

where. Ironworking was more localized, and some Greek cities developed their own specializations: swords in Chalcis, helmets in Boeotia, knives in Laconia, and breastplates in Argos. Athens itself was known for the quality of its pottery, and fine pieces were prominent among its exports. Masons and sculptors were numerous and highly skilled, but it does not appear that any attempt was ever made to burn bricks, though ceramic tiles were used on public buildings. Lead was used with the dowels which held pieces of masonry together, but, apparently, not in water-supply systems. That was left for the Romans.

No other city had the variety of crafts to be met with in Athens, though Corinth exported bronzes and pottery; Chalcis and Sicyon, metal goods; and Megara, coarse clothing. The cities of Magna Graecia each had their specialized industries, of which potting, weaving, and ironworking were the most important. But the chief center of the ancient iron industry was Etruria. Its focus was Populonia, lying on the coast opposite the island of Elba which supplied the best iron ore, as it continued to do into the nineteenth century. Smelting was largely carried on in the interior of Tuscany, where charcoal was more abundant.

The same range of crafts was practiced by the Celtic peoples north of the Alps. Bronze continued to be employed in the art of the Celts, but for more serious purposes iron alone was used. Methods of smelting and refining were closely similar to those employed and illustrated by the Greeks. A few furnaces have been excavated, and the great extent of slag heaps of the period, especially near Siegen in northwest Germany gives some idea of the scale on which the industry was carried on.

Mining and quarrying were clearly important both to Mediterranean and to northern peoples. Greece itself was poorly mineralized. Some gold was obtained from alluvial deposits in the north; there were pockets of iron ore, which were quickly exhausted, and also important reserves of copper in Cyprus. But the most important were the silver-lead deposits of Laureion, near the southeastern tip of Attica. The mines were worked with slave labor by individuals who leased them from the Athenian state. Individually the mines were very small, but together they yielded large quantities of silver and may have employed twenty thousand slaves. Methods were primitive and labor-intensive; much of the ore was wasted and it proved profitable in the nineteenth century to rework the tailings from the ancient mines for the silver they still contained.

Iron ore was obtained from countless small deposits, which were quickly exhausted and abandoned. Ores, however, varied greatly in quality, and even at this date the metal from certain areas like Tuscany, the Siegerland, and the eastern Alps was particularly valued.

Copper was mined and smelted in the Kitzbühel Alps of Austria, which must have yielded immense quantities of metal. Other deposits were also exploited at this time in Hungary, the Ore Mountains of Bohemia, and the Harz. Without an admixture of tin, copper could not easily be hardened, and tin was one of the least widespread of metals. Some was found in the Ore Mountains, but the only significant sources were northwestern Spain, Brittany, and Cornwall. It is likely that much of the tin used in the fifth century came from Cornwall. Diodorus Siculus, writing in the first century B.C., is quite explicit on the matter. It was panned from the valley gravels and shipped from an offshore island known as *Ictis,* probably St. Michael's Mount. It is likely that his account would have been no less accurate four centuries earlier, but who the merchants were, whether Greek, Carthaginian, or Celtic, we do not know.

Trade

At a time when most communities were largely, if not entirely self-sufficing, long-distance trade was limited in volume and restricted in its range and variety. That carried on by the Greek *poleis* was by far the largest and most diverse. "It is almost impossible," wrote Plato, "to found a state . . . where it will not need imports."[10] The nature of this trade is known, but not its volume. The latter has become a matter of debate, some arguing that the Greeks carried on an exchange, on a very considerable scale, of their own manufactures for grain and raw materials from less-developed regions. To Athens and a few other city-states trade was important, but the great majority could have had no exportable surplus of anything with which to requite any imports there might have been. And at Athens the only large-scale trade was the import of breadgrain. This came partly from Sicily, Euboea, Thessaly, and Macedonia, but mainly from the shores of the Black Sea by

10   *Republic,* II, 370e.

way of the Bosporus and Dardanelles. The trade was controlled at its northern end by the Scythians, who received in return for grain some of the finest Athenian pottery and metalwork. Indeed, pottery of identifiable Attic origin has been found over much of the Mediterranean basin and is evidence of close and continuing commercial contacts. It is probable that such items were received in return for grain.

Athens was the largest, but not the only importer of cereals in the Greek world. Corinth, Sicyon, and Argos also had to satisfy part of their needs by overseas trade. A number of other cities seem, at least occasionally, to have had recourse to trade in order to maintain their own food supply. Only the cities of Magna Graecia had no reason to fear food shortages, largely because of the great extent of their cultivable land. At the time of the Second Persian War, Gelon of Syracuse offered "to provision the entire Greek army for as long as the war may last,"[11] a claim which was fortunately not put to the test. It is a measure of the dependence of some city-states on grain imports that part of their strategy in the Peloponnesian War consisted in blockading the food supply of others.

Breadgrains and pottery loom large in the trade of classical Greece, but they were by no means the only commodities shipped into and out of the ports. There was a trade in wine and olive oil; in wool from western Greece and flax from the Black Sea; in skins and hides. Fish was caught in abundance around the Aegean shores and, dried or salted, was sent to the cities. Anthedon, according to Dicaearchus, was peopled largely by "fishermen, living by their hooks, by the purple shell [murex, source of "purple" dye] and by sponges."[12]

Athens in the fifth century was the focus of this varied commerce. Everyone, wrote Xenophon, "who would cross Greece. . . . passes Athens as the center of a circle, whether he goes by water or by road,"[13] and its port of Piraeus was a natural entrepôt, whose activity he sought to expand. Athens had the great advantage of a deep, sheltered harbor, around the shores of which covered "ship houses" were built for the construction and repair of ships. Jetties were sometimes built of large stones, but often the small ships were merely dragged up the beach, as in Homeric times, beyond the reach of the waves of this almost tideless sea.

Very much less is known of trade in the western Mediterranean than in the Aegean. In volume it was probably far larger than would appear to have been the case from historical sources. Immense quantities of Attic pottery have been excavated at the Greek colony of Massilia (Marseilles), but what they contained and how they were paid for is far from clear. In the end, however, Greek trade was largely driven from the western Mediterranean by the Carthaginians, who continued to dominate its commerce until they in turn were ousted by the Romans. It was probably the Carthaginian control of the sea and, from their port of Tartessos, the biblical Tarshish, of the Straits of Gibraltar that led to the development of a trade in Cornish tin *across* France. Certainly the commerce of the Greeks began to

11   Herodotus, VII, 158.
12   *Geographi Graeci Minores,* I, 104.
13   *On the Revenues,* I, 6–7.

penetrate central Europe after their exclusion from the western basin of the Mediterranean Sea. This trade was probably not large. It may have embraced furs and skins, but its most important items were amber and metals, chiefly copper and iron. The Etruscans certainly shared in this trade, and may, indeed, have been the principal partners.

Trade within northern Europe was on a far smaller and more restricted scale than in the Mediterranean. We may assume that each community was self-sufficing, and that there was no trade in grain. Objects of trade were very largely the metals – iron, copper, and tin – and other materials like obsidian, from which tools were made. There must also have been a trade in salt from such salt springs as Hallstatt, and, as has been seen, amber was dispatched south to the Mediterranean. Among Celtic imports from the Mediterranean world were wine and the vessels in which to store and drink it. Celtic thirst, it has been said, was a very important factor in trade with the classical world. [14]

FROM GREECE TO ROME

In 431 B.C. war broke out between Athens and Sparta, a war which quickly engulfed the whole Hellenic world. When it ended twenty-seven years later, Athens was prostrate and Sparta severely weakened. Population had been lost and wealth destroyed. The golden age of Greek civilization had ended. The age of the *poleis,* small, jealous, and quarrelsome, was over, and hegemony in Greece passed to other powers and groupings. At first Thebes, controlling the whole of Boeotia, played this role. Then primacy passed to the immeasurably larger and stronger Macedonia which began to absorb neighboring city-states, until the Hellenic world was largely under its control.

Greek civilization had been achieved under the shadow of the Persians. This danger remained, and Alexander of Macedonia dealt with it through a course which Hellas could never have taken – by invading the Persian empire, defeating its armies, and conquering its territory. Greek influences were spread through the Middle East, and some seventy cities were founded on the Greek model. Yet neither Greek culture nor Macedonian authority were able to impose any kind of unity on this vast area which stretched from Epirus (Albania) to the Indus River. It broke up into the Hellenistic states which continued to fight and intrigue until they were overcome by the greater might and strength of purpose of Rome. Within the Greek world the will to independence of the *poleis* was ended, and they were merged into territorial states which paid scant regard to their pride and privilege.

In the meanwhile that little *polis* which had grown up beside the Tiber was following a not dissimilar line of development. It lay, like Macedonia, just beyond the fringe of the Hellenic world, and in a kind of no-man's-land between it and the Etruscans. The Greeks destroyed themselves; at the same time the Etruscan power was destroyed by the Romans. Rome was transformed into a territorial

14   J. M. de Navarro, "Massilia and Early Celtic Culture," *Antiquity* 2 (1928): 423–42.

state, in a world dominated increasingly by large political units. The ambitions of a city-state were limited by its restricted resources. The territorial state was less constrained. Conflict led to conquest and these encounters, first with the Italic tribes of Italy, then with Epirus and Carthage, led on – domino fashion – until Rome found itself in possession of an empire. Conquest bred conquest, and empire led only to an extension of empire in order to protect what had already been won. By the time the Roman Republic gave place to the Principate in 29 B.C., it remained only to consolidate and organize the territories conquered and to establish a definitive and defensible frontier around them.

In terms of political geography the changes that had taken place in the previous five hundred years had been profound. In other respects, however, comparatively little had changed. Population had probably increased, though of this there is little evidence. Some cities had grown greatly, like Rome, while others, including Athens, Corinth, and Syracuse, had declined in size and importance. Yet others, like Megalopolis, had been founded and had both blossomed and died within the period. Rural settlement was, in all probability, little changed before the first century A.D. Only then did the Romans attempt on any significant scale to relocate population in the provinces in order to break down their tribal loyalties and minimize their military danger.

There was a certain logic in the expansion of the Roman empire, each advance being conditioned by the circumstances of the previous conquest. The empire reached its greatest extent in Europe during the second century A.D. Over six hundred years of territorial growth then came to an end, the basic problems of the empire still unresolved. These were the question of defense against the barbarian world beyond its borders, and that of reconciling imperial rule with a sociopolitical structure which in its essentials derived from the *polis*. The Romans never really reconciled *polis* with empire.

THE ROMAN EMPIRE IN THE SECOND CENTURY

We have it on the authority of Edward Gibbon, the historian, that the second century A.D., when the Roman empire was presided over in succession by the emperors Hadrian, Antoninus Pius, and Marcus Aurelius, was one of the happiest in the whole span of human history. Contemporaries would have agreed with this judgment. Aristeides wrote of the profound and unbroken peace which prevailed, and Tertullian, commenting on what we would call "economic growth" wrote that "cultivated fields have overcome the forests; the sands are being planted, the rocks hewn, the swamp drained; there are as many cities today as there were formerly huts."[15]

This picture is, without question, overdrawn. Peace was broken along the frontiers. There were internal revolts against Roman rule, and economic growth was very slow. Techniques of production developed little, if at all, in part because the

15 *De Anima,* 30.3.

aristrocratic cast of mind of the ruling classes did not readily concern itself with invention and in part because there was an abundant supply of slave labor. Yet much of Europe nevertheless enjoyed a more lasting peace than had been experienced before, and the Roman conquest brought a style of urban living to regions which had previously known only the rude self-sufficiency of the village community. "Men ought to draw together into cities," wrote Cassiodorus,[16] and, despite literary expressions of love for rural life, it was urban living which attracted the Romans and which they sought to impose on their subject peoples.

The Romans never wholly abandoned the concept of the *polis*. The cities which they created throughout their empire were centers of consumption and foci of administration for their local regions. The empire became, in effect, "a vast federation of city-states."[17] Ease of movement within the empire, both of people and of goods, opened up every corner of it to outside influences. If the *forum* in every small town represented the cultural legacy of Rome, the temple of Mithra and the Christian church reflected the external influences which Rome was gradually absorbing and assimilating. But cultural influences were not all in one direction. Trade preceded the advance of empire, and Roman artifacts were to be found far beyond its limits.

Political geography

Augustus left as his testament for his successors the advice to keep to the current bounds of empire. On the whole they followed his advice. In Britain the boundary was stabilized along the lines of Hadrian's Wall. In continental Europe the line of the Rhine and Danube was adopted, and excursions beyond it were limited to the so-called *Agri Decumates*, between the upper reaches of the two rivers, and Dacia (Romania). The former was protected, like northern Britain, by a physical wall with forts and towers. No such barrier was possible elsewhere, and it was difficult, amid the shifting channels of the Rhine mouth or of the Danube delta, to know where the limit of Roman authority lay.

Within these limits the empire was divided into provinces under the direct control of either emperor or senate. Within each were *civitates* or city-regions, the Roman equivalent of the *polis*. Many corresponded, if only approximately, with earlier tribal areas. The Roman process of detribalization was nowhere complete, and in many areas the urban central-place was heir to the pre-Roman tribal center. In some cases it was moved, as from high ground to low. In Britain there were a dozen such "tribal" cities, most retaining the name of the tribe which they represented, as at Isca *Dumnoniorum* (Exeter) and Calleva *Atrebatum* (Silchester), belonging respectively to the *Dumnoni* and the *Atrebates* (Fig. 2.8). In Gaul, according to Tacitus, there were sixty-four, though the true number was probably greater. In Spain their number was a great deal higher, and most were excessively small. In the Balkans, by contrast, the mountainous terrain and sparser population dictated

16   *Letters,* ed. T. Hodgkin (1886), VIII, 31.
17   M. Rostovtzeff, *The Social and Economic History of the Roman Empire* (Oxford, 1926–57), I, 135.

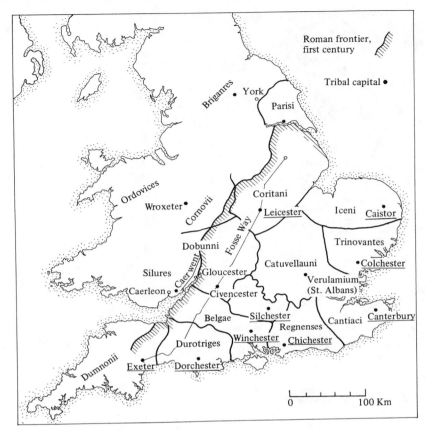

2.8. The tribal areas of Roman Britain and their capitals, as established by the Romans

units which were larger and fewer than in the west. It was the policy of the Romans to allow the city to be an expression of the individuality and pride of the local *civitas,* but also the medium for its Romanization. Even in Italy, which had been under Rome's control for centuries, the legacy of the Italic tribes was apparent in the "several hundreds of fairly independent town territories."[18]

Peoples of the Roman empire

The empire was from the start ethnically diverse, and its internal conditions encouraged the movement of people within it. There was little racial prejudice within the empire, though aristocratic citizens of Rome expressed their grave misgivings at the influx of easterners. "I cannot endure a Rome that is full of Greeks," wrote Juvenal, and Seneca wrote disparagingly of the footloose swarms who were at-

18 Rudi Thomsen, "The Italic Regions," *Classica et Medievalia Dissertationes,* IV (Copenhagen, 1947), 11.

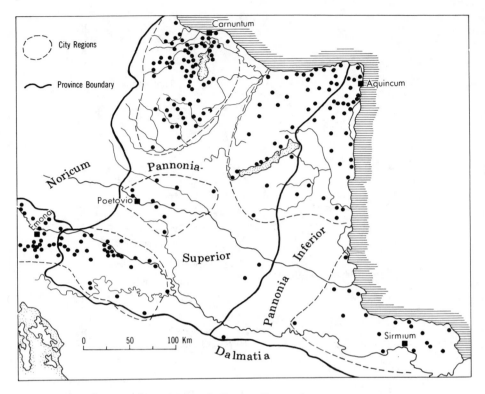

2.9. The distribution of inscriptions in Roman Pannonia

tracted to the city by the prospect of comfort or profit. "The Syrian [river] Orontes," wrote Juvenal, "has long since poured into the Tiber."[19] Rome had, in fact, become a great, cosmopolitan city, and the same was probably true of all the larger urban centers. Inscriptions which have survived show an increasing proportion of names of Greek or Middle Eastern origin.

The empire was, in a sense, the "melting pot" of the ancient world, in which varied groups lost their individuality and merged to make a Roman people. This process of migration and assimilation was always continuing and never complete. Within the European empire the process of Romanization was diffused from its urban centers. It never fully reached remote areas. "There were always barbarians within the Roman Empire, left to themselves in remote mountains and deserts, or recently incorporated by conquest."[20] Most acquiesced to Roman rule, provided that it did not interfere with their traditional way of life. They valued the peace it ensured and the occasional artifact that came their way. Figures 2.9 and 2.10 illustrate from the province of Pannonia, very roughly Transdanubian Hungary, two aspects of Romanization, the use of Latin inscriptions and the building of

19 *Satires*, III, 62.
20 Ramsay MacMullen, "Barbarian Enclaves in the Northern Roman Empire," *L'Antiquité Classique* 32 (1963): 552.

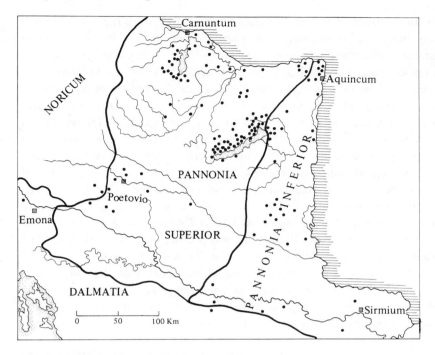

2.10. The distribution of villas in Roman Pannonia

rural villas. Both occur in clusters, each cluster centering in a Roman city. Between the clusters lay open spaces which, on this evidence, had been little influenced by the civilization of Rome.

Such a pattern was repeated in every province. Nowhere was there a uniform leveling up of cultural standards, only islands of progress which expanded slowly, in some places imperceptibly, into the cultural realm of the last Iron Age. There is no means of knowing the extent to which Latin displaced Celtic and other languages. It probably did so only to a small degree, and every province, barring perhaps Italy, remained multilingual. In the third century the validity of legal documents written in a Celtic language was accepted, and there is the statement by St. Jerome that the *Treveri,* a people whose tribal capital was the important city of *Augusta Treverorum* (Trier), still spoke Celtic in his day.[21] The Celtic language had certainly not disappeared from western Britain, and perhaps not even from eastern.

Lastly, peoples, collectively known as "barbarians," were continuously filtering into the empire, attracted by employment and higher standards. Some were invited by the Romans who needed the labor they could provide. Many were enlisted in the legions. Sometimes whole tribes were settled within the empire, and Marcus Aurelius himself admitted some three thousand of the *Navistae* tribe.

21 Patrologia Latina, XXXVI, col. 382.

The line of defense which stretched from northern Britain to the Black Sea was no ordinary boundary. It separated two worlds. Trade crossed it, and goods of Roman origin found their way deep into barbarian territory, but standards of living and of conduct differed sharply on each side. The Danube and Rhine were the Rio Grande of the ancient world. Beyond this line clan and tribal organization prevailed, but ethnic patterns were no more clear-cut than within the empire. Linguistically speaking, one may say that a Celtic people was being intruded upon by a Germanic, while to the east the emergent Slavs were very slowly advancing eastward into the Russian forests. But no one people ever completely displaced another. They merged and fused, the invaders sometimes constituting a kind of "feudal" elite. Nor were the languages they spoke clearly distinguished from one another. There were without question tribal dialects, so that language ceased to be a valid basid for classifying peoples. Although Tacitus named some tribes, he rarely indicated their linguistic affinities; he was probably not aware of them. The tribal organization which he described was fluid. Tribes would merge and divide, and some of those named by Tacitus disappeared from history not long afterward. He did, however, recognize the Germans as a cultural group, the chief characteristic of which was that they lived in permanent settlements. They were, indeed, a settled agricultural people, but one which periodically pulled up its roots and migrated.

East of the Germans lived the Slavs, a settled agricultural people of the northern forests. Tacitus's *Venedi* were almost certainly Slav, and he distinguished them from the Germans, though for the wrong reasons. Their settlements were sparse, so that migrating Germans could pass through them as if by a kind of osmosis. Tacitus peopled the vast area to the north of the Danube with a number of tribes. Some were almost certainly part of the great outward movement of the Celts; others were probably Germanic, ancestors of those who invaded the empire in the fifth century. Yet others, the *Iazyges* of the Pannonian plain, for example, were related to the Scythians of southern Russia and were still seminomadic pastoralists. Apart from the latter, these were mostly a settled farming people, who used iron tools and tilled the soil with light wooden plows. Farther north, and east of the Baltic Sea, were agricultural peoples, ancestors of the Baltic peoples, who, in Tacitus's words, "seldom use weapons of iron." Clearly the Iron Age was just beginning to dawn. Beyond them lived the Fenni. "They eat grass, dress in skins and sleep on the ground. Their only hope is in their arrows, which for lack of iron, they tip with bone."[22] These were preagricultural people who, in cultural terms, belonged to the Mesolithic and lower Neolithic phases of the Stone Age.

Population

The population of Europe was unquestionably larger in the second century than at any time previously and, in all probability, bigger than at any subsequent time

22 Tacitus, *Germania,* 46, 3–4.

before the end of the Middle Ages. The urbanization of Roman society, the rising level of welfare, the extension of agriculture, and the volume of specialized production and trade are all both evidence for and explanation of this increase.

The Romans were accustomed to holding regular censuses, the results of which are, in part, recorded by Livy. Their value is, however, severely limited by our ignorance of who it was who was actually being counted. The city of Rome presented the greatest concentration of population that Europe had up to this time known. Yet there is no acceptable measure of its size; less is known of it than of Athens six centuries earlier. The most promising line of enquiry seeks to elucidate the density of housing within the city. This varied very greatly. Large areas were occupied by public buildings. The district beyond the Tiber – known today as Trastevere – was characterized by low density villas of the rich. By contrast, densely inhabited apartment blocks or *insulae* covered a considerable though uncertain area. The most reasonable estimates, based on such data, range from 800,000 to 1.2 million. Wherever the truth lay, the population was large enough to present immense problems in housing, food supply, and entertainment. Down the Tiber from Rome lay the city's port, Ostia. Here one can come closer to an answer, because much of it has survived, albeit in ruins. Nevertheless, estimates of its size vary from 27,000 to 60,000.

On the basis of agricultural resources and the known level of technology, the population of the Italian peninsula has been put at 6 to 9 million, and that of Sicily more reliably at 600,000 to a million. Evidence for Gaul consists of little more than Julius Caesar's estimates of the size of the tribes. An estimate between 6 and 10 million seems plausible but cannot be substantiated. Southern Spain was densely populated, but the north and west very much more sparsely. The total for the Iberian peninsula may have been between 7 and 12 million. Britain may have had up to 2.5 million, and the Danubian and Balkan provinces each between 3 and 6 million. The total population of the Roman empire within Europe is likely to have been between 27 and 47 million, but these figures, it must be emphasized, are no more than intelligent guesses.

Beyond the bounds of the empire there is no evidence for the size of the population. We can only say that the resources of the land and the level of technology together set an upper limit. Such an argument suggests some 3 to 5 million in central Europe, and a great deal less in eastern and northern.

Settlement

Urban development was very much more advanced than six centuries earlier. Overall, cities were more numerous and had spread to the outer limits of the empire. There were cities along the Rhine and Danube, outposts of urbanism on the very edge of barbarism. The government encouraged their foundation. In Britain, according to Tacitus, the governor, Agricola, "gave private encouragement and official assistance to the building of temples, public squares and private mansions" and, in the jaundiced view of Tacitus, "the Britons were gradually led on to the amenities that make vice agreeable – arcades, and sumptuous banquets."[23] When all allowance is made for Tacitus's prejudice, it does appear that the Roman city had little more than a civilizing function, that it had developed no basic economic functions other than agriculture, which could as easily have been carried on from village settlements.

Nevertheless, the empire came to be made up of discrete *territoria,* each with its urban central-place. These were the building blocks of which the empire was made. Wherever possible the Romans took tribal areas as the basis of these units (see Fig. 2.8), relocating the central city where this seemed desirable, or even founding a new one. This process of urban foundation continued into the second century, and the period of the Antonines can be regarded as marking the climax of Roman urbanism. Thereafter cities ceased to grow in number and size, and many actually declined in population. Their status varied with their origin and degree of self-government. The Romans were faced, as we are today, with the problem of defining the city. Many of those in Spain, wrote Strabo, "are the points. . . . from which and to which the people carry on their traffic, not only with one another but also with the outside world." Their basic occupation was commerce. But in his treatment of the Meseta of central Spain he wrote that some claim "that there are more than one thousand cities" (he used the Greek term *poleis*), but added that they did so "by calling the big villages cities; for, in the first place, the country is naturally not capable, on account of the poverty of its soil or else on account of the remoteness and wildness of it, of containing many cities, and, secondly, the modes of life and the activities of the inhabitants . . . do not suggest anything of the kind."[24] Strabo was remarkably perceptive. Legal status did not always agree with economic function, and we who think of a city as an essentially nonrural scene of specialized activities have a false view of the Roman town. Its primary role was its civilizing mission. In the later years of the empire this role wore thin and in some instances the city was left an empty shell.

Of one kind of urban settlement, however, there can be no doubt. The military fort, rigidly planned and encompassed by a wall, was constructed for a specific purpose, and the need for it tended to increase rather than diminish. Close to the military fort was commonly a civil settlement, or *cannaba,* which existed to satisfy the needs of the legions. In some instances the civil settlement acquired urban status in its own right. *Corstopitum* (Corbridge) in northern Britain thus served the garrison on the Roman wall, and *Mogontiacum* (Mainz), *Brigetio* and *Aquincum* (both on the Danube in the Hungarian plain), and *Carnuntum* (Petronell) in lower Austria, all in origin military stations, grew to be civilian towns.

In some instances a pre-Roman fortress, or *oppidum,* was forcibly abandoned, and its inhabitants and functions were relocated on a more approachable or less defensible site. The classic examples are the desertion of the Gallic sites of *Bibracte* and *Gergovia* in favor of respectively Autun and Clermont, and in Britain, of Maiden

23   *Agricola,* 21.
24   Strabo, III, 2, 5; 4, 13.

Castle and Bagindon for *Durnovaria* (Dorchester) and *Corinium* (Cirencester). Most Roman towns, however, continued to occupy the sites of pre-Roman tribal centers, and inherited whatever functions the latter had performed. In the Greek world, most of the urban central-places of the fifth century continued to be occupied, though time had dealt harshly with some of them. Their semi-independent status had ended and some had been merged in a grand act of synoecism to create a new city, just as Augustus had founded Nicopolis from the remains of many local *poleis*.

Because the definition of "city" is so variable, it is almost impossible to estimate their number. The map in Figure 2.11 is only tentative. Where cities were numerous, as in southern Spain, central Italy, and Greece, they were in general very small. Where they formed an open and fairly even pattern, as in Gaul and the Balkan provinces, they are more likely to have been relatively large and deliberately planted. In many instances the urban area can be measured because its walls have survived, but some defenses were not built until late in the imperial period, when conditions were more disturbed, and are not a true reflection of urban size in the second century. Some were large cities by any standard before the nineteenth century. *Nemausus* (Nîmes), *Vienna* (Vienne), and *Augustodunum* (Autun) — all of them in Gaul — each covered 500 acres or more, whereas there were other undoubted cities in Gaul which had less than 25 acres. With the onset of invasions at the end of the third century, the walled area of the larger cities was contracted in order, presumably, to make their defense easier. In a few instances the reduction was drastic: Nîmes from 550 to 20 acres; Autun from 494 to 25. This is a measure of how insubstantial were the functions which some of these cities performed.

The city had to be supported by its surrounding territory, and its public buildings rested on the surplus income of its inhabitants. To this extent they reflected the level of private wealth in their regions. But what if the local elite chose not to invest or live in their central-place? Rivet has pointed out that in Britain villas were more numerous around small towns than near the larger and more important ones. Can one argue from this that in the one case surplus was invested more readily in villas than in town houses? And was there a change in the later years of the empire, with more people opting to live on their estates? In all probability there was, and this was an important factor in the late Roman decay of the city.

The cities of the Roman empire, like Hellenic cities before them, provided a contrast between rigorous planning and totally unplanned growth. The camps of the soldier and the *coloniae* in which time-expired veterans were settled were both arranged in orderly fashion around two main streets which intersected at right angles. The idea was quickly applied to civil foundations. Pompeii was one of the earliest non-Greek cities to exhibit such a plan. It suited the Roman disposition toward order and discipline, and in some degree it was incorporated in the layout of a great many towns in Italy and the provinces. But it called for the exercise of authority, and where this was not present the city plan quickly lapsed into disorder. Outside Italy, where cities were more often founded by the Romans than

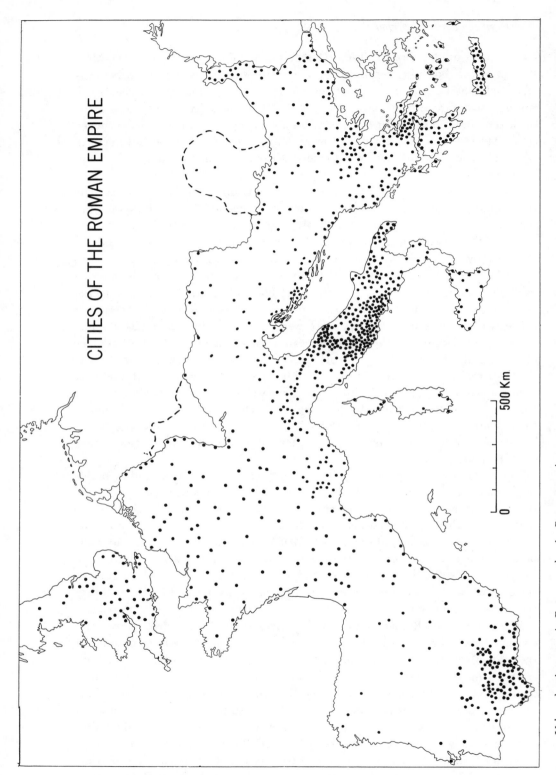

CITIES OF THE ROMAN EMPIRE

500 Km

2.11. Urban development in Europe under the Roman empire

developed from earlier settlements, a regular plan was imposed on urban growth. In a few instances, where the Roman site was subsequently abandoned and never reoccupied, the street patterns have largely been recovered, as at *Venta Icenorum* (Caistor-by-Norwich), *Calleva Atrebatum* (Silchester), and *Aventicum* (Avenches in Switzerland). In others as far apart as Cordoba and Ljubljana, Nîmes and York, street patterns remain recognizable if distorted, but one would be hard put to find a Roman plan in the streets of London or Vienna.

The Roman town was, first and foremost, a place for civilized and urbane living, where the wealthier provincials might live in comfort, taking some part in local administration but, above all, posing no threat to the authority of Rome. The smallest had necessarily some commercial functions, if only because their citizens had to be supplied and fed. There must also have been craftsmen who worked for a local clientele. In larger towns, like Lyons, Nîmes, and London, these functions were conducted on a bigger scale and served a wider area. In very few indeed was there any form of specialized manufacture serving the needs of distant and unseen markets.

City buildings varied greatly in style and density. Some cities were made up largely of spacious villas; in others rows of buildings which combined the functions of dwelling and workshop lined the streets. The ground-floor room opened onto the street by a wide-arched opening. These were *tabernae,* shops, in which the craftsman both made and sold his wares. Only a little altered in the course of eighteen centuries, *tabernae* continue to characterize the older quarters of Naples, Dubrovnik, and many other cities, and ossified, they can be seen still at Pompeii and Ostia. Urban building rarely ran to more than two stories. Only in Rome and Ostia were tall apartment blocks known. Urban building was usually of stone, with tiled roofs. Brick was coming into general use, sometimes as a facing for walls built mainly of a kind of concrete. The danger of fire was great, and wood construction was generally avoided in the more densely built cities. In many of the smaller, of which Silchester is perhaps the best example, dwellings were often freestanding and incorporated a spacious *atrium* plan. Such luxurious accommodation was also found on the periphery of larger and more congested cities.

Public buildings were as necessary a part of the Roman *civitas* as of the Greek *polis.* The forum and basilica, temple and baths, amphitheater and gymnasium were designed to make the city attractive and to bring people together. They covered much of the central urban area, and in small towns must have dominated the whole. The stadium, like its lineal descendant the Spanish bullring, and the theater were sometimes placed out on the fringes of the city for the greater convenience of crowd control. Every city had a temple dedicated to the deified emperor. It transcended local cults, and its altars were a symbol of loyalty to the unity and spirit of the empire.

A feature of Roman cities was the care lavished on the engineering works which supplied them with water and, less conspicuously, discharged its waste. The Romans made heavy demands on water, and there were few large cities which were not obliged to draw their supplies from distant sources. Arles was supplied by an

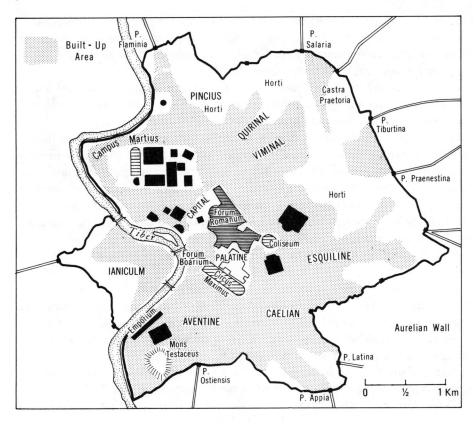

2.12. Rome under the empire

aqueduct of about 30 miles, which included the Pont-du-Gard, one of the most impressive works of hydraulic engineering that have survived. The total length of the aqueducts which supplied Lyons was 110 miles, and even Roman Paris had one of 15 miles. Segovia, on the dry Meseta of Spain, drew its supply from the distant Sierra de Guadarrama, and the works included the giant aqueduct which still survives.

Military settlements were of course protected by defensive walls and fortified gates. In the second century these were generally not considered necessary in cities except those close to the frontier. But in the following century the threat of Germanic invasion led to the construction of walls, often in a very hasty fashion, using whatever materials from public and private buildings were available.

City of Rome. To many of these generalizations Rome was an exception. It had grown gradually over many centuries. No attempt was made to plan or control its growth. Public buildings were planted wherever an emperor wished and land was available (Fig. 2.12). The immense size of the city, without any regular means of transport, led people to crowd toward the center, where speculative builders had erected apartment blocks which were tall, congested, and above all dangerous.

Who, asked Juvenal, at Praeneste or Tivoli "was ever afraid of his house tumbling down. . . . Here we inhabit a city supported for the most part by slender props; for that is how the bailiff holds up the tottering house, patches up gaping cracks in the old wall, bidding the inmates sleep at ease under a roof ready to tumble about their ears."[25]

This was the city which burned one dry summer's day in A.D. 64. "The city's narrow winding streets and irregular blocks encouraged the progress of the fire," wrote Tacitus,[26] and when it was over the devastated areas were cleared, and the rubble carried down the Tiber and dumped in the marshes at Ostia. A new Rome grew from the ashes of the old. Its streets were wider and straighter. The new buildings were of masonry – tufa or travertine, which occurred locally – or of brick and concrete, but they rose, story on story, and people continued to suffer from the stench, noise, and congestion, if no longer from the fear of imminent collapse. These *insulae* are represented in a city plan, the *forma urbis,* which in the third century was engraved on marble and exhibited in the forum. Fragments have survived (Fig. 2.13) and show how correct Suetonius was when he spoke of *immensus numerus insularum* (the huge number of apartment blocks). If we only knew how numerous they were we might have the means of estimating the city's population; unfortunately the fragments are too few for that.

The supply of food and water, of building and industrial materials posed problems for city government. The surrounding Campagna had never been a significant source of food. Most had to be imported. It was brought to the port of Ostia, transferred to barges, and borne up the river to the city. An enormous fleet of barges was used. Warehouses or *horrea* lined the Tiber downstream from the lowest bridge. Here the grain and other foodstuffs, including olive oil and wine, were stored. The broken *amphorae* were heaped in the *Mons Testaceus* which still rises almost 150 feet, made up entirely of broken pots. Vegetables were brought in from the Campagna by cart or pack animal, and lumber was floated down the Tiber from the hills.

Water supply posed an even more difficult problem in this climate of dry summers. The oldest aqueduct had been built more than four centuries earlier to bring water from the nearby Campagna. As the city grew, sources ever more distant had to be tapped. Most lay in the Anio valley to the east of the city (Fig. 2.14). By the second century A.D. nine separate systems, with 264 miles of aqueduct, were in use. The earliest of them entered the city at a relatively low level, but as buildings spread over the higher ground to the east it became necessary to supply them with aqueducts built high above the ground. The last major work, the Claudian aqueduct, took its water from springs more than 30 miles to the east, and strode across the Campagna on giant columns, the ruins of which still stand. The Romans were justifiably proud of their water supply system. It was a precondition of the city's growth, and the most elaborate and successful in the western

25 *Satires,* I, 3, lines 190–8.
26 *Annals,* XV, 38–41.

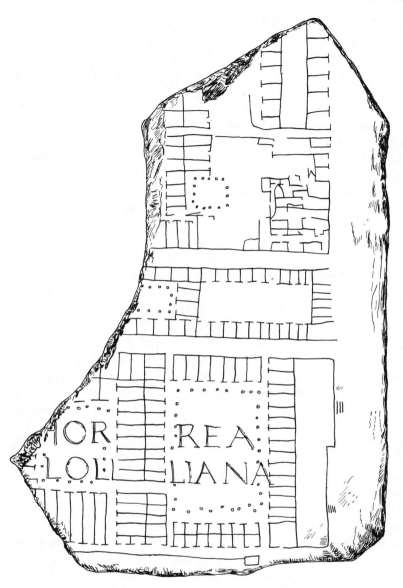

2.13. Fragment of the *forma urbis,* showing the *horrea lolliana,* a granary

world before the late nineteenth century. It is, however, of some interest that their engineering skills never ran to the construction of holding reservoirs.

Rome could not have grown without the Tiber. In fact it was the only great city of the classical Mediterranean which actually lay on a navigable river. Supplies were brought by river. The river gave protection to the early city, yet it was a dangerous and turbulent neighbor, and its frequent floods were disastrous. Augustus ordered the river to be cleared of the rubbish which choked it and the

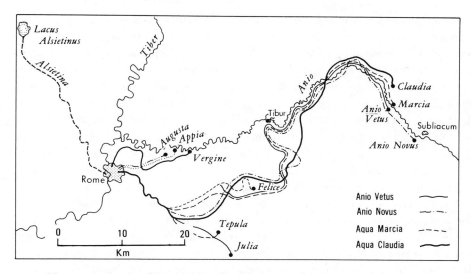

2.14. The water supply of Rome. The Aqua Felice is a Renaissance work which appears to have followed the Aqua Alexandriana, constructed by the Emperor Alexander Severus in the third century. [Based on Thomas Ashby, *The Aqueducts of Rome* (Oxford, 1935) and Frontinus (Loeb edition).]

buildings which interrupted its course. The danger was reduced, but not eliminated, because it sprang chiefly from denudation and erosion in the upper valley. Twenty-four miles downstream from the city was Ostia which grew with the expansion of Rome. Quays along the river ceased to be adequate for its commerce, and a great floating basin, still discernible, had been built, making Ostia "not merely the harbor of the world's largest consuming center, but an important link . . . in the great trade route from the east to west."[27] Ostia became the world's first port for the bulk handling of commodities.

Rural settlement. In the study of rural settlement we find a dichotomy between the pattern imposed by Rome and that which had survived unchanged from the later Iron Age. "The natives of southern Britain," wrote O. G. S. Crawford, "lived very much the same life as before."[28] Yet rural settlement was in the process of continuous change. Native *oppida* were broken up and their population dispersed. Land ownership was being concentrated and large estates formed. Villas were intruded among the villages and hamlets, and no doubt many of the native population began to emulate the ways of their new masters.

The villa was an instrument of the Romanization of the countryside. Some villas were merely luxurious country residences, of which Hadrian's villa at Tivoli was one of the grandest. Most, however, were the working farms of large estates. They probably employed slave labor, and many incorporated workshops, including a weaving shed. Whether these produced for the market or were part of a self-

27 Russell Meiggs, *Roman Ostia* (Oxford, 1960), 61.
28 "Our Debt to Rome," *Antiquity* 2 (1928): 173–88, 174.

subsisting community is not clear. Alongside the villa-estates were the small farms of free peasants, though their number had been declining, perhaps since the devastation of the Carthaginian Wars. Evidence for rural settlement is most abundant in southern Etruria. The region had long been occupied, but under the empire settlement had become very much denser, and peasant homes lay thick on the ground. In this region villas and villa farms *(villae rusticae)* appear from the archaelogical evidence to have been relatively common. Farther south, especially in the Naples district, they were very numerous indeed, and were an important source of wine, olive oil, and fruit for the urban markets. Estates were large and family farms relatively few. This was one of those areas of Italy where the rich landowner had gobbled up the peasant farmer.

The pattern of rural settlement showed everywhere the influence of authority, but nowhere more conspicuously than in the centuriated landscape of parts of northern Italy. Public land was surveyed and divided into regular plots, separated by roads or paths, which were then allocated to settlers. The system, so similar to American "township and range," was practicable only where thinly peopled land had been brought under government control. Such an area was the plain of northern Italy, and here two broad belts of centuriated field-systems, one on each side of the floodplain of the Po, are still visible in the landscape today.

In much of Europe it was in the villa system that the impact of Rome was most conspicuous. Some villas had tessellated or mosaic floors, hypocausts, and workshops for weaving and cloth finishing. Most appear to have been built by well-to-do provincials. Near Mayen, west of the Rhine, a villa site has been excavated which had been occupied continuously for three centuries, during which it had grown from a small thatched hut of the pre-Roman Iron Age to an elaborate, if not luxurious mansion. We are far from having a map of villas during the empire, but where the land has been thoroughly examined, they are found to cluster near the larger urban centers, which probably served as markets for their surplus.

Little is known of the settlements of the humble peasants of the Roman provinces. No doubt some aspects of Roman culture rubbed off on them, but basically they differed little from those of the pre-Roman Iron Age or contemporary settlements beyond the Roman frontier. Of the latter Tacitus wrote that "they live apart, dotted here and there. . . . Their villages are not laid out in Roman style, with buildings adjacent and interlocked. Every man leaves an open space around his house."[29] Most houses were of wood and clay. One must visualize small, loosely nucleated settlements scattered through the forests, the more permanent of them encircled by a palisade and ditch.

Agriculture

Agriculture was of basic importance to the Roman empire. "By far the greatest part of its national income," wrote A. H. M. Jones, "was derived from agricul-

29 *Germania*, 16.

ture,"[30] and, despite the number of villa estates, the peasant farm was fundamental. Rome, a few large cities, and garrisons stationed along the frontier were dependent on distant sources of food, but in the rest of the empire local communities were basically self-supporting.

Cereals made up the bulk of the diet of most people. Wheat was the chief breadgrain in Italy, barley in the Balkans and in much of Europe north of the Alps. Rye and oats were beginning to be cultivated in their own right and not merely as weeds of the wheat field. The pulses were widely cultivated and were a source of protein. In addition, turnip and fodder crops were grown and also flax and hemp for weaving and rope making.

Wine and olive oil were among the necessities of life in the Mediterranean region. Then, as now, ordinary quality wine and oil were produced for local consumption, higher quality for the market. The Latin writers and their public were discriminating in their tastes, and the best wines and oils fetched a high price. There was necessarily a trade in olive oil, because it could be produced only around the shore of the Mediterranean Sea. Wine was produced more widely, but it was the Romans themselves who advanced the frontier of viticulture across Gaul until by the third century it had reached Paris and the valleys of the Moselle and Rhine. This was to remain the frontier of viticulture until the nineteenth century.

Animal farming was of limited importance in the Mediterranean region owing to the difficulty of keeping stock through the summer. There were no fodder crops which could be stored for future use, and transhumance offered the only means of using many parts of the region. The practice of moving animals with the seasons had developed many centuries earlier and continues to be practiced on a restricted scale. A Roman law of 111 B.C. had provided for the maintenance of *tratturi* or migration paths, though there is good evidence that sheep – and perhaps their shepherds – were sometimes reluctant to keep to them. The basic problem was the lack of meadow. The animals reared were chiefly sheep and goats. Cattle were less important, but were used as draft animals, and donkeys and mules were used for transport. North of the Alps animals were more important in the farm economy, and cattle and pigs were relatively more numerous.

The cultivated area undoubtedly increased during the classical period with the growth of population. This was probably most marked in frontier regions, where grain was needed to feed the military garrisons. It is likely, on the other hand, that arable contracted in Italy with the formation of large estates. How numerous and how big these were is an open question. They had probably been increasing since the wars of the third century B.C. which devastated much of the south. Pliny thought them the "ruin of Italy." They were worked by slaves, and probably extensive areas were given over to transhumant animals. There was a decline in the number of peasant farmers both in Italy and in most of the provinces, and there can be little doubt that large areas were absorbed into estates which carried on a more or less specialized agriculture for the market. To what extent this was

30 *The Later Roman Empire* (Cambridge, U.K., 1964), II, 770.

due to the import of food grain from Egypt and the Middle East is uncertain. There was unquestionably a "flight" from the land to the glamour of the cities. Perhaps the Roman policy of urbanizing the empire was too successful, drawing to the cities a peasant population which would have been better left on their small farms.

The Roman agronomists who produced a series of handbooks on farming were writing for wealthy patrons who grew the olive, vine, and exotic fruits on their lands. They tell us nothing about the basic problems of plowing, sowing, and harvesting; their readers were not interested. The result is that we know very little about fields and plows. We can be sure that the light *aratrum* continued to be used, but clearly modifications were made. A coulter was sometimes added, and it was occasionally so heavily built that it had to be supported on wheels, thus anticipating the medieval plow (see Chap. 3, under "Agriculture"). One cannot say how widespread was the use of the heavy plow, but one can be sure that it called for a large team, beyond the means of the peasant farmer. So also was one of the few technical innovations, a kind of harvesting machine, a cart with teeth along its forward edge, which was *pushed* through the fields of grain. There is evidence not only for forest clearance, but also for land drainage in the Po Valley of northern Italy as well as in the marshes southeast of Rome.

There was without question a wide gulf between the farming practiced on the *fundi*, or estates, and described by Columella and that of the peasant farmer. But of the latter almost nothing is known. Beyond the boundary of the empire we may be sure that a simple, subsistence agriculture prevailed. Germany, wrote Tacitus, was "fertile in grain crops," but, and in this he reflected his Mediterranean background, "unkind to fruit trees." The Germans practiced a shifting pattern of cultivation, changing their cultivated fields frequently. Their plow was probably a light one, not dissimilar to that in use farther south. The crops which they grew were the basic breadgrains, the wheats and barley, and, on an increasing scale, rye. The land was "rich in flocks," and excavated sites confirm that cattle, sheep, and pigs were abundant in the diet.

Manufacturing and mining

Manufacturing was of increasing importance during the empire, and archaeological evidence is eloquent testimony to the growing volume of consumption. Yet the craft industries were pursued more in the countryside than in the towns. This was due in part to the bulky nature of their raw materials: clay, ores, soft iron, and wool. There were few specifically urban industries, other than milling grain and preparing foodstuffs.

Best known of Roman craft industries was potting, and nothing illustrates more clearly the rise in material standards than the widespread use of superior quality ware. Foremost was the so-called Samian or Arretine ware. Its manufacture spread through Italy and Gaul, and the output of its standardized designs was immense. But outside Italy the manufacture of coarser pottery in the native, Celtic tradition

2.15. A relief showing Roman miners, from Linares, Spain

never ceased, and late in the empire, demand for such wares increased. The manufacture of glass was introduced from the Middle East and spread through the western provinces. Related to the ceramic industry was the manufacture of bricks and tiles, used almost universally in better quality buildings.

Mining, smelting, and metalworking were important, though highly localized. Metalliferous ores, as a general rule, belonged to the state which leased the mines to private individuals. Slaves provided most of the labor force. Conditions in the mines appear to have been harsh, and the mortality rate among miners high. The Romans made no significant advance in the technology of mining. Iron ores were worked and smelted most widely. The Tuscan industry, which derived its ore from the island of Elba, remained active, but the chief source of iron for Italy was the rich, iron-bearing region of Noricum, which has retained its importance till the present. On the authority of Cassiodorus, Dalmatia also provided weapons. Other important sources of iron ore and refined iron were central Spain, the lower Rhineland, and parts of the Balkan provinces (Fig. 2.15).

The Romans worked all the nonferrous metals known at this time. Most important of them was lead, in heavy demand for the hydraulic engineering works met with in most cities. Britain was one of the chief sources of lead, but it was also worked in Spain and the Balkans. Copper, chiefly from Spain, was used for bronze founding, and it is presumed that the tin used to alloy with the copper came from Cornwall. There is, however, little evidence here for any large-scale tinworking. The precious metals were worked and used for decoration and jewelry. The silver mines of Laureion continued to be used, but their output was small. Most of the silver now came from the mountains of southern Spain. Gold, much of it alluvial, was also found in Spain, the Alps, and the Balkans, as well as in deep mines in central Wales.

Nonferrous metals were smelted close to the mines, as they lost much of their mass in the process. The refined metals, especially copper, lead, and the precious metals, were sent in their refined state to be used by urban craftsmen. Some cities, notably Rome, Capua, and Corinth, were centers for working in bronze, and there were goldsmiths and silversmiths wherever there was a wealthy clientele to employ them.

The metalworking crafts were practiced on a smaller scale and in a less sophisticated manner beyond the imperial frontier. Iron smelting was the most widespread, and there was a smelting complex of considerable proportions in the Holy Cross Mountains of southern Poland.

Commerce

Aristeides in the second century A.D. represented Rome as the focus of trade in the known world. The world's products could be seen in its markets. What he failed to note was that the ships which brought their cargoes to Ostia sailed away empty, for Rome had almost nothing to export. It was a vast consumer, parasitical on the rest of the empire. Apart from the traffic of Rome there was little long-distance trade in the empire. The latter was made up of self-sufficing communities, and in each local area most of the trade was internal.

It is sometimes assumed, because the Romans built a unified road system spanning the whole of their empire in Europe, that there must have been a regular and rapid flow of goods. This was not the case. The roads were built by the legions to satisfy military needs. Their layout was not adjusted to civilian needs, and, indeed, proved subsequently to be of small commercial value. Most roads available for local trade are unlikely to have been much more than tracks and the greatest use was in fact made of the rivers, especially in Gaul and the Rhineland. The rivers of Italy, with the exception of the Po, were of little value, and even the Tiber below Rome was regularly navigated only by small barges. Road traffic was by four-wheeled wagon where possible, but by pack animal over the rougher ground. Numerous bas-reliefs show transport both by road and river, the river barges being towed by the boatmen wherever necessary.

Much has been written about the unity of the Mediterranean basin and the supposed ease with which commerce and communications could be maintained between its opposite shores. There was, indeed, a vigorous traffic carried on mainly in small sailing ships, few of which were of more than 150 tons displacement, and navigation was largely in the summer half year. Rome's large import came mostly from a small number of major ports, of which Alexandria and Carthage were among the most important. In the Aegean Sea, and along the coasts of Italy and Sicily and probably also of Spain there was a local traffic from cove to cove, small port to small port, as, indeed, there continued to be until modern times when traffic was drawn to the improved roads.

The commerce of the Roman empire was made up, first and foremost, of foodstuffs, especially breadgrains, and secondly of manufactured goods, most of them lightweight and of relatively high value. Cereals were transported to Rome and a few other large cities, as well as to military bases along the frontier. Olive oil and wine also entered into long-distance trade. But the evidence – literary, epigraphical, and archaeological – can only lead to the conclusion that the total volume of trade was small. Apart from the food supply of Rome and of military garrisons, commerce seems to have satisfied only the whim and appetite of a small and rich minority. The excavation of Silchester, abandoned at the end of the empire and not again occupied, revealed only a handful of goods from beyond the local area.

There is no quantitative evidence for the study of Roman trade. It appears, however, that apart from the grain trade, the greatest volume of long-distance trade was between Italy and southern Spain, with Gaul running a close second to Spain. If trade within the empire was very largely in luxury goods, that between the empire and the barbarian world beyond its northern frontier was almost exclusively so. Bronze, silver, glass, and large quantities of the brown Arretine pottery have been found across the plain of Germany and Poland, and in smaller amounts as far away as Scandinavia and the eastern Baltic. These were probably the means by which the Romans paid for cattle, forest products, and slaves which they obtained from beyond their frontier.

SELECT BIBLIOGRAPHY

On the Greek world

General:
Bolkestein, H. *Economic Life in Greece's Golden Age.* Leiden, 1958.
Ehrenberg, V. *The Greek State.* Oxford, 1960.
French, A. *The Growth of the Athenian Economy.* London, 1964.
Michell, H. *The Economics of Ancient Greece.* Cambridge, U.K., 1940.

Urban development:
Collis, J. *Oppida: Earliest Towns North of the Alps.* Sheffield, 1984.
Haverfield, F. *Ancient Town Planning.* Oxford, 1913.
Pounds, N. J. G. "The Urbanization of the Classical World." *Annals of the Association of American Geographers* 59 (1969):135–57.
Wycherley, R. E. *How the Greeks Built Cities.* London, 1962.

Social and economic conditions:
Applebaum, S. "The Agriculture of the British Early Iron Age, as Exemplified at Fighel-dean Down, Wiltshire." *Proceedings of the Prehistoric Society* (1954): 103–14.
Clark, J. G. D. *Prehistoric Europe: The Economic Basis.* London, 1952.
Ehrenberg, V. *The People of Aristophanes.* Oxford, 1951.
Finley, M. I. *Studies in Land and Credit in Ancient Athens, 500–200 B.C.* New Brunswick, N.J., 1951.
Glotz, G. *Ancient Greece at Work.* London, 1926.
Gomme, A. W. *The Population of Athens in the Fifth and Fourth Centuries B.C.* Oxford, 1933.
Singer, C., E. J. Holmyard, and A. R. Hall. *A History of Technology.* Vol. 1. Oxford, 1954.
Tod, M. N. "The Economic Background of the Fifth Century." In *Cambridge Ancient History,* vol. 5, 1–32. Cambridge, U.K., 1953.

On the Roman world

General:
Frank, T. *An Economic Survey of Ancient Rome,* vols. 3 and 5. Baltimore, Md., 1937–40.
Frere, S. S. *Britannia.* London, 1967.
Jones, A. H. M. *The Later Roman Empire.* Cambridge, U.K., 1964.
Millett, Martin, *The Romanization of Britain,* Cambridge, U.K., in press.
Rivet, A. L. F. *Town and Country in Roman Britain.* London, 1958.
Rostovtzeff, M. *The Social and Economic History of the Roman Empire.* Oxford, 1926–57.
Walbank, F. W. *The Decline of the Roman Empire in the West.* London, 1946.
Wheeler, Mortimer. *Britannia. Rome beyond the Imperial Frontiers.* London, 1954.

    Population:
Boak, A. E. R. *Manpower Shortage and the Fall of the Roman Empire in the West.* Ann Arbor, Mich., 1955.
Brunt, P. A. *Italian Manpower 225 B.C.–A.D. 14.* Oxford, 1971.
Gimbutas, M. *The Slavs.* London, 1971.
MacMullen, R. *Enemies of the Roman Order.* Cambridge, Mass., 1966.
Wacher, J. S., ed. *The Civitas Capitals of Roman Britain.* Leicester, 1966.

    Urban development:
Loane, H. J. *Industry and Commerce of the City of Rome.* Baltimore, Md., 1938.
Meiggs, R. *Roman Ostia.* Oxford, 1960.

    Commerce:
Charlesworth, M. P. *Trade-routes and Commerce of the Roman Empire.* Cambridge, U.K., 1926.

PART II

The Middle Ages

It has rarely happened in the course of human history that a material culture has sunk to the point at which skills have been lost, technologies forgotten, and a whole way of life lowered. Of course there have been recessions when the level of prosperity declined, but on such occasions nothing was irretrievably lost. The decline which ended the Roman empire in the West was of the former kind. Life was reduced to a lower plane, from which mankind had again to struggle upward. The Middle Ages, taken as a whole, was such a period of regrowth, though the pattern which emerged at the end was a very different one from that which had been eclipsed with the decline of the Roman empire.

Any discussion of the end of the empire and the beginning of the Middle Ages must take into consideration that it was only the western empire which "fell." The eastern empire, with its focus in Constantinople, continued its sometimes precarious existence for another thousand years before it succumbed to the Turks. The western empire ended in a formal sense in 476, but economic and social decline had been apparent long before this in the dwindling size of cities, the drying up of trade, and the diversion of the empire's energies and resources to protecting its frontiers in north and east.

Attacks by Germanic tribes were not new, but they became more intense. Small groups had previously been settled within the empire; now whole tribes broke through barriers of the empire and spread south toward the Mediterranean. They had not come primarily to destroy — though there was immense destruction — but to inherit. They wanted the riches of the empire and, above all, its well-tilled fields for themselves. It was the wealth of the empire which attracted them across the Rhine and the Danube.

But the invaders, nonetheless, brought with them a different scale of values and a lower material culture. They were not city dwellers; indeed cities as the Romans conceived them were unknown in their Germanic homelands, and their arrival was followed in varying degrees by urban decay. They practiced a self-sufficing agri-culture, so that where they settled commerce was little needed. Their material demands were more restricted and the manufacture and trade in artifacts was greatly reduced. Material standards, as judged by the traces of Dark Age settlements that have been excavated and by the primitive household goods of their inhabitants, fell to levels not very different from those which prevailed before the Romans conquered much of Europe.

The geography of Europe which emerged as the invaders settled and took possession of the land was a very different one from that which had existed at the height of Roman prosperity. Yet not everything was lost. Decay could not remove the evidences of former Roman greatness: ruined cities, broken aqueducts, and a road system which guided the invaders to the next city. Nor was the folk memory of Rome wholly erased. During the Dark Ages the legend of Roman peace and prosperity took a hold on peoples' imaginations, and recreating the empire was an ideal toward which they groped.

Not all of Europe suffered equally during the period of invasion. The Mediterranean coastlands, and Italy in particular, escaped comparatively well. There was little destruction, and most of the cities of the later empire continued to be inhabited and to carry on some kind of urban function. Indeed, the insecurity and depopulation of much of the countryside drove people to the relative safety of urban settlements. Urban life was attenuated, but not terminated; and in the countryside isolated villages and farmsteads and even hamlets were abandoned, but large clustered villages lived on through the Middle Ages into modern times.

Beyond the Mediterranean basin decline was more complete. Cities were reduced to villages, if, indeed, they continued to be inhabited at all. Some decayed, never to be revived. In the countryside a new pattern of human settlement was imposed on the old, and new systems of agriculture responded to the social organization and institutions of the newcomers. Lastly, in central, northern, and eastern Europe a more simple mode of life continued, based on tribe and kinship group, in most respects entirely self-sufficing and totally devoid of urban life. It was here that the peoples of western and central Europe took up the task which the Romans had interrupted in the second century – that of diffusing the material culture of the empire through the forests of northern Europe.

This threefold division of Europe is not susceptible of precise definition on a map, but it underlies the revival of European society during the rest of the Middle Ages. It is pointless to say when the progress of medieval recovery again reached the level attained under the Roman empire, if only because the new structure of civilization was fundamentally different from that which had been destroyed during the invasions.

Three aspects in which medieval society differed from classical lay in its feudal structure, its relationship to the land, and its attitudes to cities and urban growth. Medieval society was feudal. This meant that central government was relatively weak and that part – in many instances a large part – of its functions were taken over and discharged at the local level. Administration was intimately bound up with the holding of land. The landholder, baron, or lord had been granted land, or was assumed to have been given it, in return for service to his king, lord, or master. In order to perform these services he himself granted part of his land to others who in return assumed obligations to *him*. At the lowest level in this feudal hierarchy was the peasantry which held its land of its lord and repaid him by services; plowing, reaping, carrying. Society was held together by mutual service and protection. It was, at least in theory, a rigid structure. People could not move freely because that would interfere with the discharge of their obligations. They were locked into a particular place in society with little opportunity for social or geographical mobility. In reality social structures were less rigid than this implies, and, in any event, tended to break down, especially when services came to be exchanged for a money payment.

Nevertheless, the geographical pattern of feudalism did acquire a certain rigidity, with interlocking services and obligations, which left an unfortunate legacy into modern times. In brief, the rural community was tailored to the provision of the goods and services which its lord demanded. This perpetuated field and cropping systems long after they had become outmoded and constituted, perhaps, the supreme example of social restraint on technological progress.

The city, as the Romans knew it, was almost entirely absent from much of Europe during the early Middle Ages. Urban life, essential if there were to be specialized crafts and trade, had to be rebuilt. Cities fitted awkwardly into a feudal system based on land tenure, but were tolerated and then encouraged because there was profit to be had from them by those on whose land they were built. But there was an essential difference between the urbanism which evolved during the Middle Ages and that which had existed in classical times. The latter represented an intimate relation between town and country, between the central-place and its region. They were two parts of a whole, the *polis* or *civitas*. The medieval city was cut off from its rural environment and at most controlled the fields which lay beneath its walls. The countryside was feudal, the city belonged to the bourgeoisie, and the relations of the two were never simple and often strained. Only in Italy, where the legacy of classical organization was strongest, did the city control its *contado* or region. And only here did the landowning aristocracy live mainly in the city and not on its estates in the countryside.

The first chapter of this part is concerned with the decline of the western empire, the decay of its cities and trade, and the changes which took place in settlement and agriculture during a period of great insecurity and instability. Its organization is broadly similar to that of Part I: first the political geography of Europe, with which is closely linked the course of the German and barbarian invasions and settlement. A discussion of population change is rendered impossible by the lack of data, but the changes in the pattern of human settlement consequent upon urban decay and rural insecurity are examined.

These changes were arrested at some time between the seventh and the tenth centuries. The Carolingian empire of the late eighth and ninth centuries marked a brief period of relative stability within western Europe and of advance along its eastern borders as, for the first time since the second century, the West resumed its eastward march. One can again make estimates of population and of its distribution; one can get a momentary picture of a changing structure of agriculture, of the new pattern of settlement, and of the rudimentary craft manufactures which had survived through the Dark Ages.

Yet the Carolingian period was but an interlude before renewed invasion and external pressures again afflicted Europe. It nevertheless opened a window through the haze which covers the Dark Ages, allowing us to glimpse a little more clearly agriculture and settlement at this time. The picture which we see was changing relatively quickly, as new forms of agriculture and settlement were being developed to match developing social structures. This picture of Europe in the ninth century must necessarily be less complete than that for the climax of either Roman or medieval civilization, because the sources on which it is based are scanty. This age has left few records and little literature. Its buildings have mostly perished and the period as a whole has, until recently, not been a favored one among archaeologists. In fact, the light shed by the evidence plays most intensely on the northwest European heartland of the Carolingian empire, and even here illuminates mainly those lands which had passed into the possession of the church.

Chapter 5, which follows, is in some ways the complement of Chapter 3. It is a record of rapid change in those elements in human society with which this book is concerned, but it is one of growth rather than of decay. The expansion of society and economy during the Middle Ages would probably be found, if it could be expressed in percentage terms, to have been more rapid than at any other time before the nineteenth century. There was growth and change in the spatial pattern of every element examined in this book – population and settlement, urban life, agriculture, the crafts and trade – but growth was, it must be emphasized, from a relatively low level.

The period of medieval expansion culminated in the early fourteenth century. By that time population had probably ceased to grow in much of the continent, and the network of cities and towns was complete except in the east and the north. Chapter 6 looks at Europe at that date, before the Great Plague and subsequent epidemics cut back on population, and settlements were abandoned for lack of people to inhabit and cultivate them.

The last chapter in this part surveys the later Middle Ages, approximately the two centuries from the early fourteenth to the early sixteenth centuries. This period is often conceived as one of gloom and despondency, in contrast with the brightness of the thirteenth, but this is to overstate the case against the later Middle Ages. Repeated outbreaks of the plague kept the spectacle of death prominently in everyone's mind. Storm and flood were more frequent – or more frequently recorded than in earlier times. But there is good evidence that ordinary people fared no worse than before. In fact, the slight easing of the pressure on land meant that the peasant could be more selective in what he cultivated. Poorer soils were abandoned, yields increased, and there is good reason to suppose that the food supply of the ordinary person was increased marginally. If one still has doubts about the general level of welfare in the later Middle Ages, one has only to look at the scale of building activity, not only on the part of the great landowners but also of the humble people who gave of their possessions to build the great churches which were erected at this time in both cities and rural parishes.

A feature of the closing centuries of the Middle Ages was the wider diffusion of all forms of economic activity. In the early fourteenth century there was an axis from southeastern England and the Low Countries, through the Rhineland to northern Italy, along which a high proportion of the great cities was to be found, and through which much of Europe's internal commerce flowed. By the early sixteenth century this corridor had been broadened to include central Germany, Bohemia, and the Alpine system. The more easterly mountain passes had been opened up to trade, and Vienna and Prague, Dresden and Kraków had been brought within the trading system of the West. The frontier of mining and commerce was pushed eastward to the Carpathians and Transylvania and northward into the hills of Sweden. Western civilization had clearly passed far beyond the limits established by Rome.

3

From the second to the ninth century

The seven centuries which elapsed between the rule of Hadrian and that of Charlemagne saw profound changes in the geography of Europe. The Roman empire,
at the height of its power and prestige in the second century, faced increasing
difficulties from late in the third. It was under pressure from without. Germanic
peoples were threatening its frontiers in Europe, while to the east the empire never
succeeded in defining its boundary against the Parthians and other peoples of the
Middle East. Within the empire the constitutional role of the emperors was not
defined, and no law of succession was ever promulgated. Some emperors nomi-
nated their successors, but their choice was always liable to be challenged or over-
thrown by the unruly soldiery. There were times when one might say that the
choice of emperor devolved upon the praetorian guard, a pampered corps of elite
soldiers which was stationed just outside the walls of the city of Rome and served
as an imperial guard.

POLITICAL GEOGRAPHY

The vast extent of the empire, from northern Britain to the Euphrates and from
the Danube southward to the Sahara, would have posed profound problems even
without dangers from barbarian enemies without and from weak and incompetent
rulers within. In the later centuries of the empire, its resources were stretched to
the limit. Its old provincial structure was with only minor changes retained, but
for administrative purposes the empire was divided into two – at one time even
into four – parts, with as many coequal emperors. This was an unsatisfactory
device, and under Diocletian (284–305) the empire was formally divided into a
western and an eastern half, a division which, except for short periods, as under
Constantine, was to prove permanent. A line was drawn through what, in demographic and economic terms, was a no-man's-land, from the Danube near Sir-
mium, through the thinly peopled Dalmatian Karst to the sea. From here the
boundary of the western and eastern empires was conceived as running due south
to the Gulf of Tripoli, where the Sahara Desert comes closest to the Mediterranean
Sea. From an administrative point of view the line of partition could not have been
chosen more wisely. There were fundamental differences between the two halves
of the empire. The western was the more sparsely peopled and less developed

economically, but was more exposed to the attacks of the Germanic peoples. The eastern empire had the physical protection afforded by the lower Danube as well as by the mountains of the Balkan peninsula, and was less exposed to the casual raid. At the same time, however, it had to face the attacks of the Parthians of Persia, against whom there was no physical line of defense. It had proved impossible from Rome to direct the fighting which ebbed and flowed along the Fertile Crescent, and a more easterly control point became essential.

Under Constantine the small Greek city of Byzantium, strongly and strategically placed on a bluff overlooking the Bosporus and commanding the land route from Europe to Asia and the sea route between the Black Sea and the Mediterranean, became the eastern capital. It was rebuilt between 325 and 330, grew rapidly with its new administrative and military functions, and remained unconquered, except for its occupation by the Crusaders in 1204, until it fell.to the Ottoman Turks in 1453. Rome remained the capital of the western empire, despite its distance from the northern frontier on the Rhine and Danube, until in the fourth century the emperors took up their residence at *Mediolanum* (Milan), long the administrative center of northern Italy. In 402, in the face of Gothic invasion, the capital was moved to Ravenna, behind the protective marshes of the Po delta.

There was little significant change in the provincial divisions of the empire, though the political boundary was altered at several points to make its defense easier. The *Agri Decumates,* between the upper courses of the Rhine and Danube, were abandoned about 263, and the large province of Dacia, lying north of the Danube and difficult to defend, soon afterward. In Britain the boundary across central Scotland, established by Antonius Pius, was given up late in the same century in favor of the older defenses erected by Hadrian (Fig. 3.1).

The population of the Roman empire in Europe was certainly in decline during its later centuries, though there are no statistical data whatever. There was a growing shortage of recruits for the army; Diocletian introduced a kind of conscription, and Germans and others from beyond the frontier were recruited in growing numbers. Some of the latter, especially the *foederati* who served under their own barbarian leaders, were highly unreliable. The vast empty spaces of the European provinces could readily be infiltrated by peoples from beyond the frontier, and at times large numbers were settled on land within the empire. At the same time people from the Levant, variously described as Syrians and Jews, spread westward and mostly settled in the towns as merchants and tradesmen.

It is very difficult to identify the causes of the population decline. That it was related to rural conditions seems to be clear. Great estates continued to grow at the expense of small, peasant holdings. They seem in general to have been worked by slaves who thus displaced the free peasantry which had previously tilled the land. The tax burden on the rural population was heavy and growing heavier. Most cities of the empire, Rome itself above all, had no basic industry to employ their population and support the vast superstructure that had been developed. They were supplied with food which had been paid for by taxes on the provincials.

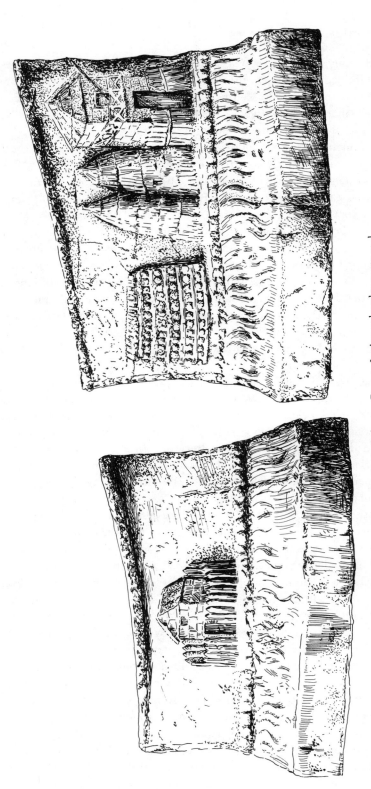

3.1. The Roman frontier, as shown in a relief carving on Trajan's Column, Rome. It shows border posts and a beacon ready to be lighted in the event of an attack

The burden of supporting the army also fell on the small landowner. In good years and bad he had to pay his land tax, which tended to increase in real terms, and if he could not, he ran into debt or abandoned his holding. From the third century imperial edicts frequently noted the extent of abandoned fields, *agri deserti,* and required that they again be brought under cultivation. The decay of the country-side was both the cause and the consequence of the declining population. The point was reached early in the fourth century when the peasant was forbidden to leave his land. He became *adscriptus glebae,* bound to the soil, as unfree in this respect as the serf during the Middle Ages. Large estates and a servile peasantry long before the end of the empire in the west were just two of the ways in which the Romans anticipated the feudal structure of landholding of the later Middle Ages.

THE INVADERS

In the last resort it was the barbarians who brought about the decline and fall of the empire. Without them the immense military expenditure would not have been necessary; there would have been no conscription; taxation could have been lower, and the plight of the peasantry less desperate. What led to the invasions which brought an end to the western empire and gravely threatened the eastern we do not know. The invaders were pushed, it has been claimed, by the Huns, a Tartar people from the central Asiatic steppe. What, then, drove the Huns westward? Was it the "pulse of Asia," the alternating wet and dry periods in the heartland of the Old World? Was the population of the barbarian tribes increasing beyond the ability of their lands to support it? Unlikely, as all subsequent evidence points to a very sparse population in central and eastern Europe. Was it warfare between the Germanic and other tribes which drove the weaker of them to find refuge within the empire? Again, there is no evidence to support such a view. Or was the motivation of the barbarians nothing more than greed for the spoils of the empire. Such may well have been the case. The empire had long carried on trade with the barbarian peoples. Roman artifacts, chiefly bronzes and pottery, have been found in vast numbers as far away as southern Norway and central Sweden. The barbarians had clearly developed a taste for the Roman way of life, and as the Roman ability to resist diminished, so they pressed across the imperial frontiers.

There are two points to note. In the first place, there was nothing new in barbarian attempts to invade the empire, and, secondly, the numbers involved were relatively small. The Celts from central Europe had attacked Rome itself in 390 B.C., and in 102 B.C. Italy was saved from the Cimbri and Teutones, who, after a circuitous route from the Baltic, were finally defeated and annihilated by Marius at *Aquae Sextiae* (Aix), in Provence. If there were no significant invasions by the barbarians during the next two or three centuries, this was only because the Romans built strong and effective frontier defenses. But by the later second century these were being tested to the utmost, and Marcus Aurelius spent much of his time as emperor campaigning along the Danube. In the third century,

Germanic bands penetrated far into the empire, and cities were hastily fortified to resist them. Walls were thrown around open cities and some, already enclosed by walls, had their perimeter shortened to make it more easily defensible. In Britain, forts were built in the fourth century along the "Saxon Shore," the coast facing the European continent, to guard against invasion by sea from northwestern Europe.

The numbers involved in all these invasions was small. They made up tribal communities. They moved very slowly, with their fighting men, families, animals, and wagon trains. They were too numerous to be able, as a general rule, to live off the land they were passing through, and so paused in their movements to till the soil and take a crop. The more vigorous activity among the Germanic tribes in the late fourth century was probably due to the Huns. These, like the Scythians before them, raided into eastern Europe from the south Russian steppe. The brunt of their attack was taken by the Goths, who moved westward and southward away from them. These people derived from Gotland, in Sweden, several centuries earlier. They had made their home first in what would now be called Poland, and then in Dacia and the western Ukraine. It was here that they divided into the Visigoths, or western Goths, and the Ostrogoths or eastern Goths. Under the impact of the Huns the Visigoths crossed the lower Danube into the Roman province of Moesia. They appear to have come more as refugees than as invaders, but the attempt of the eastern emperor, Valens, to turn them back led to his defeat and death. They remained in the Balkans for a generation, before again moving around the head of the Adriatic Sea and into Italy, where they attacked Rome. But again they withdrew, crossed the Alps, and entered Gaul. Here they settled in Aquitaine, making *Tolosa* (Toulouse) the center of the first of the barbarian kingdoms. From here they spread across the Pyrenees and into Spain.

The Ostrogoths followed almost a century later. They crossed Dacia, the Pannonian or Hungarian plain, and reached Italy. Here they stayed, imposing their rule on the Romans and replacing the last emperor in the West, Romulus Augustulus, with their own chieftain, Theodoric. The Ostrogoths disappeared as a separate, Germanic people. They merged with the incomparably larger population of Italy and within a generation or two their language and culture were gone. Other Germanic peoples, the Swabians and Alamanni, moved from central Germany southwestward to the region of the upper Rhine and Danube; the Vandals moved from eastern Germany, across Gaul and Spain to North Africa, where they eventually settled near Carthage; the Burgundians, in origin a Baltic people, settled in the middle Rhineland and southwestward in the province which still bears their name; and the Franks, a federation of Germanic peoples living to the east of the Rhine, crossed the river and spread into Gaul. Lastly, the Saxons, Angles, and Jutes from northwest Germany and the Danish peninsula, crossed the North Sea to Britain and slowly carved their way across the land.

The wanderings of the empire's Germanic invaders seem to be utterly without pattern or purpose, except that all came from beyond the limits of the empire and settled within it. No argument based on land hunger or flight from the Huns can

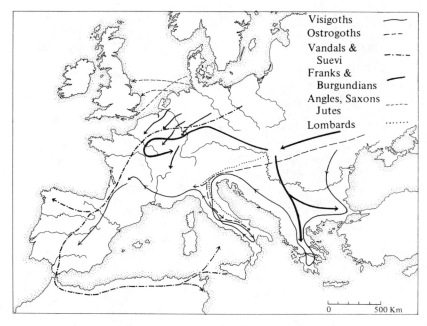

Visigoths
Ostrogoths
Vandals & Suevi
Franks & Burgundians
Angles, Saxons Jutes
Lombards

0   500 Km

3.2. Routes followed by the Germanic and barbarian invaders in the fifth and sixth centuries

explain the extraordinary meanderings of the Vandals. The events of the *Völkerwanderung* can only suggest that these people coveted the wealth of Rome and what they supposed to have been the easy life of the Romans, but that they had little idea of how this could be achieved or of the routes to be taken.

A map of the great invasions (Fig. 3.2) suggests that few parts of Europe were untouched by them, that a great swirl of peoples passed over the continent, by implication destroying cities and extinguishing civilizations. This was very far from being the case. The numbers involved were relatively small. It is unlikely that the largest of the Germanic peoples, like the Visigoths or the Ostrogoths, numbered more than a hundred thousand, and the smallest, such as the Alamanni or Burgundians, probably numbered fewer than twenty thousand. The number of Germanic settlers in Gaul could not have been more than 4 or 5 percent of the total population, easily assimilable under conditions of near self-sufficing agriculture.

The Ostrogoths were not the last of the Germanic invaders of the lands which formerly belonged to the empire. They were followed, almost a century later, by the Lombards. This people appears to have originated in the Bardengau, in eastern Germany. Here they remained until, in the mid-sixth century, they went to war with the Gepids, a Gothic people who had remained in the Pannonian plain when the Ostrogoths left for Italy. The Gepids were destroyed and, inflated with victory, the Lombards invaded Italy. They conquered and settled the northern plain

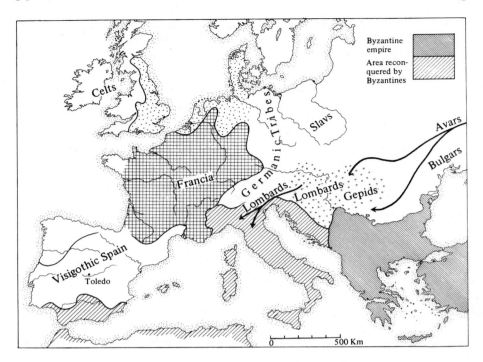

3.3. Europe at the time of the Emperor Justinian, mid-sixth century

which still bears their name, and raided southward far into peninsular Italy. The Lombards were culturally and politically among the least developed of the Germanic invaders of imperial territory, and the state which they ruled from their capital, the former Roman city of Pavia, was in effect a loose, anarchical congeries of tribal territories. Nor did it embrace the whole peninsula. With the abdication of Romulus Augustulus in 476, sovereignty was claimed by the surviving emperor, the emperor in the east, who ruled from Constantinople. Significant parts of Italy, chiefly those most readily accessible from the sea, were regained, and remained throughout the period of Lombard rule outlying territories of the eastern empire (Fig. 3.3). In the meanwhile the Lombards themselves, who cannot have been very numerous, were absorbed into the already confused ethnic mixture of Italy.

Yet another people – the Slavs – appeared on the central European scene at this time, and may, in fact, have contributed to the migration of the Germans. The fact that their language is an early form of the Indo-European language group strongly suggests their independent existence amid the forests and marshes south of the Baltic Sea from an early date. When they began to spread southward is far from clear. The Polish scholar, Jażdżewski, represents them as occupying most of eastern Europe in the sixth century. If indeed they did inhabit this area, they undoubtedly shared it with other peoples, including Germans, the Balts, ancestors of the Lithuanians, and Tartar peoples from the Russian steppe. For a period they were held back by the lower Danube, a wide river difficult to cross without a fleet of boats. But cross it they did, and during the seventh century they spread across the Balkan peninsula, and even sent bands southward into Greece where they established a Slav colony in the Peloponnese. The eastern or Byzantine emperors fought a losing battle to restrain them. The rapid spread of the Slavs was undoubtedly facilitated by the fact that incessant invasion and warfare had depopulated much of eastern and southeastern Europe. Whatever pressures may have urged them forward, the Slavs were undoubtedly attracted by the prospect of vast, depopulated lands to settle and cultivate. They imposed their language, so that today the common roots of Polish and Macedonian are apparent. But they could not have found the lands which they occupied entirely devoid of people. Judged by ethnic criteria, the southern Slavs are distinct from many of the northern. They are brachycephalic, or broad-headed, whereas their northern kinsmen have the Nordic characteristic of dolichocephaly, or long-headedness. This would suggest that the incoming Slavs intermarried with the native peoples, imposed their culture, but were racially assimilated.

Behind all the invasions from the fourth to the sixth century stood the Tartar peoples of the steppe. They were nomadic, and their lives were bound up with their flocks and herds. What gave their movements a westerly turn is uncertain. It may have been a progressive desiccation of central Asia; it may, more likely, have been the feuding between the Tartar peoples themselves. Their pressure had long been felt by the settled peoples of eastern Europe, but the first major incursion was that of the Huns. They were a horse-riding people, and made up in their ferocity and speed of movement for the relative sparsity of their numbers. They set the Goths in motion; they burst into the Pannonian, or Hungarian plain late in the fourth century and for some fifty years were uncomfortable neighbors of the Romans. Then, in 451 they set off under Attila on the western expedition which ended with their complete defeat on the "Catalaunian Plain," somewhere to the southeast of Paris. But they were not destroyed. They still had sufficient resources to invade Italy, ravage much of the northern plain, and raze the large and important Roman city of Aquileia. Then they returned to the Hungarian plain, where they lost their cohesion and strength. It required an almost superhuman quality of leadership to bring together the quarrelsome Tartar clans. This is what Attila possessed, and after his death Huns who remained resumed their nomadic, pastoral life in the plains of the middle Danube basin, uncomfortable neighbors but not particularly dangerous.

The Hunnish invasion was followed by at least three other waves sweeping in from the steppe. First came the Avars who had previously lived around the lower Volga. They raided indiscriminately in eastern Europe before settling in the Danube basin from which they ousted the Lombards. From this base, like the Huns before them, they raided into northern Italy and southward into the Balkans where they even attacked Constantinople itself. But their main body remained in the Hungarian plain, threatening the Germanic peoples to the west and the Slavs to north and south, until Charlemagne, about 790, ended their power and their depredations.

After the Avars came their neighbors on the steppe, the Bougars or Bulgars. They moved around the northern shore of the Black Sea and down to the lower Danube. Here they overwhelmed the Slavs and defeated the army of the eastern empire which tried to resist them. The Bulgarian state which was thus created centered in the platform lying to the south of the lower Danube, and spanned the lowland between the Carpathian and the Balkan mountain ranges, with its capital at Pliska. None of the invading Tartar peoples were numerous, and they inter-married with the native peoples and were quickly assimilated. The Bulgars lost their identity, and even their language disappeared, replaced by the Slavic which had come to prevail south of the Danube. In the Hungarian plain, however, the Tartar element was reinforced by the Magyars who came in at the end of the ninth century. They too were absorbed ethnically by the complex population which they found there, but culturally they remained dominant, and the present language of the region, Hungarian, derives from the Asiatic steppe rather than the forests and marshes of Poland. The last great eruption of the steppe peoples, the Tartar inva-sion of 1241, is discussed in Chapter 5 under "The invasions."

The only other great invasion of the Roman world came from the south and east, and was made up of Islamic people under Arab leadership. The extent of their conquests and settlement and their impact on Europe are discussed in this chapter under "Islam and the Mediterranean."

The eclipse of the Roman empire in the west was followed by the creation of a kaleidoscopic pattern of Germanic states. They were tribal in origin, their bound-aries were fluid, and few of the invading peoples possessed the institutions and traditions necessary to create a stable, territorial unit. Burgundians, Visigoths, Ostrogoths, Swabians, and Lombards each created a state within the limits of the western empire, and the Germanic invaders of Britain formed the many small kingdoms of the Anglo-Saxon "Heptarchy." Some states were conquered and ab-sorbed by their more powerful neighbors – the Swabians by the Visigoths, the Burgundians by the Franks. The Lombards replaced the Ostrogoths in Italy, and in Britain the many tribal kingdoms were first reduced to three – Wessex, Mercia, and Northumbria – and ultimately to the kingdom of England. Beyond the for-mer boundaries of the empire, conditions were even more fluid. In Germany, the Slav lands of the east and southeast, and in the Tartar-dominated region of the Danube basin, tribal "kingdoms" grew and contracted, were born and disap-peared. The kingdom of the Franks, most extensive and most durable of all the barbarian kingdoms, was divided and subdivided among the heirs of its founder, Clovis, whom the French count as King Louis I. The interminable wars between these petty Merovingian rulers reflect nothing more than family feuds and jealou-sies, which were fortunately ended when a stronger and more virile house, the family of Charles Martel, reunited the fragmented Frankish state and laid the foundations of a renewed empire of the west.

One can divide Europe very broadly into three zones, according to the degree to which they inherited the institutions of imperial Rome. First was the eastern empire, the empire of the "second Rome" or Constantinople. Throughout the period discussed in this chapter it embraced the whole of Asia Minor, Greece, and the southern Balkans, as well as most of the islands of the Mediterranean. Its command of the sea allowed it to make landings almost anywhere on the Mediterranean littoral and to advance as far inland as its resources permitted. It regained for the empire the Vandalic area of North Africa, as well as southern Italy and other enclaves, including the Exarchate of Ravenna, around the coast of the Italian peninsula. The cultural and commercial ties between these outliers of the Byzantine empire and Constantinople were close. They are reflected in art and architecture, and endured until command of the sea and of seaborne communications was gained by the forces of Islam.

The second zone was that within which barbarian kingdoms were created to fit into the framework of Roman provinces. Frankish, Gothic, or Lombard "law" replaced Roman, though not without considerable influence from the latter. Their rulers thought of themselves as heirs of the Roman empire, and it was entirely in keeping with their ideals that one of them, Charlemagne, revived the concept of the western empire in the year 800.

The third zone lay in the main outside the former imperial limits. It covered all central and eastern Europe and the Balkan peninsula except where Constantinople maintained an effective control. It was, politically and economically, the most backward region of Europe. Its organization was tribal, and though certain tribes and their leaders asserted at times a hegemony over extensive areas, the states which they formed, at least before the tenth century, had nothing permanent about them. Change came only as concepts and institutions — feudalism, kingship, and the Christian organization of land and people — spread eastward and northward from the states which comprised the second zone.

Islam and the Mediterranean

A feature of the Roman empire, we are told, was that it embraced the whole Mediterranean Sea, which thus became an internal lake, *mare nostrum,* "our sea." A corollary of this was that the sea provided an internal means of transportation and communication, holding all parts of the empire in a single functional unit. An extension of this idea, which is associated, in particular, with Henri Pirenne, is that any interruption of the seaborne commerce of the Mediterranean upset this delicate balance of mutual dependence. The European provinces then turned in upon themselves, ceased to depend on commerce with Africa and Asia, and became self-sufficing. This, Pirenne argued, marked the real end of the Roman empire, not the Visigothic capture of Rome or the abdication of Romulus Augustulus.

This breach in the unity of the Mediterranean came in the seventh century. The Middle Eastern peoples had always been a problem for the empire, but until this time they had never posed a threat. There had been no unity of purpose among them, but the rise of Islam altered this. Its foundation is ascribed to the flight of the prophet Mohammed from Mecca to Medina in 610. The faith which he preached was quickly adopted by the desert Arabs, and passed by them to the non-Arab peoples of the Middle East and North Africa. At once these varied peoples had a common cause, for Islam became a militant and proselytizing creed. Its leadership for a time remained Arab, but its manpower was recruited from all over North Africa and the Middle East as far as Persia. Under the caliphs, successors to the "prophet," the forces of Islam spread through the Middle East and Anatolia and in 670–7, unsuccessfully attacked Constantinople itself. In 640 they invaded Egypt and during the next half century spread through North Africa to the Atlantic. In 711 they crossed the Strait of Gibraltar and invaded Spain. The Visigothic state crumbled before them; they crossed the Pyrenees and advanced across France until, at Tours in 732, they were defeated and turned back by the Franks. They retreated across France, and by 800 their frontier lay just to the south of the Cantabrian Mountains and Pyrenees of northern Spain.

The Pirenne thesis, despite its simplicity and elegance, has come in for rigorous criticism. He undoubtedly exaggerated the seaborne trade of the Mediterranean during the later years of the empire. The European provinces had been sliding into self-sufficiency long before the Moslems cut off trade across the inland sea, and the "economy of no markets" began to take shape in the fourth, not the seventh century. If he exaggerated the volume of commerce carried on under the later Roman empire, he also minimized that of the seventh and eighth centuries. There was no impenetrable barrier between Christian Europe and Moslem Middle East and North Africa. Trade continued in the intervals between military campaigns, much of it in the hands of Syrians and Jews, themselves Middle Easterners. It was probably more precarious than before. Moslems made piratical raids on shipping and even on the coasts of Europe itself, but Middle Eastern goods continued to find their way to the west, and cloth, tin, and other products of western Europe reached the east. Above all, the Byzantines maintained their hold in Sicily, Calabria, Crete, and the islands of the Aegean, with all of which communication could be maintained only by sea.

POPULATION AND SETTLEMENT

The question has long been debated: Did the Germanic and barbarian invasions mark a turning point in the history of population and settlement? Did they lead to a widespread abandonment and destruction of towns and villages, so that a fresh start had to be made? The "Germanist" view was that the change was profound, that the landscape of the seventh and eighth centuries was by and large the creation of the Germanic invaders. The Romanists countered with the claim that much of the population lived on, and that previously inhabited places continued to be inhabited. There is truth in both opinions, depending on the area studied. Most is known of the fate of the cities of the empire, since their number is very approximately known and it was difficult, almost impossible to destroy them utterly. The number of places recognized by the Romans themselves as urban must have reached some 600 in the western provinces. Half of these would have been in Italy, and more than 100 in Gaul. Britain, according to Gildas, had 28, though most

historians would have put the number somewhat lower. The eastern provinces of
Europe had fewer, though Pausanias, in a kind of tourists' guide to Greece, enumerated no fewer than 140 in the peninsula. Cities were few in the Balkan peninsula. Most were small, and the largest were route centers and military bases. What
then happened to a grand total of close to 1,000 cities as the invaders swept across
the continent and crossed to Britain? No city was protected from the invaders; all
were captured, some after long and damaging sieges. What was their fate once the
invaders had settled down?

In the first place, the newcomers had, as a general rule, little use for cities and
lacked the resources to maintain them. The urban structure of the empire was, as
has been seen, superimposed upon the rural provinces, whose taxes built and supported them. The cities had little economic function and, as centers of culture and
polite living, would have had no great appeal to the invaders. To this generalization Italy and perhaps southern Spain were exceptions. Despite destruction, such
as that of Aquileia, and the general contraction in the volume of trade, urban life
continued. Italian cities continued to focus the life of their small territories, and
the invaders of Italy quickly became Romanized enough to make their homes and
the seats of their governments in them. Rome, Ravenna, Pavia, Milan continued
to be, as they had been before the invasions, centers of government.

The disappearance of the emperors and of their urban and provincial officials
left the field clear for another category of leader to arise – the religious. Christianity had been spreading through the empire from the first century, and in 323 it
became its official creed. It was an urban religion in the first instance. Its missionaries established themselves in the cities, no doubt in a clandestine fashion, but
from early in the fourth century more openly. The church developed its hierarchy
of officialdom to parallel that of the state. A bishop was established in each city,
and its *civitas,* or city-region, became his diocese. This was true, not only of Italy,
but of most of the western provinces. Other urban functions of the city might
cease, but that of being the location of the bishop and his *cathedra,* or seat, remained. With the decay of civil functions, the officials of the church were left in
many instances to manage the city, to supervise its defenses, maintain its food
supply, and even negotiate with the barbarian invaders. Of no city was this more
true than of Rome, whose bishop achieved ever greater power within and acquired
more and more extensive lands beyond its walls. The popes, as the bishops of
Rome came to be called, were helped by the fact that after 476 there was no
emperor in the west, and the eastern emperors were distant and ineffective. The
popes in the eighth century tacitly assumed control over the lands which the
Byzantine emperors had continued to hold in Italy, and subsequently justified
their actions in the forged Donation of Constantine. In this document they claimed
that it was the great emperor himself who had given them temporal power over
these lands. No other bishops ever made such extravagant claims, but none other
had the opportunity.

The continuity of urban life was also maintained in the south of Spain until the
Moslem invasion of 711. In the rest of the western provinces it suffered severely.

Many towns were burned by the invaders; many more were abandoned by most of
their remaining inhabitants. An Anglo-Saxon poem, commonly called *The Ruin,*
describes graphically what a Roman city, almost certainly *Aquae Sulis,* or Bath,
was like in the seventh century:

> the work of giants moldereth away.
> Its roofs are breaking and falling; its towers crumble in
> ruin. Plundered those walls with grated doors — the walls
> white with frost. Its battered ramparts are shorn away and
> ruined, all undermined by eating age.

Trier, chief city of the Gallic province of Belgica, was taken and plundered no less
than three times, but evidently life returned after each attack. Sidonius Apollinaris, after a career as a petty civil functionary, became bishop of Clermont in
central France. From here he wrote to a friend "from within the narrow enclosure
of half-burned and ruined walls, with terror of war at the gates."[1] Yet he and his
retinue continued to live here, and Clermont survived the Visigothic wars. Elsewhere, especially in northern France, where the depredations of the Frankish invasions were greatest, cities were reduced to mere villages, but as inhabited places
they managed to survive. At Vienne, on the Rhône, as Gregory of Tours makes
clear, even the Roman aqueduct was maintained in the sixth century. At Tours he
described streets of shops, and at Paris, Lyons, Toulouse, and elsewhere some kind
of urban life continued through the period of the invasions and expanded in the
quieter times which followed.

  Southern and southeastern Spain was among the more highly urbanized parts of
Europe, and here too life continued in at least the larger and more important
cities. It survived the Visigoths, who in fact made *Toletum,* or Toledo, the capital
of their state. Nor were the Moslem or Moorish invaders deliberately destructive,
and the damage to cities and urban life largely resulted from the warfare between
the Moors and the Christian states to the north. The destruction of urban life was
on a far greater scale along the empire's northern frontier and in the Balkan peninsula. These regions suffered for centuries from barbarian attack and invasion, and
the purpose of most cities was primarily military. Many were destroyed and totally
abandoned, like *Augusta Rauracorum* (Augst in Switzerland) and *Carnuntum* (Petronell in Lower Austria), so that their physical remains can still be seen today.
Aquincum is inhabited now only because it has been embraced within the expanding suburbs of Budapest. Along the lower Danube, where the Romans had built
numerous small towns and legionary forts, urban life came to an abrupt end, and
when the invading peoples came to create towns for themselves, these were on
sites which the Romans had never used. In the interior of the Balkan peninsula,
wrote Procopius, the few towns "were captured by the Slavs and now stand uninhabited and deserted, and nobody lives in them."[2]

1   *Letters,* III, no. 2.
2   Procopius, IV, 3.

One can trace the rise and decline of Roman urbanism in Britain more clearly than elsewhere. Towns were fewer and their record, both archaeological and literary, more abundant. Of some twenty-five cities only five ceased to be inhabited places, and seven subsequently became the seats of bishops. Of those which were totally abandoned, one, *Verulamium,* was after the lapse of a considerable time replaced by the town and monastery of St. Albans on the hill a mile to the north. The others – *Calleva Atrebatum* (Silchester), *Viroconium Corrnoviorum* (Wroxeter), *Venta Icenorum* (Caistor-by-Norwich), and *Venta Silurum* (Caerwent) – ceased to be inhabited places, and their sites have remained free for excavation. They decayed slowly as their inhabitants withdrew to their farms and villages. In all other cities there was some kind of continuity. Some became places of refuge during the Scandinavian invasions of the tenth century. Others, London and York among them, redeveloped commercial functions suited to the new conditions of the early medieval west.

Rural settlement was more vulnerable than urban. It was less solidly built and, if abandoned, quickly crumbled. The immense number of Roman sites, both villas and *vici* or hamlets, that have been found away from later settlements suggests a widespread abandonment. But what this does not show is how many continued to be occupied, with new buildings erected as the old decayed. It is impossible to excavate beneath inhabited village sites to find the date of the lowest strata of human settlement, and the archaeological evidence must underestimate the extent of continuity between the classical and medieval worlds. The degree of continuity was probably greatest in Italy, but here, long before the end of the western empire, the number of individual settlements was tending to decline. Intensive field work in an area of Etruria near Veii has shown that a total of 307 known settlements in the second and third century had declined to 93 by the fifth, and to 46 by the sixth. This appears to have been the result in part of the continuing concentration of land in the hands of the owners of great estates, in part of the tendency for settlements to become fewer and larger for security in these disturbed times. The inhabited sites were no longer in the open countryside but on any hilltop that could be fortified and defended. But this seems to have been the extent of change. The peasant made a longer journey to the fields, as indeed he continued to do until recently. But, aside from this, "one is startled" wrote J. Ward-Perkins, "by the conservatism of the patterns of everyday life in the face of seemingly overwhelming political change."[3]

Elsewhere in western Europe there was either a tendency to abandon small and isolated settlements, or to establish a refuge, a *Fluchtburg* where their inhabitants could withdraw in time of war and invasion. This is reflected in a statement of Isidore of Seville that a town was only a place "where life was safer." One inevitably asks where the invading peoples settled when their wanderings ceased. Did they dispossess the earlier peoples, or create new villages of their own? Unfortu-

3 "Etruscan Towns, Roman Roads and Medieval Villages: The Historical Geography of Southern Etruria," *Geographical Journal* 128 (1962): 389–405, 402.

nately the data are slight and ambiguous, and in the absence of archaeological evidence most reliance has to be placed on the names of places. But the name of a place is a far from infallible guide to those who founded it. Who gave a place a name: those who inhabited it, or those outside who needed some kind of handle with which to refer to it? Take, for example, the numerous English place-names which incorporate the elements *Wal-* or *Wael-* or *-ton*. They are generally taken to mean the "township of the Welsh" or Celts. It is improbable that such a name would have been chosen by the "Welsh" themselves. Almost certainly it would have been first used by newcomers who came and settled in the vicinity, and needed a name to define an existing village. If such was the case, one can perhaps assume that the "Waltons" are evidence of continuity. But what about the names adopted to designate the settlements of the newcomers themselves. In Britain, where place-names have been studied more intensively than anywhere else, the earliest adopted by the Germanic invaders incorporated a personal element followed by *-ingas* or *-inga*. *Hoestingas,* which later became "Hastings," denoted *Hoest's* people. Most such names arose soon after the invaders had taken possession of the land. The addition of the suffix *-ham,* indicating home or settlement, probably came later. Walsingham thus denoted the "ham of Woels's people." In a rough kind of way one can follow the movement of the invading people across the land. But did they create the settlements which bear their names? Of this there can be no certainty. It is highly probable that they did occupy land which was already cleared. They would have been foolish not to do so, but whether they built their huts on the sites which had been previously occupied we cannot say without excavating the sites themselves, and even then the evidence may be far from clear. A village is different from a city. It is easily destroyed and razed to the ground. If, and when, new buildings were erected they *could* have been built on the same foundations or have used the same postholes. More likely they would have been put up elsewhere on the same plot or toft, or on an adjoining piece of land, or even a hundred yards away. If this may be said to constitute continuity of settlement, then it is likely that the "conservatism of the patterns of everyday life" was no less marked in Britain than it had been in Etruria.

The well-publicized case of Withington, in Gloucestershire, is a case in point. Here the medieval village and its parish were heirs to a late Roman villa-estate. The village itself was established a bare half mile to the north of the villa site, on the best agricultural land in the district. The sub-Roman owners of the land may have perished in fighting with the Anglo-Saxons, but their half-servile tenantry lived on. They were probably Celtic-speaking, and it is significant that a place-name incorporating the *Wal-* or "Welsh" element occurs in the parish. Here, indeed, is continuity in population and in the occupation of the land, even though the villa site was razed and another settlement founded either contemporaneously or later not far away. The idea that the Anglo-Saxon conquest of Britain "involved a complete break with the agricultural past" is surely too extreme a view, though it is rare for continuity to be as clearly demonstrable as at Withington.

The situation is similar in continental Europe. Clearly villages were destroyed;

population became more concentrated for security and protection; Germanic peoples settled among the Romanized Celts of Gaul and Spain. Some of the latter doubtless fled and abandoned their lands. But over most of the land there was continuity both of population and of settlement. The changes claimed by the Germanists would have required the invasion and settlement of Germanic people on a massive scale for which there is no evidence whatever.

The cultural results of the Germanic and barbarian invasions are no less difficult to assess. An invading people is likely to impose some elements of its culture upon those among whom it settles. At the very least the latter are likely to take over loanwords. The extremes of complete cultural absorption or assimilation on the one hand and complete dominance on the other are never likely to be experienced. Language changes are the easiest to identify. In eastern Europe Slavic replaced Germanic languages north of the Danube, and Thracian to the south. The Slavs were culturally strong enough to assimilate the Bulgars and perhaps the Huns and Avars, but not the Magyars, whose language continues to be spoken over the Hungarian plain. Their relationship to the Romance-speaking peoples of the Balkans — the Vlachs and Romanians — is complicated by the subsequent migrations of the latter, but these descendants of the Romanized Thracians seem locally and in part to have resisted the cultural influence of the Slavs. In western Europe the Germanic peoples advanced the boundary of their language to a line which ran from northern France across Belgium and southward through Luxembourg and Lorraine to the Jura Mountains and thence across Switzerland to the Alps. That the Germanic peoples, notably the Visigoths, Burgundians, and Franks, settled far beyond this line is apparent both from recorded history and current place-names, but linguistically they were assimilated by the native Romano-Celtic population. One can only guess at the factors which led to the superimposition of German in one area and its assimilation in another. Clearly the relative numbers of the invading and the native people were one, but so also were the kinds of social and economic stratification which emerged. Place-names of Germanic origin are found, generally in clusters, over all of France except Brittany in the northwest and Provence in the southeast, but no trace of the German language is to be found. Locally the French language has regained territory lost by its Romano-Celtic predecessor during the invasions, but substantially the language boundary stands today where it was established by the invaders of the fifth and sixth centuries.

AGRICULTURE

Agricultural practice in Europe during and after the great invasions is almost a closed book. In southern Europe one presumes a continuity in field systems and methods of cultivation from Roman to medieval times. Elsewhere there was undoubtedly change. A new type of plow, foreshadowed in imperial times, was widely adopted. It was heavily built of wood, was supported on wheels, and had a moldboard, which turned the sod, as well as a coulter (see Fig. 3.4). It was pulled by a large team, difficult to manage and to turn at the end of a furrow. It called for

3.4. The heavy medieval plow. After the Jenštejn Codex (Prague) of the fourteenth century

the combined efforts of a village community and for a kind of field which minimized the number of times this clumsy apparatus had to be turned. The social and
economic consequences of the heavy plow were considerable. Its use spread probably from south Germany, where Pliny had first noted its use, but how fast there
is no means of telling. There is no literary evidence except certain drawings of the
eleventh century, and the plows themselves have long since crumbled to dust.

There is little identifiable change in the pattern of crops. In the Mediterranean
region wheat and barley continued to be cultivated on a two-field system with
alternating cropland and fallow. The vine and olive were grown, but, in view of
the contraction of trade in wine and oil, probably on a smaller scale than in late
Roman times. North of the Alps, the principal grains were varieties of wheat,
particularly spelt and einkorn, and rye. It is likely that the Germanic peoples
extended the cultivation of rye to the west. The very scanty evidence suggests that
barley and oats were less important than they had been in the Iron Age or would
be in the later Middle Ages. Vegetables were grown almost everywhere, and the
vine was cultivated still in those areas where the Romans had introduced it. Animal husbandry was important, and the polyptyques (surveys of monastic lands) of
the ninth century and Domesday Book in the eleventh show that cattle and sheep
were very numerous indeed.

TRADE AND INDUSTRY

Long before the end of the western empire the great estates in both east and west
were moving toward self-sufficiency. They were selling less of their produce off
the land and manufacturing at the villas more and more of the goods they needed
for themselves. Though Europe was progressing toward an "economy of no markets," there was always some trade in necessities like salt, and in luxuries like
glass and ornaments for churches, and expensive cloth. Much of the long-distance
trade in the west appears to have been in the hands of people from the Levant,
variously called Syrians and Jews. Priscus the Jew, for example, was described by
Gregory of Tours as a servant of King Chilperic of the Franks (c. 570) "whom he

helped . . . in the purchase of precious things."[4] Another chronicler, Notker, referred to the spices, unguents, and medicaments which were brought from the east, and Pavia, seat of the Lombard kings, was becoming an emporium for such goods which were probably imported through Venice. Nevertheless, commerce was dangerous and difficult and was probably restricted to expensive goods which alone could bear the cost of such transportation. Under the empire much of the trade had been by coastal shipping. This was abandoned as the seas became less safe, and goods were carried between Italy and France by way of the Alpine passes.

Manufacturing was of slight importance, and the artifacts that survive show that the quality of their workmanship had declined sadly since the days of the Roman empire. Pottery was coarser, metal goods less refined, and cloth unquestionably of poorer quality. Almost all such goods were made for local consumption. There was little or no long-distance trade in the goods of everyday life.

The routes used by traders and others were, in general, those which the Romans had created. They were well built, and despite the lack of maintenance, did service until well into the Middle Ages. They formed a network linking the chief towns of the empire, and these continued to be the chief centers of what production and trade there was.

SELECT BIBLIOGRAPHY

Bury, J. B. *The Invasion of Europe by the Barbarians*. London, 1928.
Finberg, H. P. R. *Roman and Saxon Withington*. Leicester, 1955.
Latouche, R. *The Birth of Western Economy*. London, 1961.
Moss, H. St L. B. *The Birth of the Middle Ages 395–814*. Oxford, 1935.
Olsen, M. *Farms and Fanes of Ancient Norway*. Oslo, 1928.
Russell, J. C. "Late Ancient and Medieval Population." *Transactions of the American Philosophical Society,* vol. 48, pt. 3 (1958).
Ward-Perkins, J. "Etruscan Towns, Roman Roads and Medieval Villages: The Historical Geography of Southern Etruria." *Geographical Journal* 128 (1962): 389–405.

4 *The History of the Franks*, ed. O. M. Dalton (Oxford, 1927), I, 175.

4

Europe in the age of Charlemagne

On Christmas Day in the year 800, Charles, King of the Franks, was crowned emperor by Pope Leo III. Whatever the politics which surrounded this event, it was hailed by contemporaries and also by posterity as the re-creation of the empire in the West. Charles or Charlemagne was heir, after a lapse of 324 years, to Romulus Augustulus. And the empire thus reestablished was to last until, in 1806, it lapsed without a murmur, absorbed into the empire of Napoleon. The short-lived Carolingian period occupied a gap between the first wave of Germanic and barbarian invaders and the second, characterized by the incursions of the Norse and the Avars, and by renewed activity of the Moors. The period of Charlemagne was one of relative peace, and was marked by a renaissance of art, literature, and learning, only to be snuffed out before the end of the ninth century.

POLITICAL GEOGRAPHY

The political geography of Europe at the beginning of the ninth century was dominated by two empires, the western of which Charlemagne had just been crowned emperor and, eight hundred miles to the east, that which derived in unbroken succession from Diocletian and Constantine. Both claimed universal rule and carried on only a frigid diplomacy with one another. They had no direct contact. Between them lay the Germans, the Avars of the Hungarian plain, and the Balkan Slavs. This was a frontier into which both hoped to expand.

The lands which Charlemagne had inherited were those which the Franks had conquered in the fifth century and had settled, however sparsely. They extended from the Pyrenees to the Rhine, and beyond the upper course of that river they included much of south Germany (Fig. 4.1). The Frankish state had little cohesion. Its nucleus lay in the lower Rhineland. There was no capital in the formal sense. Charlemagne had several palaces – at Ingelheim near Mainz, at Nimwegen and Héristal in the Low Countries, and above all at Aachen, where his palace was adorned with marbles looted from Ravenna and Rome. He was constantly in motion between them, but never strayed far from Austrasia – roughly the Low Countries and lower Rhineland – which was the area of densest Frankish settlement and the basis of his power. The remoter areas of the west and southwest had little affinity with Austrasia, and the peninsula of Brittany never accepted Charle-

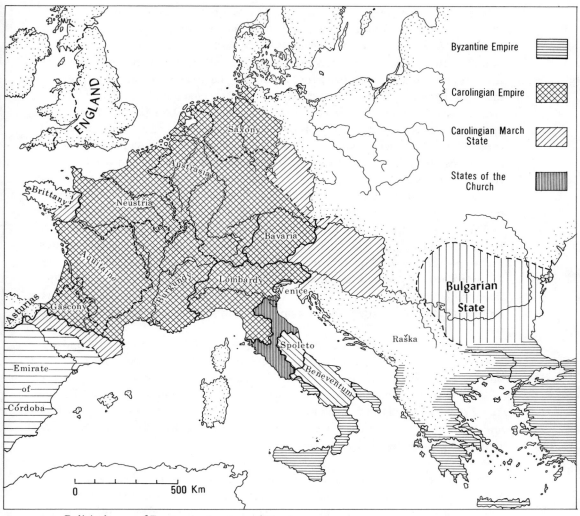

4.1. Political map of Europe in the time of Charlemagne

magne's rule. The unity of the Frankish realm was the achievement of Charlemagne's grandfather, Charles Martel, and of his father, Pepin. It had previously been a number of fluctuating states, ruled by members of the quarrelsome and ineffective Merovingian dynasty. Traditions of independence died hard in much of this area, and it required great tact and judgment to hold the empire together. This Charlemagne possessed in full measure, and he ruled with discretion and firmness. He maintained control by dividing the empire into a large number of "counties" or *Gaue*. In each was an appointed count or *Graf* who exercised the royal power on behalf of Charlemagne. The system was successful only as long as there was a strong emperor to supervise it – and this was only as long as Charlemagne lived.

The empire was ringed with enemies. The Moors had been driven south of the Pyrenees, and here, from the Bay of Biscay to the Mediterranean, was the Spanish March, a frontier province established to protect the Frankish state in this direction. The Bretons had never been conquered by the Franks, but their numbers and resources were too small to constitute a danger. The greatest threat came from the east. "Except in a few places," wrote Einhard, Charlemagne's biographer, "where large forests or mountain ridges intervened and made the bounds certain, the line between ourselves and the Saxons of northwest Germany passed almost in its whole extent through an open country so that there was no end to the murders, thefts, and arsons on both sides."[1] Incessant frontier warfare led in 772 to the Frankish conquest of Saxony. Thirteen years later, the boundary of the Frankish state was pushed east to the Elbe and Saale rivers, and beyond this line a number of frontier or "march" provinces was established.

The Tartar Avars had been living in the Hungarian plain for some two centuries, and had used this base for raiding up the Danube valley into south Germany and across the eastern Alps into Italy. This danger also was terminated. In a series of campaigns in 791–6 Charlemagne broke the power of the Avars, and annihilated them so that "to perish like the Avars" became a saying among the Slavs. As a result of these campaigns, Bavaria and the Alps were incorporated into Charlemagne's empire.

Charlemagne's relations with Italy were more peaceful. The decline of Lombard power had left it a political vacuum, only partially filled by the pope's secular authority over the patrimony of St. Peter. Charlemagne came into Italy in defense of the papacy, and was rewarded first with the crown of Lombardy, and then by being crowned emperor. South of the lands of St. Peter lay the duchies of Spoleto and Benevento, both of them previously part of the Lombard kingdom, but now remote dependencies of Charlemagne.

While Charlemagne was thus establishing his control over a large part of western and central Europe, the eastern empire was contracting on all sides before the blows of nothern and Middle Eastern peoples. All that remained to it at the beginning of the ninth century was Anatolia and those parts of the Balkans which were accessible to Byzantine sea power (Fig. 4.2), but in its capital city of Constantinople it had an incalculable advantage. Its massive defenses gave it protection on the landward side, and the steep bluffs on which it was built protected it from the sea. It could be provisioned by ship, and whatever the political and military situation, was always able to obtain supplies. But the empire over which it presided had few elements of unity. Added to its initial ethnic diversity there were varied peoples whom the empire admitted and moved about like pawns within its territory. Greek was the language of its efficient bureaucracy, but it never succeeded in imposing it on the bulk of the population. On the other hand the church, which was gradually diverging in doctrine and practice from that of Rome,

1   Einhard, vii.

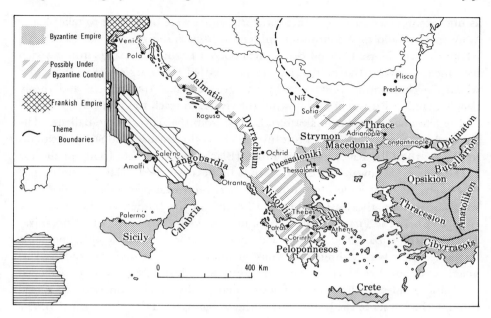

4.2. The Byzantine empire and the Balkans in the ninth century. Themes were administrative divisions of the Byzantine empire

gave to the empire such unity as it was ever to know. Indeed, religious orthodoxy became the empire's peculiar kind of nationalism.

The Byzantine empire continued to hold precariously the southern part of the Italian peninsula together with Sicily and Crete which were under increasing pressure from the Moors of North Africa. The Dalmatian coast from Albania to Istria, a narrow strip between the sea and the Karst, remained under Byzantine control, together with the Greek peninsula and islands and the coastal region of Macedonia and Thrace. One last possession, held only in virtue of Byzantine sea power, was the southern shore of the Crimea, from which Constantinople was able to obtain part of its food supply.

Britain, Scandinavia, and the Slav lands lay beyond the control of either the western or the eastern empire. In Britain the Anglo-Saxon and Jutish invaders had advanced across the country and had consolidated their control of all except the mountainous west and north. The many small tribal kingdoms, which are commemorated still in local place-names, had been reduced to three, Northumbria, Mercia, and Wessex. About 800 the dominant among them was Mercia, whose ruler, Offa (d. 796), was the only European ruler, apart from the pope, who could deal on equal terms with Charlemagne. Even so, he had no authority in Wessex and Northumbria, and very little in East Anglia.

Scandinavia was sparsely settled by Germanic peoples. Their organization was into tribal units, but in the lowlands of central Sweden and on the Danish islands, as in contemporary Britain, larger territorial units were beginning to take shape. Why there should be a continuing migration from Scandinavia is far from clear. About 800 the Norse raids on Britain had not yet begun, but bands from Sweden had already crossed the Baltic Sea and had settled along its eastern shore from which, in the coming century, they were to penetrate the forested and thinly peopled land of Russia, and, following the rivers, to reach the Black Sea.

The Slavs had spread across eastern Europe from the Baltic to the Balkans. The chronicler Adam of Bremen wrote in the eleventh century that Slavia "extends from . . . the Elbe River to the Scythian [Black] Sea, and . . . from our diocese of Hamburg . . . toward the east . . . in boundless expanses."[2] He was right. The Slavs were the most widespread if not the most numerous people in Europe. They were also among the least developed. Except on the borders of the Byzantine empire, where the First Bulgarian "empire" covered a large area, their organization was still tribal. The Russian chronicler Nestor mentioned by name some fifteen Slavic tribes, adding that "thus the Slavic race was divided, and its language was known as Slavic."[3] The expanding Slavs had by 800 almost enveloped the Baltic peoples, with whom they were linguistically closely akin, and had spread through the forests to the headwaters of the Volga River. Here they farmed village communities, awaiting Norse leadership to weld them into a state.

By and large, the Slavs occupied the belt of deciduous and mixed forest which extended eastward as far as the Urals. To the north were the still nomadic ancestors of the Finns and Lapps. To the south was the steppe with its population of Ural-Altaic tribes. They checked the expansion of the Slavs in this direction and posed a threat to all the settled peoples of eastern and southeastern Europe. At this time the Khazars, who lived to the northeast of the Black Sea, were the most powerful of the steppe peoples. Beyond them were the Pechenegs, Kumans, and Polovtzi. Warfare was endemic, and attack on one people and its enforced migration might lead to a wholesale reorganization of the steppe peoples. The Pechenegs, for example, defeated by the Khazars, moved westward and, in turn, dislodged the Magyars who crossed the Carpathian Mountains and settled the Hungarian plain, vacated by the Avars, where their descendants still live. The Arab traveler ibn Rusta described them as living "during the summer on the Steppes, moving with their tents wherever they found a better pasture for their horses and cattle. They even tilled some land. But with the coming of winter they went to the river to live by fishing."[4]

The Slavs had already spread south of the Danube, and some of their number had even reached southern Greece where they were in time assimilated by the local people. Only in Bulgaria was their predominantly tribal society absorbed into any

2   *History of the Archbishops of Hamburg-Bremen,* trans. and ed. F. J. Tschan (New York, 1959), 64–5.
3   *The Russian Primary Chronicle,* ed. S. H. Cross, *Harvard Studies in Philology and Literature* XII (1930): 52–3.
4   As quoted in *Cambridge Medieval History,* IV, 197.

larger territorial unit, and here the invading Bulgars from the steppe had created a state which was a severe challenge to the Byzantine emperors.

The forces of Islam had control of much of the Mediterranean Sea, but only in Spain had they by 800 secured a foothold within Europe. The high-water mark of their advance had been achieved in the previous century, and about 800 their frontier lay across northern Spain. To the north the native peoples had maintained some form of independence within the Cantabrian Mountains, and here the petty states of Leon and Asturias had emerged. To the east lay the Frankish Pyrenean March, but the rest of the peninsula made up the Emirate of Córdoba and owed loyalty to the distant caliph of Baghdad.

POPULATION

Little can be known of the population of Carolingian Europe. It is generally assumed that the decline which marked the later years of the Roman empire continued, and it seems reasonable to suppose that invasion, war, and destruction would have prevented any recovery. The only statistical data consists of the surveys of monastic lands known as polyptyques. The enumerated population on the twenty-five estates of the Parisian house of Saint-Germain has been used as a starting point. But these lands had good soils and were probably more densely settled than the rest of France. On this evidence France may have had a population of not more than six million. The data for other parts of Europe is even less satisfactory. The slender evidence drawn from Moorish taxation records suggests that the Córdoban emirate had some four million. Italy may have had a not dissimilar population, but for the rest of Europe there is no quantitative evidence whatever. Everything points to a small and thinly scattered population. Of the Slavs Procopius wrote that "living apart, one man from another, they inhabit their country in a sporadic fashion."[5] Polish and Hungarian historians have adopted a density of about twelve to the square mile as the maximum that could have been supported by this semi-nomadic way of life. On this basis the Slav lands may have had six million people, and a similar argument would allow some four million for Germany and Scandinavia. The British Isles may have had two million or perhaps more. It must, however, be emphasized that these totals result from intelligent guesswork, and that they have no real statistical support.

The linguistic pattern of modern Europe had, by and large, been established by the early ninth century, and the only significant changes since then have been the eastward advance of the Germanic languages at the expense of Slavic, and the arrival of the Magyars in the Pannonian plain (Fig. 4.3). Languages themselves were far, indeed, from assuming their present forms, but the basic divisions between Romance, Germanic, Celtic, Slavic, and Ural-Altaic languages were already present. There was, however, no correspondence between language groups and

5 Procopius, VII, 14, 29–30.

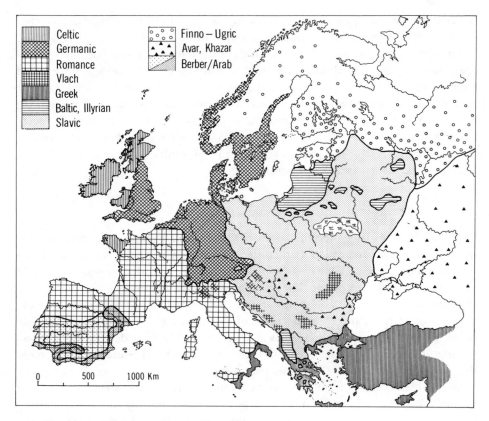

4.3. Ethnolinguistic map of Europe in the ninth century

strictly ethnic criteria. Measurable physical characteristics are of very little value in distinguishing between cultural groups. The Anglo-Saxon conquest of England had no appreciable effect on racial aspects of the population, and the same is broadly true of the invasions and folk movements of continental Europe. The bearers of new languages seem in most cases to have been few in number and were racially absorbed, leaving little measurable inheritance in the physique of the population.

SETTLEMENT

The decay of urban settlements and the changes in rural which had taken place during the previous five hundred years have already been summarized. Although some Roman cities had been abandoned and had crumbled to ruin, the majority were at the beginning of the ninth century inhabited places. Some, especially in southern Europe, had never ceased to be settled. In many instances the Roman street plan had been distorted or even obliterated, but whether this was due to complete destruction followed by rebuilding or to the "disrupting influence of a continuous and comparatively dense occupation through a period of indifferent civic discipline"[6] is far from clear. But, whatever the level of destruction, the walls usually survived and did service throughout the Middle Ages. They set constraints on the rebuilding of the city. In particular the small number of gates through the walls insured that the new street pattern would not differ greatly from the old. This is well shown at Winchester. The street pattern is Anglo-Saxon, but the axes of the city conform closely with the Roman plan, since the Roman gates continued to be used.

Commerce and manufacturing, of no great importance in most cities even in the later Roman empire, continued to decline. But they never disappeared, and the "economy of no markets" is a figment of the imagination of Henri Pirenne. The evidence is fragmentary but nonetheless convincing that, despite their reduced population and ruinous condition, many cities retained that essentially urban function, the conduct of trade. To this vestigial role another was added, the ecclesiastical functions of cathedral and monastery. The Christian bishop had established himself in the city because it was Roman, and a city without a bishop was a very poor city indeed. To the church of the bishop was added in very many instances that of a community of monks. Monasticism had begun, as its name implies, as a retreat from the world, and most early and many later monastic foundations were in remote, rural areas. But they tended also to grow up in or adjoining the cities. There were few significant cities in the ninth century which did not have a settlement of monks following the Rule of St. Benedict. Sometimes they enclosed an area within the walls. More often they built just beyond them, as at St. Augustine's Canterbury, Saint-Germain at Paris, and Saint-Rémi at Reims. Doubtless the city gave them a certain security, just as its ruins provided a quarry for their building.

Urban life declined less in Italy and Spain than elsewhere. The small Italian cities tended to concentrate the population of their surrounding areas. Their population may have declined less than in the northern cities, but it became overwhelmingly agricultural. The Moorish invaders of Spain had a stronger urban tradition than other invaders of the Roman empire. In consequence the cities of the Spanish peninsula remained as centers of trade and of craft industries more fully than those of France. At the same time the looseness which characterized Moslem administration allowed housing to encroach on the streets, reducing them to the narrow, twisting alleys which have continued to be a feature of many Spanish cities.

The two imperial capitals, Rome and Constantinople, showed strongly contrasted lines of development. Rome was grossly oversized for the functions which it performed. The Palatine and Capitoline hills and the Forum were abandoned during the early Middle Ages and for that reason are a rich treasure house of Roman architecture today. Population became concentrated in the Campus Martius, the flat ground to the north of the old city center, and agriculture spread

---

6   R. E. M Wheeler, "Mr. Myers on Saxon London: A Reply." *Antiquity* VIII (1934): 443–7, 291.

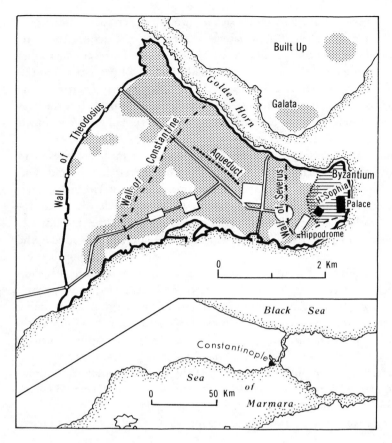

4.4. Plan of Constantinople in the ninth century

over the eastern and southern hills of the imperial city. Many of the great Christian churches of the city, like St. John Lateran and Santa Maria Maggiore, were built in areas which had been virtually depopulated. Constantinople, by contrast, was the largest and most prosperous city in Europe. It covered a triangular promontory between the creek known as the Golden Horn and the Sea of Marmara (Fig. 4.4). The area enclosed by the wall of Theodosius, whose gigantic ruins survive today, was about 4.5 square miles. Within the city a large area was – and still is – occupied by the Hippodrome, around which the ferocious chariot races were conducted, and by Hagia Sophia and other churches. The older parts of the city must have been densely built, mainly with wooden houses, but to the west, between the wall of Constantine and the later wall of Theodosius, were large open spaces, across which the Roman aqueduct brought water from the hills beyond to the brick-built cisterns which are still one of the attractions of the city.

Thessaloníki, Corinth, and Athens also remained large and important. All lay on or about the coast and carried on trade with Constantinople, and along the west coast of the Balkans urban life continued because the cities "obtained their livelihood from the sea."[7] The Byzantine empire was more truly a "sea state" than the Mediterranean empire of Rome had ever been. The Byzantines made a belated effort to urbanize the Balkan peninsula, founding cities both to civilize the region and to constitute fortified places for its defense. Justinian, for example, had developed his home village in the Kossovo region, surrounding it "with a wall . . . in the form of a square with a tower at each corner."[8] He provided it with an aqueduct, stoa, agora, and fountain, but despite these benefactions it, like most other Byzantine urban foundations in the Balkans, failed to survive the Slav invasions.

Rural settlement appears to have been modified almost everywhere. Hamlets and isolated settlements were abandoned, and the rural population concentrated in larger villages where some kind of defense was possible. The morphology of settlements was at one time taken to be an indication of the cultural affinities of those who founded them. Such a view is no longer held, and it is more likely that the forms assumed by settlements were related to social and economic conditions. Rural settlement took the form mainly of hamlets and villages, with a tendency for the former to grow larger and the latter to send out colonies to create new settlements when they became too big. Most were unplanned clusters of huts, and it is impossible to see in the later village the plan of its early medieval predecessor. Huts were of wood and thatch, combustible and short-lived, and the positions and interrelations of the buildings were continuously changing. Even the site of a village might shift without any break in its continuity as a settlement.

Outside the former limits of the Roman empire the Germanic peoples probably lived, as they had done when Tacitus described their way of life, in small villages of roughly built, rectangular huts, which they were prepared to abandon at a whim. German villages were probably not defended. The Slavs, on the other hand, appear to have had some form of communal protection. The Moslem traveler Ibrahim ibn Ja'kub noted the circular defenses which they built of earth. Over 250 such *grody* have been identified in Poland alone, and they were also numerous in eastern Germany and to the east in Russia. They probably served as refuges for a local population which lived in less troubled times in surrounding villages. The latter may have included small wooden huts, but probably consisted at this date mainly of crude pit dwellings, roughly covered with wood and turf.

In southern Scandinavia there was a large settled population living in forest clearances. They appear to have lived in hamlets, like that which has been excavated at Vallhagar on the Baltic island of Gotland (Fig. 4.5), but, when danger threatened, to have sought refuge in the neighboring forts. This pattern of hamlets clustered near an earthwork fort seems to have been common to much of Europe beyond the Roman frontier, as it was in Britain before the Romans came (see Chap. 2, under "Rural settlement"). Huts were often built of the stones which were abundant in the boulder clay and were roofed with timber and branches.

7   Constantine Prophyrogenitus, XXX, 143.
8   Procopius, VI, 1.

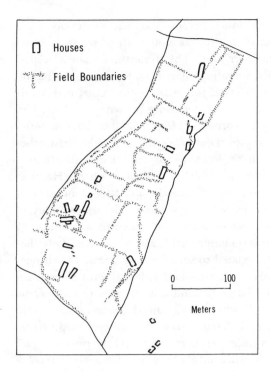

4.5. Vallhagar, a settlement on the island of Gotland of the age of the migrations

Most were elongated and were in both form and function similar to the long houses of western Europe. Along the west of Scandinavia settlement was restricted by the terrain. Hamlets occupied the narrow "strandflat" between the steep hills and the sea. The Norse sagas represent them as made up of extended, patriarchal families. They were crowded; there was a shortage of cultivable land, and their population was obliged both to rely on the sea fisheries and to use the marginal resources afforded by summer grazing on the high fjeld. The population pressure generated in this harsh environment probably led to the Scandinavian migrations of the ninth and tenth centuries.

AGRICULTURE

Not until the ninth century is a window into agricultural conditions opened by the polyptyques, or registers of land and tenants of certain Carolingian monasteries. The tradition of making such records derives from the cadastres of the later Roman empire and was continued in the English Domesday Book. Seven such records survive, as well as a number of fragments which are too incomplete to be of much use. Each describe a group of scattered monastic lands, but they are not strictly comparable in form and content, nor can it be said that they were typical of conditions of landholding in the Carolingian empire in the ninth century. It is likely that much of the agricultural land was held in small units by free peasants. Indeed, one of the polyptyques, that of Saint-Pierre of Ghent, is in effect a cata-

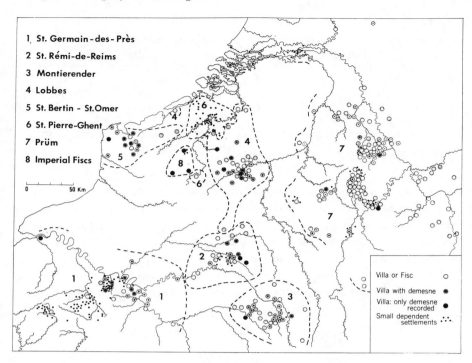

1. St. Germain-des-Près
2. St. Rémi-de-Reims
3. Montierender
4. Lobbes
5. St. Bertin - St.Omer
6. St. Pierre-Ghent
7. Prüm
8. Imperial Fiscs

0 ___ 50 Km

Villa or Fisc   ○
Villa with demesne ◉
Villa: only demesne ●
recorded
Small dependent   ⋰⋱
settlements

4.6. Bipartite villas on monastic estates in the ninth century

logue of donations of land, most of them quite small, to the monastery. There was a strong tendency for small holdings to be absorbed into large estates, probably by the gift of their owners who deeded the land either to a monastery or to a lay landowner in return for protection.

In each survey the lands were grouped into *villae* or fiscs. Most, especially the larger ones, were bipartite, and the land was divided into demesne, which was cultivated on behalf of the monastery, and dependent tenures, cultivated by the peasantry in return for labor services and payments in kind. The bipartite manor was common on the lands of Saint-Germain, Saint-Rémy, Lobbes, and Saint-Bertin, which lay mainly on the good soils of the Paris basin and northern France (Fig. 4.6), but was rare in the Low Countries and in the Ardennes and Eifel. One can only deduce from this that the feudal process had made more headway in France than in its eastern borderlands. The size of *villae* cannot always be gauged with accuracy. In the Paris basin and northern France, they appear to have been large and probably centered in nucleated villages. But to the west of Paris, in Flanders, and in the Ardennes-Eifel they were in general small. In the case of the last, this was probably a consequence of the poor soil and rough terrain.

On the matter of field systems and crops the polyptyques are tantalizingly vague. It is evident that agricultural systems were in process of development, slowly progressing from their infinitely varied origins toward a common form with de-

Table 4.1

Manor	Fall sown	Spring sown	Fallow	Total
A	5	6	5	16
B	10	10	10	30
C	16	16	16	48
D	5	5	5	15

Note: Units are in bonniers (about an acre).

mesne, tenant land, and labor dues. Only in one case, that of the very small polyptyque of Saint-Amand, is there evidence of what is commonly assumed to have been the typical medieval field and cropping system. On four separate manors the areas sown are recorded as shown in Table 4.1. Such equality between fall sown, spring sown, and fallow land surely denotes a simple three-course system with, in all probability, wheat or rye sown in the fall, and oats or barley in the spring. On five manors belonging to the monastery of Lobbes the amounts of grain sown were

$$
\begin{array}{ll}
\text{Spelt} & 2{,}172 \text{ measures (\textit{modii})} \\
\text{Oats} & \left.\begin{array}{l} 1{,}028 \\ 630 \end{array}\right\} \; 1{,}658 \\
\text{Barley} &
\end{array}
$$

The approximate equality between crops normally sown in fall and spring is again suggestive of a three-course system. On the other hand, the total amounts of grain sown on the demesnes of Saint-Rémy and received as rent present in this respect a picture of utter confusion (Table 4.2). The predominance of spelt – over 80 percent of the cereals cultivated – suggests strongly that there was no regular rotation, such as was assumed above for Saint-Amand. The same can be said of many of the manors of Prüm, where oats was the only recorded crop; and at Aldenselen, in the Netherlands, was a tract of land which took oats "whenever" it was sown. There is no evidence of a quantitative nature for other parts of Europe, and one can only assume that elsewhere too the formation of estates and demesnes was followed by a kind of streamlining of their administration, aimed presumably at securing a regular supply of appropriate cereals.

   Grain crops provided most of the food supply, but a wide range of vegetables was grown, probably in garden plots. The chief drink was beer, brewed from malt which had been made mainly from oats. Wine was produced in only a few well-favored areas, foremost among them the Seine valley near Paris, in the vicinity of Reims and along the valleys of the Moselle and Rhine. The Reims region was, as it remains, the most northerly wine-producing region of significance in France, and some northern monasteries acquired small estates there in order to insure their supply. Some of the tenants of Lobbes, which had few vineyards of its own, were required each year to make the long journey to Reims with their carts to fetch wine for their masters. The most northerly vineyards recorded were near Lille and

Table 4.2

	Sown on demesne	Received as rent
Wheat (*frumentum*)	150	55.5
Rye (*sigillum*)	586.5	53.5
Barley (*ordeum*)	6	271.5
Spelt (*spelta*)	7,256	2,024.0
Oats (*avena*)	0	15.5
Grain (*annona*)	988	60.0

Note: Units are in *modii* (approximately a bushel).

Ghent, where their cultivation can have been justified only by the difficulty and cost of bringing wine from better sited but more distant vineyards.

Most of the manors listed in the polyptyques possessed meadow which could be cut for hay, but amounts were generally small. Only on the damp soils of Flanders was meadow really extensive. Rough grazing land played an important role in the economy of the Carolingian *villae* since it alone provided animal feed throughout the year. But it was rarely mentioned in the polyptyques, perhaps because it was abundant and was taken for granted. The record is strangely silent on the subject of farm animals. There must have been oxen for the plow and sheep to supply wool for the small cloth manufacture, but the only beast of which we have numerical record was the hog. On a single *villa* near Lille 1,025 grazed the woods and there were 645 *baccones,* or sides of bacon, salted down. In addition, immense numbers of poultry were kept if one may judge from the chickens and eggs, which formed part of the rents. Not only did the abundant woodland support pigs, the chief source of animal protein, but it also supplied wood for a multitude of purposes, from construction timber – rafters, roofing shingles – to barrel staves and vine poles, as well as oak bark for tanning. Inroads were being made in the forests for settlement and cultivation. Their extent cannot be known, but at one *villa* of Saint-Germain enough land had very recently been cleared to sow sixty measures of wheat.

East of the Rhine field systems were even more rudimentary than in northwest Europe. Population was less dense and a system of shifting agriculture was probably used. The chief crops were rye, the breadgrain of the Germans, oats, barley, and garden vegetables. Animals were relatively more numerous, as is demonstrated by the numbers of bones found at excavated sites. Cattle were especially numerous in the northern plain, and sheep in the hills. The farther north one went, the more important did pastoral activities become, until in Sweden and along the coast of Norway, cattle, supplemented with fishing, provided the greater part of the food supply. The Norse sagas portray a society in which cutting and drying the hay were the chief events of the farming year. In such a marginal environment the greatest possible use had to be made of the land, and the high fjelds were grazed in summer by transhumant animals.

Agriculture was more precarious in southern Europe owing to its climatic regime, and was more easily interrupted. The insecurity resulting from the great invasions had led the population to concentrate in large villages. Coastal plains were in some measure abandoned. They became marshy in winter or were grazed by transhumant flocks which migrated to the hills in spring. Southern Italy was slowly slipping into the condition of backwardness and depression which was to characterize much of it until modern times. A greater prosperity marked central and northern Italy. Here the popes attempted to establish farms in the Campagna, and in the north there were monastic estates as well managed as any in northern France. The monastery of Bobbio, in the northern Apennines, for example, controlled a vast area and received each year far more grain, hay, wine, and animal products than were necessary to support the house. It even possessed olive groves beside the distant shores of Lake Garda, since the olive would not grow in its hilly environment. Another monastery, St. Julia at Brescia, held extensive lands in the northern plain, where its tenants grew cereals, olives, and the grape vine and sent their animals up into the Alps in summer. Here cheese was made and used to pay rents due to the monastery.

Coastal parts of Italy were exposed to Moorish raids, which restricted development, but in Spain the Moors had themselves settled along the Mediterranean coast. Here they repaired and extended the irrigation works of the Romans and developed an intensive agriculture which lasted until their expulsion from the peninsula early in the seventeenth century.

Little is known of agricultural conditions within the Byzantine empire. A document known as the *Farmer's Law,* and probably relating to Macedonia or Thrace, shows a society of peasant farmers cultivating small parcels of land intermixed with one another, growing the grapevine, and keeping large numbers of animals. The cultivators were probably in the main descendants of the Slavs who had invaded this region some two centuries earlier. Among their products was almost certainly the grain which they shipped along the coast to provision Constantinople.

Anglo-Saxon England, like much of continental Europe, was in the early ninth century moving slowly toward a feudal mode of landholding. Estates were being formed, cultivated by dependent peasants who owed specific obligations. At the end of the next century an English document, known as the *Rights and Duties of all Persons,* defined with considerable care the obligations of the unfree and half-free peasants. On some estates the *gebur,* "boor" or villein had to work "two days at week-work at such work as is bidden him . . . and in the harvest three days . . . and from Candelmas [February 2] to Easter [the period of spring plowing and sowing] three."[9] One is reminded of the peasants' lament in Aelfric's dialogue: "I work very hard; I go out at daybreak, drive the oxen to the field and yoke them to the plow. Never is winter weather so severe that I dare remain at home; for I fear

---

9 In A. E. Bland, P. A. Brown, R. H. Tawney, *English Economic History: Select Documents* (London, 1930), 5–9, 6.

my master. But when the oxen are yoked to the plow and the share and coulter fastened on every day I must plow a full acre or more."[10] Evidently he used a heavy, moldboard plow, able to turn the sod and bury the weeds. But what he grew is far from clear. Breadgrains were without doubt the chief crop, and barley was in all probability the most cultivated. This is confirmed both by the evidence of place-names and the impressions left in the rough, hand-thrown pottery made by the Anglo-Saxons, but wheat, oats, and rye were also grown.

MANUFACTURING AND MINING

Manufacturing industries were at a very low ebb during the Carolingian period. Most were carried on within the context of a manorial economy. Their products were consumed locally, and very little entered into trade. Archaeological evidence for manufacturing is negligible and there are very few references to it in literary sources. Yet there had to be craft industries. Cloth was woven, leather tanned, and iron smelted. Without such industries even the low level of welfare which did exist could not have been maintained. Masonry construction was important, at least for church buildings, and there was humble timber construction for the mass of the population and on a grander scale in the palaces of the emperor. Craft industries were small-scale and were probably carried on domestically.

Most widespread was the spinning and weaving of flax and wool. Pieces of cloth were submitted to some of the monasteries by way of rent; Prüm received at least two hundred pieces of cloth a year and, in addition, had cloth woven in its own *gynaecia,* or women's workroom. This was far more than was needed to satisfy even the most extravagant demands of the monastery, and we must assume that the surplus was sold into the market. Aelfric included in his dialogue a "shoemaker" who, in addition to preparing hides and skins, made "slippers, shoes and gaiters; bottles, reins and trappings; flasks and leathern vessels; spurstraps and halters, purses and bags. None of you," he added, "could pass a winter without the aid of my craft."[11]

Iron was used in house construction as well as in tools and weapons. "Where would the farmer get his plowshare," asked Aelfric's blacksmith, "or mend his coulter when it has lost its point, without my craft? Where would the fisherman get his hook, or the shoemaker his awl, or the tailor his needle, if it were not for my work?"[12] Ironworking was as widespread as the occurrence of the ore. It was smelted, probably in a simple "wind furnace," to a plastic mass of impure iron, which was then hammered to the required shapes. There is little evidence for the location of ironworking, but tenants of one of the Saint-Germain manors owed one hundred pounds of iron – presumably a small bloom – as rent, and a considerable amount of iron was among the assets of St. Julia of Brescia. The laws of King Ine of the West Saxons recorded a thegn who was accompanied when he

10 *Aelfric's Dialogue,* in Robert S. Lopez, *The Tenth Century* (New York, 1959), 29–30.
11 Ibid., 32.
12 Ibid., 33.

traveled by his smith. Ironworking was evidently something that could have been carried on anywhere by the retainers of the rich.

Even less is known of the mining and smelting of nonferrous metals. Lead was used for roofing large ecclesiastical buildings but was evidently scarce. Abbot Lupus of Ferrières, for example, appealed for a supply to King Ethelwulf of Wessex where lead was probably being mined in the Mendip Hills. Lead may also have been mined in France, but the great German mines had not yet been opened up. Copper and tin were used on a very small scale, but how they were obtained is quite unknown. For saltworking, on the other hand, there is abundant evidence, and salt entered into long-distance trade on a larger scale than any other mineral substance. There were salt pans on the Mediterranean coast, where brine was evaporated by the sun's heat, and they served as the basis of the early prosperity of Venice. There were salt springs in Lorraine and doubtless elsewhere, but here fuel must have been burned to evaporate the brine. Distant monasteries, including Prüm, obtained rights in the Lorraine salt springs.

The later Roman empire had been noted for the production of elegant but functional pottery. This manufacture ceased with the invasions, and a coarse, hand-turned ware became the rule. Glassmaking, technically more difficult than potting, continued to be practiced, and when Benedict Biscop was building his churches in northern England he was able to obtain glass and the services of glaziers from continental Europe, but the craft may have died out in Britain soon afterward.

The construction industry was important in most of Europe. Most building was in wood, very little of which has survived. But monastic foundations and other religious buildings called for masonry construction. Good building stone was difficult to obtain, and Charlemagne, as mentioned above, had masonry brought from Roman sites in Italy for his construction projects. How the building industry was organized is unknown. Tenants on some monastic lands owed their services as builders, even though their skills, as we may guess, were minimal. The lack of competent masons may be a reason for the relative paucity of masonry construction.

To these generalizations, the eastern empire provides a partial exception. The principal cities did not decay like those in the west, and Constantinople was an important manufacturing center. In the ninth century the regulations of its craft guilds were codified in the *Book of the Prefect*. It prescribed in detail how craftsmen were to conduct their business. Linen weavers, leatherworkers, saddlers, the makers of soap, candles, and perfumes; butchers and bakers were all separately organized, and they were forbidden to sell to the barbarians anything that might have a military value. The greatest prestige attached to the silk weavers and dyers. The sale of their best products was an imperial monopoly, and only silks of poorer quality were allowed on to the market.

Manufactures within the Byzantine empire were in the main of a luxury nature. Some were sent to the west, but most were absorbed by the rich landowners and the citizens of Constantinople and of other large cities. The scale of production was probably small but was carried on largely by freemen. In southern Greece, however, a manufacturer of cloth and carpets is said to have employed no fewer than three thousand slaves, but whether this was an incipient factory system we have no means of knowing.

TRADE

The vigor of manufacturing and trade in the Byzantine empire was in sharp contrast with the decline in the west. This was largely because the eastern empire had in large measure retained its control over its seas. This was easier to do than in the western Mediterranean. The barbarian peoples who pressed against the Black Sea never took to maritime activities, and, in the other direction, the Aegean was protected from the ships of the Moors by the island of Crete. Maritime trade in the eastern empire was continuous; in the western Mediterranean and Atlantic it was intermittent. Long-distance trade was mainly by water and was carried on largely in luxury goods. Despite the hazards of travel, Byzantine silks, leather from southern Spain, and spices of the Middle East continued to reach the west. Their volume was minute but so also was the demand. The merchant in Aelfric's dialogue in answer to the question "What do you bring us?" replied, "purple goods and silk, precious gems and gold, strange raiment and spices, wine and oil, iron and brass, copper and tin, sulphur and glass, and the like."[13] It was exclusively a trade in luxury goods.

There was also a commerce in goods of lesser value. The formation of the large and widely scattered estates of the greater monasteries led to the development of a not inconsiderable movement of goods between one villa and another. Trade was organized and controlled, not by the market, but by the monasteries themselves. Servants were sent with wagons to fetch salt from the brine springs and wine from the vineyards, and, as is implicit in the polyptyques, cloth, and iron and timber for building. These journeys were short compared with the long and hazardous voyages to Constantinople or the Middle East, and they were concerned mainly with goods of low value. One must not underestimate the volume of short-distance movement of the goods of everyday life. It is clear, also, that some of the monasteries were receiving more of some items – cloth for example – than they could consume. The surplus, we must assume, was sold into the market. The monastery of Saint-Gallen in Switzerland received *pallia fresonica* – Frisian cloth – which, it was claimed, was brought up the Rhine by merchants. It is highly improbable that the Frisians of the North Sea coast wove cloth for export, though they may well have engaged in the trade. It is likely that the cloth handled by the Frisian merchants was in reality the surplus produced on the lands of the monasteries and paid as rent.

Much of this internal trade was probably by water, as it had been during the later Roman empire. The abbey of Stavelot-Malmédy, in what is today Belgium, was in 814 granted exemption for its boats from tolls on the Rhine and Moselle.

13   Ibid., 31.

What is remarkable is not the fact that the monastery operated a fleet of riverboats, but that there was enough traffic on these rivers to warrant the setting up of tolls. If cloth from the Low Countries moved up the Rhine to Switzerland and perhaps across the passes which led to Italy, wine was certainly carried in the opposite direction. Another route linking northwestern Europe with the Mediterranean was that which ran up the Meuse valley, through Verdun to Dijon and the Rhône valley. No doubt waterbourne transport was used for much of this distance, and Verdun on the Meuse was evidently a well-known focus of this trade, as *Virdunenses negociatroes* – merchants of Verdun – were quite well known. Trade across the Alps to Italy was probably more important than that directly with southern France and the Mediterranean, if only because it was not exposed to the hazards of sea travel. It focused on Pavia, the chief emporium of the plain of Lombardy. The passes most often used were the Mont Cenis from the Rhône valley and the Great St. Bernard and, perhaps, the Septimer from the upper Rhône in Switzerland. The passes themselves presented little difficulty. The greatest danger lay where the roads ran through the defiles, or *clusae,* between the foothills. This is where travelers were most likely to be molested, and the Carolingian rulers took especial care to keep these "narrows" under their own control.

The Carolingian empire also carried on trade with the Germanic tribes to the east, and with the Slavs, Avars, and other peoples beyond. The Rhineland cities, notably Mainz and Cologne, served as foci for this trade, which followed both the loess belt through Saxony to Silesia and the Main valley to Bohemia and the Danube. These routes continued eastward to the Black Sea and the Russian steppe. Traders, Jewish or Arab mainly, covered this long and dangerous route, and some of them have left valuable accounts of conditions in eastern Europe. Charlemagne sought to control this trade, to limit it to a few trading points along the eastern frontier of his realm (Fig. 4.7), and to prohibit the sale of weapons to potential enemies. Very few finds can be related to this eastern trade, and very little currency was in circulation.

Carolingian commerce was most active to the north and northeast. Here there were active markets and a much more intensive circulation of coins, as finds in recent years have shown. Much of this trade was seaborne and was carried on through a small number of ports, of which Quentovic, near Etaples in northern France, and Duurstede (Dordrecht) in the Rhine delta, were the most important. From here trade was carried on with Britain and also with Scandinavia. The small ships in use did not need a well-appointed port. They could be hauled upon a beach to be loaded and unloaded. Nevertheless a small number of "ports" came to dominate the trade. In southern Britain they included London and *Hamwih,* close to the later Southampton. Trade with Scandinavia followed the coast of the North Sea to the base of the Danish peninsula, which it crossed at its narrowest point to reach Hedeby, on the river Schlei, which is in reality a fjord opening into the Baltic Sea. Here the western merchants made contact with those who traded with the Baltic ports and markets, like Birka, and with the Russian lands. Hedeby and

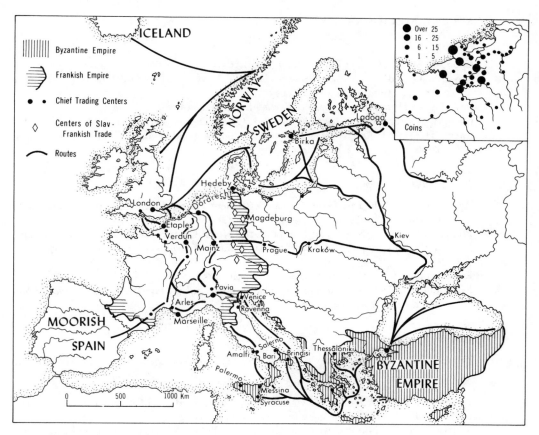

4.7. Trade and trade routes in Europe in the early ninth century. The inset shows the distribution of coin finds of the period

Birka developed in the ninth century into permanent commercial centers with shops and warehouses. This region and its trades were described to King Alfred by Othere, who was one of them.[14]

Along the eastern shore of the Baltic Sea, Scandinavian traders met those who had come by way of the great Russian rivers from the Black Sea (see Chap. 5). Byzantine control of the Black Sea was undisputed, and from its trading stations in the Crimea and at the mouths of the Russian rivers its merchants, many of them Middle Easterners, traveled overland to Poland and the west, as well as up the Dnepr toward the Baltic. They carried with them the products of Byzantine crafts. They returned with skins and other forest products. The volume of this trade was certainly small in the ninth century, but upon it in part depended the industry of Constantinople.

14   See Henry Sweet, ed., *King Alfred's Description of Europe* (London, 1906).

SELECT BIBLIOGRAPHY

General

Coon, C. S., *The Races of Europe.* New York, 1939.
Cross, S. H., ed. *The Russian Primary Chronicle,* Harvard Studies in Philology and Litera-
    ture, 12. Cambridge, Mass., 1930.
East, G. *An Historical Geography of Europe.* London, 1935.
Gregory of Tours. *History of the Franks.* Ed. O. M. Dalton. Oxford, 1927.
Sweet, Henry, ed. *King Alfred's Description of Europe.* London: Early English Text Society,
    1906.

Population and settlement

Applebaum, S. "The Late Gallo-Roman Settlement Pattern in the Light of the Carolingian
    Cartularies." *Latomus* 23 (1964): 774–87.
Pounds, N. J. G., "Northwest Europe in the Ninth Century: Its Geography in the Light
    of the Polyptyques." *Annals of the Association of American Geographers* 57 (1967): 439–
    61.
Runciman, S., *Christian Constantinople.* London, 1952.
Russell, J. C. "Late Ancient and Medieval Population." *Transactions of the American Philo-
    sophical Society* 48 (1958), pt. 3.

Economic development

The Cambridge Economic History of Europe. Vol. 1, *Agrarian Life of the Middle Ages,* 2d ed.,
    Cambridge, U.K., 1966. Vol. 2, *Trade and Industry in the Middle Ages,* Cambridge,
    U.K., 1952.
The Fontana Economic History of Europe: The Middle Ages, ed. C. M. Cipolla. London, 1972.
Latouche, R. *The Birth of Western Economy.* London, 1962.
Morrison, K. F. "Numismatics and Carolingian Trade: A Critique of the Evidence." *Spe-
    culum* 38 (1963): 403–32.
Ostrogorsky, G. "Agrarian Conditions in the Byzantine Empire in the Middle Ages." In
    Cambridge Economic History, vol. 1, 205–34. Cambridge, U.K., 1966.
Pounds, N. J. G. *An Economic History of Medieval Europe.* London, 1974.
Slicher van Bath, B. H. *The Agrarian History of Western Europe A.D. 500–1850.* London,
    1963.

5

From the ninth to the fourteenth century

The centuries from the early ninth to the early fourteenth saw the rise and splendor of medieval civilization. They saw also the emergence of a political organization of the land which underwent little fundamental change before the end of the eighteenth century: an increase in population which stretched to its limits the agricultural resources of Europe, and the development of a pattern of cities, that remained almost unaltered until the Industrial Revolution. Not until the nineteenth century do we encounter again a period of comparable development and change.

THE INVASIONS

The period began with another wave of invaders from beyond the core areas of western and central Europe. These came from Scandinavia, westward from the fjords of Norway and the plains of Denmark to the British Isles and France, eastward from Sweden to the shores of Russia and overland to the Black Sea (Fig. 5.1). The first of these sea raiders reached the shores of western Europe before the death of Charlemagne; the last landed on those of northern Britain two and a half centuries later. Their raids were but an episode in European history, but they had, locally at least, far-reaching consequences. The sudden explosion of Nordic peoples in the ninth century is as enigmatic as that of the Tartar peoples during previous centuries. It has been attributed to political struggles within Scandinavia, to overpopulation, and to environmental change in this climatically marginal land. None of these explanations fits all the facts, though each may have relevance somewhere within the region. One can say for certain that the Nordic peoples set their eyes on such wealth as had been accumulated in western Europe, and profited from the political weakness of the latter to seize it. They gathered booty, which they transported back to Scandinavia. But stolen property cannot be allowed to accumulate endlessly, and the Vikings sold much of it within the Baltic region. The divide between freebooting raids and legitimate trade was a narrow one, and the Nordic peoples crossed it many times. The early raids took place in summer, but before the end of the ninth century the raiders were establishing camps in Britain and western Europe, where they began to spend the winter. This led on to permanent settlement. Norse from the Norwegian coast – the true Vikings – made perma-

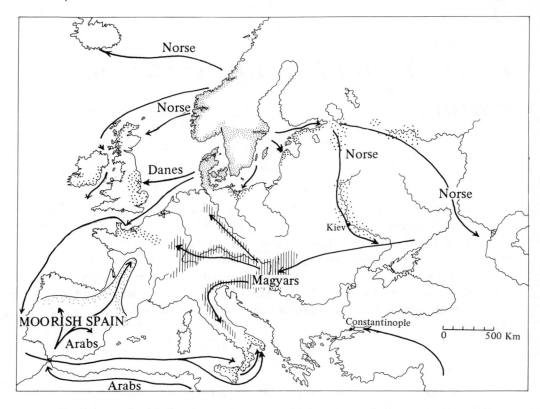

5.1. Norse, Arab, Magyar, and other invasions of the ninth through eleventh century

nent homes in northern Britain, Scotland, and Ireland. *Eboracum* became the Viking city of *Jorvik* – hence its modern name of York. Dublin was founded by the Vikings, and eastern England became the Danelaw, the region where Danish custom prevailed. This area was characterized in the eleventh century by a much greater degree of personal freedom than the rest of the country, and this was in turn attributable to the strong-minded settlers from Scandinavia. They also reached Iceland and settled it, and from here they explored Greenland and may have reached the shores of North America (Fig. 5.2). In 910, after decades of raiding along the French coast, the Norsemen settled around the lower Seine, in Normandy, creating a region as distinctive as the English Danelaw. It was from Normandy that a band of Norman-French adventurers a century later seized Apulia and extended their control to the whole of southern Italy and the island of Sicily. In 1066, Normans, by this time more French than Nordic in both language and culture, invaded and conquered England and spread from there into Wales and Ireland.

Norse expansion across the Baltic Sea to its southern and eastern shore was no less important. The Norse established the trading center of Jumna at the mouth of the Oder and numerous settlements along the coast as far as Finland. There was

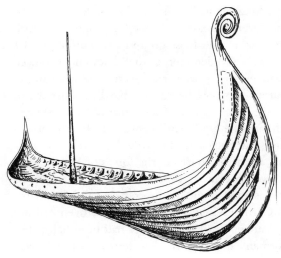

5.2. A Norse boat, such as was used in the invasions of Britain and Iceland

little booty to be had here. The land was poorer and more primitive than their own and they turned to a more legitimate exploitation of its resources and to trade with its hinterland. This commerce had begun well before the ninth century and extended by way of the Baltic rivers to the Volga, Don, and Dnepr. The Norsemen followed these rivers southward; indeed, most of their travel seems to have been by water. Their earliest contacts, as revealed by finds of coins, were with Persia. Then they appear to have taken a more westerly course and, by way of the Dnepr, to have reached the Black Sea and then Constantinople itself. The Byzantine chronicler Constantine Porphyrogenitus described how they built boats along the headwaters of the Dnepr and sailed them past Kiev and through the rapids to the sea.

The Vikings, or *Rus* as they were called, made Kiev the center of a loosely organized state, which embraced other Viking settlements at Smolensk, Vitebsk, Chernigov, and elsewhere. But the Norse settlers were quickly assimilated by the local Slavs, as they had been in Normandy by the French. Norse trade later lost its importance, and Kievan Russia, lying on the border of the steppe, was itself first ruined by the Kumans and then destroyed by the Mongol and Tartar peoples. It was, in a sense, replaced by Muscovite Russia, lying farther north and protected in some degree from the steppe nomads by the forests which surrounded it. Here the Principality of Rostov, lying between the upper Volga and its tributary, the Oka, became the focus of a new state, Muscovy; and its people, Great Russians, were formed by the intermarriage of the Slavs with the native Finno-Ugric peoples. Here Russian society acquired those features which were to characterize it until the nineteenth century.

The Magyars were moving into the Danube basin at the time when the Norse were settling in France and Britain. Their numbers may have been greater than those of the Norse invaders, but their impact was less, because they fitted into an environment only recently vacated by the Avars and pursued a similar arable and pastoral economy. Their raids into south Germany and northern Italy were contained, and by the tenth century the Magyars had established a stable state in the Hungarian plain. They were not, however, the last of the steppe people to disturb central Europe. In 1240 the Tartars, part of that loose grouping of Turkic peoples under Mongol overlordship, known as the Golden Horde, took Kiev and advanced west into Poland and Hungary. Wherever they went they were as devastating as the Huns had been. But central Europe was now better organized to resist them. Political changes within the Horde called them home. They returned to the steppe, where their descendants continued into the eighteenth century to be a thorn in the side of Russia and eastern Poland, but they ceased to trouble central Europe.

Europe was still being threatened from the south by the forces of Islam. They continued until the middle of the twelfth century to straddle the Iberian peninsula. They occupied Sicily and other islands of the Mediterranean, and for a time in the tenth century even occupied Garde Freinet, on the coast of Provence, from which they led raids up the Rhône Valley. But their advance had been held; they were driven from Sicily by the Normans and were in slow retreat in the Iberian peninsula before the Christian states of the north: Leon, Castile, Navarre, Aragon, Barcelona. At the end of the century Europe took the offensive against Islam. In 1099 the Crusaders captured Jerusalem; they lost it half a century later and battled to regain it for the next century. The Crusades were many things, of which the attempt to regain a place of Christian pilgrimage was only one. They had marked commercial overtones. The Italian merchant cities took no part in the warfare, but provided ships – for a rent – and set up trading posts in the areas conquered by the Crusaders. Despite momentary setbacks, the expansion of Europe continued during the rest of the Middle Ages.

THE POLITICAL MAP

The Carolingian empire barely outlasted the reign of Charlemagne's son and successor. It was partitioned first at Verdun in 843 and subsequently at Meersen. At the former, the empire was divided into a western Francia, an eastern Germania, and in between, a sort of no-man's-land called Lotharingia from the name of Lothair who inherited it (Fig. 5.3). The Meersen treaty partitioned this extraordinary piece of political planning, separating off the kingdom of Italy and dividing the rest between France and Germany. This division of western and central Europe, endlessly modified by changes of boundary and loyalty, lasted into modern times.

Even these kingdoms were too large for effective, centralized administration. They broke up into provinces, counties, *Gaue*, in each of which a local magnate exercised quasi-royal functions which had been, in theory if not also in reality, delegated to him by the king. This was one aspect of feudalism; the other was the mode of land tenure in return for service. The course of development in Britain and France was very different from that in Germany and Italy. In the former the central government gradually asserted its authority and gained a measure of control over the provinces. In England this process of political unification had made some progress under the later Anglo-Saxon kings and was, in effect, completed

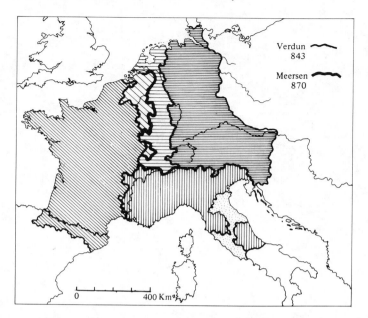

5.3. The partitions of the Carolingian empire in the ninth century

under their Norman successors. In France it was slower. In 987 the last of the descendants of Charlemagne gave way to the first of the Capets. Hugh Capet was count of Paris, effectively the ruler of a small region which surrounded Paris. From this focus his descendants and successors, slowly and with many setbacks, extended their real authority over counties and provinces whose dependence on them had previously been only nominal. For example, in 1204 the king of England *ceased* to be duke of Normandy, though he long kept the title, and the province was absorbed into the domain of the king of France, followed by the counties of Champagne and Blois, of Poitou, Marche, and Perche. But by the early fourteenth century the process was very far from complete. The French king had direct control over less than half his country and, ill omen for the future, significant areas were still in the hands of the king of England (Fig. 5.4).

Much has been written about the supposed centrality of Paris and of the role of the city in the spread of royal authority. The radiating pattern of the rivers which converged in the Paris basin, it has been said, led the kings outward to seize control of peripheral areas of France. The rivers in their courses, it has been said, fought for the king of France. They did nothing of the kind. If the center of Hugh Capet's power had been in Lyons or Toulouse, there would be some who would see in the expansion of royal authority the same kind of geographical inevitability. In fact, the policy of unifying the country politically was pursued only intermittently and was dependent on marriage and inheritance to bring the semi-independent fiefs of France under the king's direct control.

The autonomy of some French fiefs was buttressed by other factors. Flanders,

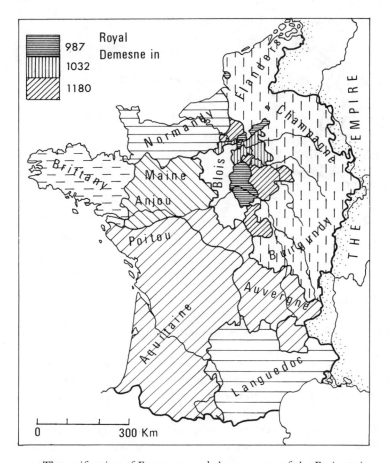

Royal Demesne in
987
1032
1180

5.4. The unification of France around the core area of the Paris region

for example, was becoming the richest and most developed region of Europe, and its resources were such that it could defy the king; Guyenne (Aquitaine) in the southwest and Ponthieu on the Channel coast were held by the English kings; Brittany was remote, culturally distinct, and had never been incorporated even into the empire of Charlemagne.

The course of political development in Germany and Italy was the reverse of that in England and France. Central authority, instead of intensifying its control over the provinces, actually disintegrated, leaving a vast array of quasi-sovereign states, whose independent role was not effectively terminated until the nineteenth century. The imperial title, which Charlemagne had revived in 800, was tossed among his successors and ultimately lapsed. When it was again revived by Otto I, duke of Saxony and king of the eastern Franks, it was, despite its universal pretensions, effectively restricted to Germany and marginally to Italy, and even there became an empty title, without substance or power.

The boundary between France and the German empire was first delimited at

Meersen. It was never demarcated or established on the ground. It was conceived as the line of the "four rivers": Scheldt, Meuse, Saône, and Rhône, but had, in fact, been blurred by conflicting feudal loyalties. No one knew where it lay, and there were no maps on which to represent it. People who lived close to the boundary determined themselves in many instances the side to which they wished to belong, and were influenced more by matters of loyalty and convenience than by any physical or nationalist considerations. Nevertheless, the trend was toward regularizing the boundary, reducing it to a line, known and recognized by each side. As disputes regarding allegiance arose and were settled in the frontier zone – and they were frequent – so a tract of boundary was firmly established.

This European core area was enclosed by incipient states. Most began to emerge in the tenth century. Each had, as a general rule, a core area characterized by relatively dense population, with a central authority in effective control. In Sweden such a territory could be distinguished around Lake Malaren even before the Carolingian period. The fertile island of Sjaelland became the core of the Danish state. South of the Baltic Sea, the Polish state emerged in the tenth and eleventh centuries with its focus in the region of Poznań (Posen) and Gniezno. A Bohemian state developed with Prague as its center; a Hungarian state, with Buda and Székesferhérvár; a Serbian, within the mountains and basins of Raška; and a Bulgarian in the Danubian plain between Trnovo and Pliska. Lastly, a Russian state, replacing Kievan Russia, emerged around the headwaters of the Volga River. It was made up of a number of shifting principalities which vied with one another for the title of "Great Prince." All the while the Tartars of the steppe, under their Mongol masters, exerted pressure on the Russian statelets, reducing them to a tributary status. It was under these circumstances, early in the fourteenth century, that the princes of Muscovy came to the fore. In 1328 the seat of the Metropolitan of the Russian church was shifted from Vladimir, to which it had moved from Kiev, setting a seal on the predominance of Muscovy. At the same time, the Golden Horde was beginning to disintegrate, and the threat to the incipient Russian state from this direction was relaxed.

In the period up to the early fourteenth century all these states developed politically and expanded territorially into the "frontier" which lay between them. As in western Europe, boundaries gradually became firmer, and capital cities developed as centers of administration (Fig. 5.5).

In the meantime, the Byzantine empire was contracting before the blows of the Slavs, the Moslems, and, strange though it may seem, of the Crusaders and their Venetian allies. In 1204 the latter seized Constantinople which they held until 1261. At the same time much of Greece passed under their control and the Venetians mopped up islands and trading stations in the Aegean basin.

POPULATION

The five hundred years from the ninth to the fourteenth century saw the most rapid increase in population that the continent had yet known. There was no

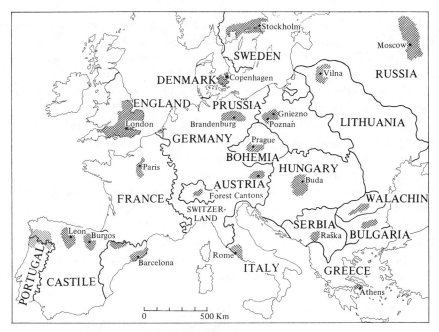

5.5. Core areas of the states of medieval Europe

comparable increase before the late eighteenth century. Yet this increase, so apparent in the growth of cities, the extension of agricultural land, and the increase in wealth, is very difficult indeed to measure. The idea of a census would have been foreign to the medieval mind, and governments would have lacked the administrative skills to carry it out. The evidence for the size of the population comes mainly from tax records, from manorial accounts which contain lists of tenants, and from ecclesiastical records estimating the number of "souls." All are difficult to interpret. It is never clear whether they include children and paupers. In a great many instances, it is not people but "hearths" or households which are enumerated, and it is almost impossible to establish with any pretension to accuracy the average size of a medieval household.

It is not known when the size of the European population began to recover after the recession of late Roman times and the losses of the period of the great invasions. Invasions continued on a smaller and more localized scale until late in the eleventh century. Growth was probably very uneven between one part of Europe and another. One could not expect a rapid recovery in areas of southern Europe exposed to raids by the Moors, nor in the east where the Tartars were uncomfortable neighbors. Nor can it be said to have been continuous anywhere. Growth, if later and better documented ages are any guide, was interrupted by epidemics and famine crises.

Estimates of population at the beginning and end of the period have been arrived at by two processes: by extrapolation from the very few areas for which there is firm data, and secondly, by computations based on the quality of the soil and the methods of exploiting it. The latter method can, at best, suggest a maximum population, above which, it is supposed, some form of Malthusian check would apply. On the basis of such arguments as these, the total population of Europe has been estimated to have been about 45 million in the early ninth century. Similar calculations, for which the basis is even more slender, have suggested a total of 52 million in the year 1000, 61 million in 1200, and 86 on the eve of the Black Death. On this basis the population is held to have approximately doubled in the course of five centuries, an average annual rate of increase of only a fraction of 1 percent. Such a rate of increase, which may well appear negligible in the circumstances of the twentieth century, could have been serious when not matched by improvements in technology and an increase in the area of cultivable land.

It is impossible to know, even for small and restricted areas, when population took an upward turn. It may have been in the tenth or eleventh centuries, but the rate of change was so slow that, even with sources far fuller and more abundant than actually exist, it would have been extraordinarily difficult to detect. Population increases when the birthrate is consistently higher than the death rate. What, one may ask, were the factors which favored such a condition? The cessation of the great invasions and a lower incidence of both epidemic disease and famine crises resulting from harvest failure may have been such conditions. But the relatively few references in contemporary sources to famine and disease may be illusory. Epidemics were, however, almost certainly less serious than in the later Middle Ages, because, in the first place, the bubonic plague had not yet appeared in Europe, and secondly, the much lower level of mobility meant that infection was spread a great deal less rapidly. A factor of no small importance in the growth of population, at least in the earlier part of the period, is that there was an abundance of land awaiting clearance and cultivation. The evidence for the number of new settlements is overwhelming, and most appear to have been made with the good-will of the territorial lord who expected to receive an increased revenue from them. Abbot Suger of Saint-Denis, near Paris, reported in the record which he wrote of his administration of the abbey's estates that "we have laid out a township . . . and caused land which was uncultivated to be brought under the plow . . . there are already there about 60 tenants. . . . The place before . . . had more than two [square?] miles of barren land, and was of no profit at all to our church."[1] One may assume that conditions such as these permitted a peasant to have a holding and a home of his own at an earlier age than he would have done if he had to wait until he could inherit. His completed family would thus be likely to have been larger. How long this surplus of agricultural land lasted is unknown. One must assume that there was little space for "assarting" by the early fourteenth century, and that this influenced the slower rate of growth of population.

By this date, also, there is evidence for famine crises, notably that of 1315–17

1 Suger, *De rebus in administratione sua gestis,* chap. X in *Oeuvres complètes de Suger,* ed. A. Lecoy de la Marche (Paris, 1867), 164–5.

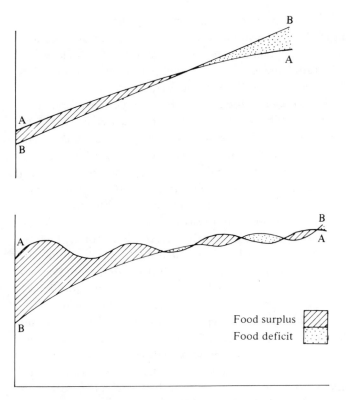

5.6. Growth of population in relation to growth of the food supply: (A) the Malthusian model, (B) a probable course of development, taking into consideration the probable fluctuations in the harvest

which was experienced over much of western and central Europe. The reason probably lay in the unstable climatic conditions, which led to wide divergences from the expected weather pattern. Does this amount to a condition of overpopulation? Was there a Malthusian crisis in the early fourteenth century? Population was, without question, pressing hard against available resources and the great majority of the population lived close to the margin of subsistence. In good harvest years they lived adequately if not well. In poor years they scraped by, but a harvest failure was disastrous and many died. Hardship and hunger did not increase by small increments year by year. A few years of relative plenty might be interrupted by famine and the death of thousands. We must think not of a population rising slowly until it reached a limit set by a static level of food production, but rather of a fluctuating food supply which at intervals dipped below the requirements of the population (Fig. 5.6).

The population of England is better documented than that of most other European countries. Not only does Domesday Book of 1086 provide the basis for a meaningful estimate, but tax rolls of the fourteenth century can also be used, along

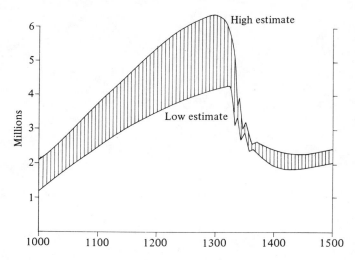

5.7. Growth of the population of England. [After J. Hatcher, *Plague, Population and the English Economy 1348–1530* (London, 1977).]

with a great deal of manorial records, to estimate population at later dates. Not that these sources give unambiguous answers; they do not, and the totals one obtains depend on the allowances one makes for the categories which are not included in the records. The margin of error is wide. Domesday population is likely to have been between 1.5 million and 2.25 (Fig. 5.7). The figure one accepts for the early fourteenth century depends on whether one assumes that population continued to grow, albeit at a reduced rate, until the Black Death of 1349, or began to decline under Malthusian pressures before this. On this question there are very strong opinions, but no firm answers.

CITIES

Growth

The development and spread of urbanism in the classical period has already been described. Most classical cities were still in the ninth century inhabited places, many had become cathedral towns, almost all served as markets for their local areas. During the five hundred years from the ninth to the fourteenth centuries, existing cities for the most part increased in size and diversified the functions which they performed. Furthermore, their ranks were joined by an even greater number of "new" towns. Town foundation became significant during the eleventh century and increased sharply during the twelfth and thirteenth, and then, the potentialities for new foundations exhausted, tapered away (Fig. 5.8). Very few new towns were created in the later Middle Ages. It is difficult to formulate any estimate of the number of places with urban pretensions. In central Europe there may have been three thousand, in England, three hundred, and considerably more

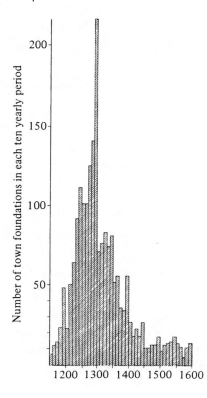

5.8. Town foundation in central Europe. [After W. Abel, *Geschichte der deutschen Landwirtschaft* (Stuttgart, 1962), 46.]

in France. If we add those in southern Europe, which had mostly survived from classical times, and the very much less dense urban network in eastern and northern Europe, we have a total which could not have been less than six thousand and was possibly considerably more.

Medieval urbanism differed fundamentally from classical. In ancient times the city was the focus of its city-region, its *civitas* or *polis,* with which it was intimately linked. The citizen was free to live in the central-place, or in its region, and to move between them. The urban center was an administrative and cultural focus. It was not a place for carrying on manufacturing and commercial activities. The medieval city was different. It was cut off from its surrounding countryside and exercised no authority over it. It lived by a different law from that which prevailed in the rural areas. Its citizens were free. They could come and go as they pleased; they could take up crafts and engage in trade. Not so the peasant who was over much of Europe at this time "bound to the soil," unfree and unable to move legally to the city, though, of course, many of them did. The medieval city was, in fact, an intrusion into a feudal world based on landholding and tenurial relationships. It introduced a new class, the middle class, which engaged in commerce and the crafts, and was destined in time to supplant the feudal class.

The rights of a city and its citizens were paid for dearly. These were granted and guaranteed by a charter from the king or the local territorial lord, but in return the citizens usually paid a rent. In England this commonly consisted of either an arbitrary sum for the whole city, or an individual rent for each building plot, known as a burgage. In addition, the lord often retained the right to levy tolls on goods sold in the local market and to receive the profits, that is, the fines levied, in the local courts. Towns were profitable. That is why so many were founded. Indeed, so many were established, with charters and burgage plots, that they could not all be supported by the volume of local business. More than sixty were established in the single English county of Devon. In each case, a lord was trying to profit from the kinds of business which a town would be likely to attract. Most lords in Devon and many elsewhere were disappointed. No business developed. There was no stream of potential burgesses, eager to take up burgage plots, and the town market attracted few goods. It remained a particularly privileged village.

Devon was exceptional in its number of lapsed towns, but they can be found in every county and every country. Most successful cities, whether newly founded or not, satisfied a need. They grew, attracted business, surrounded themselves with a circuit of walls, and developed the apparatus of urban self-government.

The broad similarity of cities and towns in the thirteenth and early fourteenth centuries hides the variety of their origins. A minority — indeed, a very small minority outside Italy — derived from the cities of the later Roman empire, and could show some degree of continuity of settlement, if not also of urban life. Their walls may have been extended, their street plan distorted, and parts may have fallen to ruin and not been rebuilt. The Christian church had intruded into the city. Many had become the seats of bishops, and all had, within their walls or close by outside, monasteries, friaries, and a vast number of parish churches, far greater in many instances than was warranted by the size of the population. The larger cities in western and southern Europe, with very few exceptions, of which Venice is one, derived from a Roman foundation. This is not surprising. The cities which survived from the Roman empire had immense advantages. Each was served by a network of roads; it had walls to protect it; and masonry buildings which, if ruinous, could still provide the materials for later construction. Lastly, an aura still clung to them and was reinforced by the institutions of the church.

Then there was a group of towns which owed their origins to the special needs of the Dark Ages. Most were fortified refuges for people in those troubled times. The so-called Slavic Chronicle relates that in Holstein, when danger had passed, people "came out of the strongholds in which they were keeping themselves shut up for fear of the wars. And they returned, each one to his own village."[2] The urbanlike settlement had some form of protection and served as a *Fluchtburg,* a place of refuge. Such settlements usually protected by ditch, bank, and palisade, were common in central Europe. In England, where raids by Scandinavian peoples were a danger, outlying settlements are believed to have maintained buildings and doubtless also stores and supplies within such fortified sites. Such "towns" were

2 *The Chronicle of the Slavs by Helmold,* trans. F. K. Tschan (New York, 1935), I, 34.

also created for military or strategic reasons. The Anglo-Saxon Chronicle records under the year 913 that the Saxons "went . . . to Tamworth, and built the fort there . . . then that at Stafford; in the next year, that at Eddesbury . . . and at Warwick. Then in the following year that at Chirbury and that at Warburton, and . . . before midwinter that at Runcorn."[3] Most of these grew into towns in the later Middle Ages, but the speed with which they were built does not suggest that they were very elaborate. Not all such places have retained any kind of urban status, and in continental Europe the majority are represented only by earthworks in the fields. But some acquired permanent inhabitants and gradually developed truly urban functions.

At the same time settlements of traders and craftsmen appeared. They may have developed from the casual or regular meetings of traders. Several such "towns" emerged in the Baltic region, not all of which proved to be permanent. Often such settlements gathered round a nucleus, a building or institution which attracted settlers and perhaps gave them some degree of protection. The city of Bruges thus grew up near the castle of the count of Flanders. A chronicler described, retro-spectively, how "there began to throng before his gate near the castle bridge trades and merchants selling costly goods, then inn-keepers to feed and house those doing business with the prince. . . . The houses increased to such an extent that there soon grew up a large town which in the common speech . . . is still called 'Bridge,' for Bruges means 'bridge.' "[4] Similar developments were taking place over all of western Europe. The Domesday Book (1085–6) recorded that at Tutbury there were forty-two merchants *circa castellum* (around the castle) and at Ewyas Harold, on the Welsh border, there were just two tenements in *castello* – evidently in the courtyard of the castle.

A monastery could also perform this role of nucleus, as at Fulda in Germany, Cluny and Corbie in France, and Bury St. Edmunds and Glastonbury in England. Domesday Book records the rapid growth of the borough of Bury St. Edwards in the years immediately following the Norman conquest.

But not all "new" towns had such a nucleus around which they grew. Many were "planted" in open country; streets were planned and tenements allocated to settlers. Such planted towns were common in central Europe, southern France, and Great Britain. Their origin is often discernible in their plans. The planted town was commonly made up of streets intersecting at right angles to make a gridiron pattern, the whole surrounded by wall or palisade. By contrast, the castle town often consisted of a broad street extending down the slope from the castle which commonly stood upon rising ground. One finds also hybrid types, combin-ing both these elements. Kraków, in Poland, for example, consisted of a nucleus, the *Wawel* or castle, and below it the somewhat irregular "Polish" town. Adjoining this to the north there developed the planned "German" town (Fig. 5.9). The names commonly used to designate these two contrasted quarters of the city have

3 *Anglo-Saxon Chronicle*, Everyman ed. (London, 1912), 78–9.
4 *Annales Sancti Bertini*, quoted in R. Latouche, *The Birth of the Western Economy* (London, 1961), 248.

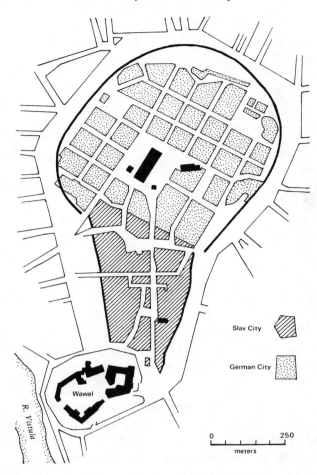

5.9. Plan showing the organic (Slav) and planned (German) elements in the city of Kraków

no ethnic connotation; they indicate merely the customs or "laws" by which each part lived. Sometimes urban growth was yet more complicated. The city of Hildesheim (Fig. 5.10) had as its nucleus a *Fluchtburg*, which developed into the "old" city (Altstadt). Adjacent to it was a small suburban settlement, a sort of "castle" town which was itself enclosed by a palisade at an early date. Southeast of the latter, a cathedral was founded and itself became the nucleus of another settlement, while to the north yet another grew up around the monastery of St. Michael's. Lastly the "new," planned town was added in the thirteenth century, and a century later a wall was built to enclose the whole. The complexity of Hildesheim can be paralleled at many other cities in central Europe. Occasionally, as at Nuremberg and Prague, the city spread across a river which separated its distinctive "quarters." A monastic suburb was built outside the walls of several cities of Roman origin, such as Toulouse, Reims, and Arras.

The creation of the "German" city of Kraków was part of the eastward progression of urban institutions. In many instances a new town was merely added to the

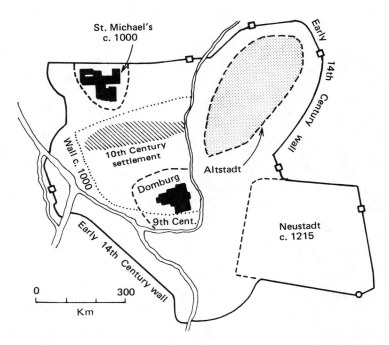

5.10. Plan showing the discrete elements around which the city of Hildesheim developed. The Neustadt was a planned town of the early thirteenth century

earlier fortified enclosure, known as *Burgwalle, grody,* or *hrady.* Sometimes the latter was developed into a castle. Occasionally it provided a secure site for the institutions of the church, and a cathedral was built within it. Most often the new town was planned and planted without any preurban nucleus. Hundreds of such cities and towns were founded in central and eastern Europe. Figure 5.11 shows in highly generalized form how medieval urbanism spread across eastern Europe.

This discussion suggests that there were, from the point of view of urban development, three zones, based upon the ways in which cities evolved. In southern Europe there had been no interruption in urban life. Cities had ceased to grow in size, and many, like Rome itself, became smaller. A few, like Aquileia, were destroyed, and a small number, like Venice and Alessandria, were founded, but the urban map in the twelfth or thirteenth century was very similar to that of the later Roman empire. There were, however, changes in their relative importance. They had declined in southern Italy, but had grown more important in Tuscany and the north Italian plain, where commerce and crafts were developing steadily from the eleventh century. Southern Spain also remained highly urbanized, and during the early Middle Ages Córdoba may have been the largest city in Europe after Constantinople.

The second zone consisted of the remaining provinces of the Roman empire. Cities declined in importance; many were depopulated and some destroyed. In this region urban life had to be rebuilt, but the renewed growth of cities was a selective

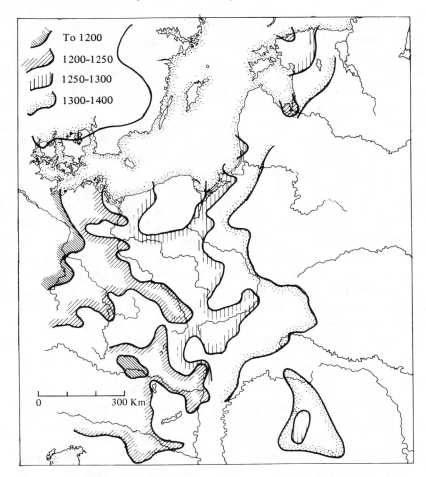

To 1200

1200–1250

1250–1300

1300–1400

0   300 Km

5.11. The spread of towns in eastern Germany and east-central Europe

one. Some grew to a size far greater than under the Roman empire; others failed to prosper and remained small. In addition, a large number of new towns was founded, most of them for commercial reasons, a few for military or strategic.

The last zone was made up of the rest of Europe. Though there were fortified refuges by the hundred, there was no tradition of urban life, and all cities were the creation of the years from the ninth to the thirteenth centuries. Urban growth was a response to contemporary factors and occurred as a general rule where commercial conditions were most favorable. With the development of commerce between the south and the north of Europe, the Rhineland became the chief avenue of trade and also one of the most highly urbanized areas of Europe. At the same time the natural routeway, variously known as the loess belt and as the Hellweg, from the Low Countries and lower Rhineland eastward through Germany to Poland, developed a chain of cities which reached from northern France to Silesia.

The general region of the southern Low Countries and lower Rhineland, where these two major routeways met, began to develop by the ninth century. There were "Frisian" merchants trading up and down the Rhine, and among the goods they handled was cloth. This may at first have come from the monastic estates of the region, but, after the Viking raids had ceased, cloth manufacture appears to have developed also in the incipient towns. No doubt, too, the local rulers in the west of this region, the counts of Flanders, assisted and encouraged the process.

During the eleventh century a network of cities, reaching from Tournai and Valenciennes in the west to Bruges and Ghent in the east, had emerged. It is difficult to point to any physical advantage possessed by the region, other than the relative ease of transportation both within and from it. Perhaps the existence of a kind of infrastructure made up of routes, shipping, and some kind of informal organization of traders, which brought them together at regular fairs, was the chief factor in the evolution of the chief manufacturing and commercial region for cloth-working outside Italy. This development occurred on the outermost fringe of the second of the three urban zones in an area which the Romans had scarcely settled. It owed almost nothing to Roman urbanism. Most of the cities had grown up beside castles; only Arras owed its origin to a Roman city. By the thirteenth century this had become the most highly developed urban region north of the Alps and contained the largest cities outside Mediterranean Europe.

Size and function

It is probably true to say that most cities increased in size until late in the thirteenth or early in the fourteenth century. This growth can be measured in a few instances by the construction of successive lines of walls, as at Cologne (Fig. 5.12). It is more difficult to count the number of citizens. It is evident that the great majority of cities remained very small. Many of the new towns covered only a few acres within their walled perimeter, and their population can only have been numbered in hundreds. On the other hand, some cities were very large. Although there is no head count for any, excepting the listing of "mouths" in some late medieval Italian cities, we do have the number of tradesmen in some of them. At Toulouse, for example, there were 177 butchers near the beginning of the fourteenth century, and in other cities the number of bakers ran to hundreds. This must imply a population of many thousands.

While precision is impossible, one can suggest that by the mid-thirteenth century a small number of giant cities had emerged, each with a population in excess of fifty thousand. Their growth had largely occurred in the previous century. The list would certainly have included Milan, Venice, Genoa, and Florence and, north of the Alps, Paris and possibly Ghent. Córdoba in Moorish Spain and Constantinople would also have reached this size. A much greater number of cities would at this time have had populations between twenty-five and fifty thousand, including several in northern Italy, the southern Low Countries, and northern France, but in Britain only London would have belonged to this category. Cities of inter-

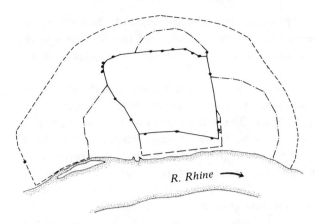

R. Rhine →

5.12. An example of the extension of a city's walls with the growth of urban population: the city of Cologne (Köln)

mediate size, from, let us say, ten to twenty-five thousand, were scattered not unevenly through northwestern Europe, northern Italy, and southern France, but were almost wholly lacking throughout eastern Europe.

The functions which these cities performed were related to their size. All were in some measure agricultural. They were surrounded, like any village, by their own fields, to which the citizens journeyed daily. For the rest, they were market centers, serving the needs of market areas so small that peasants were able to make the market journey and return home within a day. The presence of a market attracted craftsmen, particularly those, like the smith and the leatherworker, whose skills had some relevance to rural life. Large cities distinguished themselves from small by their possession of a wider range of services and, usually, by becoming the centers of administration, either lay or ecclesiastical.

Cities grew during these centuries very largely by immigration. Feudal control of the land and of its rural population was never so restrictive that none escaped from it. There were many footloose peasants, younger sons with no expectation of an inheritance, and those who were free to go to whatever lord they wished. These were likely to flock to the nearest town which offered any prospect of employment.

AGRICULTURE

During the five hundred years surveyed in this chapter the medieval agricultural systems gradually took shape and, before their end, had begun in some areas to decay. Over most of Europe agriculture was conditioned by the fact that breadgrains constituted the greater part of the human diet. Animal proteins were of minor importance, and over much of the continent animals were not kept primarily for food. The maximum production of cereals was achieved by a system of taking two grain crops, followed by a year when the land was left idle. Such a system was foreshadowed in Carolingian Europe (see Chap. 4, under "Agriculture"). During the following centuries it was gradually extended over much of northwestern Europe. We have no means of discovering how it came to be diffused, but it is reasonable to suppose that the monasteries, with their close associations with one another, played a role in the spread of the three-course system. Certainly, by the thirteenth century it was in use from northern England to Poland.

A feature of the system, as it took shape during these years, was the alternation of fall-sown grain – normally wheat or rye – with spring-sown – usually oats or barley – with fallow following the latter. This was adjusted to the plowing routine and, furthermore, gave the opportunity for fallow grazing, when animals, chiefly sheep, were turned out to nibble whatever growth there was. The farming community came to rely on this rough grazing, and from it the land derived most of its manure. Southern Europe never developed a three-field system. Over much of the region spring-sown cereals could not grow and ripen before the drought and heat of summer withered them. Here a fall-sown crop – almost always barley or wheat – alternated with fallow, à system which was used from classical times to the nineteenth century.

The emergence of the three-course system of cultivation was closely linked with that of the open fields and the use of the heavy plow. The three were not necessarily inseparable. Open fields were characterized by long cultivation strips designed to minimize the number of times the plow had to be turned (Fig. 5.13). These implied the use of a heavy plow drawn by a large team. This, in turn, called for the collaborative efforts of a farm community of several households, each contributing some element to the team, for it is clear that a large team of six or eight oxen or other draft animals lay far beyond the resources of a single peasant family. The whole system of plowing, crop rotation, and fallowing called for an element of control within the community which appears to have been best supplied under a feudal system of landholding. One must assume that the several elements which made up this system of cultivation were assembled gradually and over a period of time which may have lasted from the ninth to the twelfth centuries. But, once put together, their interdependence made the system so durable that as late as the nineteenth century it remained in parts of Europe an obstacle to agricultural progress.

Beside the open-field system was one of small fields, enclosed probably by wall or fence, and cultivated with a lighter plow, which could be turned more easily at the end of the furrow and was drawn by perhaps a single animal. In a sense this was a prehistoric or classical mode of cultivation. It had survived chiefly in areas which were unsuited to the open-field system. The latter called for a community large enough to supply the plow and team, but in large areas of Europe the intensive agriculture which this implied was precluded by conditions of climate and terrain. Among these were the highland areas of "Atlantic" Europe, as well as many hilly regions in central Europe. Islands of such "enclosed" cultivation also appear to have survived within the broad region of open-field agriculture, wherever the discipline of the open-field system had not been imposed. In southeast England the trend toward the imposition of the three-course, open-field regime was halted,

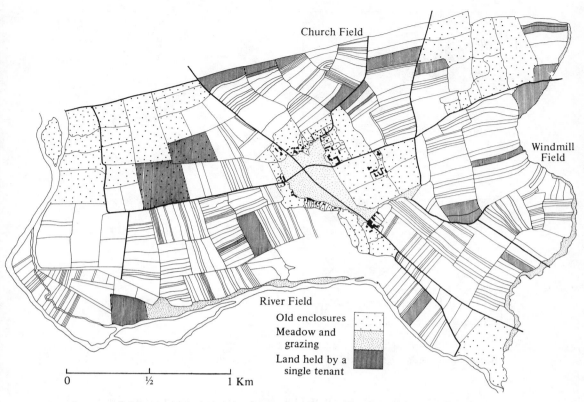

5.13. An open-field system, as it survived into the nineteenth century

possibly for social reasons linked with inheritance practices and control over land use.

In few places can the three-course, open-field system have been developed in its textbook simplicity. One of them was the Cistercian grange at Veulerent in the Paris basin. Here a thirteenth-century record shows the areas cultivated to have been

1. Wheat (fall-sown)	365 ½ arpents
2. Mixed grain (probably oats and barley – spring-sown)	323 arpents 9 perches
3. Fallow	333 arpents 10 perches

The arpent was a somewhat variable land measure, varying from 0.75 to 1.25 acres. This grange was managed in its entirety by the monastery and was cultivated by its lay brothers. The result was one of the most streamlined examples of manorial exploitation to be found. The object was to achieve as steady a flow of farm produce as was practicable, and to this end an approximate equality between fall- and spring-sown crops was desirable. There were many places at which this

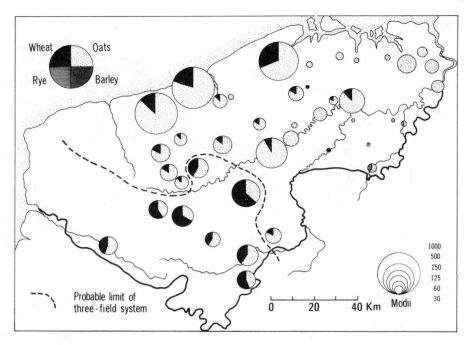

5.14. Cereal cultivation in Flanders in the twelfth century. [After A. Verhulst and M. Gysseling, eds., *Le Compte Général de 1187* (Brussels, 1962).]

parity was not achieved. On a manor belonging to the Belgian abbey of Saint-Trond this disequilibrium was extreme. In all, 980 measures of fall-sown grain were harvested, but only 55 of spring-sown. It is evident that in parts of the southern Low Countries the irregular cropping systems shown in the ninth-century polyptyque of Saint-Pierre at Ghent continued, little modified by the trend toward three-course cultivation, into the thirteenth century (Fig. 5.14).

Animal farming can never have been of great importance in open-field Europe. The system provided little feed, apart from fallow grazing. Cattle were bred for the plow and wagon, and sheep were kept where the demand for wool was high, as in parts of England and the Low Countries. But the meadowland which supplied much of the feed for cattle and horses was always short and, as a general rule, represented the most valuable part of a community's land. Animals were of greater importance in areas of enclosed fields. They were a means of using land which was too poor or too rough for regular cultivation. Pastoral Europe was, by and large, the humid northwest and north and the hilly regions of the center. In southern Europe dry grasslands and scrub were used for sheep grazing, chiefly because there was no other practicable use for them.

Animal rearing in such marginal areas was often transhumant. One does not know to what extent the practice of transhumance survived the period of migrations. It certainly developed again during the more settled period which followed. From the Norwegian fjords to the Spanish Meseta and the hills of southern Italy, the seasonal movement of animals became important. Austrian monasteries derived rent, paid significantly in cheeses, from the rough Alpine lands which they controlled, and in upland areas of western Britain hill grazing was regularly used in summer.

MANUFACTURING AND MINING

Mining and the smelting of metals were at a low ebb in the ninth century. Iron was worked for making weapons and tools, but it continued to be smelted on the hearth or in a primitive wind oven throughout the period. The description in *Egil's Saga* could have been paralleled in much of Europe:

> Skallagrim was a great iron-smith and had great smelting of ore in winter time. He let make a smithy beside the sea . . . the woods lay not over far away. But when he found there no stone . . . to beat iron on . . . he found one and bore the stone to his smithy . . . and thenceforward beat his iron on it. That stone lieth there yet, and much burnt slag nigh.[5]

In the course of the eleventh and twelfth centuries ironworking became more widely diffused. Domesday Book suggests that in England ore was mined and iron smelted and fabricated in many places, but that the yield of each was small. In continental Europe the craft of ironworking was spread particularly by the monastic orders, which would have needed metal in the construction of their houses. By the thirteenth century demand for iron and steel had greatly increased and was beginning to be satisfied increasingly from a few areas which had acquired a reputation for the quality of the metal they produced. The Carthusian monks had opened up the rich Allevard ores in Savoy. The Pyrenees, the Siegen district of western Germany, and the eastern Alps, where the Romans had obtained much of their best iron, were all in production. Swedish ores were beginning to be exploited in the twelfth century, and in Britain both the Weald and the Forest of Dean were increasing their output.

There was, however, little technical progress during the period. Most iron production was by the so-called direct process, in which a soft, but very impure iron was produced directly from the ore on a low hearth, which resembled that used by a blacksmith. At the same time a low-shaft or wind furnace, not unlike that used for making tile or pottery, was used. The problem was to maintain a strong draft, and for this reason the furnace was often built in an exposed position, where the wind could blow into it.

Lead was the nonferrous base metal in greatest demand, and was used in building, glazing, and making pipes and vats. The Rammelsberg mine in the Harz Mountains of central Germany was opened up before 1000. Domesday Book records lead mining in the southern parts of the Pennine Hills, and it developed soon afterward in the Mendip Hills of Somerset. Tin mining had probably lapsed in

5 *Egil's Saga,* trans. and ed. E. R. Eddison (Cambridge, U.K., 1930), 57.

Cornwall and Devon. It is not clear when it was revived, but mines – almost certainly alluvial or drift workings – had been opened by the twelfth century. Copper was worked in southern Spain and, from the later thirteenth century, in Sweden. But it was the precious metals which were most sought after. Deposits in Europe were few and small, and gold was decidedly rare. Silver was found most often in association with lead, notably in the Harz Mountains, from which the metal for much of Europe's coinage must have been obtained.

The five centuries covered by this chapter saw the emergence of specialized manufacturing industries which supplied distant markets with goods of high quality. Most widespread and important were the textile industries. In the Carolingian period cloth production, both woolen and linen, had been the unspecialized activity of peasants everywhere. Cloth appears to have been made in large quantities in northern France and the southern Low Countries, and, coarse though it may have been, was shipped to other parts of western Europe. At the same time, southern Britain may also have been producing a surplus of cloth. The industry was rural, carried on in the cottages of the peasants, but around 1100 it began to move to the small but growing towns of northwest Europe. Here cloth weaving became a specialized craft. The skills of the weavers and the volume of production increased, so that the "clothing cities" of the Low Countries and northern France became the foremost industrial region in thirteenth-century Europe. Local wool from the marshland villages of Flanders and the open-fields of northern France at first sufficed for their needs. This then began to be supplemented by the best English wool from the limestone "scarplands" of the East Midlands and from the Welsh border. By the thirteenth century wool had become Britain's chief export.

A comparable industry was growing up at the same time in the cities of northern and central Italy, particularly Milan and Florence. The Italians appear to have been engaged in the cloth trade before they became manufacturers on a significant scale. In the course of the twelfth century they developed the import of cloth from northwest Europe, much of it by way of the great fairs which were developing in eastern France (see this chap., under "Transport and trade"). They then further refined the cloth by fulling, dyeing, and embroidering it. The Low Countries and Italy did not by any means account for all the cloth that was being traded in thirteenth-century Europe. Many a city in France and England was producing fabrics whose reputation transcended the local region, without ever developing the reputation of Ghent or Florence. In addition, the narrow loom in the peasant's cottage continued to produce coarse homespun which clad the bulk of the laboring population.

Spinning and weaving did not exhaust the processes in the cloth industry. Linen was bleached and dyed, and woolens were fulled to thicken them, sheared to give a smooth surface, and dyed. By the thirteenth century these had become specialized and highly skilled branches of the textile industry. To the traditional textile industries silk weaving was added in the course of the period. The industry, introduced into the Byzantine empire from Asia, had prospered, because demand continued high for silks of quality. From here the craft was taken to Sicily, probably by the Arabs, and thence was diffused through the peninsula. In the thirteenth century it was adopted in Lucca (Tuscany) which then became one of the leading centers for silk manufacture, and from which the craft spread to Venice and to France.

Linen weaving, the humblest branch of cottage industry, was developing during this period into an important branch of textile manufacture. Linen from south Germany and Switzerland was marketed in the Mediterranean region, where it was better suited to the climate than heavy woolens. Cotton was also beginning to be used. It was imported from the Middle East, and a small quantity was grown in Sicily, where it had been introduced by the Arabs. It yielded a weaker thread than modern cotton and in Europe was employed along with wool or flax to make a "mixed" fabric, called fustian or barchent. As a general rule it was used as weft, while the tougher thread served as warp.

The tanning of leather and the manufacture of leather goods – footwear and gloves, harness, bottles and other containers – was carried on throughout the period almost everywhere that skins and hides and a supply of oak bark for tannin could be had. The volume of production must have increased, but there was little change either in the methods used or the location of the industry.

Potting was also a universal craft, practiced wherever clay and fuel were available. Regions differed only in the customary forms of their pots and in the artistry displayed in their manufacture. Pottery furnaces were small and simply built. Their lives were generally short, and they were readily abandoned. The number of potteries and the volume of their output increased. Pots were carted around Europe, chiefly in the baggage of travelers, and since their broken fragments are almost imperishable, they are often a measure of the intensity of human movement. Tiles for flooring and roofing began to be made in the twelfth century, and soon afterward larger kilns began to be built for burning bricks. The Roman craft of brickmaking had died out. It was revived in northern Europe in the twelfth century and became important in those areas, chiefly near the coast of the Baltic and North seas, where there was little good building stone. The earliest recorded use of brick in medieval England was about 1160, but it became important only in the east of the country.

Building construction was one of the more important branches of industry, and one which grew in relative importance throughout the period. In the ninth century almost all building construction was of wood. Masonry was little used except in religious building. After 1000 this began to change. Stone came to be used increasingly in castles, palaces, fortifications, and even in private homes. Building skills developed rapidly. Romanesque gave way to the Gothic style in the later years of the twelfth century and was diffused from the Paris basin where it originated. The greater refinement of building styles called for stone of higher quality. Quarries were opened on an immense scale in those areas, such as the "limestone belt" of England and the plateau of Brie in France, which provided the best, free-cutting stone; and in the thirteenth century, a period of the most intense building activity in much of Europe, stone was transported by road, river, and coasting vessel over great distances. If its architecture was the crowning glory of the thirteenth century, it owes this as much to the quality of the stone as to the skills of the masons.

TRANSPORTATION AND TRADE

These centuries marked a fundamental change in the nature of Europe's commerce. In the ninth century the volume of trade both within Europe and between Europe and non-European lands had been very small. There was some internal movement of cloth and of necessities like salt and wine, but external trade consisted of the import of luxury goods such as silks, precious metals, and religious objects from the Byzantine empire and the Middle East, requited by the export of primary goods like skins, furs, metals, and even slaves. Western Europe had a dependent, almost a "colonial" status in relation to the richer and more sophisticated Islamic world. By the fourteenth century this had changed. It was Europe, or at least western and central Europe together with Italy, which was exporting manufactured goods. Of these, fine cloth from the Low Countries and Italy was most in demand, but exports also included pewter, ironware, and leather goods.

Roles had in some measure been reversed, and the turning point may have been about the time of the Crusades of the twelfth century. The capture of Jerusalem and the formation of the Latin states of the Levant was accompanied by the setting up of trading bases along the coast. First to profit from them were the commercial republics of Venice and Genoa. These were heirs to Amalfi which in the tenth and eleventh centuries had dominated the overseas trade of Italy. Now the city-republics of northern Italy began to serve as intermediaries in the growing trend between the Mediterranean and the northwest of Europe, sending their goods by way of either the Rhône valley or the Alpine passes to Paris, the Low Countries, and the lower Rhineland.

This change in the nature of extra-European trade was accompanied by a reorganization of internal trade, by the development of an infrastructure which eased transport and travel and made the activities of merchants more predictable. A system of markets and fairs evolved and continued to play a vital role in Europe's trade until the nineteenth century. Markets served the needs of local communities. Permission to hold a market — most often weekly — was granted or, in some instances, merely confirmed by a feudal lord. Some such institution existed in the ninth century, but markets became very much more numerous in the eleventh and twelfth. Domesday Book recorded altogether sixty markets in England, but this was only a fraction of their total number, which cannot be known. Several of these markets were specifically described as "new," and new markets continued to be established until the fourteenth century, by which time Britain had in all probability more markets than it could profitably use. The creation of markets in continental Europe followed similar, though less well documented lines. Many just grew up in response to local needs, and their existence was merely authorized after the event. At the same time there were markets which failed and were abandoned for lack of business. It was possible to have too many markets, too closely spaced to one another.

Fairs differed from markets in being less frequent, in attracting merchants and goods from a far greater distance, and, as a general rule, in their specialization in a narrower range of goods. They began with periodic gatherings of merchants. Monasteries appear to have played an important role, holding such events on the name day of the dedicatory saint. The fair at Reims began as a wine sale in the fall. The very important Lendit fair, near Paris, was created and "owned" by the abbey of Saint-Denis, which received the tolls paid by merchants. Cloth fairs emerged at an early date in the southern Low Countries, linked in all probability with the sale of cloth from the manors of the region (see Chap. 4). The Vikings themselves contributed to the growth of fairs in northern Europe, since they used them to dispose of the loot which they had gathered on their raids. Late in the eleventh century the most important fairs in Europe, those of Champagne, had begun to take shape. We do not know how they originated, whether they began as markets or as the seasonal sale of particular commodities. Nor is there any good reason why as many as four cities of the region – Provins, Troyes, Lagny, and Bar-sur-Aube – should have developed fairs. Lagny was very close to Paris. They had the advantage of waterborne transportation, and they were staging points on the routes – there were several of them – linking northwest Europe with the Mediterranean. It was here that, by habit or mutual agreement, merchants agreed to meet at prearranged times during the year. The cycle of fairs grew up and reached its greatest importance and prosperity in the thirteenth century.

There were other fairs in Europe – cloth and wool fairs in England at Stamford, at Stourbridge (near Cambridge), and elsewhere; and in various parts of France and Italy – and in the twelfth and thirteenth centuries, a network of fairs was spreading eastward through Switzerland and Germany. The thirteenth century saw the climax in the development of western Europe's system of fairs. Thereafter business began to decline. Some were ruined by war, others succumbed to the competition of the cities, and part of the commerce which had moved by river and road across Europe began to travel by ship along the coasts of western and northern Europe. As the fairs declined, so did the great ports – Venice, Genoa, Marseilles, and Barcelona – and in northern Europe, London, Antwerp, and Lübeck began to develop.

Travel and transportation in medieval Europe were beset with difficulties. Even if the Roman road system in western and southern Europe had survived in usable condition, it would have been found to be of little value. New needs called for a new system of routes, at a time when central authority was incapable of providing and maintaining them. Waterways were used, even those which today would be considered too small to have much value. They were particularly important in the movement of bulky goods like wool, timber, and wine barrels, but most people and much of the lighter and more valuable merchandise traveled by road. The rich and mighty rode on horseback; others walked. Routes were broad ribbons within which travelers picked their way as best they could. River crossings presented a

serious problem. Most often they were crossed by ferries or fords. Bridges were
few before the later Middle Ages, and where they existed they led to a convergence
of routes.

Most long-distance travel, especially that between northern and southern Europe, necessitated the crossing of high mountains. Complaints of the dangers and
difficulties of Alpine travel were frequent, but despite the depth of snow and the
frequency of avalanches, the Alps were crossed at all seasons of the year. The
Emperor Henry IV made his journey to Canossa in January. The most used passes
before the thirteenth century were the western passes which led from Italy to the
Rhône valley. Then about 1236 the St. Gotthard Pass was opened. The "opening"
consisted in the improvement of the approach road up the Reuss valley to the
north. The importance of the St. Gotthard Pass was that, in a single ascent and
descent, it gave access from northern Italy to the Swiss plateau and the navigable
river Rhine. It quickly became one of the most used passes, and the prosperity
which it brought to the mountain valleys along its route contributed to the rise of
the Swiss Confederation.

The more easterly passes led to the valleys of the upper Rhine and Inn, a tributary of the Danube. They were, in the main, easier than the western passes, but
came into general use only with the economic development of central Europe (see
p. 181).

The commercial axis which was developing during these years between the north
Italian cities and those of northwest Europe was the most important but not the
only avenue of trade. The Crusaders several times used an overland route from the
Albanian coast, through Macedonia to Constantinople, and this continued to be
used and to be supplemented by others across the Karst plateau of Dalmatia. At
the same time, the routes, foreshadowed in the decrees of Charlemagne, between
his empire and eastern Europe, grew in importance. They took off from the Rhine
at Cologne and Mainz and ran eastward respectively to Magdeburg and to Prague
and Kraków. Early travelers, many of them Jewish or at least Middle Eastern in
origin, wrote in the highest terms of the commercial cities along these routes. One
must not, however, overrate the volume of trade which followed them. It was, at
least in the earlier centuries, minute. Few goods could bear the high cost of land
travel, and when demand arose in the west for the grain, flax, timber, and metals
of eastern Europe, these goods moved down the great rivers to the sea and then
along the coast.

In the meantime, Mediterranean seaborne trade increased greatly in both volume and variety. The Jews played an important role in this trade, at least until,
in the twelfth century, it passed into the hands of the Venetians and Genoese.
Benjamin of Tudela enumerated no fewer than forty Jewish communities between
Seville and Constantinople, and all of them engaged in some degree in trade. Islam
proved no barrier; Amalfi and Salerno were the chief intermediaries in the tenth
and eleventh centuries, carrying on trade with Moslem Sicily and North Africa.
But Amalfi never recovered from its capture in 1077 by the Normans under Robert
Guiscard, and its commercial role passed to the port cities of northern Italy. If the

trade of Venice was primarily with the Aegean Sea and the Levant, Genoa inherited Amalfi's role in the western Mediterranean.

Earlier centuries had seen the development of an important if not large trade by way of the great Russian rivers between the Baltic Sea and the Black. The driving force in this trade had been Scandinavians from Sweden, and it was under their auspices that Kievan Russia became a focus of trade. The routes across the steppe, on which it relied, were in the tenth century cut by the Pechenegs and Kumans. Trade was brought to a standstill. Kievan Russia was destroyed, and its people were driven back within the forest belt, where, protected from the horse-riding nomads, they built up the state of Muscovy.

SELECT BIBLIOGRAPHY

General

The Alexiad of the Princess Anna Comnena. Trans. E. A. S. Dawes. London, 1928.
The Chronicle of the Slavs by Helmold. Trans. F. K. Tschan. New York, 1935.
Dopsch, A. *The Economic and Social Foundations of European Civilization.* London, 1937.
Egil's Saga. Trans. E. R. Eddison. Cambridge, U.K., 1930.
Herlihy, D., R. S. Lopez, and V. Slessarev, eds. *Economy, Society and Government in Medieval Italy.* Kent, Ohio, 1969.
The Itinerary of Benjamin of Tudela. Trans. M. N. Adler. Oxford, 1907.
Ladurie, E. Le R. *Montaillou.* London, 1978.
Luzzatto, G. *An Economic History of Italy from the Fall of Rome to the Beginning of the Sixteenth Century.* London, 1961.
Pounds, N. J. G. *An Economic History of Medieval Europe.* London, 1974. "The Origin of the Idea of Natural Frontiers in France." *Annals of the Association of American Geographers* 41(1951): 146–57.
Vives, J. V. *An Economic History of Spain.* Princeton, N.J., 1969.

Population and settlement

Beresford, M. *New Towns of the Middle Ages.* London, 1967.
Brown, H. F. "The Venetians and the Venetian Quarter in Constantinople to the Close of the Twelfth Century." *Journal of Hellenic Studies* 40 (1920): 68–88.
Pirenne, H. *Medieval Cities.* New York, 1956.
Rörig, F. *The Medieval Town.* Berkeley, Calif., 1967.
Russell, J. C. *Late Ancient and Medieval Population. Transactions of the American Philosophical Association,* vol. 48, pt. 3 (1958).

Economic development

Bloch, M. *French Rural History.* London, 1966.
Darby, H. C., ed. *A New Historical Geography of England.* Cambridge, U.K., 1973.
Duby, G. *Rural Economy and Country Life in the Medieval West.* London, 1968.
Slicher van Bath, B. H. *The Agrarian History of Western Europe A.D. 500–1850.* London, 1963.

6

Europe in the early fourteenth century

By the early fourteenth century the period of medieval economic growth was over; the population of Europe reached its peak at about this time, and the spatial pattern of cities was to develop no farther before the nineteenth century.

POLITICAL GEOGRAPHY

The political map of Europe had assumed a form which, with minor changes, it was to retain into modern times. Only in the Balkan peninsula, where the Byzantine empire was clinging desperately to its last foothold, were major changes still to come. In most of Europe political control was becoming more centralized, and kingship more absolute. Feudalism, as a mode of government, was weakening, though its outward symbols were as conspicuous as ever. Only in eastern Europe and Russia were feudal relationships tending to strengthen.

In the Spanish peninsula the southward advance of the Christian states had reduced the Moorish kingdom of Granada to the Sierra Nevada and neighboring coastlands. To the north, Castile, having absorbed Léon and other petty states, reached from the Biscay coast in the north to the Strait of Gibraltar (Fig. 6.1). It dominated the Meseta, while around its periphery lay Navarre and Gascony, Aragon and Portugal. Only Castile still had a boundary with the Moors and still continued its centuries-old crusade against them. Portugal and Aragon were casting their eyes beyond the seas and were beginning that commercial expansion which was to take them to Asia and the New World.

In 1328 the Capet dynasty of France ended, and the crown passed to the house of Valois. The Capets had succeeded in converting a nominal kingship over France into an effective control over much of it by eliminating intermediate dukes and counts. But they had not pursued this objective with the singleness of purpose that has sometimes been assumed. No sooner did they get possession of a duchy or county, but they alienated it, most often as an *apanage* to a member of their own family. Sooner or later control of it returned to the king, though not always, as the cases of the duchy and county of Burgundy show, without untold trouble for France. In 1328, the duchy of Brittany continued to be ruled in almost complete independence, and the duchy of Gascony was held by the English kings, who, far from admitting the overlordship of France, claimed the crown themselves

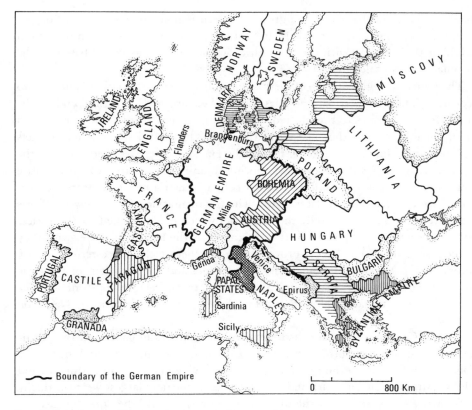

6.1. Political map of Europe in the early fourteenth century

as heirs of the last Capet. There were other provinces, among them the county of Chartres and duchy of Anjou, whose allegiance to the king of France was entirely nominal.

The eastern boundary of France derived from the partitions which brought the Carolingian empire to an end. There had been endless territorial disputes between the French kings or their subjects on the one hand, and their eastern neighbors on the other. As each was settled, an attempt was made to establish an incontrovertible boundary and thus to make further dispute impossible. The only way seemed to be to align the boundary along an unchanging feature of nature, a mountain crest or a river. In eastern France, rivers were most convenient and so the boundary came gradually to approximate to the line of the four rivers: Scheldt, Meuse, Saône, and Rhône.

The county of Flanders was thus brought within the territorial limits of France, though its counts pursued a remarkably independent policy throughout the Middle Ages. Beyond the line of the river Scheldt lay Brabant and Hainault, no less, theoretically, parts of the German empire. The boundary was blurred, not only by the independent stance of the feudal units which bordered it but also by the fact that the whole area had become a great industrial region, the foremost in Europe, with the exception only of northern Italy. Power in Flanders, as also in its eastern neighbor Brabant, lay with the great cities whose wealth was firmly based on the manufacture and sale of cloth.

The political fragmentation of Germany had been growing apace for almost two centuries. The great "tribal" duchies had broken up, and, since the end of the Hohenstaufen in 1254, the elected emperors had been feeble, ineffective, and totally unable, even if they had wished to do so, to control the hundreds of fiefs and free cities. In 1273 Rudolf I, first of the Habsburg dynasty, had assumed the imperial title, and, without even attempting to unify the empire, set out to create a patrimony for his own family. To the duchy of Austria he added Styria, Carinthia, Carniola (Krain), and later Tyrol. The fragmentation of Germany itself was complete. It embraced not only the territories which made up the Low Countries, but also Lorraine; that part of Burgundy known as the Franche-Comté, which lay to the east of the Saône; Savoy; Provence; and northern Italy. Its eastern boundary embraced the Marches of Bradenburg and Lausitz and the kingdom of Bohemia with its dependencies, Silesia and Moravia. In this direction the limits of the German empire remained almost unchanged until it was snuffed out by Napoleon in 1806.

Within Germany few states had the size and resources to command the obedience and respect of the others. But among them at this time was the kingdom of Bohemia, ruled by the house of Luxembourg and embracing also Moravia and Silesia. After the Luxembourg and Habsburg lands the next largest were the duchy of Bavaria and the estates of the many German bishops. At the opposite extreme were diminutive states of only a few square miles, but among them were the forest cantons of Switzerland, each little more than a single mountain valley, which in 1291 joined to throw off their allegiance to the Habsburgs and declare themselves independent.

Across the center of the Italian peninsula, from the Po delta on the east to Terracina on the west, lay the patrimony of St. Peter, more or less as it was five centuries earlier, when Charlemagne recognized the bogus claims of the papacy. Between it and the Alps lay the kingdom of Lombardy to which, since Charlemagne, the German emperors had laid claim. They had no power base in Italy, and their rule was barely recognized and totally ineffective. Northern Italy had fragmented even more than Germany. It seemed to be reverting to the Roman pattern of city-states, with the important difference that these were wealthy, powerful, and in constant conflict. Foremost among them were Milan, Verona, Padua, Lucca, Pisa, and Florence, but on the coasts of, respectively, the Adriatic and Tyrrhenian seas lay Venice and Genoa. Both were expanding along their neighboring coasts; both had developed trade within the Mediterranean which brought them wealth and power; and both were effectively beyond any control by the emperor in whose territory they theoretically lay.

South of the Papal States were Sicily and the Kingdom of Naples. They had been inherited by the Hohenstaufen, but the popes had called in the French to protect them from the German emperor. This the French continued to do but had, in 1282, lost possession of Sicily (the "Sicilan Vespers"), which was absorbed into the growing maritime state of Aragon.

Ever since the Carolingian period the Germans had been advancing their settlements eastward into lands which had hitherto been occupied by the Slavs. And close behind the German colonists came German political control. By the early years of the fourteenth century the limit of both lay well to the east of the river Oder, and Germany's frontier states were Pomerania, Brandenburg, and the province of Silesia, which at this time passed from Poland to Bohemia and was therefore conceived as part of the German empire. Across the isthmus of eastern Europe, from the Baltic Sea to the Black, lay what remained of Europe's tribal kingdoms: Poland, Hungary, Serbia, Bulgaria, and the vast, inchoate state of Lithuania. The German fighting orders, the Teutonic Knights and Brethren of the Sword, had settled along the east Baltic coast and had cut a swath into the interior from the lower Vistula to the Gulf of Finland. Their conquests had been at the expense in part of the Christian Poles, in part of the still heathen Lithuanians, who provided the excuse for their missionary depredations. To their south lay the Polish state with its capital at Kraków, and to the east the grand duchy of Lithuania, which was at this time extending its territory through the forests of Russia toward the headwaters of the Volga and on the south into the steppe. Beyond the loosely held lands of Lithuania were the Russian principalities of Novgorod and Moscow. To all these predominantly Slavic states the Tartars of the Golden Horde were an ever present danger. In 1241 they had erupted into central Europe in raids which resembled the invasions of the Huns and Avars. Their power was somewhat diminished in the fourteenth century, but their unruly presence was a grave danger to all states which bordered the steppe, and they even exercised a kind of suzerainty over Muscovy.

The Kingdom of Hungary also had the steppe peoples as uncomfortable neighbors but gained some protection from the arc of the Carpathian Mountains. The Hungarians, like the Poles, thought of themselves as guardians of the west against the pagan Tartar and the orthodox Slavs, a claim for which there was a measure of justification. South of the Danube the Slav population of the Balkan peninsula had formed a series of states whose mutual boundaries reflected their political fortunes. During the previous century the second Bulgarian empire had spread across the peninsula from the Black Sea and the lower Danube to the coast of Albania. But in the fourteenth century its power was weakening, and at the same time the tribes of Raška and Kosovo were building up a Serb state. To the northwest, Bosnia, divided internally by the Bogumil heresy, was invaded and conquered by the Hungarians. On the fringes of the Balkan peninsula lay the pathetic remnant of the Byzantine empire, now reduced to little more than the Marmara region and the Aegean shore of Greece. That it was able to endure so long was due entirely to its control of the sea, by means of which it supplied its capital city and maintained contact with its outlying members. But even here it was in retreat, and the Venetians were snapping up Aegean islands and coastal bases and absorbing them into their own maritime empire, while to the east the shadow of the empire of Islam was creeping ever nearer.

Scandinavia, like the Balkans, lay on the fringes of European civilization. Three states had emerged: Denmark, Sweden, and Norway. Each centered in a relatively fertile and populous region, its "cove area," from which its authority reached outward to an ill-defined frontier. Denmark was the most advanced both politically and economically. It was open to cultural influences from central Europe, the ships of the Hanseatic merchants regularly sailed through its waters, and in the island of Sjaeland it had a fertile and productive land base. Not so Sweden and Norway. Both were mountainous and infertile, incapable of supporting a dense population or of maintaining many cities. The focus of Swedish authority was the lowlands around Lake Mälaren, where Stockholm was beginning to develop as its capital. Norway was at this time no more than a string of settlements built on the narrow shelves of land between its rugged interior and the sea. The lowland around Christiania (Oslo) Fjord was the most extensive, and contained the capital of this very fragmented state. The north of Scandinavia was almost wholly unpopulated, and only the coastal areas of Finland, loosely linked with Sweden, held any economic significance.

England was at this time the most centralized and most successful monarchy in Europe. It had developed an efficient bureaucracy. The administration of justice was being concentrated in the royal courts and an equitable system of taxation was yielding the revenue to sustain the central government. In England itself, despite local variations, there was a common culture, and a man might feel equally at home in Devon or in Durham. Only in Cornwall did a separate — and Celtic — language continue to be spoken. Wales had long been under pressure from England. Much of the country had been overrun and brought under English control, and the last area of Welsh political resistance had succumbed to invasion in the closing years of the previous century.

Similar attempts to incorporate Scotland into a "united kingdom" had failed. Environmental factors favored the Scots, as they did not the Welsh. The focus of their power, the Central Lowlands, was protected from invasion by the Southern Uplands; and control of the sea, used so effectively against Wales, was of little importance in the Scottish campaigns. The English seemed at first to have made more progress in Ireland. Here they met with no united resistance, and were able to claim sovereignty over the whole island. But real control was restricted to the "Pale" of English settlement, as Dublin and its immediate hinterland were called, and the rest of the country was divided into "tribal" territories. Irish society had been infiltrated by Anglo-Norman barons, but they had been, by and large, assimilated into Irish society, becoming, in the current phrase, "more Irish than the Irish themselves." A theoretical English sovereignty over the island was not translated into effective political control.

POPULATION

It is generally assumed that the early years of the fourteenth century marked the culmination of a long period of population growth, and that pestilence and famine then combined to reduce the total to a fraction of what it had been when the century began. When population took this downward turn is far from clear. Did it begin with the disastrous harvests of 1315–17, or with the spread of the Black Death in 1349, or were its roots more subtle, the growing pressure of population on agricultural resources, malnutrition, and disease? In all probability these all played a role, and the plague of 1349 only intensified a movement which had already begun.

Evidence for the size of population is indeed scanty. A census in any formal sense would have been inconceivable, and we are obliged to make whatever use is possible of surrogates like "hearths" or households, communicants, poll tax records, even the numbers of urban craftsmen. The problem is always to discover by how much the given figure has to be multiplied to yield an approximation to the total population: How large, for example, was the typical household; what allowance must be made in tax records for paupers and the very young? And everywhere one encounters the problem of clergy, who did not pay lay taxes and were excluded from most categories of population.

Death rates were high, and the average expectation of life was short. A large proportion of children died before reaching maturity, and a high birthrate was necessary even to maintain a stable population. Birthrates were highest in rural areas and death rates highest in cities. This was due in part to poor environmental conditions, but also in part to the fact that much of the urban population had migrated from the countryside and tended to marry relatively late. Without a continuous inflow from rural areas cities could not even have maintained – much less increased – their population. More is known, generally speaking, of urban than of rural population. It acquired property; it was taxed; many citizens belonged to guilds whose records have survived, and in some Italian cities periodic counts of *bocche* – "mouths" – were conducted in order to estimate the grain requirements of the city.

For a number of rural areas hearth rolls have survived, consisting in general of lists of inhabited places with the numbers of "hearths" in each. If one could arrive at an estimate of the size of the average household, one could estimate, if only approximately, the size of the population. As a general rule, the household in western Europe consisted only of the nuclear family of parents and children, though occasionally one finds evidence for the extended family, embracing also grandparents, aunts, uncles, and yet more distant relatives. This clearly distorts the demographic picture presented by the simple catalog of hearths. To convert hearths to total population a multiplier of between four and five has usually been used. Four is probably too low, and five may not be large enough for areas where the extended family was at all common.

Tables of the number of hearths survive for several parts of France from the years before the Black Death, and there are several series for the Burgundian lands in the fifteenth century (see Fig. 7.5). That for the county of Rouergue, which spanned the more southerly part of the French Central Massif, is apparently one of the most complete of such records. It was compiled in 1341 and gives the number of hearths

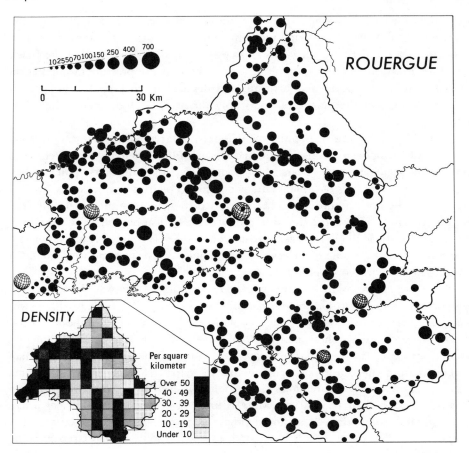

6.2. The distribution of population in the province of Rouergue (*département* Aveyron), France, 1341. (Globes indicate large towns.)

in each of 578 parishes. Its aggregate figures are confirmed by a record of the numbers of parishes and hearths of 1328 in each of the units which made up that part of France which was subject directly to the French king. The settlements recorded in the survey of Rouergue (*département* Aveyron) are shown in Figure 6.2. It is not easy to translate these data into terms of population density. The method used has been to superimpose a grid on the map, and then to calculate the density within each square. The result is shown in Figure 6.2, and ranges from fewer than 10 to the square kilometer to more than 50. The overall density was about 30 to the square kilometer. This is closely similar to the *present* density of about 32. Given the fact that soils were in general poor and agricultural techniques backward, it cannot be said that Rouergue was anything but overpopulated on the eve of the Black Death.

Unfortunately such hearth lists are lacking for most of Europe, at least for the years before the Black Death. The excellent series of records of the Low Countries, compiled by the dukes of Burgundy, do not begin until after the Great Plague, but they continue into the sixteenth century (see pp. 187–91). Using the same method as that employed for Rouergue on the Burgundian materials, one finds a belt of dense population extending across the Low Countries from near Saint-Omer in the west to Liège in the east. Over large areas of the plain of Flanders, Brabant, and Hainault densities of well over 130 to the square mile were to be found. On the other hand, densities rarely exceeded 75 in northern France and were consistently below 50 in the hilly province of Luxembourg and over the infertile heaths of north Brabant. The province of Burgundy and the diocese of Lausanne (western Switzerland) showed similarly low densities. The evidence on which these estimates were based was compiled *after* the first and most savage visitations of the Great Plague, and we may assume that densities were considerably higher during the first half of the century.

There is little comparable evidence for Germany, only a few hearth lists for relatively small areas in the east. Their evidence should not be pressed too far, but it indicates a very low overall density – fewer than ten persons to the square mile – in this predominantly rural and forested region. The same can be said of Poland. A list of the numbers of communicants in each parish in the diocese of Kraków suggests that on the best soils along the river Vistula density did not exceed fifty per square mile, and that it sank to well under ten in the mountains of the south. This is confirmed by the evidence for the payment of Peter's Pence to the papacy, which shows an average density of fewer than ten over most of Poland. The Slav lands of the east clearly offered abundant scope for German penetration and settlement.

If evidence for eastern Europe is scanty, that for southeastern is nonexistent. The same can be said of Lithuania and Russia. Bearing in mind the poor quality of the soil, the frequency of warfare, and the ever present danger of invasion from the steppe, it would be surprising if the population of these areas greatly exceeded 12 million.

Italy, by contrast, was both densely peopled and well documented. The country was highly urbanized, and its burgesses were literate and kept good records. In particular, the need to keep their cities well provisioned led to periodic counts of the number of "mouths." A survey of the *contado* of the Tuscan city of Pistoia in 1344 revealed surprisingly high densities. In the lowlands along the Arno River densities of 120 to the square mile were reached, and in the hill country to the north – much of it terraced for vineyards – an average of 160 was reached. Even the Apennines had more than 25 to the square mile. The neighboring *contado* of Florence is said to have had an overall density of 168. There is little quantitative data for the northern plain, which also appears to have been densely peopled, though much of the land near the river Po, now among the most fertile and productive, was then ill-drained and little used. Densities appear to have been lower in central and southern Italy, though the evidence is less satisfactory than in the north. War and misgovernment had taken their toll, and the relative paucity of true urban development was reflected in the less intensive use of the countryside.

In the Spanish peninsula information is available only for Catalonia, and this dates from the period after the Great Plague. As for the Balkans, any estimate of population can be nothing more than an intelligent guess. For Scandinavia and the vast and almost empty lands of the north there is no concrete evidence, and one can only postulate a level of density which matches their resources and the extensive economy practiced there.

For much of Britain we are on safer ground, but even here the sources are susceptible of a wide variety of interpretation. The chief sources are a tax return of 1334, based on local wealth, and a poll tax levied in 1377 on all aged 14 and over, excepting only clergy and paupers. The latter is the more useful document, even though the problem of allowing for the excluded categories and also for evasion is not easily solved. Estimates of the total population of England in 1377 range from a low of 2.3 million to a high of 3 million. The discrepancy here is relatively small. The problem is rather to project these figures back through the Black Death to the higher totals earlier in the century. There is absolutely no evidence for the overall mortality rates in the Great Plague of 1349–50 and in the subsequent severe outbreak in the 1360s. There were communities which largely escaped, others which were almost obliterated. The average may have been between 20 and 30 percent. Where population was sparse mortality appears to have been a great deal lower, because the vectors of the plague were able to make fewer contacts and infected a smaller number of people. The difference is between those who argue for a high mortality rate and those who assume that it was low, and this gives a range of between 2.5 and 6 million for the population of England before the Black Death. There is no satisfactory evidence for the population of highland Britain — Wales, Scotland, and Ireland. Densities could not have been higher than those met with in southwestern England, where physical conditions were not wholly dissimilar. There the density was no more on average than forty to the square mile. It would have been a great deal less than this in the mountains of Wales and Scotland and over much of Ireland.

The total population of Europe, including Russia, during the half century preceding the Black Death is thus likely to have been between 75 and 80 million. Table 6.1 incorporates the differing estimates made by two distinguished demographic historians, Julius Beloch and Josiah Cox Russell. The estimates of population suggest that densities ranged from 150 and more to the square mile in highly urbanized regions like Flanders and Brabant to fewer than 10 to the square mile in the Alps and Central Massif. They appear to have varied from 60 to 100 on good loess soils, like those of the Paris basin and Saxony, but rose above this level where the urban population was considerable. There is a degree of consistency in estimates for the plain of eastern Europe, where soils were in general of only mediocre quality and towns were few and mostly small: in general between 20 and 30 to the square mile. It was almost certainly a great deal less than this in heavily

Table 6.1. *Estimated population, in millions*

	Beloch's estimate	Russell's estimate
British Isles	4.0	5.3
France	14.0	19.0
Low Countries ⎫ Germany ⎭	15.0	11.0
Scandinavia	1.9	0.6
Spanish peninsula	6.0	9.5
Italy	11.0	9.3
Eastern and south- eastern Europe	15.0	15.0
Lithuania and Russia	8–10.0	8–10.0

forested areas like Lithuania and Russia. But one must beware of reading too much into the nature of the terrain and the quality of the soil because agricultural production was not the only factor influencing the density of the population. To say that it was would be to admit that there was a persistent Malthusian crisis throughout Europe. This was clearly not the case, except in a few areas within western Europe and Italy. In eastern Europe there was, even in the early fourteenth century, abundant land to attract the land-hungry peasant from the west. Nevertheless, in the absence of quantitative data one can only ask how many people could have been supported by land of a particular quality at a given technological level. The map of Europe in Figure 7.5 is a very tentative attempt to answer this question.

By the early fourteenth century the great migrations had ended. No longer did great bodies of people sweep across the continent; the Tartar invasion of 1241 was the last. Henceforth the movement of peoples was on a smaller scale and over shorter distances. They were still spreading – always in small groups – from well-cultivated and densely peopled lands into those which offered them greater scope. Much of this migration was only from the village into nearby woodland or waste, but some was over greater distances, from central Germany, for example, to the frontier of settlement in the German east or in Poland. This longer distance movement was coming to an end as population pressure eased in western and central Europe, and after the Black Death it ceased altogether.

Much of the migration was of agricultural population. At the same time, however, there was migration from rural areas – and not necessarily crowded ones – to the cities. The reasons were varied. There were footloose younger sons with no expectation of ever inheriting a farm holding, as well as victims of accident and misfortune. The city appeared to be a place of opportunity. Serfdom was unknown, and successful escape to the city marked the end of villein status and personal obligations to a lord. On the other hand, the city had to recruit citizens in this way if it was to survive. Urban mortality was high because disease traveled fast through its crowded houses and markets, and birthrates were low because immigrants took time before they could make homes and establish families. All cities, and especially the largest, needed a continuous inflow from rural areas if they were even to maintain their population. Much of this migration was over only relatively short distances. A study of immigrants to four French cities shows that half of them had traveled no more than fifteen miles, and that only 7 percent came from places more than fifty miles away. Acute rural overpopulation, such as could be found in parts of northern France, the Low Countries, and northern Italy might be expected to lead to a more intense migration to nearby cities, and thus to a large body of paupers and mendicants. This was indeed the case, and it contributed to urban unrest and popular movements of a broadly economic order. Hearth registers which distinguish between those able to pay the taxes and those unable almost always showed an increase in the latter.

THE LANGUAGE MAP

The linguistic map of Europe had by the fourteenth century very nearly assumed its modern form. Language boundaries were becoming sharper, as minorities on one side or the other were gradually assimilated. At the same time dialect differences within each country were beginning to weaken, and in each a dominant form was asserting itself. This was most notable in Britain and France. In Britain the dominant language, English, had largely replaced the Norman-French, brought by the Norman conquerors, and was spreading in the west at the expense of Celtic. French had acquired the status of a national language in all areas except Brittany, which retained its Celtic tongue, and the south, where the related Romance language "Languedoc" continued to be spoken into modern times. The use of French was spreading, at the expense of Germanic dialects in north and east, and of Romance languages and dialects in the south, but almost everywhere a local patois continued to be spoken into the nineteenth century.

In the Low Countries Flemish was taking shape in Brabant and very slowly displacing local and regional dialects. A similar process was, however, barely distinguishable in Germany, where local tongues, loosely grouped into Low Middle and High German, continued to be used without any of them gaining any kind of broader acceptance before the sixteenth century. The eastern limit of German speech was a great deal less clear than its western. The German tongue was carried eastward by settlers who made their homes among people whose native speech was a form of Slavic. There was no clear boundary. Language was a matter of class as it was wherever immigration was important. In this eastern borderland German remained until the twentieth century the language of the landowning and managerial classes; Polish and Czech were the languages of the peasantry. This was reflected in the structure of the cities, where the older nucleus (see Chap. 5, under "Growth") remained Slavic while the newer additions — the *Neustädte* — were German in their institutions and perhaps also in language. There was, however, always a tendency for the humbler, Slavic language to be abandoned in favor of German, the mark of social upward progress.

Islands of Romance speech grew smaller within the Alps but, in the form of

Romansh, still survive today. In Italy the Tuscan dialect was becoming a refined literary instrument and was being adopted increasingly in central and northern Italy. The tendency toward linguistic unity was very much less marked in the Spanish peninsula. Castilian Spanish was taking shape on the northern Meseta but was making no headway against the peripheral Romance languages: Catalan, Galician, and Portuguese, or even the Valencian and Andalusian dialects of the south. And Basque, a pre-Roman language of the peninsula, continued to demonstrate its obstinate capacity for survival.

The Slav languages were spoken over an immense area which extended from the Elbe River in the west to the Volga in the east, and from the Baltic Sea to Macedonia. Their original continuity was interrupted by the Ural-Altaic language brought by the Magyars to the plain of the middle Danube, and by the related Szeklers to Transylvania. Theirs was an instance of the superimposition of an immigrant culture upon a people who had been culturally Slav and ethnically Thracian, Dacian, and Avar. The situation in the former Roman province of Dacia is far from clear. The Romanian claim that the region was culturally "latin" and that it had retained a Romance language since Roman times is difficult to support, especially as Romanian incorporates a good deal of Slavic vocabulary. Groups of Romance-speaking pastoralists had survived in the Balkan peninsula since Roman times. In origin they were probably Romanized Thracians who had sought refuge from invaders in the mountains while invading peoples swirled around them. These were the Maurovlachs or Vlachs. They were a scattered but numerous people and were politically powerful. It is generally assumed that the leadership in the second Bulgarian empire was, at least in its earlier stages, Vlach.

Greek remained the language of the Byzantine empire and was spoken throughout Greece, the Greek islands, and the Marmara region. To the north, the pre-Roman language of the peninsula, Thracian, had not been entirely supplanted by Slavic. It could be found in remote and inaccessible regions and, with a strong admixture of later languages, survived in Albanian.

The Slav languages of eastern Europe were in the end reduced to some ten regional tongues, but in the later Middle Ages they were represented by a large number of local dialects. Two of these, Sorb in eastern Germany and Kaszub in northern Poland, have retained some importance into recent times. North of the Slavs were the Balts, of whom the Prussians formed part. Their language, which survives in Lithuanian and Latvian, was closely akin to the Polish variant of Slavic, and many were culturally absorbed by the Poles. Yet farther north was the very sparse population of Finno-Ugric peoples, distantly related by language to the Tartars.

Scandinavia was Germanic, and the German language of central Europe derived from here (see pp. 78–9). Here also a variety of local dialects was being assimilated into two main tongues, Danish and Swedish. The English language derives from the dialects carried by the Anglo-Saxon-Jutish invaders of the fifth and sixth centuries. This was carried across the English plain and into the borders of Wales and Scotland and, supplemented by the Old Norse of the later Scandinavian settlers and the French of the Normans, was in the fourteenth century ripening into English. This period saw the beginnings of a truly national literature. The western boundary of English, like the eastern boundary of German, was far from clear-cut and reflected social standing rather than any progress of the English conquest.

SETTLEMENT

At least 80 percent of the population of Europe – considerably more in some areas of the north and east – lived in the countryside and worked on the land. They lived in villages, hamlets, and isolated homesteads which reflected both social and historical conditions and also the technical requirements of agriculture. Almost all such settlements that appear in the landscape today were present in the early fourteenth century. Only a fraction have since been "deserted" and ceased to exist as inhabited places. Except in a few marginal areas, such as northern Scandinavia and parts of the Spanish peninsula and the Balkans, the period of expansion was over; the European "frontier" was closed.

The pattern of settlements and the morphology of the settlements themselves had, generally speaking, been established in the earlier Middle Ages and showed a remarkable durability. The basic settlement type in western and central Europe and over much of eastern was the compact or nucleated village. Houses were grouped irregularly. There was often a central space or green, usually overlooked by the church. The area given over to yard or garden was relatively small, and the visible evidence of communal life in the form of common land, burial ground, and church were conspicuous. Around lay the open-fields, divided into plots and strips and cultivated, if not communally, at least according to a common format by the villagers. The great antiquity of such a settlement type is beyond question. Clustered villages commonly occupied the best land, occupied by the first settlers. As population grew it began to colonize the extensive areas of forest and waste (Figs. 6.3 and 6.4). The new settlements often differed fundamentally from the earlier and more traditional forms because they were established under different social conditions. Family groups, or even single individuals, moved into the forest, made a clearing, and established an isolated homestead. The single farm might grow into a small group of cottages, but very rarely did it approximate a large nucleated village. On the other hand settlers might migrate in a group, usually under the leadership of a *locator* who had already found a site and was paid for bringing settlers to it. Such settlements implied a degree of organization and control not found in scattered farmsteads. Most often settlers were each allocated a length of frontage on a road, with permission to clear a narrow strip of land behind it, reaching to whatever boundary may have been determined. Such was the "street" or "forest" village found in Germany, but above all in the area of German colonization to the east (Fig. 6.5).

The zone of early conflict between German and Slav, between the lower Elbe valley and the mountains which enclosed Bohemia, was characterized by the *Rundling,* or "ring fence" village. The cottages were placed in a circle, facing on to a

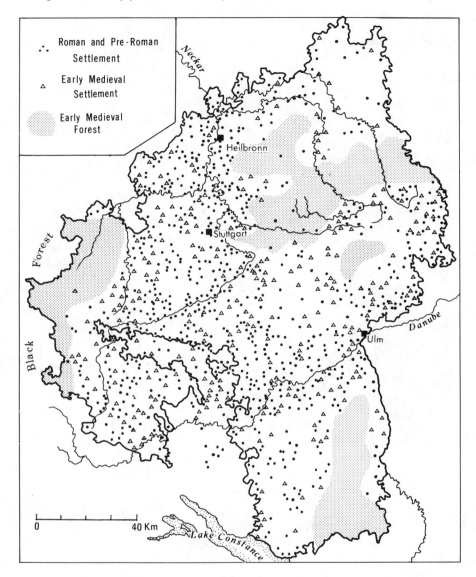

6.3. Settlement in Württemberg. [After Robert Gradmann, "Die ländlichen Siedlungs-formen Württembergs," *Petermanns Mitteilungen* 56 (1956), folding maps.]

central "green." There can be little doubt that this open space was designed for corralling farm animals and implies a degree of insecurity. A compromise between this and the street village was achieved when the double row of cottages in the latter drew back from one another to leave an elongated open space. Even the clustered or nucleated village sometimes had a centrally located place or "green." It was usually land held in common by the community. It served a variety of social

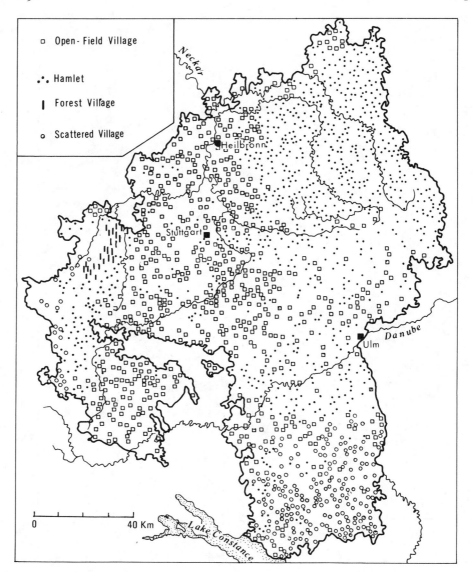

6.4. Village types in Württemberg. The correspondence is close between nucleated, open-field villages and the longest settled areas. New settlement is largely in the form of hamlets and scattered farmsteads. [After Gradmann, "Die landlichen Siedlungsformen Württembergs."]

and economic purposes, in addition to providing a little grazing, and is today frequently preserved as a very desirable open space.

In much of Europe the tendency for village settlements to grow was restricted by the fact that the journey to the most distant fields would become too great. In southern Europe this consideration does not appear to have hindered the growth

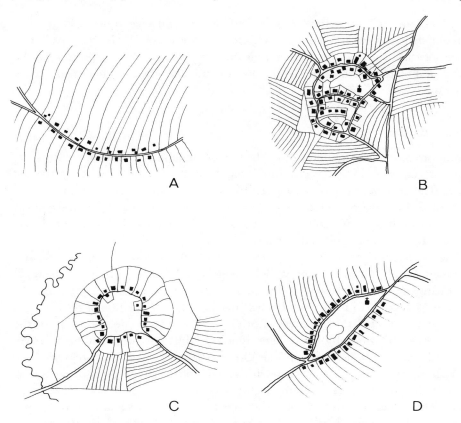

6.5. Village types: (A) forest village, (B) nucleated village or *Haufendorf,* (C) round village or *Rundling,* (D) spindle-shaped village or *Angerdorf*

of giant villages. The reason was probably in the overriding need for protection. Through the earlier Middle Ages scattered homesteads and small hamlets were being abandoned, and their inhabitants were concentrating at sites which lent themselves to defense. Usually they were located on hilltops; sometimes the houses were built so that their outer walls formed an almost continuous line. Not until modern times did the villagers begin to resume their former practice of living amid the fields which they cultivated.

It is impossible to exaggerate the importance of the need for security in the planning and development of villages. They were rarely fortified in any formal sense – that was a prerogative of cities – but they not infrequently erected some kind of defense, if only a palisade and a ditch. The dangers to which they were exposed came mainly from small marauding bands. Sometimes a village grew up in the outer courtyard of a castle. Sometimes the church – often the only masonry construction in the community – was the last refuge of the villagers. From Scotland to Transylvania churches were built specifically for defense, or the churchyards were enclosed by a crenelated wall and entered by a fortified gatehouse. The

French chronicler Jean de Venette described how, within a few miles of Paris, "the peasants dwelling in open villages, with no fortifications of their own, made fortresses of their churches by surrounding them with good ditches, protecting the towers and belfries with planks as one does castles, and stocking them with stones and cross-bows."[1]

Urban settlement

The most conspicuous changes which had taken place in the landscape during the previous centuries were the clearing of land for cultivation and the growth of cities. The two were linked insofar as urban growth could not have taken place without an increase in the food base. Urban growth was also a consequence of the growth of both local and long-distance trade and of craft industries. These were the *basic* functions of cities and towns.

The fourteenth-century city was compact and well defended. Except in England it was invariably surrounded by walls, though small towns occasionally made do with bank, ditch, and palisade. The walls were also symbolic. They cut off the free inhabitants of the town from the half-free or unfree population of the countryside. They protected these centers of privilege in the harsh, feudal world of the Middle Ages. This highlights the very significant difference between the medieval city and that of classical times. The Greek or Roman city stood in symbiotic relationship with its surrounding territory. The inhabitant of the villages was as much a citizen, enjoying the same rights, as one who dwelt beside the *agora* or *forum*. The feudal structure of society changed this. The jurisdiction of the medieval city scarcely extended beyond its walls. It was an exception to its environment, not, as in the classical world, part of it. The medieval city stood outside the feudal order. Nevertheless, it was sometimes invaded by that order which it strove to hold at bay. This was particularly the case in Italy. There is a passage in the writings of the monk Fra Salimbene in which he described the progress of the French king, Louis IX, through the town of Sens. The women who greeted him along the streets, he wrote, were "for the most part like handmaids; yet, if the king had passed through Pisa or Bologna, the whole flower of the ladies would have gone out to meet him. Then I remembered that this is indeed the custom of the French; for in France it is the burgesses only who dwell in the cities, whereas the knights and noble ladies dwell in the villages and on their estates."[2] He was right. In southern Europe the landowning aristocracy had never abandoned the classical practice of maintaining a dwelling within the city. But it was no longer a villa. More often than not it was a tall tower, such as survives in Bologna and San Gimignano, and it was between these urban *turri* rather than rural castles that Montagues and Capulets maintained their perpetual feuds.

The variety of city plans in the fourteenth century reflected the differing ways

---

1   *The Chronicle of Jean de Venette,* trans. Jean Birdsall (New York, 1953), 85.
2   As quoted in G. G. Coulton, *From St. Francis to Dante* (London, 1907), 140.

in which they had originated and developed. In almost all, with the exception of many in England, the existence of town walls placed a constraint on growth. Most were congested, with narrow streets which became even narrower as buildings encroached on them. In many cities of Roman origin one could still detect the gridiron pattern of Roman streets, twisted and distorted by time. In some of more recent origin the rectilinear plan was more regular. Where planners, either classical or medieval, had not imposed their ideas on the shape of the city, the street pattern was more irregular. Sometimes, as at Hildesheim, and Kraków and several other cities of central Europe, a planned "new city" has been added to an older and unplanned (see Figs. 5.9 and 5.10). Sometimes the town seemed in plan to be nothing more than a large village, an axial street widening into an oval marketplace, with a wall cast around the whole. Many cities existed in intimate relationship with castle or monastery, beneath whose shadow and protection they had developed. In such cases the town wall was often made to abut against that of the latter. Sometimes the city grew from two or more such nuclei – castle or palace, monastery, cathedral, trading settlement – each imposing its own plan on its particular quarter of the city. This compartmentalization was apparent in Hildesheim, Brunswick, and Magdeburg before their destruction in World War II. In such instances the built-up area of the city was continuous. It might, however, have been interrupted by a river. There are several examples of such "double" cities, of which Prague, London, and Paris may serve. In such cases, the two sectors of the city were often seen to have radically different functions. In Prague and Budapest the royal or governmental quarter lay on one bank, the commercial and manufacturing on the other. In the case of Paris, the "royal" city occupied an island in the Seine, with business activities largely on the north bank and the university quarter on the south. Even cities as small relatively as Bristol, York, and Nuremburg occupied both banks of a river. Such a situation raised an acute problem when the city came to be enclosed by walls. In the case of large cities the two parts were usually treated as separate entities, but in the case of small cities and narrow rivers, the walls were sometimes carried across the latter by a kind of bridge.

It was clearly desirable to keep the length of a city wall as short as possible. Ideally it should be round in plan. This was rarely practicable, though there are examples at Nördlingen and Soest. Usually the wall was built to take advantage of every accident of the terrain in order to make it as secure as possible. In many instances the walled area of the city became as tightly built up as was practicable, and the city could grow only by expanding beyond the line of its walls. In this way successive lines of walls were built, enclosing ever larger areas. Figure 6.6 shows how Prague expanded on both sides of the river. At Cologne there were no fewer than three successive lines of defense. In most instances the outermost walls were built during the fourteenth century, when the city had already reached its greatest extent before modern times. Its builders had no means of estimating the future size of their city. In fact, growth had in most instances already ceased, and the newest walls continued until the nineteenth century to enclose large areas which were used only as gardens and orchards.

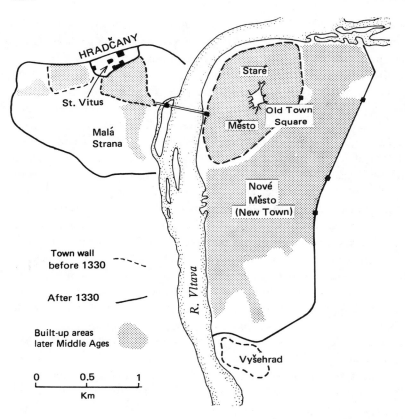

6.6. Prague, showing the "royal" city on the west (left) bank of the Vltava and subsequent stages in the growth of the commercial city on the right bank. The bridge (Karluv Most) was not built until the fourteenth century

Every city had a marketplace, for commerce was its primary function. Here stalls were set up for the weekly, sometimes twice weekly market, and sometimes also for an annual fair which attracted more exotic goods and brought merchants from greater distances. In or near the marketplace there may have been a "hall" or commodity market, where goods could be stored before sale. This was most likely to be so if the city had become an emporium for a particular commodity such as cloth. The Cloth Hall at Ypres and the corresponding Sukiennice at Kraków are cases in point. Nearby, too, there would have been a town- or guildhall, which served the needs of administration. The *Rathaus (Ratusz)* at Breslau (Wrocław), the *Bargello* at Florence, and the Guildhall at London are surviving examples. The scale of these buildings varied with the size and wealth of the city. In the smallest cities, those struggling to retain their urban status, they were diminutive, and may even have been absent. In the largest they were elaborate structures, the expression of municipal pride, even of arrogance.

The church was a prominant feature of every city. Most of the larger cities were the seats of bishops, and many more had monastic foundations, friaries, and numerous parish churches and private chapels. The Renaissance engravings of cities invariably show a skyline of soaring towers and spires. The cathedral in southern Europe was an inheritance from the later Roman Empire, and it was, as a general rule, conspicuously sited on the central square of the city. It was indeed heir to the temple of the deified emperor. In cities of more recent origin the church was more self-effacing. Merchants' buildings took pride of place, and the cathedral may have been tucked away behind the facades of their houses. Monastic buildings lay sometimes within, more often without the walls, where they served as the nucleus of a suburb. From the middle years of the thirteenth century several orders of friars began to establish themselves in the cities. Indeed, they were the social workers of their age; they established few houses in rural areas, and the number of friaries in a city was a very rough measure of its significance. They consisted usually of very large churches, since preaching to the laity was one of the chief functions of the friars, with very small claustral buildings. They were often located on the periphery of the built-up area, since it was only there that they were, as a general rule, able to acquire land. Parish churches served the spiritual needs of the townspeople. Though very small towns might have only one parish with its church, most had several, and in the largest there might be thirty or more parishes, each with its parish church. It was the multitude of parish churches that dominated the medieval townscape.

The medieval city, even at the peak of its prosperity, was small by modern standards; it was small even in comparison with the smallest cities of the Roman Empire. A city of 50,000 was very large indeed, and there were few of this size: Paris, Florence, Bruges, the commercial cities of Genoa and Venice, and very few others. Large cities of 10,000 to 20,000 were more numerous. They included the clothing towns of the Low Countries, most of the important cities of northern Italy, and several of the Hanseatic cities of northern Germany. Nuremberg may have had 20,000 inhabitants and London perhaps 30,000. Below these were cities of intermediate size, with from 2,000 to 10,000 inhabitants. Some of these cities had commercial and industrial functions which served areas far wider than their local regions, but at their lower margin towns of this size were little more than local market centers. Small towns, lastly, made up the great majority. Their population was less than 2,000, and most numbered only a few hundred. They were small market and craft centers. Their townsfolk owned and cultivated the surrounding fields, and in many of them agriculture was as important as commerce and the crafts. The small town of Rheinfelden, on the south bank of the Rhine upstream from Basel, can have had few more than a thousand inhabitants and its walls enclosed no more than twenty-five acres. Yet it served the simple needs of a relatively large area of about a hundred square miles on both banks of the Rhine (Fig. 6.7). Such small towns were very numerous in Germany and Switzerland (Fig. 6.8). In France they were fewer, possibly because their functions had in part been preempted by the older cities of Roman origin. It must be recognized that the categories of town size adopted here are arbitary, and that it is impossible in many instances to know even approximately the size of their population in the

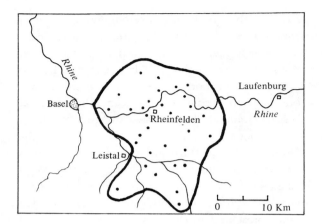

6.7. The service area of the small Swiss town of Rheinfelden

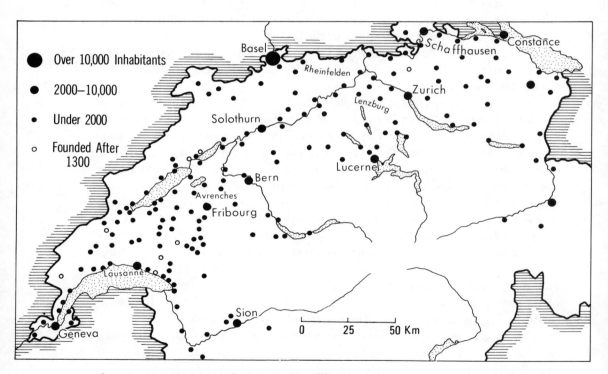

6.8. Towns in Switzerland in the later Middle Ages

fourteenth century. Table 6.2, showing the number and size of cities in northern
Europe, from the Low Countries to Poland, must be regarded as only an approximation.

By the fourteenth century, a network of cities had spread across Europe from
Spain to Poland, but it was a very uneven network (Fig. 6.9). In the plain of

Table 6.2. *Number and size of cities in northern Europe*

	Number	Estimated population
Giant cities (population over 50,000)	1	c.90,000
Very large (25,000–50,000)	8	240,000
Large (10,000–25,000)	38	570,000
Intermediate (2,000–10,000)	220	1,100,000
Small (less than 2,000)	3,000	2,250,000
	3,267	4,250,000

eastern Germany and Poland even small towns were widely scattered, and south of the Danube they were almost nonexistent. Only in France, the Rhineland, and northwest Germany, in addition to northern and central Italy, was there a close urban net with a hierarchical arrangement of medium-sized and large cities. Within this more highly urbanized region of Europe two areas stood out – northern Italy and the belt of territory which stretched from Flanders eastward to the Rhine. The first dervied from the cities of the later Roman empire. One can, in fact, point to only two whose origin dated from after the end of the western empire: Venice and Alessandria. Although some of intermediate size and most small towns were mainly agricultural, the larger cities were engaged primarily in commerce and manufacturing. The largest, without question, were Florence, Milan, and the port cities of Genoa and Venice, with Pavia and Bologna probably running close behind. Rome was no longer in the first rank of European cities, and its built-up area was only a fraction of that enclosed by the wall of the Emperor Aurelian. Several cities of southern Italy, notably Naples and Palermo, were large, but their size was in part due to the fact that they had become the refuges of the poor and dispossessed, as in fact, they have remained until recent times.

The second highly urbanized region included Flanders, much of Brabant, and Liège, and extended eastward to the Rhine at Cologne. Beyond the river, a line of cities dotted the belt of fertile country which lay between the hills and the northern plain. With very few exceptions these cities owed nothing to Roman urbanism, everything to the manufacture and trade in cloth. They were essentially manufacturing centers and were dependent on the import of wool and of other materials and the export of cloth. Without exception they were located on waterways which were then navigable. Whereas most of the Italian cities showed some evidence of Roman planning in the layout of their streets, those of northwest Europe were irregular. They had grown from small trading settlements into large cities without any overall control over their development. All had large marketplaces, as befitted their commercial importance, and in most the role of the church was subordinated to that of the merchant.

Over the rest of France, in western Germany, and in lowland England, there was a lighter scattering of cities, most of them of small or medium size. But over the rest of Europe – highland Britain, Scandinavia, eastern and southeastern Eu-

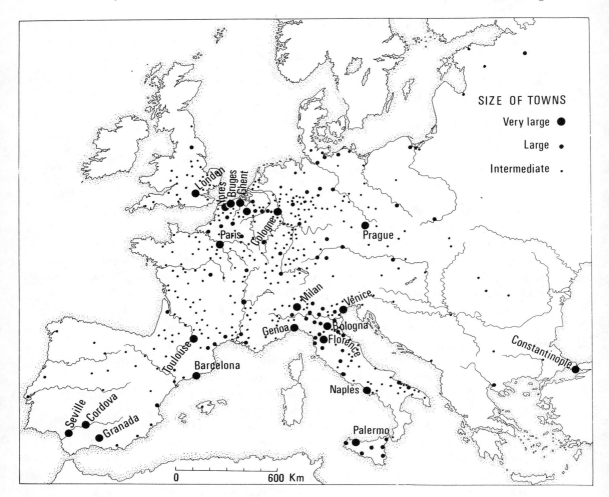

6.9. Distribution of the larger cities of medieval Europe

rope, and parts of the Mediterranean region — cities were few. Southern Spain and Italy provided a partial exception to this generalization. In the former the Moorish tradition of urbanism had led to the growth of some formerly Roman cities to a greater size than had ever been known under the Roman empire. In southern Italy also there was a number of large cities, but, as has been noted, their functions were not necessarily those normally regarded as urban.

The functions of the medieval city were more narrowly circumscribed than those of classical cities. Urban control extended only a very short distance from a city's walls. Beyond, feudal control of land prevailed. The city did, however, have a relationship with its region. It was a market center. No city was without a right to hold a market, to which countryfolk brought their surplus produce and at which they bought such necessities as they were unable to make for themselves. The possession of a market was basic to the medieval city; it was a place of trade.

Second in importance were craft industries. But cities did not have a monopoly of manufacturing. Many industries were rural, including ironworking and cloth finishing. Nevertheless urban crafts were numerous and varied. Boileau's *Livre des Métiers* listed a hundred, each organized in its guild. They ranged from tiny crafts like th. : of making shields with heraldic decoration and the pressing of oil-bearing nuts and seeds, to the very large crafts of tanners, weavers, and dyers. Only the largest cities could boast so great a range, and the more obscure were to be found only in the higher-order places. But even the smallest towns had their weavers and cloth finishers, their dyers, tanners, and woodworkers. In all cities there were crafts which specialized in the preparation of food, and one is constantly surprised at the immense numbers of bakers and butchers. The former were very numerous because few homes had an oven for baking purposes.

Agriculture, lastly, was always an urban function. There were garden plots within the city, and the fields beyond its walls tended to pass into the possession of the citizens. Indeed, land purchase was one of the few forms of investment available to them. At Toulouse, a relatively large city, half the population is said to have owned at least a plot outside the city. The suburban fields seem in general to have been cultivated intensively and were an essential source of urban food supply.

The size of a city was always restricted by the availability of food. Small towns could as a general rule satisfy their needs within their local regions. Larger cities had to draw on distant resources, and for this waterborne transportation was desirable if not absolutely necessary. Paris, for example, had to rely on small town markets over a large part of the Paris basin. The head counts which were made in the Italian cities during the later Middle Ages (see p. 189) were for the purpose of ensuring an adequate food supply. The supply was always precarious as much for political as logistic reasons, and not a few of the military conquests of the Italian city-states were for the purpose of gaining possession of wheat-growing land. Florence, Rome, and other Italian cities were heavily dependent on supplies from Romagna, southern Italy, and Sicily.

The medieval city had fewer amenities than the Roman. There was little provision for water supply and almost none for the disposal of sewage. Water was obtained from wells sunk within the city – or dipped from the river – and distributed by water carriers. Only monasteries showed any disposition to construct piped water-supply systems, which they are known in a few instances to have shared with the townspeople. Sewers were almost nonexistent. The larger houses often had cesspits, sometimes masonry-lined, which were emptied at intervals. For those less fortunate, there were public toilets, sometimes built over the town wall and discharging into the ditch below. London, for example, had at least sixteen public toilets. Monasteries usually built those offices, euphemistically termed reredorters, over a stream which carried away the effluent. Such conveniences were very rare in cities. Such a level of sanitation and water supply was bearable in the villages, but toilets were never developed during the Middle Ages to meet the more exacting requirements of city living.

Urban refuse was commonly thrown into the streets where it was at intervals collected and removed. Although some cities – London among them – appear to have been kept relatively clean, the burden of street cleaning does not appear to have weighed heavily on most urban authorities. Urban living was clearly fraught with many difficulties, of which dirt and smells were among the most obvious, and exposure to various infections, the most dangerous. A high urban death rate was to be expected, and conditions underwent no radical change before the nineteenth century.

AGRICULTURE

At least 80 percent, in some areas closer to 90 percent, of the population lived in villages and worked on the land. The great majority cultivated holdings which, under medieval technical conditions, were barely adequate to provide a family livelihood. In return they paid a rent or provided labor on the lands of their lord, and it was the latter which provided most of the breadgrains which entered into trade and supplied the cities. But in the organization of fields, the systems of cropping, and the tools used there was an almost infinite variety. Each was a function of so many variables – soil and climate, tools and technology, social structure and local traditions – that it would be strange if this were not the case. Nevertheless, great landowners, dependent on rents and services from a number of sometimes widely scattered manors, tended to organize and manage them all in a uniform manner. Agricultural systems thus tended to become more uniform, without ever achieving that uniformity which is implicit in the textbook models of the medieval manor.

There could have been no consistency, even within restricted areas, in the ways in which peasants organized and cultivated their fields. Too many cultural traditions were involved. Nevertheless, by the end of the Middle Ages three broad field systems could be distinguished. None was spatially distinct; each merged into the other, and there were many compromises and transitions between them. The open-field system was the most extensive in northwestern and central Europe. A number – commonly three – of great fields were each divided into long, narrow, and slightly sinuous strips. Each is assumed originally to have represented a day's plowing with a heavy plow, but purchase and inheritance of strips on the one hand, division between heirs on the other, quickly destroyed any primitive equality there may have been between them. Each of the great fields was cultivated in unison, according to a common plan. One was plowed and sown in the fall, the next in spring, and the third was allowed to lie fallow for a year, its stubble grazed and manured by the animals of the community. This system dictated an approximate equality between fall-sown grain, wheat and rye, and spring-sown, oats and barley. These were likely to crop differently, but there might, nevertheless, be expected an approximate equality in the volume of fall- and spring-sown crops. The example of Veulerent has already been mentioned (see p. 133) but Veulerent belonged to a Cistercian monastery, unusually well placed to impose this kind of discipline on its lands. Usually there was a far greater inequality in the size of fields; their number might be considerably greater, and the sequence of crops less regular. This three-course system is commonly assumed to have developed from a two-course, with alternating cropland and fallow. More likely both derived from earlier and more complex and irregular systems. It is not known to what extent a two-course system was once used in northern Europe. It was known in the Rhineland, and it survived until the nineteenth century in Poland.

In contrast with the open-fields, with their intermixed strips all cultivated in unison, were the lands with enclosed fields, each belonging to a single peasant who was free, as we are led to believe, to cultivate whatever he wished. This system of "several" characterized western Europe, the highland region of the British Isles, as well as extensive areas, most of them apparently of rough terrain and poor soil, within the open-field region of western and central Europe. In addition, the whole of southern Europe appears to have been characterized by small, enclosed fields. The barrier between "open" and "enclosed" was less absolute than might appear to be the case. The one could be changed into the other and both could sometimes be found within the limits of a single community. On the lands of the Belgian abbey of Saint-Trond, the tenants of newly cleared land were permitted for six years to grow whatever they chose, but thereafter "they will observe the common custom of sowing, so that in one year they sow wheat or rye; in the second, barley or oats or whatever spring crop was usually grown; and in the third they will sow nothing."[3] Of course, this tells us nothing about the fields themselves, but it is highly improbable that if these were open-fields, the peasants would have been left to their own devices for six years.

Enclosed fields belonged as a general rule to very small settlements or to isolated farmsteads. These are unlikely to have had the resources to operate a heavy plow, and this precluded the cultivation of the land in long, narrow strips. On the other hand, small, roughly square fields were more suited to the light plow which would have been generally used. The relative freedom to cultivate his lands as he pleased, enjoyed by the peasant in areas of enclosed fields, allowed him to develop the so-called in-and-out system. The fields lying close to the house and its outbuildings might be manured from the farm and cultivated continuously. Farther afield, land might be broken up and cultivated for a few years, as and when it was required, and then be allowed to return to the waste. Such a system was well adapted to regions of poor soil and heavy rainfall, such as western Britain and Brittany, but it was one which lent itself to endless variation.

The contrast between open-field agriculture and that carried on in small, enclosed fields was well-known to medieval people. They even had a legal phrase to describe it: *in plano et in bosco*. They recognized the landscape of hedges and hedge-row trees of the one and the sweeping lines and bare horizons of the other. They

3 *Le Livre de l'Abbé Guillaume de Ryckel (1249–1272)*, ed. Henri Pirenne (Ghent, 1896), 232.

recognized also that these two constrasted landscapes marked a sharp difference in social structure and personal status. To Wace in the twelfth century the association was clear:

> Li paisan et li villein
> Cil des bocages et cil des plain

> [The peasant and the villein;
> the one of the "bocage" and the
>   other of the open country.]

The third type of field system was that associated in particular with the pioneer settlements of eastern Europe, though sometimes found elsewhere. The houses and farm buildings lay along a "street" or road, and the land belonging to each stretched back from the road in a narrow strip until it reached whatever terminal barrier there may have been. The peasant was free; he owed no labor services, and there was, in fact, no demesne on which he could have performed them. He was free to cultivate his single enormous strip as he wished. This field system developed from the social and physical conditions prevailing in eastern Europe, but was also to be found in several forested areas which had been opened up to settlement in the course of the Middle Ages.

Beyond Europe's pioneer fringe, in the forests of Scandinavia, Finland, and Russia, a primitive system of cultivation survived. It was characterized by an abundance of land. The peasant could have as large a plot as he had energy to cultivate. His tools were simple, and we must assume that fields were small and compact. The prevailing type of agriculture, sometimes called "slash and burn," consisted in cutting and burning the forest and tilling the soil, enriched by the ashes, as long as its fertility lasted. It was then abandoned, and a fresh break made elsewhere. Agriculture was clearly supplemented to an important degree by hunting and fishing, for which the environment offered far greater resources than were to be found in most of western and central Europe.

Cereal crops were the basis of human diet and dominated the cropping systems. The preferred cereals were wheat and rye. They were better suited, owing to their gluten content, for bread making than others, but were more exacting in their demands. They required a longer growing period and were normally sown in October. Wheat in particular did not grow well on poor, acid soil or in a cool, wet climate. It was well suited to southern Europe and to the rich loams of western Europe. Rye was more tolerant but made a dark and rather bitter bread. Oats and barley grew fairly well in poor soil, and oats in particular were tolerant of harsh conditions. These were the crops of hilly and mountainous areas and of the northern frontier of agriculture. These crops, together with certain primitive forms of wheat, were combined in countless ways to suit conditions of cultivation and the demands for food.

Manure was always desperately short, and continuous cropping impracticable except in some areas of enclosed fields, where the infield could be supplied directly from the farm. In open-field agriculture it was necessary to leave the land idle every two or three years, when the stubble was grazed and manured by the animals. These practices crystallized into the system, already described, of taking a fall-sown crop, followed by a spring-sown crop, and then leaving the land fallow. Under these conditions it was impossible either to increase the area under wheat and rye or the frequency with which they were sown. This restriction did not apply to farms with small enclosed fields, but these usually lay in areas which were unsuited at least to wheat. The grazing of the fallow field after harvest came to be locked into the system. Not only did it supply manure, but it afforded the means of keeping stock through the winter, and it was for the latter reason that it survived far into the nineteenth century, when fertilizer had begun to supply the needs of the soil. It is apparent that the ratio of fall- and spring-sown cereals was roughly constant. It is no less clear that the production of the more palatable "winter" grains was insufficient for human requirements. Indeed, there were many areas where they scarcely grew at all. Barley and oats thus entered very largely into the human diet. Both were used for malting and brewing but, more importantly, were cooked into flat cakes or made into a kind of soup or gruel. The porridge of Scotland is a survival of what was at one time the principal article of diet. It often happened that the peasant was obliged to grow wheat in order to pay his rent in kind, but was himself obliged to eat mainly oats or barley. Diet was a matter of status. The abbot of St. Pantaleon at Cologne received a large amount of oats as rent, which were used to feed the lord abbot's horses and any casual visitors who claimed the monastery's hospitality. Meanwhile the lord abbot himself ate wheat or rye bread.

Cereals were sown thinly, and the return on the seed was always low and unpredictable. The ratio of crop to seed can be calculated for a great many places from the accounts kept by the stewards. Thierry d'Hireçon, a fourteenth-century landlord in northern France, was able to get an eightfold return and sometimes more, but this was exceptional. The peasant was usually happy if he could get a fourfold return. The yield ratios were usually lower for oats and barley, in part because they followed wheat or rye. On the lands of the bishop of Winchester in southern England a 3.9 ratio for wheat, 3.8 for barley, but only 2.4 for oats was achieved on average. There were times when the harvest yielded little more than was required for the next year's sowing. Yield ratios seem to have been highest in lowland England and the southern Low Countries, but were a great deal lower in much of France and over the great plain of Germany and Poland. Crop failures were more frequent than in modern times. Usually they arose from the weather, especially heavy rainfall in autumn, winter, and spring, which prevented plowing and sowing, sometimes from storms in summer which flattened the crops and caused their seed to rot. Severe cold seems in general to have been less damaging than excessive moisture. The medieval farmer had no devices for draining wet land. At most he could hope that the ridges which he plowed would lift part of his crop above the standing water. "Plow your ridges high," urged Walter of Henley at the end of the thirteenth century, that the water may flow away.

The evidence suggests that bad harvests came frequently. There was on average a poor harvest every four or five years, and a disastrous harvest, a real *crise de subsistence,* at longer intervals. The crisis of 1315—17 is well known. It afflicted much of western and central Europe and was attributed to prolonged and heavy rain in both winter and summer. Crops were destroyed in the ground, and there was famine and high mortality.

Diet did not — indeed, could not — consist wholly of cereals. These were supplemented by a range of vegetables — peas, beans, roots, and cabbages — most of which were grown in the garden plots attached to the peasants' cottages. The onion was much used for adding flavor to the bland diet of cereals. Meat was eaten very sparingly because most farm animals, the hog excepted, were bred for other purposes than food. Cheese and butter were consumed but were really important in the diet only in the wetter areas of the west where pasture and meadow grass grew well.

A number of regions of specialized agriculture had either survived from the Roman period or had been developed since. Foremost were the vine-growing areas. In Italy and Greece viticulture could be practiced almost anywhere, and wine was both an important local drink and an export. Wine from southern Greece was beginning to play an important role under the name of "Malmsey." Viticulture was driven from southern Spain by the Moslem prohibition of wine. At its northern margin the cultivation of the vine was declining. It had almost ceased in England and was in retreat in northern France and the Low Countries. On the other hand, vine growing seems to have been expanding in those areas, like the Rhineland and Aquitaine, where the vintage was good and export to northwest and northern Europe easy. In fact, those areas which were subsequently to become renowned for the quality of their wines were at this time beginning to establish their reputations. Vine growing was also increasing in central Europe, especially in south Germany, in Bohemia, and in the Alpine foothills of lower Austria and Sytria. A poor quality wine was even made in Poland.

Olive oil, by contrast, was less important than in classical times. This was due, in part, to the increasing use made of animal fats, but also to the fact that olive groves, destroyed in warfare, were not easily reestablished. A number of industrial crops was grown, foremost among them flax for linen and hemp for rope and coarse cloth. Attempts to grow cotton, made in southern Italy and Spain, met with no great success. Vegetable dyestuffs, notably wood, weld, and madder, tended to be grown in a few specialized areas, from which the chief clothworking regions were supplied.

Pastoral farming was closely linked with arable and was overall of far greater importance than in classical times. Animal rearing was in many parts of Europe an important means of using marginal land. Farm stock was the only source of manure, small though it was, and animals provided essential raw materials, notably wool and hides. Cattle and horses and, in southern Europe, donkeys and mules were used for both transport and draft purposes. Without a team the land could not be plowed, and the knight would have seemed incomplete without his horse.

The food which domestic animals provided might seem of secondary importance. The problem with all forms of animal husbandry was the provision of food during that season of the year when their natural feed was unavailable. In much of southern Europe this was the summer, when, in the lowlands at least, the scanty grass was burned by the heat. North of the Alps, the season of shortage was the winter, when there was little grazing. This problem was not to be solved before the eighteenth century, but various partial remedies were adopted, including grazing the fallow, transhumance, and the slaughter of animals, notably pigs, at the onset of winter.

There was a gradation in the importance of animal husbandry between areas of "high" arable farming, where animals, except for draft purposes, were relatively unimportant, and the cool, humid regions of the west and north, where they were more important than crop growing. But local variations were so great that it is difficult to generalize. Sheep were important – but always for their wool – in areas where dry pastureland was abundant: in central Spain and Italy; on the open-field regions of western Europe, where they grazed the fallow; and sometimes in the hills, as for example in western and northern Britain. Cattle were reared for draft purposes almost everywhere, but dairy produce was important in its own right only in areas where their natural food, meadow grass and hay, were most abundant. These were, in the main, "Atlantic" Europe and the mountains of central Europe. The records of Austrian monasteries show that they possessed a very large number of small holdings within the Alps, the rents of which were paid in cheeses. The number of hogs varied with the extent of the woodland in which they foraged for acorns and beech mast, a highly seasonal food, which necessitated the slaughter of large numbers in November or December.

The practice of transhumance had continued in southern Europe, probably without interruption, from classical times. In Italy animals, chiefly sheep, wintered on the lowlands which fringed the peninsula, and went for summer into the mountains. The practice was, however, most developed in the Alps, where cattle moved up the mountainside in spring, leaving the lowland grazing free to grow a crop of grass for hay. In southern France, it was chiefly sheep and goats which made the longer journey to the mountains. In Spain a more "horizontal" pattern of transhumance developed as the Moors were driven south of the Meseta. Here the sheep wintered in the southern parts of the plateau and passed the summers in the northern. In the late thirteenth century the association of shepherds, known as the Mesta, was formed, and they were guaranteed the right to use their migration paths, or *cañadas*, without interruption. Transhumance was used on a smaller scale in northwestern Europe. In Britain regional contrasts were not really great enough for it to acquire an importance comparable with that in Spain, Italy, or the Alps. Nevertheless, short-distance migration was of some importance in western Britain. A doggerel poem, written in Cornwall in the seventeenth century, explains why:

Our best neighbour – and he's choice and good –
Is the wild moor; there's the best neighbourhood.

> It keeps vast herds of cattle, I profess,
> And flocks of sheep even almost numberless.
> Thus we our stock do summer on the Down,
> And keep our homer grass till winter come.[4]

The medieval peasant in much of Europe lived surrounded by the forest. It supplied his fuel, timber for building, charcoal for smelting, pannage for his hogs, and even greenery for cattle and goats and covert for game. Yet by the early fourteenth century the woodlands had long been in retreat. Charcoal burner and goat had combined to destroy much of the forest cover in southern Europe (see pp. 16–17). In northern Europe, the destruction of the woodlands was beginning to give cause for alarm. The count of Champagne ordered a survey to be made of woodland remaining in one part of his lands. In England attempts were made to restrict the peasants' fuel to dead trees and branches torn down by the wind. But charcoal burners in the depths of the forest faced little restriction and were powerful agents of destruction. Venice was hard put to it to find timber for ship building, and in all mining and smelting areas the forests were rapidly disappearing. They remained a great deal more extensive in eastern and northern Europe, but transportation of lumber to areas where the need was greatest was not really organized before the seventeenth century.

MANUFACTURING

Most communities were as self-sufficing in manufactured goods as they were in foodstuffs. Many requirements, such as that for coarse cloth and footwear, was satisfied within the village if not in the home, and long-distance trade was restricted to luxury goods.

The cloth industries

The weaving of cloth and making of clothing was, after food production, the chief activity of medieval people. Every cottage had its handloom, and the stench of the tanyard was a fact of life. Cloth was spun and woven chiefly from flax and wool. Hemp was sometimes used for coarse fabric as well as for rope. Cotton was used in Italy and south Germany, and silk was coming to the fore as the supreme luxury cloth. There was a two-tier cloth industry. The largest production was of rough "homespun," commonly made from flax or the coarsest wool, and dyed some shade of brown with local dyes. It provided the clothing of three-quarters of the population. It was probably woven on a narrow, vertical loom, since the cottage could contain nothing larger, but comparatively little is known about it since both fabric and looms have decayed leaving only the faintest trace in drawings and documents. On the other hand, our knowledge of the superior types of cloth is very considerable. It was made by specialist weavers, finished by dyers, fullers, and other crafts-

4 *The Spoure Book*, manuscript in Cornwall County Record Office, Truro, Cornwall.

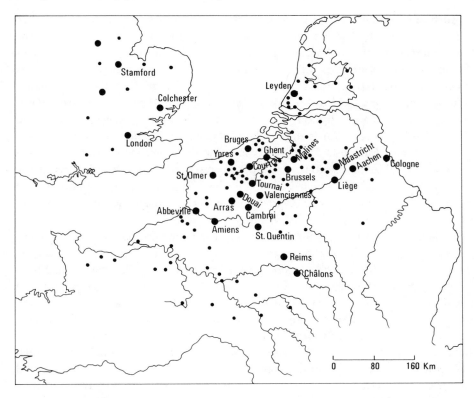

6.10. The northwest European cloth-making region in the fourteenth and fifteenth centuries

men, and marketed by merchants. The records of the later Middle Ages are full of references to the more sophisticated forms of cloth production.

Although much of the superior cloth was made of wool, some use was also made of flax, which was abundant in some areas where wool was scarce and was technically easier to use. On the other hand, flax lacked the felting qualities of wool and could not be thickened to form a warm fabric for northern climes. A compromise, adopted in parts of Germany, was to use flax for the warp and wool for the weft. The result was a mixed cloth, sometimes called "barchent" or fustian.

There were two regions in which the manufacture of superior cloth assumed great importance, the Low Countries and northern Italy. The former included northern France and part of northwestern Germany. It had the advantage of locally produced raw materials, a network of waterways for internal transportation, and ports for external. A specialized cloth industry may have originated in the early Middle Ages (see p. 197). It came to focus in the three great *villes drapantes* of Ypres, Bruges, and Ghent in Flanders, but in fact spread very much more widely – to Amiens, Saint-Quentin, and Reims in the south, and Brussels, Liège, and Aachen in the east (Fig. 6.10).

Much of the wool used for the best cloth came from Britain, but wool of more than average quality was grown throughout the region. The basic product of the older centers of industry was a heavy, well-fulled broadcloth. Its processes of manufacture were intricate and costly, and a demand was growing for a good, but less expensively produced cloth for the middle range of the market. The older manufacturers, with conservatism bred of success, resisted the change, and the newer manufactures — mainly lighter woolens commonly called "serges," "says" and "kerseys" — began to be made in peripheral regions, in Brabant, Hainault, northern France, and England. Many of these "new draperies" were woven in small towns and rural areas in order to escape the restrictive guild regulations of the older centers. England, which had not formerly engaged in the production of better quality cloth, now turned to its manufacture on an increasing scale and began to restrict the export of raw wool.

The second cloth-manufacturing region of fourteenth-century Europe was central and northern Italy. Although there was a long history of cloth making, the production of quality cloth had come relatively late to Italy. The market had been supplied from northwest Europe, by way of the Champagne fairs, and the industry began in Italy, principally in Florence, only when the merchants undertook the finishing and embroidery of cloth imported from the Low Countries. This became a monopoly of the *Arte di Calimala* of Florence, where it was carried on in workshops situated in a street of that name. It was a prestigious but small-scale industry, greatly exceeded in volume of production by the *Arte della Lana,* which used wool from Mediterranean countries to weave a sound cloth for the growing urban market. Such cloth was also made in other cities of Tuscany and Umbria, as well as in those of northern Italy.

The Low Countries and Italy were the foremost centers of the woolen cloth industry, but there were many others: Paris, Bourges, Barcelona, and other cities of France and northern Spain, as well as throughout the Rhineland. Good quality cloth from the Low Countries and Rhineland was sold throughout Germany, Poland, and beyond, while the coarser cloth woven in these latter regions moved in the opposite direction and was bought by the humbler classes in the west.

Flax growing and the weaving of linen cloth were important in many parts of northern Europe. Linen was an article of peasant dress, but in south Germany and Switzerland a better quality linen was made. Sometimes cotton from Italy or the Middle East was used for the weft, and the resulting mixed fabric was sold back into Italy.

The most esteemed fabric in the later Middle Ages was, without question, silk. It was woven in the Middle East and in Constantinople (see pp. 136–7). The rearing of silkworms had been introduced into Sicily, and silk weaving spread to central Italy, notably to Lucca. Lucchese silks were sold at a very high price in northwest Europe. The industry then spread to Venice, Avignon, and other places in France where there was a market for so expensive a commodity.

The cloth industry called for other materials than the thread it used. It required mordants, dyestuffs, and the materials for fulling and dressing. Dyes were of vegetable origin and yielded only a narrow range of colors. Most important of them were woad and madder, yielding respectively blue and red, but saffron and weld were also grown, and indigo and brazilwood were imported by way of the Middle East. Without mordants the dyes could not be made to adhere to the wool. Several mineral substances were used, but the most satisfactory was alum. This complex chemical was obtained from a number of places in western Europe, but the best quality alum was found at Phocaea, on the west coast of Asia Minor, and was imported to western Europe by the Genoese. In addition, fuller's earth was used as a detergent and for thickening woolen cloth, and teasel heads for raising the nap.

The tanning of leather was almost as widespread as the weaving of cloth, but was carried on most intensively where cattle rearing assured a supply of hides. Oak bark was used to supply the tannin. There were many ways of handling the skins and hides, some yielding a thick leather for boots and saddlery; others, a thin, soft leather for slippers, purses, and bookbindings. The latter were obtained by scraping the skins and treating them with alum and other chemicals and dyes. The result was a very pliable leather commonly called cordovan from Córdoba in Spain where it was at one time made.

The metal industries

Mining and metalworking faced great difficulties and little progress had been made by the fourteenth century beyond the levels reached in classical times. The precious metals were in universal demand. Gold was obtained from alluvial workings, in, especially, the hills of central Europe, but much came from sub-Saharan Africa and was brought by caravan across the desert. Silver ores were more abundant and were being mined in the Harz, the Ore Mountains of Saxony, the eastern Alps and Carpathians, and in the Balkans. In some mines it was associated with lead.

Ferrous ores occurred very widely and were worked and smelted in most parts of Europe. Ironworking tended to be carried on in remote areas where charcoal was abundant, since the early refineries were extraordinarily extravagant of fuel. This helps to explain why the industry is so poorly documented, and it is impossible to formulate any estimate of the volume of production. It must have been considerable in order to supply metal for armor and weapons, the tools of agriculture, and the needs of building construction. The blast furnace was unknown, and the ores were smelted in low furnaces and on hearths of very varied designs. The temperatures reached were low and the metal was never separated fully from its slag. Quality iron and steel for weapons and tools were the product of prolonged remelting and manipulation of the metal. Some areas acquired a high reputation for their "steel," including Toledo in Spain, the Milanaise in northern Italy, the eastern Alps, and the lower Rhineland. The industry was also developing at this time in central Sweden, strongly influenced by the German entrepreneurs and merchants who shipped the *osmund* iron in bars to the west. At the same time iron of lesser quality was being produced in not inconsiderable quantities in northern France, Burgundy, the Alps, and the Pyrenees, in each of which distinctive hearths and processes were used.

The iron was passed in bars and blooms to the craftsmen who worked it up into the articles required by commerce. In small towns there might only be a smith who wrought everything from nails to coulters, plow tips, and horseshoes. In a large city the iron-using crafts were organized into highly specialized guilds. Paris had no fewer than eight, whose skills ranged from blacksmithing to forging swords and armor. Some places enjoyed a high reputation for the quality of their iron and ascribed this to the consummate skill of the craftsmen. This may, indeed, have been so, but some of the credit must in most instances be given to the quality of the ores from which their metal was derived. A trace of manganese and the absence of sulfur made all the difference to the iron from Sweden or Siegen or Styria.

The nonferrous metals — lead, copper, and tin — were mined as widely as resources permitted. Lead, used primarily for roofing large buildings, making pipes for water supply, and, alloyed with tin, for pewter, was in great demand. It came chiefly from northern England, the Eifel, Harz, and Ore Mountains. Copper ores were mined in the Harz and at Mansfield, in Saxony, the Ore Mountains, and the Balkans and southern Spain. After smelting, generally in a low-shaft furnace, it was usually hammered into sheets, or alloyed with tin or zinc, and made into bronze or brass. This was not a large industry, but it had one important center, Dinant on the Meuse, which was famed for the production of copper and brass wares, known as *dinanderie*. Tin was chiefly used in making pewter and bronze. Most was obtained from alluvial workings in southwestern England. Zinc was not a metal known to medieval people. They were for technical reasons quite unable to smelt it (see pp. 200–1), but they did know that its ore, calamine, yielded brass when added to a molten bath of copper.

The fourteenth century was a period of intense building activity — churches great and small, castles, city walls and gates, and domestic construction. Vast numbers must have been employed in quarrying stone, cutting it to the shapes required, and transporting it to the building sites. Much of the labor was unskilled, but at every building site skilled masons were usually working under the direction of a master of works who was, in effect, the architect. Building stone varied greatly in quality and greatly influenced the character of the building. Good stone, capable of being carved and used in elaborate tracery, was sometimes conveyed great distances. Caen stone from Normandy was much used in southern England, and within Britain fine stone from the quarries of the east Midlands was transported by riverboat and coasting craft to many parts of the country. Paris relied heavily on the limestone from the plateau of Brie to the east of the city; the Cloth Hall of Ypres was built of stone from quarries in Hainault, sixty miles away; and Venice imported stone by sea from quarries along the Dalmatian coast.

All good construction required mortar, and one of the first steps in erecting a large building was to construct a limekiln on the site. This in itself sometimes necessitated the transport of rough limestone over great distances.

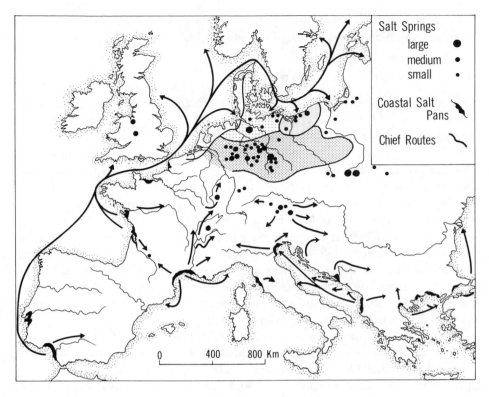

6.11. Salt production and the salt trade in late medieval Europe

Other minerals were extracted and used: marble and alabaster for monumental sculpture and decoration, clay for pottery and bricks, sand for glass, and salt for seasoning and preserving food. Most of the salt was obtained either by evaporating seawater in salt pans or by boiling the solution obtained from salt springs (Fig. 6.11). The former called for hot, dry summers and was important around the shores of the Mediterranean Sea. The most northerly salt pans at this date were near La Rochelle, from which salt was shipped all over northern Europe.

FUEL

Wood was the universal fuel, either in its natural state or as charcoal. The latter was used almost exclusively for metallurgical purposes. The influence of this on the woodlands has already been mentioned. Peat was of great importance in some lowland areas, notably eastern England and the Low Countries, and peat cutting sometimes left a landscape of shallow lakes or meers. Coal was known, but there were important reasons for not using it. It was, in general, unsuitable for metal-working, its fumes excluded it from the domestic hearth, and problems of transport ruled it out for most other purposes. It was, however, used occasionally, especially in England, for burning lime and bricks.

TRANSPORTATION AND TRADE

Despite the prevailing self-sufficiency of the local region, there was a not inconsiderable volume of long-distance commerce. The bulk of the trade continued to be handled at the level of the local community; peasants sold in their nearest market and the goods they purchased came mainly from local craftsmen. The number of markets had in recent decades been increasing rapidly, until Europe had a close net. In England, where the right to hold a market was conferred by charter, an inquiry was often made of the distance of the nearest existing market. It came to be assumed that they should not be closer to one another than 6 $\frac{2}{3}$ miles. Nevertheless, too many market privileges were in fact granted, and many markets succumbed in the later Middle Ages to the competition of their neighbors. The pattern was most dense in good agricultural country like the Paris basin and lowland England. Markets were very much more widely scattered in mountainous and thinly populated areas like the Alps and eastern Europe. Here the peasant might have to make a very long journey to market.

The market was commonly held each week. The fair, which often existed alongside it, was held once or twice a year and usually lasted for several days. Fairs were part of the mechanism of long-distance trade; in general, they handled goods a great deal more valuable than those bought and sold in the local markets; they were frequented by merchants who used the occasion not only to buy and sell goods, but also to meet, discuss their business, and settle their accounts. Many fairs were highly specialized, like the wine fair at Brixen in northern Italy and cloth and horse fairs in eastern Europe, and some served the needs of very large areas. That of Frankfurt was used by merchants from the Low Countries and most of Germany. Very many fairs were established; most failed to attract any significant volume of business, declined, and eventually ceased to be held. In western Europe the business of fairs was tending to pass to the cities, and merchants found other and more efficient means for transacting their financial business. The great Champagne fairs were now of only slight importance, but fairs retained their importance in central and eastern Europe, in part because the urban net was less developed. The Nördlingen fair was the most important in south Germany, and that of Zurzach in Switzerland had grown in response to the increasing traffic across the Alps (Fig. 6.12).

The fairs declined as commerce became a regular, year-round occupation rather than a seasonal activity. Their diminished importance mirrored the increased activity of the towns. Even the local markets declined, as small-town craftsmen opened their shops throughout the week. Interurban trade was increasing in volume. Much of it might have seemed unnecessary. Strasbourg and Freiburg, on each side of the upper Rhine, sold cloth to one another. In fact, cities prided themselves on the texture and color of their fabrics which were peculiar to them-

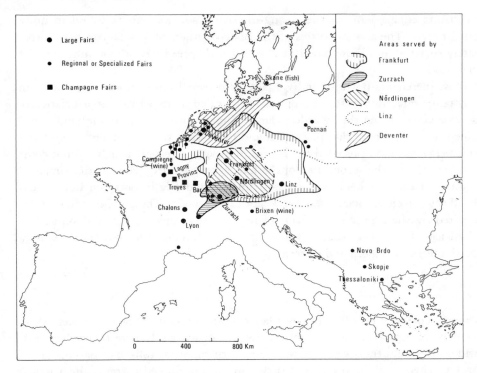

Large Fairs

Regional or Specialized Fairs

Champagne Fairs

Areas served by
Frankfurt
Zurzach
Nördlingen
Linz
Deventer

Skåne (fish)
Poznań
De Winter
Compiègne (wine)
Lagny
Provins
Troyes Bar
Frankfort
Nördlingen
Linz
Chalons
Zurzach
Brixen (wine)
Lyon
Novo Brdo
Skopje
Thessaloniki

0   400   800 Km

6.12. European fairs in the fourteenth and fifteenth centuries and the areas they served. The Champagne fairs were of little importance by this date

selves. The cloths of Strasbourg were different from those of Freiburg, and in each city there might be a demand for the product of the other.

A century or two earlier merchants had traveled with their goods, sharing the dangers and difficulties of travel. In the fourteenth century there were, of course, countless petty hucksters who transported their wares from fair to market and vice versa. But trade had also become big business, and there were trading houses in Italy and the Low Countries where merchants rarely left their counting houses and, instead, maintained agents or factors in important commercial centers to look after their interests. The Peruzzi of Florence had in 1336 no fewer than 88 such agents in 17 different cities, and their rivals, the Acciaiuoli, had 53. Italian merchants, sometimes known as Lombards, had bases for their activities in Paris, Bruges, and Ghent, and in London they are commemorated in a street name in the heart of the present financial district. They combined the buying and selling of commodities with banking and the transfer of money by means of bills of exchange and even invested in extractive industries like saltworking. It was, in effect, an early instance of vertical integration.

The Florentines and "Lombards" dominated long-distance trade within Europe, but it was the Genoese and Venetians who, with the merchants of Barcelona, Marseilles, and a few other cities, controlled Europe's Mediterranean trade. But merchants engaged in complex, long-distance trade were to be found in quite small towns. The account books of the Bonis brothers of Montauban have fortunately survived and show how intricate and widespread were the ramifications of their trade.

Most merchants operated individually or in small associations, some of them only temporary. In northern Europe, a broader and more permanent association of merchants developed the so-called Hanse of merchants trading to Gotland. They joined together for mutual protection and to advance their commercial interests. This personal union preceded the Hanseatic League of cities, which did not come into being until the second half of the fourteenth century. The chief commercial business of the merchants was the distribution and sale in northern Europe and the Baltic of cloth, wine, salt, and fabricated goods. These commodities were requited by the export to the west of lumber, flax, metals, furs and skins, and salted fish. It was essentially a trade between a developed western Europe and a less developed northern and eastern.

Trade routes and travel

The movement of people and goods faced severe difficulties. Not only were there dangers from robbers and natural accidents, but the roads were themselves bad, bridges few, and transportation was beset with countless tolls and man-made obstacles. There was, however, a road system, an interlinked pattern which joined cities and ports with one another. Despite the fact that some Roman roads had survived and were being used, most were merely ill-marked tracks, from which deviations had continually to be made according to the depth of the mud or the condition of the bridges. Little attempt was made to maintain the roads. Where they ran over limestone or gravels their surface was likely to be dry much of the time, and roads were often diverted to take advantage of such conditions. Where they were obliged to cross areas of clay, conditions were very different. In the plain of Flanders, it was reported, "the land was so soft in winter that it was impossible to transport food and merchandise by cart from one city to another."[5] These conditions were to show little improvement before the nineteenth century. In England the law placed the maintenance of the "King's Highway" squarely on the local landowner. It does not follow, however, that the obligation was adequately discharged. Not until the seventeenth century were local authorities charged with the maintenance of public roads. The building and repair of bridges was also necessary for long-distance travel. Small rivers were commonly forded, but across larger there were infrequent bridges, generally of masonry. They often constituted nodes in the network of routes and contributed to the growth of cities. Their construction and endowment was often a charitable act, like founding schools and hospitals. Nevertheless, they were endangered by floods and ice and were often in poor condition.

5   *Recueil des Ordinnances de Pays-Bas,* ed. Charles Laurent, 2d Series, I, 444 (author's trans.).

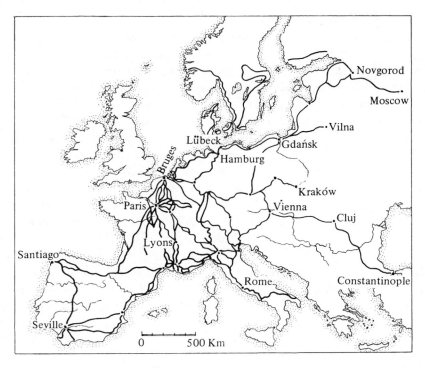

6.13. The *Itinerary of Bruges*, a thirteenth-century roadbook, describing routes from Bruges

Travelers often moved in groups which included carts, wagons, horsemen, and those who just walked. There was safety in numbers, but such "convoys" were reduced to the speed of the slowest among them. Nevertheless, they might hope to cover fifteen or more miles in a day, and sometimes as many as thirty. By the fourteenth century handbooks were available for the guidance of travelers. The *Practica* of Pegolotti told the merchants the best routes to use, and the so-called *Itinerary of Bruges* of the later fourteenth century is an elaborate roadbook describing the routes which radiated from the city (Fig. 6.13).

A bundle of routes ran from northwestern Europe to the Mediterranean by way of either the Rhône valley or the Alpine passes, and these were probably the most used in Europe. The passes had the effect of concentrating traffic on a single road across each. Several, including the Little St. Bernard and Mont Cenis between the Rhône valley and Italy, and the Great St. Bernard, Septimer, and Reschen-Scheideck across the central Alps were among the most used. To these the St. Gotthard was added in the mid-thirteenth century. It had the immense advantage of allowing the central Alps to be crossed more directly, but the northern approaches to the pass had been extremely difficult and were made passable for commercial traffic only by elaborate road and bridge construction. The journey across a pass was commonly more than could be accomplished in a day, and some form of shelter and accommodation was desirable near its summit. The most used passes are likely to have been those best provided for in this respect. The tendency in the fourteenth century was for the more westerly routes which crossed France to decline in importance, and for those from Italy, across the central Alpine passes to the Rhineland to increase. The latter had the immense advantage of converging on the navigable Rhine, which bore the merchants and their commerce northward to the Low Countries.

Rivers were used for travel and transport as much as possible. Boats were propelled by sail and oars, and were towed by man and beast. No river could be used without a towpath, and a flood which swept it away was enough to bring navigation to a stop until it had been repaired. The difficulties facing navigation were different from but no less serious than those which confronted the traveler by road. On most navigable rivers, notably the Rhine and Seine, there were tolls levied by the local landowner. Some Rhineland cities demanded that all goods passing along the river be offered for sale, and their journey continued only if there was no demand for them. In others the cargoes had to be transshipped to another vessel, allegedly better suited to the next section of the river. Then there were hazards from floating mills and fishnets. On some rivers the speed of the current at certain times of the year was so great that downstream travel was dangerous and upstream impossible. On the other hand, there were periods when the water level was too low for ordinary boats. Some rivers, on which navigation was difficult, were used only for floating rafts of timber downstream from the mountains. Nevertheless far more rivers were regularly used than would be thought navigable today. In the Low Countries, which relied heavily on waterborne traffic, sluices were used to raise and lower boats between two water levels. There was scarcely a river in western and central Europe which was not used, if only by local market boats. Only in southern Europe was river navigation of little or no importance. There were exceptions, like the Po and Guadalquivir, but most Mediterranean rivers were torrents in winter and almost dry in summer. Long-distance travelers often used boats for short segments of their journeys, as, for example, on the Swiss lakes. The *Itinerary of Bruges* actually prescribed a boat journey on the Po in its route to Venice.

Despite the difficulties, an intense use was made of some waterways. In Flanders transport by water seems to have been far more important than that by land. In a period of 122 days in 1297 no fewer than 3,250 small sailing boats and 87 market boats were pulled over a sluice or *overdraghe* near Ypres. At this time, at least one boat a day passed Meulan on the Seine below Paris. On the Loire, 1,397 boats passed the toll station at Champtoceaux, above Nantes, in a year.

There was no effective means to control the proliferation of toll stations on the rivers. In 1273 the *Parlement de Paris* had forbidden the creation of more tolls, but its regulation does not appear to have been effective, and landowners continued to raise toll stations – many of them fortified – and to charge whatever the traffic would bear. There are said to have been thirty-five on the Rhine, at least as many on the Elbe, and thirty on the Weser. Tolls were no less obstructive on the Po and most other rivers. Tolls were also levied on road traffic but were commonly less effective since the traveler could often avoid them by a detour.

Seaborne trade

Maritime trade in the fourteenth century centered in two areas: the Mediterranean and northwest Europe and the Baltic, with but a tenuous link between them. In the Mediterranean there was a long-distance trade, largely controlled by the galleys of Genoa and Venice, and a short-distance, coasting trade which by and large took the place of transport by land. The long-distance trade was distinguished more by its quality than its volume. All the ships of Venice, it has been said, could have transported only two thousand tonnes in a year, and those of Genoa probably no more. The wealth of the east which made its way to Italian ports could have amounted to no more than five thousand tonnes. But it was a rich cargo. The only bulky commodities were alum from Phocaea, wine from Greece, and cotton from Egypt. The rest was made up of spices, sugar, silk, decorative woods, dyestuffs, and precious and ornamental stones. Both Venice and Genoa traded chiefly with their Aegean dependencies, but they had bases in Constantinople and the Crimea, as well as in Egypt and the Levant.

The commerce of the Italian ports with northwestern Europe was largely overland, in part because their oar-driven galleys were unsuited to the heavier swell of the Atlantic. Toward the end of the thirteenth century they began to sail direct to the Low Countries, but it was not until the later fourteenth that the sailings of the "Flanders galleys" became at all regular. Their cargoes certainly contained the luxury goods commonly associated with the eastern trade, but it was the humble alum which made up much of them. The return cargo consisted largely of cloth and wool.

In Flanders the Mediterranean trade met that of northern Europe and the Baltic and also that which followed the Rhine from the Alpine crossings. Very broadly, three streams of maritime traffic converged on the Low Countries in addition to the infrequent galleys from the Mediterranean. From the Bay of Biscay came wine and salt; from Britain, wool and tin; from the North Sea and and Baltic ports, flax, lumber, fish, metals, and poor quality cloth, much of it linen. In the ports of Flanders these goods were sold and exchanged, and most of them reexported. The eastern trade of the Low Countries was largely in the hands of "easterners" or merchants of the Hanse. The Baltic trade was described as *in mit solt unde ut mit roggen* – "in with salt and out with rye." These were certainly important commodities, but trade was far more complex than this, and it also included French wine, Swedish iron, and furs from the forests of Russia.

The commodities of trade

The commodities of local and short-distance trade were in the main the products of the fields and farms and the manufactured goods made by local craftsmen for the needs of their neighboring peasantry. Long-distance trade was somewhat more varied. It can be grouped into foodstuffs, raw materials of industry, and the products of manufacturing.

Although the trade in grain was carried on mainly at the local level, there was nevertheless some long-distance trade. In the west there were grainmongers or dealers who bought up local surpluses and transported them to the cities. They were often able to anticipate scarcity and to hold the grain in store until prices rose. Grain was not of a high enough value to warrant long-distance transport except by water, and the mechanism of the market could not always be relied upon to provision the larger cities. For this reason the city fathers always kept a watchful eye on the store of breadgrains in hand and available. This was especially the case with the cities of Italy and the southern Low Countries. The local regions were usually quite inadequate to supply the grain required, and in both a heavy reliance was placed on distant areas: Apulia and Sicily in Italy, and northern France and the Baltic in the Low Countries. A fierce struggle was fought between the cities of Flanders for the grain which was brought by boat down the rivers which flowed from northern France to join the Scheldt. In the end, it was the rye of the north German plain, brought westward by the merchants of the Hanse, which satisfied the needs of the Flemish cities.

There was never any question that Constantinople could satisfy its needs in grain from its immediate hinterland, and the city had always relied on imports by sea. At this time the chief source was the coastal regions of the Black Sea, particularly Moldavia which lay to the north of the Danube mouth.

If the grain trade resulted from the growing concentration of people in cities, the wine trade stemmed from the fact that wine production was strictly localized. The "export" vineyards lay close to river or maritime ports from which the wine could be shipped to consuming centers in the north. Immense quantities were sent from Gascony both to England and the Low Countries, from which some traveled on by sea to the Baltic. Wine was also carried northward from Burgundy by the rivers of the Paris basin and from southwest Germany by the Moselle and Rhine. There was a vigorous local trade in wine in southern Europe, for wines differed greatly in quality and some vintages became fashionable and greatly in demand. The papal court, for example, acquired a taste for Burgundy. Another fashionable wine in northwest Europe was Malmsey, a heavy wine like Madiera, which was made in southern Greece (cf. Monemvasia) and brought to the west by the Venetians.

Salt was a bulky, low value component of long-distance trade. It could be made most economically in southern Europe, where summers were hot enough to evaporate the brine. Northern Europe at this time imported almost all of its not inconsiderable consumption.

The raw materials of manufacturing were too bulky and of too low a value to enter significantly into long-distance trade. Ores were smelted, clay was burned to make pots and bricks, and hides tanned wherever they occurred. The only exception was the raw materials of the textile industry. Silk was imported from the Middle East for the Italian industry. Even flax was transported over considerable distances in northern Europe. Alum and dyestuffs were highly localized and had become important articles of trade. But the most important item by far was wool. Although sheep were reared in most parts of Europe, the quality of their wool varied greatly. Even in England it ranged from the "Le'mster ore" (Leominster "gold") of the Welsh border down to Cornish "hair," and prices varied accordingly. At a time when dress was the foremost mark of rank and status, the quality of the cloth worn, and thus of the wool used, was of great importance. The best quality and most highly priced wools were in great demand. Pegolotti's handbook listed the best English wools and indicated the prices which they might be expected to fetch. English wool — the staple export par excellence — sold in the weaving centers of the Low Countries and was shipped to Italy, even though Italian wool, especially that from Tuscany, was reckoned to be of high quality. Lastly, Spanish wool was beginning to come onto the market, though not yet in large quantities.

Manufactured goods were, by contrast, prominent in fourteenth-century trade. Foremost among them was cloth, on which the rich spent an inordinate amount. But a market was developing at this time among the rising middle class for fabrics intermediate between the fine cloth of the rich and the peasant's coarse homespun. The "new draperies," which were beginning to be made in the Low Countries, satisfied this demand and were just entering into trade on an increasing scale. Silk was, like fine cloth, made at only a few places, and was distributed widely but in very small amounts.

Ironware, like cloth, came in varying qualities, and the best, used for weapons and armor, entered into long-distance trade. Nonferrous metals were even more significant, because they were smelted and fabricated at even fewer sites. Articles of copper and its alloys, as well as lead, were significant in fourteenth-century trade. In addition to these primary categories there was an immense range of manufactured goods which entered into commerce, many of them more decorative than useful. The anonymous author of the *Libel of English Policie* roundly condemned the unequal exchange of good English products for these ephemeral goods:

> Thus these galeys for this licking ware,
> And eating ware, bare hence over best chaffare:
> Cloth, woll, and tinne.

SELECT BIBLIOGRAPHY

General

The Cambridge Economic History of Europe. Vol. 1, *Agrarian Life of the Middle Ages,* 2d ed., Cambridge, U.K., 1966. Vol. 2, *Trade and Industry in the Middle Ages,* Cambridge, U.K., 1952.
Darby, H. C., ed. *A New Historical Geography of England.* Cambridge, U.K., 1973.
The Fontana Economic History of Europe. The Middle Ages, ed. C. M. Cipolla. London, 1972.

Population and urban settlement

Charanis, P. "A Note on the Population and Cities of the Byzantine Empire in the Thirteenth century." *Jewish Social Studies,* vol. 5. New York, 1953.
Herlihy, D. *Medieval and Renaissance Pistoia.* New Haven, Conn., 1967.

Hilton, R. H. *A Medieval Society*. London, 1967.

Lewis, A. R. "The Closing of the Medieval Frontier." *Speculum* 33 (1958): 275–83.

Postan, M. M. "Some Economic Evidence of Declining Population in the Later Middle Ages." *Economic History Review* 2 (1950): 221–46.

Postan, M. M. *The Medieval Economy and Society*. London, 1972.

Russell, J. C. *Medieval Cities and their Regions*. Bloomington, Ind., 1972.

Whaley, D. *Medieval Orvieto*. Cambridge, U.K., 1952.

Economic development

Bishop, T. A. M. "The Rotation of Crops at Westerham, 1297–1350." *Economic History Review* 9 (1938–9): 38–44.

Dollinger, P. *The German Hanse*. London, 1970.

Gras, N. S. B. *The Evolution of the English Corn Market from the Twelfth to the Eighteenth Century*. Cambridge, Mass., 1915.

Lennard, R. "The Alleged Exhaustion of the Soil in Medieval England." *Economic Journal* 32 (1922): 12–27.

Lopez, R. S., and I. W. Raymond. *Medieval Trade in the Mediterranean World*. Oxford, 1955.

Mertens J. A., and A. E. Verhulst. "Yield-Ratios in Flanders in the Fourteenth Century." *Economic History Review* 19 (1966): 175–82.

Postan, M. M. "The Trade of Medieval Europe: The North." In *Cambridge Economic History*, vol. 2, 119–256. Cambridge, U.K., 1952.

Pounds, N. J. G. *An Economic History of Medieval Europe*. New York, 1976.

Roover, R. de "The Organization of Trade." In *Cambridge Economic History of Europe*, vol. 3, *Economic Organisation and Policies in the Middle Ages*, 42–118. Cambridge, U.K., 1963.

Slicher van Bath, B. H. *Yield Ratios, 810–1820. Afdeling Agrarische Geschiedenis Bijdragen* 10 (1963).

7

The late Middle Ages

The two centuries from the early fourteenth to the early sixteenth form one of the more enigmatic periods in European history. It was one of continuous warfare and civil disturbance, yet it saw the birth of humanism and the beginnings of the Renaissance. It has been represented as a period of economic depression, while at the same time the peasantry in some parts of Europe enjoyed a higher material living standard than at any other time in the Middle Ages (Fig. 7.1). It was an era of extreme bigotry, intolerance, and superstition, and at the same time of reason and enlightment. Its art showed a preoccupation with death, and at the same time it could display the lightness and grace which we associate with the Renaissance. These many contradictions spring from the horrific experiences of the Great Plague and its subsequent recurrences. The bubonic plague reached western Europe in the ships of the Genoese at the end of 1347. It came from the Crimea in the bloodstreams of infected rats, having been brought to the Crimea in the baggage of merchants from the Far East. Wherever the ships called, the pathogens of the plague went ashore with the crew and spread rapidly through the local population. Their vectors were the black rat and the flea, the former carrying and nurturing the bacillus, the latter distributing it to all whom it bit. Crowded, dirty, and rat-infested homes were ideal for its diffusion. It spread fast. Within six months it had covered much of France (Fig. 7.2). In 1348 and 1349 it spread through the British Isles and western Germany, and in 1350 it died out in Scandinavia and eastern Europe.

POPULATION

No one knows how many perished. There were places where whole communities were wiped out, and others where, quarantined by distance or by physical barriers, mortality was slight. The papal court barricaded itself in the vast Château du Pâpe at Avignon and escaped. There were also areas in Poland which the infection did not reach. But everywhere else mortality was heavy. Overall, a quarter of the population, perhaps more, may have died.

After about seven years the plague returned, less severe than on its first visitation because part of the population had acquired an immunity. Thereafter it remained endemic, breaking out into localized epidemics, until its last occurrence

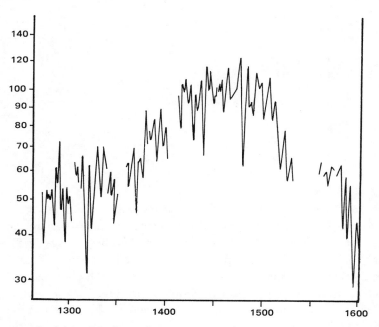

7.1. Real income of a craftsman, expressed in the volume of consumables that he could buy. [After E. H. Phelps Brown and Sheila V. Hopkins, "Seven Centuries of the Prices of Consumables, Compared with Builders' Wage-rates," *Economica* XXIII (1956): 296–314.] (Scale: Index number, 1451–75 = 100.)

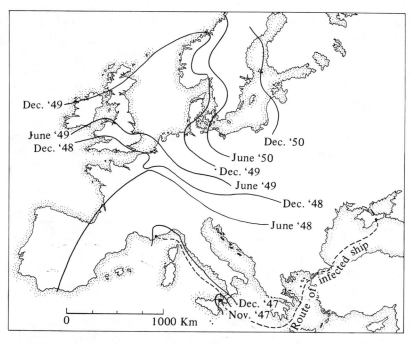

7.2. The spread of the Black Death. [After E. Charpentier, "Autour de la Peste Noire," *Annales: Economies-Sociétiés-Civilisations* XVII (1962).]

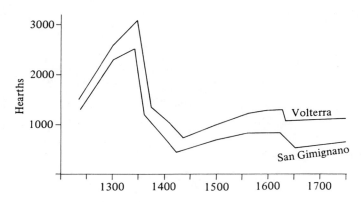

7.3. The number of hearths at Volterra and San Gimignano (Italy) before and after the Great Plague. [After E. Fiumi, *Studi in Onore di Amintore Fanfani* (Milan, 1962, 249–90.]

in Britain in 1665, and in western Europe in 1720. The threat of the bubonic plague hung like a cloud over late medieval Europe, as that of nuclear war has done over the more recent past. It contributed to a mood of gloom and despondency, but it also led some to indulge in a reckless hedonism and to live only for the moment.

But the most significant consequence of the plague was the drastic reduction of the population and the shift which resulted in the balance of supply and demand. The evidence from European cities – and most of the evidence is urban – indicates a sudden and catastrophic drop in population. Figure 7.3 shows the number of hearths, or households, in two Italian cities, Volterra and San Gimignano. Their number continued to fall into the next century and then recovered only slightly. The continued decrease must have been due in part to later outbreaks of the plague, but a contributory factor is likely to have been the very high mortality recorded among children, who would have become the householders and parents of the next generation. The dukes of Burgundy conducted a series of inquests for tax purposes into the number of hearths in the towns and villages of their domains. The evidence of these surveys indicates a population at best stable, at worst slowly declining until the end of the first quarter of the fifteenth century (Fig. 7.4). By contrast, the population of Poland, which suffered little from the plague, appears to have enjoyed an uninterrupted growth.

The population of much of Europe had, during the early years of the fourteenth century, been pressing against the available food resources. Farm holdings had, on average, been reduced to an uneconomic size and cultivation had spread to land of marginal quality. Nevertheless, the losses of the years 1347–50 led to an acute labor shortage in many areas. Court records showed tenancies vacant with no prospect of anyone to take them. The peasant found his services in demand as never before, and raised his price accordingly. His lord, on the other hand, tried to exact services which had been commuted or even forgotten when labor was abundant and cheap. The result was peasant unrest, inspired as much by rising expectations as by real distress.

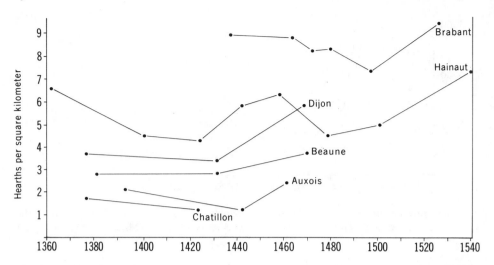

7.4. Population of Burgundy in the late Middle Ages, as expressed in the number of hearths (households) per square kilometer

The reduced population led to a smaller demand for foodstuffs. The price of cereals declined, and marginal land passed out of cultivation. Indeed, whole villages were abandoned, not only in England, which is in this respect well documented, but also over much of western and central Europe. The peasant holding is likely to have become somewhat larger and more economic. Many, through the premature deaths of parents or relatives, inherited land and set up home at an earlier age. The market in land — small parcels bought and sold among the peasantry — increased. The wage earner could command a higher price at a time when foodstuffs were becoming cheaper. This has been called "the golden age of the workers," but it was not so everywhere. Renewed outbreaks of plague and recurrent war ruined the bright prospects for many. Bad weather, floods, and harvest failure were more frequent than earlier in the Middle Ages, and the English poet William Langland, who represented the gloomy view of society, could write in the *Vision of Piers Plowman:*

Ere five years be fulfilled such famine shall arise
Through floods and through foul weather fruits shall fail.

Many were the lords who sought to profit — and succeeded — from the afflictions of the time. If demand for breadgrains was reduced, that for woolen cloth was increasing. Wool fetched a good price, and there was profit in converting land from crops to pasture. Some at least of the deserted villages had been cleared of their few remaining inhabitants to make way for sheep. Animal husbandry became more important in other respects. More cereals became available for horses and cattle, and there is some evidence that meat and milk products increased in human diet. Gilles le Bouvier, in fifteenth-century France, pointed repeatedly to the large production of animal foods in western Europe.

There is no consistent and continuous record of population in any part of Europe for these two centuries. At best we have records, some of them very detailed and generally reliable, for particular places or areas at specific times. These can be extrapolated to other areas and other times only with considerable risk. They do, however, confirm a catastrophic drop in population at the time of the Great Plague, followed by a less precipitate fall until well into the next century. For much of the fifteenth century population fluctuated, but it seems in general to have taken an upward turn near the end of the century or early in the next. The total population which had stood at between 75 and 80 million before the Great Plague, fell by at least 25 percent in those areas most affected by it. If, however, allowance is made for the smaller mortality level in the sparsely populated areas of northern and eastern Europe, including Russia, the total *may* have been reduced about 1425 to some 60 million. By the early sixteenth century the recovery of the closing decades of the previous century had probably taken the European total (including Russia) to 70 to 75 million.

The distribution of population changed little during the period. The area of densest population continued to be the narrow belt which reached across the southern Low Countries, from Artois in northern France to the Rhine near Cologne. An area of lower density extended beyond the Rhine toward Soest, Paderborn, and Brunswick. The plain of the upper Rhine, in Alsace and Baden, and the inner parts of the Paris basin also had a moderately high density, but the only regions of Europe which could rival the Low Countries were in Italy – Tuscany and the plain of Lombardy. Even here the dense rural population which surrounded the large cities was interrupted by areas of low density, like the marshy flood plain of the Po. Figure 7.5 has been compiled from the hearth rolls and other such records. The data relate mainly to the late fourteenth century and the first half of the fifteenth and have been extrapolated for those areas for which such information is not available. The sources are inadequate for the extension of the map in this degree of detail to other parts of Europe, with the exception only of England, where tax records show a relatively dense population in the southeast and sparse elsewhere.

URBAN DEVELOPMENT

There was little change in the urban map of Europe during these two centuries. By the early fourteenth, so many towns had been founded and endowed with charters of privilege that there was little scope for more. Only in the plains of Poland and in Scandinavia did towns continue to be planted. In fact some towns, already established, disappeared from the map, destroyed in war like Dinant in the Low Countries, or decaying for lack of business like many in Britain and some in central Europe.

The bubonic plague was particularly devastating in cities, where squalid conditions and close personal contacts favored its spread. In the few instances where records are available, the urban population is seen to have fallen catastrophically

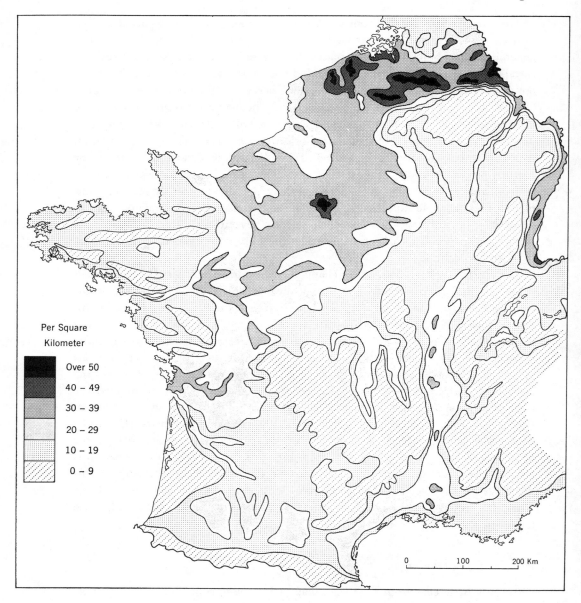

7.5. Distribution of population in the Burgundian lands, fifteenth century. Based, with extrapolations, on hearth taxes

during the years when the ravages of the plague were most severe. To some extent this may have been offset by migration, and some cities, in fact, quickly regained their earlier size. But urban growth was a highly selective process in the later Middle Ages. The great majority of cities and towns were no larger in the late fifteenth century than they had been during the decades following the Great Plague.

Dijon, for example had about 2,350 in 1376 and about 2,500 a century later. Zurich actually declined from about 6,000 in 1357 to fewer than 5,000 in 1470. Sources for urban population in central Europe and Italy are far from reliable but are consistent in showing for the majority of cities no significant change between the late fourteenth and early sixteenth centuries. There were, however, exceptions. The really large cities continued to grow. Some, like Rome and Paris, were the seats of government, and, in the words of Giovanni Botero, "the greatest means to make a city populous and great is to have supreme authority and power; for that draweth dependency with it, and dependency concourse, and concourse greatness."[1] But most of the rapidly growing cities were ports, at a time when a growing proportion of Europe's trade traveled by sea. London, which combined the functions of political capital and leading port, was increasing rapidly in both size and economic importance during these years. The expansion of Antwerp was even more rapid. In 1374 it had barely 5,000 inhabitants. By 1440, this had increased to 20,000, and by 1500 to 50,000, reflecting the growing concentration of the seaborne trade of Flanders and Brabant. Other cities which grew, though less rapidly, were Lübeck and Danzig, both deeply involved in the expanding Baltic trade. In Italy the great port cities of Venice and Genoa increased their population, and Venice approximately doubled from about 65,000 in 1363–8 to about 130,000 in 1540, at a time when most inland cities of Italy remained more or less stable. Barcelona may have increased marginally, but Lisbon, focus of the expanding Portuguese maritime empire, certainly grew. Only one great port city declined in size – Constantinople. Its significance had been greatly reduced when it was seized by the Crusaders in 1204. During the next hundred years the Ottoman Turks landed in the Balkans, cutting off the city from its hinterland, and seizing the coasts and islands of the Aegean with which much of its seaborne commerce was carried on. Constantinople had been the largest city in Europe, but when it was taken by the Turks in 1453 it was largely depopulated.

RURAL CONDITIONS

The decline in population in the second half of the fourteenth century was reflected in agriculture and the pattern of rural settlement. The widespread abandonment of settlements has already been noted (see this chap., under "Population"). In England, no fewer than 2,500 "deserted" village sites have been enumerated, of which at least half were abandoned during the later Middle Ages. In Germany and the rest of central Europe the situation was similar. In Württemberg alone there is evidence for over a thousand deserted settlements, and at about half of them the abandonment took place in the fourteenth or fifteenth centuries. In Denmark extensive areas of cultivated land reverted to waste. France has not been the subject of so intensive a search for "lost" villages as England and Germany, but here they

---

1 Giovanni Botero, *A Treatise Concerning the Causes of the Magnificency and Greatness of Cities*, trans. R. Petersen, in *The Reason of State*, ed. P. J. Waley and D. P. Waley (New Haven, Conn., 1956), 241.

were in all probability no less numerous. The consequences of the plague were reinforced by the ravages of the Hundred Years' War, with English armies campaigning up and down the country and living off the land. Froissart and other contemporaries wrote that in some parts of France the land was totally devastated and depopulated, and this is confirmed by the evidence of the fifteenth-century hearth lists for the Burgundian lands.

It is probably true to say that the village settlements which were totally abandoned were in general quite small. Their population might be reduced to the point at which they could no longer muster enough animals to pull the plow. This was the time to join forces with those of another diminished village community. What the data do not tell us is how many large villages were gravely reduced in size but not extinguished. The evidence from court rolls and accounts is overwhelming. There were losses everywhere, and the reason why deserted villages were rare in southern Europe was that small villages and hamlets were not initially common.

The abandonment of some settlements and the contraction of others were accompanied by the retreat of cultivation from marginal land. The population growth of previous centuries had led to the plowing up of inferior land, much of which was on clay. Some of this land was allowed to revert to pasture, a process which was intensified by the fact that the climate appears, at least in northern Europe, to have become appreciably wetter, thus making it even more difficult to till clay soils. Across the clay lands of the English Midlands one can today trace the sinuous ridges of the medieval plowlands, as they were when cultivation ceased and grass for sheep was allowed to cover and freeze them into the landscape.

There is little evidence for any radical change in cropping patterns, apart from the general contraction of the cultivated area. Such evidence as there is suggests that the more palatable breadgrains – the wheats – grew in relative importance, though in some areas there was a marked increase in barley production. The cultivation of pulses and of vetch and other "artificial" grasses, grown as cattle feed, also increased. The pervasive three-course husbandry with fallow was beginning to be abandoned for more flexible systems of cultivation. This could only happen where the open fields did not exercise their tyranny over crops and cultivators, and this was, in the first instance, in the Low Countries. It was here, where fields were generally small and many were enclosed, that the practice of fallowing was first abandoned. The earliest evidence for taking a catch crop on what had previously been fallow dates from the mid-fourteenth century. The practice spread, and the Flanders rotation systems became the envy of later agronomists.

These developments in cropping were intimately bound up with animal husbandry. The fodder crops were fed mainly to cattle, and the rotation grass which sometimes entered into the system was used for intensive cattle grazing. The greater number of animals led to a more generous provision of manure, while the pulses contributed to the nitrogen content of the soil. This in turn brought about the small increase in yield ratios of cereal crops, which became noticeable in the later Middle Ages. These advances were highly localized. They were conspicuous before

the end of the Middle Ages only in the southern Low Countries but were beginning to spread into northern France and southern England.

Evidence for the increase in animal farming at least in western and central
Europe is overwhelming. In Great Britain there was a large increase in sheep
rearing, and the common accusation leveled against landlords, that they enclosed
land and depopulated villages in order to increase the area of grazing, may not
have been universally applicable but nevertheless had an element of truth. A famous preacher declared before King Edward VI in the mid-sixteenth century that
"whereas have been a great many householders and inhabitants there is now but a
shepherd and his dog."[2] In the Low Countries the expansion of animal husbandry
took the form rather of an increase in cattle rearing and milk production. Little
attempt, however, seems to have been made to breed animals suited to the production of milk or meat. They remained undersized, and their milk yield relatively
small. The increased use of cattle was in part accounted for by the diminished
importance of hogs. The bones of pigs at excavated sites became fewer, as those of
cattle became more numerous. The reason lay in the diminishing area of land left
under woodland, which provided much of the food for these half-wild creatures.

Although there may have been very little visual alteration in the landscape of
open-field Europe, the pattern of ownership and control of the land underwent
more considerable changes. These were most far-reaching in Great Britain and the
Low Countries. Here the bipartite manor, divided into demesne and peasant-held
land, the latter providing labor for the former, had, by and large, disappeared.
Labor dues had ceased to be performed. The demesne was "farmed," leased at a
fixed rent to a well-to-do peasant who worked it with hired labor. Of course, such
change spread only slowly. There was little evidence of it in much of France and
central Europe, and elsewhere none at all. Yet such a change was a prelude to the
consolidation and enclosure of peasant lands, to the abandonment of fallow, and
the introduction of more flexible and more productive cropping systems. It also
underlay the increase in animal husbandry and the dietary improvements which
flowed from it.

There were no significant innovations in the technology of agriculture during
these years, despite the shortage and relatively high cost of labor. The older methods of plowing, sowing, reaping, and threshing continued unchanged. At most,
one can point to the introduction in the Low Countries of a lighter plow, drawn
by a smaller team than the old and more easily turned at the end of the furrow,
and the slow replacement of the sickle by the scythe for reaping.

MANUFACTURING

The demographic changes of the later fourteenth century contributed to significant
shifts in the pattern of industrial production and the nature of demand. Matteo

2   *Sermons by Hugh Latimer*, Everyman ed. (London, 1906), 84–5.

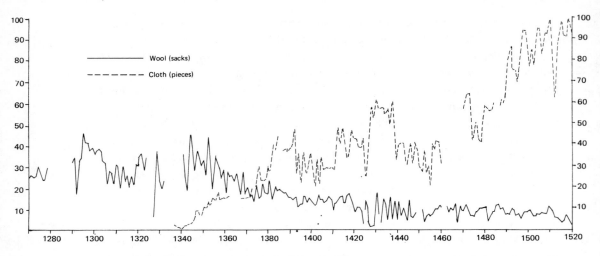

7.6. The export of wool and cloth from England

Villani, writing in Florence soon after the plague, noted that "the common people by reason of the abundance and superfluity that they found would no longer work at their accustomed trades; . . . children and common women clad themselves in all the fair and costly garments of the illustrious who had died."[3] Conditions in the decade or two following the Great Plague were exceptional. Large numbers of people had inherited or otherwise acquired wealth, but those who found their services in greater demand and thus more highly rewarded were far more numerous. The peasant had marginally more to spend on consumer goods; the urban population paid less for its food supply; and both contributed to the increased demand for cloth, leather, decorative and luxury goods, and for better quality building. And the taste for extravagance, engendered during the years following the plague, continued into the Renaissance. Inevitably, however, in a time of social change, many lost in the process. The number of "paupers" appears to have increased, and in some of the tax records of the dukes of Burgundy the total of households too poor to pay the hearth tax rose almost to a quarter of the whole.

   The cloth industry remained the most important, satisfying the largest demand and employing the greatest number of people. Yet there were significant changes within the industry, with the decay of some producers of traditional types of cloth and the emergence of new manufacturing areas. Public taste was, in fact, turning from traditional fabrics to lighter cloths with different weaves and types of finish. Foremost among the changes of these years was the emergence of the English cloth industry. Before the Black Death England had been the foremost exporter of wool in Europe. After about 1360 the volume of wool shipped to continental Europe began to decline, and by 1500 it was only a quarter of what it had been a century and a half earlier (Fig. 7.6). At the same time the manufacture and export of cloth

3   *Croniche di Giovanni, Matteo e Filippo Villani* (Trieste, 1857), bk. 2, chap. 94.

increased, and more than six times as many pieces of cloth were sold abroad about 1500 as in the decade following the plague. Within England cloth weaving was carried on almost everywhere, but two areas emerged as the leading centers for the production of good quality fabrics. These were the west country – essentially Gloucestershire, Somerset, and Devon – which produced woolen cloth, and East Anglia, which became noted for its worsteds and light woolens.

Much of the English wool export had gone to the Low Countries, where in the "clothing cities" of Bruges, Ghent, Ypres, and others much of it was woven into heavy broadcloth. This cloth was in turn exported to Italy where some was further finished before being marketed. It was a complex system of manufacturing and trade, susceptible to changes in taste as well as to shifts in the pattern of trade. The events surrounding the Great Plague merely hastened a process which was inevitable. The cloth industry decayed in the ancient "clothing cities." The number of pieces of cloth made fell irregularly, but by the end of the fifteenth century was quite small in the traditional centers of production.

This was, however, compensated to some extent by the rise of the "new draperies." These were lighter fabrics. They used longer "combing" wool and were only lightly fulled. Craftsmen who wove the traditional woolens did not readily take to the new materials, with the result that the manufacture of the latter developed most in the small towns and rural areas. It spread eastward into Brabant and westward into west Flanders and Artois. In the course of the later fourteenth century small towns like Ath and Lier began to develop a cloth industry, and, more important, the weavers of Hondschoote received a grant of privileges and protection in 1374. Hondschoote, in west Flanders, was typical of the new weaving centers. It grew to a considerable size, without achieving urban status, and was ultimately destroyed during the wars of the later sixteenth century. Its products were light woolens, serges, and "says," which were beginning to command a market in the cities (see Fig. 6.10).

The linen industry also expanded in response to a growing demand. The cultivation of flax increased on the peasant farms of Flanders, and its preparation and weaving were added to the domestic crafts throughout the region. Courtrai in west Flanders became a focus of the linen industry. At the same time other branches of textile production, including the making of carpets and rugs at Ghent and of tapestry at Arras, were developed. The so-called decline of the textile region of Flanders was, in fact, far more a diversification of production and a diffusion of the industry into the small towns and rural areas.

The other important area of cloth production was Tuscany and northern Italy. Here too, traditional fabrics were in decline. Florentine production, which had amounted to 70,000 pieces of cloth a year before the Black Death, had fallen to 19,000 pieces by 1373 and was about the same in 1382. During this time, however, a less traditional industry was developing in the cities of the northern plain. Its principal centers were Bologna, Verona, and Mantua, but it could appear almost anywhere. Skilled weavers moved from one city to another, often attracted by the offer of special privileges. English wool continued to be imported for the better quality cloth, but increasingly wool was obtained from Spain and North Africa.

At the same time cotton began to be used in the Italian industry. Some was grown in Sicily, but most was imported from the Middle East. Pure cotton cloth was not often made, perhaps because of the weakness of the shortstapled cotton available. More often it was woven with a warp of flax or wool. The resulting mixed fabrics became quite popular during the later Middle Ages. This manufacture spread to south Germany, where flax often replaced cotton in the manufacture of fustians and barchents.

The cloth industries which emerged in England, the Low Countries, and Italy were the most renowned in Europe, but it would be wrong to exaggerate their scale. Spinning was invariably a domestic activity, carried on mainly by women. Weaving was, at least in these areas, a full-time occupation for men. But the number of weavers was small. The whole English cloth industry, it has been said, employed only some fifteen thousand persons in 1400, and at Bologna, one of the most important centers of the Italian industry, textile workers numbered only five to six hundred. The output of these major clothing regions was supplemented by that of numerous less important centers. Pegolotti in the mid-fourteenth century listed a number of French cities which each produced a serviceable cloth.

In most other branches of manufacture there was little technological development or locational change during these years. Tanning and leatherworking, the making of pottery and glass, the milling of grain, and the fashioning of clothing were almost unaltered. There was expansion in crafts associated with the building industry. Timber construction, at least in churches and the homes of the better-off, became more complex, calling for a higher level of skill among woodworkers. There was a greater provision for comfort in the home, more tapestry, wainscoting, and furniture, and, above all, a growing use of masonry. Stone tended throughout the period to replace wood, and there was a rapidly growing use of brick throughout those areas of northern Europe and eastern Britain where good building stone was scarce. Lübeck, Danzig, and many smaller cities of the Baltic region came to be built largely of brick, and in Britain brick was used increasingly in public buildings and large homes.

Ironworking continued to be practiced in most parts of Europe, and its scale increased during the period. It was, furthermore, the only branch of industry in which a significant technical advance was made during the period. The primitive wind furnace, which was built in an exposed position and relied on the wind to supply a draft, disappeared near the beginning of the period and was replaced by the hearth or bloomery. This made use of bellows to supply its draft. It could have been operated by man- or animal-power, but in fact it was usually worked by a waterwheel. This brought about the relocation of works close to streams and further emphasized the importance of hilly areas where waterpower was more readily available. In the fourteenth and fifteenth century the hearth, already in use in the eastern Alps, spread through western Europe and Scandinavia. It was adopted in all ironworking areas which produced for the market, but older methods continued in use in remote areas where smelting was carried on only to satisfy local needs.

A second technological innovation was the blast furnace. It is not known where or precisely when it appeared, probably because its development from the hearth was a slow and gradual process. The walls of the hearth were first raised so that it could contain more ore and charcoal. This in turn necessitated a stronger draft, which raised the temperature and produced a more fluid metal. The advantages were obvious in the large production of metal, its greater freedom from slag and ease of working. It remained only to build the walls of the hearth high, to line it with fireproof brick, and to leave a taphole at the base through which the fluid iron could discharge.

It seems probable that the blast furnace evolved in the course of the fifteenth century, most likely in the hills, long noted for their ironworking, which bordered the lower Rhine. Its use spread to southeast England before 1500, and it was adopted in particular in the Weald. The blast furnace appeared to offer great advantages over the bloomery. It allowed much larger quantities of metal to be produced in a shorter period of time. But there were also grave disadvantages, which were to show themselves in the next century. It was inordinately extravagant of fuel at a time when in western Europe the forests were severely depleted. Secondly, the higher temperature at which smelting took place produced a more fluid metal but also permitted it to take up a great deal of carbon from the fuel that was being burned. The result was cast iron, very hard, incapable of being forged or welded, and, above all, very brittle. The metal would flow into molds, and iron castings, chiefly pots, stoves, and firebacks, became increasingly decorative, elaborate, and numerous. But demand was not so much for castings as for steel for tools, weapons, and armor, and for soft, that is, very low carbon iron, which could be forged and used in building construction. For these purposes cast iron was useless. It could be refined on the hearth and the carbon "burned" out of it, but it was cheaper in terms of both labor and fuel to revert to the older, "direct" method. Not until the eighteenth century were the problems inherent in the use of cast iron overcome.

The growing scale of ironworking in the later Middle Ages led to a concentration of production. Of course, small refining hearths – even wind furnaces – continued to be used in isolation, but one can see the emergence of a small number of regions in which ironworking was the major industry. In Great Britain, the Wealden district became the foremost iron-producing region, and was the first to use the blast furnace. The Forest of Dean had long been an ironworking area and was especially important as the source of iron arrowheads. In continental Europe the hills of eastern France and western Germany developed a reputation for their iron products which survived into the nineteenth century. It was probably in this general region that the blast furnace evolved. Even before the end of the Middle Ages iron from the Eifel and the Siegerland was supplying the toolmakers and weaponsmiths of Liège, Cologne, and places even farther afield. At the same time the Pyrenean region and the Alps of Savoy and northern Italy continued to supply metal to the smiths and armorers of Milan, Toledo, and elsewhere. The eastern Alps, which had retained their classical reputation for iron, increased their output and were among the first areas to adopt the bloomery. But the most rapid expansion during these years was probably in central Sweden. An industry, founded on the exploitation of the nodules of limonite, or bog ore, found in the marshes, expanded when deposits of high-grade ore began to be worked in the later Middle Ages. The industry was located in the district known as *Bergslagen,* lying to the west of Stockholm. The ore was reduced to bars of soft iron, known as *osmund,* which was exported in considerable quantities to western and central Europe, where its quality, due to the presence of manganese and the absence of sulfur and phosphorus, was reckoned to be higher than that of German iron.

The outstanding quality of some iron, such as that of Siegen, Bergamo, Styria, as well as of Sweden, was due as much to the quality of the ore as to the skill of the craftsmen who made it. There was, during the later Middle Ages, no question of the exhaustion of the ores — overall production was too small for this — but there was concern for the supply of charcoal. The bloomery consumed immense quantities of charcoal, and as early as the fourteenth century in England bloomeries were abandoned for lack of fuel. The situation was not dissimilar in parts of France, but in Germany the forests were more extensive, and one hears less of the scarcity and high price of charcoal. The abundance of the forests, as well as the quality of the ore, was an important factor in the prosperity of the Swedish industry.

The iron industry was very important in late medieval Europe, but it is easy to exaggerate its scale. The bloomeries customarily worked only for part of the year, if only because the flow of water, which operated the bellows, often ceased in winter. There are also instances of summer drought bringing work to a halt. The winter was usually the season when the workers went into the forests to make charcoal. It is difficult — almost impossible — to form any estimate of the output of any particular works or groups of works because so few records have survived from this period. It has been estimated, on the basis of the number of bloomeries likely to have been in operation, that the output of bar or soft iron was of the order of 25,000 to 30,000 tons in Europe about 1400, and that this rose to 40,000 tons by 1500.

The mining and smelting of nonferrous metals appears to have increased during the later Middle Ages and to have spread to mineralized areas not previously exploited. The profitability of mining was increased by the fact that two or more minerals were sometimes in joint production. Silver was often associated with lead and lead with zinc. Apart from the precious metals, the most sought after were lead, copper, and tin. Calamine, an ore of zinc, was used in making brass, but metallic zinc was not, for technical reasons, produced before the eighteenth century. Lead was the most malleable of the common metals, and thin sheets were commonly used for roofing large buildings and for making pipes and vessels for holding water. Alloyed with tin, it became hard and, in the form of pewter, was used for making table and other decorative ware. Indeed, the demand for pewter was increasing sharply in the fifteenth century among those who could afford it.

The chief sources of lead continued to be the highlands of western and northern Britain, the Ardennes-Eifel, the Harz, and Bohemia, where it was closely associated with silver. Copper was less widespread, but it was also mined in central Germany, Bohemia, and the mountains of Slovakia, which became in the fifteenth century a major source. The metal was either sent down the Vistula to the Baltic Sea, where it was handled by the merchants of the Hanse, or across Hungary and the Dinaric Mountains to the ports of the Adriatic where it was received by the Venetians. But the most abundant source in the fourteenth and fifteenth centuries was the great Swedish mine of *Stora Kopparberg,* near Falun, in the hills to the northwest of Stockholm. Small quantities were also worked in southern Spain and the Balkan peninsula.

Calamine was not treated as a metallic ore because it had never been smelted. Instead it was legally an "earth" and, as such, began to be mined in the Ardennes and Harz and to be used as an alloy in making brass a major industry at Dinant, on the Meuse. Tin, lastly, had a very restricted occurrence and was really important only in southwest England. It was mostly obtained from alluvial deposits in the moorland valleys. The volume of production was increasing, despite the approaching exhaustion of the stream workings, and in the later Middle Ages the Cornish miners were beginning to turn to the mineral-bearing lodes within the rock.

Metalliferous mining was beginning to face a crisis in the fifteenth century. Ores, with the exception only of tin ore, were deep mined. The task of breaking up the rock with simple hand-tools was difficult. In Swedish copper mines "fire setting" – the practice of building a fire against the rock and of then fracturing it by pouring water over it – was used. The chief problem was not, however, the harness of the rock but the fact that, as mining progressed, it reached a water table. Mining at the Rammelsberg, in the Harz, was in fact halted, until the water could be exhausted by means of an adit. Elsewhere primitive forms of pump, such as those illustrated by Georg Agricola,[4] were used. The increasing difficulty and rising cost of mining were driving the prospector farther afield, and in the later Middle Ages three areas were opened up on a significant scale. Metalliferous mining had long been carried on in the Ore Mountains of Saxony and in neighboring Bohemia. Silver provided the greatest attraction, but lead and other ores were found in association with it. There were many mining sites in the fifteenth century, but foremost among them were, without question, Kutná Hora, Příbram, and Jáchymov (Joachim*stal*), where the first silver *täler,* or dollar, was minted in 1519.

From Bohemia mining, especially for silver and copper, spread eastward to the mountains of Slovakia, where, at the very end of the fifteenth century, another mining region emerged, centered in Kremnica and Bánska Bystrica (see p. 214). Lastly, mining developed in the Dinaric Mountains of the Balkans. It was checked by the Ottoman invasion, but revived in the late Middle Ages. Its chief centers

---

4 Georg Argicola, *De Re Metallica* (Basel, 1556). English trans. H. C. and L. H. Hoover (New York, 1950).

lay in Bosnia and southward toward Macedonia. Silver, copper, and lead were mined and sent by pack animal across the mountains to the Adriatic coast and the waiting Venetians.

The only nonmetallic mineral in regular demand was salt, sodium chloride, obtained ultimately from seawater. Its uses, too numerous to catalog, included the salting of meat and fish and the preservation of leather. Most was obtained by evaporating seawater, and since this was best done by the heat of the sun, much came from the southern coasts of Europe. It continued to be made on the English coast in the later Middle Ages, but in this cool and cloudy climate it was necessary to boil the brine. The most northerly point at which natural evaporation could be relied upon was the Bay of Bourgneuf, on the Biscay coast of France, and "The Bay" was throughout the period the chief source of supply. But inland salt springs were also used (see p. 108), notably those at Lüneburg in north Germany, at Halle in Saxony, and at Wieliczka in southern Poland. At these sites the salt had to be extracted by boiling. Salt became one of the more bulky articles of trade but was, nevertheless, widely distributed from the coast salines and the inland salt springs.

TRANSPORTATION AND TRADE

A feature of the closing centuries of the Middle Ages was the increasing complexity and importance of long-distance trade. The same modes of transportation continued in use. The peasant carried his produce to market on packsaddle and in wagon. The merchant used waterborne transport wherever he could and roads when he had to. In fact, if it were possible to calculate the ton-miles of freight transported, it would be found that by far the greater part moved along the roads, however bad they may have been. There was, however, a shift in the relative importance of road and water. Small boats were used increasingly to convey people and goods to town markets, and the *Marktschiff* (market boat) played an increasingly important role on the Rhine. At the same time the sea route from the Mediterranean to northwest Europe began to supplement the overland route between northwest Europe and Italy. The oar-driven galley, in common use in the Mediterranean, was poorly suited to the rougher seas and longer swell of the north Atlantic and was, in general, replaced by a shorter vessel, broader in the beam, and propelled entirely by sail. From the destination of the Italian ships in London and the Low Countries, vessels of the league of German trading cities, the Hanse, sailed the northern seas as far as Russia. In the early Middle Ages Europe's internal trade had been overland, using river transport only when it was convenient and maritime transportation scarcely at all. In the fourteenth and fifteenth centuries a significant part of Europe's commerce made its way to the coast – by river if possible, by road if necessary – and thence along the coast to other parts from which it was distributed overland.

In the early years of the fourteenth century the great fairs which had developed to the east of Paris ceased to focus the trade of western Europe. Merchants no longer needed to meet face-to-face in order to settle their accounts. This was now done by means of more sophisticated financial instruments. Goods were becoming standardized to the point at which they could be ordered and paid for unseen by those who purchased them, and the business of buying and selling was, in western Europe, becoming a continuous process carried on in the cities rather than an intermittent business at fairs. While the importance of fairs was declining in western Europe, it was increasing in central. There was an eastward shift in the routes taken between northern Italy and the Low Countries. The passes of the central and eastern Alps were opened up to normal traffic. The opening of the St. Gotthard in the thirteenth century had consisted of the dramatic construction of a road up the Reuss valley. Other passes had no such obstacle. Their difficulty lay rather in the absence of shelter for travelers and their animals over the cold, windswept summits. This was remedied by the construction of hospices where the arduous journey could be interrupted.

At the same time a system of fairs developed in Switzerland and south Germany, comparable with those which had recently decayed in eastern France. The most used of these fairs were held at Geneva and Zurzach in Switzerland and at Nördlingen and Frankfurt in Germany. To some extent they were cloth fairs at which the products of cottage looms in south Germany and the Swiss plateau were marketed, but they also handled the animal products of the Alps and the weapons, tools, and other metal goods from the workshops of Italian craftsmen. But in the end, the German and Swiss fairs went the way of those of Champagne. Traffic declined as business moved in the fifteenth century to shops and commercial houses in the cities. The fate of the Nuremberg fair illustrates this course of development. In 1423–4 the city, hoping to profit from the supposed prosperity of fairs, obtained imperial permission to hold one. It failed to compete with establishments already active in the city and closed shortly afterward. Meanwhile, newer fairs were set up yet farther east at Leipzig, Poznań, Gniezno, in a region of Europe where commercial cities were few and the infrastructure of commerce undeveloped. A similar process was taking place in the still undeveloped region of the northern Low Countries. Urban development remained slight to the north of Antwerp and for a time fairs at Dventer, Utrecht, and Bergen op Zoom served the same role. But during the fifteenth century they declined before the growing importance of the Antwerp market. At Antwerp itself an earlier fair became continuous and merged with the regular activities of the city.

At the end of the Middle Ages fairs retained their earlier importance only in Scandinavia and eastern and southeastern Europe. They were a feature of the earlier phases of commercial development, and after long-distance and international trade had passed to the cities, they had no significant role to play.

MEDITERRANEAN TRADE

The failure of the crusading movement and the advances of the Ottoman Turks restricted but did not terminate the activities of the Italian commercial cities throughout the Mediterranean basin. The "empires" of the Venetians and Genoese consisted of a large number of strategically placed bases. Most were small – the city republics lacked the resources to hold extensive territories – and served only to store merchandise while it was being bought and sold. The Venetians continued until the late fifteenth or early sixteenth centuries to possess bases on the Greek islands and even on the coast of the Peloponnese (southern Greece). The Turks made little effort to dislodge them, probably finding their commerce useful. Until late in the fifteenth century "malmsey" wine continued to make its way from Monemvasia in southern Greece to western Europe. Genoese trade in the eastern Mediterranean, never on as large a scale as Venetian, suffered more severely. The bubonic plague had been brought to Europe in the ships of the Genoese from Caffa on the Black Sea coast, but this port was taken by the Turks in 1475. The trade in alum from Phocaea on the coast of Asia Minor had almost been a Genoese monopoly, but this was ended by the Turkish conquest, with important consequences for the European cloth industry.

Venice's control of the Adriatic Sea was almost unchallenged, even after the Turks had overrun the Dinaric region to the east, and, despite frequent interruptions they continued to trade, especially in metals, with the interior of the Balkan peninsula. Zara, Dubrovnik (Ragusa), and smaller ports like Budva and Trogir became autonomous dependencies of Venice.

Genoa predominated in the commerce of the western Mediterranean. The Moslems held the northern coastlands of Africa, as well as the kingdom of Granada in southern Spain, but the islands remained firmly in Christian hands, and Islam in the western Mediterranean lacked the missionary zeal which had characterized it in the east. Genoese trade was mainly in bulky cargoes of relatively low value rather than in the spices and silks which were the staple of Venetian trade. Wheat from North Africa, salt from the coastal marshes, Spanish wool, and Byzantine alum filled their ships. Nor did the Genoese have the seas to themselves. In 1406 Florence conquered its coastal neighbor, Pisa, and, shortly afterward, opened the port of Livorno (Leghorn) and developed a fleet of galleys. Barcelona and the small ports of the coasts of Spain and southern France, as well as of the Balearic Islands, also participated in this trade, and the Genoese from early in the fourteenth century began to send their ships on summer expeditions to northwest Europe.

The Italian city-republics received goods, chiefly cloth, furs, and metal goods from beyond the Alps, and reciprocated by sending raw cotton from the Levant, alum, spices, and other products of their oriental trade. Merchants from central Europe regularly crossed the passes to the Italian plain. They had their bases in the cities, just as the Italians had theirs in the ports of the Levant. The Germans, indeed, established their "factory," or place where their "factors" or agents lived, in the *Fondaco dei Tedeschi,* or "German Foundation," close to the Rialto Bridge in Venice. But it was the Italians who excelled in commerce. Only they understood the ramifications of international trade, the complications of making payments by bills of exchange, and the varied and conflicting units of measurement and currency in use. They compiled handbooks for the guidance of merchants, of which Pegolotti's *Practica della Mercatura* of about 1340 was one of the most comprehensive and well-known. Only the Italian merchants learned at this time to sit in their counting houses in Florence, Venice, and elsewhere, manipulating the markets and watching their profits accumulate.

Northern Europe

The trade of northern Europe contrasted with that of the Mediterranean. Whereas the southern trade was with a sophisticated even if sometimes hostile partner, that of the north was with the least developed region of Europe, the north and northeast. Here European merchants obtained forest products – timber, furs, and skins – flax and hemp, honey and wax, which they paid for with salt and the more refined products of the west – cloth, wine, and metal goods. Trade developed with the eastward spread of German settlement. Ports were established along the Baltic coast as far as Königsberg (Kaliningrad) and Riga. Their merchants shipped the products of the Baltic hinterland to the west. Their trade consisted essentially of an import of western manufactured goods, including salt, and an export of primary products of field and forest. At the center of this Baltic trading sphere lay the island of Gotland, and the commercial city of Visby. Though under Swedish sovereignty, it became a gathering place for German merchants in the Baltic trade, who here formed an association or Hanse for their own protection and mutual assistance in this hostile environment. At the same time German cities formed alliances, among them the substantial group of Wendish (Mecklenburg) cities, both to protect themselves from their princely neighbors and to further their commercial interests. From such seeds the Hanseatic League grew in the fourteenth century. In 1356 representatives of a large number of North German and Baltic cities formed the Hanse of cities, so-called to distinguish it from the earlier Hanse of merchants. The alliance remained informal and the number of its members fluctuated between seventy and eighty. Those cities were members which sent representatives to the irregular meetings of their *Hansetag,* or "parliament." The advantages of membership were great. Most of the cities were small, but collectively they had a very considerable political power. They successfully fought the kingdom of Denmark over trading privileges and rights of passage for their vessels through the Danish Straits (see Chap. 11); they suppressed piracy within their own sea; and in those countries, notably Flanders, England, and Russia, in which they could exercise no political control, they were able to maintain Kontors, establishments like the German Foundation in Venice, where they could live and keep their merchandise secure.

The titular head of the League was Lübeck, at whose initiative the *Hansetäge* were summoned. Its membership extended from the lower Rhineland to Riga and Reval, in the eastern Baltic, and embraced not only the many small port cities of the Baltic but also a large number in Westphalia and lower Saxony, which had no direct access to the sea and but little commercial importance in the Baltic. No doubt membership was of political value to them. Around the margin of its trading sphere, at London, King's Lynn, and Boston in England; at Bruges, Sluys,

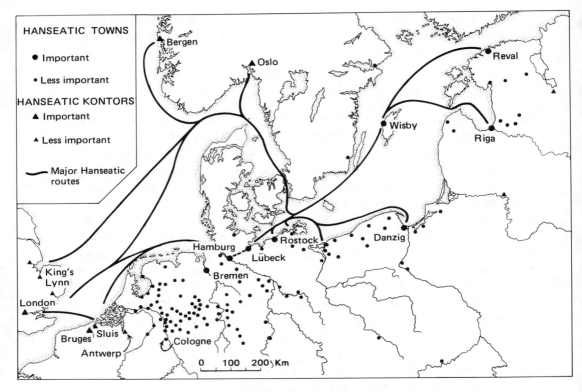

7.7. The Hanseatic League in the fourteenth century. Its composition changed later

and Antwerp in Flanders; at Bergen and Oslo in Norway; at Kaunas in Lithuania and at Novgorod – "the Great," to distinguish it from Nizhni Novgorod – in Russia were ports used by the League but not full members of it. In London the League's *Kontor* or market-house was the semifortified *Steelyard,* which retained its privileges until it was suppressed by Queen Elizabeth I. The League was at the height of its prosperity and power in the late fourteenth century (Fig. 7.7), when its commercial privileges were confirmed by its defeat of the Danes. In the next century the strength and prosperity of the League weakened. Territorial states, particularly Sweden, Russia, and Poland, increased their power over the cities, and trade itself suffered from war, more or less continuous, in the east Baltic region. The number of cities represented at the *Hansetäge* diminished, and other peoples, notably the Dutch and the English, began to intrude into what had previously been the closed trading sphere of the German Hanse.

The Low Countries

Flanders lay at the focus of trade in western Europe. It was here that the northern trade met the Atlantic trade, and from here the routes by road and river ran across France and Germany to the Alps and the Mediterranean. The eastward shift in the

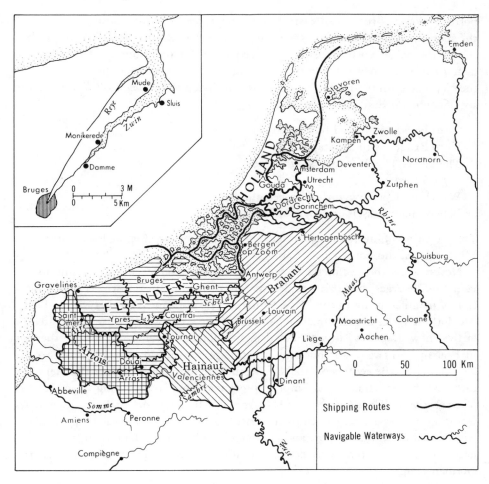

7.8. The Low Countries in the fourteenth century, showing ports and the chief water routes

avenues of commerce, from Champagne to western Germany, made little difference. They still impinged on that area of northwest Europe which lay between Flanders and the Rhine, and here was to be found the greatest concentration of commercial cities and trading activity to be found outside Italy (Fig. 7.8). As the rhyming poem of the fifteenth century, the *Libel of English Policie*, put it:

> The little land of Flanders is
> But a staple to other lands ywis.

Yet there were significant changes in the trading pattern during the last centuries of the Middle Ages. The industry of Flanders was dependent on trade. The wool came from England. The cloth was sent by road and later by sea to Italy and France. A somewhat naive view of the situation represents English wool as imported through Bruges and distributed from there to other clothing cities. Furthermore, it is often said that the silting of the river Zwin, on which Bruges lay, ruined the trade, with devastating consequences for the industry of Flanders. In fact, Bruges was never a port for seagoing vessels; the nearest they could get to the city was Damme, four miles downstream. The *Libel of English Policie* was quite specific when it described merchandise as

> Unto Flanders shipped full craftily,
> Unto Bruges as to her staple fayre:
> The Haven of Scluse (Sluys) *hir haven*
>   *for her repayre*
> Which is cleped Swyn tho shippes giding
> Where many vessels and fayre are abiding

The haven was Sluys, near the mouth of the Zwin, and this, at least during the Middle Ages, did not silt irreparably.

Nevertheless the commerce of Sluys and of the river Zwin did decline in the later Middle Ages, but this was due mainly to changes in the structure and location of manufacturing in the Low Countries. The traditional industry of the Flemish clothing cities became smaller, both relatively and absolutely, with the growth of the "new draperies" in west Flanders and northern France and also to the east in Brabant. Antwerp was not only a better port than Sluys; it lay closer to the developing textile centers of Brabant. In the late fourteenth century the Flemings captured the city in a vain attempt to prevent it from contributing to the success of their rivals. They failed. In 1406 Antwerp became part of Brabant, and its future growth was assured. Until its destruction by the Spaniards in 1576, Antwerp remained the chief port and commercial focus of the Low Countries, destination of the Mediterranean fleets, and site of one of the major *Kontors* of the German Hanse.

Links between the Low Countries and the Rhine were increasingly important in the later Middle Ages, as urban and industrial development spread eastward. From Antwerp it was possible to navigate the waterways of the Rhine delta, then very much wider and deeper than they became in modern times, and thus to reach the Rhine. Cologne and the cities of the Rhineland were reached in this way. At the same time the river Scheldt carried goods inland to Antwerp's hinterland in Hainsault and Brabant.

Across the sea to the west the port of London was developing during these centuries into the leading British port, handling not only the greater part of an increasing export of cloth, but also the import of wine from France and the Rhineland, metals, pottery, even bricks and fine cloth. London was drawing away from its rivals. The importance of Boston and King's Lynn had been based upon the export of wool, which was declining. Bristol, Exeter, and Southampton developed an export of cloth; Southampton was an occasional port of call for Italian ships from the Mediterranean; and there was also a vigorous coasting trade, much of it tributary to the small number of more important ports.

SELECT BIBLIOGRAPHY

General

The Cambridge Economic History of Europe, Vol. 1, *Agrarian Life of the Middle Ages,* 2d ed., Cambridge, U.K., 1966. Vol. 2, *Trade and Industry in the Middle Ages,* Cambridge, U.K., 1952.
Darby, H. C., ed. *A New Historical Geography of Europe.* Cambridge, U.K., 1974.
Dollinger, P. *The German Hanse.* London, 1970.
Duby, G. *Rural Economy and Country Life in the Medieval West.* London, 1968.
The Fontana Economic History of Europe. The Middle Ages. ed. C. M. Cipolla. London, 1972.
Hay, D. *Europe in the Fourteenth and Fifteenth Centuries.* London, 1966.
Slicher van Bath, B. H. *The Agrarian History of Western Europe A.D. 500–1850.* London, 1963.
Slicher van Bath, B. H. *Yield Ratios, 810–1820. Afdeling Agrarische Geschiedenis Bijdragen* 10 (1963).

Population and settlement

Beresford, M.*The Lost Villages of England.* London 1954.
Ladurie, E. Le Roy. *The Peasants of Languedoc.* Urbana, Ill., 1974.
Ladurie, E. Le Roy. *Time of Feast, Times of Famine.* New York, 1971.
Pounds, N. J. G. "Overpopulation in France and the Low Countries in the Later Middle Ages." *Journal of Social History* 3 (1970): 225–47.
Pounds, N. J. G. "Population and Settlement in the Low Countries and Northern France in the later Middle Ages." *Revue Belge de Philologie et d'Histoire* 49 (1971): 369–401.
Pounds, N. J. G. and C. C. Roome. "Population Density in Fifteenth Century France and the Low Countries." *Annals of the Association of American Geographers* 61 (1971): 116–30.
Russell, J. C. *British Medieval Population.* Albuquerque, N. Mex., 1948.
Russell, J. C. *Medieval Regions and Their Cities.* Bloomington, Ind., 1972.
Ziegler, P. *The Black Death.* London, 1969.

Economic development

Bridbury, A. R. *England and the Salt Trade in the Later Middle Ages.* Oxford, 1955.
Carus-Wilson, E. M. *Medieval Merchant Venturers.* London, 1954.
Gimpel, Jean. *The Medieval Machine.* London, 1977.
Klein, J. *The Mesta.* Cambridge, Mass., 1920.
Lopez, R. S. *The Commercial Revolution of the Middle Ages.* Cambridge, U.K., 1976.
Origo, I. *The Merchant of Prato.* New York, 1957.
Postan, M. M. *Essays on Medieval Agriculture and General Problems of the Medieval Economy.* Cambridge, U.K. 1973.
Postan, M. M. *The Medieval Economy and Society.* London, 1972.
White, L. *Medieval Technology and Social Change.* Oxford, 1962.

PART III

Modern Europe

Modern history, we are taught, began with the Renaissance. This was indeed a time of intellectual rebirth, a return to the speculative freedom of the Greeks. Mental horizons were broadened. The earliest steps in the development of modern science and medicine took place at this time, and the great voyages of the Portuguese, Spanish, French, and British extended the geographical horizon and made some Europeans aware of the peoples and resources of other parts of the world. But on essentially spatial aspects of European economy and society this new awakening had very little impact. In the *material* things of life the great break came, not with the intellectual reawakening of the late fifteenth and sixteenth centuries but some two centuries later, when an accelerating technical progress turned a preindustrial into an industrial society.

Nevertheless, the Renaissance was not without its impact on the spatial structure of the continent. There developed a new outlook on the environment. More and more people showed an interest in the land in which they lived. Books began to be written which combined geography with a somewhat biased account of the country's history. This new interest in the land was part of a broader concern, that with the nation. This was the time when people began to see themselves as part of a wider society than the community or kinship group. There had been "nations" during the Middle Ages, but they were groups independent of the soil, such as those met with at the "international" universities. Now people began to identify themselves with a particular country or region, whose distinguishing qualities were commonly language, customs, and common experience. There was thus a trend, which reached its fullest development in the nineteenth century, toward the formation of the "nation-state," a people, coherent and autonomous, occupying a clearly distinguishable tract of land.

The emergence of the nation-state accompanied the decay of the feudal structure of society. It is relevant to the subject matter of this book because it provided a framework within which human activities could be organized and directed. A government, once in secure control of all parts of its territory and of all orders of society, set about regulating its economy and protecting certain branches of manufacturing and agriculture. Governments met with varying degrees of success, but at the least they modified the distribution of settlement and economic activity.

For this reason Part III opens with a discussion of the new attitudes toward the territorial composition of the state. This is followed by an examination of the same components of human geography that have been discussed earlier. And the differences between the sixteenth and the fourteenth century are found not to be as great as the change in intellectual climate might have led one to suppose.

Chapter 9 follows the changes in these components between the early sixteenth and the end of the eighteenth century. This period of almost three centuries was a prelude to the rapid growth of the nineteenth century. It was characterized by an accelerating rate of change. Population, after the fluctuations of the sixteenth and seventeenth centuries, began to increase in the eighteenth, and, when that century ended, was growing faster than at any previous time. This was matched by a slow but selective expansion of cities, some of which had by 1815 attained a size never before reached in Europe.

Change in agriculture and rural settlement was slower, because, in large measure, of the inbuilt social controls which greatly restricted the possibilities of change. Nevertheless improvements were made, especially in the Low Countries and England, in methods of preparing and tilling the soil, in rotations, crops, and field management, and these innovations were slowly diffused into France and central Europe. The result was an increasing volume and variety in food production and a very slow improvement in diet.

Most significant for the future of developments of this period were those achieved in craft industries. These, from metalworking to weaving and cloth finishing, became more concentrated spatially. The scale of the individual enterprise grew larger until it approximated a factory, and production ceased to be largely for the local market. This necessitated the intervention of the merchant capitalist who supplied materials, controlled the several branches of any particular manufacture, and gathered and marketed the product. This phase of industrial production has come in recent years to be called *protoindustrial*. It marked the transition from the simple craft industry of earlier times, in which the craftsman dealt directly with his public, to the factory system. It encouraged the concentration of industry in areas well favored by the factors of production, and one can begin to speak of "industrial regions." Not all regions, however, which evolved under the protoindustrial system were to retain their preeminence under changing conditions in the nineteenth century.

The gradual concentration of manufacturing on the one hand and the rise of large, urban centers of population on the other necessitated a growing volume of trade in both foodstuffs and raw materials and products of manufacturing. But the infrastructure of commerce was to show little improvement before the nineteenth century. Roads were to remain bad, and a heavy dependence was placed on waterborne traffic and the coasting trade around the shores of at least northern and western Europe. Periodic fairs were at last giving way to the permanent commercial operations of the larger cities.

The dominant feature of the geographical change during this period was a growing interregional dependence and an increasing level of commerce and communication between the several parts of a country or of the continent. Despite the theoretical concept of the unity of medieval Christendom, it was during this period that a *functional* unity began to evolve, and it was this that permitted the rapid diffusion of innovation during the next century and the consequent rapid development of every branch of technology.

8

Renaissance Europe

Europe in the early sixteenth century was still in many respects medieval. Its population was rural and agricultural to the extent of about 80 percent. Cities remained small; craft industries were small-scale and most were carried on domestically. Technology had made little advance during the previous thousand years, and there were few industrial and agricultural processes that would not have been understood by the year 1000. Over much of Europe the rural population was still unfree, bound to the soil and subject to heavy and arbitrary labor demands. One of the complaints made in the German Peasants' War of 1524–5 was of "labor services which . . . daily increase and daily grow." Yet there was change; people were becoming more critical and enquiring. It is too early to speak of a scientific attitude, but institutions and beliefs were being questioned; new forms of organization were being adopted, and, in a slow and halting way, a spirit of innovation and experimentation was beginning to develop and spread.

NATIONALISM AND THE POLITICAL MAP

One of the most important intellectual developments of the age of the Renaissance was the emergence of a new attitude to the state and to public administration. The impact of central government during the Middle Ages had been slight. Its authority was mediated through the ranks of a feudal hierarchy. But now governments – in Britain, France, Spain, and Scandinavia – were beginning to reach down through this feudal structure and to control affairs at the local level. The greater desire and ability of governments to govern at all levels was reflected in a growing desire of people to belong – and be seen to belong – to the corresponding "nation." A spirit of nationalism, both rising from below and imposed from above, was beginning to permeate society.

A prerequisite of this newly developing nationalism was a greater precision in political boundaries. In 1546 the emperor Charles V, when passing along the eastern bank of the river Meuse, noted the city of Villefranche on the opposite shore. "Whose is it," he asked, "mine or the king of France's?" Then "the records of the district . . . were brought and examined, and it was shown that the inhabitants . . . were subjects of the French king."[1] It was typical of medieval kingship

1 *Mémoires de Martin et Guillaume du Bellay,* ed. V. L. Bourilly and F. Vindry, Société de l'Histoire de France, 4 (Paris, 1908), 1325.

that the limits of its authority were in many areas uncertain or unknown, and when questions arose, it was usual to ask the local population to whom they owed loyalty. Such uncertainties were one by one cleared up as they arose, but some remained until the eighteenth century.

It was difficult to define boundaries, except in physical terms. Those between local communities and estates might be described in terms of woodlots and roads, but these could not serve as national boundaries. It was usual, when international boundaries were delimited, to choose some permanent and immoveable feature of the landscape, a river or a mountain range. The trend was always to bring boundaries into harmony with physical features and to reduce to a minimum such phrases as "a line from A to B."

Despite the many surviving instances of vagueness and uncertainty, rulers in the sixteenth century could be expected to have a considerable knowledge of the lands which they ruled. Maps which were something more than a schematic representation of a theoretical world began to be printed. They had some pretension to accuracy; they located cities precisely and showed boundaries as lines. At the same time panoramic views of cities began to be produced. Even though these were in the first instance probably intended for artillery masters who might be called upon to lay siege to the cities, they also revealed much about the cities' internal relations. More people were traveling; they learned more about the land, and this encouraged a desire to read about it.

In the 1540s John Leland "was totally inflamed with a love to see thoroughly all those parts of this opulent and ample realm" of England, and left, in consequence, an *Itinerary* which is a mine of information.[2] Aeneas Sylvius (Pope Pius II) had written a description of Germany, and Gilles le Bouvier in the 1460s had the English and French heralds debate the wealth and resources of their respective countries. From France to Poland books were being written extolling the virtues and resources of individual countries and embellishing their histories. Such writings were most numerous in Germany and Italy, countries in which political divisions ran deepest. This raised the question of what were the criteria of nationhood, what brought people together and made them want to be fellow members of a state? Answers varied. Johann Stumpf sought to define Germany in terms of "customs, character and language." To Ulrich Mutius, Germany was where "the German language or any of its dialects was spoken." This emphasis which was given in Germany to language led to a sense of *Germania irredenta* – that part of a true Germany which was still controlled by others. "Our famous harbor, Danzig, is held by the Pole," wrote Celtis, "and the gateway of *our* ocean, The Sound, by the Dane," while to the east were communities "separated from the body of our Germany . . . like the Transylvanian Saxons who also use our racial culture and speak our native language."[3] It is not easy to recognize that this was written about 1500 and not in the 1930s.

2 *The Itinerary of John Leland*, ed. Lucy Toulmin Smith (London, 1907), I, xli.
3 *Selections from Conrad Celtis, 1459–1508*, trans. L. Forster (Cambridge, U.K., 1948), 47.

The same sentiments were being expressed in Italy, though in general more elegantly. The Alps were described as the God-given boundaries of Italy. Machiavelli called for the expulsion of the barbarians (French and German) from Italy, and Guicciardini could hope, before he died, to see "three things . . . a well ordered republic in our city Florence, Italy liberated from all the barbarians, the world delivered from the tyranny . . . of priests."[4] In the major territorial divisions of Europe, a single language was beginning to absorb provincial dialects – in Italy, the Tuscan speech of Dante, and in Germany, the *Mittelhochdeutsch* of Luther, while in France, the *langue d'oil* of the Paris basin became the official language. But this did nothing to diminish the use of local patois or dialects.

If a common language was the most important force making for national unity, another was a common emotional experience, like a war for independence or survival. This had been the case in Switzerland; French unity was forged in the Hundred Years' War with the English; Spanish in that with the Moors; Bohemian in the course of the long struggle with Austria; and, late in the century, Dutch in the revolt against Spain. Even linguistic diversity could be subsumed in the emotional unity which sprang from successful revolt, as Switzerland had shown.

The dominant powers in Europe were Spain and France, and around these two most were grouped. The Habsburgs, who in 1519 inherited the joint crowns of Castile and Aragon, already possessed Austria with Bohemia and Silesia, and after 1526 what remained of Hungary, as well as Burgundy and the Low Countries, which were acquired when the last of the Burgundian dukes was killed before Nancy in 1477. The Austrian emperor thus came to possess almost a quarter of continental Europe to which he added what power derived from the Spanish empire overseas and from the title of Holy Roman Emperor (Fig. 8.1). Superficially regarded, the power of the Habsburgs was overwhelming. They could control most of the land routes from the Mediterranean to northern Europe, as well as that by sea. They controlled much of Europe's metal production as well as the sources, both European and American, of most of the gold and silver, with which they could pay whatever armies they wanted. Never, it might have seemed, had so many of the determinants of power been united in the hands of a single ruler since the end of the Roman empire. Yet this power was in some respects illusory. The Habsburg lands were scattered; movement between them was sometimes difficult. There was social unrest in Spain and Germany, particularism in the Low Countries, and hostility in Bohemia and Hungary. Added to these disruptive forces was the Protestant Reformation which had by the middle of the century split Germany into two. The Habsburg empire did, indeed, have feet of clay.

The boundary which divided the German empire from France ran along or close to the "four rivers" – Scheldt, Meuse, Saône, and Rhône – though it was complicated by the feudal dependencies of each which lay on the other side of the line. French kings had pursued a ruthless, even if only intermittent, policy of drawing authority over the provinces into their own hands (see pp. 142–3). It was, how-

4   *Maxims and Reflections of a Renaissance Statesman,* trans. Mario Domandi (New York, 1965), 144.

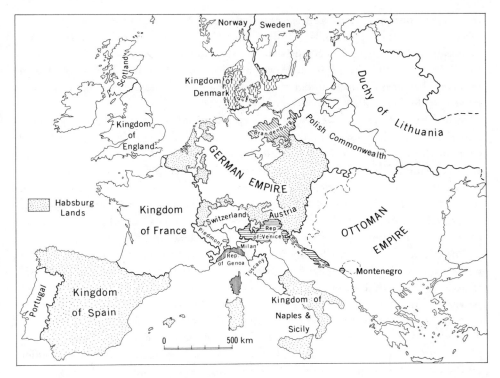

8.1. Political map of Europe, about 1530

ever, crowned with success when the ducal title of Brittany was merged with the crown, and there ceased to be any overly great feudatories to threaten the unity of the state. In 1539 the dialect of the Paris region became the official language of France. Yet the south was not wholly reconciled to rule from the north and was to resist it in many ways.

Italy was divided into more than a dozen principalities, mutually hostile and all of them prey first to the French, then to the Imperialists, who in 1527 sacked Rome with far greater fury than the Visigoths had shown in 410. To the east of Germany lay the tumultuous commonwealth of Poland, and beyond it the more primitive grand duchy of Lithuania, the two bound together in a personal union under the Jagiełło dynasty. Beyond Lithuania, and even less developed, lay the vast inchoate mass of Muscovy. It lay within the forest belt but extended indefinitely eastward. Its resources were only potential, yet its princes were beginning to make the kind of universalist claims to power that had in the west been put forward by the Holy Roman emperors. Moscow was the "third Rome" and the last, heir to both Rome itself and Constantinople. A body of myth and legend grew up around this claim, accepted implicitly by the Orthodox Church, but spurned or ignored by the west.

The Scandinavian states were beginning to emerge from their obscurity. Denmark, the most populous and advanced among them, embraced both southern Sweden and Norway, which was linked with the Danish crown. The former gave Denmark control over The Sound, the most easily navigated of the entrances to the Baltic Sea, and the political power and tolls which resulted. Sweden was at this time becoming united under the Vasa dynasty and was developing a political power on the basis of its iron and copper resources.

While European states were advancing overseas and conquering vast areas in the Americas and Asia, they were under threat from the east. The Ottoman Turks had overrun the whole of the Balkan peninsula and in 1526 defeated the last king of an independent Hungary, and even threatened Vienna. The duchy of Austria resumed its ancient role of defender of Europe from invasion from this direction. Not only did the Ottomans flood across the Hungarian plain, they also crossed the lower Danube into Walachia and Moldavia and, advancing round the outer arc of the Carpathian Mountains, threatened southern Poland and the steppe.

The countries of eastern Europe were at this time being drawn into ever closer relationship with those of central and western. Europe was becoming smaller; news traveled faster; the barrier of distance was being overcome, and west European powers, notably France, were becoming more deeply involved in the affairs of eastern Europe. The Protestant Reformation spread to Poland, Hungary, and Transylvania, and the art styles of the Italian Renaissance were diffused to England, Slovakia, and Poland. The sphere of European civilization was made smaller by the Ottoman conquests, but it was becoming more unified.

POPULATION

In the early sixteenth century the population of Europe was beginning to increase after the decline of the fourteenth century and the fluctuations of the fifteenth. Epidemic disease may have been less fatal than previously, but for no country, except perhaps England, is there an adequate statistical basis for estimating population. The hearth lists, which continued to be compiled for parts of the Low Countries, were losing their value, as the hearth became more a notional unit of taxation than a measure of real population. And similar records are very scanty for other parts of Europe. Only for England can there by any pretension to accuracy. Here the parish registers, which were ordered to be kept from 1538, provide a record of baptisms, marriages, and burials, and though they are far from complete for the sixteenth century, they do provide the means for making a reliable estimate of total population.

On the basis of aggregate totals derived from the registers, E. A. Wrigley estimates that the population of England alone, when registers began to be kept, was of the order of 2.75 million. There was a belt of dense population across the Low Countries and extending to the Rhine. Areas of moderately dense population extended southward to embrace much of the Paris basin and up the Rhine valley to Switzerland. Similar densities were to be found over much of the Swiss plateau,

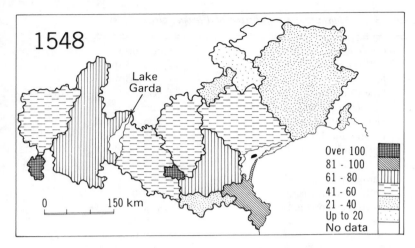

8.2. Population density in Venezia, mid-sixteenth century

but population was very sparse throughout the Alps and the hilly regions of southern France. The north European plain varied greatly in the density of its population. All the evidence points to very sparse population in the glaciated areas but a much denser population on the good soils of the loess belt of Saxony, and there were islands of dense population also around mining centers in the Harz and Ore mountains. Densities fell off toward the east, in Poland, Lithuania, and Russia, and southward beyond the Danube into the Balkans, where the settled population had been greatly reduced by the Turkish wars. The evidence points to severe devastation and depopulation in the plain of Hungary, and probably also in much of the Balkan peninsula.

Mediterranean Europe was better documented and certainly more populous. Cities were large and numerous, and their local regions intensively cultivated. But only central and northern Italy could show densities comparable with those met with in the Low Countries. Records of the Republic of Venice allow population densities to be calculated for 1548 (Fig. 8.2). Over much of Venezia there were more than 50 to the square kilometer, and comparable densities were probably found in Tuscany and the lands of several other city-republics. A visitation of the diocese of Bergamo by its bishop was accompanied by a listing of the number of "souls" in each parish. This suggests a total population of about 150,000 and a density of over 130 to the square mile. Densities were appreciably lower in the Spanish peninsula, and there were strong regional variations between populous Catalonia and Old Castile, on the one hand, and the thinly peopled, almost deserted conditions on the plains of Estremadura and La Mancha.

Any estimate of the population of Europe in the first half of the sixteenth century, like all earlier estimates, can only be tentative. Such evidence as there is suggest the totals given in Table 8.1.

Table 8.1. *Approximate population of Europe, circa 1530*

Great Britain	4,000,000
England	{2,750,000}
France	13,000,000
Low Countries	1,500,000
Germany (including Austria)	12,000,000
Swiss Confederation	800,000
Poland and Lithuania	3,000,000
Poland	{2,500,000}
Czech lands	2,000,000
Hungary	2,000,000
Balkan peninsula	1,200,000
Spain and Portugal	8,524,000
Italy	11,000,000
Scandinavia	1,600,000
Russia	6,000,000
	66,624,000

The urban pattern

Regions of really dense population were also highly urbanized. While it is probably true that no more than 15 percent of Europe's population lived in cities and
towns, the percentage was very much higher in areas like central and northern
Italy and the southern Low Countries. Urbanization is, however, difficult to measure because many towns were in fact nothing more than large and highly privileged villages. All were in some degree agricultural, and the small towns were
largely so. Such a town was Lenzburg in the Swiss canton of Aargau. It covered
six acres within its walls and held a population of no more than five hundred, most
of whom were engaged on the land. It had a market which served the needs only
of its immediate area. There were hundreds of such towns in central Europe. In
England they would probably have reverted to the status of villages, like the
decayed boroughs in Devon and Cornwall.

The appearance and even the plan of sixteenth-century cities were in many
instances preserved for posterity in the drawings and engravings of Dürer, Sebastian Münster, and late in the century, of Braun and Hogenberg. These represented
towns as walled, with gates and towers. Within were narrow streets and closely
spaced houses, dominated by a few public buildings, such as a guildhall, and by
the towers and spires of the city churches. Most were tightly packed, and the only
considerable open spaces were provided by marketplaces and the cemeteries which
enclosed some of the churches. Some, however, were greatly overextended as far
as their walls were concerned. These were built when population was still increasing, but the abrupt cessation of growth in the mid-fourteenth century left wide
spaces within the outermost line of walls, occupied, as contemporary drawings
suggest, by gardens and orchards.

The jurisdiction of most cities extended only a short distance, the *Bannmeile,* beyond its walls. Nuremberg was exceptional in controlling an area of twenty-five square miles. The citizens themselves, however, had often bought rural land at a considerable distance from the city as an investment, sometimes cultivating it themselves, more often leasing it at a rent or as sharecropping tenancies. One among many reasons for the failure of cities to develop adequate systems of water supply was their inability to control land and resources more than a short distance beyond their walls.

There must have been some five to six thousand cities and towns in Europe in the early sixteenth century, ranging from a few giant cities of over one hundred thousand down to thousands as small as Lenzburg. Their distribution was markedly uneven. There was, in western and central Europe, a fairly regular pattern of small towns, because their chief function was as market centers and their spacing was dictated by the length of a marketing journey. Even so, they were to be found less frequently in thinly peopled regions like the Central Massif of France, the Meseta of Spain and the glacial plain of northern Europe. Most of the truly large cities lay in either northern Italy or in northwest Europe (Fig. 8.3). The categories of cities by size formed a kind of pyramid with very few of giant size and increasing numbers in the smaller-size categories. The pattern of cities exercised one of the keenest minds of the age, Giovanni Botero. What, he asked, were the causes of "the greatness of a city." The first, he said, was "the commodity of the site and the fruitfulness of the country." A dense urban pattern, he realized, required a fertile and populous countryside to support it, but, he went on, there were some provinces "and they very rich, that have never [had] a good city in them." He cited Piedmont in northern Italy as an example. Clearly there were other factors than the fruitfulness of the soil. He clearly conceived of regional capitals able "to draw people to our city," attracted by "some good store of vendible merchandise." This might be assisted by a "store of navigable rivers . . . and good havens of the sea." But he was quick to note that the excellence of a harbor did not in itself make a great port. "What port is more safe or more spacious than the channel of Cattaro [Gulf of Kotor, on the Dalmation coast], and yet is there not any memorable city in that place." Botero was no determinist and recognized the importance of subjective influences. The sites of religious cults and "the commodity of learned schools are of no small moment to draw people." Above all, he added, large cities owed their size to "supreme authority and power," for government "draweth dependency with it, and dependency concourse, and concourse greatness."[5] Botero was correct; the political capitals were, almost without exception, the largest cities in their respective countries, though the evidence did not confirm his claim that the size of a capital was directly related to that of the country.

Figure 8.3 shows the distribution of the larger cities, here defined as those with a population of more than five thousand. It is likely that Moscow and perhaps Novgorod were also of this size. The largest of them were probably growing dur-

5 Botero, *Magnificency and Greatness of Cities,* 241.

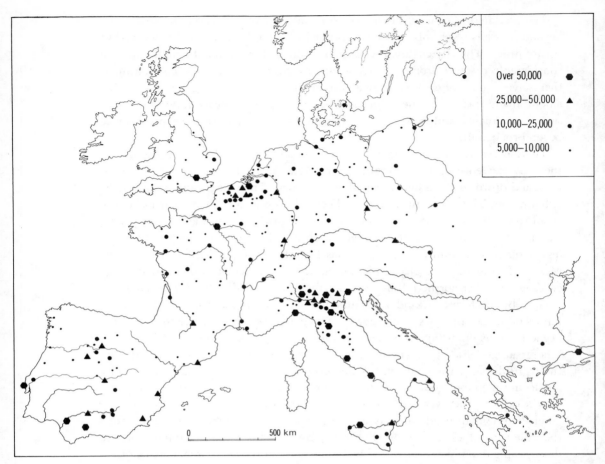

8.3. The chief cities of Europe in the first half of the sixteenth century

ing the sixteenth century, though for most of them there is very little specific information. Capital cities grew fastest, because government had ceased to be peripatetic and was taking on an increasing range of functions and employing a growing body of royal servants. At the same time, the royal courts were attracting vast numbers seeking profit or employment, or merely wishing to bask in the royal presence. The wealthier of these hangers-on of the royal courts built palaces and town houses, such as survive in considerable numbers in Warsaw and once existed in London, Paris, and elsewhere, and in turn gave employment to shop-keepers and craftsmen.

Paris became the archetype of the capital city. It had always in some sense been a capital, since the Capets had first been counts of Paris, with a palace on the crowded Ile de la Cité. In the sixteenth century this was replaced by the Louvre on the right bank of the river. The city itself overspread both banks; in the early sixteenth century it covered more than a thousand acres within the walls built by Charles V at the end of the fourteenth century and housed some two hundred thousand people. It was by far the largest urban agglomeration in Europe, with the possible exception of Constantinople. Except where land had been cleared for royal building, it was extremely congested. Houses ran to five stories or more and were built largely of wood and plaster. Streets were narrow and dirty, and the whole city was insanitary. The richest quarters lay on the right bank, to the north of the Louvre. Some of the poorest and most crowded quarters were on the left bank between the river and the university, the area known later as the Latin Quarter.

So large a city placed a heavy strain on the systems which supplied food, fuel, and even water. The city drew on a very large area, much of the Paris basin, in fact, and without its rivers a steady flow of goods could never have been maintained. As it was, timber for building construction and fuel was floated down from as far away as the Central Massif. Much of the breadgrain came from the Beauce, to the southwest, and the best of the building stone from the plateau of Brie to the east. All were unloaded on the quays which lined the Seine and were transported by an army of porters to the markets which were scattered about the city. Paris was a great consumer, but it was not at this time a great producer. Like classical Rome (see p. 59) it had little basic industry, and its vast consumption was paid for by the tax revenue of the kings and the rents paid to nobles who lived there. An underemployed population, without basic industries to employ and support it, was in some degree a feature of most capital cities at this time.

Until 1561, the capital of Spain was Valladolid. It lay in the plains of Old Castile, without the convenience of navigable waterways. It was at this time a city of about forty-five thousand, with little to support it except the business of government. In 1561 it was abandoned as the seat of government for Madrid, a site which had even less to recommend it, beyond the doubtful virtue of centrality within the Iberian peninsula.

In Italy and Germany political fragmentation had prevented the emergence of large capital cities, though Milan, Turin, and Florence, as the chief cities of their respective duchies, were large and growing. Only Rome was a capital of more than provincial importance, but it owed its size and importance, as Botero observed, "to the blood of the martyrs, to the relics of saints, to the holy consecrated places, and to the supreme authority in beneficial and spiritual causes."[6] Nevertheless, the city was only a fraction of the size it had once been under the Roman emperors, and most of its population crowded onto the Campus Martius, close to the Tiber, and into the Trastevere suburb beyond. The city held about fifty-five thousand inhabitants when, in 1527, it was ravaged by the soldiery of the emperor Charles V. It was probably the most visited city in Europe; countless guides were prepared for the use of travelers, and in 1526, there were no fewer than 236 inns, hostelries, and taverns. But the city was at this time being transformed. Work had begun on

6   Ibid.

St. Peter's, beyond the built-up area west of the river, in 1506; the Vatican became the residence of the Popes, and palaces began to be built for those who
attended the papal court.

Brussels had been the chief seat of the Burgundian dukes in the fifteenth century, but at the end of the century ultimate control of their lands passed first to
Vienna and then to Valladolid. Brussels had grown to be a city of ninety thousand
by the beginning of the century, second only to Paris, but "supreme authority and
power" now deserted it, and Brussels grew no more until the nineteenth century.

There were no great cities among the capitals of the German states, not even
Munich or Vienna. Most splendid of them was probably Prague, at the center of
the rich province of Bohemia. It spanned the river Vltava, with the "royal" city,
the Hradčany, on its hill to the west, and the university and aristocratic quarters
straggling down the hill below it; across the Karlův Mos, the magnificent late
medieval bridge, lay the commercial and artisans quarter. But Prague ceased to be
a royal seat in 1526, when its last king, Lewis, perished at Mohacs, and the crown
was given to Charles V of Habsburg.

The capital of Poland at this time was Kraków. Like Prague, it had grown up
in the shadow of a royal castle and cathedral, but it never became a "social" capital,
like Prague and Paris. This role was reserved for Warsaw, to which the seat of
government was transferred in 1596. The Scandinavian capitals were, in the early
sixteenth century, small, timber-built towns with no great pretensions, either
administrative or architectural. Their period of rapid growth and rebuilding was
not to come until late in the century.

The only city which could have exceeded Paris in size and magnificence was
Constantinople. It had been reduced to a population of no more than eighty thousand at the time of its capture in 1453 by the Ottoman Turks, but it quickly
revived and by the mid-sixteenth century may have had half a million. It had filled
out the space within the Theodosian Wall (see Fig. 4.4) and had overflowed beyond the Golden Horn to Galata. The former imperial palace became the Topkapi,
residence of the sultans, and Hagia Sophia, the crowning architectural glory of the
city, became one of the hundreds of mosques, whose minarets rose like shafts above
the city's skyline. But much of the city remained congested and dirty; its many-
storied wooden houses jetted out over the streets. Fires were frequent and had
every opportunity to spread rapidly across the very narrow streets. There was, in
fact, only one wide road, that which ran from the Topkapi westward to the principal gate in the Theodosian Wall. Constantinople was a busy, commercial, and
cosmopolitan city. It traded by sea, as indeed it had to, with the rest of the
Ottoman empire, and its population was made up, in addition to Turks, of Greeks,
Armenians, Syrians, and peoples from all provinces of the Ottoman empire, as
well as Sephardic Jews from Spain.

Beside the great capital cities of continental Europe, London and Moscow must
have seemed little more than small towns. London was still enclosed within its
medieval walls which, by and large, had been rebuilt on Roman foundations. It
lay on the north bank of the tidal and navigable Thames, along the shore of which

were quays and warehouses. A single bridge, the dangerously overbuilt London Bridge, linked the city with its south bank suburb of Southwark. At the southeast corner of the city stood the Tower, London's castle and still officially a residence of the monarch. Against the river in the southwest was Baynard's Castle. Between lay St. Paul's Cathedral, a vast gothic pile on top of the gravel-capped Ludgate Hill; an immense number of city churches, monastic houses, and friaries; the Guildhall; the Steelyard – London depot of the Hanseatic League; and the crowded homes of some thirty-five thousand Londoners. London was more balanced in its development than other capital cities. It was not merely a center of government. It carried on an important commerce, both national and international, and was highly significant for its craft industries. It was already attracting those who wished to be among the king's retinue. The Tower had been abandoned as a royal residence in favor of the palace of Westminster, and the homes of the rich and powerful, as well as centers for the study and practice of the law, were spreading between the western gate of the city and its Westminster suburb, a mile and half to the southwest.

Moscow, capital since the beginning of the century "of all the Russias," lay on the small but navigable Moskva River. At its center was the Kremlin, at this time a strongly walled enclosure of seventy acres. It contained the palace of the grand dukes, but it was far more than this. In it were churches, an orthodox monastery, and the town houses of the boyars or nobles, as well as a considerable resident population. Like the Wawel at Kraków and the Hradčany at Prague, it was castle, palace, church and city. But Moscow had already spread beyond the Kremlin walls. The so-called Red Square – *Krasnaya Ploshchad* – lay outside its gates to the northeast, and was the focus of commercial activity, and around the Kremlin were the quarters of specialized craft industries. It is difficult to estimate the population of Moscow at this time. It fluctuated and the suburbs were liable to be destroyed in war, as they were by the Tartars late in the century.

Another category of city which was growing rapidly at this time was the port city. Throughout the later Middle Ages the chief ports of the Mediterranean – Venice, Genoa, Barcelona – had been among Europe's largest cities. Venice had spread over its island; its housing had encroached on other islands as well as the mainland, and its population in the early sixteenth century was at least a hundred thousand and possibly nearer a hundred fifty thousand. It was a commercial city par excellence. Its harbor was shallow but sheltered. Its ships could tie up along the quays which bordered the main island between the palace of the Doge and the Arsenal, but their commerce had ceased to expand, as trade passed from the Inland Sea to the oceans, and Venice lost its Mediterranean empire to the Turks.

Genoa was in some respects less favorably located. Its harbor was the shallow Gulf of Genoa, and behind the city the Apennines made transport to the plain of northern Italy difficult. It lost its Mediterranean possessions, except Corsica, and in the 1490s fell under the control of the French. In 1528 this was thrown off in the course of the revolt of Andrea Doria, but by this time the trading preeminence of Genoa had ended. Barcelona, never as large or important as Genoa, suffered

8.4. The ports of Portugal and southwestern Spain in the sixteenth century

even more severely in the commercial revolution of the sixteenth century, as trade passed to Spain's southern and western ports.

The trade which was beginning to pass through Europe's Atlantic ports dwarfed anything that Venice and Genoa had handled. "Compared with all other traffic flows of the period," wrote Chaunu, "the Spanish-American trade was enormous,"[7] and with it the Atlantic ports of the Iberian peninsula grew. They lay in two groups, near respectively the mouths of the Guadalquivir and the Tagus (see Fig. 8.4). Cadiz, with an excellent harbor and poor links with its hinterland, lay south of the mouth of the Guadalquivir. Seville, more than fifty miles upriver, was the largest port and one of the most rapidly growing cities in Spain. It was the focus of Spanish trade with the New World, and the *Casa de Contratación*, the department of government which managed this trade, was established here in 1503. In 1530, its population had reached about forty-five thousand, and continued to grow through the century. Lisbon, at the mouth of the Tagus, had the advantage of the finest natural harbor on this coast, and its trade with the east led to a growth as rapid, in all probability, as that of Seville.

The other great port cities of Atlantic Europe lay in the Low Countries and around the North Sea. Le Havre de Grace had been founded in about 1520 by Francis I of France but was still small and relatively unimportant. In Flanders, Bruges remained a great city of perhaps thirty thousand, but ships had deserted its silting river Zwin, and trade had largely passed to the Scheldt. Here Antwerp, located on the right bank of the river within easy reach of the sea, was becoming the chief port city of the Low Countries. By 1531 when a new bourse was built, its population had probably reached fifty thousand, and Guicciardini in the mid-

7   H. Chaunu and P. Chaunu, *Séville et l'Atlantique (1504–1650)*, I (Paris, 1966), 12.

century described its wide streets and handsome buildings, as well as the variety
and volume of the goods which were loaded and unloaded along the quays which
lined the river in front of the city. Antwerp's future rival, Amsterdam, was at this
time little more than a small port, engaged mainly in the local and coasting trade.

Within the circuit of their walls, the street plan of most cities differed in no
way from that of two centuries earlier. Streets were narrow; few were paved, and
all were the repositories of domestic waste thrown into them from adjoining houses.
Urban building was more often of wood and clay than of stone, and few cities had
adequate supplies of building stone at hand – Paris and Rome being conspicuous
exceptions. Brick construction, introduced into urban building several centuries
earlier, had become important only in the cities of northern Europe. Lübeck was
in some degree a city of brick, and brick was also much used in the northern Low
Countries and around the Baltic. Tall building was the exception. Few houses rose
more than two or three stories except in cities, like Genoa and Venice, where space
was at a premium. Fires were frequent and destructive. The journal of a burgess
of Mons recorded a fire in 1518 which, he claimed, destroyed thirteen hundred
houses in Armentières, leaving only three standing. Four years later twelve hundred
houses burned in Valenciennes, and in the next year much of Reulx was leveled.
Almost every city had its catalog of fires.

No advances had been made in the supply of water and the disposal of sewage
since the fourteenth century. Most cities relied for water on springs within or
nearby, and the water was often fed to elaborate and colorful fountains which
belied the quality of the water they dispensed. Many drew their supply from the
nearby river, at most holding it in tanks for the coarser sediment to settle. There
were no sewers, and rivers were so polluted by human as well as industrial waste,
like the drainings from tanyards and butchers' shops, that their water was totally
unfit for consumption. It is not surprising that fevers and diseases of the digestive
system were endemic and that the death rate from these causes was high.

Few cities could have maintained themselves – certainly they could not have
grown without a steady immigration from the countryside. Data on this movement are scanty, but it was large. At Lyons, in 1529–31, over 60 percent of those
adults for whom there is evidence had been born outside the city. Cities attracted
immigrants; they did not always succeed in holding them, and many who failed
to establish themselves in one city moved on to another. Small towns drew mainly
from their local areas; large, from very much more extensive areas. After the first
quarter of the century the direction of migration was strongly influenced by religious affiliation. A Catholic would have been unlikely to settle in a town like
Zurich or Geneva, or a Protestant in Cologne or Strasbourg.

Only the smallest towns could count regularly on a food supply from their
immediate district. All larger cities relied upon distant sources, and the larger the
city the farther it had to go to procure an adequate supply. Botero had postulated
"the fruitfulness of the country" as a precondition of major urban development,
and, in fact, most large cities could derive a part of their supply from their local
regions. Seville derived its food from the plain of Andalusia, Valladolid from the

grain-growing region of Old Castile. The north Italian cities had the productive plain of Lombardy at their doorstep, and the Rhineland cities used water transport to bring grain from surplus areas along the river. But there were exceptions. Geneva, hemmed in between the lake and the boundary of France, experienced recurring difficulties, and the cities of the Low Countries were beginning to organize a grain trade import from the Baltic.

Most of the larger cities and many of the smaller had a basic industry whose products in some degree paid for the city's imports. Most often it was a branch of the textile industry. Within the cities the manufacture was strictly controlled, ostensibly in order to maintain standards, more often, in fact, to preserve the monopolistic position of the masters of the craft. The effect was to encourage industry, especially weaving, in rural areas beyond the control of the city authorities. This led in turn to the growth of industrial villages, urban in size and function, but lacking urban status. These were particularly numerous and large in West Flanders and northern France, where the city fathers of Ypres and other clothing towns were powerless to touch them, and they included such straggling, half-urban settlements as Hondschoote, Armentières, Tourcoing, and Neuve-Englise, all of them noted for their production of the "new draperies," lightweight woolen fabrics, despised by the weavers of traditional broadcloths.

AGRICULTURE AND RURAL CONDITIONS

Just as two centuries earlier, the rural and agricultural sector of the population made up about four-fifths of the whole, less in areas like the southern Low Countries, northern Italy, and probably southeast England, but appreciably more in eastern and northern Europe. The agricultural sector supported the rest. In theory, it received protection, the products of craft industries, and the blessings of the church. In fact, the rents, taxes, and tithes of the agricultural population paid for the extravagant building and costly entertainment which the rich allowed themselves. Very little, indeed, was at this time plowed back into agriculture, except in the southern Low Countries and parts of the Lombardy plain, where the burgesses themselves invested in and improved the land. A model devised by Wilhelm Abel, admittedly for a somewhat later period, represents about 40 percent of the gross output of peasant agriculture as disposed of in services, taxes, tithes, and other seigneurial obligations and a further 20 percent as sold off the land, leaving little more than a third as the net income of the peasant. Such conditions are more than sufficient to explain peasant unrest generally and the revolts in Germany in particular. The Memmingen Articles of 1524, drawn up by the German peasants, show how onerous the lord's exactions were seen to be. In eastern Europe, where conditions had been improving, burdens on the peasants were reimposed and even increased, a movement commonly called the "second serfdom" (see pp. 275–6).

At the beginning of the sixteenth century most of the land belonged to the lay aristocracy or to the church. The lands of the church were extensive. In most of western and central Europe they made up from 10 to 20 percent of the land, and in some areas, Bavaria for example, they amounted to half. It is important to know what land was in the hands of the church because ecclesiastical landlords were in general among the least progressive. Comparatively little land was held by the churcn in the Low Countries and northern Italy where agriculture was most advanced. Relatively little of the land was cultivated directly by those who owned it. Most was leased in small peasant holdings or "farmed" in larger units. Only in eastern Europe did extensive lands remain in demesne, and here, as the possibility of selling grain into the western market developed, the lords began to exact to the full the labor dues of their peasantry.

The size of estates varied greatly. There were some in most parts of Europe which were little bigger than a substantial peasant holding, and in Poland the "barefoot" *szlachta* (gentry) differed from the peasantry only in their status and their pride. While there were estates – in Spain, France, and Germany, especially the east – of tens of thousands of acres, most ran only to hundreds, and much of the land in very large estates was under forest and contributed comparatively little to their owners' income. The peasantry made up at least three-quarters of the population of Europe, and more in eastern Europe and Russia, but they formed a far from homogeneous group, and the gulf between the rich peasant and the poor was as great as that between the peasant and the landowning class. Peasants differed, in particular, in their personal status, in the size of their holding, and in the nature of their title to it. The biggest barrier was, of course, that between the unfree and the free, the serf or villein and the free farmer. In much of western Europe this was tending to vanish as servile obligations ceased gradually to be exacted and the villein was assimilated into the class of free, landholding peasants. In Britain villeinage had almost disappeared; little trace remained of it in the Low Countries, Switzerland, and northern Italy, and it had never been of great importance in much of Scandinavia. It was in retreat in France, leaving behind it only a few small, though irritating personal obligations. In Germany serfdom was still widespread and important, and the authors of the Memmingen Articles of 1525 declared that God had made all men free.[8] But, alas, the princes and the church combined to defeat the aspirations of the peasants in one of the most savage of peasant wars. At the same time the reformer Zwingli secured the abolition of serfdom in Switzerland. In eastern Europe, on the other hand, peasant obligations had been relatively light, but at this time they were intensified and remained for at least two centuries the most onerous in Europe.

Peasant obligations took many forms. Serfs lacked personal freedom, which meant that they belonged to and could be sold with the land they cultivated and were not free to abandon it. Such a restriction was difficult to enforce, and if peasants had not been able to escape from the land, urban growth would have been very small. The second burden on the peasant was the obligation to work on his

8   A. F. Pollard, "Social Revolution and Catholic Reaction in Germany," *Cambridge Modern History,*
    II (Cambridge, U.K., 1903), 179–80.

lord's demesne for a certain period each week. Sometimes he had himself to provide plowing oxen and tools of cultivation. These obligations were heaviest at
seedtime and harvest when the peasant would have wanted to give all the time he
could to his own plot. In much of western Europe demesne farming had been
abandoned. The lord had leased his demesne to a "farmer" at a fixed rent and was
happy to commute the labor dues of his peasants for a rent in money or in kind.
Only in eastern Europe was this trend being reversed, with the lord demanding
the performance of labor services to the full. To the east, in the Principality of
Moscow and the recently annexed Principality of Novgorod, serfdom was being
imposed for the first time. It never had any legal basis such as existed in the
reciprocal obligations met with in western feudalism. Servile duties were nonetheless heavy, especially during the short summer, when most of the work on land
had to be performed. Russian serfdom, unlike western, was not restrained by local
custom, and the rights of the lord were often enforced by the might of the prince.
On the other hand, serfdom was not universal. It was rare in the northern forests
where the lords stood to gain more from a money rent than from labor services,
but it was being intensified on the border of the steppe, where the good, black
soil offered richer rewards.

The other obligations of the European peasant were, relatively at least, of minor
importance: grinding at the lord's mill, baking in the lord's oven, contributing
eggs or a capon at certain periods of the year to the lord's table. These continued,
as a general rule, to be exacted until modern times. Peasant servitudes were least
important in Great Britain, the Low Countries, and northern Italy, and these were
precisely the areas where the middle class was most developed and economic growth
had been most vigorous.

The size of peasant holdings varied greatly. Though there is little precise data
before the eighteenth century, the average size would appear to have been considerably under twenty-five acres, and in some areas less than half of this. The same
constraints prevailed as in the Middle Ages. Cultivation was in open-field strips
in much of western and central Europe, and the peasant, whatever his status, was
tied to the cropping routine of two cereal crops and fallow. Little progress had
been made in enclosing fields, except in those advanced areas, such as the Low
Countries, where the peasant servitudes had largely disappeared.

Although gradual change was taking place in the crops generally cultivated,
the breadgrains still held pride of place in the fields and in the diet of all classes.
Fall- and spring-sown cereals continued to be grown in very roughly equal amounts,
but there was a tendency, where climate and soil permitted, for wheat to replace
rye as the winter crop. The reason, of course, lay in the fact that it fetched a higher
price in the market and could bear the cost of long-distance transport more easily
than rye. Wheat nevertheless remained the chief crop only on the good soils of the
Paris basin and of the north European loess belt. In southern Europe where a cereal
crop, as a general rule, alternated with fallow, only wheat and barley were grown,
with barley prevailing in the drier areas. Oats and barley, usually spring-sown,
were important throughout northern Europe, in part because they fitted into the

cropping system, in part because they were suited to poor soils and cool moister climates.

Agriculture in the sixteenth century was marked, as it had been throughout the Middle Ages, by a grave shortage of manure. Both yields and yield ratios were low, but, in the few areas for which statistics are available, there appears to have been a small improvement in both respects. Except in poor harvest years, a yield ratio of at least four could be expected for wheat and rye and usually rather less for the spring grains. It is difficult, however, to draw conclusions since the spring grains alone were sown on some poor, acidic soils, and there were parts of Scandinavia where oats were the only cereal crop.

The range of plants cultivated in garden plots was probably increasing in western Europe; turnips and other root crops were becoming more common and were important because they could be stored through the winter. About 1530, corn, the first New World crop to be adopted in the Old, was being grown in Castile. Books on gardening, such as Olivier de Serres's *Maison Rustique,* presented long lists of vegetables and herbs, but these manuals were for the guidance of the rich. Few new plants appeared in the garden plots of the peasants.

The cultivation of the grapevine was in slow retreat. The principal reason in all probability was not any fluctuation in climate, but the increasing ease with which wine could be supplied from areas like Gascony, Burgundy, and the middle Rhine Valley to markets in the northwest and north. Viticulture was disappearing from the southern Low Countries; it was in retreat near Cologne and in the Paris basin. But it appears to have been gaining in importance in Austria and around the margins of the Hungarian plain. The wine export from Greece lapsed with the Ottoman conquest, but viticulture was spreading in the Iberian peninsula, not only along the Mediterranean coast, but even on the plains of Old Castile, where wine became an important commodity at the fairs of Medina del Campo.

Olive groves continued to be extensive close to the Mediterranean Sea. They had the advantage that they would flourish on soils too dry for other crops. But olive oil was less important than it used to be, replaced increasingly by animal fats, and as groves died or were destroyed they tended not to be replaced.

Industrial crops, on the other hand, were probably grown more widely. Flax was of great importance from Brittany to the Baltic. The increase in shipping called for increasing supplies of hempen cordage, and, at the opposite end of the scale of textile materials, the cultivation of the mulberry and the rearing of silkworms were spreading in Italy and southern France.

Vegetable dyes continued to be grown, and the import of indigo and other dyestuffs from Asia and the Americas had made no significant impression on the market at this date. Hops were cultivated increasingly in the Low Countries and northern Germany to flavor beer, which remained the chief fermented drink in all areas where viticulture was not practiced extensively. In northern France the decline in wine growing gave some encouragement to apple growing for cider, but this was generally considered to be a lower-class drink.

It is impossible to point to any significant change in the tools of agriculture

since the late Middle Ages, except that iron had become somewhat more conspicuous in the manufacture of some of them. Olivier de Serres recommended the use
of a roller fitted with metal spikes to harrow and compress the soil after sowing,
but there is no evidence that such a machine was ever widely adopted. The efficiency of labor remained low. Plowing and harvesting were very slow, and calculations have shown that the cultivation of a family-sized holding left very little
time for other agricultural pursuits, least of all for labor on the demesne.

The sixteenth century was a period when the area under cultivation increased in
response to rising demand for breadgrains. Waste was reclaimed and some progress, notably in the Low Countries and northern Italy, was being made with re-
claiming the coastal marshes (see p. 282). Only in Great Britain does the cropland
which went out of cultivation during the later Middle Ages appear, as a general
rule, to have been left under grass. Indeed, it would appear that land was continuing to be converted, if only on a small scale, from crop husbandry to pasture.
The primary reason here was the high price of wool, which still contributed to the
profitability of grazing. This, however, was not the case in continental Europe.
Here the evidence is clear; there was a not inconsiderable expansion of the area
under crops during the century. The increased demand for breadgrains is shown
by the rising grain prices and the attempts made to reclaim and improve land,
and it is confirmed by the increasing percentage of cereal pollen trapped in marsh
peat.

The pattern of rural settlement had changed only in detail during the closing
centuries of the Middle Ages. In England a substantial number of villages and
hamlets had been abandoned during the fourteenth and fifteenth centuries, principally in the East Midlands and south-central England. It was in all probability
only the smaller settlements which were deserted, and a very high proportion of
those which survived into the sixteenth century have remained until today. The
same is broadly true of the continent. There is no difficulty in locating settlements
named in the latest of the Burgundian hearth lists in the present-day landscape.

The general stability in the pattern of settlements was not matched by any
comparable permanence in their internal arrangements. The cottages of which they
were made had comparatively short lives, and they were not necessarily rebuilt on
the same sites or even close by. Many villages were transformed. This was happen-
ing especially in the east where villages might be completely realigned in the
supposed interests of efficiency or of closer feudal control. Even in England village
plans continued to change, as one part of a village decayed and another grew, and
street villages were transformed into "green" or rounded villages, and vice versa.

The importance of animal rearing varied greatly from one part of Europe to
another. In open-field Europe it was restricted by the area of grazing land and the
amount of fodder available. In western or "Atlantic" Europe, the practice of agriculture was tipped toward animal husbandry. It is impossible to formulate any
estimate of the numbers of animals kept. Cattle were few in open-field Europe,
because it was difficult to keep them through the winter. Sheep fared better and
could pick a living from the fallow fields and waste. In the west, however, from

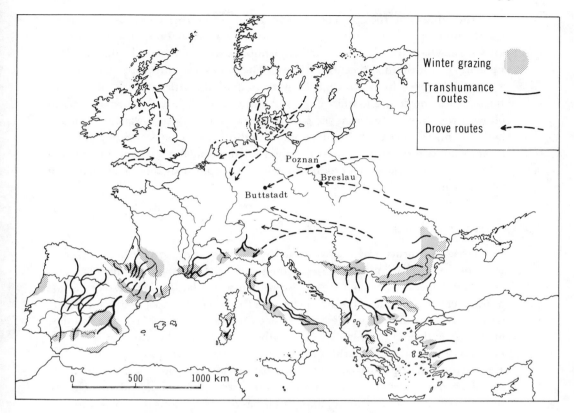

8.5. Transhumance and drove routes in Europe in the sixteenth century

northwest Spain to Norway, cattle were relatively more numerous because the growth of hay to keep them through the winter months had become generally more abundant. Pigs continued to be important only where the woodlands were extensive enough to support them.

The very important role played by transhumance has already been examined (see pp. 171–2). In the early sixteenth century its importance was tending to increase, and in many parts of Europe the balance was tipped from arable to pastoral farming. In the Alps, rents once paid in cereals now began to be rendered with cheeses, and in Switzerland, mountain pastures were proving a profitable investment for wealthy townspeople. The more intensive rearing of animals led to a greater use of marginal land and thus to an increase in the practice of transhumance. It gained in importance throughout the Alpine Zone, from the Pyrenees to Romania and Bulgaria, and was probably intensified in the hill country of Atlantic Europe. At the same time long-distance migrations were developing on the Spanish Meseta and between Provence and the French Alps, though the animals which took part were mainly sheep and their purpose was to produce wool. Figure 8.5 shows the principal areas of transhumant agriculture in the sixteenth century.

At the same time the sparsely populated areas of northern and eastern Europe lent themselves to animal rearing with or without a seasonal migration. In southern Scandinavia, Poland, and the lower Danube basin, cattle were being reared for the market in western and central Europe. They moved in droves toward the fairs of central Europe, from which they were sold to the cities. Herds of up to a thousand had made the journey in spring and fall. Even in Britain smaller herds followed the drove roads from the hills of the west and north toward the London market. This reliance of the more populous and urbanized parts of Europe on very distant sources for part of its meat supply is further evidence for both the growing specialization in agricultural production within the continent and for an increasing economic unity.

MANUFACTURING AND MINING

The sixteenth century was marked more by changes in the structure and organization of manufacturing than in the technologies used. Demand for manufactured goods was increasing, with a slight rise in living standards. The relative decline in urban crafts continued throughout much of northern Europe, and manufacturing increased in rural areas. To some extent this was inevitable, because mining, quarrying, and brickmaking, all essentially rural in their location, were among the growth industries, but the shift to the countryside was also encouraged by other factors: the rigid organization of urban guilds and their inelasticity in the face of changing demand, the unruliness of urban craftsmen, and the relative cheapness of unorganized rural labor. It all has a very modern ring. Even so, the growth of rural industry would have been impossible without the emergence of a class of merchant capitalists who provided the capital which the rural craftsman lacked; supplied the materials which he needed; and collected, finished where necessary, and marketed the products.

Textile industries

These developments were most marked in the textile industries. There had, of course, always been a rural manufacture of coarse cloth for peasant use. But now, under the influence of merchant capitalists, the manufacture was being upgraded to cater primarily for a middle-class market. This trend toward rural weaving — spinning had always been largely in the villages — began first in England and had made most progress there. In the early sixteenth century much of the cloth, of whatever variety or weave, was made in the countryside. Even the names given to it — kerseys, worsteds, coggeshalls — were those of villages. The chief cloth-weaving regions — East Anglia, the Cotswolds, and the west country as far as eastern Devon — developed and expanded the manufacture of middling- to high-quality woolens, which, by and large, satisfied the domestic market and left a considerable surplus for export. Britain had the advantage of an adequate supply of wool of good quality, and the expanding woolen industry left comparatively little available for export.

In the Low Countries the trend was similar. The broadcloth industry was almost extinct in the weaving cities of Flanders, killed off by their interminable disputes, changes in fashion, and the competition of rural areas. The cloth industry had, in fact, migrated only a relatively short distance, but enough to escape the jurisdiction of the cities. It spread westward into western Flanders and northern France, and eastward into Brabant, Liège, and the lower Rhineland. This was not, in general, a physical movement of the weavers themselves. Instead, the merchants who handled the cloth trade transferred their custom from the old to the new manufacturing areas. A lighter cloth was woven in the villages of west Flanders, less demanding in the quality of the wool used, and in increasing demand. Such were the "new draperies." The chief center of the industry was Hondschoote, an unincorporated village without guilds or any other restraints on trade. It had grown by this time into a vast, semiurban sprawl of some fifteen thousand people. Other rural areas developed similarly: Bergues-Saint-Winnoc, Armentières. In all these overgrown villages an industrial proletariat was emerging, dependent on the merchant for thread, in some instances for the loan of their looms, and for marketing their products.

The clothing industry had also spread southward into northern France, where Arras, Cambrai, Amiens, Abbeville, and, above all, Reims became important centers. The urban industry survived better here because these cities had not been previously identified with a single type of cloth and were better able to adjust to changing currents of demand. The development in the towns of Brabant was similar. The industry of the southern Low Countries had formerly relied heavily on English wool. The supply was now greatly reduced, and they were obliged to use local wool from the polders and heaths of the Low Countries and from the Ardennes, supplemented by imports from Spain.

The Italian cloth industry had maintained its position more fully than the traditional Flanders manufacture. The Italians proved to be more flexible in their methods and in the structure of their industry. They adapted more readily to changing demand and were not above introducing flax and cotton into their cloths in order to produce different qualities and textures. The Italian industry also remained more narrowly urban, and, though spinning was an occupation of the countryside, weaving was largely carried on in the cities.

The cloth industry was widespread in France. In the cities of the north and of Champagne it benefited from the decline of the Flanders industry, and Reims, in particular, grew into an important clothworking center. The lower Seine valley and southern France were clothworking areas, some of it urban, but most carried on in the cottages as a part-time industry supplementing the income from agriculture. There was an urban cloth-weaving industry in Spain, but it had declined, like that of Flanders, and for much the same reasons. East of the Rhine woolen cloth was less important, and linen proportionately more so. This was in part due to the poorer quality of the wool that was available. In Switzerland and southern Germany wool was mixed with other materials to give the fustians and barchents for which many German cities were noted.

Linen manufacture was growing in importance throughout northern Europe. The raw material was grown locally; the preparation of the flax – the retting and scutching – was a part-time peasant occupation, and linen had the great advantage that, unlike woolens, it required no "finishing" apart from bleaching. Whenever the woolen industry was interrupted by war or by a shortage of wool, the peasant turned to flax, and the linen industry appears to have been the net gainer from every crisis that swept this region. From Brittany to Silesia linen weaving was gaining in importance. In Switzerland and southern Germany linen was made for the Mediterranean market; in the lower Rhineland and across the north German plain, it was satisfying ever more of the local demand for cloth, and the best-quality linens were exported to the west.

The manufacture of cotton fabric was still insignificant. Cotton was grown on only a minute scale – in Sicily – and import from Egypt was costly and unreliable. The industry continued, though on a very small scale, in northern Italy. Silk weaving on the other hand was of growing importance, though the volume of silk cloth produced was probably less than that of cotton and cotton mixtures. The silk-weaving industry continued to be practiced in the Italian cities of Lucca, Genoa, and Venice. The French king had in the fifteenth century enticed Italian weavers to settle in France and, by the sixteenth century, Lyons had developed the silk industry which it still retains. But it was a luxury industry par excellence, dependent on the patronage of king and nobility, and was moved about the continent at their whim.

The leather industry was similar in some respect to the textile. It used a raw material – skins and hides – which was available almost everywhere, and it produced a commodity fully as varied in quality as the textiles themselves. Another consumer-oriented industry was potting, though it was not quite as widespread as tanning. Its raw material, clay, was not found everywhere, but where it was, a coarse, wheel-turned pottery was made. The related manufacture of bricks was increasing during the sixteenth century, especially in northern Europe, and brick construction was becoming increasingly common in eastern England, the Low Countries, and around the North and Baltic seas. Glassmaking was even more localized. It called for higher skills than potting, and its basic materials, silica sand and potash, were not often to be obtained in close proximity to one another. The Italians, especially the Venetians, had a high reputation for the quality of their glass, and the manufacture was also important in the Low Countries. Not a few English churches, including Fairford parish church and King's College Chapel, Cambridge, were glazed at this time with stained and painted glass from Flanders.

Another consumer good which was at this time being produced in ever-increasing amounts was paper. Parchment and vellum, the latter being a superior quality parchment obtained by scraping and preparing both sides of the skin, were expensive, and a cheaper means of preserving records and printing books was highly desirable. But it was not until the later Middle Ages that paper began to be made on a considerable scale by pulping rags. The industry derived from the Moors and was first significant in southern Spain and Italy. From the former the manufacture spread to France, and from Italy it spread to Germany in the fifteenth and sixteenth centuries. But the chief manufactories were in the cities of central and northern Italy, which supplied paper to much of Europe.

Metal industries

These formed a group second in importance only to textiles. They were concerned primarily with ironworking, but lead, pewter, and bronze were all of importance, and there was in Europe at this time a growing output of silver.

Ironworking tended to be small-scale and ephemeral. Iron ore, in its many chemical forms, was by far the most widespread of the metalliferous minerals. So abundant was it that deep mining was generally unnecessary; sufficient ore could be obtained from shallow bell pits, which were abandoned as soon as extraction began to look hazardous. It might even be said that the chief constraint on the iron industry was the availability of fuel. Charcoal was used almost exclusively; the hearth and furnace were voracious consumers, and the more accessible forests were being rapidly depleted.

Although the blast – or "high" furnace – had been developed during the previous century, most of the iron made continued to be smelted on the hearth or bloomery by a "direct" method. The blast furnace derived from the low-shaft furnace. It had developed gradually during the previous century (see p. 199). It produced iron in quantity but the usefulness of the metal was limited. Refining it was difficult, but the high-carbon metal lent itself to casting. Cast iron was first employed on a significant scale in casting cannon, which had previously been made by welding bars of soft iron. Other forms began to be cast, some of which could never have been made by forging: pots for cooking, for example, and the decorative firebacks used to protect the domestic hearth from the heat of the fire.

Most of the iron smelted in Europe in the early sixteenth century was marketed as soft or bar iron. It had countless uses and provided material for an immense variety of craftsmen such as the cutlers, lorimers (swordsmiths), armorers, and smiths, who forged simple ironware, from hinges and locks to nails and horseshoes. Among the skills developed was that of case hardening or "steeling." Steel is a form of iron in which the amount of carbon has been reduced to a level intermediate between that of cast iron and soft or wrought iron. This would be achieved by burning out some of the carbon from cast iron, but it was more usual to add carbon to soft iron. This was a skilled craft, even though most of its processes had been developed empirically. The quality of the "steel" which resulted depended on how much and how well the carbon had been absorbed, and also on the way in which the resulting metal had been tempered. But there were other factors. The presence of traces of substances, such as sulfur, phosphorus, and manganese, could have a deleterious or beneficial effect on the metal. In this respect a very small percentage of manganese in the ore was of great importance in producing an iron good for steeling, whereas phosphorus and sulfur tended to make the metal brittle or "short." Ores which contained manganese had long since been recognized for their superior qualities, though no ironmaster could possibly have known what it was that gave the ore its value.

Some ores, and the metals smelted from them, enjoyed a high reputation for their quality. Among them were the ores of the Basque region of northern Spain, which continued in demand until late in the nineteenth century; the more scanty deposits found in the Italian Alps in the province of Bergamo; the Siegen district of the lower Rhineland; the eastern Alps of Austria, especially the province of Styria; and, lastly, central Sweden. In each of these districts were ores which in general lacked the deleterious elements and possessed at least a trace of manganese. The metal made from them could be "steeled" to make blades and armour, and it supplied weaponsmiths and armorers established nearby. Milan and some cities of the lower Rhineland, especially Cologne, and of the southern Low Countries were noted for the quality of their smiths' work. Bar iron from these districts was traded widely. The merchants of the Hanse brought Swedish bar iron to England and the Low Countries; that from Styria was exported to Venice and north Italy; and iron from Siegen was transported up and down the Rhine.

But there were many other centers of iron smelting which produced a serviceable metal suited for agricultural implements, masons' and carpenters' tools, and the hardware used in the construction industry. Prominent among them were Burgundy and Champagne in eastern France, where an ore of passable quality occurred widely in the limestone beds (Fig. 8.6). Iron from this region was distributed, mainly by river, to consuming centers in the Paris basin and northern France. Another important ironworking area lay in the hills of the Ardennes and Eifel, and yet another in the hills of Thuringia, the Upper Palatinate, and northern Bavaria. Ores from the Italian island of Elba were brought to the mainland of Tuscany to be smelted with charcoal from the local forests. In England there was an abundance of ore but a growing shortage of fuel. The most important region was the Weald of Kent and Sussex where forests remained thick and a number of the new blast furnaces had by this date been built and were active in producing metal for gun founding.

The fabrication of metal goods was almost exclusively an urban occupation, and here the metalworking crafts were highly specialized. "One smith, " wrote Biringuccio, "is master only of massive iron things, such as anchors, anvils, well-chains, or guns; another of plowshares, spades, axes, hoes and other similar tools for working the earth and for reaping the harvests. Others are masters of more genteel irons such as knives, daggers, swords, and other arms for wounding with the point and edge. Others again make scythes and saws; others gauges, chisels, hatchets, drills, and similar things, including locks and keys. Still others make crossbows and muskets, and others make armor for protecting and arming the various parts of the human body. . . . There are as many kinds of special masters as there are

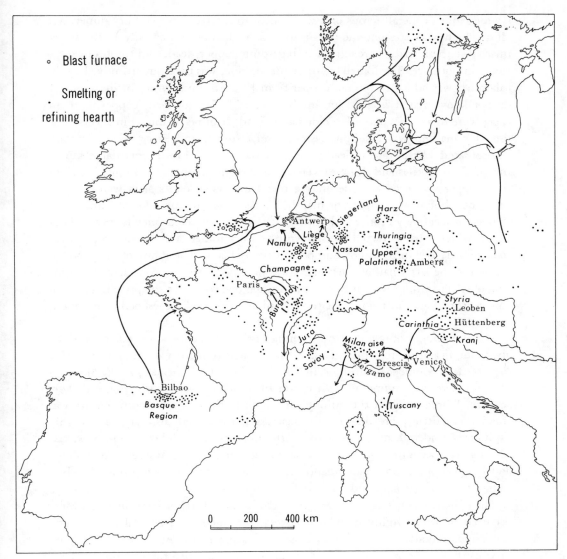

8.6. Ironworking in Europe in the sixteenth century

things that are made or can be made of iron."[9] All the larger cities had specialized workers in iron and steel, and in some, notably those of northern Italy and the Rhineland, their skills were of a very high order.

The mining and metal industries include the production and smelting of the ores of the nonferrous metals. The writings of Biringuccio and Agricola show that

---

9   *The Pirotechnia of Vannochio Biringuccio,* trans. and ed. C. S. Smith and M. T. Ghudi (New York, 1959), 370.

a wide range of metalliferous ores was known to the sixteenth-century miner, not all of which were of economic importance. Some had been used only by the alchemist. But these writers are agreed in regarding copper, lead, and tin as of exceptional importance. The fourth common metal, zinc, was used unwittingly. Its ore, calamine, was added to molten copper to make brass, and, wrote Biringuccio, "I do not know that it is good for anything else."[10] But for lead, copper, and tin there were many uses and a large demand. Lead, hammered into thin sheets, was used for making water supply systems and cisterns, and every urban fountain incorporated a great deal of lead piping. It was also used for roofing large buildings, for which tiles and shingles were considered unsuitable, and in making pewter. Copper was used as a decorative metal and some of its slats were used as pigments, but it was important mainly for alloying with tin and calamine (zinc) to make respectively bronze and brass. Yet it was the precious metals, particularly silver, which most attracted the sixteenth-century miner, and the search for them took him deeper into eastern Europe and the Balkans. The influx of New World bullion in the latter half of the century was preceded by a very considerable expansion of silver mining within Europe, and when one considers the price inflation of this century, one must not omit the contribution made by the flood of European silver.

The importance of metalliferous mining during the century was reflected in the abundant literature to which it gave rise. In addition to two major works, *The Pirotechnia* of Vannoccio Biringuccio (1540) and Georg Agricolas's *De Re Metallica* (1556), there were numerous editions of little handbooks on assaying – *Probierbuchlein*. While much of the mining carried on in the early sixteenth century was small-scale, little more than family businesses, there were also large and highly capitalized undertakings, especially in the mountains of Bohemia and Slovakia. Mining was becoming big business, as the activities of the Welsers, Mannlichs, and Fuggers of Augsburg abundantly testify. It was among such people that Biringuccio and Agricola found markets for their books.

The nonferrous metals were very restricted in their distribution (Fig. 8.7). Most occurred in a few highly mineralized areas, in which, as a general rule, several nonferrous metals would occur in close association in the mineral-bearing lode. Frequently two or more ores were in joint production, with the pricing problems which inevitably arose. Mining was active in the sixteenth century in six such areas. The hills which lay to the south of Liège, the Ardennes, and Eifel were a considerable source of lead and calamine. Far greater importance attached to the Harz region in Lower Saxony. There were few metalliferous ores which were not obtained here, but copper was especially important, and this region supplied metal to the coppersmiths of the Rhineland and Low Countries. In addition, silver and lead continued to be of great importance. The Ore Mountains which separated Bohemia from Saxony were similarly endowed, with silver the most important product in the sixteenth century. It was in the mines near Freiberg that Agricola

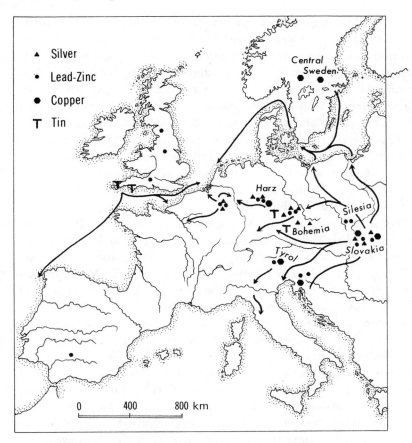

8.7. Nonferrous metal production in Europe in the sixteenth century

gained his knowledge and experience of mining. Far to the east, in Slovakia, was one of the newest of Europe's mining regions, the central part of the Carpathian Mountains. The large reserves, mainly of silver-lead and copper ores, had recently been opened up by German entrepreneurs under the overall control of the south German banking houses, which transported and marketed the metal. The impact of the German miners can still be seen in the architecture of the small towns which they developed and inhabited: Kremnica, Banská Bystrica, Banská Štiavnica and, farther to the east, Levoča, Prešov, and Košice. The eastern Alps, particularly the province of Tyrol, were chiefly important for copper, and copper was also the chief nonferrous ore produced in central Sweden.

COMMERCE IN THE SIXTEENTH CENTURY

The commercial revolution which was taking place in the early sixteenth century brought about far-reaching changes in the pattern of European trade. The commerce of the later Middle Ages had been predominantly one between the Mediterranean basin and northwest Europe. Commodities from as far away as south Asia were gathered to the Mediterranean ports and from here were sent – mainly overland – to western and central Europe. The products of Europe north of the Alps made up a return flow of merchandise. Only to a small extent had shipping by way of the Atlantic replaced the slow and costly movement of goods between the Italian commercial republics and the cities of the Rhineland and Low Countries.

This system lasted well into the sixteenth century, but only two years before that century began Vasco da Gama had sailed into the India port of Calicut and loaded onto his ships a cargo of spices which would otherwise have been transported by way of the Red Sea to Egypt and the Mediterranean. The Portuguese brought their spices to Lisbon, from which they were taken, again by sea, to Antwerp and London. But trade with Asia by the traditional route did not end abruptly; too many people had an interest in perpetuating it, and as late as the mid-century most of the Asiatic spices handled in the Antwerp market had traveled overland from the Mediterranean. But other aspects of the Mediterranean trade fared less well. The Turkish conquest of the Aegean and the Balkans brought an end both to the trade in alum from Phocaea and in wine from the Peloponnese. It was not the oriental spices which were disappearing from the Mediterranean markets but a host of less esoteric and more bulky goods which had provided much of the cargo in Mediterranean ships.

If Mediterranean trade was not suddenly extinguished, that of the Atlantic did not spring suddenly into being. It was already there. For almost a century the Portuguese had been exploring the west coast of Africa and settling the Atlantic islands. Wine was already being made in Madeira when the trade in Malmsey was closed down by the Turkish conquest. Italian merchants were already active in the Atlantic ports of Spain before Vasco da Gama brought back the first cargo of spices from the east; sugar from the Atlantic islands was being sold in the Antwerp market, and the Bretons and Normans were fishing Icelandic waters and trading as far afield as Norway even before Columbus set sail in 1492 from Palos for the New World.

It is impossible to exaggerate the volume of trade carried on in little ships along the shores of Atlantic Europe. Most carried no more than thirty *tonneaux,* the measure of capacity derived from the "tun" of wine. A *tonneau* would have been about 50 cubic yards. Much of this trade in the Bay of Biscay was in the hands of the Bretons, but the English from ports like Dartmouth, as a surviving port book shows, also played an important role. They brought iron and wool from Spain; canvas from Brittany and Normandy; wine from the Gironde; and salt from the "Bay," and returned with cloth, metals, and salted fish.

The ports of the British coast were organized in a kind of hierarchy, with a small number of "head" ports, each with several "members." Those of continental Europe functioned in a similar fashion, though their organization was less formal. Bilbao, La Rochelle, and Rouen; Exeter, Southampton, and London were "head" ports, to and from which the ships of the little ports, coves, and creeks conveyed their freights. The great "cogs" of Flanders, or even the long galleys of the Mediterranean trading cities made their occasional visits to the former, but would, generally speaking, have been quite incapable of entering and coming alongside in the latter. To some extent, the intense traffic between the small ports of the western coasts was an alternative to a more difficult and dangerous journey by land. It was, for example, usual to travel from London and the southeast of England to Devon and Cornwall by sea. A similar busy coasting trade was carried on along the shores, both English and French, of the English Channel and around at least the more southerly part of the North Sea. The Zuyder Zee which formed a kind of "inland sea" for the northern Low Countries was lined with small ports, with Amsterdam at their "head." The Baltic Sea was similar, with dozens of ports tributary to Lübeck, Stettin, and Danzig. In this respect the Baltic resembled the Mediterranean, with, however, one very significant difference. In the latter, Europe traded with the developed region of the Middle East, whereas in the Baltic it was Europe itself which was the more developed partner, trading with the underdeveloped or pioneer fringe to the north and east. This was reflected in the commodities of trade. The Baltic region, especially Scandinavia, Lithuania, and Russia, supplied primary materials; timber, especially timbers for masts and ship building; wood ash for making soap and glass; furs and skins; grain and salt fish. Its imports, apart from the salt which it could not produce, were made up of wine, cloth, and other products of west European industry.

This northern trade had formerly been dominated by the merchants of the Hanse (see pp. 205–6), but their organization had long been in decline. Outsiders, the Dutch in particular, were intruding into the Baltic. The demand for Baltic "naval stores," wood ash, and, above all, grain was increasing. There is little evidence for the volume of this trade. Neither port books nor the records of the Sound dues have survived for this early period, but the qualitative evidence that is available suggests a steady growth in the export from Riga and Königsberg of flax and ships' timber and, from the ports of the south Baltic coast, of grain, especially rye.

Water transportation was preferred for the movement of all except the most valuable of goods. Coastwise shipping, we have seen, was of immense importance around all parts of the European coast. But river transport was also used wherever practicable to gain access to the hinterlands. It is difficult to name an important maritime port that did not lie at or near the mouth of a navigable river. Rivers which would now be judged unnavigable were regularly used, and where the current was too great or the depth of water too shallow, timber rafts at least could be floated downstream. Much of the timber supply for the larger cities arrived in this way. But the opportunities for river navigation were limited. Road had to be used even to gain access to the rivers, and such "feeder" roads gave rise to important transshipment points. Such an inland port developed at Kazimierz Dolny, where the route from the grain-producing loess belt of southern Poland reached the river Vistula. Here the grain was stored in the stone-built granaries, many of which survive, before being loaded onto river craft for the downstream voyage to Danzig. There were similar points on the Seine and Rhine systems where land transportation was abandoned for water.

Although the natural speed of the current was relied upon for floating timber rafts from the mountains to the plain, propulsion was sometimes a great deal more difficult where the rivers flowed deep and slow. Three methods were used. Boats were rowed, driven by sail, and pulled by the strength of man and beast. Rowing was commonly used for short trips, and sixteenth- and seventeenth-century city engravings often show the rivers alive with rowboats. Sails were of use only on the larger rivers, wide enough for boats to tack and turn. Sails, it is said, were much used on the Loire for upstream traffic, since the river flowed *into* the prevailing wind. But, whether equipped with mast and sails or not, a boat had often to be towed, and every river had, of necessity, its *Leinpfad,* or towpath. Its condition was a persistent source of dispute between boatmen and the owner of the land through which they voyaged. The legal obligation to maintain the towpath was never clearly established and continued to bedevil river shipping until, in the nineteenth century, mechanical means of propulsion were adopted.

There were other problems in river transport besides those of propulsion. The boats themselves were often temporary and ill-built. It was not uncommon to build a rough boat near the head of navigation, to load it and sail it downstream, and then to break it up and sell the timbers when it had reached its destination. There were shipwrecks, even on the sheltered banks of rivers, and cargoes were often lost or damaged because the boats leaked. An allowance was always made when salt was shipped up the Loire from the Bay of Biscay for part of the cargo being dissolved by the river water.

Rivers, furthermore, were encumbered with man-made obstacles: mills, fish-weirs, and, above all, tolls. The Rhine was probably the most heavily encumbered, perhaps because there was more to tax than elsewhere. There were eighteen toll stations in some sixty miles on the lower Seine. Further impediments, most burdensome on the Rhine, were the "staple" and "transshipment" rights exercised by some riverine cities. So obstructive were they that they were at this time hastening the decline of the land route between Italy and northwestern Europe in favor of that by sea.

In the Low Countries, on the other hand, waterborne traffic was increasing in importance. In the vast deltaic region of the Meuse and Rhine, road building was in any case extremely difficult, and waterways were numerous and navigable. It was easier to improve the latter than to construct the former. In the later Middle Ages the Dutch and Flemings in particular had begun to build chamber locks in order to lift boats from one water level to another. By the early sixteenth century a few artificial canals were in use to supplement the natural waterways.

The whole of Europe was crisscrossed by roads, which formed a dense net in England and northwestern Europe but were fewer in central, eastern, and south-eastern Europe. In a very few instances they were well-built causeways. More often they diverged into competing tracks, between which the traveler chose according to the weather or season. A few derived from the road system left by the Romans, especially in England. None were properly maintained, and their quality varied with the bedrock which they traversed. Areas of clay or alluvium might be impassable for much of the winter, and diversions were often made to take advantage of the easier going over land floored with limestone.

The increasing use of roads was reflected in the appearance of roadbooks, of which the prototype was that published in 1553 by Charles Estienne for France. These showed direct routes between most cities of medium or large size. The network was dense in northern France, the southern Low Countries, Rhineland, and western Germany. Everywhere, however, its usefulness was conditioned by bridges. Bridges or, alternatively, ferries were the fixed points from which routes radiated. Building bridges was a task for which no authority assumed responsibility, though many a city constructed a bridge across its local river. Even London had only one bridge across the Thames until modern times, and in Hungary, Buda was not linked with Pest until the mid-nineteenth century (see Chap. 11, under "Urban growth"). Routes also converged on mountain passes. They were still viewed with a certain awe, and the roadbooks sometimes gave careful instructions on how to approach them. But the biggest problem in traversing them, as has been noted, was often not the roughness of the path or the depth of snow, but the infrequency or even lack of overnight accommodation.

Speed of travel varied greatly. News could be carried by horse and rider very quickly indeed, up to sixty and more miles in a day. But the ordinary traveler moved more slowly. Charles de Bernenicourt traveled from Flanders to Naples in 1532 in forty-four days, at an average speed of twenty-two miles a day. Wagons carrying merchandise and trains of pack animals moved more slowly and were more at the mercy of bad roads.

As a general rule only the more valuable commodities traveled by road, and then often in convoy for security. The spices were still most prominent in the overland traffic from Italy to the northwest. Pepper made up much of the freight, but there were also significant amounts of ginger, cloves, and cinnamon. Textiles were also important, but only the more valuable were worth the cost of transport halfway across a continent. The Mediterranean region at this time offered a large market for lighter fabrics, many of them barchents and fustians, woven north of the Alps. Part of this export from Swabia and Bavaria was handled by the well-documented company of merchants of the small south German city of Ravensburg. But their traffic was not restricted to cloth. They also dealt in spices, skins, leather, and metal goods.

Countless consumer goods were entering into long-distance trade – pewter, brass, and metalwares; dyestuffs, fancy cloth, and leather; artwork; ornaments of all kinds; and even printed books – but in terms of volume the chief groups of commodities were iron and ironware, salt, and cereals. The sources of bar iron have already been discussed (see this chap., under "Metal industries"). It was a

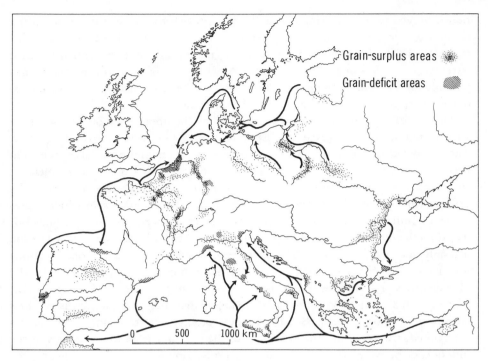

8.8. Grain-surplus and grain-deficit areas and the grain trade in the sixteenth century

prominent commodity in the ships of the Hanse, which brought Swedish iron to the west. The Bretons carried iron from northern Spain, and it was distributed by boat over the Paris basin and the Rhineland.

The nonferrous metals, increasingly important in eastern Europe, were conveyed, by riverboat where possible and elsewhere by wagon, to the Baltic ports from which they were shipped to markets in northwestern Europe. Even the precious metals came by this route, sometimes ready minted for use. The first of the silver "dollars," the "Joachimsthäler," began to be minted in 1549 at Jáchymov in the Ore Mountains.

Salt was in universal demand, on a small scale for industrial purposes, but chiefly for preserving food. The making of salt by evaporating brine called for abundant fuel, which was becoming increasingly scarce in the more populous areas of sixteenth-century Europe. This tended to force salt production to concentrate in those areas where the heat of summer was sufficient to evaporate seawater without the use of fuel, and this, in effect, meant places lying to the south of the Loire mouth. Salt was carried from the Biscay coast, from the Bay of Bourgneuf, the "Bay" par excellence, to northwest Europe and was distributed by the Hansards wherever it was needed for preserving meat and salting fish. Inland salt springs were important but faced the problem of evaporating the brine they yielded. Nevertheless, the salt of Lüneburg in northwest Germany and of Wieliczka in

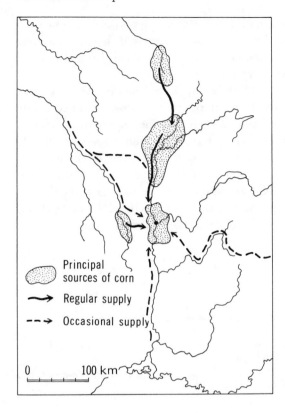

Principal
sources of corn

→ Regular supply

- -→ Occasional supply

0   100 km

8.9. The grain supply of the city of Lyons. [After A. P. Usher, *The History of the Grain Trade in France 1400–1700* (Cambridge, Mass., 1913).]

southern Poland was in demand in inland areas inaccessible from the northern ports. It was all a matter of pride.

The trade in foodstuffs is impossible to quantify. Much of it was over only short distances, from village and farm to local market, within a broadly self-sufficing market area. But some moved more widely. The trade which was developing from the great estates of the east, by way of the Baltic rivers and the ships of the Hanse to the consuming centers of northwestern Europe has already been mentioned (see pp. 205–6). Every large city was dependent upon a supply of breadgrains from distant sources, and this trade was a condition of their growth. Yet grain was, in proportion to its value, a very expensive commodity to move. As with all other bulky goods, waterborne transport was used wherever practicable. Grain moved around the coasts of Europe from surplus areas like the plains of southern Italy, northern France, and eastern Europe (Fig. 8.8). River transportation was used for the supply of Paris and the cities of the southern Low Countries and Rhineland. Lyons, one of the larger consuming centers in the west, received much of its grain by the rivers Saône and Rhône (Fig. 8.9), drawing from as far afield as Berry and Burgundy.

The problems of grain supply were even greater in southern Europe. Tuscany could grow less than half of what it needed, and Venice and Genoa were even more heavily dependent on imports. Breadgrains for the Italian city republics came from as far afield as Albania, Sicily, and Cyprus. Other seriously deficient areas were central Portugal and Constantinople, the latter continuing its traditional practice of drawing on the region of the lower Danube.

The only other foodstuff to enter significantly into long-distance trade was wine. The contraction of the area within which the grapevine was grown was necessarily accompanied by an increase in the volume of trade in wine. Apart from trade in specialized vintages within the wine-growing areas, the commerce was essentially an export from the south to the north. The chief sources of wine for the tables of northern Europe were Gascony, Burgundy, and the Rhineland. Other wine-growing areas were, however, developing an export trade, among them the borders of the Hungarian plain, southern Spain, and the Portuguese island of Madeira, which had inherited the role of southern Greece and its Malmsey wine.

SELECT BIBLIOGRAPHY

General

Braudel, F. *The Mediterranean and the Mediterranean World in the Age of Philip II.* 2 vols. London, 1972–3.
The Cambridge Economic History of Europe. Vol. 3, *The Economy of Expanding Europe in the 16th and 17th Centuries.* Cambridge, U.K., 1967.
The Fontana Economic History of Europe. Vol. 2, *The Sixteenth and Seventeenth Centuries,* ed. C. M. Cipolla. London, 1974.
Kamen, H. *The Iron Century.* London, 1971.
Koenigsberger, H. G., and G. L. Mosse. *Europe in the Sixteenth Century.* London, 1968.
North, D. C., and R. P. Thomas. *The Rise of the Western World.* Cambridge, U.K., 1973.
Strauss, G. *Sixteenth Century Germany: Its Topography and Topographers.* Madison, Wis., 1959.

Population

Faber, J. A. "Population Changes and Economic Developments in the Netherlands: an Historical Survey." *Afdeling Agrarische Geschiedenis Bijdragen* 12 (1965): 47–113.
Glass, D. V., and D. E. C. Eversley, eds. *Population in History.* London, 1965.
Laslett, P., ed., *Household and Family in Past Time.* Cambridge, U.K., 1972.
Wrigley, E. A. *Population and History.* London, 1969.

Urban settlement

Botero, G. *A Treatise Concerning the Causes of the Magnificency and Greatness of Cities.* In *The Reason of State,* ed. P. J. Waley and D. P. Waley, New Haven, Conn., 1956.
Strauss, G. *Nuremberg in the Sixteenth Century.* New York, 1966.
Walker, M. *German Home Towns: Community, State and General Estate.* London, 1971.

Agriculture

Blum, J. "The Rise of Serfdom in Eastern Europe." *American Historical Review.* 62 (1956–7): 807–36.

Klein, J. *The Mesta.* Cambridge, Mass., 1920.

Partner, P. *The Lands of St. Peter.* London, 1972.

Slicher van Bath, B. H. *The Agrarian History of Western Europe* A.D. 500–1850. London, 1963.

Vries, J. de. *The Dutch Rural Economy in the Golden Age, 1500–1700.* New Haven, Conn., 1974.

Manufacturing

Hatcher, J. *English Tin Production and Trade before 1550.* Oxford, 1973.

Singer, C., E. J. Holmyard, A. R. Hall, and T. I. Williams, eds. *A History of Technology,* Vol. 3. Oxford, 1957.

Commerce

Boyer, M. N. "Roads and Rivers: Their use and disuse in Later Medieval France." *Medievalia et Humanistica* 13 (1960): 68–80.

Dollinger, P. *The German Hanse.* London, 1970.

Lane, F. C. *Venetian Ships and Shipbuilders of the Renaissance.* Baltimore, Md., 1934.

Pounds, N. J. G. "Patterns of Trade in the Rhineland," *Science, Medicine, and History,* ed. E. Ashworth Underwood, Vol. 2, pp. 419–34. Oxford, 1953.

Roover, F. Edler de. "The Market for Spices in Antwerp, 1538–1544." *Revue Belge de Philologie et d'Histoire* 17 (1938): 212–21.

Usher, A. P. *The History of the Grain Trade in France 1400–1700.* Cambridge, Mass., 1913.

9

From the sixteenth to the nineteenth century

The three centuries from the early sixteenth to the end of the Napoleonic Wars saw changes of fundamental importance in the ways in which European peoples viewed themselves, their continent, and the world. When this period began the emperor Charles V had just triumphed over the French at Pavia (1525) and, in the minds of many, was about to restore an empire, both holy and Roman, and to unify Europe. When it ended, the bid for continental dominance by Napoleon had been shattered at Leipzig (1813) and Waterloo (1815), and Europe was set for a century of nationalism and economic growth.

A NEW WORLD

The changes which were achieved during this period can, for our purposes, be listed and discussed under five heads. First was the concept of nationalism, which was slowly and unevenly taking shape at this time. A nation is a body of people held together by a sense of belonging together. A common language and culture were important bonds. So also were a common historical tradition, the occupation of a well-defined territory, and, often enough, a common enemy. Many a nation has been forged in conflict with another and perhaps more powerful state. The Dutch nation, for example, "was born because, during the second half of the sixteenth century, a state came into existence, within whose territory men lived and strove together, and shared experiences so crowded and so intense that they found themselves overnight where it had taken the people of other national states centuries to arrive."[1] The Dutch nation was created by the long struggle (1569–1609) against Spain; the Swiss by their revolt against the Habsburgs; the Czech, Polish, Hungarian nations by their experiences at the hands of Austrians, Russians, and Prussians. These heroic achievements were apt to take on a romantic aura and to be exaggerated to epic proportions. They became part of that body of myth and legend through which popular groups saw themselves.

In the sixteenth century there were only faint stirrings of national consciousness in Germany, but already a sense of Italian nationhood was being expressed by such well-known figures as Machiavelli and Guicciardini. In some parts of Europe the

1   G. J. Renier, *The Dutch Nation: An Historical Study* (London, 1944), 10.

new nationalism took the form only of an intense provincialism, as in Flanders, Castile, Catalonia, and parts of France. Elsewhere, as in Sweden, both state and nation were being created at the same time, as political control was gradually extended outward from a "core area," in this case the Uppland area of east-central Sweden. It was not, however, until the French Revolution and the revolutionary and Napoleonic wars which followed that nationalism became articulate in much of Europe, and not until the "year of revolutions," 1848, did it begin to triumph (see p. 348).

The second force for change was the Protestant Reformation. Nationalism and Protestantism, between them, tore to shreds the "seamless web" of medieval Christendom. There had been religious protest long before the sixteenth century, but it had been individual and local. With the possible exceptions of the Cathars in southern France and the Hussites in Bohemia, protest was not identified with specific regions or peoples. The effect of the Protestant Reformation in all its manifestations – Lutheranism in Germany, Zwinglianism in Switzerland, Calvinism in France, Scotland, and Geneva – was to create a variegated pattern of religious affiliation. The Augsburg settlement of 1555 in Germany recognized the right of each prince to determine the creed of his people, as, in fact, Henry VIII had already done in those parts of Britain under his control. No prince could compel adherence to his particular beliefs, but most were able to make life difficult for any who openly touted the new ecclesiastical regime.

In some parts of Europe religion became an aspect of nationalism: Anglicanism in England, Lutheranism in Sweden, Calvinism in Scotland. On the other hand, the concurrent rise of nationalism and Protestantism confirmed some peoples in their traditional adherence to the Roman Church. Ireland remained predominantly Catholic in the face of England's Anglicanism, and in Poland loyalty to Catholicism further served to differentiate the Poles from their archenemies, Lutheran Prussia and Orthodox Russia. A crusading spirit was reintroduced into Europe. Wars acquired religious overtones, as, for example, those between Spain and the Low Countries, Poland and Russia, and Sweden and the forces of the German empire. Not until the mid-seventeenth century were wars less overtly concerned with religion and more with power and resources.

The effect of the Reformation was to produce a threefold division of Europe. The south, including Italy, the Iberian peninsula, and most of France remained Catholic, and Austria and Hungary, very largely so. Switzerland and Germany were divided. In the former, the urban cantons by and large accepted the Reformation, and in Germany, the southern states and the church lands in the northwest (Cologne, Münster, Paderborn) kept to the Catholic faith. Bohemia and Silesia were regained for the Catholic Church after the Reformation, and in the Low Countries the arbitrament of war determined that only the northern provinces – approximately the present Netherlands – remained by and large Protestant.

Beyond Poland and Hungary the prevailing religious affiliation was to the Eastern or Orthodox Church. Attempts to bridge the gap, both liturgical and theological, between the Orthodox Church and the Church of Rome had failed, and from the sixteenth century there was only hostility between them. The Orthodox Church commanded the loyalty of the bulk of the population in the Balkan peninsula and in Russia and the steppe. In the former it was dominant in areas under Turkish control, and in the grand duchy of Lithuania a Catholic land-owning class lorded it over an Orthodox peasantry. Religious affiliation thus became a mark of class and status. The Ottoman conquerors of the Balkans were Moslem, as also were the Tartar peoples of the steppe. But in Europe the Moslems abandoned their proselytizing activities. After all, if the Christian *rayas* were converted to Islam, they would no longer pay taxes or work as serfs on Moslem-held estates. Nevertheless some of the native Slav peoples of the Balkans were converted to Islam, notably the Bosniaks of Bosnia, the Pomaks of Bulgaria, and some of the tribes of Albania. But, these aside, the Ottoman population of the Balkans remained relatively small and chiefly urban.

A third factor in Europe's development was that Europe was no longer self-contained and self-sufficient. At the beginning of the sixteenth century, two states, Spain and Portugal, had acquired possessions in Asia, Africa, and the Americas, which were to become a great deal more extensive before the century ended. In the course of the century other European states, notably England and France, were each to secure a foothold overseas. The consequences of European imperialism were twofold. The dependencies were to receive a number of immigrants from their parent countries, small in the case of England and France, dangerously large in that of Spain. Secondly, these new possessions were to supply Europe with a large and growing number of commodities, not only their traditional exports – spices, dyestuffs, ivory, tropical hardwoods – but also a range of cultivated plants which were to be acclimated in Europe and in the course of time to make a very important contribution both to diet and to farming systems.

Among the commodities shipped from the New World to Europe was bullion, gold and silver looted in the first instance from Aztecs and Incas. It came in quantities sufficient to fuel the inflationary trend of the sixteenth century. It also provided the means by which the Spanish Habsburg paid their mercenary armies in the Low Countries and Italy. Through this expenditure New World silver and gold passed into general circulation. The possession of colonial dependencies helped to modify the balance of power within Europe itself, and the strength of Spain derived in part from her control of the resources of much of the New World. Other colonial powers – France and England – were drawn into the struggle for colonies largely because of their political and economic value. The New World was, indeed, brought into being to redress the balance of the Old.

The other factors which helped to transform medieval Europe into modern belong more to the field of intellectual history. They were the gradual development of a critical attitude to the material world and a willingness to experiment and innovate. Alchemy gave way to chemistry and physics. Previous ages were not wholly static, but innovation was, more often than not, the consequence of accident, not of a conscious and deliberate search for new materials and new methods to supplement or replace the old. Scientific advance was assisted by a tendency to pursue basic research as distinct from improving and extending technologies. Inquiries began to be made into the nature of material things. Hypotheses were enunciated and tested, and "laws" established. Without this, the practical advances which led up to the Industrial Revolution could not have been made.

The last factor in the changes which created modern Europe was the revolution in communication, without which the other factors would have been ineffective. Not only did people and goods become more mobile, knowledge spread faster than ever before. There was, in fact, little change in the physical means of travel and transportation before the early nineteenth century. Roads remained bad, and the speed of travel remained that of the horse. The same reliance continued to be placed on waterborne freight, and boats continued to encounter the same obstructions that they had always done. Nevertheless, more people did travel, and their journeys were better organized. What may be called the infrastructure of travel – inns, roadbooks, maps, coach services – began to develop. People began to travel for pleasure, as well as for profit, and to record for their friends and contemporaries – and incidentally for posterity – their impressions of the places and peoples whom they met.

This new knowledge, together with scientific and theological speculation, was disseminated through the printed word. The printing press was invented and came into widespread use in the fifteenth century. In the course of the sixteenth, the number of printed books increased exponentially. It was a revolutionary change without precedent, though it is sometimes forgotten that it could not have taken place without a simultaneous expansion in the manufacture of paper. The number of presses in Europe increased from a handful at the beginning of the sixteenth century to hundreds before its end. Print runs were small, and there were no public libraries. Nevertheless, those who wanted to could gain access to books, and to new books as they were printed. The range of subject matter found in printed books was continuously broadening. From history, theology, and politics it was extended to travel, geography, and what may be called the useful arts. A significant feature of books in the eighteenth century was their increasing concern with agriculture, technology, and craftsmanship. That these were intended for the practicing industrialist and artisan is apparent from the nature of their illustrations and technical details. Very little knowledge was hidden to those with an ability to read.

To printed books were added in the late eighteenth century newspapers and periodicals. Most were content to retail the news with whatever embellishments their editors chose to add, but among them were technical publications intended for a more select public. The earliest concerned themselves with agriculture, perhaps because the landowner was most likely to be literate. Then came journals devoted to mining and manufacturing. Among the very first was the *Journal* (later the *Annales*) *des Mines,* put out from 1794 by the revolutionary government in France. It was concerned with all aspects of mining and metallurgy. It was followed by comparable journals in Germany, Austria, and Great Britain. All aimed to describe business conditions and to present recent advances in technology in such detail that specialists could understand them.

THE POLITICAL MAP

The map of Europe changed little between the accession of the emperor Charles V in 1519 and the beginning of the revolutionary wars in 1792. Two powers dominated the continent throughout this period, France and the Habsburg empire, with others – Great Britain, Prussia, Russia, and the Ottoman empire – standing off in the wings, intervening periodically in the drama played out by the two principal protagonists. The reason for the relative stability lay in the fact that France and the Habsburg empire were fairly evenly matched, and that outside powers, principally Great Britain and Russia, intervened at intervals to preserve this balance. Such territorial changes as occurred were, with few exceptions, of minor importance. Most significant of these were the advance of France to the Rhine, the French acquisition of Alsace in 1681, and the slow march of the Austrians across the great Hungarian plain and into the Balkans at the expense of the Ottoman empire. In addition, the northern Low Countries rebelled against Spanish rule to form the United Netherlands; Sweden became united under the Vasa dynasty and then went on to control much of the Baltic, and Poland succumbed to the growing military strength of its neighbors: Prussia, Russia, and the Habsburg empire.

The extinction of the Polish state accompanied the expansion of the Russian, Muscovy, from the Suzdal region of the upper Volga. This was a fourfold movement. That toward the Arctic Ocean in the north and that to the Ural Mountains and beyond were into sparsely populated, unorganized territories, and were virtually unopposed. More important, however, was expansion southward to the Black and Caspian seas and westward to the Baltic. Not only did these add greatly to the resources of Muscovy, they put it into closer touch with the more advanced civilizations of the west. By the end of the sixteenth century Muscovy had occupied the northern forest belt and in 1553 made contact through the newly founded settlement of Archangel with the British traders of the Muscovy Company. A few years later the Russians crossed the Ural Mountains into Siberia and began that eastward advance which was to take them in the mid-nineteenth century to the Pacific Ocean.

Advance to the west and south was very much slower. The Gulf of Finland was reached in 1702 in the course of the Great Northern War, and in the next year Tsar Peter founded the city which he dedicated to his name saint, St. Petersburg (Leningrad). Karelia was occupied in 1710 and the east Baltic region in 1721 (Fig. 9.1). To the south the Tartars of the steppe and the Russian frontiersmen, the unruly Cossacks, presented a more formidable obstacle. But in the early eighteenth century, the plains of the lower Volga and the Don were overrun; the Caucasus Mountains were reached, and the city of Azov planted where the Don flows into

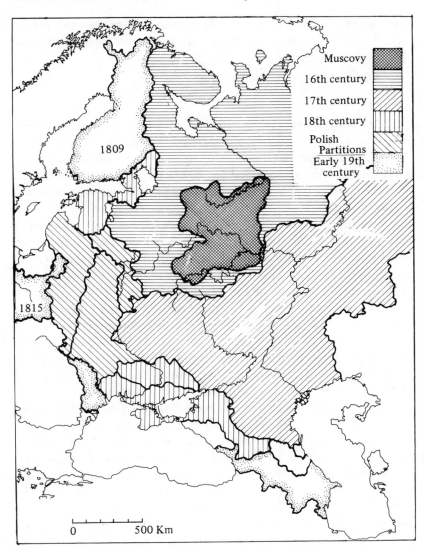

Muscovy
16th century
17th century
18th century
Polish Partitions
Early 19th century

1809

1815

0   500 Km

9.1. The expansion of Russia

the arm of the Black Sea known today as the Sea of Azov. Late in the century the western Ukraine and the Crimea were occupied and Lithuania and eastern Poland were taken in the course of the Partitions.

Many have seen in this outward expansion of the Russian state from its nuclear area in Suzdal the workings of a kind of manifest destiny, a policy of reaching for "salt water" and the benefits of maritime commerce. There can be no question that Tsar Peter the Great founded St. Petersburg as his "window on the west." The Black Sea, however, was of less immediate value, and access to it was closed by the Turkish control of the Straits. The acquisitions in the Ukraine, Lithuania, and Poland were inspired in the first instance by the desire to restrain the Tartars and Cossacks, and later by the need to keep up with the ambitions of Austria and Prussia.

POPULATION

An important factor in the balance of power in Europe was population, and hence the size of the armies which each contestant possessed. The political dominance of France was due, at least in part, to the fact that its population was the largest in Europe after Russia. Similarly, the political and military decline of Spain from the end of the sixteenth century was not unrelated to the fact that its population was either stable or declining.

The population of Europe, including that of European Russia, was of the order of 68 million in the early sixteenth century. One can say with a somewhat higher level of probability that this population had increased to about 175 million in 1815 (see Chap. 11, under "Population"), an increase of two and a half times in the course of about three centuries, or an annual rate of growth of considerably less than 1 percent a year. In fact, most of this growth occurred in the sixteenth and the latter half of the eighteenth centuries. The intervening period was, in general, one of contraction. In southern Europe population had ceased to grow by the end of the sixteenth century. In Sicily it appears to have remained more or less constant for a century, but in northern Italy it is estimated to have fallen by 10 percent by 1650, and in peninsular Italy by more than 20 percent. In Spain the decline was catastrophic. Parts of the Meseta were almost depopulated. The decline was less severe and came a decade or two later in Portugal and the coastal regions of Spain, but all parts of the peninsula experienced it. In northern Europe the decline in population was less marked, and in some areas, notably Great Britain, the United Netherlands, and Scandinavia, a slow growth continued through these critical years. In Germany and parts of France warfare took a heavy toll. The Thirty Years War, it is claimed, reduced the population overall by 40 percent. Losses in southwestern Germany, as well as in the northeastern provinces, devastated by the Swedish armies, were 50 percent and more. Wars continued to decimate the population long after the Thirty Years War ended in 1648. In France, the Fronde was particularly destructive, and the ravaging of the Rhenish Palatinate by Condé turned a prosperous province of Germany into a wilderness. It is difficult to say when the decline in population ceased and a recovery set in. It is likely that by 1700 much of Italy had regained its level of a century earlier, but improbable that there was much growth in Spain, Germany, and perhaps eastern Europe until well into the eighteenth century.

The fluctuations in total population in early modern times are difficult to measure and even more difficult to explain. One can only list and evaluate the parameters of these changes. Their relative importance must have varied from place to place and from time to time. The sixteenth-century litany of the English church prayed:

From plague, pestilence and famine
  Good Lord deliver us.

These seemed to contemporaries the most significant of the factors governing population growth and decline, and their importance cannot be questioned. The specter of famine was always present; harvest failure was something the peasant had to live with. Most often it was due to events beyond human control, very wet conditions at the time of winter plowing and sowing, and cool, wet summers which prevented the grain from developing and ripening. There is little instrumental evidence of weather before the nineteenth century, but the qualitative information available suggests that most famine crises were associated with wet, not with cold or dry weather.

The seriousness of famine crises tended to diminish during the eighteenth and early nineteenth centuries, not because inclement weather ceased to occur, but because adverse weather in one area tended to be compensated by more favorable conditions in another. Food could be moved to relieve the worst shortages. Nevertheless, there were disastrous famines, most of them localized, in the course of the seventeenth century and, less frequently, in the eighteenth. One can point to the crisis of 1692–3, which was particularly severe in northwestern Europe. The weather was very wet over a long period of time; crops rotted in the ground, and harvests were miserable. The *Intendants,* or French provincial governors, whose reports are a mine of information on conditions during this crisis, are explicit on the subject. There were parts of France where grain supplies were totally exhausted, and the population subsisted on chestnuts and other wild plants.

Mortality during a famine crisis was always intensified by the activities of dealers, who anticipated shortages and bought up whatever grain was available. Prices were raised, putting breadgrains beyond the reach of much of the population. "Three out of four mortality crises," wrote J. P. Goubert, "occurred immediately after sharp rises in grain prices."[2] Attempts of governments to intervene met with very little success, and every bad harvest was followed during the succeeding winter and spring by a very high mortality.

The English litany was right to associate plague and pestilence with famine; a population weakened by hunger was particularly vulnerable to disease. One can speak only in very general terms of the incidence of most diseases. In only a few instances, notably plague and smallpox, was the cause of death reliably given. In most, the records speak of fevers, without any clear determination of their nature. Yet the seasonal pattern of death is clear from parish registers kept by parish priests in many parts of Europe. Mortality was greatest in winter and early spring and then declined to a low in late summer, before increasing again in the fall. The regularity of this typical cycle of mortality was, however, broken at times by a sudden and severe mortality in late summer and early fall. This period of very high mortality, superimposed on the normal pattern, can, as a general rule, be taken

2 "Le phénomène épidémique en Bretagne à la fin du XVIIIᵉ siècle (1770–1787)," *Médecins, climat et épidémies à la fin du XVIIIᵉ siècle* (Paris, 1972), 240.

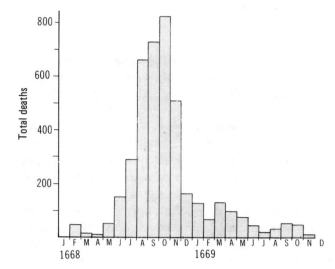

9.2. The pattern of mortality in a plague year: Brussels, 1668–9

to indicate plague. An equally sudden outbreak of high mortality in winter can, with a much smaller degree of assurance, be ascribed to typhus. But this was a season when bronchial infections were common, and any nonclinical attempts to assess the cause of death must be suspect.

The plague, which had been endemic in Europe since the fourteenth century, flared up into localized epidemics. These were especially numerous and widespread in the late sixteenth and early seventeenth centuries, and most severe in cities (see p. 189). Not a major city in western Europe escaped. In the 1630s a pandemic crept across Germany from the Rhineland to Prussia and Poland, spread by the Swedish and Habsburg armies. It is impossible to separate the population decline of the early seventeenth century from these recurrent and devastating outbreaks of plague. But an end was in sight. The last outbreak in Scotland was in 1645–7, and in England, the Great Plague of London of 1665. It was carried to the Low Countries, where Brussels is reported to have lost 10 percent of its population (Fig. 9.2). The last outbreak in western Europe was in Provence in 1720, but the disease remained endemic within the Ottoman empire. Although very little was known of the etiology of plague, the Habsburgs did maintain a rudimentary quarantine system, and were successful in excluding the plague from the rest of Europe.

There is no ready explanation for the abrupt cessation of the plague in the west. Improved building construction and personal hygiene must have played their parts. So also may the disappearance of the black rat. But it is surely no coincidence that the disappearance of plague coincided with a clearly marked increase in population.

The plague may have been the most fatal and most widespread disease in pre-industrial Europe, but there were others which reached epidemic proportions and resulted in very high mortality. Among them was smallpox, so called to distin-

Table 9.1. *Size of family according to woman's age at marriage*
(*percentages*)

No. of children	20–4	25–9	30 and over
0	2	5	10
1–3	6	12	27
4–6	17	39	57
7–9	43	40	6
10 and over	32	4	0
	100	100	100

guish it from the "great" pox, or syphilis. It first became significant in the seventeenth century. It was passed from person to person, without the intervention of a vector – an important factor in its eradication. It was often fatal, but its depredations were reduced first by the practice of inoculation with pus from an infected person, and then by vaccination. But there remained a large number of febrile diseases of which typhus, typhoid, and "scarlatina" were among the most widespread and important. Typhus, diffused by the body louse, was a disease of crowded and dirty conditions and was also known as "gaol" fever. It is impossible to assess the importance of bronchial and chest complaints, but their importance is implicit in the high mortality of winter and early spring.

Warfare was another case of high mortality. Not only were losses high in combat and from wounds, but marching armies themselves devastated fields, devoured stores of food, and spread the diseases with which they were infected. The appalling losses in Germany in the course of the Thirty Years War have already been mentioned. Other wars during the century were hardly less destructive. After the seventeenth century, it has been said, warfare became "in some ways more humane." Armies were better provisioned and better controlled, and war, by and large, lost the religious element which had previously made it so ferocious.

The structure of family and society exerted an influence on population trends no less marked than the factors already discussed. The size of a family was due more to the age of the partners at marriage than to any other factor. Late marriage, particularly on the part of the woman, resulted in a smaller completed family than early marriage. This is well shown in figures derived from an analysis of the parish registers of Crulai in northern France (see Table 9.1). Where parish registers have been analyzed, it appears that the age at marriage was relatively high, often 28 or older for men and 25 or older for women during the seventeenth and early eighteenth centuries, though there were many exceptions to such a generalization.

The intergenesic period – the time between successive births – was in general from two to three years, with an average of about thirty months. Postponement of marriage by five years might reduce the size of the completed family by two births. Age at marriage was governed by many factors, which included the inheritance or acquisition of a farm holding or the practice of a domestic craft. It seems certain that marriages were earlier and completed families larger where it was possible to pursue a craft industry like linen weaving than where the peasant had to wait until he had gained possession of land to support a family. A system of partible inheritance also seems to have encouraged earlier marriages by excluding the category of landless younger sons. The little evidence that is available suggests that there may have been a slight diminution in the average age at marriage in the course of the eighteenth century.

Mortality was high, but especially so among the young. Studies of two French districts show respectively 29 and 20 percent of children dying during their first year, and only 48.9 and 58.4 percent respectively reaching their twenty-first birthdays. Birthrates were high, as, indeed, they had to be in order to maintain the population under these circumstances. The population increase of the later eighteenth and nineteenth centuries came, not through an increase in the birthrate, but through a decline in those factors which had contributed to the very high death rates.

There were advantages in a high birthrate, apart from its importance in maintaining the population in the face of famine, disease, and war. Parents expected to be supported in their old age by their children, and children provided a supplementary labor force on the land and in craft industries. It was normal for the peasant household to consist in the early years of marriage of the nuclear family of parents and children, and later to grow to include grandparents and even grandchildren. The household expanded and contracted, consisting in turn of nuclear and extended family groups. In extreme cases it consisted of a permanently extended group, like the *zadruga* of the Balkans, which also embraced collateral relatives in a large communal society. There was everywhere a young population. Expectation of life at birth was nowhere more than thirty years, and in some parts of Europe it must have been a good deal less. The population pyramid for France (Fig. 9.3) shows a very broad base and small age groups for the older population.

The age structure of local populations would have shown distortions due to migration, both seasonal and permanent. The poverty of the peasantry in many parts of Europe obliged peasants to work elsewhere for at least part of the year. They went to the forests in winter to cut timber and make charcoal. Those of Burgundy helped with the grain harvest in France, and the *Intendant* of Limoges, on the margin of the Central Massif, reported in 1695, that "almost all who are able to work leave their homes in March and go to work in Spain and in every province of this kingdom."[3] This region was a prolific source of masons and of other construction workers in every growing city of France. In the mountains of Dauphiné the men left home for the winter. The season of migration depended upon local circumstances. In the mountains of the Auvergne, it was said, "the subsistence of half the population was dependent on the seasonal migration of the

3   Quoted in M.-A. Carron, "Prélude à l'éxode rural en France: les migrations anciennes des travailleurs creusois," *Revue d'histoire économique et sociale* 43 (1965): 301.

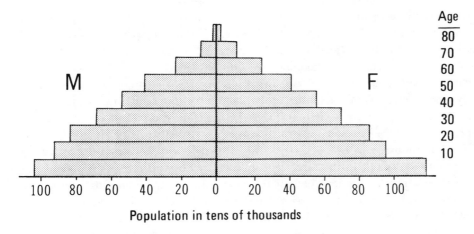

Age

80
70
60
50
40
30
20
10

Population in tens of thousands

9.3. The structure of population in France in the eighteenth century. The pyramid shows the number of people in each ten-year age group.

other half."[4] Such seasonal migrations of workers, as distinct from transhumant pastoralists, was present throughout the mountain belt of central Europe as well as in Italy. In the course of time much of this seasonal migration, particularly that for work in the cities, became permanent. In some quarters of Paris, late in the eighteenth century more than half the population was made up of immigrants from elsewhere.

Contrasted with the regular movement of seasonal workers was the flight of refugees from war and persecution. Immense numbers of people were forced to migrate in early modern times, and the cultural and economic consequences of their migration have been immense. The largest group of such refugees was without question the Moriscoes (Moors), forced out of Spain in 1609–10. They are said to have numbered some three hundred thousand. Next, in all probability, came the Huguenots – perhaps two hundred thousand of them – expelled from France in 1685. Others were the Iberian Jews who migrated to Britain and the Low Countries, and the Serbs who moved from Raška to Hungary in the 1690s. More important in the long run than these large and precipitate movements of people were the slow, sustained migrations of peoples from areas which seemed deprived into others which appeared to offer greater opportunity. Swiss mountaineers drifted into areas of Germany depopulated during the Thirty Years War, Savoyards moved into the Rhône valley, French into Catalonia, Poles from the Vistula basin into Lithuania; and from the surrounding mountains, people moved into the Hungarian plain, "deserted and uncultivated" after the Turkish wars. Parts of the plain even today are an ethnic mosaic as a result of these movements. Similar migrations, mainly from mountain to plain, took place in many parts of the Balkans.

4   *Correspondence des Contrôleurs-Généraux des Finances avec les provinces,* ed. A. M. de Boislisle (Paris, 1874), vol. 1, no. 312.

To these movements within Europe should be added the overseas migration of European peoples. This affected mainly Great Britain, France, and the Iberian peninsula, but only in the last did it represent a significant loss of human resources. Some two hundred thousand are said to have left Spain for the New World during the sixteenth century alone, and migration from Portugal was proportionately even larger. France supplied only about fifty thousand, mainly to French Canada. Great Britain's contribution, at least before the end of the nineteenth century, was of the order of 1.75 million, mainly to North America.

For few countries in Europe is it possible to trace with any degree of assurance the population trends in the three centuries covered by this chapter. England and France are without question the best documented, largely because the authorities in, respectively, 1538 and 1539 ordered the parish clergy to keep a record of baptisms, marriages, and burials. These records were for a long period inadequately kept, but they, nonetheless, provided a basis for estimating population. Indeed, in England, by analyzing a large sample of parish registers, totals have been projected back to the time when registers were first kept.

On March 9–10, 1801, a census was held in Great Britain, and 8,893,000 persons were counted in England and Wales, and 1,608,000 in Scotland. No census was held in Ireland. The totals were almost certainly too low, since many were omitted or evaded the count. The population of Great Britain could have been as high as 10.75 million, and that of Ireland about 5 million. Several attempts had been made to project these totals back to the seventeenth and earlier centuries, the most recent and sophisticated being that by Wrigley and Schofield. The population, on this basis, is said to have increased from 2,773,857 in 1541 to 8,893,000 – the census total – in 1801. At this time the Welsh population was 541,546. No census was held in Ireland until 1821, when the total was 6,802,000 (see Chap. 10, under "Population").

In France, population grew through the sixteenth century and is estimated to have stood at about 14 million in 1600. It was then struck by a series of crises, and even before the famine conditions of the 1690s some in France were gravely concerned that their population was declining. Proposals to hold a census came to nothing, but the *Intendants* offered a great deal of more or less reliable information in their reports. During the first quarter of the eighteenth century, Saugrain produced a kind of unofficial census for much of France, and this has been used for the map of French population (Fig. 9.4). The evidence points to a total of about 19,000,000 at the death of Louis XIV (1715). A number of studies of French population were made during the eighteenth century. It is evident that the total increased steadily, and the most reasonable estimates put the total at about 27,350,000 at the end of the century. At this time there were four areas of relatively dense population (Fig. 9.5): the whole of northern France from Brittany to the Low Countries, the Paris area, Alsace, and the Lyons district. Apart from a few islands of moderately dense population, the whole south of France was sparsely inhabited. It should be noted that dense population did not always accord with areas of productive soil. In fact, some of the higher densities were to be met with

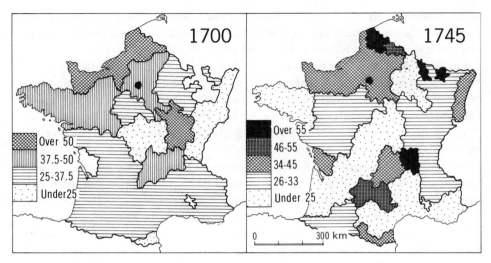

9.4. The population of France (inhabitants per square kilometer) in 1700 and 1745

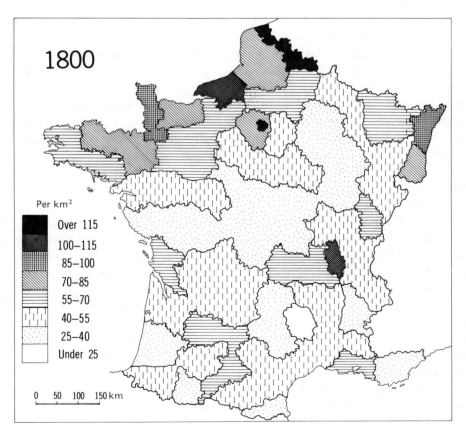

9.5. The population of France, about 1800

on the infertile soils of western Normandy. The reason probably lies in the fact that in such areas of small holdings and enclosed fields, domestic crafts, particularly linen weaving, employed a significant labor force.

The southern Low Countries suffered severely during the wars of the later sixteenth century. The Spanish (later the Austrian) Netherlands became a depressed area; its chief port, Antwerp, closed, and part of its population fled to the north. The northern Low Countries, now the United Provinces, enjoyed by contrast a period of high prosperity which lasted through the seventeenth and much of the eighteenth centuries. The growth of population was most marked in the western or maritime provinces, where Amsterdam grew to be one of the largest cities in Europe, and the population of the province of Holland became more than half urban. Growth was slower in the eastern provinces until here also the expansion of domestic industry served to complement the scanty rewards of agriculture. The population of the Netherlands rose from less than a million at the beginning of the sixteenth century to about two million at the beginning of the eighteenth, the fastest rate of growth to occur in Europe in this period.

German population rose steadily during the sixteenth century and may have reached 15 million before the Thirty Years War. There is no doubt at all that it then suffered disastrously. In 1637 General von Werth described the Rhineland as "a country where many thousands of men have died of hunger and not a living soul can be seen for many miles along the way."[5] The total population had probably been reduced to 10 million or less by the mid-century, though the extent of the losses varied greatly from one part of the country to another. But when peace returned, the population grew rapidly, as was often the case when there was an abundance of unoccupied land and the peasant could have a family holding for the asking. Nevertheless, parts of Germany, especially in the northeast, remained depopulated until well into the next century. Overall, the eighteenth century was one of growth, and by 1800 the population of Germany may have reached 20 million.

The Alpine region enjoyed a natural protection from the horrors of the wars which ravaged Germany, and the chief constraint on population growth was scarcity of cropland. Switzerland and neighboring Austria both suffered acutely from famine crises. Population pressure was in some measure relieved by migration to Germany and France, but the chief outlet for the Swiss mountain population, as for the Scottish, was service in foreign armies. At any one time, it is said, 50,000 to 60,000 Swiss were serving abroad, and 900,000 to a million were killed in other peoples' wars. Nevertheless, the population of Switzerland had probably risen to a million by 1600; to 1,200,000 by 1700; and to 1,680,000 by 1800. Denmark suffered disastrously during the wars of the seventeenth century, and the rest of Scandinavia lay so close to the margin of cultivation that famine crises were unusually frequent and severe. Population remained small until the eighteenth century, and rapid growth did not come until after 1800. Scarcity of land was not

5 Quoted in Henry Kamen, *The Iron Century* (London, 1971), 42.

an inhibiting factor in the lands of the Polish crown and in Russia, though losses in the wars of the later seventeenth century were heavy. The plains of the middle Danube were also fought over in the seventeenth and early eighteenth centuries, and parts were virtually depopulated. The eighteenth century was everywhere a time of resettlement and growth.

In Russia population was increasing very rapidly, especially during the eighteenth century. The abundance of land, especially in the steppe which was being colonized at this time, was matched by the encouragement which the lords gave to their peasants to marry early and raise large families. The population has been put at 14 million in 1727 and at 41 million in 1912.

The demographic history of Italy is better known than that of most other countries, largely because its city-republics kept records and, for their own administrative purposes, made head counts. The increase in population during the sixteenth century was greatest in peninsular Italy, and the decline in the century following most marked in northern Italy, where there was a series of disastrous outbreaks of plague. The population increase after 1700 was one of the most marked in Europe − 33 percent in the course of the century, and more than 45 percent in Sicily. Figures 9.6 and 9.7 show in rather greater detail than is usually possible the changing population densities in Italy during the period 1550–1790. A feature of these maps, apart from the continuing density in northern Italy, is the growth of population in southern Italy and Sicily, where the consequences of gross overpopulation in certain areas were apparent well before the nineteenth century.

The population of the Iberian peninsula began to decline before the end of the sixteenth century. The considerable out-migration from the Meseta to the coastal regions ceased to be compensated by a high birthrate, and Spain began to develop the vast empty heart, which by and large has continued to characterize the Iberian peninsula. When in the eighteenth century population again began to increase, growth was largely in the peripheral regions of the peninsula. This sharp decline has been attributed to a number of factors: the severe plague epidemics of the late sixteenth century, the large celibate population, and the systems of land tenure on the Meseta which did not encourage early marriage. Migration to the New World, furthermore, was also a factor, but the numbers involved were not great enough to account for the steepness of the decline.

THE PATTERN OF CITIES

The map of cities in 1815 did not differ greatly from that of three centuries earlier. Nor, if one could visit them, would their size and plan be very different, for these centuries were not characterized by urban growth. Many cities in 1815 still retained their medieval walls and gates, though these were now little more than decorative. Some had grown beyond the line of their walls, but just as often the space within the walls was far from fully built up. Cologne, for example, still had in 1815 as great an area of garden and orchard within its walls as in 1600. Merian's engravings of cities of the mid-seventeenth century consistently showed walls,

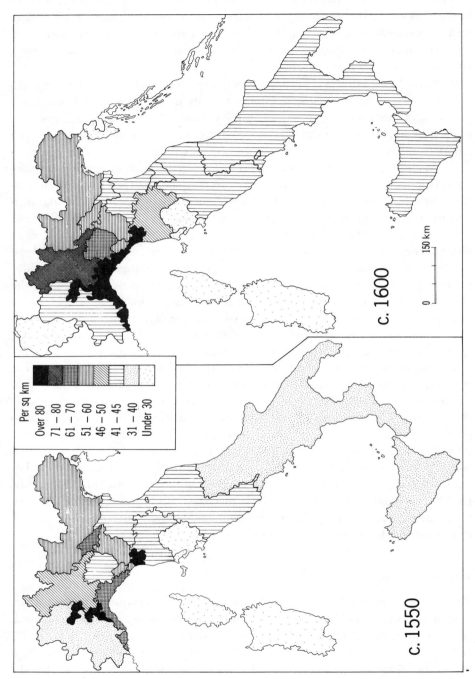

Per sq km

Over 80
71 – 80
61 – 70
51 – 60
46 – 50
41 – 45
31 – 40
Under 30

c. 1600

0   150 km

c. 1550

9.6. Population distribution in Italy, about 1550 and 1600

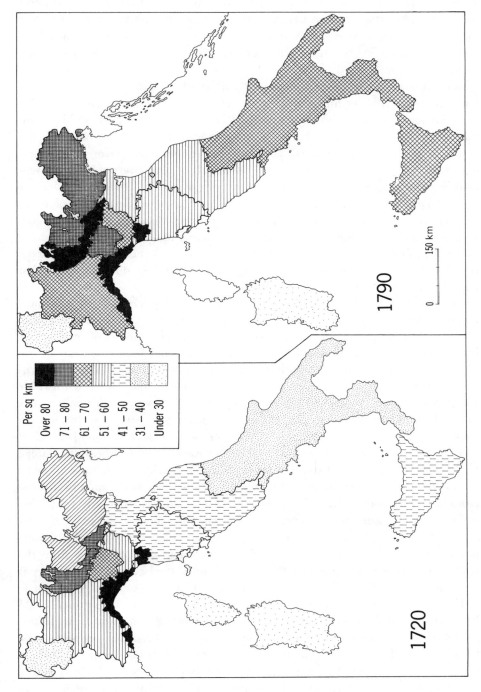

Per sq km

Over 80
71 – 80
61 – 70
51 – 60
41 – 50
31 – 40
Under 30

150 km

0

1790

1720

9.7. Population distribution in Italy, 1720 and 1790

gates, and towers. Some had been adapted to the needs of artillery, with lower walls, gun platforms, embrasures, and arrow-shaped redoubts or ravelins. These called for the services of military engineers and were, as a general rule, beyond the resources of most cities. In any case few felt any need to turn themselves into fortresses.

Within the walls, the street plans of the sixteenth century survived, with very few exceptions, into the nineteenth. Streets were narrow. Little progress was made with paving them or with keeping them clear of rubbish and filth. Public fountains were the chief – often the only – source of water, and sanitary needs continued to be met chiefly by cesspits dug wherever there was convenient space. There was, furthermore, no means of keeping the supply of drinking water rigidly separate from such means of sanitary disposal as were available. There were few cities in which these conditions did not continue little changed into the nineteenth century. A feature of all of them was the large number of stables and coach houses within their limits. They were as necessary as garages today. They generated large quantities of excreta, some of which was sold to gardeners and smallholders in the suburbs, but much was left in the streets, to be cleared in due course by what passed as an urban cleansing department.

In the sixteenth century much urban building was in wood. Timber continued to be widely used until the nineteenth century, but masonry construction was increasingly common. It is probably safe to say that city centers of most of the large continental cities were in stone, often stuccoed and highly decorated. The old city of Warsaw, now beautifully restored, is a superb example of seventeenth- and eighteenth-century urban construction. As a general rule, timber with wattle and plaster between the studding continued to be more common in smaller cities where there was less wealth to pay for expensive masonry construction. In southern Europe, where timber was generally scarce and stone relatively abundant, most cities were largely of masonry. But throughout eastern and southeastern Europe timber construction prevailed in the towns, as indeed it still does in many of them.

The gradual replacement of timber construction with masonry must have made cities safer and more healthy. Nevertheless, they remained particularly vulnerable to epidemic diseases which could be spread through their congested and ramshackle buildings. Most of the seventeenth-century outbreaks of the plague were urban. Figure 9.8 shows the population of the Italian city of Verona from the sixteenth century to the nineteenth. Its growth until the late sixteenth century is apparent, but in 1632 it was reduced to less than half by an outbreak of plague.

Under these conditions few cities, and certainly none of the larger ones, could have maintained their population without a steady influx from rural areas. Immigrants to the cities came from an every-widening area. Paris, for example, drew not only from the whole Paris basin, but also from the Central Massif; Lyons from both the latter and the Alps of Dauphiné. Many of those who made for the cities were younger sons with no hope of inheriting a farm holding, and migration was greatest where there was little opportunity for supplementary activities such as domestic crafts.

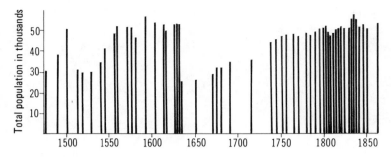

9.8. The population of Verona. Note the very slow recovery from the plague outbreak of 1632

Urban planning

Urban planning exercised some of the best minds of the age, but there was little opportunity for them to practice their art. The rediscovery in the sixteenth century of the work of the Roman architect Vitruvius stimulated many ingenious plans either for sweeping away existing cities and rebuilding them along more functional or aesthetic lines, or for superimposing new streets and buildings on the old. Opportunities for building wholly new, planned cities were few indeed. Most were fortress towns, built to defend the frontiers of France. Their streets were planned accordingly to Vitruvian models but were subservient to the needs of defense. Around each, holding the town in a tight embrace and allowing no scope for growth, were the defenses which were the only reason for its existence. Among such planned towns were Marienbourg and Philippeville in the French Ardennes, Neuf Brisach in Alsace, Longwy in Lorraine, Palma Nova in Venezia, and Naarden in the Netherlands.

A few new ports were developed to meet the expanding needs of commerce, like Le Havre in the sixteenth century and Brest and Lorient in the seventeenth. But there were few opportunities to build any other kind of city from the beginning. Vitry-le-François was built and named for Francis I of France to replace one which had been destroyed in war. Other "new" towns were built as *Residenzstädte,* semi-urban settings for princely palaces. One of the earliest was Charleville, built in 1608 on the river Meuse by Charles de Gonzaga, duc de Nevers. It was an Italian-ate city of regular blocks enclosing a vast, arcaded central square. Cardinal Richelieu founded the town of Richelieu, and Louis XIV, Versailles. The Hague was a *Residenzstadt,* built around the *Binnenhof* of the counts of Holland, but such cities were most numerous and most ambitious in central Europe. Mannheim and Karlsruhe, both on the upper Rhine, were founded near the beginning of the eighteenth century for, respectively, the elector Palatine and the margrave of Baden. Karlsruhe departed from the common practice of building rectangular blocks by establishing a radial street pattern which also derived from Vitruvius. Small *Residenzstädte* were founded in many of the small German principalities.

More often an elegant, planned suburb was added to an existing city. At Nancy

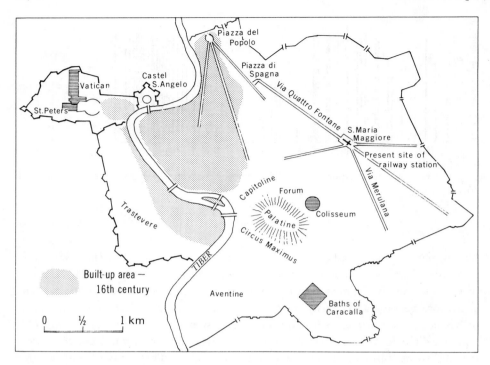

9.9. Rome after the planned rebuilding of the sixteenth century

the duke of Lorraine laid out the *Place Stanislas* as the focus of a planned development. At Warsaw, a new but less carefully planned suburb, embracing the palaces of the Polish aristocracy, was built to the south and southwest of the old city, and at Dresden, Würzburg, Weimar, and Stuttgart a *Residenzstadt* was added to the core of a medieval city. Another example of an elegant, planned development of the eighteenth century is to be found at Bath, England, where it owes nothing to the concept of a *Residenzstadt,* and everything to the taste and cultural aspirations of the middle class.

It was rare for authority to be able to superimpose a new pattern of streets on an existing city, as Haussmann did in Paris in the nineteenth century (see p. 379). The best example is the rebuilding of Rome by certain of the sixteenth-century popes. Their vision outran their resources, and the plan to cut straight roads radiating from points like the Piazza del Popolo and St. Maria Maggiore (Fig. 9.9) was left unfinished. Similar though less ambitious schemes were applied at Vicenza by Palladio and at Milan, Bologna, and some other Italian cities.

Urban functions

The preindustrial city was, first and foremost, a place of exchange, and its life focused on its marketplace. It was also a center for craft industries, though these

Table 9.2. *Prussia's cities*

Size	Number	Total population
Over 10,000	26	836,079
3,500–10,000	136	765,936
2,000–3,500	194	508,933
1,000–2,000	407	597,947
Less than 1000	258	186,937
Total	1021	2,895,832

were tending to move to rural areas. The network of small market towns which for one day a week became the center of economic life remained much as it had been at the end of the Middle Ages. They grew little, if at all. They embraced a handful of craftsmen, a few professional people, and a number of rentiers who drew their income from the neighboring fields and villages. Their society was backward looking and unchanging. "The aspect of the feudal age could be recaptured here," wrote Honoré de Balzac, whose eloquent portrayal of the small town is unequaled. "One could not walk without sensing at each step the ways and customs of the past; every stone spoke of it; the attitudes of the Middle Ages survived there as superstition."[6] Many such towns survived, outwardly little altered, into the nineteenth century or even the twentieth, only because there was little economic need to rebuild or extend them.

The existence of an urban hierarchy had already been discussed (see p. 163). Small market towns were very numerous. Above them there were, in diminishing numbers, medium-sized, large, and very large cities. The establishment of such a hierarchy is made difficult by uncertainty about their size and the problem of selecting thresholds between size categories. Cities which in western Europe might be classed as of only medium size might in eastern Europe pass as large. But here even the small towns were more widely spaced than in the west. According to a size classification adopted by Mols, there were in France about 1720:

Very large towns (over 40,000)	5
Large towns (20,000–40,000)	11
Medium-sized towns (5,000–20,000)	100
Small towns (2,000–5,000)	385

In Germany, on the evidence of Büsching, there was a smaller number of large cities and a proliferation of small and very small. The same was true in Prussia (see Table 9.2). Italy, especially northern Italy, had always been highly urbanized, with a higher proportion of large cities than elsewhere. Urban population declined somewhat in the seventeenth century but was increasing again in the eighteenth, and by 1800 no fewer than thirty-five cities belonged to the category of "very

6 *Beatrix,* 1941 ed. (Paris), 319–23 (author's trans.).

large." There was, however, very little urban growth south of Rome, with the sole exceptions of Naples and Palermo which, as early as the sixteenth century, were developing into vast, overextended, underemployed cities, growing by the influx of peasants from the poor and backward *Mezzogiorno*.

Medium-sized and large cities had more complex social structures and fulfilled more varied functions. They were, of course, market centers for their immediate areas, but they were also seats of government, centers of education and culture, and places where more costly and exotic goods were made and sold. In Catholic Europe priests and members of the religious orders made up as much as 5 percent of the total urban population. At Bayeux it was 6 percent, and at Louvain in the late sixteenth century the religious together with the university accounted for 17 percent. Every local or regional capital also had its quota of professional people, including lawyers and doctors. In addition, the gentry and aristocracy had town houses, where they spent part of the year.

Manufacturing activities were very varied in the larger cities. At Dijon, craftsmen were organized in no fewer than 130 different occupations. Some of these were esoteric in the extreme and had only a handful of members. Others, like the butchers, bakers, shoemakers, and tailors, were very numerous. But there were very few cities in preindustrial Europe which had a manufacture which might have been termed basic, in the sense that it made goods for distribution and sale far beyond its city-region. There was no trade in Dijon, which ranked as a large city, "that was not strictly proportionate in size to local needs . . . none that would be of interest to a more general and more distant market."[7]

There was an immense number of poor and destitute. They were attracted to the city, but few occupations were open to them beyond those of servant and retainer. In the medium-sized city of Vannes, in Brittany, a thousand of its population was classed as *mendiants* or *indigents*. Over half of those on the tax lists of Bayeux, according to O. H. Hufton, "hovered dangerously on the fringe of destitution."[8] This was the urban condition throughout Europe. Almost all who have left accounts of their travels commented on the extremes of wealth to be found in the cities and on the abject condition of the poorer segment of their population.

Urban growth continued to be conditioned by urban food supply. Small towns could, as a general rule, satisfy their needs from their own local regions, but larger cities had to draw on the resources of distant areas. The city-republics of Italy, the urban cantons of Switzerland, and some of the Free Imperial cities of Germany were each able to control an extensive hinterland and were thus assured of a food supply. There were, however, many exceptions. Geneva, squeezed between the boundaries of France and Savoy, always had difficulty in purchasing sufficient food, and this, in Jean-François Bergier's words, "posed the most severe problem in its economic history."[9] Augsburg also had almost no territory which it could control.

7   G. Roupnel, *La Ville et la campagne au XVIIe siècle: étude sur les populations du pays dijonnais* (Paris, 1955), 158.
8   *Bayeux in the Late Eighteenth Century* (Oxford, 1967), 58.
9   "Genève," in *Città mercanti dottrine nell'economia europea*, ed. A. Fanfani (Milan, 1964), 155.

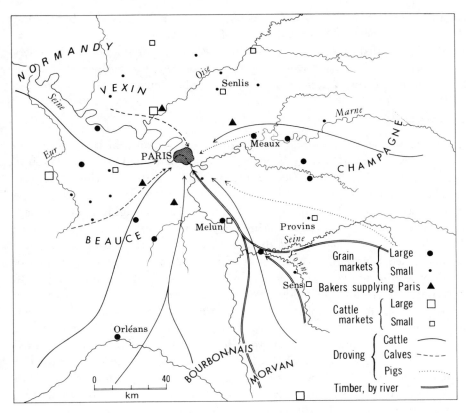

9.10. Food supply of Paris, late seventeenth century. [Based on Vauban, "Description géographique de l'élection de Vezelay," in *Mémoires des Intendants*, I (1881).]

As a general rule the jurisdiction of north European cities extended little beyond their walls, and they were dependent on market forces for the supply of basic foodstuffs. In the more highly urbanized areas of Europe, notably northern Italy and the Low Countries, there was always a scramble for breadgrains, which at times degenerated into a kind of piracy.

In many cities, especially Italian, an official was charged with the task of ensuring a supply of cereals. In Paris, the largest city in western Europe, the problem was especially great and was the subject of a memoir prepared by the *Intendant* in the 1690s. The grain supply was especially critical, and buyers were dispatched to small-town markets throughout the Paris basin. Figure 9.10 incorporates data presented by the *Intendant* regarding the sources of the city's food supply.

In eastern Europe and Russia cities were, with very few but significant exceptions, small and very restricted in their functions. Most resembled those to be met with in the west in the earlier Middle Ages: a fortified kremlin or *gorod* on rising ground; below it a small congested town with its own enclosing wall; and, beyond the latter, the elements of an expanding suburb. Few had a population of more than a thousand or two. They had markets, but craft industries served only local needs. A few, among the Riga, Vilna, and of course Moscow, were larger, and St. Petersburg, founded in 1703, grew rapidly as Russia's capital and chief commercial link with the rest of the world. By the end of the eighteenth century it was the largest city in Russia with perhaps 336,000 inhabitants.

AGRICULTURE

Agriculture was at the mercy of the weather to an extent which is difficult to visualize today. A weather diary kept by the owner of a small estate in Poitou in 1754–6 shows the kinds of problems experienced. The weather during these years was far from abnormal. The winter of 1754–5 was cold and wet, and the spring plowing was delayed. A warm April was followed by damaging frosts in May. Growth was hindered by drought during early summer, and a wet August almost ruined the wheat crop but spared the oats because very late spring sowing had postponed their harvest. Autumn was dry for the fall plowing, but the winter of 1755–6 was mild and very wet, "so wet that no ground could be tilled, nor could any carriage [cart] go to the fields." Spring and summer were cool and wet, and "weeds . . . got the better of the wheat."[10] Wheat had to be harvested so damp that it heated in the barns, and much was ruined. Grass grew well, but the weather was too wet for making hay. Roads were so wet that wood could not be carted from the forest, and this essential task had to be postponed until the fall, when it interfered with plowing. Modern technology would allow a farmer to cope with most of these difficulties, but if one considers these conditions as close to normal, one wonders how life could have been sustained when they were bad. Early in the nineteenth century, William Jacob, a kind of latter-day Arthur Young, wrote of Westphalia that "the surplus of the production of the soil in the best years so little exceeds the consumption, that there is no store on hand to meet such years of scarcity as will sometimes occur."[11]

Weather was not the only factor influencing the quality and volume of production. The husbandman was restricted by conditions of his tenure, by village custom, shortage of good land, lack of manure and above all, of capital. He was locked into an institutional framework in which vested interests made change and improvement difficult if not impossible. The French Revolution went some way toward giving the peasant ownership of his land but did almost nothing to reform agricultural practice.

Conditions of land tenure

In the sixteenth century most of the land belonged to the aristocracy or the church. Comparatively little was managed directly by its owners; it was leased in a variety of ways to "farmers" and peasants. A high proportion of the land, amounting to

10 A farming diary, in Duhamel de Monceau, *Practical Treatise of Husbandry* (London, 1759), 473–90.
11 W. Jacob, *Second Report on the Agriculture and Corn of Some of the Continental States of Europe, 1827* (London, 1928), 13.

56 percent in Bavaria and more than 15 percent in much of Catholic Europe, was held by the church. This is important because ecclesiastical landowners were among the least progressive. Most of the rest was held by lay landowners and was subject to the uncertainties of inheritance. Most was still organized into manors, but the demesne, worked by the labor of the peasantry, was a thing of the past in much of Europe. Most demesnes were leased to farmers and the duty of cultivating them had been commuted for a money payment or conventional rent. Other aspects of feudal dependence, such as the obligation to grind at the lord's mill and to make payments at specified times of the year, tended to survive till the French Revolution or even into the nineteenth century.

There was a general tendency for the size of estates to increase in eastern Germany and Poland, and southern Italy and Spain, but even in these lands of "great estates" there were many of very small size, and in France there were, by contrast, some of vast extent. That of the Saulx-Tavanes covered some 8,100 acres, two-thirds of which was made up of forest. In all parts of Europe there were estates not much larger than good-sized peasant holdings. The situation in Russia was not dissimilar. A small number of families held very large estates and were immensely rich. But most held no such wealth, and many were as poor as the Polish *szlachta*. In 1777 nearly two-thirds of the landowners had each less than 20 "souls" or serfs, the common measure of an estate, and only 16 percent had more than a hundred. A feature of these estates, especially of the larger ones, was that they were broken up into small units and were widely dispersed, a consequence of tsarist policy. There was never any question of entail such as existed in Prussia. Instead, the lords were free to alienate their lands as they chose, and they adopted in fact a form of partible inheritance which tended to increase the number of small and very small estates.

The situation was, however, continuously changing. There was always a market for land and, except where the law of entail applied as it did in much of eastern Germany and Spain (see pp. 329–32), estates were always being broken up and reconstituted by purchase and inheritance. Urban merchants and manufacturers acquired rural estates, sometimes by marriage into noble families, sometimes by foreclosing on lands mortgaged by their noble owners, and sometimes by simple purchase. By the end of the seventeenth century, all land in the vicinity of Dijon, with the exception of that which lay in the "dead hand" of the church, had been snapped up by prosperous citizens. In this way the bourgeoisie is said to have acquired almost a third of the land of France before the Revolution.

Feudal modes of land tenure disappeared from Great Britain and the Low Countries; they were of no great importance in Scandinavia and were declining in France. They remained important in Germany until the eighteenth century and in eastern Europe until the nineteenth. The reasons were simple. Demand was increasing, especially in the cities, for the breadgrains produced in eastern Europe. Far from relaxing feudal controls over their peasants, the landowing classes intensified them, using peasant *corvée* to clear and cultivate ever broader acres, and taking peasant holdings into their own hands. Only by cultivating large areas were they able to acquire a surplus for sale to the merchants, who shipped it to the west. All the same, the nobles could never have had their way if there had been a strong central government willing to restrain them. The process was carried on most vigorously in Poland, which had easiest access by sea to the markets of the west. It was less important in the Czech lands and Hungary, probably because it was more difficult to market the surplus, but reached its peak in the Romanian principalities after seaborne trade had developed from the Danube mouth (see pp. 432–3).

At least two-thirds of the population of Europe belonged to the peasantry. They formed a far from homogenous group, with a strongly marked internal stratification. Serfdom had by the eighteenth century largely disappeared from western Europe and was of no great importance in central Europe. It had in some degree been reimposed in the east and in the Balkan lands under Ottoman rule, and it prevailed in Lithuania and Russia. Vestigial feudal obligations survived in France until the Revolution and much longer in some parts of central Europe, but, by and large, the peasant had secured some kind of title to his land, and he could not, as a general rule, be evicted from his holding at the will of a lord.

The status of the peasant derived from the extent of his holding. The well-to-do peasant might have fifty acres with the stock and equipment that went with a farm of this size. Such peasants were most numerous in northern France, but might be found almost anywhere. The rich peasant or *kulak* was well-known in Russia. The average peasant cultivated from twenty to fifty acres, more or less adequate according to local soils and cropping conditions. Below them in the peasant hierarchy were the *brassiers* and cottagers, men who had an acre or two and a garden plot, but who had to offer the service of their arms *(bras)* to their richer neighbors. At the bottom of the peasant heap were the virtually landless laborers. Most peasants, though usually not those without holdings, had variable rights in the woodland and rough grazing land. At Duravel, in the Central Massif of France, where conditions for agriculture were at their poorest, no less than three-quarters of the holdings were of fewer than five hectares (12.35 acres). In a valley in Savoy, 87 percent of holdings had fewer than five hectares, and more than half had under one. Countless examples might be cited. Everywhere the poverty of an appreciable part of the peasantry was beyond description. The peasant, wrote Robert Darlington early in the seventeenth century, "fareth very hardly and feedeth most upon bread and fruit."[12]

The peasant was both overtaxed and underemployed. His holding was generally too small and his labor obligations and their commuted value too great. Most paid some form of quitrent to their lord; all paid tithe to the church. In southern Europe the practice was developing during these centuries of holding land *en métayage,* or sharecropping. The lord provided land, and often tools and farm animals, and in return received a proportion, usually half, of the produce. It was a system calculated to discourage initiative or investment on the part of the peasant but to spread the losses during very bad years. The system became widespread in Italy and southern France.

---

12 *The View of France, 1604,* Shakespeare Association Facsimiles, 13 (Oxford, 1936).

The crops

There was little change during these centuries in either crops or cropping systems. The breadgrains were cultivated almost everywhere but varied with soil and the nature of demand. The three-field mode of cultivation called for alternation of fall- and spring-sown grains. Rye was the most actively cultivated of the former, but oats and barley provided much of the peasant's diet. Vauban, with the *élection* of Vézelay in mind, noted that only the better-off were able to eat rye bread. When wheat was grown it was usually sold off the land to pay the rent. Wheat always commanded a high price, often 40 percent above rye, and twice as much as the coarse grains. But it was more exacting in its soil requirement than other cereals and sometimes cropped less heavily. In southern Europe, where a two-course system continued to be normal, wheat or winter-sown barley continued to alternate with fallow.

Buckwheat was eaten in areas of poor soil and also when the breadgrains failed. Garden vegetables were always important but had the disadvantage that, apart from roots, they could not be kept through the winter. The great value of the potato was not so much its food value but the fact that it would keep.

The cultivation of fallow was restricted by the fact that fallow grazing was almost the only way in which land could receive manure. The first breach in the traditional alternation of crops and fallow came in the Low Countries, with the cultivation of pulses and artificial grasses. Its effect was to increase the amount of legumes for human consumption and of fodder for animals, which in turn made more manure available. The practice of taking a catch crop on the fallow spread to Britain and to central Europe, but Arthur Young found little evidence of such progressive agriculture in the late eighteenth century. Such a departure from tradition was hindered not only by the innate conservatism of the peasant, but also by the fact that in many instances his lease called upon him to take two cereal crops and then leave the land under fallow. The fallow, furthermore, was institutionalized. The whole community had the right to turn their animals onto it, and it would have been quite impractical for any peasant to plant crops on his own parcels of fallow land.

The choice of cereal crops in any area was determined by soil, by the market, and above all by tradition. The dominant cereals changed from one locality to the next (Fig. 9.11). In the Paris basin it was wheat wherever possible and rye elsewhere; in Brittany, rye and buckwheat; in the Central Massif, rye and oats. On sandy soils buckwheat sometimes replaced oats or barley as a spring crop. There was a tendency, especially in the eighteenth century, for the area under wheat to increase, but only because it fetched a higher price. In Germany and eastern Europe comparatively little wheat was grown. The winter crop was rye. On the good soils of Bohemia wheat and rye were more evenly balanced. Rye became more important again in the mountains of Austria and Hungary but gradually disappeared in the Balkans in favor of wheat and barley, the common breadgrains of southern Europe.

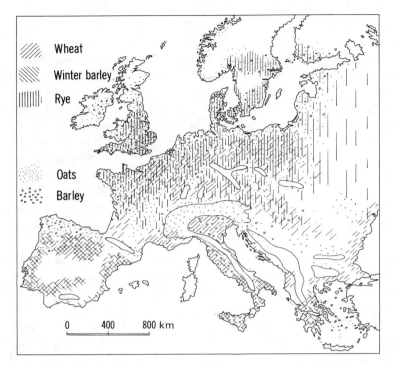

9.11. Cereal crops in Europe in the eighteenth century

The peasant's holding was not only small; its yield was low, whether measured in bushels to the acre or as a ratio to the seed used. Yield ratios are sometimes determinable from estate accounts. They were consistently highest in Great Britain and the Low Countries (Fig. 9.12), where they improved sharply between 1500 and 1800. In France, Spain, and Italy there was little improvement, and in central, northern, and eastern Europe ratios remained very low indeed. In the sixteenth century average yields of between fourfold and fivefold might be expected, or at least hoped for. The ratio rose to ten by 1800 in the most progressive areas, but remained below four in the more backward. The improvement in yield ratios in northwest Europe must be taken as a major factor in raising the living standards.

The breadgrains were everywhere supplemented by legumes, green vegetables, and roots. The turnip, in particular, was increasingly popular, but the only change of fundamental importance was the introduction and spread of corn (maize) and the potato. Both were brought from the New World in the sixteenth century and were first grown in Spain, to which neither was particularly suited. Corn spread to southern France and northern Italy. There was a prejudice against it, chiefly because it could not be cooked and eaten like the breadgrains, but its advantages were obvious. It yielded heavily and, as John Locke observed, "serves poore people for bred. That which makes them sow it, is not only the great increase [yield],

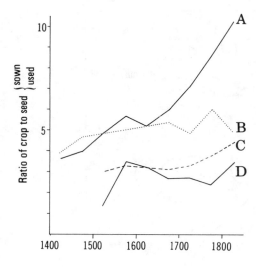

9.12. Growth of crops in yield ratios: (A) Great Britain and the Low Countries; (B) France, Spain, and Italy; (C) central Europe and Scandinavia; (D) eastern Europe

but the convenience also which the blade and green about the stalk yields them, it being good nourishment for their cattle."[13] Corn required, however, a hot and moist summer and became really important only in the Hungarian plain, the Balkans, and the more humid parts of the Mediterranean basin.

The other "new" crop was the potato, the "success story" of modern agriculture. It was being eaten in southern Spain in 1573, was a luxury in France in 1616, and shortly afterward appeared in Germany. Yet it was a rare crop before the eighteenth century. Like corn, it could not be fitted conveniently into any cropping system and was at first grown as a garden crop. Not until cereal prices rose sharply in the mid-eighteenth century did the peasant begin to accept the potato as a regular part of his diet. It appeared in Ireland about 1750 and quickly established itself as the staple food of the poorer classes. Frederick the Great ordered it to be grown in Brandenburg-Prussia, where the famine of 1771–2 led to a healthy respect for the heavily cropping potato. It began to be grown in Scandinavia in the late eighteenth century, in part because it lent itself to the distillation of liquor. The potato could become a field crop only after the tight communal control of cropping systems had been lifted, and this did not really begin to happen before the French Revolution.

There was one other "new" crop which had begun to spread before 1815 – the sugar beet. Unlike corn and the potato, it was native to Europe, but its sugar content did not become generally recognized much before the end of the eighteenth century. It acquired some importance during the Napoleonic Wars, when the import of sugarcane was cut off by the British blockade, but was not widely grown until late in the nineteenth century (see p. 383).

The grapevine, by contrast, was in retreat (Fig. 9.13). Vineyards were abandoned along the lower Seine, in northern France, the Low Countries, the Lower

13 *Locke's Travels in France 1675–1679,* ed. John Lough (Cambridge, U.K., 1953), 236.

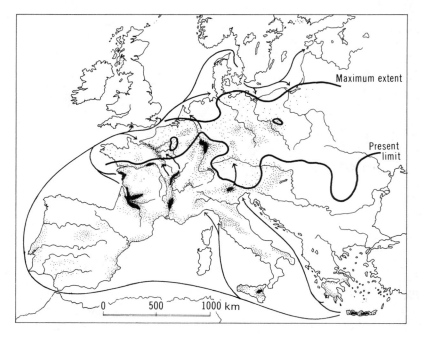

9.13. The retreat of viticulture and the abandonment of marginal vineyards since the end of the Middle Ages

Rhineland, and north Germany. The reason was that these regions were climatically marginal, and, with improving means of transportation, a better wine could be obtained from lands farther south. Here viticulture was increasing in areas well suited to it, especially Burgundy, the Rhône valley, southern France, and the middle Rhineland. Fortified and specialized wines began to be produced, such as "port" from the Oporto district of northern Portugal, Champagne from Reims, "hock" from the Rhine-Main district, and sherry from southwestern Spain. Viticulture was also spreading in the eighteenth century in Australia and, in the wake of the retreating Turk, in the Hungarian plain.

The olive, which with wheat and wine had once been the pillar of the human diet in the Mediterranean basin, was in retreat throughout these centuries. As olive groves were killed by frost or destroyed in warfare, little attempt was made to replant them (see p. 170). In Provence their area declined steadily between the sixteenth century and 1800. Only in southern Spain did the olive retain its old importance. The fact that southern Europe was able to dispense with the olive was due in the main to the greater availability of animal fats.

Industrial crops, on the other hand, were of growing importance. Most widespread and important of them was flax, grown primarily not for the oil contained in its seeds, but for the threads in its long stalk. It was a crop of the humid north of Europe and was grown from Brittany to the eastern Baltic. Its preparation, spinning, and weaving were cottage industries (see pp. 174, 340), a significant supplement to the peasant's income and a source of exports of no small importance. Hemp was a garden crop, grown in order to make rope and cordage. It appears to have been more widely cultivated than flax, and was particularly important in coastal regions like Brittany, where rope was used in outfitting ships. A number of plants, including varieties of *brassica,* were grown for the oil contained in their seeds. Arthur Young commented on the use of windmills in northern France for crushing oilseeds to extract the oil which had acquired a number of industrial uses.

If brewing and distilling can be counted as industries, their raw materials can be reckoned to be industrial crops. Weak beer, "a harmless and healthy drink in an age when water was commonly impure,"[14] was brewed in most areas where wine was unimportant. It was fermented from oats, barley, or even rye, and the practice was spreading of using hops as a flavoring and preservative. Cider, commonly regarded as a plebeian drink, began to assume some importance in northern France from the sixteenth century and later became more socially acceptable. The practice of distilling fermented drinks in order to increase their alcoholic content developed rapidly during these centuries. It derived from medieval alchemy and seems first to have been applied to wines. Cognac became an export of France in the eighteenth century. Gin was developed in the Netherlands (hence its name of "Hollands") in the seventeenth century, and the production of whisky in Scotland and Ireland began on a domestic scale in the eighteenth.

Tools and technology

There was very little development in the tools of agriculture before the nineteenth century. The eighteenth-century plow was not recognizably different from that of the fifteenth except that a metal coulter and tip to the share became more common. Harrows were made with iron teeth, but sickle, scythe, and flail were as they had always been. Seed continued to be sown broadcast, and an appreciable part of it was devoured by birds. Cereals were still harvested with the sickle. The jointed flail was the only means of threshing cereals. But the quern disappeared from all except remote areas, and mills – both water and wind – became larger and mechanically more efficient.

Farming techniques also underwent little change. Plowing, sowing, harvesting, and threshing consumed the greater part of the peasant's time. Little use was made of manure, and there were those, like Duhamel du Monceau, who followed Jethro Tull in condemning it as injurious to the crop. But the peasant knew better; only a shortage of animals prevented him from making greater use of manure. No attempt was made to drain damp clay lands, except by cutting ditches to take the water, or to irrigate dry land, except by the creation of water meadows in the eighteenth century.

Yet agricultural conditions were not wholly static. Yield ratios in parts of

14 R. J. Forbes, "Food and Drink," in *A History of Technology,* ed. Charles Singer et al., III (Oxford, 1957), 11.

northwest Europe improved greatly, and Europe was able to feed at the end of the eighteenth century a population some two and a half times as great as three hundred years earlier. One cannot point to any single innovation that could have brought about so great an improvement. Instead it was the accumulation of very small incremental changes in tools and methods and management.

Land use

Lands abandoned during the later Middle Ages were, by and large, brought back into profitable land use in the course of the sixteenth century, though in England much of it remained under grass. In some parts of Europe land values were high enough to encourage extensive land-reclamation projects. In the United Provinces of the Netherlands the drainage of coastal marshes continued throughout the period (Fig. 9.14). The Venetians drained marshes at the Po mouth, and elsewhere in northwest Europe coastal marshes were reclaimed. The fenland of eastern England was drained, and progress was made elsewhere. Many of these projects reached fruition at a time when population had ceased to expand, but other attempts at reclamation accompanied the resumption of population growth in the eighteenth century. They were not restricted to marshland. There was some extension of cropland into forest and waste. In France, for example, it is estimated that the area of agricultural land was increased by about 2.5 percent during the century.

This increase was achieved in part at the expense of the forest. Forest was essential to preindustrial societies, providing for most people essential fuel and building materials. It was in the late eighteenth century still abundant in eastern Europe and Russia, where population was less dense and the demands on it smaller. But in France there was, locally at least, a timber scarcity. Réaumur, involved as he was in the iron-smelting industry, expressed his concern at the growing scarcity, and Buffon went farther, claiming that there was not enough for basic needs. Figures 9.15 and 9.16, based, respectively, on the reconstructions of Michel Devèze and the *Carte de France* of 1758, show, if only in a very general way, how woodland had contracted in the Paris basin.

The biggest demands made on the forests were for industrial uses, for smelting and refining iron, making glass, and burning bricks. These uses almost exhausted the forests near which they were carried on. Forges were obliged to close in the Pyrenees for lack of fuel, and the furnace at Allevard in Savoy could operate for less than half the year. Germany was better off, but even here timber was scarce in the more populous areas. In Great Britain the shortages had shown themselves very much earlier. Replanting of trees was legally required from the late sixteenth century, and ships' timbers were imported in increasing quantity from Scandinavia and the Baltic. Even in Sweden which might have been thought to have a superabundance, limits were set to ironworking to conserve the forests. In Mediterranean Europe the forests had almost disappeared. Only in Lithuania and Russia was there no danger of a shortage, but even here those forests which lay close to waterways had already become overexploited.

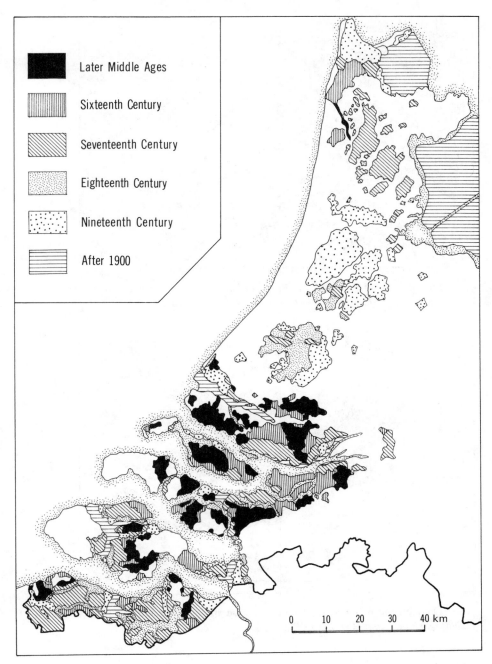

9.14. Land reclamation in the Netherlands

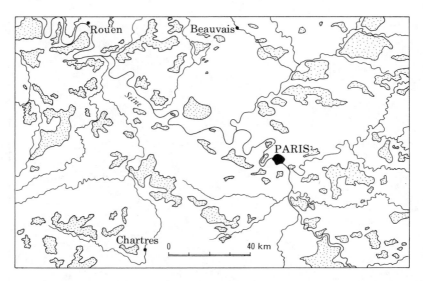

9.15. Distribution of forest in the Paris region in the sixteenth century. [After Michel Devèze, *La vie de la foret française au XVIIe siècle* (Paris, 1961).]

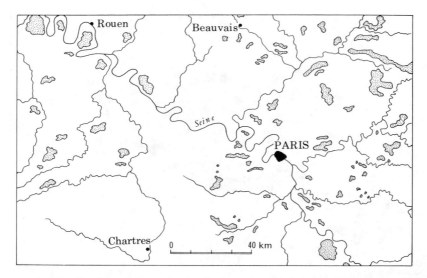

9.16. Distribution of forest in the Paris region in the eighteenth century. [After R. J. Julien, *Carte de France* (Paris, 1758).]

Pastoralism

There was no part of Europe where farm animals were not kept. Even in areas of intensive cereal growing, oxen were reared for the plow, horses for the harrow, and sheep were expected to spread their droppings over the fallow. Nevertheless, animals were, compared with the nineteenth century, few in number and poor in quality. With the exception of pigs, they were not kept primarily for meat or even milk, though these were significant by-products. Sheep were valued for their wool, horses for riding, and cattle for their brute strength in drawing the plow and wagon.

In the eighteenth century this began to change. The number of animals had been restricted by the difficulty of keeping them through the winter. But the cultivation of so-called artificial grasses on at least part of the fallow began to remove this constraint. More animals meant more manure and also the provision of more milk, milk products, and meat. Very slowly the predominantly cereal cultivation shifted in the direction of mixed farming. This process began first in England and the Low Countries and spread into France and Germany. The change was hastened on the one hand by urban demand for animal products, and on the other by the low cereal prices which prevailed in the late seventeenth and early eighteenth centuries. In France the area of grazing land and the number of animals increased appreciably. Parts of Normandy became cattle country, selling live animals to Paris and developing the cheeses which have since been among the specialities of the region. Even in central and southern France the balance was tipped toward animal farming. In the Low Countries and Great Britain the process was even more rapid, and in the Netherlands almost 80 percent of agricultural land was used for grazing by 1700. Arable farming was also in retreat in many areas of poor soil, like the Ardennes, Jura, and Alps, and even in such dominantly arable areas as the provinces of Anjou and Maine.

The development of long-distance trade in agricultural products was leading to a very slow adaptation of farming to the physical environment. If the Dutch could give so much of their land over to cattle, this was only because they were able to import part of their breadgrains from the Baltic. And in the Alps of Switzerland and Austria it proved more profitable to raise good dairy cattle than to grow inferior cereals. *La victoire du bétail sur le blé* was gained quite early in the modern period, and Swiss cattle, butter, and cheese found markets as far afield as western Germany and the north Italian cities. Cattle droving was a means of getting animals to the market, from Scotland or Wales to London, or from Scandinavia, Poland, and Hungary to markets in central and western Europe. Cattle droving reached a peak at the beginning of the seventeenth century, was cut back by wars, but developed again in the eighteenth.

The new agriculture

Long before the end of the eighteenth century a new agriculture had appeared in England. Innovation was assisted by the disappearance in the course of the eighteenth and early nineteenth centuries of the open fields and their replacement by "several" or the system of enclosed fields. Fallow was abandoned; artificial grasses and, above all, roots were introduced, and variable rotations, adjusted to soil, climate, and market, were adopted. The increased production of fodder crops allowed more animals to be kept, and the use of enclosed fields encouraged more scientific breeding. Cattle, sheep, and even pigs began to be bred carefully in order to obtain or to strengthen certain qualities. Innovations were first made on the lands of the gentry and were publicized in books and journals for others to learn.

To some extent the innovations adopted in England in the eighteenth century had been anticipated in the Low Countries a century earlier. They spread to France in the later eighteenth century, but only a small minority of landowners were aware of them or showed any desire to emulate the English example. Arthur Young could find little evidence of improved agriculture in the 1780s. On the other hand English – or Dutch – example spread into northwest Germany. George III was interested in adopting the new methods on his lands in Hanover. Frederick the Great approved of them and sent young Prussian farmers to study them in England. In Sweden, legislation encouraged the enclosure of open fields and prepared the way for agricultural progress, but elsewhere in Europe advance had to await the very different circumstances of the nineteenth century.

MANUFACTURING AND MINING

The system of manufacturing which the sixteenth century had inherited from the Middle Ages remained almost unchanged technically and but little modified in structure and organization until the latter half of the eighteenth century. Yet there were changes in this period. There was decay in many traditional industries. Italy declined in the seventeenth century from "one of the most advanced of the industrial areas of western Europe [to] an economically backward and depressed area."[15] The cloth manufacture of the northern cities and the silk of Como and Lucca almost disappeared. In the southern Low Countries industrial decay began yet earlier. The cloth industry was virtually extinguished in the Spanish wars and the port of Antwerp was effectively closed. Business shifted to the northern Low Countries; Leyden became an important center for the cloth industry, but the business of the United Netherlands remained commerce rather than manufacturing.

The industrial decline of the seventeenth century was less marked in Germany because the previous advance had been less rapid. In Britain manufacturing grew steadily, and from the late seventeenth century an increasing proportion of the goods produced was exported. The cloth industry concentrated increasingly in East Anglia and the west country. At the same time the making of hosiery and other textiles, of paper, soap, and furniture and the smelting and fabrication of ferrous and nonferrous metals all expanded at a steady pace.

The industrial expansion which had characterized Great Britain in the later seventeenth century spread to much of continental Europe during the eighteenth. In France "a wave of prosperity" overtook the country in the 1740s. In Germany recovery from the Thirty Years War was complete, and a run of good harvests increased marginally the peasant's purchasing power. A mass demand for manu-

15   Carlo M. Cipolla, "The Decline of Italy: The Case of a Fully Matured Economy," *Economic History Review* 5 (1952–3): 178.

factured goods was slowly emerging, first in England, then in the Low Countries, northern France, and the Rhineland. Arthur Young, commenting in the 1780s on the ill-clad and underequipped peasantry of France, remarked that "the wealth of a nation lies in its circulation [i.e., trade] and consumption; and the case of poor people abstaining from the use of manufactures of leather and wool ought to be considered as an evil of the first magnitude . . . a large consumption among the poor being of more consequence than among the rich."[16] British manufacturers had such a mass market at home and even overseas. This sort of market could not really develop in continental Europe until agricultural reforms had endowed the peasantry with a greater purchasing power. And this did not really come about until after 1815, and in eastern and southeastern Europe not until even later.

Nevertheless, attempts were made in continental Europe as early as the seventeenth century to establish manufacturing industries on some kind of factory basis. Colbert established a cloth factory at Sedan in eastern France, the Gobelins founded their tapestry-weaving shops near Paris, and many works were set up, often under princely patronage, to make porcelain or weave silk. But many — perhaps most — of these manufactures catered only to the expensive tastes of the rich. There was no mass demand for these goods, and in the end most failed.

The factory

A feature of the slowly growing industries of the late seventeenth and eighteenth centuries was the factory as a mode of organizing production. It displaced the domestic system very slowly, and even in the early nineteenth century most industrial production was in the cottage or domestic workshop. A factory was defined by Max Weber as "a capitalistically organized production process employing specialized and co-ordinated working methods within a workshop and utilizing vested capital."[17] It was not necessarily powered by machinery, though mechanical power became increasingly important in Great Britain in the eighteenth century and in continental Europe by the mid-nineteenth. How a factory differed from a workshop is a matter of definition: the size of the work force and the degree of discipline imposed upon it must be the deciding factors. Factories were far from new in the eighteenth century. William Stumpe, clothier, had turned Malmesbury Abbey in southern England into a cloth factory in the 1540s. Colbert established such a factory at Sedan, and some ironworks were of so great a size by this time that they might also qualify. It was in Britain, however, that the factory first came into its own. In itself it offered few advantages over domestic craftsmanship; standardized quality and work discipline were perhaps the most important. But if mechanical power was used, its advantages were immense. One tends to think of the factory as steam powered. In fact, most early, mechanically operated factories were worked by waterpower. Again, one thinks of the factory as an urban insti-

16 *Travels in France during the Years 1787, 1788, 1789* (London, 1915), 27.
17 As quoted in *Ciba Review* 1 (1968): 4.

tution; in fact, most were rural, both to escape the kind of regulation which urban authorities still exercised and to profit from available sources of waterpower. One of the earliest, if not the very first, authentic factory of modern times was built in 1719 on the banks of the river Derwent in northern England. Its purpose was to "throw" or prepare silk for weaving, and it was operated by a large paddle wheel turned by the river's current. It was, by the standards of those days, an enormous building. It was six floors high and five hundred feet long. Within a few years the factory was adapted to cotton spinning and by the middle of the century a number of giant factories were operating in the valleys of the Pennine hills of England.

There was a limit to the amount of energy which could be generated by a single stream and to the number of streams that could be used, and by the 1770s there was little scope for further development. Factories had of necessity to turn to steam power. An effective steam engine had been developed by 1712 by Newcomen and Savory, but it was a slow, extravagant machine, and for almost half a century its chief use was for pumping water from mines. In the 1760s, however, James Watt adapted his improved steam engine to rotary motion. It became a source of motive power for factories, and from the 1770s most new factories were designed to use steam power. This freed them from reliance on flowing streams, but gave them a new kind of dependence – on the coalfields. At once the coalfields began to attract industry, and industry drew people to it, so that new towns sprang up. The new industries were not attracted to the towns; rather, towns were attracted to the industries.

Development in Great Britain was sufficiently rapid in the latter half of the eighteenth century to have earned the name of the "Industrial Revolution." Its twin features, large-scale factory production and the use of mechanical – especially steam – power, characterized first the textile industries, then ironworking, and lastly consumer industries like brewing and milling. This industrial expansion was concentrated in a few areas which offered the advantages of access to coal and the ports, for much of the raw material was imported from overseas. Few rivers were navigable, and the largest ports like London and Bristol had no important coalfield nearby. Only Liverpool combined proximity to a large coalfield, a good harbor, and a developed seaborne trade, and it was on the Lancashire coalfield, in Liverpool's hinterland, that the cotton industry took root and flourished (Fig. 9.17). The woolen industry developed on the other side of the Pennine hills, in the West Riding of Yorkshire, where there had long been domestic cloth weaving. Coal was available, and the rivers, which flowed down to the Humber and the port of Hull, put this cloth-producing region in touch with the rest of the country and the world (Fig. 9.18). By 1800 the iron industry had, with very few exceptions, abandoned its earlier woodland sites and had concentrated on the coalfields of the West Midlands, South Wales, Yorkshire, and Nottinghamshire (Fig. 9.19). Manufacturing continued to increase through the period of the Napoleonic Wars, and when they ended, Great Britain was not only the largest industrial power in the world, it had more than half of the world's productive capacity.

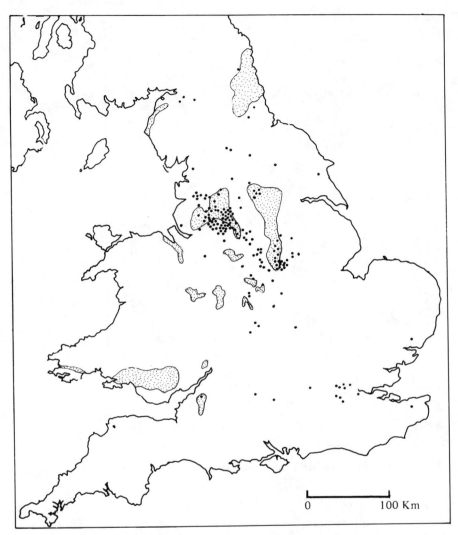

9.17. The cotton industry in Great Britain, about 1800. The coalfields are shown stippled

Why, one may ask, did the Industrial Revolution take place in Great Britain, and not in France, or the Low Countries, or northwest Germany? These enjoyed physical advantages not dissimilar to those of Great Britain and were far better endowed with the means for internal transportation. Great Britain had two advantages in greater measure than any continental country. The first was a willingness to accept innovation and change, and the other was a mass market for ordinary consumer goods. Clapham, commenting on the rise of the woolen industry in Yorkshire, noted that it was "the ordinary case of a pushing, hardworking locality

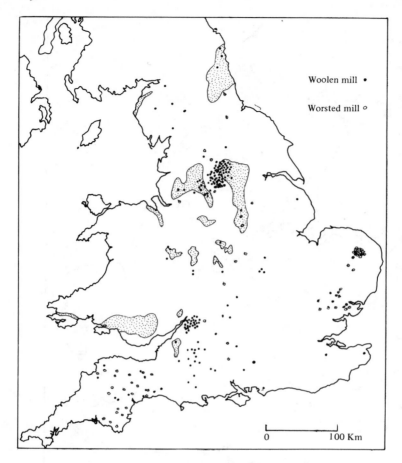

Woolen mill •

Worsted mill ○

0   100 Km

9.18. The woolen industry in Great Britain, about 1800. The coalfields are shown stippled

with certain slight advantages, attacking the lower grades of an expanding industry."[18] This is what the Industrial Revolution was about, for the same could have
been said a couple of generations later of the millworkers of Lille, Elberfeld,
Chemnitz, and Łódź. But traditional manufactures were not suddenly extinguished. There continued to be a market for their more refined and more expensive
products. In England, the cloth industry of East Anglia and the west country
lingered on through the nineteenth century, though declining both relatively and
absolutely.

A feature of manufacturing during the preindustrial period was the growing
importance of rural as distinct from urban industry. The reasons for the migration
of manufacturing to rural areas were complex. In the cities guilds imposed petty

18   Evidence given before *Royal Commission on the Distribution of the Industrial Population*, HMSO
     (London, 1940), 32.

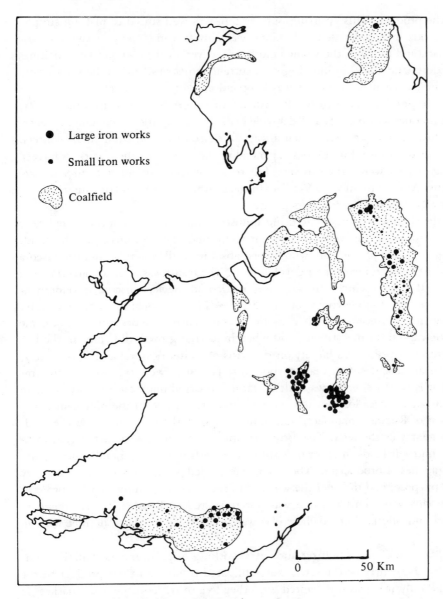

- ● Large iron works
- • Small iron works
- ⬡ Coalfield

0   50 Km

9.19. The iron industry in Great Britain, about 1800

and burdensome restrictions on craftsmen, preventing them from adapting their production to a changing market. At the same time, rural labor was cheaper and more flexible; it could make use of waterpower; in some branches of manufacture it could produce its own raw materials. Rural, domestic manufacturing came into its own when merchants began to supply the craftsmen with materials, sometimes even tools – for the rural worker always lacked capital – and collected and marketed the product. This "putting-out" system was well suited to making simple, coarse goods in popular demand. Linen was almost a monopoly of the domestic craftsman, and much of the woolen cloth was woven in the cottage. Lace making, embroidery, and stocking knitting were cottage industries, and in the seventeenth and eighteenth centuries the list was long and growing.

A few cities were able to break with urban traditions and to make a coarser, cheaper product which commanded a wide market. Among them were Lille, Amiens, and Beauvais, but their craftsmen always faced competition from rural workers. In a few instances rural industries expanded to the point that their workers formed settlements that were urban in size, but totally without urban restraints and restrictions. Among them were Verviers in the southern Low Countries and the large industrial villages of the Flanders plain.

The development of manufacturing industries in Russia took a course radically different from that in western and central Europe. The reasons were threefold. First was the role of the tsar, who owned absolutely all resources and exercised a monopolistic control over their development. The result was a certain arbitrariness in imperial policy which, in any case, tended to view industrial development exclusively from the viewpoint of military needs and national security. Secondly, there was no significant middle class from which entrepreneurs might have come and little capital for investment, and when industrial growth did come in the late nineteenth century it was largely on the basis of western capital and skill. Lastly, there was an absence of free labor, though serfs — such were the peculiar circumstances of Russia — sometimes built up large industrial undertakings, without, in many instances, ever losing their servile status. Until late in the nineteenth century most of Russia's manufacturing industry was in the hands of either the landowning gentry or the serfs. The former established factories — in fact, large workshops — on their lands in order to employ their serfs in textile, metal, leather, and other branches of production. They even transported groups of serfs across country for this purpose, and many of the workers in the Urals iron industry were brought there in this way. This practice was not restricted to Russia. It was known in Bohemia and Silesia, but nowhere else was it practiced on the scale met with in Russia.

The "factories" and smelting and metalworking establishments, whether controlled by the gentry or the serfs, were obligated to offer all their product to the state, and only if it was not wanted were they free to trade in the open market. It is indeed remarkable that there was any industrial growth at all under such a system of controls and restrictions. In fact, several relatively industrialized areas emerged during the eighteenth century. The number of manufacturing establishments increased more than tenfold, and when the century ended some seventy-five thousand were employed in textile and related industries, and there were more than eighteen hundred "factories." Most were concentrated in the towns of the Moscow region with a smaller number near St. Petersburg. Many produced woolen cloth and linen, though a small number were already engaged in cotton spinning and weaving.

Textile industries

Throughout these centuries the textile industries employed more people and produced goods of a greater total value than any other industrial sector. They were both urban and rural, and between these two there was a fluctuating and uneasy balance. Spinning was very largely rural and was carried on almost exclusively by women. Weaving was also increasingly a rural pursuit, but bleaching, dyeing, fulling, and other branches of the finishing industries were largely carried on in the cities. The textile industries may themselves be grouped into four categories: woolens, linen, cottons, and mixed and luxury fabrics. They were not spatially distinguished, and only in Britain can one speak of a cotton region quite distinct from that which made woolens or linen, and this distinction was not applicable to Scotland. Most textile regions and centers in Europe carried on the manufacture of most if not all types of fabric. There were factories which switched production from one type of fiber to another, and even some in which more than one process was carried on at the same time. Textiles were, of course, woven in every part of Europe, but in most they were used within the family which made them and did not enter the market. Commercial cloth production was located mainly in the Low Countries, France, central Europe, Italy, and, of course, England.

The traditional broadcloth manufacture of the Flemish cities declined through the sixteenth century and was replaced by the "new draperies" – mainly worsteds and serges – in the industrial villages of the Flanders plain. These developed strongly during the century, but their manufacture suffered a severe check in the wars late in the century. Hondschoote, the chief center of their manufacture, was destroyed in 1582. Although it revived later, it never regained its earlier prosperity and importance. The beneficiaries of the decline in Flanders were the Netherlands, Brabant, and the Liège region. The province of Holland and, in particular, the city of Leyden were the first to develop the industry. Helped by refugees from the south, Leyden established one of the largest cloth industries in Europe and was itself, in the seventeenth century, among the fastest growing cities. Leyden used wool from Spain and exported *lakens,* a light fabric similar to that once made at Hondschoote. The cloth industry spread to other cities in the western Netherlands – Delft, Gouda, Haarlem, Utrecht – and also to the eastern Netherlands, where it was carried on as a cottage industry.

A second area which profited from the decline of the Flanders manufacture was the Liège region. Here, on the northern edge of the Ardennes, a woolen industry grew up. Its chief center was Verviers, an unincorporated township. Much of its labor came from Flanders and its wool from Spain. Its chief advantage was that there were no institutional restraints on either the craftsmen or the merchants who supplied their wool and marketed their cloth. The manufacture spread in the eighteenth century across the hills to Eupen, Burtscheid, and other small towns of the northern Eifel. This region gained in importance from its incorporation within revolutionary France since it could now exploit the whole French market. In 1799 machine spinning was introduced by the Cockerills, and the Vesdre valley, in which Verviers lay, became one of the earliest continental scenes of the Industrial Revolution.

The regrowth of the woolen industry in the Low Countries was accompanied by the expansion of the traditional linen manufacture. Flax was grown and prepared by the peasants who wove it, and the merchants of the Flanders cities, it was said, handled as much linen as cloth. The cotton industry came late, and it was not until the closing years of the eighteenth century that the first mill was erected at Ghent and cotton textiles began to replace linen as the leading textile in Flanders.

The textile industry was universal in France but mostly yielded little more than coarse cloth for the local market (Fig. 9.20). Attempts by the government, particularly by Colbert, to develop the manufacture of quality cloth met with little success. The cloth industry of northern France was an extension of that of Flanders, producing mainly light woolens at Amiens, Beauvais, Abbeville and, above all, Reims. The industry in southern France was carried on by the peasants in the villages and hamlets of the Cevennes, "when they are not working on the land," as the *Intendant* noted. Spanish wool was used for the better-quality cloth and local or North African for the poor. Much of the fabric made was exported to Africa and the Middle East.

Linen weaving was second only to woolens and was carried on throughout northern France, where it was "the only occupation of poor families," and without it much of the rural proletariat would have perished. It was closely bound up with agriculture. In the northwest, flax was woven into sailcloth, and canvas was exported on a not inconsiderable scale. The chief threat to the linen industry came from cotton. It was of no importance until the 1740s when the industry was established in Rouen, and it was not until John Holker introduced British textile processes in the mid-eighteenth century that the industry began to thrive and to spread through the valley of the lower Seine, then to the Lille district and to other parts of France. From the first, spinning was carried on in small factories, but weaving remained a cottage industry well into the next century.

In central Europe linen weaving was the most widespread textile industry, supplying much of the clothing worn by the peasants. In Germany a traditional cloth industry was carried on in the cities, but only in the small Rhineland towns was it expanding. It was of far greater importance in Bohemia and Moravia, where it was established on the estates of the nobles, often in small, factorylike workshops manned by unfree labor. The industry owed much to immigrant craftsmen from the Low Countries, who built small mills, notably at Jihlava and Brno, during the eighteenth century.

The linen industry predominated in the plain of northern Europe (Fig. 9.21) and was especially important in Westphalia – Minden, Bielefeld, and Ravensburg being its chief centers. Spinning and weaving were cottage industries and supplemented a backward agriculture. Northern Switzerland and southwest Germany also formed part of the linen-working region of central Europe. The industry revived after the Thirty Years War and began to produce linen of a superior quality, notably at St. Gallen. A third area which developed a linen industry of consider-

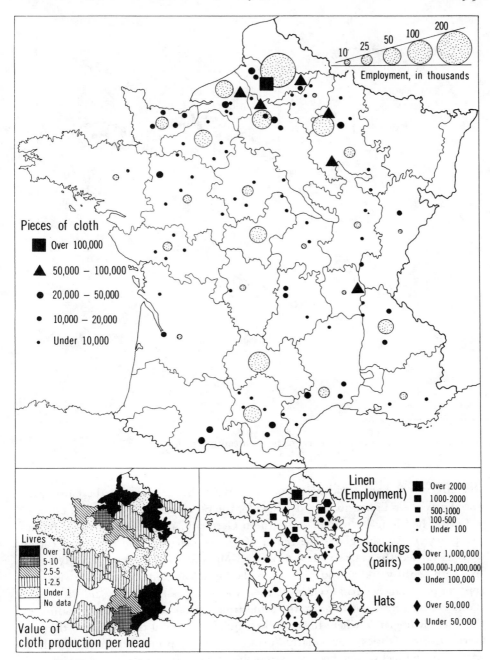

9.20. Clothworking in France in the early eighteenth century

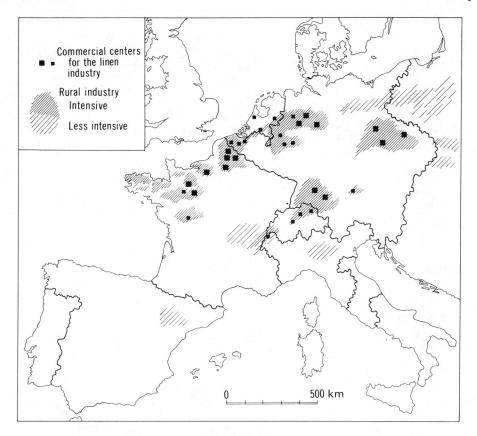

9.21. The European linen industry in the eighteenth century

able size was Bohemia and neighboring Silesia, where, however, the fabric produced was of a rougher quality, destined for the peasant market of eastern Europe.

Cotton had long been used in southern Germany, most of it in mixed fabrics (see p. 173). Augsburg was the center of its manufacture, and from here cotton weavers carried the craft to Chemnitz (Karl-Marx-Stadt) in Saxony as early as the sixteenth century and spread it through the Ore Mountains. Cotton weavers, according to Mirabeau, had even made their way as far as Pomerania and Prussia by the late eighteenth century. At the same time cotton weaving was spreading in the lower Rhineland, where linen workers quickly adapted their skills to the new fabric. Cotton fabrics, particularly "prints" made by printing patterns on them with wooden blocks, soon became extremely fashionable and competed with linen.

In southern Europe the chief centers of the cloth industry at the beginning of the period were Spain and northern Italy. The industry declined in Spain, largely because of its guild restrictions and its failure to adapt to new commercial conditions. Attempts were made in the eighteenth century to establish "royal" factories to make woolens and tapestries, but they collapsed under the weight of the officialdom which controlled them. Only in Catalonia did attempts to revive the ancient weaving industry achieve any success. A cotton-weaving industry was established in the mid-eighteenth century and spread through the hinterland of Barcelona. Spinning was carried on in small, waterpowered mills, while weaving remained a cottage industry.

The Italian cloth industry, which produced in the main quality fabrics, remained generally prosperous until the second half of the eighteenth century. The Mediterranean and north European markets were lost, manufacturing was interrupted by wars, and the industry was reduced to the production of cheap fabrics for a peasant market. Its revival did not come until late in the nineteenth century (see p. 405).

Luxury fabrics

Throughout this period silk was the elite fabric at a time when rich clothing was a mark of social distinction. There were few countries where attempts were not made to weave silk and even to breed silkworms. Buffon attempted – and failed – to establish mulberry trees in Burgundy, and those planted by Frederick the Great in Prussia succumbed to the frost. Nevertheless, the weaving of raw silk imported from southern Europe was established successfully. The first craftsmen were generally Italian. The foundation of the Lyons industry (see pp. 405–6) was followed by those of Zurich, Paris, and Tours. In the eighteenth century craftsmen from the hidebound industry at Lyons moved to Saint Etienne, which became a center for ribbon weaving. The van der Leyen family established it at Krefeld in northwest Germany, and silk mills were erected in Brandenburg, Saxony, and Bohemia, and at Spittlefields in London. Not all these branches of the industry proved to be long lasting, but those of London, Krefeld, and Saint-Etienne were well established by the end of the eighteenth century.

Another textile industry which catered to a wealthy clientele was tapestry weaving. The craft derived from Italy but in the sixteenth century was established in the southern Low Countries. In 1601 Flemish tapestry weavers took it to Paris, where they established themselves at the Gobelins. In 1664 their industry received royal patronage and continued to operate until the Revolution. Weavers from the Gobelins were enticed to carry their skills as far as St. Petersburg.

The metal industries

The second important group of manufacturing industries was concerned with mining and smelting and the fabrication of metal goods. At the beginning of the period the blast furnace (see Chap. 8, under "Metal industries") came into use, and by the eighteenth century there were few areas where the older direct method continued to be used. The blast furnace, as has been seen, produced a high-carbon, fluid metal, excellent for the castings which were coming increasingly into use. For other purposes the iron had to be refined on the hearth. Ironworking in all its

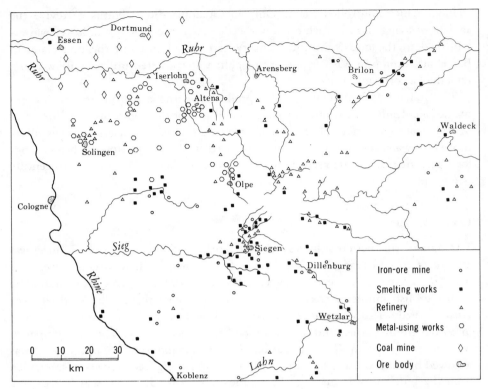

9.22. Ironworking in the Siegerland and neighboring areas, about 1800. [Based on F. A. A. Eversmann, *Die Eisen und Stahl Erzeugung auf Wasserwerken zwischen Lahn und Lippe* (Dortmund, 1804), and A. M. Heron de Villefosse, *De la richesse minérale* (Paris, 1819).]

branches made heavy demands on both charcoal and waterpower, and this led to a wider dispersion of these branches of manufacturing. Figure 9.22 shows the concentration of smelting in the hills near Siegen and Dillenburg, where the best ore was obtained, but the refining process was carried on farther to the north where there was less competition for charcoal and waterpower. The manufacture of articles of ironware was even more widely diffused. It was the problem of charcoal supply rather than the availability of iron ore that led to the very wide dispersion of primary ironworking. There were few areas from Spain to Russia that did not have small iron works (Fig. 9.23).

Demand for soft or bar iron was increasing at a time when constraints on smelting and refining were becoming more rigorous. The consequences were twofold. On the one hand the industry expanded in areas where the shortages of ore, fuel, and waterpower were less severe, and, on the other, a search began for alternative methods of refining. The former led to an increase in iron production in Sweden and, somewhat later, in Russia. The alternative remedy was to find other sources of fuel, ore, and power. Attempts to use coal instead of charcoal as a blast furnace

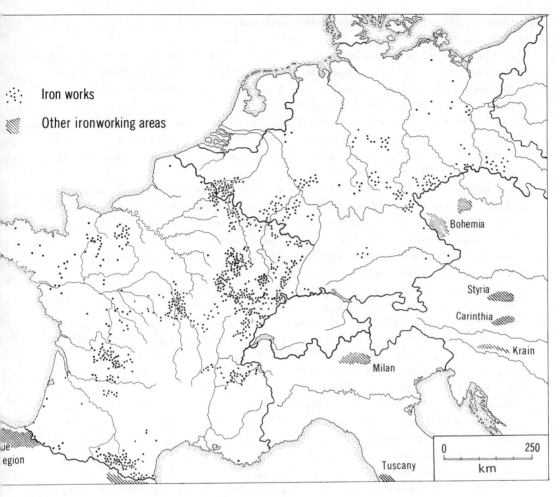

Iron works

Other ironworking areas

Bohemia

Styria

Carinthia

Krain

Milan

ue egion

Tuscany

0   250
km

9.23. The European iron industry in the later eighteenth century

150 fuel had been made in the seventeenth century, but it was not until 1709 that
151 Abraham Darby achieved success at his Coalbrookdale works in Shropshire, En-
152 gland. The innovation was not, however, welcomed as might have been expected,
153 because it still left unsolved the problem of refining the metal. High-carbon iron
154 from the blast furnace had few industrial uses. Great Britain, despite this inven-
155 tion and the possession of immense reserves of coal, even found itself importing
156 bar iron in increasing quantities from Sweden and Russia.
157   The second and complementary innovation came in the 1780s, when Henry
158 Cort adapted a type of oven, known as the reverberatory furnace, to the refining
159 of pig iron. Not only could it use coal instead of charcoal, it could also melt down
160 and recycle iron scrap. This was the so-called puddling process, which continued
161 to be used into the present century. It was the puddling oven, rather than the

blast furnace that pioneered the modern iron industry and led to its location on or very near the coalfields.

Steel, an alloy with a carbon content intermediate between that of soft iron and pig iron, was in growing demand for tools, weapons, and other purposes during the eighteenth century. It had chiefly been made by carburating soft iron, or forcing it to take up carbon. But the resulting metal was very uneven in quality, and in the mid-eighteenth century Benjamin Huntsman, a watchmaker who needed steel of fine and even quality for his work, developed a method of producing "crucible" steel. "Huntsman" steel quickly acquired a high reputation, and its output increased both for domestic production and for export.

Thus the vital innovations in the production of soft iron and steel had been made in Great Britain before the beginning of the revolutionary wars. Attempts were made in continental Europe, with varying success, to use coal or coke as fuel in the blast furnace, but the other innovations were either unknown or, at least, not used before 1815. The gulf between British and continental technology in the iron and steel industry was steadily widening.

The most important ironworking region in the seventeenth and eighteenth centuries was probably central Sweden, with Russia overtaking it late in the period. The Swedish industry was at first based on the rich ores of Dannemora in Uppland province, but later spread westward and northward into Varmland and Dalarna. Ore was smelted in masonry-built furnaces and refined on the hearth. The resulting bar iron was Sweden's most valuable export, comprising in some years three-quarters of the total. The volume increased fivefold between 1600 and 1750, to the point at which the Swedish government became alarmed for the forest and ore resources and imposed restrictions on production. Sweden never developed comparable iron-using industries. After the 1770s the Swedish industry began to decline, in part because of the technological advances made in Britain, but mainly because of the competition of the Russian industry.

In Russia, ironworking was the foremost industry during the late seventeenth and the eighteenth centuries and provided the most valuable export, apart from grain. The total output is said to have been about 15,000 tons in 1700. By 1800 it had increased to about 160,000, making Russia the largest source of pig and bar iron in the world. The earlier centers of ironworking had been in the Oka valley, near Tula. But the Ural Mountains, with their unlimited resources in ore and charcoal, overtook the older centers. Ekaterinburg (Sverdlovsk) and Nizhne Tagil were the centers of the industry, which was in fact spread through the southern Urals and over the plains of the upper Volga to the west. The industry was controlled by the families which owned the resources; labor was mostly servile and working conditions appalling. Much of the bar iron was exported by way of Archangel or St. Petersburg to the west.

The nonferrous metals were particularly important during this period. The chief sources of lead were the hills of western England, the Ardennes, the Harz Mountains, and the mining districts of Bohemia and Slovakia. The latter were more important in the sixteenth century for the silver content of their ores, and when the silver-lead ores were exhausted later in the century, mining declined in importance.

Copper was obtained from the Harz Mountains, Slovakia, and, above all, Sweden. In the Carpathian Mountains of Hungary copper came to replace silver-lead as the chief mineral product, but it declined in its turn in the seventeenth century. Slovakia was then replaced by Sweden as Europe's chief source of copper. The main deposit – Stora Kopparberg – was at Falun, northwest of Stockholm. Mining was carried on by a large number of small enterprises but was rigidly controlled by the crown. Copper was by far the most important Swedish export, until this role was taken over by bar iron. Europe, it was said, was "flooded with Swedish copper," and Swedish military enterprises in central Europe were largely paid for by the copper export. In the late seventeenth century the mines were nearing exhaustion, and by the eighteenth Swedish domination of the copper market was over, and henceforward Europe derived its supply from Spain and the Harz and the Ore mountains, with Britain supplying an increasing share from Cornwall and the Amlwch mine in Anglesey.

One must not exaggerate the volume of metalliferous ores produced in the preindustrial period. It is doubtful whether the total amount of iron, both pig and bar, exceeded 100,000 tons a year before 1800. Sweden at the peak of its production smelted no more than 3,000 tons of copper a year, and Upper Silesian zinc in the early nineteenth century amounted only to about 100 tons a year.

Coal

Europe possessed immense reserves of coal, without which the industrial expansion of the nineteenth century could not have taken place (see p. 413). They occurred in a great many fields, most of them quite small, scattered through most parts of Europe except Scandinavia and the Mediterranean. It is difficult to know how many of these basins were exploited and the volume of the coal obtained before the nineteenth century. There were strong objections to the use of coal. Medical opinion opposed it; it was forbidden in Paris, and in England John Evelyn wrote a virulent tract condemning it. Nevertheless, there is evidence that most of the coalfields were worked in the sixteenth and seventeenth centuries, if not earlier. Coal was brought to London by ship from the coastal field of Northumberland, hence its name of "sea-coal." By 1670 the Rive-de-Gier mines were supplying 20,000 tons a year to the Lyons region, and even Paris, despite the prohibition, obtained coal by river and canal from the coal basins of the "Centre." The growing scarcity of wood was forcing people to turn to coal. It was used increasingly in ironworking as well as for burning lime, making bricks and glass, and for a variety of uses which had previously required wood or charcoal.

It is difficult to trace the growth of coal production in the seventeenth and eighteenth centuries. British output may have reached 250,000 tons by 1600 and 3 million a century later. Thereafter expansion was rapid, and total production exceeded 10 million tons before 1800. Output in continental Europe was very much smaller. The most productive field in France – that of Saint-Etienne–Rive-de-Gier – could not have produced more than 50,000 tons by the early eighteenth century, and total French output was under 500,000 at the mid-century. The coalfield which lay along the Meuse and Sambre valleys in the southern Low Countries was, in the opinion of a contemporary "the biggest and most richly endowed in the continent." It was, in fact, nothing of the kind, but it was accessible; coal outcropped along the valley sides, and it could be distributed by water. Hence it supplied the Low Countries and northern France, and, when in 1713 France lost control of the Mons area, a search began for its continuation in northern France. The coal basin is, however, narrow, and, as it changes direction near Valenciennes, trial bores missed the coal seams; it was not until 1734 that workable coal was struck near Anzin and not before the nineteenth century that the dimensions of the French northern coalfield were discovered.

The southern Low Countries were in all probability the largest source of coal in continental Europe. They supplied coal to the Netherlands and Lorraine and, thanks to improved waterways, to much of northern France. The total production approached 500,000 tons about 1800. Germany had the richest resources in the continent in the vast fields of the Ruhr and Upper Silesia, but this was unknown at the time, and production from the Ruhr probably did not greatly exceed 100,000 tons even at the end of the period. Silesia produced a very great deal less, and at the beginning of the nineteenth century the total production from the whole of continental Europe was not much more than a quarter of that produced in Great Britain.

Consumer goods industries

Between 1761 and 1788 H. L. Duhamel de Monceau published a series of more than a hundred studies of those branches of industrial production which he thought deserving of this attention.[19] He viewed the crafts through the eyes of the aristocracy. He tells us nothing about how coarse cloth was made. His readers' interests ran more to porcelain, cabinet making, and fine inlay work. This, unhappily, reflected attitudes at the time and accords with Arthur Young's judgment (see this chap., under "Manufacturing and mining"). Throughout much of Europe the ruling classes showed no interest in or encouragement for those industries which might have satisfied a mass demand. Great Britain and the Netherlands were the exceptions, and a few enlightened rulers like Frederick the Great of Prussia encouraged them to the best of their ability.

Yet, there were important manufacturing industries engaged in tanning leather and making saddlery, harness, and footwear; in baking bricks and tiles; and in making pottery and glass, candles and soap. Others were more localized. The manufacture of paper spread northward from Spain and Italy, where it was first established, and with it the craft of printing. There were presses in every large or

---

19 *Descriptions des Arts et des Métiers,* 27 vols. (Paris, 1761–88).

medium-sized city, and some, including Paris, Amsterdam, Basel, and Vienna became outstanding centers of book publication.

The use of soap became more general during these centuries, but the raw materials – animal or vegetable fats and wood ash – were not easy to come by. Soap manufacture tended to arise in port cities, like Marseilles and Amsterdam, where the materials could be imported. Coarse pottery was made wherever there was a suitable clay, but the production of refined china and porcelain was less widespread. In the sixteenth century the manufacture of majolica and faience (from Faenza) – coarse ware glazed and enameled – spread from Italy, and potteries were set up widely in western Europe. The mass production of standardized types of chinaware began in England in the eighteenth century. In continental Europe the emphasis was on the manufacture of porcelain, the secret of which had recently been brought from China. A number of porcelain "factories" were established, many of them deriving their skilled craftsmen from the ducal pottery of Meissen, in Saxony. Their products today command very high prices, but in their time few were either successful or long lasting.

TRANSPORTATION AND TRADE

The development of international trade was shaped by the prevailing economic doctrine known as cameralism or mercantalism. In the words of Thomas Mun, one of its many apologists, "we must ever observe this rule: to sell more to strangers yearly than we consume of theirs in value . . . because that part of our stock which is not returned to us in wares must necessarily be brought home in treasure."[20] The accumulation of bullion was seen as an objective of policy. A corollary of this is that a country should never be dependent, unless this was absolutely unavoidable, on another for any commodity. This doctrine was in general tempered by the freedom allowed to merchants to trade as they wished and by the sheer difficulty of applying the law. Only in France and Prussia was there any attempt at rigorous enforcement. Despite these restrictive principles, the total volume of trade grew sharply during the period. During the eighteenth century alone British imports more than quadrupled, and exports increased by nearly 700 percent. The foreign commerce of France is said to have grown by over 300 percent. Most of Europe's external trade was with colonial dependencies in the New World and Asia. The Dutch, in particular, made Amsterdam an emporium for oriental goods. Internal trade was hindered by the vast array of tariffs and tolls, as well as by the physical obstacles presented by bad roads and barely navigable rivers.

External trade

Mediterranean trade recovered in time from the immediate impact of the Portuguese discoveries. Both Genoa and Venice continued to act as intermediaries in

20 *England's Treasure by Foreign Trade (1664)* (Oxford, 1928), 4.

the trade between Italy on the one hand and Africa and Asia on the other. Only the commodities and, to some extent, the routes changed. Indeed, other ports, like Livorno (Leghorn), Dubrovnik, Ancona, and Spoleto (Split) began to dispute the hegemony of Venice and Genoa. But the greatest threat to the latter came from the northwest Europeans, particularly the British, who from the late sixteenth century entered the Mediterranean and did business directly with the Levant. Furthermore, the merchants of northern Europe had goods to sell in the Mediterranean. In addition to cloth and metals, they brought grain which Mediterranean city-republics needed whenever harvests were poor. In fact, the commerce of the once proud cities of Venice and Genoa, Marseilles and Barcelona declined to a local trade.

At the same time Baltic trade grew in volume and ceased gradually to be dominated by the merchants of the Hanse. Their heirs were the Dutch and the British who carried cloth and wine to the Baltic ports and returned with grain, timber, Swedish iron, and Russian flax. Great Britain wanted primarily iron and naval supplies, a collective term for timbers, masts, pitch, and hemp, but, apart from cloth, had little with which to pay for these goods. The Dutch, backed by the immense and varied trade of Amsterdam, had more to offer and came in time to dominate the northern trade. "By extraordinary enterprise and efficiency, they had managed to capture something like three-quarters of the traffic in timber, and between a third and a half of that in Swedish metals."[21]

The Baltic trade is the earliest for which we have comprehensive statistics. This is because the seaborne commerce of the region was obliged to pass through the Danish Sound, where all ships were obliged to pay toll on their cargoes. There was, of course, a degree of evasion and smuggling, but the records of the Sound "dues" give an approximate account of the nature and volume of this trade from the late fifteenth century. The dues were not abolished until 1856.

The grain trade was crucial both to Baltic commerce and to the well-being of western and even southern Europe. Its volume varied both with the amount available in the Baltic and with Western Europe's needs and was always greater during famine crises. The grain trade began to decline in the eighteenth century, probably because the west became more regularly self-sufficient. The timber trade, on the other hand, grew continuously, as ships in the west became larger and more numerous. Exhaustion of supplies in the more accessible southern Baltic forced merchants to turn to the vast forests farther north. Riga became the foremost timber port from which "great masts" − those over twelve inches in diameter − were sent to Britain and the Low Countries.

Flax, hemp, and iron were the remaining products of the Baltic region. Flax and hemp were products of peasant agriculture. Bar iron came at first from Sweden, then in the later eighteenth century, increasingly from Russia. The export of iron was closely linked with that of flax. A cargo of flax or hemp was so light that a ship had to take on ballast. Bar iron was used for this purpose, and traveled to

21   Charles Wilson, *Profit and Power: A Study of England and the Dutch Wars* (London, 1957), 41.

the west at a very low cost in consequence. The Dutch trade with the Baltic remained large and lucrative until their country was overrun by the French armies. This left the field free for the British who dominated Baltic trade until timber and iron ceased to be exported in quantity.

The Atlantic trade showed an almost continuous expansion from the time of the first Spanish and Portuguese voyages. The twin foci of the new trade were at first Lisbon and Seville, the former with the finest harbor on Europe's Atlantic coast, the latter more than fifty miles up the navigable Guadalquivir and served by a number of outports, including Cadiz. Portuguese trade consisted from the first of spices and other products of the Orient, requited with cloth and metal goods, mostly obtained from the markets of the Low Countries. Spain brought in bullion in increasing amounts during the sixteenth century, as well as corn, tobacco, and other products of the New World, and exported chiefly food and clothing for Spanish settlers. This trade declined until, in the eighteenth century, both empires were hard put to it to protect the little trade that remained from British and Dutch predators. One must not exaggerate the volume of this Atlantic trade, even at the height of its prosperity. It employed only a handful of ships, and its tonnage, it has been said, was less than that which plied with cargoes of wool and iron along the coast of northern Spain.

Seville and Lisbon were complemented by the ports of the Low Countries, where Atlantic trade met that of northern Europe. In the sixteenth century the most important was Antwerp which had replaced the silting waterways of Bruges. It had a good navigable river, the Scheldt, and a developed hinterland which included the whole Rhineland. It became the northern base of both the Italian and the Portuguese merchants. Ludovico Guicciardini described the intensity of its traffic and the variety of the goods handled in the mid-sixteenth century, incomparably greater than that which passed through the port of Seville. Then it collapsed even more suddenly than it had developed. Sacked by the Spanish soldiery in 1576, and cut off from the sea by the new boundary of the Netherlands, it languished until links with the sea were reopened by the French in 1792.

The mantle of Antwerp was assumed by Amsterdam. The latter had advantages denied to Antwerp. It possessed, together with the many small ports which fringed the Zuider Zee, a vast merchant fleet which traded throughout the northern seas. It developed financial institutions far in advance of those known in Antwerp, and it gave refuge to much of the merchant capital and many of the entrepreneurs driven from the southern Low Countries by the Spanish. It was the merchants of Amsterdam who provided the link between the northern and the Mediterranean trades of Europe, and when in 1595 the first Dutch fleet sailed to the Indies, yet another dimension was added to the trade of Amsterdam. Unlike Seville and Lisbon, Amsterdam shipped manufactured goods for sale to its dependencies and imported in return not only pepper and spices, but, more importantly, tea and coffee, tropical oils, and hardwoods, which the Dutch sold at great profit throughout the north.

Between Seville and the Danish Sound lay a multitude of ports, most of them small, but including some which could take "great ships": Bordeaux, La Rochelle, Saint-Malo, and Le Havre, each serving as the focus of local coasting trade and as intermediaries between it and the great ports. An infinite variety of goods was carried along these coasts: wool and cloth, bar iron and fabricated ironware, wood and fuel, building stone, roofing slates and lime, grain, wine, and saltfish. The Breton sailors were the most active, but the British and the Dutch also played a role. This coasting trade owed its volume in part to the badness of the roads, and it declined sharply when the conditions of overland transport improved.

Some ports grew and expanded their commerce; others declined. Those of the Seine – Rouen and Le Havre – grew with the growth of Paris and the expansion of manufacturing (see p. 338) in their hinterland. Nantes and Bordeaux, both on navigable rivers, grew as the colonial trade expanded, and Lorient was established, as its name suggests, to promote French trade with the East.

There was change and growth also in the ports and commerce of northern Europe. Trade became increasingly concentrated, and in the eighteenth century a small number of great ports emerged, while many of the small lost out in the competition. Bremen, Hamburg, Stettin, Danzig, and Riga all profited. The reason is not far to seek. These ports handled the exports – chiefly grain, timber, flax, and bar iron – brought down the rivers from their hinterlands. The short-distance coasting trade was of less importance in this underdeveloped and thinly peopled region. A branch of this northern trade which was developing during these centuries was that with Russia. This was essentially a "colonial" trade, an export of raw materials and an import of manufactured and luxury goods. At first it went by the long and hazardous route around the North Cape of Norway; later by the shorter, but politically less secure Baltic route. The ports which served Russia were Riga, which did not pass under Russian control until 1721, Tallin (Reval), Narva, and, after 1703, St. Petersburg (Leningrad). They were linked by river and lake with Novgorod, with Moscow, and ultimately with the iron-producing region of the Urals.

Internal trade

Only a small part of Europe's trade passed through its ports. Most moved by road, river, and canal, despite the many obstacles in the shape of tolls and physical impediments. The imposition of tolls led in some cases to the keeping of records, more often to evasion and smuggling, of which there is no record. Many internal tolls were reduced or abrogated in France by Colbert in 1664 and within the Habsburg lands by Joseph II in 1775. But it was not until 1790 that the "thousand bureaux scattered over [France], slowing up traffic by their inspections and bureaucratic controls,"[22] were finally abolished; in Germany such burdensome restrictions remained until the mid-nineteenth century.

The mechanics of trade changed little. They were founded on market and fair.

22   J. F. Bosher, "French Administration and Public Finance in Their European Setting," in *New Cambridge Modern History*, VIII (1965), 565–91, 579.

Fairs declined in importance in the west, as long-distance trade passed to the city merchants, but they remained significant throughout the east until late in the nineteenth century. The market was where the peasant sold his surplus produce and occasionally his homespun cloth. Fairs served a wider area, but in the seventeenth and eighteenth centuries they were becoming less important and more specialized. They were horse fairs, or wine fairs, or just the occasion for rural jollification.

Most people and much of the goods traveled by road. The network of highways changed little. Their surface remained rough, alternately deep in mud or in dust. Travelers would make lengthy detours to avoid the clay lands. Bridges, by no means as numerous as they became in the nineteenth century, were fixed points on which routes converged. Mountain roads might be steeper, but their surfaces were often of hard rock and the going was easier. Many attempts were made to improve the quality of roads. In France, Henry IV appointed a minister to improve their quality, with, it appears, little result. Colbert's efforts met with no greater success, and toward the end of the century, the *Intendants* were given the responsibility. In 1738 the obligation was placed on the peasantry to work on road improvements, and shortly afterward a corps of engineers was created for the purpose.

In Britain the obligation to maintain the roads rested on the local communities, which were loath to discharge it. In the later seventeenth century turnpike trusts began to be established, bodies empowered by law to raise capital, improve roads, and charge a toll on those using them. Hundreds of well-built tollhouses still survive along British roads. Daniel Defoe acknowledged in 1720 that turnpikes "are very great things and very great things are done by them."[23] The speed of travel and the volume of traffic greatly increased, and the industrial development of the later eighteenth century would have been severely handicapped without them.

Little was done to improve roads in central and southern Europe, and nothing in eastern. Obstacles to their improvement, apart from the unwillingness of the authorities to invest the money, were the lack of knowledge of how to construct an all-weather road and the absence from many areas of stone with which to build a firm surface. Rivers and canals provided the only alternative to roads. As means of transport they were generally safer and cheaper, but they were slow; they did not necessarily lie where they were most needed, and there were none which were not at some time during the year rendered unnavigable by flood, ice, or low water. A traveler who went in the late seventeenth century from Budapest to Belgrade used a boat; "the Road by Land," he wrote, "is seldom travell'd [because it is] full of Thieves and Boothaylers. In fair weather you may go . . . in less than eight days, but we were forc'd to stay longer upon the water, in regard of the Cold weather."[24] The distance by road would not have been above two hundred miles and could have been covered in a much shorter time. The design of boats had to

23 *Tour through England by a Gentleman* (London, 1928), II, 119.
24 *The Six Voyages of John Baptista Tavernier through Turky, into Persia and the East Indies* (London, 1677), Introduction, unpaged.

be adjusted to the conditions of the waterway, and navigation to the season. Except on the largest rivers, the capacity of boats was small, less than ten tons, and often less than five. There were no river docks before the nineteenth century; at most there were stone-built quays against which boats tied up for loading and unloading. Even the boatmen who owned and operated them were often only part-time. Not surprisingly, inland navigation was "seasonal, sporadic and intermittent."[25]

In Italy, the Po and lower Tiber were used, and in Spain, the Guadalquivir and the lower courses of Tagus, Duero, and Ebro. France was well endowed with navigable rivers, and Vauban saw in their improvement the chief means of increasing trade. Most were, however, used irregularly. The Rhône, owing to the speed of its current, was useful only for downstream traffic. The Loire was used for conveying salt inland from the "Bay." Only the Seine appears to have been used regularly, and this chiefly for the supply of Paris (see p. 182). The Seine and its tributaries were, in fact, the most used waterway system throughout this period, but the volume of traffic using it was nonetheless small. The goods passing the toll stations between Normandy and Paris in the eighteenth century could not have amounted to more than forty-five thousand tons a year.

Waterborne transport was of far greater importance in the Low Countries, because, as a traveler said of the road from Emden to Groningen, it was "only passable in Summer, for most of the Winter it is under Water."[25] Within the Netherlands much of the travel was "in large cover'd Boats drawn by Horses,"[26] which sailed with the frequency and regularity of a well-conducted bus service. Sir William Temple in the seventeenth century noted the "great rivers, and . . . Canals [which] do not only lead to every great town, but almost to every Village, and every farm-house . . . and the infinity of Sails . . . coursing up and down upon them."[27]

The Rhine, most easily navigated and potentially the most valuable river in Europe, was in a sad state of decline and neglect throughout the period. It had its natural obstacles — the swift current of the upper river, the meanders and cutoffs above Mainz, and the rocky bar at Bingen — but these were not the reason for its neglect. Rather, the river was formerly so useful that it came to be burdened with tolls and restrictive rights of riverine cities (see p. 182). These had brought river traffic almost to a halt. Goethe described its "empty stillness," broken only by the "market boat" which circulated near the larger cities. The immense potential of the Rhine's tributaries went unused before the nineteenth century, and when Goethe, in his somewhat precipitate flight from the battle of Valmy, took a boat down the Moselle, he had the whole river to himself.

The north German rivers were used by local traffic and for floating timber down from the mountains. Beginning in the seventeenth century short, linking canals

25 J.-Y. Tirat, "Circulation et commerce intérieur dans la France du XVIIᵉ siècle," *XVII Siècle,* nos. 70–1 (1966): 71.

26 William Bromley, *Several Years Travels, Performed by a Gentleman* (London, 1702), 271.

27 *Observations upon the United Provinces of the Netherlands,* ed. G. N. Clark (Oxford, 1932), 93.

were cut between them, and one — the Stecknitz Canal, between the Elbe and Lübeck — allowed the Danish Sound and its tolls to be circumvented. The early canals decayed, but Frederick the Great rebuilt those between the Elbe and the Oder and even made a link by way of the Warthe with the Vistula. The Prussian government also had a canal cut from the Oder to the Upper Silesian coalfield — the Klodnitz Canal — to facilitate the shipment of coal to Berlin. The Vistula was far from suitable for navigation, being shallow in summer and liable in winter to ice and severe floods. Nevertheless, it was one of the most used. Grain was brought by wagon to the river at Kazimierz Dolny, eighty miles above Warsaw, and taken downriver to the port of Danzig (Gdańsk). The river was also used for rafting timber. Traffic on the Vistula was interrupted by the Partitions but continued at a reduced level until taken over by the railways. The Polish magnates had a perhaps exaggerated view of the wealth to be had by exporting grain and timber from their lands in eastern Poland and Lithuania, and they cut canals linking the Vistula with the Niemen and the Prypeć. But the commercial results scarcely justified their expectations.

The sixteenth and seventeenth centuries saw great canal-building activity in France. King Francis I had ambitious plans and even discussed their implementation with Leonardo da Vinci. It was not however until the next century that canals were constructed to link the Garonne, and thus the Bay of Biscay, with the Mediterranean and the Loire with the Seine. The former — the Languedoc Canal — has been described as "the greatest feat of civil engineering in Europe between Roman times and the nineteenth century."[28] It aroused the admiration of contemporaries, and its technical and economic success led to several others, which were less successful or were left incomplete when the revolutionary wars began.

Canal building in Britain was more carefully conceived and more expertly carried out. Even here, however, not all canals were successful. The construction of canals to serve the needs of industry began in the mid-eighteenth century with short canals on or near the Lancashire coalfield. In 1761 the Bridgewater Canal, a prototype for many others, was built to bring coal to the mills of Manchester. This was followed by "trunk" canals which ran across country, linking London with the Midlands, the Severn, and the north, and the growing industrial regions with the ports. Many of these canals served a vital function, carrying coal and raw materials, and were heavily used and highly profitable until the coming of the railway age in the 1830s.

SELECT BIBLIOGRAPHY

General

Braudel, F. *The Mediterranean and the Mediterranean World in the Age of Philip II.* 2 vols. London, 1972–3.

28 A. W. Skempton, "Canal and River Navigation before 1750," in *A History of Technology,* ed. Charles Singer et al., III (Oxford, 1954), 438–70, 459.

The Cambridge Economic History of Europe. Vol. 3, *The Economy of Expanding Europe in the 16th and 17th Centuries.* Cambridge, U.K., 1967.
The Fontana Economic History of Europe. Vol. 2, *The Sixteenth and Seventeenth Centuries,* ed. C. M. Cipolla. London, 1974.
Heckscher, E. F. *An Economic History of Sweden.* Cambridge, Mass., 1954.
Kamen, H. *The Iron Century.* London, 1971.
Marczali, H. *Hungary in the Eighteenth Century.* Cambridge, U.K., 1910.
Temple, Sir William. *Observations upon the United Provinces of the Netherlands,* ed. G. N. Clark. Oxford, 1932.

Population

Berkner, L. K. "The Stem Family and the Developmental Cycle of the Peasant Household: An Eighteenth Century Austrian Example." *American Historical Review* 77 (1972): 398–418.
Clark, Sir George. *War and Society in the Seventeenth Century.* Cambridge, U.K., 1958.
Jutikkala, E. "The Great Finnish Famine in 1696–97." *Scandinavian Economic History Review* 3 (1955): 48–63.
Ohlin, G. "Mortality, Marriage and Growth in Pre-Industrial Population." *Population Studies* 14 (1960–1): 190–7.
Post, J. D. "Famine, Mortality and Epidemic Disease in the Process of Modernization." *Economic History Review* 29 (1976): 14–37.
Vincent, P. E. "French Demography in the Eighteenth Century." *Population Studies* 1 (1947–8): 44–71.

Urban settlement

Hiorns, F. R. *Townbuilding in History.* London, 1956.
Hufton, O. H. *Bayeux in the Late Eighteenth Century.* Oxford, 1967.
Kany, C. E. *Life and Manners in Madrid, 1750–1800.* Berkeley, Calif., 1932.
Kaplow, J. *Elbeuf during the Revolutionary Period: History and Social Structure,* Baltimore, Md., 1964.
Murray, J. L. *Amsterdam in the Age of Rembrandt.* Norman, Okla., 1967.
Murray, J. L. *Antwerp in the Age of Plantin and Brueghel,* Norman, Okla., 1972.
Pike, R. *Aristocrats and Traders: Sevillian Society in the Sixteenth Century.* Ithaca, N.Y., 1972.
Pike, R. *Enterprise and Adventure: The Genoese in Seville and the Opening of the New World.* Ithaca, N.Y., 1966.
Van der Wee, H. *The Growth of the Antwerp Market and the European Economy.* 3 vols. Louvain, 1963.

Agriculture

Blum, J. "The Rise of Serfdom in Eastern Europe." *American Historical Review* 62 (1956–7): 807–36.
Bourde, A. J. *The Influence of England on the French Agronomes.* Cambridge, U.K., 1953.
Forbes, R. J. "The Rise of Food Technology (1500–1900)." *Janus* 47 (1958): 139–55.
Forster, R. "Obstacles to Agricultural Growth in Eighteenth Century France." *American Historical Review* 75 (1970): 1600–15.
Goldsmith, J. L. "Agricultural Specialization and Stagnation in Early Modern Auvergne." *Agricultural History* 47 (1973): 216–34.
Goubert, P. "The French Peasantry of the Seventeenth Century." *Past and Present* 10 (1956): 55–77.

James, P., ed. *The Travel Diaries of Thomas Robert Malthus*. Cambridge, U.K., 1966.

Lough, J., ed. *Locke's Travels in France 1675–1679*. Cambridge, U.K., 1953.

Marczali, H. *Hungary in the Eighteenth Century*. Cambridge, U.K., 1910.

Salaman, R. N. *The History and Social Influence of the Potato*. Cambridge, U.K., 1949.

Slicher van Bath, B. H. "Agriculture in the Low Countries (c. 1600–1800)." In *Relazioni del X. Congresso Internationale di Scienze Storiche*, IV, 169–203. Florence, 1955.

Vives, J. V. *An Economic History of Spain*. Princeton, N.J., 1969.

Wagret, P. *Polderlands*. London, 1968.

Wyczanski, A. "Tentative Estimate of the Polish Rye Trade in the Sixteenth Century." *Acta Poloniae Historica* 4 (1961): 119–31.

Young, A. *Travels in France during the Years 1787, 1788, 1789*. London, 1915.

Zytkowicz, L. "An Investigation into Agricultural Production in Masowia in the First Half of the Seventeenth Century." *Acta Poloniae Historica* 18 (1968): 99–118.

Manufacturing

Albion, R. G. *Forests and Sea Power*. Cambridge, Mass., 1926.

Cipolla, C. M. "The Decline of Italy: The Case of a Fully Matured Economy." *Economic History Review* 5 (1952–3): 178–87.

Hobsbawm, E. J. *Industry and Empire*. Harmondsworth, 1969.

La Force, J. C. *The Development of the Spanish Textile Industry, 1750–1800*. Berkeley, Calif., 1965.

Nef, J. U. "Industrial Europe at the Time of the Reformation." *Journal of Political Economy* 49 (1941): 183–224.

Nef, J. U. *Industry and Government in France and England 1540–1640*. Ithaca, N.Y., 1957.

Nef, J. U. *Rise of the British Coal Industry*. 2 vols. London, 1932.

Nef, J. U., "Silver Production in Central Europe." *Journal of Political Economy* 49 (1941): 575–91.

Wilson, C. "Cloth Production and International Competition in the Seventeenth Century." *Economic History Review* 13 (1960–61): 209–21.

Commerce

Astrom, S-E. *From Cloth to Iron: The Anglo-Baltic Trade in the Late Seventeenth Century*. Helsinki, 1963.

Davis, R. "England and the Mediterranean, 1570–1670." In *Essays in the Economic and Social History of Tudor and Stuart England,* ed. F. J. Fisher. Cambridge, U.K., 1961.

Friis, A. *Alderman Cockayne's Project and the Cloth Trade*. Copenhagen, 1927.

Hinton, R. W. K. *The Eastland Trade and the Common Weal in the Seventeenth Century*. Cambridge, U.K., 1959.

Kent, H. S. K. *War and Trade in the Northern Seas*. Cambridge, U.K., 1973.

Oddy, J. J. *European Commerce*. London, 1805.

Pullen, B. *Crisis and Change in the Venetian Economy*. London, 1968.

Ringrose, D. R. *Transportation and Economic Stagnation in Spain 1750–1850*. Durham, N.C., 1970.

Verlinden, C. "From the Mediterranean to the Atlantic: Aspects of an Economic Shift." *Journal of European Economic History* 1 (1972): 625–46.

The Industrial Revolution
and after

A period of increasingly rapid change in the later eighteenth century was interrupted by the revolutionary and Napoleonic Wars. When peace returned in 1815
there was revealed the immense gulf separating the levels of technology in Britain
from those in a continent which had been ravaged by war.

The first chapter of Part IV surveys the levels achieved by Europe at this time.
Population in the British Isles had not ceased to grow while that in much of
continental Europe was stunted by the exigencies of war. In Great Britain the
selective growth of cities which had characterized the previous period continued
unabated, whereas there was little expansion on the continent. The slow progress
in rebuilding the structure of agriculture was halted everywhere except in Great
Britain and Scandinavia, which suffered little direct loss from the wars. But it was
in manufacturing that the relative backwardness of continental Europe was most
apparent. At a time when the factory system was spreading in Britain and account-
ing for an ever-increasing proportion of total output, the use of mechanical power
– at least above the level of the humble water mill – was rare in continental
Europe. Commerce, lastly, had to rebuild itself after the wars, though interruptions to seaborne trade had been less than might have been expected.

The expansion of the European economy during the nineteenth century and the
profound changes which took place in its spatial distribution form the substance
of Chapter 11. The economic forces which governed this evolution are only touched
upon, emphasis being given to the changing spatial patterns which resulted. Underlying the rapid changes of this period was the revolution in transport and communication. This was fundamental to the growing concentration of industry, to
the increasing specialization of production, and above all to the speed of interaction between producer and market. Not only could producers reflect every change
in popular demand, but innovation could spread with the speed of the newly
invented postal system.

Spatial developments in the European economy during the century can be summarized in six areas. (1) In the first place the use of labor was becoming less
intensive and its effectiveness increased. This was true no less of agriculture than
of manufacturing. The result was a marked increase in production thus creating at
least the potential for improved material standards.

(2) Change and growth, secondly, were least conspicuous in agriculture for

reasons which have already been elaborated (see Chap. 9, under "Tools and technology"), and traditional modes of cultivation continued in use until the end of the century in some areas. Nevertheless, there was a growing specialization in agricultural production. This was most noticeable in the growing of vegetables and fruit and in the production of milk, cream, and butter for the urban markets. Specializations owed as much to the proximity of a large market as to physical conditions. Examples are cited from greater London, the Paris region, the lower Rhineland, and the Low Countries of the effects of urban demand on rural land use. But specialization was not restricted to these branches of production. Wine growing and cheese making were other areas in which a narrow specialization went with improved quality.

(3) The great burst of innovative activity was experienced most intensely in manufacturing. Fundamental to these changes was the application of mechanical power, in the first instance with the steam engine and only later the steam and water turbine and the internal combustion engine. Coal and other forms of fossil fuel were a "gross" material, in that they were totally consumed in the process of manufacturing. In no way were they ever a component part of the finished product. The economies of transportation dictated that manufacture should be carried on as close as was practicable to the sources of fuel. During the nineteenth century this meant that manufacturing industries were attracted to the coalfields. Even the smallest enjoyed a short-lived period of prosperity. But in the long run there had to be some relationship between the scale of investment in manufacturing and the total fuel resources available to support it. It was quickly realized that many small coalfields lacked the substance to maintain a significant growth, and after a flurry of activity they were abandoned. Indeed, one can distinguish three phases of industrial activity. The first was the widely scattered craft of the artisan who used, at most, the power of the local stream. The second was characterized by larger units of production which for a period made do with small resources in fuel. France is, for example, strewn with such moribund or abandoned centers of manufacturing. The last stage was the shift – in many cases the physical transfer of whatever moveable assets the industry possessed – to sites where available resources – coal or iron ore – would not be exhausted in the foreseeable future.

This is the rationale of the growth of manufacturing on, or in the close vicinity of the coalfields. But growth begets growth. Many industries, whose dependence on mineral fuel was minimal, nonetheless moved into these burgeoning industrial regions. Many sought to use the infrastructure – transportation, banking, commerce – which had been developed. Others were attracted by the market which such an industrialized region afforded both for capital goods and for the consumer goods demanded by a large and growing work force. One would be rash to conjecture what fraction of Europe's growing manufactures had by the early twentieth century been attracted to the vicinity of the coalfields. That it was very large is apparent. It included much of Great Britain's heavy and textile industries, and a large proportion of the iron and steel industry in western and central Europe.

(4) As the century wore on a contrary tendency began to show itself. Increasing fuel efficiency made manufacturing less dependent on coal; the completion of the railroad net made it possible to deliver coal without great cost to places remote from the mines, and to a limited extent the building of large capacity canals assisted this process. Before the century's end a new, dispersed pattern of industrial production began to supplement that of densely settled industrial regions.

(5) Throughout the century Europe continued to be dotted with decaying, as well as with growing industries. Rural craftsmen did not, as a general rule, migrate with the tools of their trade from their workshops in the small towns and villages. They remained on the job, trying desperately to hold at bay the competition of factory industry by trimming their costs and making what adjustments they could. In this way, protoindustry lasted through the nineteenth century, but it attracted little new labor and became increasingly restricted to branches of production which did not lend themselves to mechanization. Toward the end of the century a high proportion of its labor force consisted of aged women practicing traditional crafts of lace making, embroidery, and stocking knitting.

(6) The increasing scale and specialization of production within Europe was matched by a growing volume of trade, both intra-European and with the rest of the world. Europe's increasing population and growing industrial production necessitated ever-increasing volumes of imported foodstuffs and raw materials. The gigantic cotton industry – aside from that in Russia – was supplied entirely from overseas; much of the wool and timber was imported, and production of the ores of both ferrous and nonferrous metals had increasingly to be supplemented by imports. At the same time, imports had to be requited by the export of manufactured goods, which in addition to paying for imports, increased the scale and marginal productivity of European manufacturers.

The consequence of these changes was the increased availability of goods but it took time for the advantages to spill over to the mass of the population. The profits of manufacturing during the first half of the century tended to be reinvested and, in the latter half, to be passed on in shorter working hours and better living conditions of the populace. In the latter respect developments in public utilities, in the diversification of food supply, and in public health were rapid in much of Europe during the last third of the nineteenth century.

In tracing the resulting changes in the spatial pattern of human activity, they have been grouped, as in previous chapters, under the following heads: population and its distribution, urban growth, agriculture, manufacturing, and commerce. But it must be emphasized that the growing integration of the continent has meant that these aspects of Europe's geography no longer existed – if, indeed, they ever did – in separate compartments. They were becoming ever more intimately bound up with one another, each influencing every other.

The last chapter is merely a summary of one which could be written on the geography of that Europe which was torn to pieces in the war of 1914–18. It marks the culmination of the several lines of development presented above. A new

Europe emerged from that conflict, with new states, changed boundaries, and different hopes and aspirations. It was no longer the "workshop of the world." It had lost markets and was soon to feel the competition of producers in Asia and the Americas. The sense of weakness and frustration led to renewed attempts by some European nations to assert themselves with consequences which were disastrous for themselves and the world. It was indeed a different Europe which emerged scarred and disfigured, from over four years of the bloodiest war Europe had known.

IO

Europe on the eve of the Industrial Revolution

The statesmen who gathered at Vienna to bring back peace to a war torn continent set themselves to restore the conditions which had prevailed before the wars began. This proved impossible; too many of the changes of the previous decades were irreversible. This was especially the case in Germany, where the number of separate and autonomous political units was reduced from more than three hundred to thirty-nine. The German empire was snuffed out in 1806, without as much as a whimper. In 1815 it was restored, no longer under the auspices of the Austrian Habsburgs, but as the German Confederation, or *Bund,* dominated by Brandenburg-Prussia (Fig. 10.1). In western Europe, political boundaries were smoothed out, and much of its feudal debris of enclaves and exclaves was tidied up. France lost marginally and, in retrospect, significantly. Much of the Saar coalfield and of the ironworking Sambre Valley were lost respectively to Prussia and the United Netherlands. Savoy and Nice were restored to the Sardinian kingdom, only to be regained in 1860. Fear of renewed French aggression led to the incorporation of the southern Low Countries, previously Austrian, in the United Netherlands, the purpose being to create a powerful buffer to French expansion. This settlement proved to be unacceptable in the southern Low Countries, which in 1831 broke away to form the kingdom of Belgium, its independence and inviolability guaranteed by the powers.

Changes were more fundamental in eastern Europe. Napoleon's Grand Duchy of Warsaw, a kind of revived Polish state created from the Prussian and Austrian shares of the Partitions, was given to the Russian tsars in their personal capacity. Not until 1864 was it fully incorporated into the Russian empire. Finland, previously a dependency of Sweden, was also given to the tsar as a semiautonomous Archduchy, while Norway was united with Sweden.

The Habsburg empire continued to be an untidy grouping of peoples. It consisted of the strictly Austrian lands, centering in Vienna; the Czech lands of Bohemia and Moravia, and those which Austria had been allowed to retain from the Partitions of Poland. These consisted of Galicia, Lodomeria or the territory of Lwów, and Bukovina. To these had been added the lands of the Hungarian crown, including Transylvania and Croatia. Along their border with the Ottoman empire the Habsburgs maintained the Military Frontier, a zone of defense separately administered from the rest of the empire, and along the shore of the Adriatic Sea,

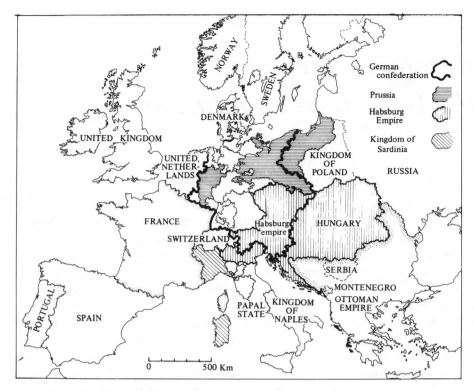

10.1. Political map of Europe after the Napoleonic Wars

Austria extended a long finger of territory almost to Dubrovnik. Lastly, the Habsburgs incorporated, as spoils of the Napoleonic empire, Milan, Lombardy, and the Venetian Republic. Apart from this and the incorporation of Genoa into the kingdom of Sardinia, there was no great change in the Italian peninsula.

The Ottoman empire had taken no significant part in the Napoleonic Wars and lay beyond the jurisdiction of the peacemakers. There were stirrings of independence among its non-Turkish population. Montenegro, Serbia, and the Romanian Principalities were effectively independent, though this status was not recognized either by the Porte, the government of the Ottoman empire, or by the great powers.

The Russian empire reached from the shores of the Baltic Sea to the farthest parts of Siberia. It included the steppe as far as the Caspian Sea, but had not yet expanded into the Caucasus region and central Asia. In the west it included the semiautonomous Archduchy of Finland and "Congress" Poland, so-called because its status had been determined by the Congress of Vienna. This vast, backward, ill-organized and poorly governed empire was a power in Europe more because of its potential than its actual resources. It was protected by its vast distances and incapable of being conquered.

POPULATION

A period of population growth had been interrupted by twenty years of warfare. It is difficult to estimate the extent of losses, both direct and indirect. France is said to have lost more than eight hundred thousand men in the military campaigns, and some other countries must have lost proportionately. Indirect losses were small in France, since the fighting largely occurred on other peoples' territory, but unquestionably they were high in the southern Low Countries, in Germany, northern Italy, and Russia. The end of the wars was followed almost immediately by a period of very bad harvests and near famine conditions in parts of Europe. Warfare and the destruction of farm equipment were contributory factors, but the chief reason was meteorological. Mount Tambora in the East Indies erupted in 1815, spreading a blanket of dust around the globe, reducing insolation and giving the coolest summer on record.

There followed an accelerating growth in population. The factors were a more assured food supply, the disappearance of major epidemics, and the appearance of social and economic conditions favoring earlier marriage. A feature of the Napoleonic Wars, in contrast with the Thirty Years War, was that it did not lead to the spread of disastrous epidemics. The plague was finished, as far as most of Europe was concerned, and smallpox, thanks first to inoculation and then to vaccination, was in process of being overcome. There is little evidence for any significant change in the birthrate. The population increase in these years was due almost wholly to a decline in the death rate, particularly that among the very young.

It is not easy to compile a population map of Europe during the years following the end of the Napoleonic Wars. Great Britain, France, and the Iberian countries had held censuses of very variable standards of accuracy, and in Scandinavia the parochial registration of births and deaths was turned into an effective instrument for recording changes in the total population. There are good estimates for Prussia and Italy, but for most of the rest of Europe there is nothing better than crude estimates of aggregate population. For much of Europe there is no detailed information before the mid-nineteenth century, and for Russia not before its end. The map, Figure 10.2, relates in the main to data collected in the 1830s. The densities shown would have been greater than those of twenty years earlier, but the general demographic pattern would have been not dissimilar.

Population data are most detailed and most reliable for Great Britain, notwithstanding the shortcomings of the first three censuses. The recorded population is shown in Table 10.1. Its distribution was markedly uneven, much higher in lowland England than in the hilly regions of the west and north (Fig. 10.3). London was already a sprawling metropolitan area of about 1.6 million and the map was beginning to show strong concentrations in the West Midlands, south Lancashire, and the West Riding of Yorkshire, as well as lesser concentrations around such growing industrial centers as Bristol, Stoke-upon-Trent, Nottingham, Coventry, and Newcastle-on-Tyne. In Scotland, a dense population was beginning to appear

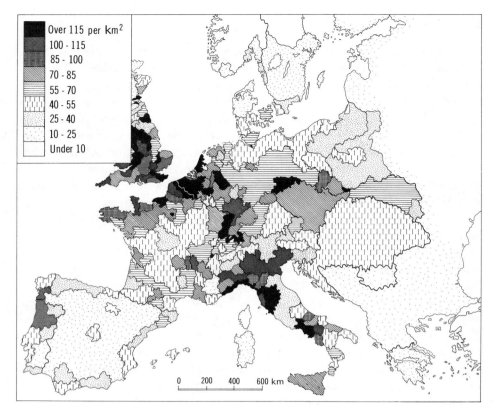

10.2. Population density in Europe, early nineteenth century

Table 10.1. *Great Britain's population in the early nineteenth century (in thousands)*

	1811	1821
England and Wales	10,164	12,000
Scotland	1,608	1,806
Ireland	—	6,802

along the lower Clyde, on the Lanark coalfield and across the central lowlands. But one of the most marked features of the map was the relatively high density over much of Ireland. Most of the areas of high density in Great Britain were due to coal mining and the development of manufacturing. In Ireland there was no such development at this time, and a dense and growing population lived almost exclusively by agriculture and in abject misery.

At the end of the Napoleonic Wars France had a population of about 30 million, the highest of any European country with the exception of the Russian empire.

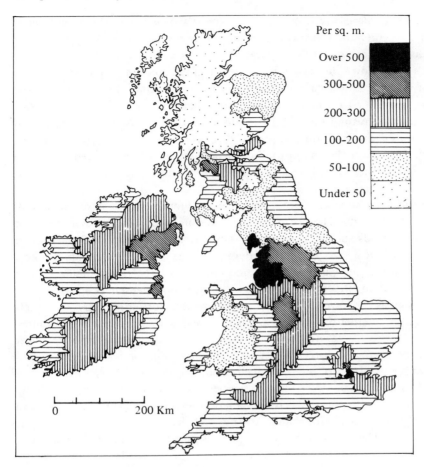

Per sq. m.	
Over 500	
300–500	
200–300	
100–200	
50–100	
Under 50	

0   200 Km

10.3. Population density in the British Isles, according to the census of 1821

But growth had been slowed, not only by wartime losses, but also by the lowered birthrate. The introduction of the *Code Napoléon,* France's civil code, has been blamed for this, because it provided for the division of farms between heirs, and the French peasant had no desire to allow his holding to be broken up. The causes almost certainly go deeper than this, and the birthrate had begun to decline long before the Code was adopted. In any case, there were parts of France where partible inheritance was the traditional practice. The reasons for the lower birthrate are more likely to lie with the social aspirations of the French peasant, with the desire to follow the practices of members of the class higher than his own. It is important that the change was not limited to France itself, but was apparent in the French-speaking areas of Belgium and Switzerland. The reduced birthrate was as much a cultural as an economic phenomenon.

The densest population continued to occupy a broad belt along the north coast from Brittany to Nord, apart from which relatively high densities were found only in Alsace and the Paris and Lyons regions. The low densities of the mountainous regions of the center and southwest were in fact becoming lower, with the migration of peasants from impoverished rural areas to the cities.

In much of the Low Countries agriculture was intensive, but employed a smaller fraction of the population than in most other parts of Europe. In fact, the United Provinces was the first country in which more than half the population was employed in nonagricultural pursuits. The prevalent craft industries, together with the beginnings of factory industry, provided the conditions for an upsurge of population which must at the end of the Napoleonic Wars have numbered about 3.4 million in the southern Low Countries, or Belgium, and 2.4 million in the United Provinces, or Netherlands.

The political fragmentation of Germany makes any computation of its population extremely difficult. The German Confederation, which included at this time both the Czech lands and Austria proper, is estimated to have had a population of about 23.5 million in 1816. The kingdom of Prussia, which made up almost a third of the area of the Confederation, and embraced large areas outside it, had about 10.35 million. Prussia embraced some of the most densely peopled areas of Germany, such as the lower Rhineland, where manufacturing industry was developing, and also much of the sparsely populated east, where great estates had hitherto been cultivated by servile labor. The kingdom of Saxony was, like the lower Rhineland, becoming industrialized, and had about a million and a third, a density comparable with that of the lower Rhineland. Population density varied greatly in other parts of Germany. The north, together with much of Bavaria, was thinly peopled, but a belt of relatively dense population reached up the Rhine valley and into Württemberg and Switzerland. Austria itself had a very sparse population, except along the Danube valley and on the margin of the Hungarian plain, but the Czech lands of Bohemia and Moravia, with their well-developed domestic manufacturing, constituted one of the most populous areas of central Europe.

With the exception of Denmark, the Scandinavian countries lay on the northern frontier of settlement and agriculture. A climatic fluctuation, which in more southerly latitudes might be nothing more than an inconvenience, would here be disastrous. The people of Norway, Sweden, and Finland lived permanently on the edge of a subsistence crisis, which was relieved only by the introduction of the potato. If spring frosts could be avoided, the potato cropped heavily and reliably, and it appears to have had a demographic influence not unlike that experienced in Ireland.

Denmark, with its more southerly latitude and generally better soils, was, in some degree, insulated from these hardships; it was by far the most densely peopled of the Scandinavian countries, with over a million in 1815. Norway's population was somewhat smaller and was spread around the coasts of the more southerly part of the country. Much of Sweden was an uninhabited wilderness, of value only for its iron ore and its timber, and even these were little exploited early in the nineteenth century. Sweden's population of about 2.5 million was to be found chiefly in the lakes region of central Sweden and in the southern province of Skåne, which in many ways closely resembled Denmark. Finland, which in 1815 had passed from Swedish control to Russian, had about a million, most of whom were to be found along the country's southern coast.

There are no satisfactory data for estimating the population of eastern Europe and the Balkans. Congress Poland may have had about 2.7 million, and Hungary, which included Slovakia, Transylvania, and Croatia, about 8.3 million, of whom some 40 percent were actually Hungarian. The area of southern Poland, known as Galicia and Lodomeria, which had been occupied by the Habsburgs in the course of the Partitions, was agriculturally rich and had a dense rural population. The birthrate was high, and, without any outlet for surplus population, this was to become perhaps the most dangerously overpopulated area in all nineteenth-century Europe.

One can only guess at the population of the Balkan peninsula. Greece had less than a million, Bosnia and Serbia perhaps a half million, and the Romanian principalities perhaps 1.5 million. The rest of the peninsula was still under Ottoman rule and, even including the capital of Constantinople, probably had no more than 5 million. Most lived in the restricted areas of lowland, particularly the plains of Macedonia and the Marica valley, and in the small mountain-ringed plains which are a feature of this region.

The population of Russia is even less susceptible of analysis than that of eastern Europe and the Balkans. It is evident, however, that it was growing rapidly during the first decades of the nineteenth century. It is said to have been about 35.5 million, including Russian-held Poland in 1800. It must have been of the order of 40–45 million in 1815.

The population of Spain and Portugal must have been much reduced in the course of the Peninsular War. That of Spain had stood at about 10.5 million before the war began, and that of Portugal at about 3 million. There is no means of knowing what the losses were, but they were probably made good within a decade of the war's end. Much of Italy suffered little during the wars, and the population continued to rise. By 1815 it had probably reached 18 million. Densities were greatest in parts of the northern plain and in Tuscany, but were increasing in southern Italy, where birthrates were high and there was no obvious outlet for the population.

It is difficult to estimate the aggregate population of European countries, and impossible to assess the regional variations in density within each. Broadly speaking, a belt of relatively high density extended across northern France, the southern Low Countries, and the lower Rhineland. It was in part related to the agricultural productivity of the region. In fact, however, there were other factors. Some regions of relatively low agricultural value, such as western Normandy, show an inconsistently high density because of the development of domestic crafts, especially those associated with textiles. In others, social conditions, among them the practice of partible inheritance, had induced a higher birthrate and a denser population than might have been expected. Mining, smelting, and metalworking industries, even though small-scale and sometimes highly localized, commonly supported a population in areas which would otherwise have been almost uninhabited. By contrast there were areas of high fertility – the Beauce is an example where density might appear abnormally low. Here the social structure, linked as it was with a three-course, open-field system of agriculture, was calculated to discourage early marriage and large families.

Lastly, urbanism contributed greatly to the population density of many areas. In earlier centuries urban population was, by and large, supported by the food-producing capacity of its local region. This set limits to the number and size of cities. By the early nineteenth century urban growth had broken through such limitations, and every large city and urbanized region was dependent on food from distant sources. This was a new phenomenon. Nineteenth-century urban growth, which was just beginning about 1815, would have been inconceivable without a supply of food, in particular of breadgrains, from areas far beyond its local region. In the course of the century, this dependence was to increase, until European metropolitan areas had come to depend on breadgrains from North America and Australia and meat from New Zealand and Argentina.

THE URBAN PATTERN

The urban map in 1815 differed little from what it had been two or even three centuries earlier (Fig. 10.4). Urban population had increased in keeping with overall growth. But this was most significant in the larger cities; there was little increase in the smaller. A feature of the urban pattern during the early decades of the nineteenth century was the rapid growth of large and, in particular, capital cities.

Great Britain was by far the most highly urbanized country in Europe. In England itself almost 30 percent of the population lived in cities of over 10,000 people. Largest, and indeed the largest in all Europe, was London. It had spread far beyond its medieval core, and its built-up area extended from Kensington in the west to Bethnel Green and Hackney in the east, and embraced Southwark and Lambeth to the south of the Thames. Most of this vast conurbation was not administratively part of London, but its population in 1815 was of the order of 1.5 million and was growing at the rate of about 2 percent a year. The expansion and mechanization of industrial production had already made considerable progress and had attracted population to the future industrial regions. Manchester and Liverpool both exceeded 100,000, and Birmingham, Leeds, and Bristol were approaching this total. In Scotland, both Glasgow and Edinburgh had populations of more than 100,000, and Dublin had reached about 175,000.

Continental Europe had not yet experienced the explosive growth of cities which followed industrialization. Paris, with the possible exception of Constantinople, was the largest city in continental Europe, but its population was barely half that of greater London. No other French city even approached the size of Paris. The largest were Lyons and Marseilles, both with about 115,000 at this time. Lyons was the regional capital of east-central France and, furthermore, had an important

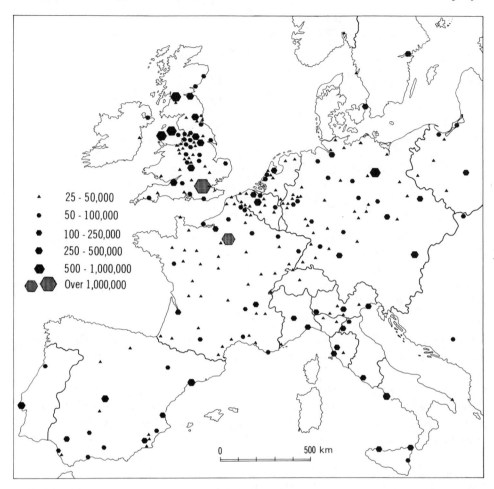

10.4. Urban map of Europe during the first half of the nineteenth century. This was a period of very rapid urban growth, and size categories can be regarded as only very approximate

basic industry in its silk weaving. Marseilles illustrated the rapid growth which characterized all major ports.

There were few large cities in the Iberian peninsula. The largest, Madrid, had grown rapidly – the only Meseta city to do so – and late in the eighteenth century a wall had been built (Fig. 10.5), enclosing 2.5 square miles, though not all this area was built up at this time. Its population was about 175,000. Barcelona, Valencia, and perhaps Seville exceeded 100,000, and Lisbon, capital city of Portugal, was approaching 200,000.

Italy, as always, had a large urban population. Milan had reached 150,000, and Venice a quarter of a million. Rome and Turin, both of them political capitals as

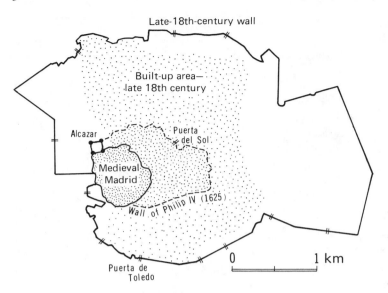

10.5. The growth of the city of Madrid

well as cultural centers, were large, and Naples, with little more than the government of the Two Sicilies to support and employ its people, had considerably over
400,000.

In the Low Countries, Brussels and Antwerp were large, but the former had
ceased to be a political capital, and the latter had been opened to seaborne shipping
only a few years earlier. In the northern Low Countries, Amsterdam had been an
important port since the early seventeenth century and now had a population of
more than 200,000.

There were few large cities in Germany and northern Europe, and most were
either ports or political capitals. Berlin had been growing rapidly. Its population
in 1815 was in the order of 200,000 and was increasing with the growth and
consolidation of the Prussian empire of which it was the capital. Its rival, both in
terms of size and political significance, was Vienna which at this time was appreciably larger with about a quarter of a million people. Other large cities within
the German Confederation were Hamburg and Prague, but regional capitals, most
of them, like Munich, Stuttgart, Dresden, and Hanover, the capitals of German
states, were of no more than intermediate size. The urban explosion in Germany
was still many decades away.

In northern and eastern Europe there were no really large cities. Capitals were
the most populous and in size far outstripped every other in their respective countries. Copenhagen had 100,000, but Stockholm, with about 80,000, was no bigger than a medium-sized English industrial city; Oslo had only about 10,000, and
Helsinki was but a large village. In eastern Europe also the primacy of the capitals
was strongly marked. Warsaw had more than 100,000 and Budapest, still administered as the separate cities of Buda and Pest, had about 60,000. In the Balkan

peninsula, Constantinople, seat of the sultan, had more than half a million but no city in the European provinces of the Ottoman empire, not even Athens, Bucharest, Sofia, or Belgrade, could possibly have had a larger population than 20,000–25,000. The Russian empire was similar: two large cities in St. Petersburg and Moscow, with respectively about 340,000 and 275,000 inhabitants. Elsewhere there were no cities larger than Kazan with some 50,000, Riga with 32,000, and Kiev with 25,000.

Cities at this time had not become the centers of industrial growth, as they were to do in the course of the century. Of course, the crafts were practiced, and domestic industry, such as the silk manufacture of Lyons, was sometimes practiced on a considerable scale. But the metal industries were, by and large, rural, and most factories, except in Great Britain, were located on the banks of flowing streams which supplied their motive power.

AGRICULTURE

The agricultural systems of Europe were in process of change. In much of the continent, the crops and farming practices of three centuries earlier still prevailed, but throughout western Europe and much of central, new methods were being adopted. To some extent these developments were a consequence of the French Revolution and of the widespread break with tradition which resulted. The revolutionaries in France had given legal title to the land to the peasants who cultivated it. This was no egalitarian step. Landless peasants and *brassiers* with only an acre or two got no extra land from estates which were expropriated. But the peasant ceased to pay *cens* or *champart,* the commuted value of his labor services, and restraints on what crops he grew and how he grew them consisted only of the powerful social pressures of his own community. Nevertheless, he could innovate and was likely to have more capital to do so. The resulting improvements in agriculture were very slow, but at least certain preconditions had been established.

The French "reforms" were also adopted in those areas, including the southern Low Countries, which had been temporarily incorporated into France. Elsewhere also the old ways received a shock. New modes were not adopted immediately; indeed, the travels of William Jacobs revealed conditions of appalling backwardness in parts of Germany. Nevertheless, change did come more rapidly in consequence of the Napoleonic experience.

Much of Europe continued to practice a three-course system, with fallow over which the community claimed the right of *vaine pâture.* Areas where the fallow was being cultivated with a catch crop were very small, except in Great Britain and the Netherlands. Most of the land was sown with cereals, the spatial pattern of which changed only very slowly. In France a survey was made by Chaptal of the cereal crops grown and of the areas sown with each. He collected data by *départements,* and his results are shown in Figure 10.6. Wheat was most important, but it covered a really large area only in northern France, the Paris basin, and the south. It was little grown in the northwest and the center. Rye, the alternative

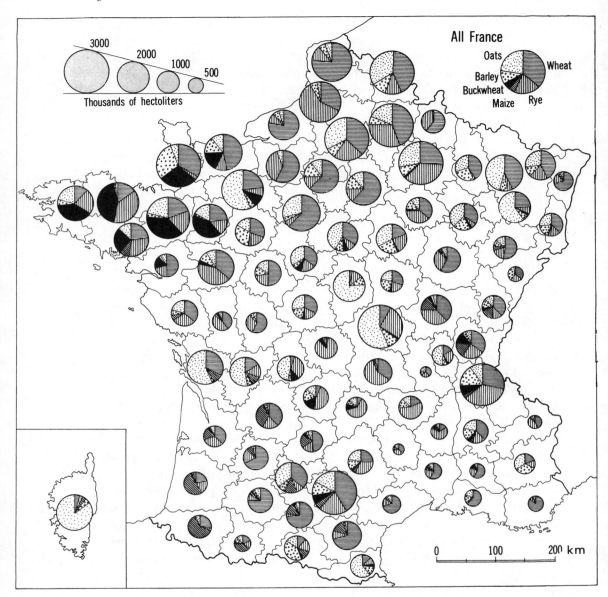

10.6. The cultivation of grain crops in France in the early nineteenth century, by *départe-ment*. [Based on table in de Chaptal, *De l'Industrie française* (Paris, 1819).]

winter cereal, was important on the poorer soils of Brittany and the Central Massif. Oats were the most widely cultivated of spring cereals. Corn was grown only in the southwest, but a feature of the map is the importance of buckwheat *(sarrasin)* in Brittany, where in some *départements* it was the most widely grown of field crops.

Only for Great Britain is there comparable data on cropping, thanks in large measure to the county monographs on agricultural conditions compiled during the previous twenty years. In Germany, rye was the most important breadgrain, and wheat diminished steadily in importance toward the east. In Prussia grain crops occupied almost 40 percent of the cropland, and much of the remainder was cultivated with fodder. In Poland cereals were even more dominant, and the situation was probably similar in northern Europe, though one has nothing more than the observations of travelers like Malthus and Jacobs as evidence.

The conditions by which land was held influenced greatly the ways in which it was used. Only security of tenure would be likely to encourage or even to justify investment in the land. The peasant, it is true, was not likely to make significant innovations, but he was capable of imitating those who did, if, in his hardheaded way, he saw some advantage for himself. The French "reforms" gave him security of tenure. They did not make him a progressive farmer; they only offered an inducement to become one. Indeed, many reverted to the status of dependent leaseholders. There was a vigorous market in land. Some was bought back by its former aristocratic owners; some was acquired by well-to-do burgesses looking for investment. In either case, the new owners leased their land to peasants, much of it on a sharecropping basis.

In western Germany the manorial system had largely disappeared. Services had been commuted for a rent; holdings were generally small, but their occupants had in fact, if not in law, a security of tenure. This, however, was not the case east of the Elbe River. Here a strict and all-embracing manorial rule had survived, together with hereditary serfdom. Indeed, the rigors of the system had been intensified, as the lords seized the opportunity to exploit their lands to the full in order to benefit from the profitable export trade in grain. Early in the nineteenth century, the Prussian government, influenced by the liberalism prevailing in Europe, freed the peasants from all servile obligations with, however, compensation to their lords. Peasants gained possession of their land, but had to sell or mortgage part of it to buy out the claims of their lords over them. In all about 2.5 million acres passed out of peasant hands. The effect was to create a class of peasants with little or no land, dependent on day labor on the estates. It has been debated whether the peasants benefited from the reforms. Some – especially those with large holdings – clearly did, but it is doubtful whether the lot of the mass was much improved, and some, especially those with very small holdings, fared badly in the liberal reforms of the Prussian government.

In Russian-held Poland and in Russia itself there was no reform at this time. Estates, both large and small, continued to be worked by the unpaid labor of the serfs in return for the right to cultivate their own holdings. Such feudal obligations had disappeared from Scandinavia, and there the land was held almost everywhere either in freehold or by long-term leases. In the lands of the Austrian crown, serfdom continued and was not in fact abolished until 1848, but it was less burdensome as a general rule than that which had prevailed in eastern Germany, perhaps because the opportunities enjoyed by the lords for marketing their produce were less. In the Romanian provinces the peasantry continued to hold their tenements by labor services on the demesnes of their lords, and this was probably the only part of Europe where the conditions of peasant tenure were in fact deteriorating. In the Iberian peninsula, the class of free landholding peasants was small and was to be found chiefly in Catalonia and the mountainous north. Over most of the peninsula peasant land was held on lease, generally short-term and onerous, and there was a very large landless class which provided labor on the estates. Attempts to reform the landholding system and to benefit the small cultivator met with little success, since the peasant was called upon to buy out the rights which the landowner had to his services. Southern Italy was also characterized by great estates, worked in much the same way as those of Spain, but much of central and northern Italy was made up of small holdings cultivated on a sharecropping basis.

Quite distinct from the status of the peasantry and the survival of burdensome feudal obligations was the size of the holding which was at the peasant's disposal. Much of the land, except in Great Britain, the Low Countries, France, and Switzerland, was held in estates. Large areas were under forest or waste and were of little agricultural value; part, especially in eastern Europe, was held in demesne and cultivated either with hired labor or with the labor obligations of a servile peasantry. The rest was in peasant holdings held under the varied conditions which have been outlined. One cannot determine the proportions in which these categories made up the totality of estates, but it is clear that a considerable proportion did in fact consist of peasant holdings, for which rent or service was paid.

There can be no question that most of these tenements were too small, though there was everywhere a small group of rich peasants. The optimum size of a holding varied with physical conditions and the varieties of crop grown. It was far larger in northern or eastern Europe than in western or southern. Its adequacy was also dependent in part on whether the peasant had the use of common grazing for his animals and common forest for cutting fuel and keeping pigs. The statistical data are very hard to come by. In France in 1826, "small landowners," with on average only 6.5 acres (2.6 hectares) made up nearly 90 percent of the peasantry and occupied nearly a third of the land. On a holding of this size the peasant may generally be said to have been underemployed and to have suffered from severe shortages. Only with a tenement of 12 to 25 acres, it was said, "does one get the beginning of a sense of security."

Estates and small, freehold tenements were to be found in all parts of Germany; only the "mix" varied one province to another. Great estates were larger and more numerous in the east than in the west, but even in Pomerania and Posen, holdings of more than 370 acres (150 hectares) made up little more than half the area. At the opposite extreme, nearly half the farms in the Bavarian Palatinate were of less than 2.5 acres, and only 5 percent had more than 25. The average peasant holding was larger in Poland, but was in all probability cultivated less intensively.

The situation within the Habsburg lands was even more varied, ranging from the large estates of Hungary, which had resulted from the reconquest of the plain from the Ottoman Turks, to the microholdings of Austrian Galicia, inhabited by what can only be called a rural proletariat. Bohemia and Silesia were characterized by large estates, many of which were broken up into small peasant holdings, the majority of less than 12.5 acres. Similar conditions prevailed in the mountains of Slovakia and in Transylvania.

In the Spanish peninsula, also, estates, many of them owned by the church and the military orders, were large, and peasant holdings impossibly small. Even in Catalonia and the northern mountain belt, where marks of servitude were less in evidence, holdings were far too small. Italy, or at least the northern and central parts, were characterized mainly by small holdings, barely adequate to support a family. Larger units were to be found in southern Italy and Sicily, and in the Tuscan, Pontine, and Po marshes, where the environment was quite unsuited to peasant farming.

It is one of the paradoxes surrounding peasant life that material conditions were probably better in some parts of the Balkans than in central Europe. In Serbia, for example, much of the land was held in units of 12.5 to 50 acres and in Croatia and Dalmatia the family holding was in general adequate. In those parts of the Balkans still under effective Turkish control conditions were far more onerous. The better agricultural land, by and large that in the plains of Macedonia, Thrace, and the Marica valley, was held by the Turks themselves in estates of varying size, cultivated by the forced labor of their Christian subjects, who lived in *chiflik* villages and produced export crops for the profit of their Turkish masters. Their own holdings appear to have been very small. In the most favored areas, *chifliks* covered more than 20 percent of the area. The rest of the land, much of it mountainous and infertile, was held by the native Balkan peasants in small holdings, for which they were heavily taxed by their Turkish masters.

In Poland and Russia most of the land was held in estates. In Poland many of these were very small indeed, less in many instances than a good-sized peasant holding and quite inadequate to support the genteel pretensions of their owners. Toward the east, however, estates were generally larger and were operated with servile labor. The bipartite manor, such as had disappeared from western Europe by the end of the Middle Ages, was still to be found, its lord exacting to the full the services which were owed to him. These obligations had to some extent been commuted for a payment – *obruk* – but the peasant did not thereby become free, and his movements remained restricted. Over much of Russia the peasant was controlled by his village community, or *mir,* far more closely than was ever the case in the west, and he might even find his lands reallocated by his community.

An important factor in the size and fragmentation of lands, whether estates or peasant holdings, was the legal basis of their inheritance. Over much of Europe, especially open-field Europe, the principle of primogeniture prevailed. The lands were inherited by the eldest son. The effect of this was to keep the holding intact. As a general rule this was what the lord of a manor wanted, because it facilitated the administration of his lands. In the case of estates this principle was sometimes extended in the form of entail, the principle by which the estate not only descended to the eldest son, but could not be partitioned or alienated. This rule applied in particular to eastern Germany and to Spain, where it was used to keep estates intact. Any thoroughgoing land reform was dependent on breaking the entails in order to liberate land for peasant farms. But when this was done in Spain the land brought into the market was snapped up by the wealthy members of the bourgeoisie and the nobility, so that it merely resulted in a reordering of estates. The Prussian law of 1807 abolishing the law of entail and creating peasant free-holds met with more success than the Spanish effort, but it left the peasant burdened with debt and obliged in many instances to sell off part of his land (see p. 387).

The other important mode of succession was the partible inheritance, by which the land and other possessions were divided between heirs. It led to the fragmentation of lands, since in many instances the individual strip or parcel was divided. This principle, which had been a local practice in some parts of France, was incorporated into the Napoleonic code of civil law. But in France the worst consequences of the system were obviated by the low birthrate among the peasantry. Elsewhere, however, in Flanders, southwest Germany, Austrian Galicia, and other areas where the principle of partible inheritance prevailed, the fragmentation of land and the increase in the number of microholdings tended to produce an impoverished rural proletariat.

Technical progress

William Jacob, who toured Europe during the years following the Napoleonic Wars, wrote that "the greater part of France, a still . . . greater portion of Germany, and nearly the whole of Prussia, Austria, Poland and Russia, present a wretched uniformity of system. . . . The fields are almost universally unenclosed."[1] In other words, the open-field system prevailed, with its communal restraints on the initiative of the individual peasant. To this Jacob attributed the backwardness which he found almost everywhere. From Spain to the Ural Mountains, with exceptions only in a few progressive areas, fall-sown grain was followed by spring-sown, and then by fallow. Yields and yield ratios were low except in the few areas where more progressive practices had been adopted. The peasant holding in these areas consisted of a number of strips and parcels scattered through the open fields, a wasteful system which limited the progress of each peasant to that of the slowest in his community. In northeast Poland such practices continued until the end of the nineteenth century. Here the area of open-field farming was about five hundred thousand acres. Of this, twenty-five thousand, or 5 percent, was made up of "balks, boundary strips, furrows, access roads." Add to this the incessant and time-wasting disputes and the labor of moving plows and teams between strips, and one has some idea of the impediment to better farming which this system constituted. By 1815 much of England and the Netherlands had been enclosed. Progress was being made in Denmark, where a law of 1781 gave to every peasant the right to consolidate his land into a single holding, and, though more

---

1   *A Report respecting the Agriculture and the Trade in Corn in Some of the Continental States of Northern Europe,* Cambridge University Library, Pamphlets vol. 10, 1828, 361–456.

slowly, in Sweden and Norway. But over most of open-field Europe the institutional and psychological barriers to change were still, even after the traumatic experiences of the preceding twenty years, overwhelming.

It might be assumed that in areas where the open-field system had never prevailed, where land had always been cultivated in compact and enclosed fields, there might have been greater opportunity for innovation and progress. These areas included the highland areas of Atlantic as well as of central Europe and much of the Mediterranean basin. But there is little evidence for agricultural progress in these areas, and the reason is not far to seek. Soils, generally speaking, were poor, and climate adverse. Yields were low, and these regions lacked the capital for any significant agricultural advances. They were, in fact, areas where the population was supported by supplementary craft industries and from which they migrated in large numbers during the nineteenth century.

The tools of agriculture were little different in 1815 from those employed three centuries earlier. The spiked roller for compressing and aerating the soil, advocated by Olivier de Serres, had not gained acceptance, and the horse-drawn hoe, which Jethro Tull developed in England to keep weeds under control, was scarcely to be found in continental Europe. A seed drill was known in England, but its use had spread no farther. Harvesting was still with the sickle even though the scythe, with its longer blade and greater sweep, was available. Manure was little used, because little was available. The peasant sometimes dug marl or burned lime for the land, but only if these were available with little effort.

The numbers of farm animals were increasing, but only in the more progressive regions of Europe, where sufficient fodder crops were available to sustain them, and where they reciprocated by contributing regularly to the fertility of the fields. In France and Germany animals are thought to have contributed from a fifth to a quarter of all farm income, but it varied regionally. It was highest in mountainous areas and in damp lowlands, which could not easily be plowed, and lowest in areas of unreformed open-field farming, where little fodder could be grown.

Transhumance, always important, probably reached the peak of its importance at this time. Sheep from Provence and the north Italian plain went into the Alps in summer probably on a scale not previously known, and short-distance, seasonal migration was regularly practiced within the Alps and in Scandinavia, western Britain, and the Balkans. In Spain, the seasonal migration of the flocks was institutionalized in the Mesta, an association of sheep owners, which succeeded in keeping open the migration routes and preventing the enclosure of cropland.

Agricultural regions

It is difficult, in a Europe in which local communities were basically self-supporting, and local specializations few, to delineate generalized agricultural regions. Nevertheless, five distinct types of farming can be distinguished:

1. *Extensive crop farming,* in which a small part of the land was cultivated on a shifting basis and almost always in a climatically marginal area.

Animal rearing – sometimes transhumant – was important. Such a system was important in much of Scandinavia, parts of Prussia, in the hill country of Atlantic Europe, as well as in hilly and mountainous areas of central and eastern Europe. "Burnbeating," the periodic burning of vegetation in order to cultivate the soil for a year or two, was a feature of this agricultural system in northern Europe.

2. *Animal rearing* with subordinate crop farming. This category included not only the transhumant pastoralism of southern Europe, but also cattle rearing on the Hungarian plain, in eastern Poland, and on the Russian steppe. Animals were also dominant in the agricultural system in much of the Alpine region, in the Central Massif, and in the marshy lowlands of the Netherlands and northwest Germany. Although animals were sometimes driven from these areas to markets in central and western Europe, they were chiefly important for the supply of wool and hides, butter and cheese. These areas were usually deficient in breadgrains which were obtained from neighboring areas, commonly in return for animal products.

3. *Mixed farming,* in which crop husbandry and animal rearing were combined and were mutually dependent. Such farming assumed many forms, but the most important was the cultivation of roots and other fodder crops on land which had previously been fallow, and feeding it to stock which in turn provided manure for the arable. In enclosed areas of Britain, northwestern Europe, and some parts of Scandinavia it called for crop rotations of increasing complexity, incorporating cereals, roots, and artificial grasses. This category embraced the most progressive areas of European agriculture.

4. *Arable farming* concentrated on the production of breadgrains and is often regarded as the typical agricultural system of preindustrial Europe. It corresponded very broadly with open-field Europe, and was most highly developed in northern France and on the north European loess belt which extended into the Russian steppe. A three-course rotation with fallow prevailed almost everywhere. Animals were of subsidiary importance; cattle or horses were kept for draft purposes, and sheep to make marginal use of the fallow, but, relative to the numbers in other agricultural systems, they were few. Agriculture was, in general, unprogressive, because hedged in by communal and institutional restraints. Nevertheless, on the best soils it was capable of yielding a very considerable grain surplus.

5. *Intensive agriculture,* in which the maximum use was made of the land, covered very restricted areas. It was usually reserved for specialized crops, including intensive produce near the cities, olive groves in Spain, and fruit and hop orchards in Britain and northern France. Along the Po Valley in northern Italy rice was grown by irrigation, and vineyards covered large areas in France, Italy, Spain, and elsewhere.

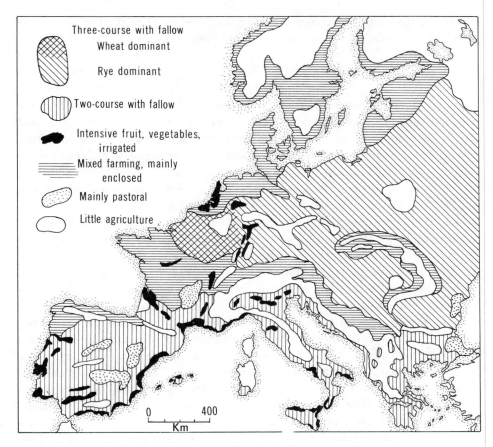

Three-course with fallow
Wheat dominant

Rye dominant

Two-course with fallow

Intensive fruit, vegetables, irrigated

Mixed farming, mainly enclosed

Mainly pastoral

Little agriculture

0   400
Km

10.7. Generalized agricultural regions in Europe in the nineteenth century

The map, Figure 10.7, attempts to show in highly generalized form the distribution of these types of agriculture.

MANUFACTURING INDUSTRIES

When the long period of wars ended in 1815, continental Europe lagged even farther behind Great Britain than in the 1780s. Advances in the textile industries, including the introduction of the power loom; innovations of fundamental importance in the refining of iron and steelmaking; and, above all, the increasing use of the steam engine had together transformed manufacturing industries in Britain. But very little of this had reached continental Europe. Napoleon had offered a reward for anyone who could produce steel comparable with that obtained by the Huntsman process. Several claimed success, among them Friedrich Krupp, but it is doubtful whether any of them had discovered "the Englishman's secret." In Britain, 150 of the improved Watt steam engines were in use, in addition to a number of the older Newcomen-type engines. It is doubtful if there were more than half a dozen altogether in continental Europe.

Great Britain

Although light industries continued to be carried on in rural areas where today one finds none, the basic industries had already concentrated in a few specialized areas. The cotton industry, which had been the leading sector in the industrial advance in the eighteenth century, was concentrated in Lancashire and the Pennine valleys. It had been attracted at first by the waterpower available, but by 1815 a high proportion of the mills was operated by steam engines, and this drew the industry toward the coalfields. The attraction of Lancashire proved to be greatest, because the raw cotton, brought in through the port of Liverpool, could be distributed by barge. Manchester, with the navigable Mersey, was ringed with industrial towns: Stockport, Oldham, Rochdale, Bury, all of them engaged in spinning and weaving cotton. Spinning was by now entirely mechanical. Power looms were in use, but at this date offered little advantage over the old handloom, so that much of the weaving was still done in the home and cottage.

Small woolen mills in Lancashire were converting to cotton, but on the other side of the Pennines the woolen and worsted industries were expanding rapidly. Leeds was the focus of production, and mills lay along the Pennine valley. As in Lancashire, steam power was replacing waterpower, and the industry was concentrated close to the coal. Cotton manufacture was virtually a new industry in the eighteenth century, but woolen cloth had been woven since early times. Western Yorkshire began to take over the role of other clothworking areas, especially the west country and East Anglia. These continued to produce a good quality cloth but suffered from the competition, and there was much unemployment.

The several branches of the iron and steel industries were growing no less rapidly than textile manufactures, and, like the latter, were concentrating in areas where factor costs were lowest. The scattered charcoal furnaces had mostly closed down; the last in the Weald was blown out a few years earlier and only a handful remained active in the Forest of Dean and northwest England. For the rest, iron was smelted in coal-fired blast furnaces, located on or very close to the coalfields. Four iron-smelting districts had developed. The oldest and still probably the largest was in Shropshire, close to where Abraham Darby had first used coke successfully in the furnace. The second lay in Staffordshire, to the west and northwest of Birmingham. A third developed on the coalfield of West Yorkshire, Derbyshire, and Nottinghamshire, and the last and most recent was in the coal-mining valleys of South Wales. All had an assured supply of fuel, and most used ore which occurred in the coal series. Much of the iron was refined to soft iron, either in the puddling furnace, which was of rapidly growing importance, or on the hearth. But castings were assuming a new significance. The cast iron bridge built across the Severn at Ironbridge, near Coalbrookdale, was a prototype of many iron structures. Even primitive rails for hauling coal were of cast iron. Of course, some of the soft iron was converted to steel, particularly in Yorkshire, where it supplied the cutlers of Sheffield, and in the West Midlands where it was absorbed by a rapidly developing engineering industry. The growing British production was making unnecessary the import of bar iron from Sweden and Russia. There are no reliable statistics of production for this date, but the best estimates suggest that pig iron production in Britain amounted in 1806 to about 250,000 tons, and in 1820 to about 400,000. To this should be added a small but significant import of Swedish bar iron, which was particularly important during the war years.

The increase in manufacturing production summarized here would have been impossible without a commensurate output of coal. British production had exceeded 10 million tons before 1800, and in 1815 was possibly of the order of 12 to 15 million. The largest output was from the West Midlands, where the iron industry was growing most vigorously. Next came the Northumberland and Durham field which lay on the coast and shipped coal to London and the southeast. Much of this growing output of coal was consumed by steam engines and in the ironworks. Both were inefficient and extravagant, and their demands were heavy. It has sometimes been assumed that Britain's early industrialization was due to the abundance of coal. In fact, however, the process of industrial growth had made much headway before mineral fuel became important. The early factories were worked by waterpower, and it was not until the latter part of the eighteenth century that coal and coke displaced charcoal on any significant scale in manufacturing.

There was one important exception to the late adoption of coal for these purposes, and that was in the metalliferous mines, chiefly in the southwest of England. The veins which bore the ores of tin and copper, lead and zinc ran deep into the crust. By the seventeenth century many mines were too deep to be drained naturally, and pumps were essential if the metals were to continue to be extracted. Primitive devices worked by horsepower or waterpower proved inadequate, and mining would have declined or even come to an end without steam-operated pumps. Until late in the eighteenth century the mines – metalliferous rather than coal – were the chief market for steam engines, and most of the improvements made in them were for the purpose of increasing their efficiency in the mines. They allowed southwest England to become by 1815 the world's largest tin producer and a significant and growing source of copper.

The Low Countries

The southern Low Countries – the future kingdom of Belgium – came closest to Britain in their industrial development. The coal resources were not the most extensive or even the best in continental Europe, but they were the most well-known and accessible. Mines along the Meuse and Sambre valleys produced about five hundred thousand tons of coal, very little of which was used in local manufactures. Steam engines were used in the mines, but had not yet been adapted to the textile industry, and iron smelting with coke still lay a few years ahead.

Manufacturing industries in the Low Countries, both Belgium and the Netherlands, still consisted primarily of textiles: linen in Flanders, cottons at Ghent, woolens at Verviers and in the Netherlands. In general it was a domestic industry and technically unprogressive, and when in 1815 barriers to imports were ended, the Low Countries felt acutely the harsh competition of British factories. But already there were signs of change. In 1799 William Cockerill, a native of Lancashire, arrived in Verviers and began to build spinning machines such as he had known in England. His success led to the foundation near Liège of the first continental works for constructing textile machinery. But the Belgian textile industry failed to emulate the British; production grew slowly, and it is symptomatic that Cockerill, who had begun in the textile industry, transferred his interests to iron and steel which was to become the growth sector of the Belgian economy.

France

France emerged from the period of the Revolutionary and Napoleonic wars with an industrial structure little changed from that of the *ancien régime*. Attempts to introduce British technology had not been conspicuously successful. Early efforts to use coke in the blast furnace had failed dismally. Machines for spinning cotton were introduced in the 1780s, but had achieved only a limited acceptance by 1815. Everywhere the hand of tradition lay heavily on French manufacturing. But conditions were ripe for change. The Revolution had swept away the whole apparatus of guilds and regulation. The peasantry was gaining a greater purchasing power, and the country was opened up to both the industrial products and the manufacturing technology which had been developed in Britain. French manufacture had to progress or succumb.

Textile manufactures were widely dispersed. There were four major areas where the woolen industry, almost exclusively domestic, was pursued. These were the valley of the lower Seine, where it centered in the towns of Elbeuf, Darnetal, and Louviers; northern France, where Lille and its neighboring towns of Tourcoing and Roubaix were developing into a major center of production; Sedan and neighboring places in Lorraine; and lastly, Languedoc, which had lost much of its Middle Eastern market and was in decline.

The other traditional textile manufacture, linen weaving, continued to be practiced across northern France, but it was even less progressive than other branches of the industry and was, furthermore, beginning to feel the competition of cottons. Cotton manufacture had increased steadily and, as in England, had concentrated where restrictions on new branches of manufacturing were least burdensome. These were the lower Seine valley, where cotton rivaled the long-established woolen industry; the Paris region; the Lille district of northern France, where cottons tended to replace linen; and lastly in Alsace and, particularly, in the city of Mulhouse, where Swiss craftsmen were active and Swiss capital was available. Raw cotton had to be imported. This was no great problem in northern France, and the Seine valley and Paris derived their material from the ports of Rouen and

Le Havre. But Alsace lay far from the sea and the raw cotton had to be transported overland by wagon. No major industry could have been located less opportunely in this respect, but the Mulhouse industrialist made up for this by his entrepreneurial skills, and Alsace became the most progressive of the French cotton-spinning and weaving districts. The cotton industry was expanding rapidly in the years immediately following the end of the Napoleonic wars, but it was still small by comparison with that of Great Britain. In 1809 its raw cotton consumption was only a fifth of Britain's but this proportion had by 1820 increased to about a third.

Cottons, woolens, and linen by no means comprised the whole of the French textile industry which ranged from silk to coarse hempen fabrics. Silk weaving continued to dominate the industrial structure of Lyons, which produced high-quality silks for export. The industry had, however, spread northwest to Saint-Chamand and then to Saint-Etienne, where, beyond the jealous control of the "masters" of Lyons, a cheaper material was produced, aimed more toward the domestic market. Saint-Etienne became, in fact, the center of a scattered cottage industry which wove silk ribbons.

As large centers of production gradually took over the production of cotton and woolen cloth, the industry began to die in the countryside and was replaced by a host of derivative industries, which included stocking knitting, lace making, and embroidery. Some of these were traditional crafts, and their adherence to accustomed styles and patterns was of great importance to their market. These craft industries were most important in the northwest – Brittany and Normandy – and in the Central Massif, where they supplemented a backward agriculture.

Central Europe

Central Europe was, with the exception of Switzerland, even farther behind Great Britain than France. Little attempt had been made to introduce the technological advances made in Britain in either the metallurgical or the textile industries. Ironworking was widely scattered, with concentrations of furnaces and refineries in the Lower Rhineland, the Harz Mountains, Saxony, and the Ore Mountains. Output was small and methods traditional. Only in Upper Silesia was any attempt made to progress beyond these levels, and this was due to the initiative of the Prussian government. Much of the small German output of pig iron was refined on hearths of local and traditional patterns to make an immense variety of metal goods. Much of the iron from the Siegerland was drawn into wire in waterpowered workshops and used to make pins, nails, and screws. Some was converted to steel for the cutlery industry which flourished in and near Remscheid; some was forged into chains and weapons. The industry was expanding but its growth was along traditional lines. The same kinds of production permeated the hills which extended through Thuringia to Saxony. Only in Upper Silesia was any technical advance being made. There had long been a small charcoal-iron industry. Late in the eighteenth century the Prussian government sought to profit from the abundance of resources to produce weapons for use in its recurrent struggles with the

Habsburgs. The traditional industry was expanded, and experiments were made with some success with coke smelting. Then, with the help of British craftsmen, a furnace was built at Gleiwitz (Gliwice) specifically to use coke, and this was followed by another – and more famous – works at Königshütte (Chorzów). These developments occurred *on* the coalfield, but this did nothing to prevent the aristocratic landowners of the region from using charcoal to fuel furnaces on their own estates. The fact is that timber was a cheaper and even more abundant resource than coal.

Germany had always been notable for its nonferrous metals and, in the years following 1815, was important for its zinc, lead, and copper. Zinc came largely from two sources, from the Vieille Montagne mines on the Belgian border near Aachen, and from Upper Silesia. Lead was worked in the Ardennes, the Harz, the Ore Mountains of Bohemia and Saxony, and Upper Silesia. Copper ores were less abundant, and the chief source was Mansfeld in the eastern Harz.

Textile industries were widely scattered. The few factories were all very small, and little use was made of waterpower and none of steam. Linen weaving was carried on in much of the northern plain and in Silesia, and woolen weaving had spread from Verviers into the Aachen region, and thence into cities like Gladbach, Rheydt, Elberfeld, and Barmen, wherever, in fact, the metal industries were not dominant. Both the woolen and the linen industries were carried on in south Germany, where they owed much to Swiss initiative.

Although cotton working had been known in south Germany and Switzerland from the Middle Ages, it did not expand greatly before the later eighteenth century. The jenny was adopted for spinning, but power weaving lay in the future. The centers of the growing cotton industry lay in the Lower Rhineland, where it was displacing linen, in south Germany, and, above all, in Saxony. Chemnitz was an important center, and the industry was spreading to Zwickau, Plauen, and many of the small towns which bordered the Ore Mountains.

The silk industry, established at Krefeld in the early eighteenth century, had grown until it dominated the city and effectively excluded other branches of textile manufacture. It had become the Lyons of northern Europe, and, like Lyons, had spawned other branches of silk weaving at nearby towns, especially at Elberfeld and Barmen.

Sweden and Russia

Only in Sweden and Russia was a traditional iron industry still practiced on a large scale. The reasons lay in the quality of the Swedish product and the cheapness of the Russian. Swedish bar iron was refined at countless small works scattered through central Sweden. Lack of fuel prevented Sweden from adopting most of the innovations made in Britain; nevertheless, bar iron continued to be by far the largest Swedish export after the collapse of copper mining, and its quality even commanded a market among cutlers and toolmakers in Britain.

Within Russia, a short-lived attempt under Catherine II to develop manufacturing – mainly of luxury goods on the French model – had withered, and the only significant industry in the early nineteenth century was iron smelting and refining. It had great advantages – the abundance of charcoal and ore, and the cheapness of the servile labor which it employed. But it also suffered from the handicap of distance. The chief ironworks were in the northern forests and beyond the Ural Mountains. The hauling of ore and fuel to the furnaces and of the metal to the ports added to its cost. Nevertheless production was of the order of 165,000 tons – the highest in the world – at the beginning of the nineteenth century. Much of it had been exported, but this trade was reduced both by the political situation and also by the expansion of British industry. For the rest, manufacturing was of negligible importance. There was no mass consumption of goods, and the demands of the nobility were largely met by imports. The government encouraged only those industries necessary for the support of the military.

Eastern Europe

There was little manufacturing in eastern Europe, from the Baltic to the Aegean, that was not carried on domestically and for local consumption. Iron was smelted on a not inconsiderable scale in southern Poland. There were furnaces and refineries scattered through the Carpathian Mountains and Transylvania, and, it is said, there were "almost one hundred smelting sites across the Bulgarian lands." All were small and backward, even by the standards of central Europe. Indeed, the only center of ironworking that showed any promise was that which had grown up on the good ores of Styria and Carinthia in the eastern Alps. But even here growth was hindered by distance from markets.

The textile industry of eastern Europe was broadly similar in that it produced a rough woolen cloth for a predominantly local market. In Poland, flax working and linen weaving were important. But within the Habsburg empire, workshops – more weaving sheds than factories – were active in northern Bohemia and Moravia. Many were built as annexes to the homes of landowning families which expected in this way to gain some profit from the labor which they "owned." Most enterprises were engaged in wool and linen weaving, but the influence of south Germany and Switzerland was showing itself in the adoption of cotton in some of the larger enterprises.

Southern Europe

The Italian and Iberian peninsulas had once been noted for the quality of their textile and metal products, but in both respects the eighteenth century saw a catastrophic decline. The cloth industry was reduced to the production of rough fabric for local consumption, and the export trade in Venetian, Milanese, and Florentine cloth had virtually ceased. In Spain an overzealous control by guild and government had destroyed a once prosperous woolens industry, which attempts to found "royal" factories had failed to restore. There was, however, one

Table 10.2. *Production of leading commodities, 1815–20*

	Great Britain	France	Total Europe (excl. Russia)
Coal (million tons)	10.5	0.5	12.0
Pig iron (thousand tons)	125.0	140.0	512.0
Raw cotton consumption (thousand tons)	48.0	19.0	80.0

exception which was significant for the future. Barcelona merchants succeeded in expanding the small, local cotton industry until at the beginning of the nineteenth century there were almost a hundred weaving sheds in the coastal towns and villages of Catalonia.

The iron industry was similarly small and unprogressive. Bar iron was made, very largely for export, in the Basque territory and the Pyrenees. In Italy, a small amount of metal of good quality was made in the Alps of Brescia and Bergamo, and ore from the island of Elba was smelted on the mainland of Tuscany.

It is difficult to evaluate the manufacturing industries of Europe in the early years of the nineteenth century. For some countries the number of spindles or the consumption of raw cotton is known, but in general one can only arrive at estimates by extrapolating from later statistics. Table 10.2 summarizes the little that is known. It shows the impressive lead which Great Britain had achieved over every other European country, except Russia. Only France's production of pig and bar iron exceeded that of Great Britain.

THE PATTERN OF TRADE

The Revolutionary and Napoleonic wars came at the end of a period of steadily increasing external trade. Trade was then reduced between European countries, and the periods of peace were too short for any significant volume to redevelop. During the later years trade was diminished yet farther by Napoleon's "continental blockade," which attempted to sever all commercial links between continental Europe and Britain. It failed because Napoleon had lost control of the sea, but it was sufficiently effective to cause grave inconvenience to continental manufacturers and consumers.

Great Britain had become the dominant commercial power in Europe, and it is only for Britain and her commercial partners that satisfactory trade statistics are available. Britain's trade, which had been growing steadily during the eighteenth century, was by the time of the Napoleonic Wars immense. It was dented, but not severely diminished, by the continental blockade, and continued its growth

Table 10.3. *British overseas trade*

	1806		1817	
	Value[a]	%	Value	%
Northern Europe	16,338	28.6	21,885	27.5
Southern Europe	5,070	8.88	12,629	15.87
Asia	5,692	9.96	10,483	13.18
Africa	1,549	2.71	854	1.07
North America	11,894	20.83	12,345	15.52
Central and South America	16,572	29.02	21,367	26.86

[a] Values in thousands of pounds sterling.
Source: Based on B. R. Mitchell, *Abstract of British Historical Statistics.*

when the wars were over. The statistics available suffer, however, from two serious defects and must be regarded as only approximations. In the first place, they necessarily omit the value of goods smuggled, at a time when smuggling was a common and almost honorable pursuit. In the second place, the valuations used tended to be those adopted many years before by the customs service and did not reflect the differential changes between commodities.

Table 10.3 shows the direction of British trade (exports and imports combined) in 1806, before the continental blockade had been imposed, and in 1817, when the immediate consequences of the wars had been overcome. Britain's trade with continental Europe increased, especially that with southern Europe, which had suffered most heavily as a result of the blockade. But overall trade with continental Europe had long been declining relatively, as that with Asia and the New World increased. One cannot use British figures to illuminate trade between continental countries and the overseas world, but qualitative evidence suggests that, except during the war years, that of France and the Netherlands had also been growing. This growth in the non-European trade of northwest Europe was achieved in part at the expense of that of Spain and Portugal.

One can speak in only general terms of intra-European trade. Overall statistics are lacking, and data are available only for Great Britain's bilateral trade with individual countries. There is no comprehensive information on the volume of goods crossing the internal boundaries of continental Europe. This would have fluctuated from year to year during the period of war, and at times it would have been brought to a halt. In any case, the obstacles to intra-European trade, both physical and fiscal, were great, and its volume small relative to that carried on through its ports with Britain and the rest of the world. This latter trade can, for convenience, be classified as "northern" and "southern." The former had been consistently the larger, because it included those two commodities essential to the maritime powers of western Europe: breadgrains and ships' supplies. To Great Britain the northern trade was of critical importance, and in 1801 a naval battle had been fought in the Danish Sound in order to keep the sea route open for British

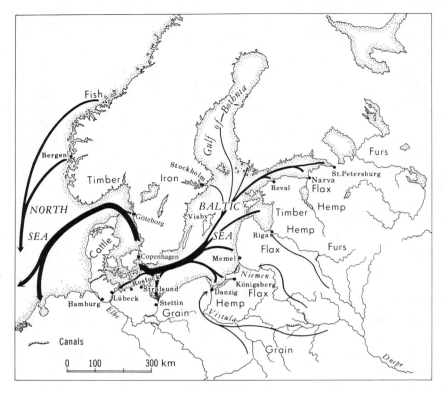

10.8. The principal directions of Baltic trade in the early nineteenth century

trade. A few years later Jepson Oddy published a treatise on British trade which, despite its title,[2] was in effect restricted to that with the Baltic region.

Britain's northern trade was little influenced by the continental blockade. Oddy showed it as dominated by timber, flax, and hemp, largely from the east Baltic region, and by cereals from the south (Fig. 10.8). The small canals which had been cut in Lithuania (see p. 432) extended to the hinterland of the Baltic ports, and hardwood from the Carpathians was even rafted down the Dunajec and the Vistula to Danzig. Much of the ships' timbers came via St. Petersburg and "the finest masts . . . by way of Riga."[3] Some of the timber came from so deep within Russia that it took up to two years to reach the Baltic coast. Transport problems were, indeed, serious. Rye from Galicia was rafted down the rivers and often arrived at the ports so wet that it had to be dried out. This trade, wrote Oddy, "is chiefly in the hands of the Jews, whose interest, one would suppose, would instruct them better." Shipments varied greatly from year to year, not, as one would suppose, with the state of the harvest, but "as the plenty of water in the

2   *European Commerce* (London, 1805).
3   Ibid., 75.

rivers for easy navigation in summer."[4] The trading sphere of the Baltic was being extended into the Ukraine, and the British even proposed to trade with the Ottoman empire by way of the Baltic Sea and the great Russian rivers, a proposal, reminiscent of some sixteenth-century projects, which never reached fruition.

Oddy dismissed Sweden as a country of little commercial importance except for the export of bar iron, and he noted that Denmark's trade, apart from transit traffic through the Sound, was very small. But he found Hamburg playing an increasingly important role as intermediary in the Baltic trade, much of which was tending to come by way of the rivers and canals of eastern Germany to the river Elbe. Norway was a source of timber, especially ships' masts, and of fish, but Oddy summarized its imports as "such necessaries, and the few luxuries that a poor people require, and such a northerly latitude does not produce."[5]

The trade of the Netherlands was interrupted, perhaps more than that of other European countries, by the French conquest and occupation. Trade both with the Dutch empire and with northern Europe was gravely hindered, and the only beneficiary of this was Great Britain. At the same time, the port of Antwerp, reopened to maritime shipping by the French in 1792, began to pose a threat to the future of Amsterdam, and the port of London grew daily. The lower Thames was congested with shipping, and the East and West India Docks were opened in 1802, and the London, Surrey, and Commercial Docks only a few years later. Elsewhere in Britain, at Bristol, Liverpool, and Hull, docks were built at this time, reflecting the rapid expansion of trade which followed the growth of the textile and metal industries. As the statistics cited above show, a third or more of Great Britain's overseas commerce continued to be with the continent of Europe. Some of this consisted of the reexport of goods, such as cotton, which had been imported into Britain from Asia or the New World. The rest of the exports to the continent consisted of manufactured goods. It was a heavily unbalanced trade. Britain's imports from the rest of Europe, consisting of timber, grain, wine, and luxury goods, falling very far short in value of what Europe took from Britain.

Trade with southern Europe was small in volume. North Africa and the Levant were a large potential market but, apart from raw cotton, supplied little that Europe needed, and the oriental goods, once handled in the markets of Alexandria and Antioch, were now brought to Europe in the holds of the British, Dutch, and French ships. The Middle East provided a market for light cloth, notably that made in Languedoc, and cotton and dried fruit formed the return cargoes. Mediterranean trade was more important for France, Spain, and Italy than for northern Europe, but for none was it of great significance, and in volume it paled before the large cargoes handled in the ports of the North Sea and the Baltic.

The growing exports of eastern Europe and Russia called for an increase in the number and capacity of the ports. The Baltic ports were already well established,

4 Ibid., 248.
5 Ibid., 297.

with Riga and St. Petersburg handling most of the trade of northern Russia. The development of the rich "black earth" soils of southern Russia was recent, and the export of breadgrains from here to the west might be expected to grow. At the end of the previous century Russia had occupied the small coastal settlement of Odessa and from 1794 developed it as a grain port. Russia had already secured from the government of the Ottoman empire the right of its ships to navigate the Turkish Straits, and the steppes soon became a major source of grain to the west. But the ports of the Danube mouth were, like their hinterland, less developed, in part because there was no assurance before 1829 that ships from the Romanian ports would be allowed to navigate the Turkish Straits.

SELECT BIBLIOGRAPHY

General

The Cambridge Economic History of Europe. Vol. 6, *The Industrial Revolutions and After,* 2 pts. Cambridge, U.K., 1965.
The Fontana Economic History of Europe. Vol. 3, *The Industrial Revolution,* ed. C. M. Cipolla. London, 1973.
Kuznets, S. *Modern Economic Growth.* New Haven, Conn., 1966.
Landes, D. *The Unbound Prometheus.* Cambridge, U.K., 1969.
Lillin de Chateauvieux, F. "Travels in Italy Descriptive of the Rural Manners and Economy of That Country." In *New Voyages and Travels.* London, n.d.

Population and settlement

Blaschke, K. "The Development of Population in an Area of Early Industrialization: Saxony from the Sixteenth to the Nineteenth Century," In *Third International Conference of Economic History,* vol. 4. Paris, 1972.
Drake, M. *Population and Society in Norway 1735–1865.* Cambridge, U.K., 1969.
Hendricks, F. "On the Vital Statistics of Sweden from 1749 to 1855." *Journal of the Royal Statistical Society* 25 (1862): 111–74.
Hufton, O. H. *Bayeux in the Late Eighteenth Century: A Social Study.* Oxford, 1967.
James, Patricia, ed. *The Travel Diaries of Thomas Robert Malthus.* Cambridge, U.K., 1966.
Mayer, K. B. *The Population of Switzerland.* New York, 1952.
Sjoberg, G. *The Preindustrial City.* New York, 1960.
Utterstrom, G. "Population and Agriculture, c. 1700–1830." *Scandinavian Economic History Review* 9 (1960): 176–94.
Walker, M. *German Home Towns: Community, State and General Estate.* Ithaca, N.Y., 1971.

Economic development

Blum, J. *Noble Landowners and Agriculture in Austria 1815–1848.* Baltimore, Md., 1948.
Jacob, W. *A View of the Agriculture, Manufactures, Statistics and State of Society of Germany.* London, 1820.
Pounds, N. J. G. *The Ruhr.* London and Bloomington, Ind., 1952.
Pounds, N. J. G., and W. N. Parker. *Coal and Steel in Western Europe.* London and Bloomington, Ind., 1957.
Scrivenor, H. *A Comprehensive History of the Iron Trade.* London, 1841.

I I

The nineteenth century

The century which elapsed between the battle of Waterloo and the outbreak of World War I saw changes more profound than in any comparable period in human history. It was one of unprecedented growth: population more than doubled; there was a commensurate growth in agricultural output; industrial production increased tenfold; and Europe's gross product multiplied six times. This growth in economic activity was accompanied by a radical shift in its location, as an older, protoindustrial pattern decayed and was replaced by another which responded to new factors of production and to changing demand. The geography of Europe, when the Napoleonic Wars ended, differed fundamentally from that which saw the lights go out in August 1914.

The intervening century was, in the main, one of peace. Most conflicts were short-lived and far from destructive. Many were related to peoples' democratic aspirations or to their demands for independence from the empires which had between them shared much of Europe. But economic growth was, nevertheless, a highly localized phenomenon. Much of the continent remained untouched by progress – industrial, agricultural, or commercial – until late in the century. At the same time, there were areas where growth was rapid and from which the new technology was diffused to other parts of the continent. The difference between central Belgium, the lower Rhineland, and the English Midlands, on the one hand, and the mountains of Macedonia and Romania, or the forests of eastern Poland and northern Russia was far greater in the mid-nineteenth century than that between the developed world and the Third World today.

NATIONALISM

The century which followed the Vienna Congress was dominated by three trends or movements: nationalism, imperialism, and economic growth. The French Revolution had opened the floodgates of nationalism, which the Congress of Vienna tried unsuccessfully to close. The century was marked by outbreaks of national sentiment, always accompanied by demands for democratic institutions through which to express these views. First came the Belgian revolt against the far from oppressive and unenlightened rule of the Dutch, then the first of many unsuccessful risings in Poland, the Czech rising against the Habsburgs, the Croatian against the Hungarians, and the Hungarian against the Austrians. Only the Hungarians achieved a measure of success, gaining autonomy under their Habsburg rulers in 1867, but refusing all concession to their own subject people, the Croats.

In Germany, meanwhile, an economic unity was being gradually forged in the successive agreements between the German states which made up the Zollverein. This unity was achieved under the auspices of Prussia. It was not at first matched by any degree of political unity, and the attempts made in the "year of revolutions," 1848, to create a united Germany failed. It was not until 1864–71 that political unity was achieved and the German empire proclaimed.

The situation in Italy was broadly similar: a number of independent states influenced in varying degrees by France and the Habsburg empire. But here unity was achieved by a move from below, the *Risorgimento*. The Habsburg empire in northern Italy was in large measure terminated, not without French help which had to be paid for by the cession of Savoy and Nice.

The most violent movements in the national awakening occurred in the Balkans. Here a small, inefficient, and corrupt Ottoman bureaucracy and army attempted to hold a vastly larger population consisting mainly of Slavs, Romanians, and Greeks. The struggle was in some degree one between Orthodox Christian and Moslem, but to a far greater extent it was between an oppressed and overtaxed peasantry and the reactionary, even feudal classes which controlled land and resources. The harshness of Ottoman rule was tempered by its ineffectiveness. In the Romanian principalities Ottoman authority was represented by phanariot[1] Greek officials, who identified themselves increasingly with the Romanians, so that Walachia and Moldavia drifted, as it were, into independence. Ottoman officials exercised little power in Albania and none in Montenegro. The first revolt came in Serbia and was followed by that in Greece, resulting ultimately in Serbian and Greek independence. In 1875 revolution broke out in Bosnia and spread to Serb lands still under Turkish rule and to Bulgaria.

The Balkans then became the scene of a three-cornered struggle for influence and control. There was Austria-Hungary, seeking to advance its authority southward from the Danube; Russia, aiming to control the Turkish Straits and access to its southern shores from the Mediterranean; and Great Britain, seconded by France, anxious to exclude any other great power from the Mediterranean basin. In the course of the struggle the Balkan nations achieved independence but, in doing so, precipitated the war of 1914.

IMPERIALISM

The second force which shaped the nineteenth century was imperialism. No fewer than ten European powers, if we include Russia among them, acquired overseas territories or extended those which they already possessed. Spain, it is true, lost much of her empire early in the century and most of what remained at its end.

---

1   From the suburb of Constantinople, known as Phanar.

Table 11.1. *Area of dependent empires, circa 1900*

United Kingdom	8,964,571 (square miles)
France	4,587,085
Netherlands	2,048,626
Germany	1,231,513
Belgium	905,144
Denmark	879,672
Portugal	808,253
Italy	245,882
Spain	132,425

Russia's empire lay not beyond the seas, but in Asia, where she was involved nonetheless in conquest and rule over non-Russian peoples. The British and French empires were very extensive, even if much of their vast extent was made up of unrewarding desert. The Belgian and Dutch empires were more restricted. The Portuguese, like the Spanish, consisted of what survived of a much greater domin- ion. The Italians and Germans came late into the race and were only "snappers up of unconsidered trifles," which had escaped the net of earlier imperialists. By 1900 the colonial dependencies of European powers covered no fewer than 19,803,171 square miles, 35 percent of the land surface of the earth. Their extent at this date is shown in Table 11.1. The motives for imperialism were mixed, but the foremost must surely have been economic. "Whereas various real and powerful motives of pride, prestige and pugnacity, together with the more altruistic professions of a civilizing mission, figured as causes of imperial expansion," wrote J. A. Hobson, who witnessed many of these events, "the dominant motive was the demand for markets."[2] All industrializing countries desired unrestricted access to the raw ma- terials and foodstuffs which they needed, and, since large-scale or mass production was a condition of their success, markets in which to sell their products were no less necessary. An empire might be expected to provide both. This was without question the case with Great Britain. Even in 1815 some 60 percent of trade was with the non-European world, and this proportion remained fairly constant until late in the century when it declined slightly.

Other European countries benefited less than Great Britain from trade with their colonial dependencies, in part because they were acquired late and remained undeveloped. Nevertheless the commercial benefit of colonies to the Dutch and French was unquestioned, and even Spain suffered acutely when much of its over- seas territory was lost in 1898, and with it an important part of the market for Catalan textiles. Colonies became less valuable commercially, as the concept of the "open door" to colonial trade gradually spread. The principle that no colonial power had an exclusive right to the resources and markets of its dependencies was first incorporated into public law in the Congo Act of 1885. Its implementation

2   J. A. Hobson, *Imperialism, A Study* (London, 1902), 113.

was slow and imperfect, but by the later years of the century not even the Dutch, most exclusive of colonial powers, were able to maintain their commercial monopoly. At the same time the volume of trade was increasing, both relatively and absolutely, with independent countries overseas, particularly with China, Japan, the United States, and Latin America.

The opening up of colonial territories occurred roughly when the construction of the railway net within Europe was nearing completion. The making of railway equipment had been an essential activity of the European iron, steel, and engineering industries (see pp. 433–4). Now this was extended at a useful level into the twentieth century. The same held good for the building of docks and ships and the opening of mines. Investment in the infrastructure of colonial territories gave a new lease of life to many a capital-goods industry in Europe. The term "periphery" has been used for this basically undeveloped region of the world which supplied raw materials and absorbed capital investment. Much of eastern and southeastern Europe can also be said to have belonged to the periphery, as did the whole of tsarist Russia. Its exports consisted largely of primary goods: grain, lumber, raw flax. These were sent to the "core area" of northwest Europe and were paid for by factory products. But there was an important difference between the European and the overseas periphery. The latter was, by and large, controlled from western and central Europe. The former was in the hands of "feudal" elements within its own society. These succeeded in manipulating production and trade in their own interests, and, though they did not prevent a degree of industrial development, they succeeded in maintaining the role of these areas as primary producers. Not until after World War I, with land reform and industrial development, did this role change significantly.

ECONOMIC GROWTH

The spectacular growth in production, and with it of employment in the tertiary or service sector, was the third important characteristic of the century. These developments can be measured by their contribution to the gross national product, but this is difficult to measure and estimates can be regarded only as the crudest approximations. The tables compiled by Bairoch are the basis of the maps used here and of the accompanying discussion. After allowance has been made for inflation, the gross national product of Europe, including Russia and the United Kingdom, was of the order of 60 billion dollars at 1960 values. Allowing a total population of about 200 million at this time, this gives an average GNP per head of about $300. But it varied greatly. In Great Britain it was almost $600; in Russia and much of eastern Europe, less than $200 (Fig. 11.1). Growth was uneven through the century, fastest in Great Britain and central Europe, slowest in southern and eastern Europe (Fig. 11.2). By 1913, the difference between the richest and the poorest countries was proportionately far greater than it had been in 1830 (Fig. 11.3).

The growth in gross national product was accompanied by a change in the

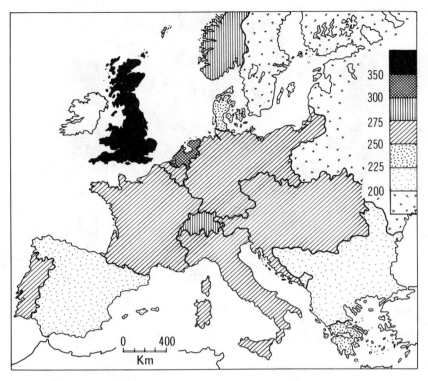

11.1. Gross national product per head, about 1830. The units are 1960 U.S. dollars. [Based on P. Bairoch, "Europe's Gross National Product, 1800–1975," *Journal of European Economic History* V (1976): 273–340.]

contributions made to it by the several sectors of the economy. Very broadly, one may say that the productivity of agriculture increased somewhat, but that employment in it fell in absolute terms, and that both employment in and the productivity of manufacturing increased both relatively and absolutely. There was an increase, large in the developed countries of Europe, small in others, in the tertiary sector. The graphs of German GNP (Fig. 11.4) and of employment in Sweden (Fig. 11.5) illustrate the trends in economic growth during the century. The rest of this chapter will be concerned with the spatial aspects of these changes.

POPULATION

The population of Europe grew more rapidly than that of any other part of the world except those which, like North America, were receiving a steady stream of immigrants. By 1815, including both the British Isles and Russia, it was of the order of 180 million. By 1910 the total had risen to about 435.5 million, an increase of about 140 percent, or scarcely more than 1 percent a year. The graph (Fig. 11.6), drawn on a logarithmic scale, shows how consistent and uniform this growth was, the only significant exceptions being the flattening of the curve for

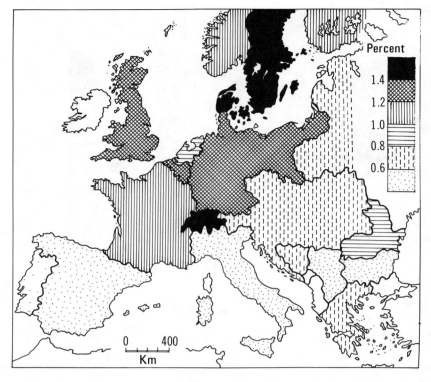

11.2. Increase in gross national product, 1830–1910, as percentage of 1830 figures, shown as percent per year

France in the mid-century, and the sharp increase in the population of Hungary about 1840.

Factors in population growth

The rate of population growth was the resultant of changes in birthrates and death rates, though it was influenced also by migration. Broadly speaking it was "falling mortality [that] accounted for the observed rate of population growth in England,"[3] and the same was in general true of the rest of Europe. Birthrates declined, but not significantly, except in France, before the last quarter of the century (Fig. 11.7). Indeed a number of countries showed a rise in the birthrate and net reproduction rates until the 1830s before declining abruptly. Death rates began to fall much earlier, and in most countries the decline was consistent from the 1830s (Fig. 11.8). The reason was, by and large, the disappearance of famine crises from Europe, the declining importance of epidemic disease, and improvements made in the material conditions of life. The result was a slow change in the struc-

3   Colin Clark, *Population Growth and Land Use* (London, 1967), 50.

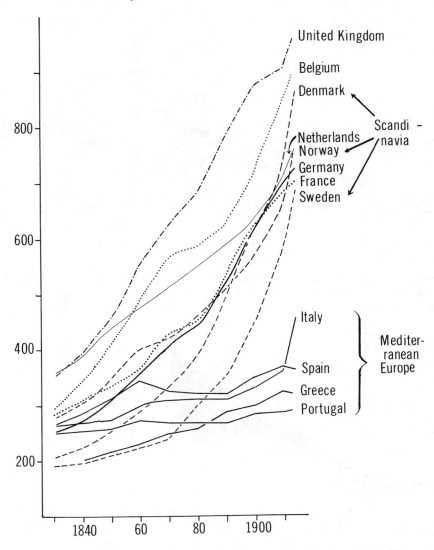

11.3. The increase in the gross national product per head in the principal European countries, 1830–1913

ture of the population, with smaller cohorts of young people and proportionately larger of old. This trend manifested itself first in France, but by the early twentieth century had appeared in most parts of the continent.

Food supply and disease. It is impossible to separate statistically the consequences of diet, disease, and bad housing. While famine ceased to be a significant factor, diet remained important, subject to seasonal fluctuations and almost always unbalanced. The last continentwide food crisis was in 1816–7, but there were more localized and less serious crises in 1830 and 1846–7; even in the 1850s poor

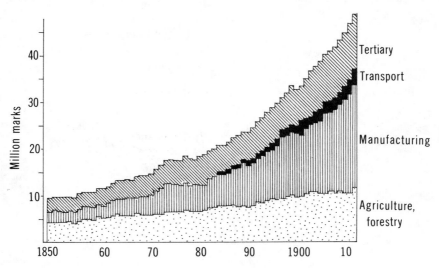

11.4. The gross national product of Germany by sector. The value of transport services was too small before 1886 to show on the graph. [Based on statistics in W. G. Hoffmann, *Das Wachstum der deutschen Wirtschaft seit der Mitte des 19. Jahrhundert* (Berlin, 1965).]

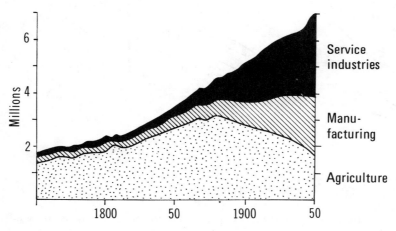

11.5. Growth of population, by employment sector, in Sweden. [After H. Osvald, *Swedish Agriculture* (Stockholm, 1952).]

harvests caused widespread distress and increased mortality. Even in good years, diet was highly farinaceous, with breadgrains predominating and a growing consumption of potatoes. The use of green vegetables was inadequate, and that of animal proteins small. Even in Normandy and the Paris basin, reckoned to be an area of heavy meat consumption, the amount eaten per head amounted to no more than about 60 pounds a year. Elsewhere the consumption of protein was very much less, and many a peasant and industrial worker touched meat only at special celebrations. Urban diet was even less adequate than that in rural areas, where at least

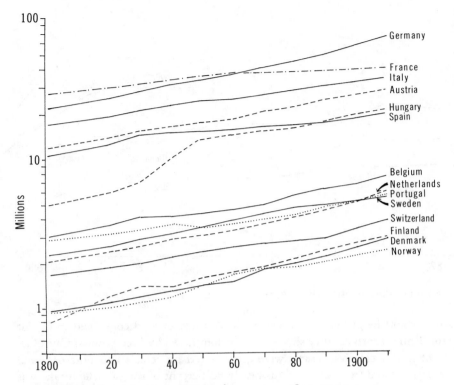

11.6. Growth of population in Europe, by country, 1800–1910

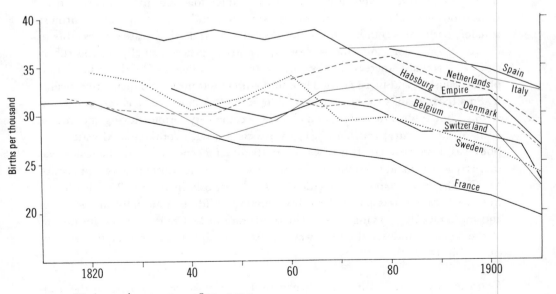

11.7. Birthrates by country, 1810–1910

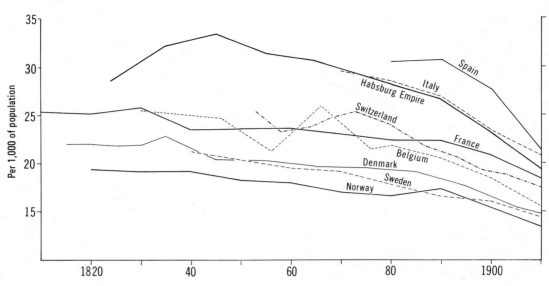

11.8. Death rates by country, 1810–1910

vegetables could be grown on garden plots. A study of food consumed in Ghent in the mid-nineteenth century showed a diet dominated by breadgrains. Out of an average of 2,435 calories, 1,479 were contributed by cereals and potatoes, and 428 by beer brewed from grain. Thus nearly 80 percent of the calorific intake was from farinaceous foods. It does not appear that the quality of the diet improved significantly before 1850, and in the cities not until after 1875.

The effects of poor diet were reinforced by bad physical conditions under which many people lived. Those least able to resist infection were most exposed to it. Conditions were always worst in the cities, where, under conditions of the utmost squalor, pathogens could be transmitted with ease. Indeed, disease attributable to crowding and poor sanitation – cholera, typhus, diptheria, smallpox, and tuberculosis – actually increased in virulence (see pp. 383–4). On the other hand, plague vanished and in 1871 the Habsburg empire terminated its quarantine against it. Smallpox, thanks to the increasing adoption of vaccination, was very much less serious, but typhus increased, and cholera became very serious during the middle years of the century, until, in fact, its association with contaminated water supplies was demonstrated. But it was more than half a century before the lesson was properly learned and uncontaminated water was piped to most cities (see pp. 374–5). On the other hand, the incidence of tuberculosis increased. The death rate from such causes was particularly high among children, especially in the larger and more rapidly growing cities. The death rate in Le Creusot, by no means one of the worst of industrial cities, was consistently higher than the French average (see Table 11.2).

Restrictions on births.   Birthrates began to decline in many countries in the mid-nineteenth century. A lower level of conceptions can sometimes be attributed to

Table 11.2. *Death rate per thousand*

	Le Creusot	All France
1851–5	33.0	24.1
1856–60	31.5	23.8
1861–5	31.7	22.9

undernourishment and epidemic disease, but, in general, it can only be explained by the decision to have fewer children. The trend toward smaller families first became apparent in France, where Le Play attributed it to the testamentary provisions of the Napoleonic code, prescribing the equal division of an inheritance between heirs. This was a powerful motive for reducing the number of children, but it was not in itself an adequate reason. A reduced birthrate first showed itself among the middle classes and was, in time, imitated by the lower. In this France only anticipated a trend which became apparent in most of Europe by the end of the century.

Migration. There had always been migration within Europe, and, in recent times, overseas migration had become significant. Migration tended to postpone marriage and thus reduced the size of the completed family. The greater part of European migration was over only short distances, to the nearest small town or regional capital, and much of it was only temporary, the migrants hoping to return eventually to their native villages. The pattern of migration was complex. Much began as seasonal movement and ended with permanent alienation from the home village. There are even instances, with the coming of steamship navigation, of seasonal migration for the harvest in the New World. Overseas migration was on a much smaller scale but is more easily measured, since most countries kept records of those who passed through their ports.

Internal migration was in the main a movement from rural areas to the cities. At first it was mainly from areas of poor soil and backward agriculture, but toward the end of the century even areas of good soil and progressive agriculture lost population as labor on the land became less intensive. Figure 11.9 shows for France the increase in urban population and the decline of rural and agricultural. Migration was at first largely from the Alps, Pyrenees, and Central Massif but after 1870 increasingly from the fertile regions of the Paris basin and the northeast. There was also considerable migration from the south of France to Algeria, especially after the outbreak of the *phylloxera* epidemic in the vineyards.

In Germany internal migration remained relatively small until after the creation of the German empire in 1871. The considerable migration at the mid-century has often been ascribed to the failure in 1848 of the movement for a unified and democratic Germany. In reality much of the migration of these years was due to crop failure and rural distress. The correlation of migration and the price of rye is close (Fig. 11.10). The development of industry in the lower Rhineland during

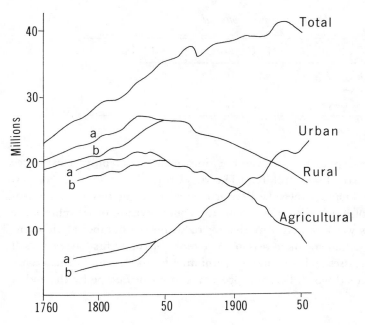

11.9. The contraction of rural population in France with the growth of towns. The difference between the "rural" and the "urban" graphs is a rough measure of internal migration; *a* = maximum estimate, *b* = minimum estimate. [After J. C. Toutain, "La population de la France de 1700 à 1959," *Histoire Quantitative de l'Economie Française* 3 (1963).]

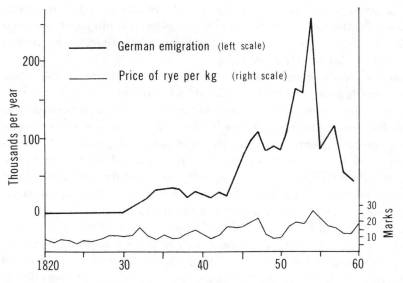

11.10. Migration from Germany, 1820–60, and the price of rye. [After Mack Walker, *Germany and the Emigration, 1816–1885* (Cambridge, Mass., 1964).]

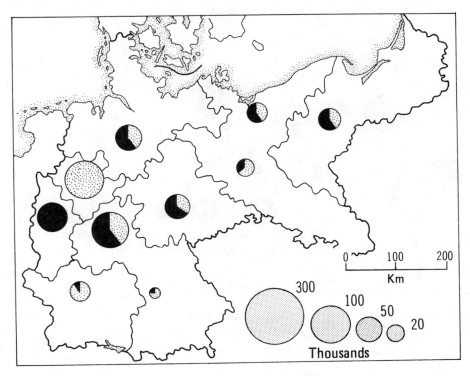

11.11. Migration within Germany to the industrial provinces of Rhineland and Westphalia, 1880. See also key in Fig. 11.12. [Based on W. Kollmann, "Die Bevolkerung
Rheinland-Westfalens in der Hochindustrialisierungsperiode," *Vierteljahrschrift für Sozial-
und Wirtschaftsgeschichte* 58 (1971): 359–88.]

the second half of the century attracted large numbers of workers to the area. At
first they came mainly from neighboring areas of western Germany. Then in the
1890s migration built up from the eastern Provinces where rural birthrates remained high and there was little opportunity for employment in manufacturing.
It was in fact so great that it even led to a labor shortage in the east, made good
by the immigration of Poles. Many Poles even made their way to the Rhineland,
and there were 250,000 in the Ruhr by 1910 (Figs. 11.11 and 11.12).

Internal migration was on a smaller scale in other parts of Europe. There was
an outward migration from the Alps and from the mountains of southeastern Europe. In Italy, peasants, especially from the south, moved to the cities, and Naples, Palermo and others grew without ever developing the functions to employ
so vast a population. Population also moved to the developing areas of the north,
but after 1900 people migrated in growing numbers to the New World (Fig.
11.13). Everywhere the extent of migration varied with the fortunes of agriculture: a good harvest, and few were inclined to leave; crop failure and scarcity, and
the peasants flocked to the ports to take the cheapest passages available across the
Atlantic. A problem for the poorest peasant was to accumulate enough money for

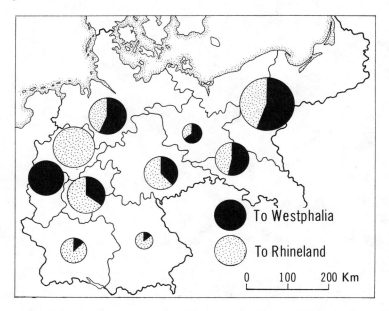

11.12. Migration within Germany to Rhineland and Westphalia. See key in Fig. 11.11

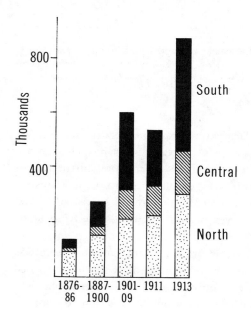

11.13. Migration from Italy, 1876–1913. Note the increasing importance of migration from southern Italy and Sicily

the passage, and it was for this reason that overseas migration afforded so small an outlet for the excess population of areas like Austrian Galicia. In the Balkans, catastrophes like the Montenegrin famine of 1890 led to widespread migration, both internal and overseas. The Scandinavian countries contributed powerfully to the stream of migration, largely because of their marginal environment. Weather

Table 11.3. *Migration from Europe, 1850–1914*

	Total migration, in thousands	As percentage of total population in 1900
Austria-Hungary	4,878	10.7
Belgium	172	2.6
British Isles	18,020	43.5
Denmark	349	13.9
Finland	342	12.7
France	497	1.3
Germany	4,533	8.0
Italy	9,474	29.2
Netherlands	207	3.9
Norway	804	36.5
Portugal	1,633	32.7
Russia	2,253	1.2
Spain	4,314	23.2
Sweden	1,145	22.5
Switzerland	307	9.3

fluctuations, which elsewhere would have led only to short-term scarcities, could here become disastrous and lead to emigration.

In terms of absolute numbers, the largest stream of migration came from Italy, followed by the Habsburg empire, Germany, and Spain (see Table 11.3). But, relative to the size of the population in the home country, Norway was first, followed by Portugal and Italy. In both respects France contributed very few migrants, chiefly because of the low rate of growth of the population.

Migration within individual countries was considerable, but there was little movement between European countries. Poles moved into eastern Germany, from which some made their way to western. Belgians, Italians, and Spaniards entered France in search of work in areas where the local population had almost ceased to grow, but there were few other examples of significance.

Jewish migration. The movements of the Jewish people form a special case of migration within Europe. They constituted the largest body of migrants, and they spread mainly from Russia to central Europe (Fig. 11.14). At the beginning of the century there were two distinct Jewish communities. The Sephardic Jews had settled (see p. 261) mainly in the western Mediterranean and, before their expulsion, had been identified primarily with Spain. From here they moved both eastward to the Ottoman empire and north to Great Britain and the Netherlands, where they tended to lose their identity. The other community had moved during the Middle Ages into central Europe, from which they were driven by Christian hostility eastward into Russia, where, in the early nineteenth century, they were settled in White Russia and the Ukraine. Here their numbers began to increase more rapidly than those of the peoples among whom they lived.

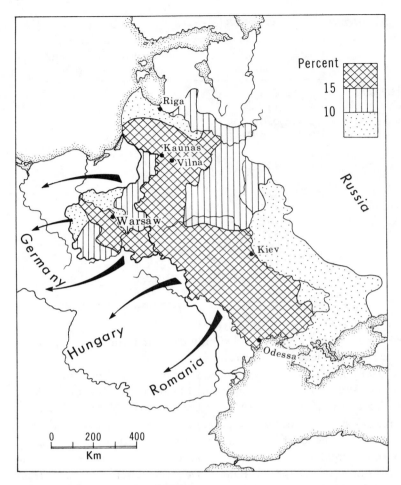

11.14. The Jewish Pale of Settlement within Russia, and the migration of the Jewish people into central and southeastern Europe. After H. G. Wanklyn, "Geographical Aspects of Jewish Settlement East of Germany," *The Geographical Journal* 95 (1940): 175–90

About 1800 most of the Jewish population of Europe lived to the east of Germany. They were forbidden to inhabit the larger cities and most lived in villages and small towns. They could not hold land and were thus excluded from agriculture and were left with crafts and petty trading as their only occupations. Within Russia they were confined by a decree of Catherine II to the so-called Pale of Jewish Settlement. From here, as their numbers mounted and local hostility increased, they drifted westward on a broad front which stretched from Prussia to the Black Sea (Fig. 11.15). Relatively few crossed the Danube into the Balkans where conditions were even more hostile than in Russia. As they migrated so the economic basis of their life slowly changed. They remained mainly rural in Poland, Galicia, and the Romanian provinces where they served as "petty shopkeepers, pedlars and

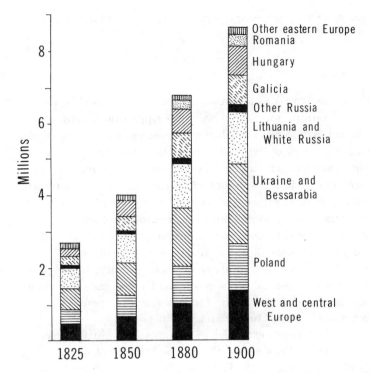

11.15. Distribution of Jewish population in Europe, 1825–1900. Based on U. Z. Engelman, "Sources of Jewish Statistics," in L. Finkelstein, *The Jews: Their History, Culture and Religion* (New York, 1949)

hawkers."[4] They took on the business of dealing in grain, furs and skins, timber, and, as production developed, petroleum. Many small towns became largely Jewish. As they moved into central Europe so their activities became increasingly upmarket. In 1867 they gained full rights of citizenship in the Habsburg empire and, in 1871, in Germany. The liberal professions were thus opened to them, and their petty trading and moneylending developed into commerce and banking.

The Jews had mainly spoken a Slavic language, but as they moved west they adopted a form of German suited to their needs. This became Yiddish and was carried back to Poland and the east as an important cultural bond between the Jewish people. Not all who left the Pale settled in central Europe. After 1870 they began to migrate to the New World. The movement was at first slow. By 1899 American Jews numbered fewer than half a million, but between 1900 and 1914 no fewer than 1.5 million left for America, most of them from Russia and eastern Europe. The Jewish migration differed from that of other European peoples in that there was no return flow, except the subsequent movement to Israel, and, secondly, the migrants were not peasants, but craftsmen and traders. They became

4   I. Cohen, "The Economic Activities of Modern Jewry," *Economic Journal* 24 (1914): 45.

urban dwellers, and the New York garment district is a lasting monument to their migration.

The ethnic pattern

In the strict sense the ethnic pattern of Europe had been established before recorded history began, and historic migrations were but ripples on its ethnic surface. Physical types varied and some areas showed a concentration of particular characteristics: pigmentation, shape of the head, type of hair. But European "races" were a discovery of the nineteenth century and became an extreme manifestation of nationalism. If "race" has little real significance in the context of nineteenth-century Europe, culture – a social rather than biological inheritance – was very important indeed. Language, the foremost expression of culture because it was the chief vehicle by which culture was transmitted, acquired great significance. Language groups acquired a deeper sense of unity, and countries within which there were different languages found them a formidable obstacle to unity. In Belgium, for example, the rift between French-speaking Walloon and Dutch-speaking Fleming widened. The division increased between the Catalan and the Spaniard of the Meseta, between Czech and German, Hungarian and Croat.

Cultural characteristics sometimes extended to patterns of familial behavior. Birthrates were low not only in France, but also in the French cultural areas of Belgium and Switzerland. In the former, the Flemings always had a higher birthrate than the Walloons and tended to migrate southward into the latter's territory, and only assimilation by the Walloon, whose material standards tended to be higher, kept the two peoples in an uneasy balance. A not dissimilar situation arose in Switzerland, where the birthrate among the German- and Italian-speaking population was appreciably higher than that among the French (Table 11.4). This marked differential led to migration into French-speaking Switzerland, but, since each canton had its own official language, the tendency was for immigrants to become assimilated fairly quickly.

Similar cultural differences existed within the Habsburg empire. The Magyar (Hungarian) birthrate was higher than that of other peoples within the Habsburg empire, but an increase of 55 percent in the Magyar population in thirty years can be accounted for only by the assimilation of non-Magyar peoples in the Hungarian plain.

The nineteenth-century pattern of population

The increase of about 140 percent in Europe's population was accompanied by its redistribution by migration and differential birthrates. Broadly speaking, rural areas either stagnated or lost population by migration; the industrializing areas gained. These changes can be traced most easily in Great Britain and France, for both of which there are satisfactory census data. In Great Britain there was an absolute loss of population in much of Scotland, most rural areas of England and

Table 11.4. *Live births per thousand married women in Switzerland*

Canton	1899	1909–12
German-speaking		
Uri	399	326
Obwalden	336	312
Nidwalden	338	303
Schwyz	304	257
Lucerne	305	262
Bern	299	246
Italian-speaking		
Ticino	293	250
French-speaking		
Vaud	242	188
Neuchatel	240	177
Geneva	150	109

Wales, and over the whole of Ireland, except the vicinities of Belfast and Dublin. There was a corresponding growth in the great cities and industrializing areas of the Midlands, the north, and south Wales. There was also a marked growth, related to the amenities of the region, along the south coast of England (Fig. 11.16).

In France the birthrate had been declining before the century began, and it received a further setback from wartime losses and the distorted sex structure which resulted. Rural birthrates remained higher than urban, and there was a steady movement to the towns, intensified by the decline of rural crafts. French historians have referred to the "ruralization" of the countryside, which tended to become exclusively agricultural. A comparison of the maps in Figure 11.17 will show where decline was most marked, as well as those areas, notably the north, and the regions of Paris, Lyons, and Marseilles, where urban and industrial growth was most rapid.

In Belgium the consequences of differential birthrates between the north and the south were disguised by migration. Two areas of dense population built up, around Brussels, Antwerp, and Ghent, and along the valley of the Sambre and Meuse, where coal supported heavy industry. The Netherlands shared the high birthrate of the Flemings, with whom they had close cultural ties. In the absence of any large-scale industrial development, much of the increase was absorbed into agriculture and the Netherlands was, in consequence, one of the few areas where the rural population showed an increase.

German population grew rapidly. Growth was greatest in four areas: Westphalia and the lower Rhineland; Berlin, Brandenburg, and neighboring provinces; Saxony; and Upper Silesia, in each of which there was vigorous industrial devel-

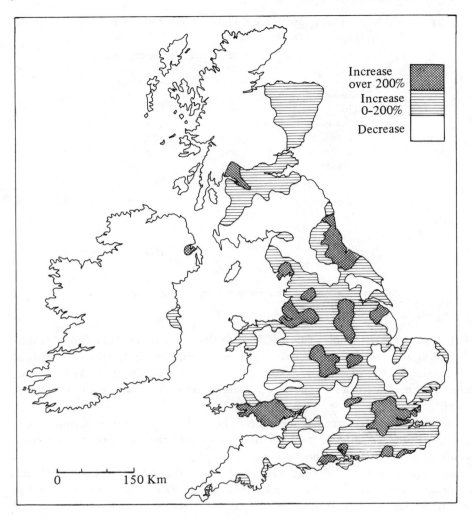

11.16. Population changes in the United Kingdom in the nineteenth century

opment (Fig. 11.18). The lowest rates of growth were in south Germany and the eastern provinces, chiefly because it was from here that migration was most active. Eastern Germany was a net loser, despite the attraction of greater Berlin.

In the pattern of their demographic behavior Poland and Russia resembled eastern Germany. A mainly rural population had a high birthrate and a steadily growing population, relieved in the one by migration to Germany, in the other to Siberia and central Asia. The population of Scandinavia increased more rapidly than might have been expected in so marginal an environment, leading to one of the highest emigration rates to be met with in Europe (see this chap., under "Migration"). The increase in population remaining there was made possible by

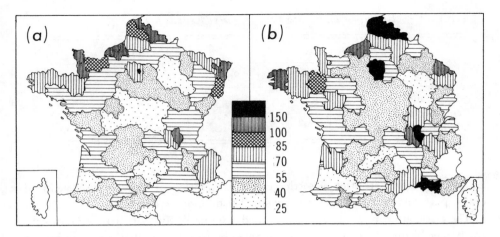

11.17. Population of France, per hectare: (*a*) 1821, and (*b*) 1911. After C. H. Pouthas, *La Population française pendant la premiere moitie du XIXe siècle* (Paris, 1956)

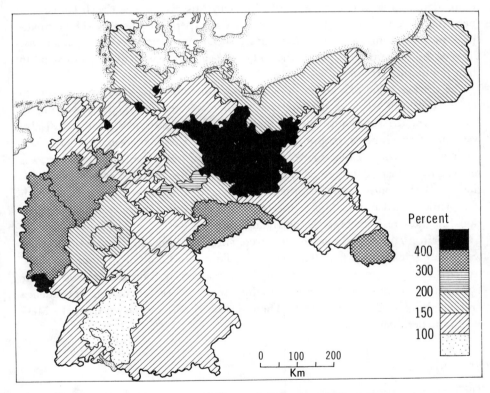

11.18. Percentage increase in the population of Germany, 1816–1914

Table 11.5. *Birthrates and death rates in Italy (per 1,000)*

	Birthrate		Death rate	
	c. 1875	c. 1895	c. 1875	c. 1895
North Italy	36.2	33.2	28.7	23.7
Central Italy	34.4	34.8	20.8	24.0
South Italy	40.8	37.2	30.8	29.0

an advance of the frontier of settlement, the adoption of more heavily yielding crops, particularly the potato, and by small-scale industrialization.

The population of Switzerland increased less markedly than that of Germany, the higher birthrate among the German-Swiss being offset by the lower rate among the French. The demographic history of the Habsburg empire and the Balkans is bedeviled by the lack of statistics and the unsatisfactory nature of those which are available. Overall both birthrates and death rates remained relatively high, though the tendency to decline became marked first in Austria and the Czech lands, and then spread slowly toward the southeast. It was experienced first by the German-speaking communities, with their higher social status and rising expectations. Parts of the Balkans remained at the end of the century essentially preindustrial in their population structure.

The demographic revolution by which low birthrates and death rates came to replace the high levels of preindustrial Europe was relatively late in coming to Italy and the Iberian peninsula. The birthrate in Italy, particularly southern Italy, was one of the highest in Europe and was reduced only marginally in the late nineteenth century (Table 11.5). In northern Italy the population pressure was relieved by industrialization; in southern Italy there was no relief except by migration, and "the south" sank into the overpopulated, underdeveloped region which it remained until the middle of the twentieth century. Central Italy was transitional in these respects between north and south.

In Spain birthrates and death rates were similarly high, but regional contrasts were more strongly marked. The rates were falling in Catalonia, the most industrialized and progressive part of Spain, but remained high on the Meseta. About 1900 crude birthrate in Barcelona province was 27.8 per thousand, but Cuenca province in New Castile had 41.6. There was inevitably migration from the Meseta to the peripheral and coastal regions.

URBAN GROWTH

The total population of Europe increased by about 140 percent during the century, but the growth of urban population was of the order of twentyfold. Preindustrial towns formed a more or less regular network. Necessarily so, for their functions were related to the needs of their surrounding districts, and the areas which they

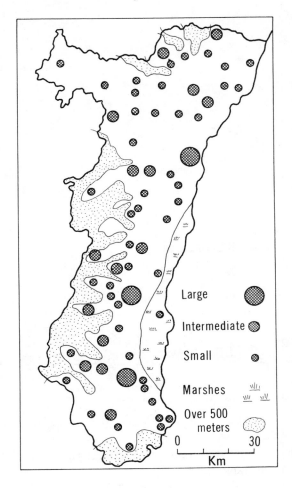

Large

Intermediate

Small

Marshes

Over 500 meters

0   30

Km

11.19. The urban net in Alsace, about 1850. Based on M. Rochefort, *L'Organisation urbaine de l'Alsace* (Paris, 1960)

could serve were in turn related to the speed of travel. Figure 11.19 shows the network which developed in Alsace. Above the many towns of small or medium size rose the three larger ones, Mulhouse (Mülhausen) and Colmar, with Strasbourg towering above and dominating the province. There was thus a hierarchy of "central-places," their functions adjusted to the areas which they served. Small towns had only low-level functions such as that of market center; the largest had administrative, commercial, and manufacturing functions which far transcended their local areas. Such patterns and urban relationships were replicated all over Europe at the beginning of the nineteenth century.

Cities grew at varying rates. Regional capital and industrializing cities grew rapidly. Others, remote from coalfields and the main avenues of transportation grew little, if at all. Yet throughout the period the cities in any particular country or major region presented a size pattern like that shown in Figure 11.20. The largest was, very roughly, twice the size of the second; the second bore a similar

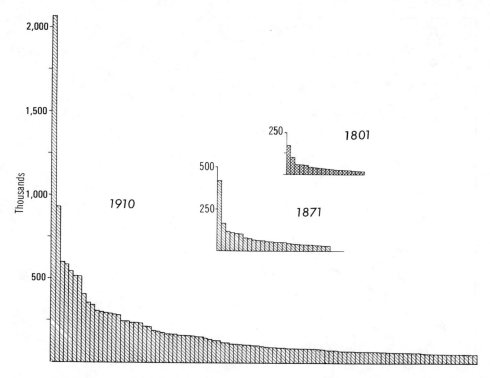

11.20. Rank–size graph of the larger towns in Germany in 1801, 1871, and 1910. Based on P. Meuriot, *Des Agglomerations urbaines dans l'Europe contemporaine* (Paris, 1897), and *Petermanns Mitteilungen* 57 (1911), i, 131.

relationship to the third, and so on. The pattern was preserved through time, even though some cities changed places in the rank order.

Some grew in the course of the century from almost nothing. They were villages when the century began, but a coal mine, a factory, or an ironworks attracted settlements; workers' housing was erected; the railway came, its depot creating a kind of focus for the amorphous growth that was taking place. Eventually the village might achieve urban status, with a town hall, a coat of arms, and municipal regalia, like any long established city, but its newness could not be disguised. It was severely working class; its service industries were reduced to a bare minimum, and most of those employed were at the mill or the mine. In Great Britain every industrial region had its new towns, like Oldham, Barnsley, Smethwick. In northern France and central Belgium they were scattered through the coalfield: in the Ruhr district, Gelsenkirchen and Wanne-Eickel; in Upper Silesia, Königshüte (Chorzów) and Kattowitz. Łódź, in Poland, was a new town, as also were the mill towns of Catalonia and those which, like Decazeville and Commentry in France, grew up around a single iron and steel works.

A special category of new town was the resort, either inland, around a spring of supposedly healing waters, or on the coast to benefit from clean air and sunshine. They were virtually unknown before 1815, and most did not develop until after

1850. They owed everything to increasing wealth and the craving, which they did their utmost to encourage, for rest and relaxation away from home. They were a middle-class institution, though humbler classes were beginning to frequent them in the years before World War I. Their growth and popularity owed less to their intrinsic merits than to the recommendation of someone of importance. King George III set his seal on Brighton on the south coast of England, and the Empress Eugenie, on Biarritz on the Biscay coast of France. Inland "watering places" from Bath in England and Spa in Belgium to Karlsbad (Karlovy Vary), Marienbad (Mariánské Lázně), and Bad Ischl acquired reputations as social as much as curative centers. Resort centers were as specialized and as narrowly based as the industrial; their business was to accommodate, entertain, and exploit their guests.

Size of cities

Estimates of the size of cities were subject to two kinds of error: uncertainty as to what constituted a city, and the fact that the legal boundaries of any large city were at intervals extended to enclose an ever greater area. In eastern and southern Europe were many settlements of truly urban size but mainly agricultural function, much of their building consisting of farm structures. Such agrarian "towns" remain a feature of the Hungarian plain. They did not, as a general rule, grow much in the course of the century. Their tendency was rather to lose population, as their farming population took up permanent residence amid the fields.

Most cities grew during the century, but the rate of growth of large cities was proportionately greater than that of medium-sized and small. The large cities absorbed an ever-increasing proportion of the population. Brussels, for example, had about 2 percent of the population of Belgium at the beginning of the century, but 10 percent in 1910. In Germany also the expansion of the larger settlements was particularly marked. The growth of the "primate" or largest single city was in every instance very strongly marked. In most instances it was also the political capital and concentrated within its limits administrative functions which increased in scale during the century. Figure 11.21 shows the size of the primate cities expressed as a percentage of that of their national populations.

Cities have always carried on three functions: agriculture, manufacturing, and services. The balance between these functions not only varied from one city to another, but changed through the century. The agricultural function of all cities declined, but there were few, even in the twentieth century, which did not retain some vestigial trace. In most, service functions increased to the point at which they dominated the employment structure. Figures 11.22 and 11.23 illustrate these trends in the cities of Toulouse and Strasbourg. Most new industrial towns would have shown an employment structure dominated by manufacturing.

Social geography of the city

The growth which took place in urban population could not have been achieved without massive migration from the countryside. There were industrial cities in

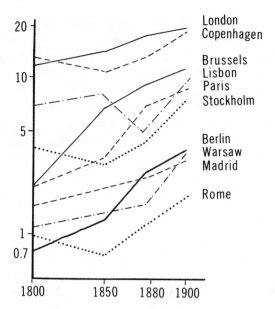

11.21. The size of the primate city as a percentage of the national population, 1800–1910

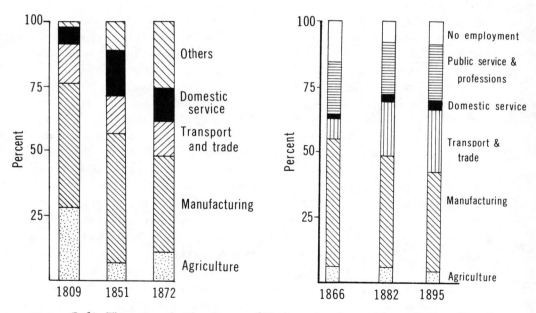

11.22. (Left). The occupational structure of Toulouse in 1809, 1851, and 1872. [Based on M.-T. Plégat "L'évolution demographique d'une ville français au XIXe siècle: L'exemple de Toulouse," *Annales du Midi* 64 (1952): 227–48.]

11.23. (Right). The occupational structure of Strasbourg in 1866, 1882, and 1895. [Based on E. Sayous, "L'évolution de Strasbourg entre les deux guerres (1871–1914)," *Annales: Economies-Sociétés-Civilisations* 6 (1934): 1–19, 122–32.]

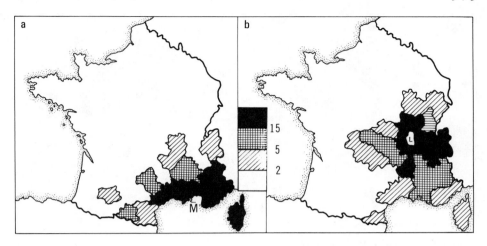

11.24. Migration to (*a*) Marseilles and (*b*) Lyons. The figures represent the number per 1,000 of population in the home *département*. [After A. Chatelain, "L'attraction des trois plus grandes agglomerations françaises: Paris–Lyon–Marseille en 1891," *Annales de Démographie Historique* (1975): 27–41.]

the late nineteenth century in which a majority of the population had been born elsewhere. Berlin and the industrial cities of northwest Germany drew heavily on the rural population of the German east. Marseilles and Lyons each drew mainly from their own mountainous hinterlands (Fig. 11.24). In the early years of the century migrants to the city came generally from its local region, but as the century wore on every large city was obliged to extend its catchment area. Figure 11.25 shows how the area which supplied migrants to Paris expanded during the century.

Both the age and sex structures of cities were usually distorted and were rarely typical of the country as a whole. The immigration of adults meant that the younger age-groups were underrepresented, and the lower expectation of life, common in cities, reduced the numbers of elderly. Sex ratios could be distorted in both directions. Many small towns, Dijon for example, showed an excess of females above the age of about fifteen. This was due to the large number of women from surrounding rural areas who took up domestic service in the towns. On the other hand, cities with dominantly heavy industry showed a preponderance of men.

Urban death rates were usually somewhat higher than national averages, in part because it was an older population, in part because conditions of public health were poorer than elsewhere. No large city was able to house its immigrant population adequately; the stock of homes was always too small. This necessitated a degree of crowding and congestion which encouraged the spread of infection. Many nineteenth-century epidemic diseases, such as typhus, tuberculosis, and smallpox, were spread by close personal contacts. At the same time sanitary arrangements remained in most cities totally inadequate until the end of the century. Domestic waste was thrown into the streets from which it was at intervals carted away.

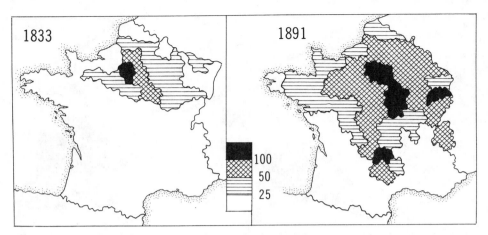

11.25. Migration to Paris: the source of migrants, 1833 and 1891. The figures represent those born in each *département* and living in Paris as the number per 1,000 of those living in the *département*. [After L. Chevalier, *La formation de la population parisienne au XIXe siècle* (Paris, 1950).]

Toilets, which were everywhere quite inadequate in number, commonly discharged into cesspits or the nearest river. Paris, as late as 1880, had no fewer than seventy thousand *fosses,* and the stench of one of them – the Maufaucon cesspit – could, it was said, be detected when the wind was right over most of the eastern quarters of the city. The inevitable result was that typhoid, dysentery, and, above all, cholera were endemic, breaking out periodically into epidemics. Not until 1894 did French law require cities to build sewer systems. Progress came somewhat earlier in Germany, but many cities in southern Europe had made little provision early in the twentieth century, and in the Balkans there was none.

Public health was closely linked with water supply. No European city in the early nineteenth century had a supply as safe and as assured as many cities of the Roman empire had possessed. They drew it from wells within their city limits and from springs beyond them, or merely dipped from the river. As late as the 1890s Hamburg was taking its water unfiltered from the river Elbe. This contributed to the cholera epidemic of 1892, after which the water-supply system was reconstructed. Most large German cities had already established reliable systems by the end of the century. Haussmann, in the course of his rebuilding of part of Paris, planned to take water from distant springs in Champagne but, for reasons of cost, had to settle for sources nearer the city. The technique of sinking very deep wells had been developed by the 1840s, when Paris was drawing some water from a depth of eighteen hundred feet, well below the level of possible infection.

In western and central Europe only the larger cities, and within them only the better-off quarters, had an improved water supply by 1850. Most of the larger cities acquired a piped supply during the second half of the century, but progress was nonetheless very uneven. It was more rapid where the economic benefits of an abundant water supply were obvious. In the Ruhr, for example, industrial needs were seen to be greater than domestic, and supplies were laid on for cooling and quenching coke long before they were made available to homes. Nevertheless, the latter benefited eventually, and by 1913 the Ruhr had an elaborate system of dams on the river Ruhr for water storage and of pipelines to supply the industrial area.

A source of energy was scarcely less important to a large city than a supply of water. Both safety and convenience required some form of street illumination, and factories demanded a motive force, usually in the form of coal. The latter was brought by river and canal barge and, from the mid-century, by rail, and its supply in general posed little problem. Illumination and the supply of energy for domestic purposes created greater difficulty. Coal gas proved to be the most flexible and convenient medium. There were gas-burning installations in the 1790s, but London became in 1813 the first city to have gas illumination, followed by Berlin in 1816 and Paris in the 1820s. But the use of gas called for a supply of coal and also a net of metal pipes to convey the gas to the consumer, a costly project, restricted, like a piped water supply, to the more affluent quarters.

The use of gas spread, at first slowly and then more rapidly. By 1850 gas was supplied to at least parts of 35 German cities; by 1860, the number had increased to 250, most numerous in areas easily accessible to the coalfields. Electricity did not begin to displace gas until the last two decades of the century. Its distribution was easier than that of gas, but large generators, suitable for a public power supply, did not begin to be built until after 1880. Berlin's first large-scale generator was built in 1884, and Paris began to use electricity for illumination in 1875. In the 1880s hydroelectricity became available in the Alps and Pyrenees, but its use was restricted by the difficulties in its long-distance transmission.

As cities increased in size, so transport within them assumed ever greater importance. Horse traction was used through much of the century, and there were coach houses and stables tucked away behind many a city home. But the problems of keeping horses within cities of ever-increasing size and congestion proved too great, and other means of conveyance were devised. The first were the horse bus and then the horse tram, the latter running on rails. The first horse "omnibus" was operating at Nantes in 1826, and similar services "for all" were operating in Paris and London soon afterward. By 1853–5 Paris had a rudimentary tramway system.

While horse-tramway systems were being installed in smaller cities, the larger were gradually converting to electrically propelled trams. In this Berlin was the pioneer, largely because of the local presence of Werner von Siemens's electrical engineering works. Elsewhere, horse trams were converted to electric power, but not generally before the closing years of the century.

The railways rarely penetrated to the centers of older towns, and only in exceptional cases, such, for example, as London and Berlin, could they serve as effective means of internal movement. But the tramway, which followed the city streets and often used the same gauge rails, could be regarded as an extension of the railway. London's Metropolitan Railway used steam power but converted at an early date to electric. It was followed by the Paris *métro,* built underground where necessary, and by the London "underground" which was, at least in the more closely built areas, wholly underground. Lastly, the motor bus, powered by the internal combustion engine, began to make its appearance soon after 1900 and proved for a time to be an adequate solution of the transportation problem.

Urban housing rarely kept pace with the growing influx of people, and congestion and squalor increased in the larger cities until late in the century. Working-class housing consisted during the early and middle years of the century of rows of terraced houses, often built, as in northern England and Belgium, "back to back." Later in the century the tenement block became the dominant form of workers' housing in much of central Europe and parts of western. An enquiry into the conditions in Germany, made by the British Board of Trade in the early twentieth century noted that the tenement block "is become more and more predominant. . . . In some of the larger [cities] these erections often resemble large barracks built round small paved courtyards. . . . Nothing could be more depressing than the sight of the huge structures which surround many of the courtyards in working-class districts . . . merely a builder's device for exploiting costly sites."[5] Such tenements came to dominate many large cities and at Königshütte "practically the whole working-class population . . . may . . . be said to live in tenements of one or two rooms," and Berlin was described as one of "the greatest tenement cities of the world."[6] Much of this industrial housing, especially in the Ruhr, Berlin, and Upper Silesia, was built by the firms whose workers lived in it. It was a means of maintaining discipline among the work force. The worst of this proletarian housing was to be found in Upper Silesia, where it sometimes consisted of nothing more than dormitories of the roughest construction. Tenements were fewer in Belgium and France, but they were an important form of housing in Paris and Lille.

Great Britain pioneered in the creation of such industrial slums. Urban and industrial growth came early, before the nature of urban problems was understood or techniques had been developed for handling them. In 1844–5 Friedrich Engels described the conditions of life in the rapidly growing industrial cities of northern Britain. He portrayed the utmost squalor, congestion, and degradation. Lack of water, sanitation, and street cleaning might not have been of great significance in a small village. Their absence from large parts of a densely packed city of a quarter of a million people, as Manchester was at that time, was a very serious matter. It was half a century before the conditions described by Engels were eradicated in Britain, and even longer in continental Europe. Figure 11.26 shows the changes which occurred in a single city block in Łódź. In less than ninety years it was transformed from cultivated strips in an open field into four acres of closely built workshops and tenements.

In time these conditions were eliminated. City authorities took steps to clean

5   *Report of an Enquiry by the Board of Trade into Working Class Rents, Housing and Retail Prices in the Principal Industrial Towns of the German Empire,* in Parliamentary Papers, London, 1910, 85.
6   Ibid., 354.

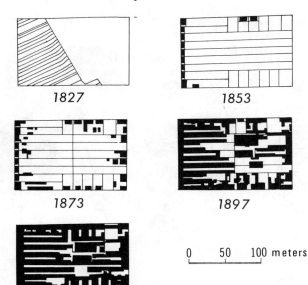

1827   1853

1873   1897

1914

0   50   100 meters

11.26. Changes in a single city block in Łódź, 1827–1914. The diagram for 1827 represents agricultural strips. [After A. Ginsbert, *Łódź* (Łódź, 1962).]

up the worst of the slums, and legislation defined minimum standards of housing. But there were places where conditions like those described by Engels lingered on until the end of the century.

In all large cities, however, there were contrasts in the quality of housing and standards of living. Some suburbs — traditionally those on the windward side — had low-density housing and were often the first to have piped water, gas mains, and electricity. Others had high-density housing and none of these amenities. The differences were apparent to the senses, and even today one can judge the standard of housing from what has survived. There are other measures of the quality of life in different sectors of the city. Figure 11.27, for example, shows the distribution of (a) domestic servants, and (b) manual workers in Paris. The two distribution patterns are complementary. Not dissimilar patterns could have been found in London, Berlin, and, in fact, in all large cities.

As cities grew larger, the problem of maintaining the flow of foodstuffs and other necessities increased. The older mechanisms of supply became inadequate, and the traditional market ceased to be held. Markets, instead of being periodic and general, became specialized and permanent, serving as wholesale rather than retail outlets. In Paris, London, and elsewhere such markets developed: *les Halles* and Covent Garden for produce, Billingsgate for fish. The local region, even though its agriculture became more intensive, ceased to be adequate except for smaller cities, and foodstuffs had to be obtained from distant provinces and even from overseas. By the mid-century flour milling, sugar refining, and oil pressing were established as factory industries, most often at the ports or at break-of-bulk points. It was the evolution of this extensive network of supply which finally ended for

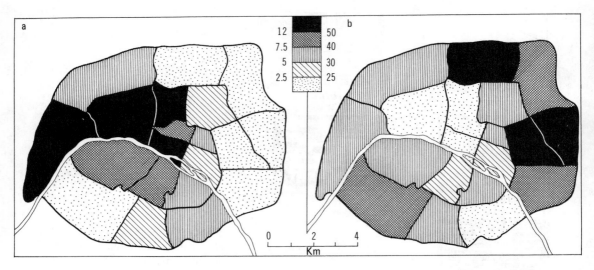

11.27. Distribution of (*a*) domestic servants in Paris (1872), and (*b*) working-class population. The figures represent percentages of total population. [After L. Chevalier, *La formation de la population parisienne.*]

highly urbanized regions the sequence of food crises which had characterized their earlier history.

The urban pattern

Figure 10.4 (see Chap. 10) shows the pattern of cities before their period of rapid growth. Fewer than twenty in continental Europe were larger than a hundred thousand. In Great Britain, where modern industry had been developing for almost a century, there were ten, but in Russia there were only two, St. Petersburg and Moscow. A highly urbanized belt stretched from northern Britain, through the Low Countries, to northwest Germany. Elsewhere cities of large or medium size were more widely scattered. By the early twentieth century the zone of dense urban development had intensified in Britain and the Low Countries and had extended across central Europe to Silesia (see Chap. 12, Fig. 12.3).

France was in some ways an exception to the general trend. Paris and a few ports and industrial cities, among them Lille, Lyons, and Marseilles, grew rapidly, but small and medium-sized cities increased at a much slower pace. This reflected the slow growth of population during the century and the low level of industrial development. Nowhere in western Europe did cities retain their links with the countryside more conspicuously than in France, nor preserve their tradition of craft industries more strongly.

Paris was, however, the scene of a more rapid urban growth than any other city in continental Europe until, late in the century, it was overtaken by Berlin. It was the seat of a highly centralized administration, a place of culture, education, and

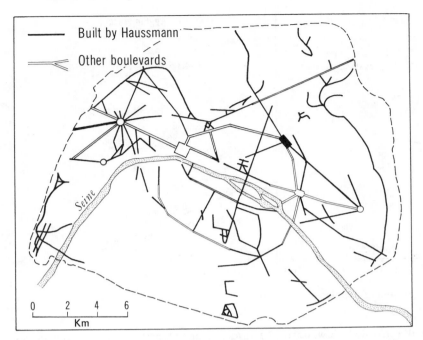

Built by Haussmann

Other boulevards

Seine

0 2 4 6
Km

11.28. Haussmann's rebuilding of Paris, 1850–6. [After D. H. Pinkney, *Napoleon III and the Rebuilding of Paris* (Princeton, N.J., 1958).]

fashion, and a large center of consumption. It attracted consumer goods industries as no other. Population grew by immigration and approximately doubled every thirty years. This growth was achieved at the expense of unbelievable squalor and congestion. Much of the working population lived in tenement blocks, approached by dark and fetid alleys. Paris was still "an overgrown medieval city," with totally inadequate systems of sewage, waste disposal, and water supply, when Napoleon III in 1852 presented his plan for rebuilding the city. His ideas owed much to recent developments in west London, and, as developed and implemented by Haussmann, the *préfet* of the Seine *département,* they consisted of a series of wide, straight streets, meeting and intersecting in large public squares. The motive was not only to eliminate slums and beautify the city, but also to allow it to be commanded by the artillery of the government. The plan aroused intense opposition and was never completed (Fig. 11.28). Behind the rococo facades of Haussmann's building still lay the squalid housing which Hugo had described.

The southern Low Countries had always been highly urbanized. Little of the new industrial growth, however, took place in the older cities; it was in new towns which grew from villages on or near the coalfield. In the Netherlands urban growth took the form very largely of the expansion of Amsterdam, The Hague, and Rotterdam and of the cities lying between them, together making up the so-called *Randstad Holland,* or ring of Holland cities.

Only in Germany did urban growth compare with that in Great Britain, but

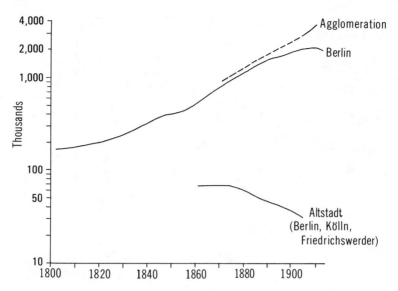

11.29. The growth of population in greater Berlin

even here it remained slow until the mid-century. Until the 1870s Berlin remained considerably smaller than Paris. Then, with the formation of the German empire (1871), growth became very rapid (Fig. 11.29), and by 1910 Greater Berlin had reached 3,709,500. In the meantime the Old City had declined, and the most rapid growth was in the suburbs, beyond the city boundary which was established in 1861 and remained unchanged until after World War I. The spread of Berlin, more like that of London than of Paris, covered a vast area within which an efficient system of public transport became a necessity. Berlin did, however, resemble Paris in its reliance on tenement blocks for housing, hurriedly built to serve the influx of people from the east.

Urban growth in Poland, like that in Germany, came largely in the later years of the century, when it was marked by the rapid expansion of Warsaw and Łódź. Throughout Scandinavia cities remained few and small, in part because industrial development was largely rural. In Russia, also, urban growth was slow except in St. Petersburg and Moscow and a few regional centers, like Kiev, Kishinev, and Saratov, and the port cities like Odessa and Riga. Odessa had reached a quarter of a million before 1914.

Town life was little developed in the Habsburg lands and the Balkans, and cities remained primarily market centers. Only Vienna showed a particularly rapid growth, increasing from less than a quarter of a million early in the century to more than two in 1910. This growth has sometimes been ascribed to its role as capital of a large empire, but government service, including the military, never accounted for more than about 10 percent of the population. The rest was supported mainly by manufacturing and commerce. The city, as befitted its frontier location, retained its defenses until the nineteenth century, and beyond them an open space, to secure a wide field of fire. In the 1850s this area was, in the face of military opposition, turned over to civilian use. It was then replaced with a series of monumental buildings, which rank, along with Haussmann's work in Paris, among the finest examples of urban redevelopment in nineteenth-century Europe.

Growth in Bohemia and Moravia was more in line with that in Germany, largely because these provinces became the industrial core of the Habsburg empire. Prague remained the regional capital, a cultural as much as an industrial center. For the rest, urban growth largely took the form of industrial "new" towns, such as Ostrava on the Moravian coalfield and the mill towns of northern Bohemia. The only other large city in the Habsburg empire was Budapest, consisting until 1872 of the administratively separate cities of Buda and Pest, on opposite banks of the wide Danube. Buda, on the steep west bank of the river, remained largely governmental; Pest, on the flat eastern bank, became the commercial and industrial heart of Hungary.

The Balkan peninsula was not noteworthy for its urban growth. Over much of the region there were no cities as these were conceived in western and central Europe, and fairs continued to perform functions which elsewhere were carried on at regional capitals. The only large city was Constantinople, capital of the Ottoman empire and its chief commercial center, with perhaps a million inhabitants. Bucharest grew rapidly at the end of the century with the development of the petroleum industry, but other Balkan cities remained small (Fig. 11.30).

There was little change in the course of the century in the urban pattern of the Iberian and Italian peninsulas. Figure 11.31 shows cities in Spain and Portugal about 1855. Their strongly primate character is apparent, with Madrid and Lisbon at least twice the size of any other in their respective countries. Italy, in line with its classical traditions, was highly urbanized (see p. 163), but many of the towns, especially in the south and Sicily, were, in fact, heavily agricultural. In northern Italy there was slow growth until the last quarter of the century, when, with Italy's belated industrial development, Milan and Turin began to increase more rapidly.

AGRICULTURE

The nineteenth century saw changes of fundamental importance in the geography of Europe's agriculture. These may be summarized as a very considerable increase in overall production of foodstuffs, resulting in the main from a more intensive use of land, and, secondly, the end of local self-sufficiency, except in a few remote areas, and the development of national, even of continentwide markets in foodstuffs. The middle years of the century, lastly, saw the end of the series of subsistence crises which had devastated preindustrial Europe.

There are no acceptable statistics of agricultural production during the early years of the century, but it is probably true to say that the increase in cereal production in the course of the century was of the order of threefold, far greater than the rate of increase of the population. Even at the beginning of the century there was a considerable net import of breadgrains – up to 12 percent of total

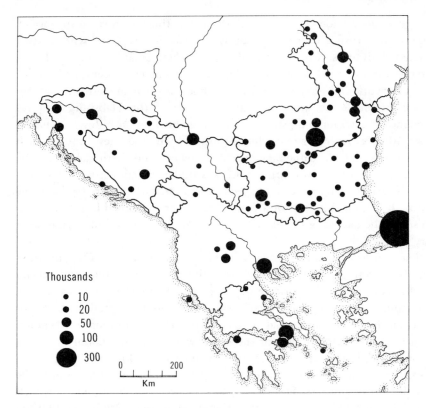

11.30. Towns of the Balkan peninsula, about 1910

demand – into western and central Europe. Despite larger production, imports had further increased by the end of the century. Western and central Europe obtained breadgrains from eastern Europe and Russia as well as from overseas. There was an increase in consumption per head; larger quantities were fed to animals, and there was a significant industrial use, for brewing and distilling.

In addition to an increased overall production, cereals showed a change in relative importance. The output of wheat increased absolutely, especially in France where there was a compensatory fall in rye (Fig. 11.32). In Germany both wheat and rye, the primary breadgrains, increased (Fig. 11.33). In Sweden, wheat production increased faster percentagewise than that of rye (Fig. 11.34). As a general rule, the cultivation of coarse grains, used primarily as animal feed and for malting purposes, increased less than that of the primary breadgrains (Fig. 11.35).

The gradual disappearance of fallow (see p. 391) gave more space for the cultivation of other crops, primarily artificial grasses and root crops. In addition, potatoes and sugar beets became increasingly important. The potato was of limited use before 1815 and was grown chiefly as a garden crop. But its food value and heavy yield made it increasingly attractive. It became a major crop in Ireland and, from the mid-century, in Scandinavia and central and eastern Europe. It was of importance in relieving famine crises and contributed to the increase in population

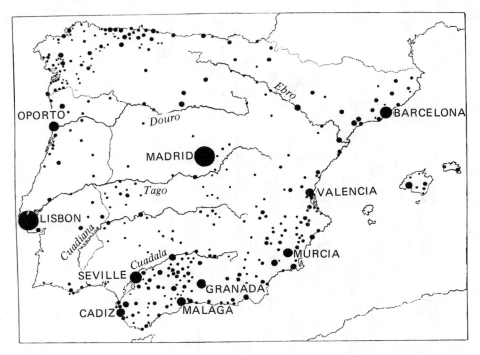

11.31. Cities and towns in Spain and Portugal, about 1855. [Reproduced from T. E. Gumprecht, "Die Stadte-Bevolkerung von Spanien," *Petermanns Mitteilungen* (1856) 303. This may be one of the earliest attempts to use proportionate symbols to represent city size.]

in those areas where it was widely grown. By the early twentieth century the area under potatoes in central Europe and Scandinavia was very considerably in excess of that under wheat.

The sugar beet was in some ways an alternative to the potato, but its cultivation was far more localized. Since it required a large processing plant to extract the sugar, it tended to be grown on a large scale or not at all. It was cultivated during the Napoleonic Wars when the import of cane sugar was reduced. Cultivation then lapsed and was not revived until the 1820s when it was grown in northern France, and later in Belgium, Germany, Bohemia, Poland, and Russia. In Germany a quite exceptional emphasis was placed on root crops, almost to the exclusion of green fodder. Roots became "the pivotal crop in sequences." They required heavy fertilization, and the reason for their popularity probably lay in the contemporary expansion of the fertilizer industry.

The structure of agriculture

The key to the great expansion of agricultural production during the century lies in the changes made in the structure and techniques of farming. In the nineteenth century feudal modes of land tenure were yielding rapidly to other more effective

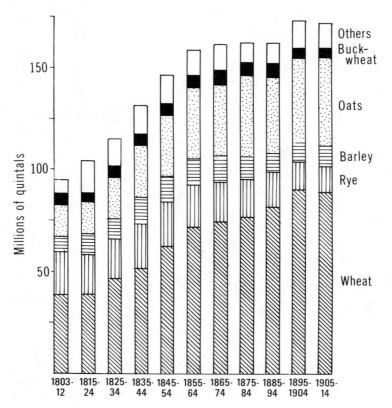

11.32. Cereal production in France. [Based on J. C. Toutain, *Le Produit de l'agriculture française de 1700 à 1958*, in *Histoire Quantitative de l'Histoire Economique Française* 2 (1961): 16.]

modes. Any discussion of the relationship of the peasantry to the land is bedeviled by the confusion between ownership and occupation. The peasant occupied and cultivated the land; only in exceptional circumstances – France after the Revolution, Serbia after the expulsion of the Turks, Poland after 1864 – did he actually own it. The magnate owned large estates in eastern Germany or Poland, but he occupied and cultivated directly only a small part of it. Most peasants held their land in return for rent or service, and most of the estates were cultivated in small units by the peasantry.

The European periphery, in east, southeast, and south, was characterized by estates, owned and exploited by people who, it is often said, were absentee and showed little interest in the progress of their lands and tenants. This is not wholly true. In the first place, the number of really large estates, running to thousands of acres, was small (see p. 330). Most were of fewer than 1,000 acres and, even in areas such as eastern Germany and southern Spain, made up significantly less than half the land. Large units (over 250 acres) made up a somewhat larger proportion of Poland – about 59 percent. Even in Hungary, so often regarded as a land of

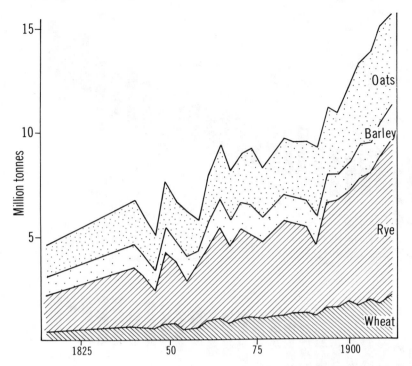

11.33. The growth in cereal production in Prussia. [Based on H. W. Finck von Finckenstein, *Die Entwicklung der Landwirtschaft in Preussen und Deutschland, 1800–1903* (Würzburg, 1960).]

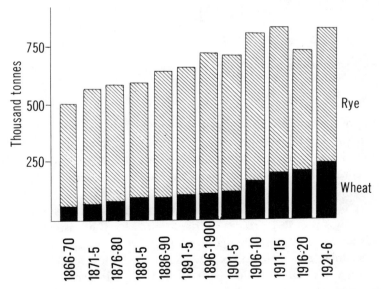

11.34. Growth in the production of rye and wheat in Sweden, 1866–1926. [After H. Oswald, *Swedish Agriculture* (Uppsala, 1952).]

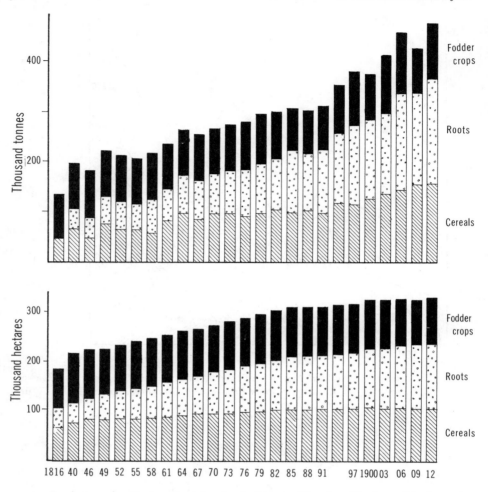

11.35. Land use and agricultural production in Prussia. (Based on Finck von Finckenstein, *Die Entwicklung der Landwirtschaft*, 329.)

great estates, a third of the land was throughout the century held in units of fewer than about 40 acres, and less than 40 percent of the area was in holdings of more than about 140 acres. There are no statistics available for the size of Spanish estates in the nineteenth century, but in 1930, those of over about 250 acres made up considerably less than half the total area.

A significant part of all large estates consisted of woodland and waste. The proportion varied and was probably greatest on the forested lands of eastern Germany. Much of this land was deliberately maintained for hunting purposes, some was exploited for its timber resources, and part was land of very low fertility.

Part of most estates was retained in the hands of the lord, who lived on it and had it cultivated for his own direct use. The rest of the agricultural land was leased in tenancies. The conditions of these tenures varied but were commonly onerous.

They still included at the beginning of the century labor service on the lord's demesne, or the commuted value of such services. The peasant had good cause to complain of his personal status and of his obligations in service or rent. These were often excessive, and stemmed from an earlier feudal relationship of lord and subject. He could complain no less of the size of his holding, which, in much of the area characterized by estates, was far too small. This was generally recognized by governments, though attempts to remedy the situation were stultified by the fact that they were often controlled by the landowners themselves, who had most to lose from change.

Land reform, which included changes in peasant status and personal obligations and an increase in the size of their farms, was a major political and social issue throughout the century. What was needed was to make more land available to the peasant either as freehold tenures or at a reasonable rent with security of tenure. Quite apart from political objections to such reform there was the important legal fact that most of the estates in eastern Germany, Hungary, and Spain, together with some elsewhere, were entailed. It took legislation to break the entails, and this was adopted in eastern Germany and Spain early in the century. The lords were allowed to offer part of their estates for sale in the unwarranted expectation that it would be snapped up by a land-hungry peasantry. It was not. Much of the land which came onto the market, especially in Spain, was bought by urban capitalists, and the peasant found that he had unwillingly exchanged a master whom he knew for an even less scrupulous landowner whom he did not. In consequence, relatively little progress was made during the century in this aspect of land reform.

Attempts to deal with the other problem – personal status and obligations – also met with only limited success. The lord had the right to receive labor and rent – often quite arbitrary – from the peasants who occupied and cultivated units of his land, and he demanded compensation for the surrender of these rights. What happened in the early nineteenth-century reforms in both Prussia and Spain was that the peasant bought out his obligations by surrendering part of his tenancy. Small farms were made yet smaller, and the poorest peasants were thus squeezed off the land and obliged to join the ranks of the landless day laborers. It was from this class that a large part of the migrants from eastern Germany came (see this chap., under "Population").

Apart from estates, the land was held in four ways. In the first place, a peasant might hold his land in fee simple or freehold. He owned it, without payment of rent or performance of labor services, and could within limits make improvements and pass it on to his heirs. He was not, however, totally without obligations; he owed taxes and was likely to be burdened with tithe payments. He was bound by custom and had often to follow the local plowing and cropping regime. He was often restricted in the ways in which he could bequeath his holding. Although primogeniture – inheritance by the firstborn son – was generally practiced, there were parts of Europe where division between direct heirs was enjoined by custom or required by law. In southwest Germany, for example, holdings were "partible" and came to be minutely divided. The same custom prevailed in parts of prerevolutionary France and was made applicable to the whole country by Napoleon's code of civil law. Testatory provisions were in various ways circumvented or overcome, but, nevertheless, the practice of partible inheritance tended to reduce the size of peasant holdings.

Leasehold tenures formed a second group of tenancies. The peasant held his land for an agreed period and at a fixed rent. This mode of tenure was the most common in Great Britain, but it was to be found in all parts of Europe. As feudal obligations came to be abandoned, they were often replaced with some form of leasehold arrangement. There was an immense variety of such tenures. Leases might be short-term – for a few years only – or long-term, up to ninety-nine years, or they might be for the lives of certain designated persons – a kind of gamble popular in England. The leases themselves might incorporate restrictions as to cropping and improvements. Short-term leases usually discouraged the tenant from making any great investment in the land, and even long-term leases were held to be less advantageous to the peasant than freehold.

Métayage, or sharecropping, the third form of tenancy, was a special case of leasehold. The tenant held for a term of years, but the lord provided not only the land, but very often the stock and tools of cultivation, and he received as rent an agreed portion – usually a half – of the produce. The system was widespread in France and general in much of Italy but was little known elsewhere. It was condemned as discouraging agricultural progress, but it had the advantage of allowing a peasant without capital to farm on his own, and it also protected him in some degree from bad harvests, in that his rent was reduced in proportion to his crop.

The only other form of tenancy was common land. This was legally one of the least precise ways of holding land. It was usually restricted to woodland, grazing, and occasionally meadow. Ultimate ownership was in many instances never defined. The community had use of it, but the limits of the community were often vague. In England, when common land came to be divided between those who could show claim to it, shares were often denied to poor cottagers who held no land in the open fields. In Poland, ownership of the common woodland was vested ultimately in the lord, who retained his rights after the peasants had gained possession of their holdings. Everywhere commons were essential to the community, providing it with the means of keeping sheep, pigs, and goats, and also with wood for building and firing, but commons were also a fertile source of dispute owing to the lack of definition of rights in them.

Even more important to the peasant than the legal right by which he held his land was the size of the holding which he had at his disposal. Everywhere there was a broad spectrum from the landless peasant and the cottager who had nothing more than a garden plot, to the tenant who had leased the lord's demesne on the most favorable terms. The size of a family holding varied with the conditions of soil, terrain, and climate, but if thirty acres is recognized as adequate, only a small minority of European peasants had enough land to support themselves, and everywhere there was a class of landless peasants in search of day labor on the lands of their richer neighbors.

Table 11.6. *Land held in estates in Germany, 1907 (percentages)*

Hectares	Prussia and Mecklenburg	Rest of Germany	Whole of Germany
0–5	8.7	21.0	16.2
5–20	21.3	41.0	33.4
20–100	29.5	29.9	29.8
over 100	40.5	8.1	20.6

In Great Britain much of the land was held by a comparatively small number of noblemen and gentry. However much the British may dislike the thought, their land was, like Prussia and southern Spain, one of "great estates," but it must be admitted that they were managed and cultivated with far greater skill and consideration. These lands were most often leased or "farmed" in relatively large units, which were in turn cultivated with hired labor. There was, in fact, no peasantry as this term was understood in most of continental Europe. This was an efficient mode of land tenure, a fact of great importance when it came to supporting a large urban and industrial population. Only in Ireland and parts of Scotland could one find a peasantry, living close to the margin of subsistence under oppressive tenurial conditions.

France, by contrast, was a peasant country. The peasantry gained possession of the land which they cultivated at the Revolution, but they lost a significant part of it after the Restoration. Holdings were on average too small, and the well-known acquisitiveness of the French peasant was justified to the extent that there were few who did not need an extra strip in the open field. In 1826, 90 percent of them had each no more than 6.5 acres, and throughout the century a majority of holdings were too small for effective management.

In Belgium the situation was worse. "The average size of holdings," wrote Seebohm Rowntree, "is smaller than in any country of Europe," and in this land of partible inheritance, "there is a steady and continuous movement towards a still further reduction in the average size of a holding."[7] About 1880 no less than 55 percent of all farm holdings could not possibly provide full employment or a family living, and they became merely a supplement to a domestic craft or even factory employment.

There were marked regional contrasts within Germany, but in all parts both very large and very small farm units were to be found. The latter predominated in south Germany; the former east of the Elbe, with a more even mix of large and small in the northeast (see Table 11.6). After 1864 Poland became a land of small to medium-sized holdings, interspersed with small estates which had managed to survive the enfranchisement of the peasants (see Table 11.7). The Habsburg lands

---

7   *Land and Labour: Lessons from Belgium* (London, 1911), 179–80.

Table 11.7. *Size of farms in Poland, 1892 (in acres)*

	Below 12.5	12.5–50	50–125	125–250	Over 250
Percentage of farms	38.85	52.77	7.02	0.34	1.02
Percentage of area	5.96	25.43	8.0	1.81	58.8

showed an immense range, from large units in Bohemia and Hungary to micro-holdings in Austrian Galicia and the mountains of Slovakia and Transylvania.

It is a paradox of peasant life that, in material terms, the peasant in the backward Balkans was often better off than the peasant in the west. This was because, with the expulsion of Turkish landowners from Serbia early in the century and from Bulgaria at a later date, the peasants expropriated the land with very little by way of compensation to its former owners. Serbia and Bulgaria and, to a lesser extent, Montenegro and Greece became lands of small peasant proprietors. Romania, with Bosnia and Hercegovina, was an exception. Though under Ottoman suzerainty, land in Romania remained in the possession of its native aristocracy who, far from participating in the liberalizing tendencies of the nineteenth century, strengthened their control and exacted labor dues to the full. The peasant servitudes were not abolished until 1864, and land reform was both late and generally ineffective. Bosnia and Hercegovina were in some respects similar. The native gentry retained their estates after the Turkish conquest at the price of conversion to Islam. Being Slavs, they did not lose their lands when Ottoman authority was withdrawn, and their peasants benefited little.

Conditions varied greatly in the Spanish and Italian peninsulas. In Spain, a peasant society had developed in the mountains of the north, and Spanish Galicia was as notorious as Austrian Galicia for the minute size of its holdings. On the other hand, the northern Meseta and the southeast were held in the main in medium-sized farms, while the southwest was characterized largely by large estates worked by hired labor. The irrigated *huertas* of the Mediterranean coastlands were mostly cultivated in small peasant farms. Overall, nearly a third of holdings in Spain were of fewer than 12.5 acres, while another third lay in estates of over 650. This polarization between the extremes of microholdings and great estates is typical of Spain and helps to explain the conflict and violence of its history.

In Italy, large units were predominant in the south, but in the north, by contrast, small and medium-sized units prevailed, with large only in areas of reclaimed land, like the Po delta, since peasants lacked the means for capital investment. In Scandinavia farm units were on average larger than in the rest of Europe. The soil was less capable of intensive cultivation, and human pressure on the land was less. In Denmark, for example, only 10 percent of farms were of fewer than 25 acres at the beginning of the twentieth century, and in Sweden and the rest of Scandinavia they were in general larger.

The techniques of agriculture

Tenurial systems and the prevailingly small size of farm holdings acted as a brake on agricultural progress. Nevertheless, progress was made, enough to increase the total production of foodstuffs by some three times over the continent as a whole. This was achieved mainly by technical advances. These can be summarized as (1) changes in field systems; (2) the introduction of new cropping systems; (3) the adoption of mixed farming; and (4) the use of improved tools and equipment.

When the century began Europe could have been divided into two regions: that of open-field agriculture, and that of enclosed. In the open fields the practice still prevailed of taking two cereal crops and of then allowing the land to lie fallow. The constraints which kept this system in being, despite the denunciations of every agronomist, have already been discussed (see pp. 332–3). Nevertheless, changes crept into it. The fallow began to be cultivated, and the scattered strips of each cultivator began to be consolidated at least into fewer and wider strips. Gradually the tyranny of the open-field system began to weaken.

In this, as in so many other respects, progress was first made in the Low Countries and Great Britain. By 1866 the practice of bare fallow had been reduced to 3 percent of the agricultural land in England, and to 5 percent of that in Wales. By 1911 it had virtually disappeared from both. It was of slight importance in the Low Countries, but remained significant in France, where a fifth of the arable was under bare fallow about 1850, and a seventh as late as 1882. The disappearance of fallow was most rapid on the good soils of the north, slowest in the hills of the west and the mountains of the center. In 1889 the practice of *vaine pâture*, the grazing of animals on cropland after harvest, was outlawed in France, and by the end of the century rights of fallow grazing had ceased to be a reason for its preservation. Progress in central and eastern Europe was slower than in western, but even there little land was regularly left under fallow by the early twentieth century.

Fallow grazing and *vaine pâture* had been the cornerstones of the open-field system. Their decay permitted both the concentration and enclosure of individual strips and the introduction of more varied rotations. Most important was the cultivation of fodder crops in place of fallow. Such crops as lucerne and clover made a direct contribution to the soil by the fixation of nitrogen; the cultivation of roots was accompanied toward the end of the century by a generous use of fertilizer; and all such crops, by allowing large numbers of animals to be kept, increased the supply of manure.

The consolidation of strips was achieved slowly. It was opposed by too many vested interests, and the practice of partible inheritance seemed to have the effect of dividing parcels of land as soon as they had been brought together. Emile Zola's novel *Terre*, which deals with peasant life in the Beauce in the mid-nineteenth century, describes the division of a peasant holding between heirs. The peasant insisted that each parcel of land, however small, be broken up, each parcener "certain that no one could have something that the other two hadn't got."[8] In Great Britain the movement to enclose the open fields began early. By the mid-century, open fields had almost disappeared from the landscape. Denmark in 1781 introduced legislation allowing individual peasants to consolidate, a step which necessarily affected all others in the community (Fig. 11.36). Sweden and Norway followed, so that by the mid-century open fields were scarcely to be seen in the whole of Scandinavia.

Little progress was made in Germany until after 1848. In some areas, notably the southwest, the fragmentation was of an order which defied human ingenuity, and here only a limited consolidation was often possible. In some parts of Switzerland fragmentation was also extreme. In 1884 the federal government offered financial aid in reshaping a community's fields, but no great progress had been achieved by 1914. In eastern Europe, the consolidation of strips was seen as part of a land reform which was not accomplished until after 1918, and then only imperfectly. In the Balkans, the tendency was in general to increase the parcellation of the land. As communal villages or *zadruge* and Turkish-owned *chiflik* estates disintegrated, they broke into an immense number of parcels. An instance has been cited of a holding of seven acres being broken into 122 separate plots. Throughout Poland, Romania, and Russia no progress at all was made in introducing a more rational system of fields.

The implements used by the farmer had changed little since the Middle Ages. Nor was there any significant development until late in the century. Traditional types of plow continued in use (Fig. 11.37). In North America a "chilled" steel plow "broke the plains," but over much of Europe a wooden plow, with at most a metal-tipped share and a coulter was used. In southern Europe a derivative of the light classical plow remained in general use, and throughout eastern Europe the primitive, spadelike *sokha* prevailed. Sowing was broadcast, the peasant "taking handfuls of grain and scattering them all over the earth with a solemn gesture, as one bestowing a blessing."[9] A harrow sometimes followed to break up the clods of earth and bury the seed, but not before part had been consumed by the birds. Harvesting was with a sickle, replaced only slowly by the scythe. In the 1870s the sickle was used almost exclusively in parts of the Paris basin, and the more efficient and economical scythe was objected to because it left too little for the gleaners to gather. In other words, it was not wasteful enough.

An American commission found that in Germany the "farmer is thoroughly conservative and clings to many ancient habits and customs which are none the better for age. With great difficulty he is brought to introduce new and more profitable practices."[10] These better practices called for different tools, and, since these were mostly made locally, it must have been at least as difficult to induce the smith to make them as it was to persuade the peasant to use them.

8   *Earth*, New English Library ed. (London, 1962), 21–2.
9   W. Reymont, *Chłopi;* English trans.: *The Peasants* (New York, 1938), Vol. 1, *Autumn*, 7.
10 *Agricultural Cooperation and Rural Credit in Europe*, Senate Document 214, 63rd Congress, 1913, 270.

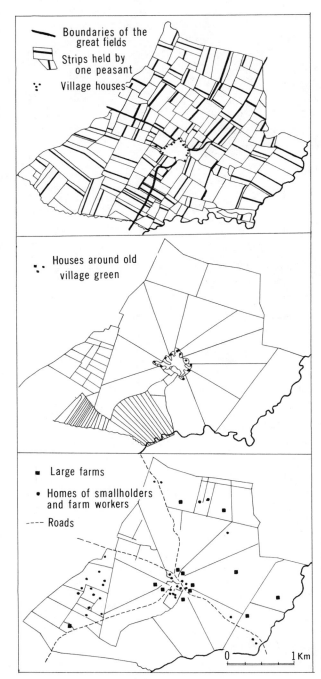

11.36. Land enclosure in Denmark. The maps relate, respectively, to 1769 (*top*), 1805 (*middle*), and 1893 (*bottom*). [After H. Thorpe, "The Influence of Enclosure on the Form and Pattern of Rural Settlement in Denmark," *Institute of British Geographers: Transactions and Papers* 17 (1951): 11–29.]

Primitive plows:

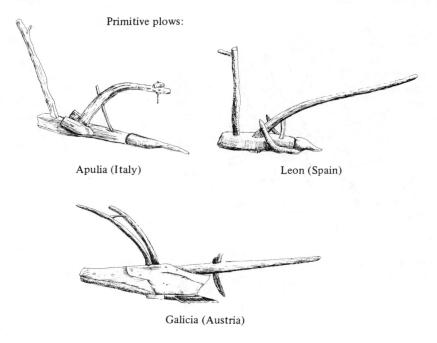

Apulia (Italy)   Leon (Spain)

Galicia (Austria)

Nineteenth-century plows:

Swing plow (England)

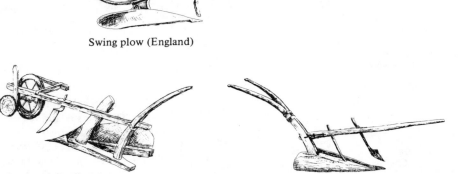

Brabant (Belgium)   Germany

11.37. Types of plows used during the nineteenth century

New practices were introduced from above, on the lands of the gentry who read the journals and visited the shows, and from them filtered slowly downward to the humblest peasant. In Zola's didactic novel *Terre,* the rich farmer is pictured as progressive, trying with little success to induce the poor to use better seed and chemical fertilizers. In Poland, Reymont's novel *Chłopi* (*The Peasants*) showed the peasant working his land in just the same way as his medieval forebears had done, but even here there was evidence of a downward percolation of new ideas. The local priest had received some new seed from Warsaw, with which he was determined to experiment!

In northwest Europe changes were occurring in other directions. In Great Britain a seed drill, first used in the previous century, began to spread; more elaborate harrows were introduced for breaking up the soil; elevators for stacking hay, threshing machines, lighter and more speedy wagons, all came into use. Later in the century horse-drawn machines for cutting hay and harvesting were introduced, and in the mid-century a steel plow made its appearance. But these advances were dependent on developments in the manufacturing industry. They were made with relative ease in Great Britain, but with very much greater difficulty in much of continental Europe. On the eve of World War I, in Poland, the flail and primitive, wooden plows prevailed on peasant farms. Only on the estates of the gentry had more sophisticated equipment come into use.

The supply of manure had always been critical and was the primary reason for the long retention of fallowing and *vaine pâture.* Peasants had learned by experience the value of manure. The cities generated large quantities, including the sweepings of stables, which were carted to suburban market gardens. There was a modest supply in areas of enclosed fields because, as a general rule, more animals were kept, but the open fields, which needed it most, were left desperately short. The situation was, however, relieved as the century wore on by the increasing use of legumes and artificial grasses on the fallow, and by the introduction of chemical fertilizers. At the same time growing use was made of lime and marl. Such developments, however, were largely restricted to western and central Europe and were almost unknown in southern and eastern. In the long run it was chemical fertilizers which were the most important, especially in Germany where they were first used on a large scale in the 1870s. At first they consisted mainly of saltpeter (KNO_3) imported from Chile, then of sulphates and nitrates from gas manufacturing and coal tar distillation, and lastly of basic slag from the steelworks and natural salts from the newly developed workings in central Germany. The greatest use was made of fertilizers in Great Britain, the Low Countries, and Germany. France used little and southern and eastern Europe almost none. The very great increase in cereal production during the century was, it has been claimed, in large measure the consequence of the increased application of nitrogen to the soil.

The slow decay of the open-field system and the introduction of catch crops on the fallow paved the way for radically different crop rotations, adjusted more closely to the qualities of the soil or the needs of the market. In regions of enclosed fields it had long been the practice, after a year or two of cropping, to grass down the

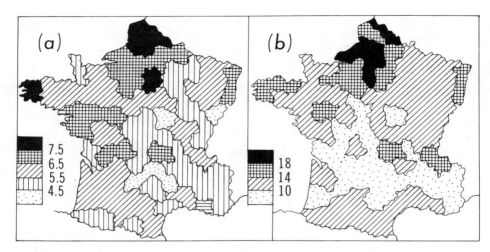

11.38. (*a*) Yield ratios, and (*b*) yields in quintals per hectare of wheat in France, about 1840. [After M. Morineau, "Ya-t-il eu une révolution agricole en France au XVIIIe siècle?," *Revue Historique* 239 (1968): 299–326.]

fields and to leave them under "long-ley" for a period. In Mecklenburg, north Germany, where von Thünen, the author of *The Isolated State,* farmed his estate of Tellow, a variable rotation covering up to nine years was introduced on his newly enclosed fields. Everywhere, progressive farmers were mixing cereals, legumes, roots, and grass, experimenting to find the best rotation for their soil and the greatest profit for themselves.

All these changes, small though many of them were, added up to the immense increase in total agricultural production that has been noted. Yield ratios, the most meaningful measure of agricultural growth, had shown only small improvements over previous centuries. They varied greatly. In France, about 1840, the best were more than twice the level of the lowest (Figs. 11.38 and 11.39). The increase in yield ratios in the course of the century went far toward explaining the increased cereal production. In Germany yield ratios were initially lower than those of France but increased sharply late in the century, with the growing use of fertilizer; they remained low throughout eastern and southeastern Europe where few technical improvements were made and no fertilizer was used.

An important feature of the developing agricultural scene during the nineteenth century was the increasing importance of animal farming. The enclosure of fields permitted better maintenance and more careful breeding. The increased production of roots and fodder improved its quality. This was accompanied by a change in the balance between animals. Sheep rearing, for which fallow grazing had been important, declined. Dairy and beef cattle became more important with increased demand for milk and meat. Most parts of western Europe became in some measure areas of mixed farming, and in those particularly suited to growing grass and fodder, the balance was tipped in favor of dairy cattle and the production of milk,

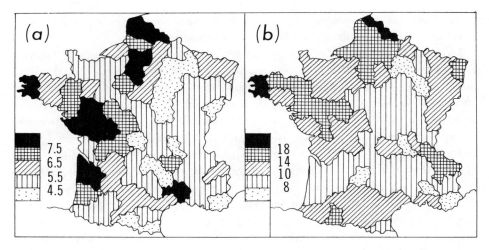

11.39. (*a*) Yield ratios, and (*b*) yields in quintals per hectare of rye in France, about 1840. (After M. Morineau, "Ya-t-il eu une révolution agricole?")

butter, and cheese. Such areas included much of the clay lands of England, Normandy, and the Netherlands. In Denmark a veritable revolution in farming turned a country which had previously produced mainly cereals in a three-course rotation into a specialized producer of dairy goods and bacon. In Switzerland there was a sharp increase in the number of dairy cattle, and the grazing lands along the Po in northern Italy became the source of Parmesan and Gorgonzola cheese. Most of these changes occurred late in the century, after rapid transportation to the cities had been developed. Broadly speaking, the most accessible of these areas marketed liquid milk; the more remote specialized in butter and cheese.

The rearing of hogs, previously half-wild creatures of the woods, was moving to the dairy country, where they consumed the by-products of butter and cheese production. Horses remained the chief draft animal, tending, for many purposes, to replace the slow-moving ox. The growing specialization of animal farming led to a decline in transhumance. The seasonal migration of sheep across the Spanish Meseta (see p. 333) was diminishing. Sheep and cattle still moved up to the "alps" in early summer, but their numbers were fewer, and they were even known to travel by train.

MANUFACTURING

When the Napoleonic Wars came to an end, Great Britain was already an industrial power. A century of innovation had transformed the technology of its textile and metal industries. The steam engine was being used increasingly to power factories and to operate mines. The greater part, as much as four-fifths, of the world's coal production was in Great Britain, and a smaller fraction, perhaps a half, of the world's iron was smelted there. Most of Europe's cotton spindles were to be found in Lancashire, gathered in large mechanically powered factories. Everywhere, the traditional craft-based industries were in retreat.

Little of this industrial technology had yet been adopted in continental Europe. Despite laws to prevent the export of machines and the migration of skilled craftsmen, knowledge of the new techniques had in one way or another reached the continent. The latter was, however, unprepared for it. Resistance to innovation, combined with a lack of scientific attitude, made it difficult for the continental entrepreneur to emulate his British counterpart. Plans could be obtained with ease. A witness before a Parliamentary Committee in 1825 declared that Cockerill of Liège had obtained engineer's drawings "from a person who was in England . . . and who has rolls of drawings of all the machinery in this country."[11] The difficulty was to find skilled labor and the machine tools to implement these plans. Nevertheless, the Napoleonic period had prepared the way for an industrial revolution in continental Europe comparable with that which was taking place in Britain. The French had swept away "a whole deadwood of time-honored institutions . . . which had been hampering economic progress"[12] – guild regulations, tolls, and restrictions on trade.

The half century following Waterloo was for much of Europe one of unaccustomed peace, growing production, and increasingly effective demand, especially in rural and agricultural sectors. This was reflected in the adoption of British innovations – the law against their export was repealed in 1846 – and a rapid increase in production, at least in western Europe, occurred after about 1850.

The factory system

Protoindustry decayed slowly during the century. In some areas it gave place to factory industry; more often it dwindled away as younger men migrated and others grew old on the job. The last practitioners of a decaying protoindustry were not infrequently aging women who made lace or turned the handle of a stocking knitter. The contribution of protoindustry to later industrial growth has to be looked for in the entrepreneurs who managed the system and, in some instances, accumulated wealth to invest in factory development. There were many reasons for the long survival of protoindustry in an age dominated by factory production. Among them were lack of capital and institutional and psychological barriers to change. But above all the system survived because if offered a viable alternative to mechanically powered factory industry. Many craft industries could not be mechanized, like expert woodworking. Others served only a local market and could not make use of the economies of scale offered by the factory, and yet others survived because they were a supplement to agriculture.

11   *Report from the Select Committee on the Laws relating to the Export of Tools and Machinery*, Parliamentary Papers, 1825, V, 115–66, 149.
12   F. Crouzet, "Western Europe and Great Britain: Catching up in the First Half of the Nineteenth Century," in *Economic Development in the Long Run*, ed. A. J. Youngson (London, 1972), 99.

The handworker fought a losing battle against the machine. He was at the mercy of the merchant capitalist, intent only to buy his product at the lowest price, and in time of depression he had no income at all. In 1848 the French sociologist A. Audiganne wrote of the "complete deprivation and deepest misery" among domestic workers, adding that hours and conditions of work in the factory were better than the working conditions of "those who work freely at home in their families."[13] The system survived longest in subsidiary branches of the textile industry, like lace making and embroidery, and in the production of small metal goods such as nails.

The essence of the Industrial Revolution was the application of mechanical power to manufacturing processes. The factory was the inevitable consequence because, in order to be economic, power had to be generated in large units. Nevertheless, the boundary between workshop and factory is hard to draw. In some of the earliest factories, processes were entirely manual, the factory building merely providing a scene for disciplined and coordinated labor. After 1815 British-made steam engines began to be used in mills in continental Europe. It was not long before they were made there, first by Cockerill of Seraing, near Liège, later in Berlin, Hanover, and the Ruhr. The steam engine was adapted to iron smelting and rolling mills and to many and varied uses in other branches of manufacturing.

Until the second half of the century industrial growth was largely in the textile and the iron and steel industries. Rising living standards were leading to an increased demand for clothing, and the necessary development of transportation and of other social overheads called for large quantities of iron and steel. Not until the second half, or even the last third of the century was the range of factory industry extended to include chemicals, glass, china, paper, and consumer goods, though these had long been produced on a small or workshop scale.

The transition from domestic to factory production was accompanied by a change in location. In Great Britain the major branches of manufacturing had migrated to the coalfields. Factory development came later in continental Europe. Sources of waterpower were more abundant, and when the use of steam power became necessary, a railroad system already existed to bring fuel to the factories. In no instance was a significant textile industry located on a coalfield because of its need for fuel. In most instances there was a gradual conversion from waterpower to steam power. This, however, cannot be said of the iron industry. The coalfields were, at least until the last third of the century, an irresistible magnet. The iron industry's fuel consumption was enormous, and part at least of its ore supply was found in the coal measures.

In the second half of the century technical and structural changes within manufacturing industries brought about some degree of relocation. Different sources of raw materials dictated new locations; the great ports became industrial centers, processing imported materials; greater economies in the use of coal led some branches of industry, notably iron smelting, to establish themselves at other than coalfield

13 *De l'organisation du travail* (Paris, 1848), 66–7.

sites. Lastly an increasing range of production was attracted toward its market, whether in the great consuming centers – the big cities – or in other branches of manufacturing which used its products. Thus, during the second half of the century every great city and every major industrial region was attracting new types of manufacturing, so that there were few branches that were not represented in Greater London, or Paris, or Berlin, or in the industrial regions of northern France, the lower Rhineland, or Saxony.

The textile industry

The manufacture of woolens was a domestic industry in most parts of Europe, but commercial production was in the early nineteenth century concentrated in a few restricted areas. Foremost among them were the woolen regions of England: East Anglia and the west country. But by the end of the century Yorkshire held a near monopoly of the British woolen industry. It was scattered through a group of towns for which Leeds served as a commercial center, but individual towns developed a narrow specialization not met with elsewhere in Europe. Worsted weaving was separate from that of woolens and shoddy. The industry lay on or very close to the coalfield, and even before the railway age it was linked by canal and river with the ports.

In no other region was the woolen industry as concentrated as in West Yorkshire. In France it was important at the beginning of the century in towns and villages in the north and in Normandy, Champagne, and Languedoc. Most had no particular advantage and their traditional craft industry slowly decayed. Only along the Seine valley near Rouen, at Reims and Sedan, and, above all, in the Lille region did it survive.

The cloth industry of the Low Countries survived at Verviers and spread across the German border to Aachen and the Eifel hills. As the domestic industry declined, the manufacture concentrated in the small towns of the region. From here it spread into the lower Rhineland and the Ore Mountains of Saxony. Greater Berlin became one of the larger centers of the cloth industry during the century, but declined in the face of competition from Saxony and the lower Rhineland. The towns of the Saxon Ore Mountains, so similar in location and physical resources to Verviers and Aachen, became in the course of the century the chief German centers for woolen textiles.

In Poland and Russia attempts to foster a cloth industry met with little success except at Łódź, and here it was subordinate to cotton (see p. 404). In Russia a woolen industry on a workshop–factory basis had been established in the previous century at Voronezh, Kazan, and Smolensk in western Russia. It expanded throughout the century but remained, in terms of organization and equipment, far behind the industry in central Europe. Indeed, the handloom remained in use here longer than almost anywhere else in Europe. In Bohemia and Moravia, on the other hand, the industry grew rapidly, stimulated by entrepreneurs from the west and the vast market of the Habsburg empire. Early in the century small factories and workshops, powered by water, sprang up. Many of the more favorably sited were converted to steam power, and Brno, Liberec, and Jihlava became centers of the cloth industry before the end of the century.

The woolen industry never achieved any great importance in southern Europe. In the course of the century a factory-based cloth industry grew up in Catalonia, in the hinterland of Barcelona, and in the Alpine foothills of northern Italy. A coarse cloth was made in the cottages of the Balkans and marketed in the Ottoman empire, and in 1836 a factory industry was established at Sliven, in Bulgaria, for the purpose of making uniforms for the Turkish army. Others followed – at Plovdiv, near Sofia, and elsewhere – but the Balkan industry was carried on in small inefficient workshops and failed to compete with superior imported cloth. The history of the woolen industry in Europe is one of very slow growth throughout the century. The market for fabrics was expanding, but an increasing share of it was being taken by cottons.

The other traditional textile manufacture was linen weaving. It was, and largely remained, a peasant industry. The peasant could himself grow, prepare, and spin the flax, weave it into linen, and bleach and dye the cloth. It was carried on during the first half of the century wherever flax grew well, and not even the spinning and weaving of wool drove it from the cottages of northern Europe. From Brittany to Poland its manufacture was the foremost of domestic crafts. It was the ideal complement to a small agricultural holding, and the loom was always busy during the dark winter days. Without it, wrote the *sous-préfet* of Mayenne in 1832, "men were reduced to idleness and families deprived of their means of subsistence,"[14] and Tennent advised the traveler in Belgium to buy linen in spring, because that was when the peasant offered his winter's work for sale in the markets. Nowhere was linen weaving more important than in Flanders, where it had completely replaced the old cloth industry. In 1843, it was said, 20 percent of the population was engaged in one way or another in its manufacture. But the market for the rough linen which was woven in the peasant's cottage was declining with the increased availability and lower cost of cotton.

The plain of Westphalia was noted for the quality of its flax, which was "almost the sole commodity which creates any external trade."[15] But here too demand languished and the domestic weaver abandoned his loom. The linen industry survived through the century only in a few factories which produced a superior fabric. The fact was that machines invented to spin and weave cotton and wool did not work well with flax. Public demand turned to cotton, and it was on cotton that the Industrial Revolution was based in Great Britain and in much of continental Europe.

The reason both for the slow growth of the woolen industry and the absolute decline of the linen was the triumphant progress of cotton. Cotton fabrics were versatile and attractive, capable of being both dyed and printed with colored de-

14 Quoted in Claude Fohlen, *L'Industrie textile au temps du Second Empire* (Paris, 1956), 164.
15 Jacob, *Agriculture and the Trade in Corn*, 91.

signs. They could be laundered easily, and their widespread adoption was itself a contribution of no small importance to personal hygiene. These advantages made cotton clothing fashionable long before factory production made it cheap. A series of innovations, beginning with the spinning jenny, had begun to spread to continental Europe before the Revolutionary wars, and the period from 1815 to 1848 saw the emergence of a factory industry in most countries. By mid-century hand spinning had disappeared from western and central Europe and the handloom remained in use in only a few backward areas. The cotton industry was fully mechanized during the second half of the century, and its motive power in almost every factory derived from steam. In Great Britain this brought about an increasing concentration near the Lancashire coalfield. In continental Europe it had no such effect. Conversion to steam power was slower, and when a supply of coal was needed, the railroads were already in existence to carry it. The cotton industry, secondly, tended to grow up where there was a significant protoindustry engaged in textile manufacture, and thus a labor supply familiar with the spinning and weaving processes. In Great Britain a kind of segregation developed between the cotton and the woolen branches. In continental Europe this rarely happened. Most textile manufacturing regions produced woolens as well as cottons, and even handled flax and silk. A single factory might work with more than one material. Mixed fabrics were more commonly made than in Great Britain, and works would switch from one fabric to another according to market conditions and the availability of materials. There was, for example, a conversion from cottons to linen during the "cotton famine" of 1861–5, when American supplies were cut off.

In France the cotton industry was established along the Seine valley between Paris and Rouen. It expanded rapidly after 1815, and almost every stream which dropped from the plateau of Caux to the river had its mill. Spinning was completely mechanized during the first half of the century, but the handloom weaver, working in his cottage and dividing his time between his loom and his smallholding, remained important much longer. The second region of the French industry was the north, where it centered in Lille and was carried on in numerous small towns of the area. The industry here was heir to the woolen industry but remained relatively unspecialized. Lille and its neighboring towns of Roubaix and Tourcoing were, in consequence of the earlier mechanization of the spinning process, more important for yarn than for woven fabrics. Indeed, Lille supplied cotton yard to weaving, hosiery, and lace making industries in much of France. The third cotton region was Alsace (see p. 338). By the mid-century the Alsatian industry was largely mechanized and in volume of production was second only to the north. In 1871 Alsace passed to the German empire. Many of its textile workers crossed the Vosges into Lorraine, where they established a rival industry at Epinal and Remiremont. Meanwhile, what remained of the Alsatian industry languished under German control and in competition with the growing manufactures of south Germany and Saxony.

The Belgian cotton industry was established in Flanders at the beginning of the century, succumbed to British competition after 1815, and then revived and be-

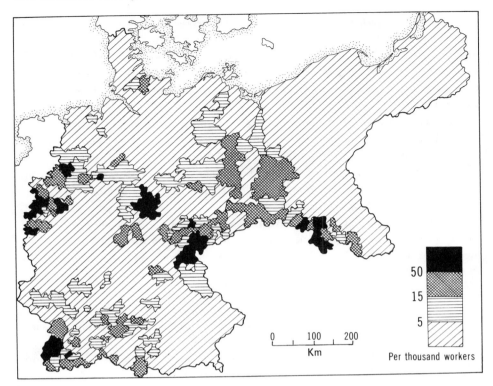

11.40. The distribution of weavers in Germany, about 1885. The principal cloth-making areas – the lower Rhineland, Baden and south Germany, Saxony and Silesia – are readily apparent. [After P. Kollmann, "Die gewerbliche Entfaltung im deutschen Reich," *Jahrbuch für Gesetzgebung, Verwaltung und Volkswirtschaft im Deutschen Reich* 12 (Leipzig, 1888): 437–528

came successful at Ghent. In the Netherlands cotton began to replace flax early in the century, but it was many years before a factory industry was established at Almelo in the east of the country. It benefited from cheap labor in this populous and agriculturally backward area and was, in consequence, very slow to mechanize.

In the course of the century three cotton-working regions emerged in Germany: the lower Rhineland and Westphalia, south Germany, and Saxony–Silesia. These are readily apparent in Figure 11.40, which shows the distribution of all weavers, among whom in 1885 cotton weavers would have formed the most numerous group. In northwest Germany cotton spinning and weaving first began to displace flax working as a domestic craft; it then became a factory industry along the Wupper valley and in Gladbach, Rheydt, and Viersen. The second region was south Germany which grew rapidly during the later nineteenth century to become the largest producer in Germany. Like Alsace, it owed much to Swiss enterprise and capital, and, like the latter, it showed how efficient management could overcome obstacles presented by lack of fuel and the long-distance transport of materials.

Saxony and Silesia formed the third region. It derived much of its inspiration from south Germany, as the latter had done from Switzerland. Chemnitz (Karl-Marx-Stadt) was its initial center, but it spread through the foothills of the Ore Mountains and into Silesia. In its more important centers it became mechanized at an early date, but in the innermost recesses of the mountains the handloom was still in use in 1912.

Switzerland was an early center of the cotton industry. Spinning mills had been established at Saint Gallen and Zurich in 1800, and by 1827 there were 106 mechanical spinneries in Canton Zurich alone. Yet the speed of this early growth was not maintained, in part because of the violent reaction of some of the weavers to the use of machines. As late as 1900 less than a tenth of the looms in Canton Appenzell had been mechanized.

The Swiss industry spread into Austria, especially into Vorarlberg and Tyrol, where it suffered from the same problems – small-scale operations and lack of mechanization. It was, therefore, Bohemia and Moravia which concentrated the cotton industry of the Habsburg empire. Small, water-powered mills spread through the hills of Moravia and northeast Bohemia. The years from about 1825 to about 1875 were a period of rapid growth. The number of spindles increased about sixfold, and it is claimed that spinning was fully mechanized by 1830 and weaving by 1872.

The chain of development, which, based on British initiative, had spread from Switzerland to southern Germany and then to Saxony, came to an end in Poland and Russia. In the 1820s a textile industry, based mainly on cotton, was founded at Łódź. Entrepreneurs came from Chemnitz, and their factories were built just within the Russian customs area in order to profit from its immense market. The industry used waterpower until the railroad was built to bring coal from Silesia, and it spread out into surrounding villages. Both city and industry grew very rapidly after about 1880, and Łódź became one of the largest and most concentrated of all centers of the textile industry. In 1864 the Russian government excluded "Congress" Poland, in which Łódź lay, from its customs area. At once the Łódź industrialists established an industry at Białystok, which lay just within the boundary of Russia proper. It never achieved any great size and met with the competition of the textile industry which was developing at this time in Russia itself.

Cotton weaving was established in Russia, chiefly in the cities of the Moscow region, early in the century. Much of the thread was imported, and it was not until the 1830s, when Russia began to receive textile machines from Britain, that the spinning industry really developed. There was a large demand for cotton "prints," and in many instances the magnates established factories and set their own serfs to work in them. The industry grew very rapidly and in 1860 employed more than any other branch of manufacturing. Growth was interrupted in the 1860s but thereafter continued to expand until World War I. The industry was not, however, fully mechanized even in its chief centers in Moscow and the Vladimir and Ivanovo districts to the northeast, until the end of the century.

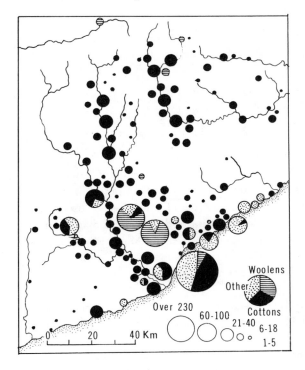

11.41. The textile region of Catalonia. [After P. Vilar, "La vie industrielle dans la région de Barcelone," *Annales de Géographie* 38 (1929): 339–65.]

Modern industry was late in coming to southern Europe. The region lacked fuel resources, and even reserves of waterpower were severely limited by the climate. In the mid-nineteenth century a cotton industry was established in Catalonia, the only region of Spain which was liberal enough to welcome industrial innovation. Nevertheless, the mechanization of spinning came slowly, and by 1850 a quarter of the spindles were hand-operated. Mechanization of weaving came later still. Industrial development took place in the hilly hinterland of Barcelona, where dozens of small mills made the most of the available resources for waterpower (Fig. 11.41). Much of the market for Spanish textiles was in the empire, most of which was lost in the Spanish-American War of 1898.

The Italian cotton industry also owed much to Swiss initiative. Spinning was mechanized at Monza, Gallarate, Busto Arsizio, and other cities close to the Alps, but, as in Spain, the handloom remained important until late in the century. In 1904 the British consul reported that a quarter of the looms were still hand-operated. Table 11.8 indicates the rapidity with which the industry grew after the unification of Italy in 1861.

The silk industry differed from other branches of textile manufacture in catering for a luxury market which was highly elastic. The raw silk was a peasant product in Italy and, to a small extent, in southern France. Silk reeling and throwing were widely diffused through the countryside, but weaving was not left to the rough hands of the peasants but was carried on by specialized craftsmen – the aristocrats of the textile industry – at a small number of centers: Lyons, Krefeld, Zurich, and

Table 11.8. *Cotton textile industry in Italy*

	Spindles	Power looms
1868	450,000	—
1876	764,000	15,517
1900	2,111,000	70,600
1914	4,620,000	120,000

Spitalfields in east London. Ribbon weaving expanded in the Saint-Etienne district of France (see p. 339) and at Basel and Elberfeld-Barmen (Wuppertal).

The decay of rural textile crafts left a legacy of manufactures which used thread – mostly cotton – to make hosiery, lace, and embroidery. These manufacturers survived in the cottages of Normandy, Brittany, the Central Massif, Belgium, and Switzerland. But before the end of the century even these were being absorbed into small factories which were able to replicate mechanically the traditional designs once produced manually.

By the mid-nineteenth century textile industries had assumed a spatial pattern which they were to retain until World War I (Fig. 11.42). A number of major centers had crystallized from the broad mass of handicraft industries. Except in Great Britain, the locations of these regions was not strongly influenced by the availability of coal. The presence of waterpower was more important. Nor, except in Britain, were these regions narrowly specialized. All processed wool and flax as well as cotton, though the balance fluctuated between them, and all grew rapidly during the second half of the century. There are no satisfactory indicators of the volume of output or the rate of growth. It seems that wool consumption increased more than three times, the number of cotton spindles increased from about 9 million in 1850 to 33 million in 1913, and the consumption of raw cotton increased three and a half times.

Iron and steel industries

Neither the technology nor the spatial pattern of the textile industries changed significantly after the mid-century. The iron and steel industry, on the other hand, underwent a series of technological changes, and its spatial pattern was in consequence in a continuing state of adaptation to new conditions.

In the years following the Napoleonic Wars there was a strong contrast between the industry practiced in Britain and that in the rest of Europe. In the former the use of charcoal had been almost completely abandoned; smelting was with coke, and the refinery had given place to the puddling furnace. The huge demand for coal had drawn the industry almost entirely to the coalfields. In continental Europe there was, with the possible exception of the "royal" works in Upper Silesia, not a single furnace fueled with coke, and the location of the hundreds of furnaces was dictated largely by the availability of charcoal.

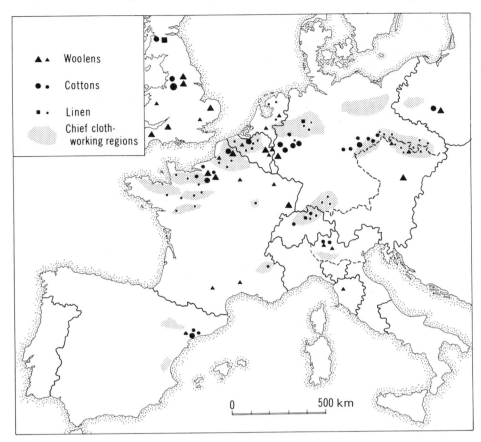

11.42. The European textile industry in the mid-nineteenth century

Technical problems in using coke as blast-furnace fuel were gradually overcome: at Liège in 1821; on the Saar and Saint-Etienne (Loire) coalfields soon after; and, in 1849, in the Ruhr district itself. This was a period of rapid expansion in the industry, and newly built furnaces were mostly established on or very close to the coalfields. Central Belgium and northern France, the Saint-Etienne district, the Ruhr and Upper Silesia became increasingly important for iron smelting and steel-making.

But the age of the charcoal furnace was far from over. Coke-smelted iron had many disadvantages. In particular, it tended to absorb sulfur and did not refine well, and the demand for charcoal iron continued, especially for quality steel (Fig. 11.43). New furnaces continued to be built, despite the scarcity of charcoal, in eastern France, central Germany, and at many places in eastern Europe. But in the latter half of the century things began to change. On the one hand the demand for charcoal could not be met; on the other, better coking ovens produced a superior quality of coke, and improvements in the refining processes overcame the

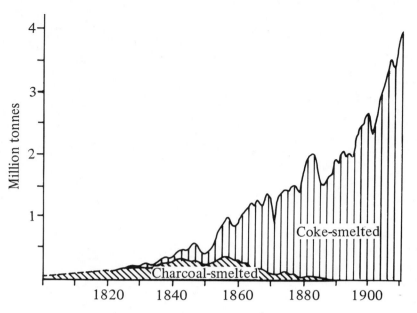

11.43. The use of charcoal and coke in the iron-smelting industry of Great Britain

deleterious qualities of coke-smelted iron. In *département* Haute Marne in eastern France, once one of the foremost producers of charcoal iron, there were seventy-five furnaces in 1864. This fell to thirty-three in 1880, to ten in 1890, and to only four in 1910. Only in Sweden did charcoal-smelted iron remain important.

High-carbon iron from the furnace was refined either on the hearth or in the puddling furnace (see pp. 336–7). Puddling was introduced into France soon after 1815, and by 1827 there were said to be 149 puddling furnaces in use. It spread quickly, to Belgium, Aachen, the Saar, the Ruhr, and on to Moravia and Upper Silesia. Charcoal-smelted iron from the forests was brought to the coalfield to be puddled, and it was the puddling furnace that first drew the iron industry to the coalfields.

Steel continued to be made by "recarburating" soft or wrought iron to the required degree. The Huntsman process (see p. 418) was perfected by Krupp at Essen, in the Ruhr, and was important also at Bochum, Saint-Etienne, and in central Belgium. There was no major technical innovation for many years, during which the demand for iron for railroad construction and ship building mounted. Blast furnaces grew in size and efficiency, especially after the introduction of the hot blast in 1831. But there was still no cheap and expeditious way of making steel. Then, about 1860, both the Bessemer "converter" and the open hearth were developed and patented. The former process consisted of blowing hot air through the liquid metal, oxidizing and removing the carbon, after which the liquid metal could be recarburized by the addition of carbon. The process gained immediate acceptance, so great was the demand for steel. On every important coalfield the converter began to replace the puddling furnace. But disadvantages were quick to appear. Minute air bubbles weakened the metal, and the process failed to eliminate phosphorus which made the metal brittle, or "cold-short" in the language of the industry. It could in fact be used only with nonphosphoric ores, with consequences of immense importance for the location of the industry.

In the meantime Pierre Martin adapted Werner von Siemen's reverberatory furnace to the needs of refining iron. It broadly resembled the puddling furnace, but it burned gas and operated at a higher temperature, melting down the iron and oxidizing the carbon. It could be used in conjunction with the coke ovens which produced gas as a by-product. But the Siemens-Martin process also failed to eliminate phosphorus from the metal.

By this time most important ore deposits were nearing exhaustion, and the largest known reserves — in Lorraine and Luxembourg, in north Germany, and in northern Sweden — were phosphoric. Experimentation was intense to find a method of "dephosphorizing" iron, and when, in 1879, Gilchrist and Thomas met with success, their process was avidly adopted. Henceforward there were no fears for an ore shortage. Nonphosphoric ores from central Sweden and North Africa lost something of their short-lived importance. The future, however, lay with the low-grade phosphoric ores of Lorraine and with the higher grade ores of Kiruna in the Swedish Arctic.

Swedish ores aside, the phosphoric ores all had a low metal content, 30 percent or less. Some were, under existing conditions, not worth mining. It was costly to transport ores, three-quarters of which might be waste. At the same time the efficiency of the blast furnace continued to be improved and its fuel consumption to be reduced. It became as profitable to convey coal to the ore field as ore to the coalfield. Furthermore it seemed practicable, if ores imported from overseas were to be used, to build smelting works at the ports where the ore was unloaded from seagoing carriers. Beginning in the 1880s the spatial pattern of ironworking began to change. The old centers — Belgium and northern France, the Saar, the Ruhr, and Upper Silesia — remained important. Some, like Saint-Etienne and Saxony, lost their smelting capacity and retained only steelmaking and metal fabrication. But most new works were either on the ore fields of eastern France or northern Germany, or at the ports. Toward the end of the period the electric furnace came into use for making steel, but its immense consumption of power limited it to areas, such as the French Alps, where hydroelectric power was abundant.

The market for iron and steel grew far faster than that for textiles and was of the order of seventy times larger in 1913 than it had been a century earlier. Demand for cast iron almost disappeared until a market developed for cast-iron pipes for municipal water and gas systems. From about 1840 the biggest consumers of wrought iron and later of steel were the railroads. A mile of track incorporated about 50 tons of metal, increasing with heavier locomotives to about 140 tons. In the mid-century track was being laid at a rate of more than 3,000 miles a year, involving an annual consumption for track alone of considerably more than 400,000 tons. If to this is added the metal used in locomotives, wagons, bridges, and other constructions, the consumption by the railroads could not have been less than 600,000 and perhaps nearer a million tons a year. And when the European systems were nearing completion, railroads were beginning to be built overseas, using mainly iron and steel from Europe. At the same time iron and later steel were being used increasingly in ship construction and in factories and mechanical equipment of all kinds.

THE SECOND INDUSTRIAL REVOLUTION

The first Industrial Revolution took place in the textile and metal industries, and it was in these that most of the technical advances were made and the vast increase in industrial production achieved. By the second half of the century another and more diverse wave of innovations was taking place. The goods affected ranged from basic chemicals to pharmaceuticals and dyestuffs; from instruments and machine tools to steel-built ships and automobiles; from paper to footwear. They included both investment and consumer goods. Most were cumulative, in the sense that any one technical advance was likely to make other advances probable. Lastly, separate branches of manufacturing interacted and promoted one another, so that progress became possible on a broad front.

During the first third of the century the chemical industry was dominated by the need to produce basic chemicals for soap, glass, and other simple products. Bleach and mordants were made for the textile industries. These called for large quantities of soda and the common acids. The chief centers of production were the great ports and existing manufacturing areas. They grew up in Britain, France, Belgium, and the Rhineland. Then, after about 1860, Germany came to the fore as the most important source of chemicals. At the same time the industry began to diversify. Coal-tar distillates became increasingly important, and in the 1870s the waste gases of the coke ovens began to be collected. Aniline dyes and pharmaceuticals on the one hand, fertilizers on the other, all derived from by-products of coking, and in these Great Britain and Germany acquired an immense lead over the rest of the continent.

France, which had at first led in the development of the modern industry, began to decline, at least relatively, a result, in part, of legal decisions regarding industrial patents, in part of the superior natural advantages of its competitors. The lead passed to Switzerland, which inherited some of France's industrial skills, and to Germany. The river Rhine became lined with chemical works, from Leverkusen in the north to Mannheim and Ludwigshafen in the south, and the chain was continued to Basel, the chief center of the Swiss industry, with its emphasis on dyestuffs and pharmaceuticals. The advantage of a river site lay in the cheap transportation which it offered for coal and other raw materials. At the same time, the discovery of the potash deposits at Stassfurt in Saxony, together with the exploitation of vast reserves of brown coal, led to the manufacture of fertilizers and basic chemicals, with important consequences for German agriculture (see pp. 395–6). In Britain the manufacture of heavy chemicals grew up in the vicinity of the salt deposits of Cheshire and near the port of Liverpool. Alongside these large and heavily capitalized industries were countless factories which produced more specialized goods: bleach, paint, lacquers, ink, soap, and cleansing materials. Many were consumer-oriented and grew up near large centers of population. Some cities, among them Berlin, Paris, and London, became noteworthy for the number and variety of their chemical-based industries. Among them was the manufacture of photographic equipment which was established at Berlin by AGFA.

The metal-using industries underwent a similar development in the closing decades before World War I. The earlier dominance of rolled steel – rails, girders, plates – gave way to an immense variety of smaller and inherently more valuable goods. In Great Britain they were very prominent in the West Midlands, where they were sometimes known as "Birmingham" wares. They were most often made in workshops or small factories, such as were to be found in the hills of the Sauerland, south of the Ruhr. Here knives, cutting tools, files, screws, and bolts were being made in a bewildering and increasing variety. Similar small metal goods were produced in central Belgium, in Saxony, and at Saint-Etienne, which acquired a reputation for its bicycles and sewing machines.

At the same time, the building of heavy machinery, including locomotives, ships' engines, cranes, and, toward the end of the century, generators and turbines, became important. It was located chiefly near the older centers of steel production: Liège, the Ruhr, western Yorkshire, but also in the great consuming centers and the ports. Berlin, for example, became the foremost center for electrical engineering, and ports like Hamburg, Rotterdam, and London and the Tyne and Clyde estuaries in Great Britain developed as the chief centers for the construction of steel ships. At the end of the nineteenth century another branch of the engineering industry, automobile construction, emerged. It was a labor-intensive, upmarket manufacture, attracted toward the public for which it catered. Paris was, almost from the start, a leading center. But the chief factor in the location of an industry as footloose as the manufacture of automobiles was, quite simply, where the entrepreneur lived: Cannstadt (Daimler) in Würtemberg, Oxford (Morris) in England, and Turin (Agnelli-FIAT) in Italy. Automobile manufacture quickly became an assembly industry, for which access to the specialized factories which made its components was the most important consideration. The same was true of the ship building industry. Steel had largely replaced wood, and this, prefabricated at Essen, Liège, or Sheffield, was, along with all other components, assembled at the coastal sites at which ship building was mainly carried on. The growing size of ships and complexity of their design brought with it a concentration at the few centers which combined the advantages of deep water for launching and easy access to materials used. The closing decades of the period saw the extinction of dozens of small ports which had once built small ships for the coasting trade.

The clothing and footwear industries underwent both diversification and concentration. With improving living standards, clothing came to be made more and more in workshops and factories and less in the home. The industry was attracted inevitably to the twin poles – the consuming centers and the cloth-making areas.

The manufacture of ready-made clothing became a major industry in almost all great cities: London, Paris, Berlin, as well as in cities, like Leeds, which lay at the focus of the cloth industry. The same happened with footwear: a growing concentration in a few large centers, similarly oriented toward either the supply of leather or to a market increasingly dominated by fashion.

INDUSTRIAL REGIONS

In the course of the century manufacturing came gradually to be concentrated in a limited number of industrial regions, all of them characterized by the range and variety of their undertakings. Most embraced either textile or iron and steel industries, but these attracted others which either used their products or supplied their components or materials. In some this range was limited. Upper Silesia and the Ruhr were dominated by iron and steel, but also included power generation and by-product industries, such as chemicals and fertilizers. The greatest variety of activity was to be found near the major centers of consumption, like the Berlin, Paris, and London regions. These regions, secondly, extended across international boundaries, so that there was little apparent difference on each side of the Franco-Belgian or the German-Russian boundary in Silesia. It was as if the forces inherent in location and natural resources overcame any conditions imposed by government.

An industrial region was made up of a number of urban centers, one or two of which usually served as regional and commercial centers. Between them were villages, slowly industrializing as their fields were overspread with factories, workers' housing, waste heaps, and the debris of industrialization. Lastly, such regions developed a complex infrastructure consisting of transportation, water- and power-supply systems, and sewage networks. These varied with the nature and density of the industrial undertakings. They were at their most complex in the Ruhr, Upper Silesia and, in England, in the West Midlands, Lancashire, and West Yorkshire. They were relatively simple in such homogeneous and dispersed regions as Catalonia and northern Italy. There is space to examine the growth of only four of Europe's industrial regions: northwest Europe, Lorraine, Upper Silesia, and southern Russia.

Northwest Europe

This was the largest and most complex. It covered an area of two thousand square miles and had a population of 8 million at the end of the century. It arose from the convergence of many lines of development: textiles in Flanders, ironworking in central Belgium, nonferrous metals near Liège, textiles and chemicals in the lower Rhineland, iron and steel in the Ruhr, and iron fabrication in the Sauerland. The region had three advantages of incalculable importance. It was already, when the century began, one of the most densely peopled and highly urbanized areas of Europe, with a well-developed agriculture. It was the scene of an important protoindustrial development, primarily in textiles but also in ironworking. Although they were of very little significance to the early development of manufacturing, the coal resources of the region – particularly of the Ruhr – were the largest and most varied of the continent and made it possible for protoindustry to develop into factory industry. Lastly, this general area was better endowed with the means of waterborne transportation than any comparable region. The Rhine, Meuse, and the rivers of the Flanders plain linked it both with the ports and with its continental hinterland, and, though overtaken by the railroads in volume of freight, the rivers, with the canals built to feed them, continued throughout the period to transport much of the bulk goods.

Coalfields. There were at least six separate, though related, coal basins, lying in an arc between northern France and the eastern Ruhr (Fig. 11.44). In the west the coal seams lay deeply buried beneath later deposits and were not fully exploited until the mid-century (Fig. 11.45). In central Belgium the field was narrow and the seams highly contorted and difficult to mine. It was nevertheless this basin which first achieved importance because coal outcropped on the sides of the Meuse valley and was easy to mine and transport. The Aachen fields were small and of no great importance, but the Ruhr was not only the largest reserve in Europe, but contained all varieties of coal. The earliest workings were along the Ruhr valley in the south, but concessions of ever-increasing size were granted as mining slowly advanced across the "hidden" field to the north (Fig. 11.46). Most of the coalfield in northern France also lay hidden beneath later deposits. It lay very deep and not until late in the nineteenth century did its extent become known (Fig. 11.47).

Figure 11.48 shows the growth of coal production in the region as a whole. It is apparent that expansion was largely in the Ruhr basin and that central Belgium showed comparatively little increase after about 1880. The Ruhr, furthermore, contained the whole range of coal types, from "hard" coal (anthracite) to "soft" bituminous, and included large reserves of the coal best suited to making metallurgical coke. Amid such abundance, the resources in brown coal (lignite) seemed almost superfluous. The so-called Ville field lay to the west of Cologne. It was worked in shallow pits from early in the century. The coal was used for making bricks and burning lime. In 1877 a plant was installed for compressing it into briquettes, burned in electrical generating stations.

The region can be divided into four principal segments: northern France, central Belgium, Aachen, and the Ruhr.

Northern France. This was the most diversified part of the whole region. Textiles were fundamental, first woolens and linen and then cottons. Waterpower was scarce and the existence of coal nearby was not even suspected in the early days of the industry. As late as 1838 almost a third of the spinning mills in Roubaix "were still running on horse gins."[16] But with the coming of the railroads the supply of fuel was eased, and spinning and much of the weaving passed to steam-operated factories. During the second half of the century the textile industry in all

16   David Landes, "Religion and Enterprise: The Case of the French Textile Industry," in *Enterprise and Entrepreneurs in Nineteenth and Twentieth Century France*, ed. E. C. Carter, R. Foster, and J. N. Moody (Baltimore, Md., 1976), 47.

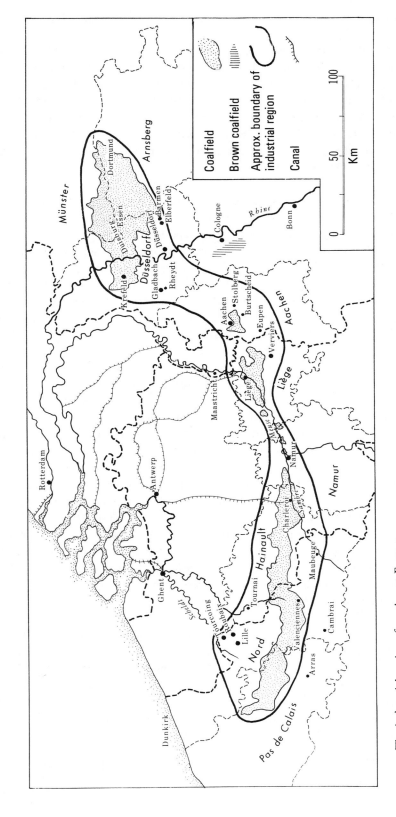

11.44. The industrial region of northwest Europe

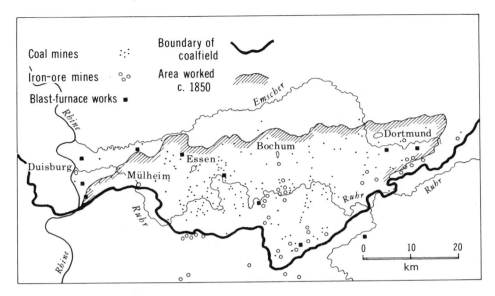

11.45. The Ruhr coalfield about 1850. [After N. J. G. Pounds, *The Ruhr* (Bloomington, Ind., 1952).]

its branches concentrated in Lille, Roubaix, and Tourcoing, which by the end of the century held some 40 percent of the spinning capacity of France.

Early in the century the iron industry spread from the Ardennes to Maubeuge, on the Sambre, where it could benefit from coal brought upriver from the Belgian field. In 1839 a smelting works and refinery were established on the French coalfield and other works followed. Labor was attracted away from the poorly organized textile industry, and the iron industry expanded on the basis of local coal and imported ore. By the early twentieth century it was second only to Lorraine (see p. 420) in the volume of iron smelted.

Central Belgium and Aachen. This was the first part of the region to develop a modern coal-based industry. With the significant exception of the woolen industry of the Verviers district, industrial growth was founded upon iron and steel. There was a declining charcoal-iron industry in the hills south of the Meuse and entrepreneurs merely shifted their activities northward to the coalfield. In 1842 there were forty-five coke-fired furnaces on the coalfield as against seventy-five smaller charcoal furnaces in the Ardennes. The latter continued to decline as smelting and puddling works multiplied in the vicinity of Liège and Charleroi. Belgian entrepreneurs in the end paid the price of being first in the field. New works elsewhere in northwest Europe were more efficient than the Belgian, and, with its ores exhausted and its coal increasingly difficult to work, the central Belgian area declined relatively to others.

The Aachen district was always less important. Its coal resources were small, but in the hills to the south there was not only a traditional ironworking industry,

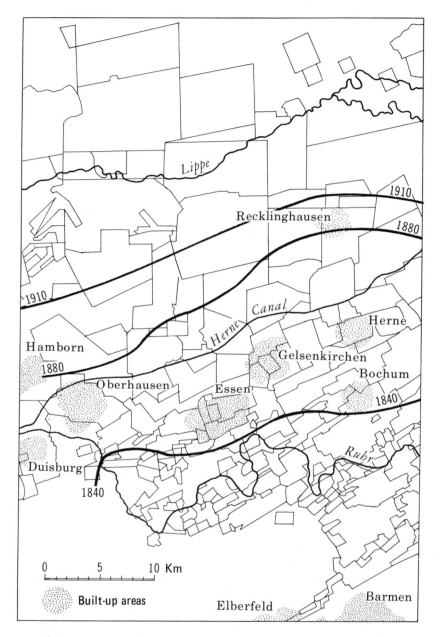

11.46. Mining concessions along a north–south transect across the Ruhr coalfield. Note the increasing size of concessions toward the north. [Based on Hans Spethmann, *Des Ruhrgebiet* (Berlin, 1933).]

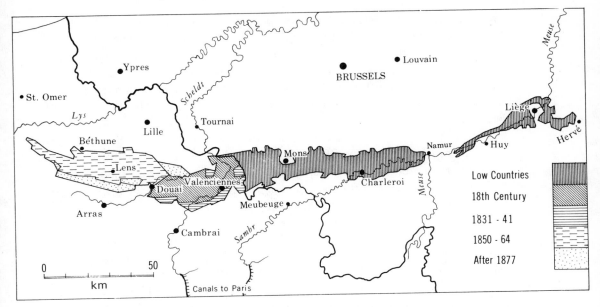

11.47. The spread of coal mining from Belgium into France with the opening up of the "hidden" coalfield

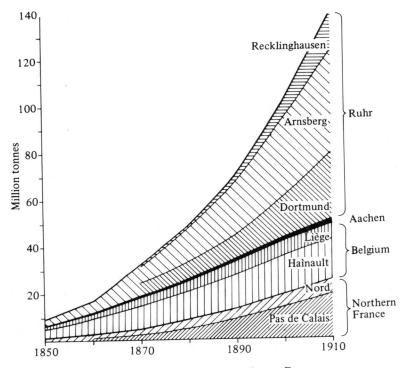

11.48. The increase in coal production in northwest Europe

similar to that of the Belgian Ardennes, but also ores of lead and zinc. The latter were worked throughout the century at Vieille Montagne until exhausted. This region owed its importance to the close proximity of Belgium. Its woolen textile industry had been promoted by entrepreneurs from Belgian Verviers. The iron industry at Aachen and Eschweiler at first puddled pig iron imported from Liège. In 1854 the German duty on imported pig iron was raised. The old pattern of industry ceased to be economic, and blast furnaces – the *Rote Erde* works – were built near Aachen. But the diseconomies of the site soon showed themselves. Ores were exhausted, the quality of fuel was poor, and there were no facilities for waterborne transportation. The industrialists one by one transferred their assets to the Ruhr or Lorraine, and the Aachen region was left with what could be salvaged from the textile and metal-processing industries.

Rhineland and Ruhr.   The plain of the Lower Rhine, together with the valleys of its right-bank tributaries, the Ruhr, Emscher, and Lippe, became in the course of the century the most highly industrialized area in the whole of Europe. The textile industries of the Rhineland cities – Gladbach, Rheydt, Viersen, Krefeld, Elberfeld-Barmen – continued to grow, and the iron and steel industries in the Ruhr region itself expanded to become the largest and most concentrated in the world. The extent and variety of the coal resources and the existence of iron ore was not known until late in the century. Until the 1840s one might have been excused for thinking that the focus of heavy industry would continue to lie in the Siegerland, well to the south of the river Ruhr. In the 1840s the English traveler T. C. Banfield could describe the environs of Essen as "poetically agricultural." But already iron, smelted in the forests of the Siegerland, was being brought down to the Ruhr valley to be puddled with the local coal. Furnaces were set up at Wetter and near Dortmund, Bochum, and Essen. There was also a small manufacture of steel by the crucible method (see p. 408). Then, in 1849, iron was first smelted with coke on the Ruhr coalfield at Mülheim-on-Ruhr. Even so, there was no immediate change, and iron continued to be smelted in the forests and puddled on the coalfield. Then, as coal mining progressed northward from the Ruhr valley into that of the Emscher, the so-called *Fettkohle* began to be mined and was found to be excellent for making blast-furnace coke. At the same time, iron ore was discovered interbedded with the coal. The volume was not large, but enough to attract smelting works to an area which could offer both ore and fuel. At least seven works were established to smelt the coal-measures ore (Fig. 11.49). This source of supply remained important for some twenty years, by which time the smelting industry was firmly established on the coalfield. There then began a search for alternative sources of ore. In the end, it proved possible to import high-grade ore from North Africa, Spain, and, above all, Sweden. At first it was brought up the Rhine from the Dutch ports. Then, between 1890 and 1899 the Dortmund-Ems Canal was cut from the eastern Ruhr to the North Sea port of Emden, and the Ruhr's future was assured. A canal, not finished until 1914, was then cut along the Emscher valley, so that ore could be distributed through the region.

The volume of production of both pig iron and steel increased steadily from the

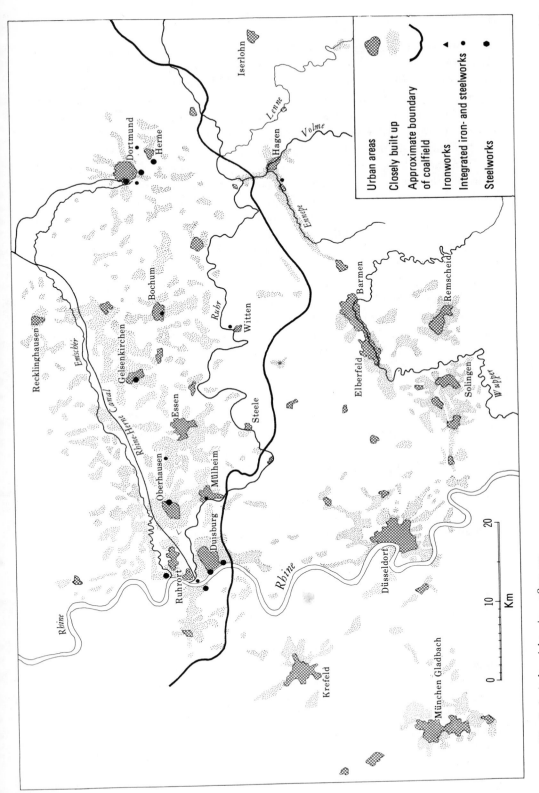

Urban areas

Closely built up

Approximate boundary
of coalfield

Ironworks

Integrated iron- and steelworks

Steelworks

11.49. The Ruhr industrial region, 1850–70

mid-century until the outbreak of World War I. In 1850 pig-iron production was about 11,500 tons, and that of steel only a few hundred. In 1913 the latter was over 8 million tons. There were a dozen large, integrated iron and steelworks, together with many works which only puddled iron or made steel. Among the latter were the Krupp works at Essen. Its reputation was at first based upon crucible steel, and later upon the making of high-quality steel for armaments in which Krupp specialized. It would, however, be wrong to think of Krupp as only an "armaments king." The Essen works was no less important for engineering and railroad equipment. The Bochum works also made special steels. Most Ruhr companies adopted the basic process, as indeed they had to in order to use Swedish ore, but tended to cling to the puddling furnace and open hearth, which yielded a better-quality metal than the converter.

The Ruhr in the narrow sense was dominated by the coal-mining and iron and steel industries, but only a few miles to the south was an area where chemicals, textiles, and light metal goods were the chief manufactures. Along the Rhine above Duisburg, the Leverkusen chemical works were founded late in the century. In Remscheid, Solingen, and the small towns of the Sauerland, cutlery, tools, and light metal goods continued to be made, and in the deep valley of the Wupper lay the textile cities of Elberfeld and Barmen, today merged into Wuppertal.

Lorraine and the Saar

The Jurassic hills of Lorraine and Luxembourg contained beds of low-grade phosphoric iron ore (minette). These deposits had long been known but were little worked because of the poor quality of the metal derived from them. During the first half of the century, a far greater importance attached to the so-called strong iron (*fer fort*), which occurred in small pockets over the surface of the hills to the west, and the even smaller ore bodies which occurred in the ancient rocks of the Hunsrück to the east. These two had once supported an industry, which declined through the nineteenth century and became extinct early in the twentieth. These ores, which had been smelted on the Saar coalfield, began to be replaced with minette from Lorraine, but the industry remained small, because of the poor quality of the phosphoric ores.

In 1879 this changed and the basic process allowed iron smelted from minette to be converted to steel (see p. 409). There was a rush by steelmaking companies to acquire concessions on the ore field, now partitioned between France, Germany, and Luxembourg, and to build smelting works. Thomas's innovation came at an opportune moment. Ores were almost exhausted in northern France, Belgium, the Ruhr, and the Saar. Most of the concessions and works in Lorraine and Luxembourg were controlled by or affiliated with companies which operated in the older manufacturing regions (Fig. 11.50). Fuel was supplied from Germany, Belgium, and northern France, and in return ore was sent to Belgium, the Ruhr, and the Saar (Fig. 11.51). Most of the ore was, however, smelted on the ore field. It was of too low a grade to bear the cost of long-distance transport, and it proved cheaper to take coal to the ore field than ore to the coalfield, with the exception of the

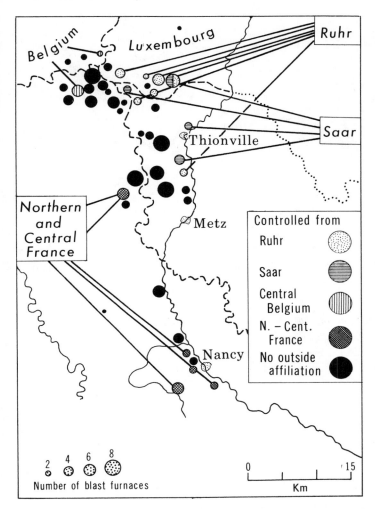

11.50. Ironworks on the Lorraine–Luxembourg ore field and their affiliation with iron and steel companies elsewhere in western Europe, about 1910

relatively short journey to the Saar. The difference between the amounts of pig iron and steel in Table 11.9 represents, approximately, the volume of iron sent for refining elsewhere.

Upper Silesia

The manufacturing region which developed on the Upper Silesian coalfield, where the territories of Prussia, Russia, and Austria met at a point known as "Three Emperors' Corner," was narrowly based on coal, iron and steel, lead, and zinc. The coalfield was larger in area than that of the Ruhr, but coal seams reached the surface over only a small part of it. Over much they lay far too deep for mining at this time (Fig. 11.52). The most easily worked coal seams lay toward the north of

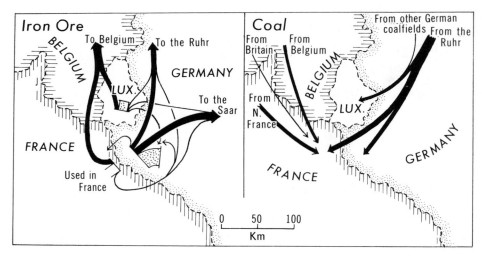

11.51. The movement of ore from the Lorraine–Luxembourg ore field and the import of coal, about 1910

Table 11.9. *Pig iron and steel production in Lorraine, Luxembourg, and the Saar, 1913 (in thousands of tons)*

	Pig iron	Steel Converter	Open hearth
Saar	1,307	1,700	300
Luxembourg	2,548	1,275	40
"German" Lorraine	3,819	1,783	150
"French" Lorraine	3,490	2,134	157
Total	11,164	6,892	647

the basin and over a small area in the south. It was in these areas that modern industry was established. Across the northern part of the coal basin lay limestone beds containing ores of lead and zinc, among the richest to be found in Europe. Reserves of iron ore, on the other hand, were small and of indifferent quality, but sufficient to support the early industry.

Upper Silesia was sparsely populated; it lacked waterborne transport and was almost inaccessible before the railway. Prospects for the early development of its resources would have been small if the Prussian government had not played a role. It was on its initiative that an English entrepreneur was brought to introduce smelting with coke. An early attempt at Małapanew met with some success and was followed by the building of furnaces on the exposed coalfield, first at Gleiwitz (Gliwice), then at Königshütte (Chorzów). Development followed a familiar course: first the puddling of charcoal-smelted iron, then smelting with coke. The first puddling furnaces were built in 1828. By 1840 there were seven smelting works,

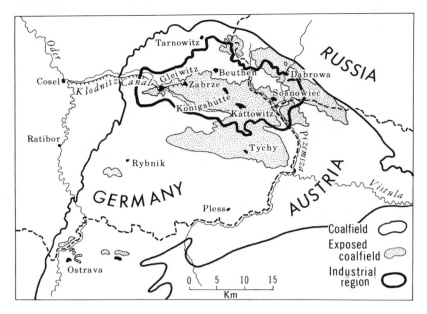

11.52. The Upper Silesian–Moravian industrial region

and a writer in a technical journal in 1842 described the development as "the equal of England and foremost on the continent of Europe."[17] At the same time coal mining spread over much of the exposed field (Fig. 11.53), and the smelting of lead and zinc grew rapidly from about 1820.

The chief problem of this, the most promising of all Europe's centers of heavy industry, was its remoteness and lack of a market. A canal, the Klodnitz (Kłod-nicki) Canal, was cut from Gleiwitz to the river Oder. Its purpose was to distribute coal as far as Berlin, but it was too small and little used. The opening of a railway to Breslau in 1846 broadened the market for metal goods, and in time engineering and other works in central and eastern Europe began to look to Upper Silesia for supplies. Prospects for the nonferrous metals were better. Lead declined in importance, but the output of zinc increased throughout the century, exceeding the production of Vieille Montagne, and making this for a period the world's leading source of the metal (Fig. 11.54). But Upper Silesia ceased to be in the forefront of industrial progress, in part because it was largely controlled by the landed aristocracy who showed no entrepreneurial flair, in part because the market potential in eastern Europe was severely limited. Everywhere west of Berlin was better served by the Ruhr.

Developments on the Prussian sector of the coalfield were followed by a similar, though smaller-scale growth on the Russian and Austrian (Fig. 11.55). Coke smelting began in Dąbrowa, the Russian sector, in the 1830s, and continued intermittently through the century, but demand within Russia was small and management of the

17 *Berg- und Hüttenmännischen Zeitung* (Leipzig), 1, 1842, 58.

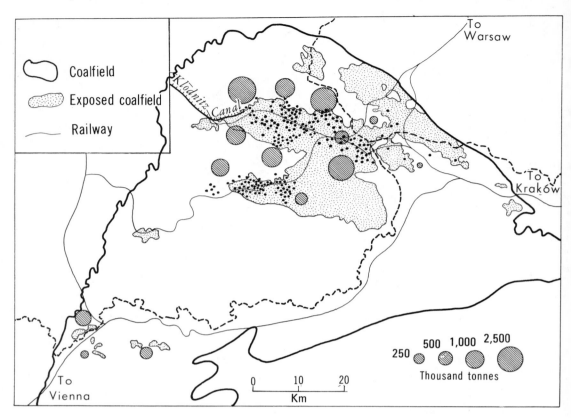

11.53. The spread of coal mining in Upper Silesia–northern Moravia; the distribution of mines about 1860

works poor. Coal also outcropped in Austrian Silesia, close to the southern margin of the basin. Puddling works were established here in 1826 to process charcoal iron from elsewhere in Austrian Galicia. Ten years later coke-fired furnaces were added, and the Vitkovice works remained throughout the century the most important within the Habsburg empire (Fig. 11.56).

Industrial growth brought with it a steady increase in population. There had been only two cities within the region before industrial development began, Gleiwitz and Beuthen (Bytom). Both were small, and even after a century of growth each had a population of fewer than seventy thousand. Other cities, such as Kattowitz (Katowice), Königshütte, and Zabrze in the Prussian sector, and Sosnowiec in the Russian, had grown from villages. Sosnowiec, on the basis mainly of coal mining, had become an ugly, sprawling city of over a hundred thousand. All bore the evidence of their rapid growth. Housing was bad, even by the standards of nineteenth-century industrial Europe (see p. 376); streets remained unpaved, and public amenities were almost wholly lacking. Population growth was largely by immigration from the prevailingly Polish-speaking countryside, but middle and

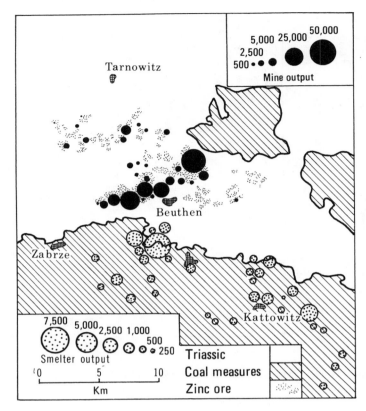

11.54. Zinc mining and smelting in Upper Silesia, about 1860

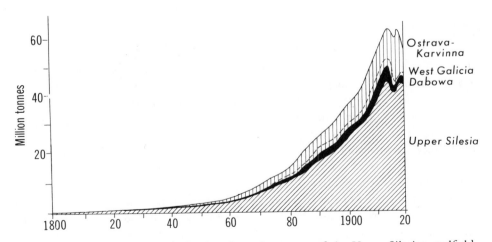

11.55. The increase in coal production from the sectors of the Upper Silesian coalfield, 1800–1920. [After N. J. G. Pounds, *The Upper Silesian Industrial Region* (Bloomington, Ind., 1958), 74.]

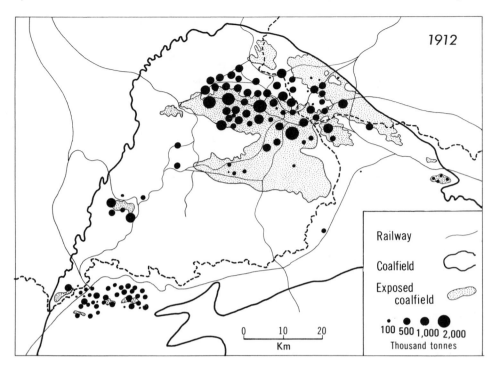

11.56. Coal mining in the Upper Silesian–Moravian coalfield, in 1912

managerial classes were mainly German. Ethnic differences were reflected in social stratification, with serious consequences for the future of the area.

Southern Russia

The last industrial region to emerge lay in the Donetz valley of southern Russia (Fig. 11.57). It was even more narrowly based than Upper Silesia and was built almost exclusively on coal mining and iron and steelworking. There had, in fact, been only two significant branches of manufacturing industry in nineteenth-century Russia, textiles and iron. The former was to be found throughout the widely scattered cities of central Russia and the Moscow region. The latter had by the early nineteenth century come to be concentrated in the Urals region and consisted mainly of an immense number of small works which used charcoal to smelt magnetite ores. It was the Urals which made Russia one of the foremost iron-producing countries in Europe. In the later years of the nineteenth century, production was increasing but was encountering serious problems. It proved difficult, after the end of serfdom (1861), to obtain sufficient labor. Ore remained abundant and of high quality, but the charcoal which served as fuel was becoming more expensive, and had to be transported over increasing distances. Technology was backward. The hot blast was little used in the furnaces, and much of the iron continued until

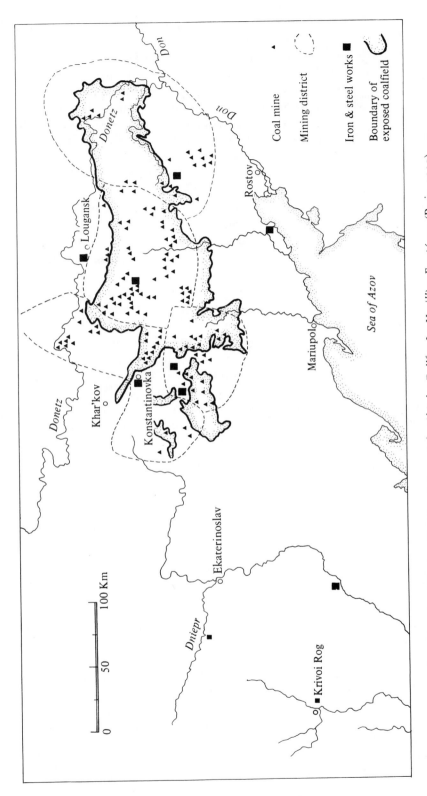

11.57. The Donetz industrial region, Ukraine. Based mainly on *Atlas Châtel et Dollfus: Les Houillères Européennes* (Paris, 1931).

late in the century to be refined in the bloomery. Furnaces remained small; many worked only seasonally, and output of pig iron never reached a half million tons. Until the end of the century iron had to be transported by river barge to the consuming centers which lay mainly in the Moscow region and central Russia.

The chief product of the Urals was bar iron, which was converted to steel at the fabricating centers. All who wrote on the Urals industry emphasized the quality and abundance of its ore but deplored the growing scarcity of charcoal and the poor quality of the sulfurous coal found locally. During the second half of the century the increasing demand for wrought iron and steel was met by imports from western Europe. The tsarist government, wishing to terminate this dependence, raised import duties on iron and encouraged the growth of the domestic industry. The obvious place for such a development was not the Urals but the Ukraine, which combined the advantages of abundant iron and coal and relative ease of transportation.

The Donetz coalfield extends mainly to the south of the river Donetz, for some 250 miles and is, at most, 100 miles wide. Its coal spans the whole coal series, with anthracite occurring mainly to the east and long-flame coal to the west. Ore occurred some 150 miles farther west in a vast deposit in the midst of which was the village of Krivoi Rog. The ores, with a grade generally of over 60 percent, occurred in thick, easily worked veins. Nowhere else in Europe did the raw materials of the iron industry occur as abundantly in such close proximity. Yet it was not until about 1870 that any attempt was made to exploit this wealth. Smelting with coke or anthracite demanded a greater capital investment and a higher level of expertise than the traditional charcoal industry. The earliest attempts to smelt the ore of Krivoi Rog with coke failed, and it was not until 1869 that a concession was granted to a Welsh ironmaster, John Hughes. The Hughes (Yuzovo) works were successful and, stimulated by high import duties, other companies, most of them with west European capital, were founded. In 1884 the railway was completed from Krivoi Rog, through Ekaterinoslav (Dnepropetrovsk), to the Donetz coal basin, and the scene was set for a rapid expansion of the industry. With works at each end of this coal–iron ore axis, there developed an exchange of materials such as was envisaged, but never really developed between the Ruhr and Lorraine.

The 1880s were a period of intensive growth. The production of pig iron in 1881 was still only 24,000 tons, but by 1892 it had increased to 274,000, and by 1905 southern Russia was producing about 2,945,000 tons, almost two-thirds of the Russian output. When the Great War began there were no fewer than 18 ironworks producing over 3 million tons of pig iron a year.

The south Russian region differed fundamentally from the older Urals region. It was based on coal fuel; its technology was relatively up-to-date, and from the start most of the pig iron was converted to steel in the open hearth. The south Russian works served a domestic market. The initiative of the tsarist government was prompted by the need for steel rails for the spreading railway net, and rolled steel remained the chief product. Little attempt was made before 1914 to diversify its industrial structure. It remained, even more exclusively than Upper Silesia, a

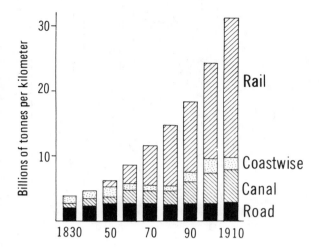

11.58. Internal transport in France. Based on J. C. Toutain, *Les Transports en France de 1830 à 1965* (Paris, 1967).

coal, iron, and steel region. Coal production increased rapidly during the thirty years before the World War and reached 16,353,000 tons in 1910. Only the largest mines, according to a writer in the mid-eighties, had a regular staff of workmen for the winter and summer seasons. The smaller mines were worked only seasonally, and the peasant was a miner in the winter, and a farmer in the summer. Ore production from Krivoi Rog increased steadily and amounted about 1910 to 70 percent of the Russian total.

TRANSPORTATION AND TRADE

The development of production during the century was, as has been seen, characterized by a growing specialization and concentration, permitted and encouraged by a transportation network of growing complexity. At the beginning of the century all passengers and most freight traveled by road. The quality of roads varied with the season and with the bedrock, and the traveler chose his route accordingly. Roads were quickly superseded by railroads in much of Great Britain, but in continental Europe they retained their importance into the 1860s (Fig. 11.58), and in eastern Europe much longer. A service of horse-drawn diligences was maintained on the main roads far into the railway age.

Difficulties of road transport encouraged the use of rivers and the cutting of canals. Rivers had long been used for freight. In eighteenth-century England they began to be supplemented by canals, which became an essential feature of industrial development. "The map of English canals," wrote R. M. Hartwell, "is the map of industrial England."[18] The same could not be said of continental Europe, if only because a primary railroad network had already been built when industrialization began in earnest. Few rivers were readily navigable without regulation,

18 "Economic Change in England and Europe, 1780–1830, *New Cambridge Modern History* 9 (1965), 31–59.

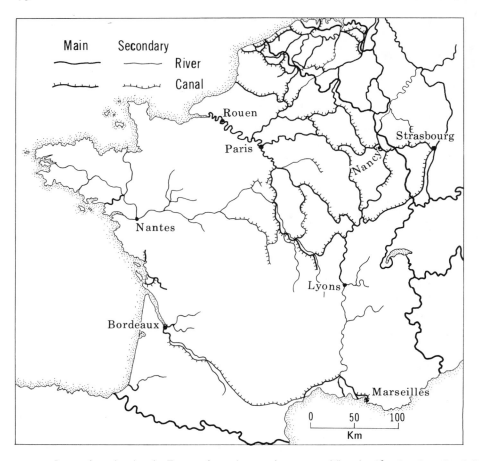

11.59. Internal navigation in France, late nineteenth century. The classification into "main" and "secondary" waterways is that adopted in the Freycinet plan. (Based mainly on *Report on Canal Traffic in France,* Foreign Office, Miscellaneous Series, London, 342, 1895.)

and on some, the Vistula, Loire, and Rhône among them, the physical difficulties were never overcome. Elsewhere improvements were made, the channel deepened and straightened, and a towpath maintained to pull the barges. In England the canal system fell into disuse as railways took over the task of carrying freight. In France a network of canals and navigable rivers overspread the northeast of the country and remained active until the middle years of the century. They then declined in relative importance until the Freycinet plan was introduced in 1879 to revive the system and standardize the sizes of locks and barges (Fig. 11.59). This was followed by a sharp increase in the volume of freight, mainly heavy, low-value goods.

No part of Europe was better suited to water transportation than the Low Countries. The Scheldt, Meuse, and Rhine were readily navigable, and the terrain lent itself to the cutting of canals. In parts of the Netherlands, waterways almost replaced roads, but their usefulness was reduced by political rivalry between Belgium and the Netherlands, and totally unnecessary canals were cut in order to preempt each other's trade.

Germany was noteworthy for its navigable rivers, of which the Rhine was the best and most used. Nevertheless, there were obstacles in its course, among them, meanders in its upper course, a rocky bar near Bingen, and the speed of the current in its middle section. These were overcome early in the century, when the engineer J. G. Tulla straightened and regulated the upper river and made it navigable up to Mannheim. The river was subsequently opened to large barges as far as Strasbourg and, early in the present century, to Basel in Switzerland. Difficulties presented by ice and, at times, by unusually low water could not be overcome and continued to hold up traffic for periods which varied from year to year. More easily removed were the human obstacles, the tolls and staple rights exercised by towns along the river. Those which were not abolished by Napoleon fell gradually into disuse until they were formally ended by the Convention of Mannheim in 1868.

In the mid-nineteenth century the volume of traffic carried on the river was growing rapidly. The size of barges was increasing and steam tugs were beginning to replace the horses which had formerly pulled them. The focus of this traffic was the ports, Duisburg and Ruhrort, which had grown up where the river Ruhr joined the Rhine. The chief cargo was coal, distributed both up and down the river. It supplied ocean-going ships in Amsterdam and chemical works in Mannheim. Iron ore was brought down the Rhine to the Ruhr, and toward the end of the century, Swedish, Spanish, and African ore was imported by way of Rotterdam. The volume of freight, though not its variety, steadily increased until the outbreak of war in 1914. Riverside quays and wharves were replaced by dock basins, where the barges could be loaded and unloaded.

The tributaries of the Rhine were of only limited value. The Ruhr itself was used by coal barges, until the northward progression of mining led to the closure of pits along the valley. The Lahn served for a time to bring iron ore down to the Rhine, but the Moselle, potentially the most valuable river of them all because it linked the Ruhr with the iron-ore field of Lorraine, was scarcely used at all. The Main and Neckar were of some value, and the former was linked from early in the century with the Danube by the King Ludwig Canal, built on so small a scale that it was almost useless.

The north European rivers, the Weser, Elbe, Oder, and Vistula, flow obliquely across the plain from southeast to northwest (Fig. 11.60). They presented greater navigational difficulties than the Rhine, were obstructed by ice for longer periods in winter, and had no cargoes like coal and iron ore to sustain shipping. Nevertheless, they served to carry goods to and from the ports of Bremen and Hamburg. A feature of the northern plain was the shallow valleys created during the closing phases of the Ice Age, which linked them with one another. These facilitated the cutting of canals from the Rhine eastward to Berlin and the Oder. Although this canal system was still unfinished in 1914, the branches which encircled Berlin and linked the city with the ports were in full use.

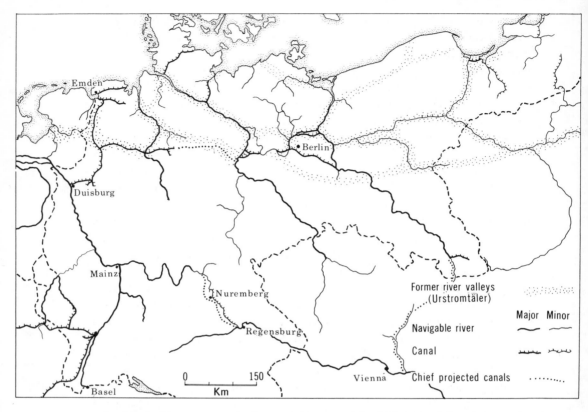

11.60. Navigable waterways in the north German plain. [After *Royal Commission on Canals and Waterways*, vol. VI, *Foreign Inquiry*, Cmd 4841 (1909): 491–735.]

The east European rivers were little used. The Vistula was shallow and difficult, and others served at most to float timber. The great Russian rivers had been avenues of commerce in earlier centuries, and even in the early nineteenth century, iron from the Ural Mountains was borne westward to the Baltic by river and lake. But the largest and most navigable of them, the Dnepr, Don, and Volga, flowed to either the Black or the Caspian Sea, and they proved to be of little significance in Russia's early industrial development.

The Danube, the longest and by far the most complex river in Europe, might have been expected to play an important role in European commerce, but it had many difficulties, including a rapid current in its upper course, a shallow and shifting course in the Hungarian plain, and gorges and rapids in the lower course. But its neglect was due to other factors: political boundaries, the fact that it discharged into the Black Sea, and the absence along much of its course of any significant freight. In fact, the most used part of the river was its delta, where three channels took most of its water into the Black Sea. Near the head of the delta lay Galaţi and Brăila, ports which developed in the nineteenth century to handle Romania's grain export. But upstream from this "maritime" Danube, there

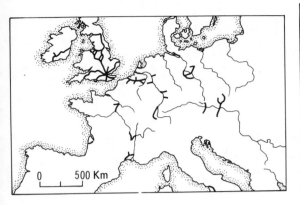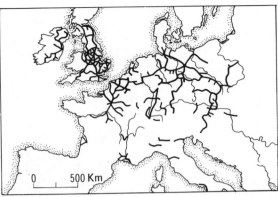

11.61 (Left). Railway development in Europe, 1840
11.62 (Right). Railway development in Europe, 1850

was very little traffic. The Iron Gate was thought to be impenetrable, though in fact small vessels occasionally weathered the rapids. Without it, wrote contemporaries, the traffic of central Europe would move to the Black Sea and the Mediterranean. It is very doubtful whether it would have done so; in fact, it never had the opportunity.

Rivers and canals were of negligible importance in Mediterranean Europe. Both climate and terrain were against their use. Many rivers ran dry in summer, and the supply of water to the few canals which were built proved difficult. In fact, it was irrigation, not navigation, that they best served.

The railway system

By 1850 a primary network linking the major cities and ports existed in north-western Europe (Figs. 11.61 and 11.62). Thirty years later it had been completed for the continent, including Russia, and only a few lines in the Balkans and the Arctic remained to be built (Fig. 11.63). Traffic moved increasingly to the railroads, leaving waterways to handle only a few bulk commodities.

The development of rail transport was greatly assisted by the fact that most European countries adopted the standard British gauge of 4 feet 8½ inches. Only in the Iberian peninsula and Russia were there significant divergences. Building a railway was a political act. Legislative authorization was necessary, and, when completed, a railroad had great political significance. The Russian system was built on a five-feet gauge, not for reasons of economy, but to prevent its use by the central powers. Only the line from Vienna to Warsaw was permitted, as a special favor from the tsar to the Austrian emperor, to be built on the standard gauge.

The building of a national railroad system was seen as a means of creating and maintaining national unity. In Germany, even before the first rails had been laid,

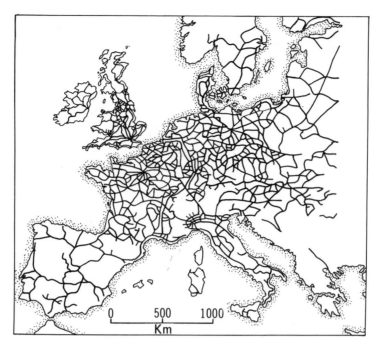

11.63. Railway development in Europe, 1880

Friedrich List had produced his plan to link every city of major importance with Berlin. And in Italy a totally uneconomic system was built as soon as practicable after 1861 as if to hold it together with sinews of steel. Nowhere was railroad building more overtly political than in the Balkans. The Ottoman empire wanted to build a line from Constantinople to the Danube, but to give no military or economic assistance to Serbia. The line remained incomplete when the Ottomans were defeated in the war of 1875–6, and when work was resumed it was, by an abrupt change of plan, made to run across Serbian rather than Austro-Hungarian territory. It was completed and the first "Orient Express" ran over it in 1888. Now it was the turn of the Habsburgs to scheme to construct a line through the Sanjak of Novipazar which would hinder the ambitions of the Serbs. This line remained unfinished when the war of 1912 postponed such projects indefinitely.

There were, on the other hand, many lines which were built to satisfy a real economic need. Typical of such was that which was opened in 1902 from the iron-ore mines of northern Sweden across the mountains to the ice-free Norwegian port of Narvik, or the lines built from Denmark's dairy farming country to Esbjerg, through which produce was exported to Great Britain. Similar needs led to the construction of lines from Trieste and Fiume (Rijeka) across the Dinaric Mountains to, respectively, Austria and Hungary, or that from the lower Danube across the Dobrudja to the Black Sea coast in order to avoid the difficult navigation of the delta.

Seaborne trade

Before the railway age seaborne trade was almost as important as that carried overland. Every country with an extensive coastline used coastal shipping for internal movement and trade. Coasts were dotted with small ports and the European seas were alive with vessels of a few hundred tons which carried freight and passengers. There was no part of the European coastline where such traffic was not important, and there were some areas, Norway and the Italian and Greek peninsulas for example, where it was almost the only way to travel. Scarcely a river reached the coast without sheltering near its mouth a small port where the commerce of its hinterland met that of the sea. In the course of the century much of this traffic was attracted to the railroads, leaving to coastwise shipping only the traffic in bulky, low-value commodities such as coal, timber, and building materials. By the end of the century the importance of coastal trade was proportional to the difficulties of land travel, great only in Norway, the Mediterranean, and the western shores of Britain. Elsewhere one would have found only decaying harbors and wooden ships, their useful life long past, slowly rotting into the mud.

There had always been great ports, through which long-distance commerce moved. They served as entrepôts, receiving the commerce of distant lands, transshipping it, and dispatching it in smaller amounts by wagon, river barge, or coasting vessel. Their role grew during the century, as they drew to themselves the commerce of their less successful rivals. Lübeck paled before Hamburg; the ports of Brittany and Normandy before Le Havre and Nantes, and the countless tiny harbors of the British coasts before London, Liverpool, Hull, and Bristol. At the beginning of the century there were hundreds of ports of some significance in Europe. By the beginning of the present century this had been reduced to barely twenty giant ports.

It was once sufficient if a ship could tie up alongside the quay to unload and load. With the growing size of ships and volume of commerce longer quays were necessary, and it became desirable to excavate docks and so to insulate ships from the rise and fall of the tide. The first such basin was that which the French constructed in Antwerp in 1803. Within a century dock basins had become a feature of all great ports except those in the Mediterranean.

All ports had to have links with their hinterlands. Most great ports lay on navigable rivers. Only in Great Britain and Mediterranean Europe was inland navigation of only minor importance – largely because the rivers themselves were too small to be of much value. Here land transport had to be used. The second half of the century saw the emergence of railroad ports. London was a railroad port; so also were most Mediterranean ports, like Genoa, Trieste, Fiume, and Athens-Piraeus, and, despite the river Rhône, Marseilles. The effective hinterlands of great ports overlapped. They changed with harbor construction, railroad building, and the improvement of waterways. That of Hamburg was through the century extending into central Europe, drawing Berlin and Saxony into its net and overcoming the competition of Lübeck, Stettin, and other Baltic ports. The building of a railroad opened up Fiume to the trade of Hungary in competition with Trieste. In the Low Countries competition was fierce throughout the century between Amsterdam, Rotterdam, and Antwerp for the trade of Belgium and the Rhineland, with the fortunes of each port influenced by canal building, the regulation of rivers, dock construction, and the policies of their respective governments. In the end Antwerp lost in the struggle for the traffic of the Rhineland and was left to dispute with Dunkirk for that of Belgium. Amsterdam had to be content, in the main, with the trade of the Netherlands, while Rotterdam went from strength to strength as the chief ocean port of the industrialized Ruhr and Rhineland.

In addition to these great ports, which handled general cargo, three kinds of more specialized ports developed during the century: the outport, the commodity port, and the "free" port. Except in the Mediterranean, none of the great ports was located on the coast. All grew up on a navigable estuary or at the head of a bay which gave them protection. A river or estuarine location came in the nineteenth century to have grave disadvantages. It restricted the size of ships, required the maintenance of a deep channel, and consumed a great deal of the ship's working time. It might be necessary to sail up to Rouen, or Bremen, or Nantes to discharge a whole cargo, but for a part cargo or a few passengers the trip was not worthwhile. It was quicker and more economical to call at an "outport" – Cherbourg or Le Havre, Bremerhaven, or Saint-Nazaire. Most great ports developed outports during the second half of the century, and in some instances, like Le Havre and Bremerhaven, it was the outport which came to handle the greater volume of traffic.

The second category of new ports was that which developed to handle a particular cargo. The iron-ore port of Narvik and the Danish port of Esbjerg have been mentioned. Other such specialized ports were Bilbao which exported Spanish iron ore, Portoferraio which did the same for the island of Elba, and those on the Sicilian coast which shipped the island's sulfur.

The "free" port, or entrepôt, developed late in the century to meet a special need. It resulted from the growing practice in great ports of importing goods, only to reexport part of them. Such a traffic would be encouraged if reexports were not subjected to customs examination and charges before being shipped out again. In practice, a zone was set aside within a port, lying outside the country's customs area. Goods could be unloaded there, held for a time in warehouses, and then be reexported almost without formality. Hamburg and Bremen retained free zones after their inclusion in the Zollverein. In 1894 Copenhagen established a free zone, and Thessaloníke set aside such a zone in order to facilitate the trade of Serbia, the goods arriving by rail rather than by sea.

The trade which passed through a diminishing number of ports and across Europe's land boundaries grew significantly during the century. France's total trade roughly doubled by 1850, and then increased fourfold before World War I. That of Germany grew only threefold between 1880 and 1913, and Great Britain showed a somewhat slower rate of growth. The trade of the Netherlands increased faster but this was accounted for in large measure by transit traffic in coal and iron ore. In most countries, the United Kingdom and Russia excepted, a high proportion of international trade was intra-European, carried on across their mutual boundaries. In the early twentieth century some 65 percent of all foreign trade of European countries was with other countries within the continent. Even the United Kingdom, with close trading relations with its overseas empire, nevertheless carried on almost half its total trade within Europe. Except in the industrializing countries of northwest Europe, the volume of trade per capita was small, a reflection of the fact that the international specialization of production had still made little progress in eastern and southern Europe.

SELECT BIBLIOGRAPHY

General

Bairoch, P. "Europe's Gross National Product: 1800–1975." *Journal of European Economic History* 5 (1976): 273–340.

Berend, I. T., and G. Ranki. *Economic Development in East-Central Europe in the 19th and 20th Centuries.* New York, 1974.

Carr, R. *Spain, 1808–1939.* Oxford, 1966.

Clark, C. *Conditions of Economic Progress.* London, 1940.

Heckscher, E. F. *An Economic History of Sweden.* Cambridge, Mass., 1954.

Hobsbawm, E. J. *Industry and Empire.* Harmondsworth, 1969.

Ladurie, E. Le R.*Time of Feast, Time of Famine.* New York, 1971.

Lampe, J. R., and M. R. Jackson. *Balkan Economic History, 1550–1950.* Bloomington, Ind., 1982.

McGowan, B. *Economic Life in Ottoman Europe.* Cambridge, U.K., 1981.

Milward, A. S., and S. B. Saul. *The Development of the Economies of Continental Europe, 1850–1914.* London, 1977.

Milward, A. S., and S. B. Saul, *The Economic Development of Continental Europe, 1780–1870.* London, 1979.

Price, R. *The Economic Modernisation of France.* London, 1975.

Rostow, W. W. *The Stages of Economic Growth,* Cambridge, U.K., 1960.

Stavrianos, L. S. *The Balkans since 1453.* New York, 1958.

Vives, J. V. *An Economic History of Spain.* Princeton, N.J., 1969.

Wanklyn, H. G. *The Eastern Marchlands of Europe.* London, 1941.

Population

Clark, C. *Population, Growth and Land Use.* London, 1967.

Coon, C. S. *The Races of Europe.* New York, 1939.

Finkelstein, L., ed. *The Jews: Their History, Culture and Religion.* New York, 1949.

Foerster, R. F. *The Italian Emigration of our Times.* Cambridge, Mass., 1919.

McNeill, W. H. *Plagues and Peoples.* New York, 1976.

Mayer, K. B. *The Population of Switzerland.* New York, 1952.

Moller, Herbert, ed. *Population Movements in Modern European History.* New York, 1954.

Post, J. D. *The Last Great Subsistence Crisis in the Western World.* Baltimore, Md., 1977.

Rosenberg, C. E. "Cholera in Nineteenth Century Europe: A Tool for Social and Economic Analysis." *Comparative Studies in Society and History* 8 (1965–6): 452–63.

Wace, A. J. B., and M. S. Thompson, *The Nomads of the Balkans.* London, 1914.

Walker, M. *Germany and the Emigration 1816–1885*. Cambridge, Mass., 1964.
Wanklyn, H. G. "Geographical Aspects of Jewish Settlement East of Germany." *Geographical Journal* 95 (1940): 175.

Urban settlement

Bairoch, P. "Urbanisation and Economic Development in the Western World: Some Provisional Conclusions of an Empirical Study." In *Patterns of European Urbanisation since 1500*, ed. H. Schmal. London, 1981.
Chevallier, L. *Labouring Classes and Dangerous Classes*. London, 1973.
Clout, H. D. "Urban Growth, 1500–1900." *Themes in the Historical Geography of France*. London, 1977.
Dickinson, R. E. *The City Region in Western Europe*. London, 1967.
Hall, P. *The World Cities*. London, 1966.
McKay, J. P. *Tramways and Trolleys: The Rise of Urban Mass Transport in Europe*. Princeton, N.J., 1976.
Pinkney, D. *Napoleon III and the Rebuilding of Paris*. Princeton, N.J., 1958.
Pounds, N. J. G. "The Urbanization of East-Central and Southeast Europe: An Historical Perspective." In *Eastern Europe: Essays in Geographical Problems*, ed. G. W. Hoffman. London, 1970.
Weber, A. F. *The Growth of Cities in the Nineteenth Century*. New York, 1899.

Agriculture

Chorley, G. P. H. "The Agricultural Revolution in Northern Europe, 1750–1880: Nitrogen, Legumes and Crop Productivity." *Economic History Review* 34 (1981): 71–93.
Collins, E. J. T. "Labour Supply and Demand in European Agriculture 1800–1880." In *Agrarian Change and Economic Developments*, 61–94.
The Consolidation of Fragmented Agricultural Holdings. F. A. O.: Washington, D.C., 1950.
Conze, W. "The Effects of Nineteenth Century Liberal Agrarian Reforms on Social Structure in Central Europe." In *Essays in European Economic History*, ed. F. Crouzet, W. H. Chaloner, and W. H. Stern. London, 1969.
Dallas, G. *The Imperfect Peasant Economy: The Loire Country, 1800–1914*. Cambridge, U.K., 1982.
Jones, E. L., and S. J. Woolf, eds. *Agrarian Change and Economic Developments*. London, 1969.
Lambert, A. M. *The Making of the Dutch Landscape*. London, 1971.
Mayhew, A. *Rural Settlement and Farming in Germany*. London, 1973.
Mitrany, D. *The Land and the Peasant in Rumania*. London, 1930.
Morgan, O. S., ed. *Agricultural Systems of Middle Europe*. New York, 1933.
Parry, M. L. *Climatic Change, Agriculture and Settlement*. Folkestone, 1978.
Perkins, J. A. "The Agricultural Revolution in Germany 1850–1914." *Journal of European Economic History* 10 (1981): 71–118.
Salaman, R. N. *The History and Social Influence of the Potato*. Cambridge, U.K., 1949.
Seebohm Rowntree, B. *Land and Labour: Lessons from Belgium*. London, 1911.
Skrubbeltrang, F. *Agricultural Development and Rural Reform in Denmark*. Agricultural Studies, F. A. O., 1953.
Thorpe, H. "The Influence of Enclosure on the Form and Pattern of Rural Settlement in Denmark." *Transactions, Institute of British Geographers* (1951): 111–29.

Manufacturing

Bythell, D. *The Handloom Weavers.* Cambridge, U.K., 1969.

Clough, S. B. "The Diffusion of Industry in the Last Century and a Half." *Studi in Onore di Armando Sapori.* Milan, 1855.

Dehn, R. M. R. *The German Cotton Industry.* University of Manchester Economic Series, vol. 14, 1913.

Elkins, T. H. "The Brown Coal Industry of Germany." *Geography* 38 (1953): 18–29.

Forrester, R. B. *The Cotton Industry in France.* University of Manchester Economic Series, vol. 15, 1921.

Henderson, W. O. *Britain and Industrial Europe 1750–1870.* Liverpool, 1954.

Mendels, F. "Proto-Industrialization: The First Phase of the Industrialization Process." *Journal of Economic History* 32 (1945): 241–61.

Mokyr, J. *Industrialization in the Low Countries, 1795–1850.* New Haven, Conn., 1976.

Montgomery, G. A. *The Rise of Modern Industry in Sweden.* London, 1939.

Pounds, N. J. G. *The Ruhr.* London and Bloomington, Ind., 1952.

Pounds, N. J. G. "The Spread of Mining in the Coal Basin of Upper Silesia and Northern Moravia." *Annals of the Association of American Geographers* 48 (1958): 149–63.

Pounds, N. J. G. *The Upper Silesian Industrial Region.* Bloomington, Ind., 1958.

Pounds, N. J. G., and W. N. Parker. *Coal and Steel in Western Europe.* London and Bloomington, Ind., 1957.

Tegoborski, M. L. de. *Commentaries on the Productive Forces of Russia.* London, 1855.

Tilly, R. *Financial Institutions and Industrialization in the Rhineland 1815–1870.* Madison, Wis., 1966.

Warden, A. J. *The Linen Trade.* London, 1864.

Wrigley, E. A. *Industrial Growth and Population Change.* Cambridge, U.K., 1961.

Transportation and trade

Beaver, S. H. "Railways in the Balkan Peninsula." *Geographical Journal* (1941): 273–94.

Bindoff, S. T. *The Scheldt Question to 1939.* London, 1945.

Boag, G. L. *The Railways of Spain.* London, 1923.

Cameron, R. E. *France and the Economic Development of Europe 1800–1914.* Princeton, N.J., 1961.

Henderson, W. O. *The Zollverein.* Cambridge, U.K., 1939.

Mance, Sir Osborne. *International River and Canal Transport.* Oxford, 1944.

International Sea Transport. Oxford, 1945.

Meyer, H. C. "German Economic Relations with Southeastern Europe." *American Historical Review* 57 (1952): 77–90.

Pounds, N. J. G. "A Free and Secure Access to the Sea." *Annals of the Association of American Geographers* (1959): 256–68.

Pounds, N. J. G. "Patterns of Trade in the Rhineland." *Science, Medicine and History.* Vol. 2, 419–34. Oxford, 1953.

Pounds, N. J. G. "Port and Outport in North-west Europe." *Geographical Journal* 109 (1947): 216–28.

Ringrose, D. R. *Transportation and Economic Stagnation in Spain, 1750–1850.* Durham, N.C., 1970.

12

Europe on the eve of World War I

A long period of steady and almost uninterrupted growth was cut short in 1914 by the "guns of August," and when these fell silent in November, 1918, Europe was a very different continent, socially, economically, and politically, from what it had been only five years earlier. In the course of the previous century population had more than doubled; gross national product had increased many times, and a continent which had on balance been self-sufficing in foodstuffs had become dependent on the rest of the world, with which it was linked in a trading network of growing complexity. Urban population, no more than 15 percent of the total when the century began, had increased to 45 percent of a much larger total. At the beginning of the century nationalism was an emotion new to many parts of the continent and unknown in others. By 1914 it was felt intensely everywhere; it sparked the most disastrous war known, and the peace settlement which followed was dominated by it.

POPULATION

In 1913 a belt of very dense population stretched from northern Britain to eastern Germany and was matched by another which covered most of Italy. Around and between these regions and dense population were others of lower density, which merged into the sparsely settled areas of "peripheral" Europe. This pattern differed only in detail from that of a century earlier. Dense population had become yet more dense, and areas of sparse population had in many instances become sparser. Growth in the one area was accompanied by migration from the other. It is natural to think of dense population as the consequence of modern urbanization and industrial growth. In many instances it was. But there are areas of moderate to high population density shown in Figure 12.1 which owed nothing to urbanism or industrialism. Their population remained heavily agricultural. There were – indeed, still are – two kinds of dense population: that exemplified by the Ruhr, central Belgium, or the English West Midlands, where the population was very largely employed in manufacturing and services; and, by contrast, areas such as Sicily, northwestern Spain and Austrian Galicia, where the density sprang from cultivating microholdings and resulted in near destitution. The one can be ex-

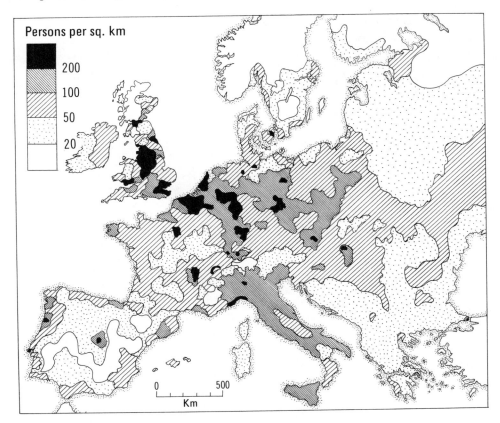

12.1. Population density in Europe, 1910

plained in terms of fuel resources, industrial raw materials, and facilities for transportation. The latter is less readily explicable.

In the first place, rural overpopulation was entirely relative. The Carpathian Mountains, with twenty to the square mile, might have too great a population; the plains of northern France, with four times the density, might not. In some areas rural population pressed against resources; in others, holdings were large enough for efficient cultivation and yielded a satisfactory standard of life. There were areas, mainly in northwest Europe, where minute holdings, fertilized and intensively cultivated, grew produce for the nearby urban markets; there were others where holdings no larger served as family farms, growing little more than coarse breadgrains. The densely settled areas of northwestern Europe were not, as a general rule, overpopulated. It was in some of the less developed rural areas that an almost Malthusian degree of overpopulation had emerged. Why, it may be asked, at a time when communication and travel were more developed than ever before, did labor not "flow" from areas which were intrinsically overpopulated to those where labor could be absorbed in secondary and tertiary pursuits? Why did labor not find its own level? There is no simple answer. There was, in fact, some

Table 12.1. *Birthrate and death rate per thousand in 1913*

	Birthrate	Death rate
High birthrate/death rate		
Bulgaria	25.7	29.0
Finland	28.8	17.1
Hungary	34.3	23.2
Austria	29.7	20.3
Italy	31.7	18.7
Portugal	32.5	20.6
Russia	43.1	27.4
Spain	30.6	22.3
Romania	42.1	26.1
Declining death rate, high birthrate		
Denmark	25.6	12.5
Germany	27.5	15.0
Netherlands	28.2	12.3
Norway	25.1	13.3
Low birthrate/death rate		
Belgium	22.3	14.2
France	18.8	17.7
Ireland	22.8	17.1
Sweden	23.2	13.7
Switzerland	23.2	14.3
United Kingdom	24.1	13.8

movement, as was shown by the depressed Polish stratum in the Ruhr. But the conservatism of the peasantry, the fear of a new environment, political restraints on migration, the problem of living among people of a different religious faith – all these served as brakes on migration and resettlement. But the most important constraint was in all probability the lack of financial resources. Moving home is an expensive business; the rural poor just could not afford it.

These overpopulated countries and regions still had very high birthrates, while their death rates were beginning to decline. A division of fundamental importance within Europe is that between countries and regions which had not yet fully experienced the "demographic transition" from high birthrates and death rates to low, and those in which the change had already taken place. Available data are on a country basis. More refined statistics would unquestionably show a broad spectrum within each country. This division is shown in Table 12.1 and in Figure 12.2. All of eastern and southern Europe still showed the preindustrial pattern of high birthrates (over 25 per 1,000) and fairly high death rates (mostly over 20 per 1,000), though this latter was tending to fall. Central Europe was marked by falling death rates, while birthrates remained relatively high. Lastly, northwest Europe, together with Sweden and Switzerland, had low birthrates (under 25 per 1,000) and generally low death rates.

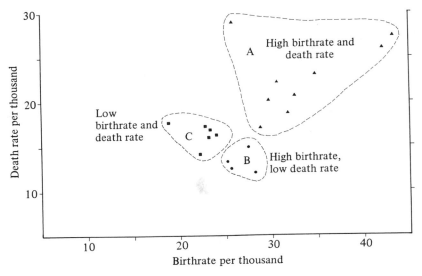

12.2. Graph showing the clustering of patterns of population behavior: (*A*) high birthrate and death rate; (*B*) high birthrate, low death rate; (*C*) low birthrate and death rate

The population of Europe was becoming increasingly divorced from the soil, with overall less than half the total employed population in agriculture. Table 12.2 shows that every country listed in Table 12.1 as having a high birthrate/ death rate appears here with more than half its active population in agriculture. Conversely, each country with a low birthrate/death rate has also a low employment in agriculture, Ireland, for which separate statistics are not available, being the only exception.

THE URBAN MAP

Changes which had taken place during the previous hundred years in the occupational structure of the population led to a rapid growth of cities in which most of the industrial and service activities were now carried on. The majority of small towns had increased comparatively little in population; growth was mainly in those which were already fairly large by the standards of the early nineteenth century. In 1913 about 43.5 percent of the total European population was classed as urban, though it must be remembered that the criteria used varied between countries (see Fig. 12.3 and Table 12.3). It is probable that the proportion of the population of the Balkans that could be regarded as urban was less than 15 percent, possibly under 10 percent.

There were at this time about 150 cities of over 100,000 inhabitants, no fewer than 40 of them in the British Isles (Fig. 12.4), representing some 43 percent of the total urban population. About 30 out of the 150 cities had each a population of more than half a million. These great cities served many functions. They in-

Table 12.2. *Employment of economically active population (in percentages)*

	Agriculture, forestry, fishing	Manufacturing	Commerce, finance, and services
Austria	56.9	21.4	21.7
Belgium	23.2	39.8	37.0
Bulgaria	81.9	8.0	10.1
Denmark	41.7	24.1	34.2
England and Wales	8.1	45.6	46.3
Finland	69.3	10.6	20.1
France	40.9	31.9	27.2
Germany	36.8	36.3	26.9
Hungary	64.0	16.7	19.3
Italy	55.4	25.9	18.7
Norway	39.6	25.1	35.3
Netherlands	28.3	31.8	39.9
Portugal	57.4	21.5	21.1
Romania	79.6	7.8	12.6
Scotland	11.0	55.7	33.3
Spain	56.3	13.8	29.9
Sweden	46.2	25.1	28.7
Switzerland	26.7	45.4	27.9

Note: No data are available for Russia.

cluded most of the political capitals; all were centers of public administration; they were the foci of transportation networks and of manufacturing industries, many of them light and consumer-oriented. The increasing concentration of overseas commerce at a relatively small number of great ports meant that these also had grown very rapidly and were, in many instances, the second largest cities in their respective countries. A feature of the urban map was the appearance of vast conurbations, in which cities and towns had physically grown into one another, leaving little or no green space between. The urban map (Fig. 12.3) fails to emphasize these vast metropolitan areas, because they were made up, in part at least, of cities whose population fell below 50,000. In England, the industrial cities of the West Midlands, of Lancashire and the West Riding of Yorkshire, together with greater London, each formed such a conurbation. Their combined populations were almost 13 million, no less than 35 percent of the population of England and Wales at this time. In continental Europe such a conurbation extended from northern France to the eastern end of the Ruhr coalfield, a distance of 350 miles, with significant interruptions only near Namur and west of the Rhine. The region contained a population of some 3.4 million in its French and Belgian sectors, and of 5.8 in the German. There were in the whole region only 10 cities of over 100,000, but between them, especially in northern France and Belgium, there lay a vast number of small mining and industrial towns, many of them little more than overgrown villages. The tendency was to absorb these smaller settlements for administrative purposes within the limits of the larger, so that the Ruhr industrial

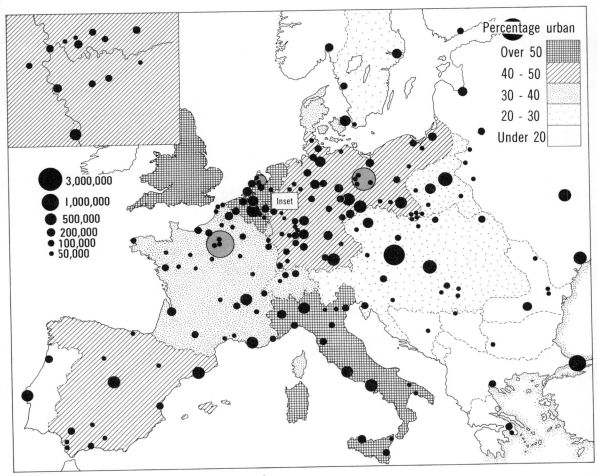

12.3. The urban population of Europe, about 1910

Table 12.3. *Population living in cities, c. 1910 (in percentages)*

Italy	62.4
Belgium	56.6
Netherlands	53.0
Germany	48.8
Spain	42.0
France	38.5
Switzerland	36.6
Denmark	35.9
Hungary	30.0
Austria	27.3
Sweden	22.6
Romania	16.0
Portugal	15.6

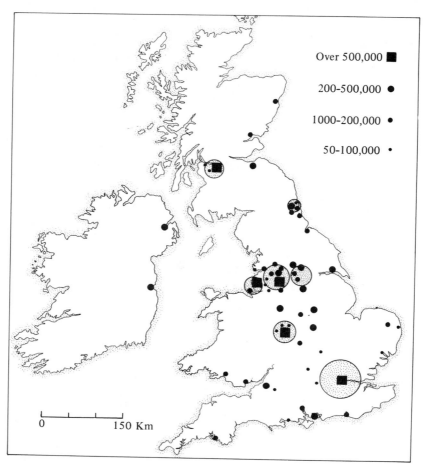

Over 500,000 ■

200–500,000 ●

1000–200,000 ●

50–100,000 ·

0   150 Km

12.4. The distribution of the larger cities in the British Isles, 1911. The stippled circles indicate the population of metropolitan areas

area had already come to be made up of a small number of *Stadtkreise,* or "city-counties."

Other such conurbations had emerged in Upper Silesia, greater Berlin, greater Paris, and in the Lyons–St. Etienne area of France. All presented the same features, large cities expanding into the countryside, linking up with and eventually absorbing small towns and industrial villages (but cf. Figs. 12.5 and 12.6).

AGRICULTURE

Agricultural output was in most of Europe larger than it had ever been, and a greater number of people were fed with a smaller input of labor. But the increasing productivity of recent years was not uniform. It was most marked in new crops, like potatoes, sugar beets, and corn; least in traditional cereals, like rye and oats.

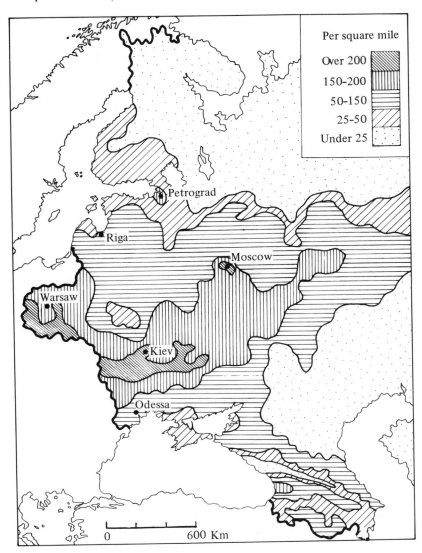

12.5. Population density of European Russia, about 1910

Overall, the more palatable breadgrains were increasing at the expense of the rest. Buckwheat was disappearing. Olive growing was in decline in the face of competition from animal fats, and, though viticulture was spreading in southern France, Spain, Italy, and the Balkans, it was in retreat elsewhere.

Despite the growing diversification of agriculture, cereals still dominated the farming system in most of Europe and occupied at least half the cultivated land. Wheat had been gaining in importance; in most of western Europe it had displaced rye and coarse grains in human diet, and it was of increasing importance in central and southern Europe. Wheat was more strongly influenced than most crops by soil

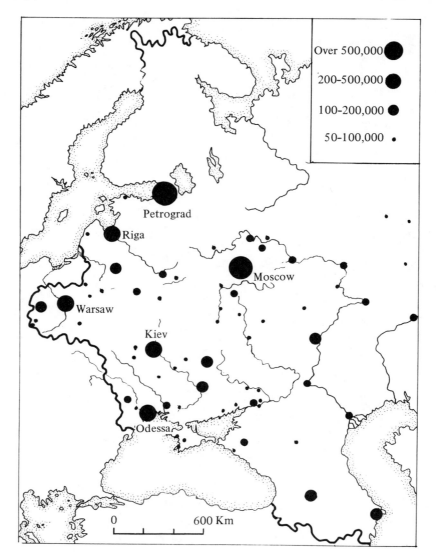

Over 500,000

200-500,000

100-200,000

50-100,000

Petrograd

Riga

Moscow

Warsaw

Kiev

Odessa

0   600 Km

12.6. Urban development of European Russia, early twentieth century

and climate and was really important in only a few restricted areas. The map
showing the area of wheat production (Fig. 12.7) contrasts with that of the volume
of output (Fig. 12.8). Yields were particularly heavy in eastern England and on
the good loess soils of northern France and central Germany, but relatively low in
most of southern and eastern Europe.

The distribution of rye was in some respects the converse of that of wheat. It
was, as Figure 12.9 shows, the crop of poor soils and damp, cool climates and was
the chief breadgrain over much of Russia and eastern Europe. The coarse grains,
oats and barley, were grown almost everywhere except in northern Scandinavia.

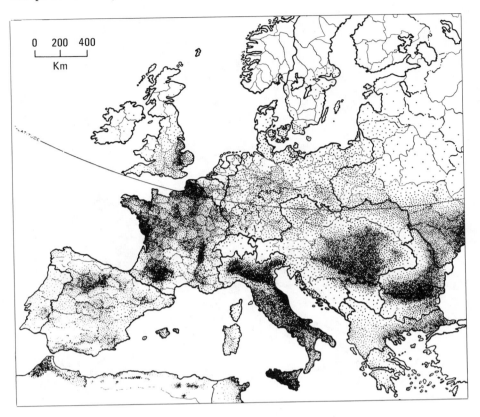

12.7. Wheat growing in Europe, about 1913. Each dot represents 5,000 acres

They were fed to animals, and barley was the favored cereal for malting and was grown wherever, as in England, Denmark, and Germany brewing was important.

The cultivation of corn had spread greatly in recent years. It cropped heavily, and for sheer volume of production it had no rival. But it required hot, humid summers, and in much of Europe summers were either cool or dry. Corn came into its own only in a few areas intermediate between north and south, such as the northwestern parts of the Iberian peninsula, northern Italy, Hungary, and Romania. It entered into human diet, but much of it was fed to stock.

Europe had long ceased to be self-sufficing in cereals, owing in part to the increase in population, in part to the growing importance of fodder crops and rotation grasses, which were grown instead of grain. Wheat, the most valuable cereal, entered most into international trade. The whole of eastern Europe had a wheat surplus, most of which was exported to central and western Europe. In the years preceding World War I, Europe as a whole imported about a fifth of its total consumption. This ranged on a country-by-country basis from under 2 percent of consumption in Spain and 4 percent in France to more than a fifth in Germany, a third in Sweden and Denmark, and almost four-fifths in Great Britain. The deficit

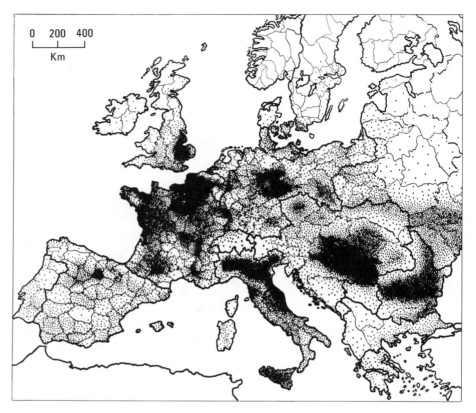

12.8. Wheat production in Europe, about 1913. Each dot represents 100,000 bushels

in western Europe was more than could be supplied by eastern Europe and Russia, and supplies from the New World and Australia were essential. There was very little international – indeed, little long-distance – trade in other cereals, which were mostly consumed close to where they were grown.

The root crops, potatoes and sugar beets, had by 1914 come to play an important role in both rotations and in diet. Both were tolerant of cool, moist weather. Neither was important in southern Europe, which was too dry, or in Scandinavia, where late spring frosts could ruin the crops. In France they were important only where the traditional three-course rotation had been abandoned, and their greatest importance was in the Low Countries, Germany, Poland, and Russia. The area of intensive potato cultivation (Fig. 12.10) almost delimits the German-culture area, where it was an important element in the diet. Sugar beets had a more restricted distribution, in part because they grew best in a deep, loamy soil, in part because they could be grown profitably only in the vicinity of a processing factory. The result is a small number of nuclear areas where sugar beets were very important indeed (Fig. 12.11).

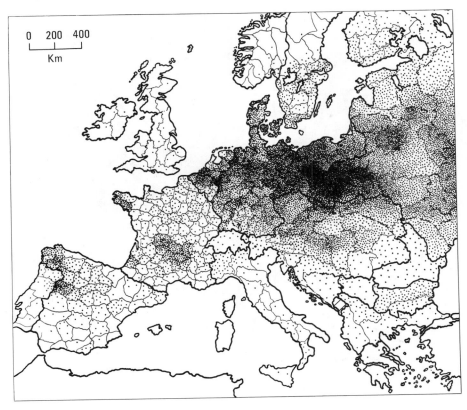

12.9. Rye growing in Europe, about 1913. Each dot represents 5,000 acres

There had been in recent years a swing from arable to mixed farming. The number of cattle was increasing and, more significant, their quality was improving. Cattle were, overall, the most numerous farm animal (Table 12.4). They had always been multipurpose animals, but in the early twentieth century there was a movement away from breeding cattle for beef and toward dairy farming. In some areas, notably Denmark, the Netherlands, northwest France, and, more surprisingly, northern Italy, farming had swung heavily toward mixed and dairy farming, and there were areas in western Britain where arable farming was almost wholly for the purpose of providing feed for cattle (Fig. 12.12).

By contrast, the sheep population was declining almost everywhere. Only in Italy and the Balkans had they retained their former importance. The reason lay in the fact that sheep had previously been raised largely for wool; milk and meat were of minor importance. Not only had the woolen textile industry, which absorbed their chief product, failed to expand greatly, but it was supplied increasingly with a superior wool from overseas, notably from Australia. But there were other reasons. Sheep had been well suited to graze the fallow after harvest; now

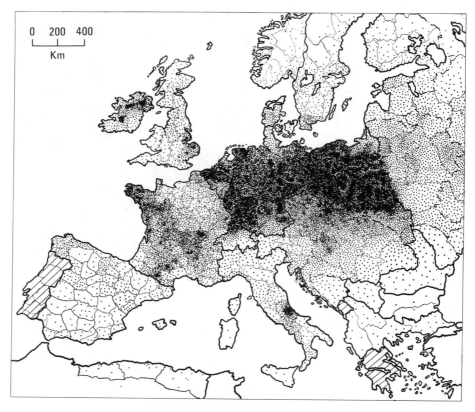

12.10. Potato growing in Europe, about 1913. Each dot represents 2,000 acres

there was in most of Europe no fallow left. The map (Fig. 12.13) shows that, apart from Great Britain and the Netherlands, only Mediterranean Europe still had a dense sheep population. In the Spanish Meseta, the Apennines, and the Balkans sheep provided the only practicable means of using marginal land.

Pig rearing had increased greatly in importance, approximately balancing the decline in sheep. It required little space and expanded with the supply of feed, chiefly coarse cereals and the waste of the dairy and city. Hogs were especially important where there was a supply of potatoes – usually those too small to be marketed – and of by-products of the creamery, as in Denmark (Fig. 12.14). The trend in western Europe and, though less strongly, in central was toward the production of high protein foods, with an increasing reliance on overseas sources for cereals.

MANUFACTURING

By 1914 northwestern Europe had become the dominant industrial region in the world. It was still ahead of the United States, and Japan at this time lagged far

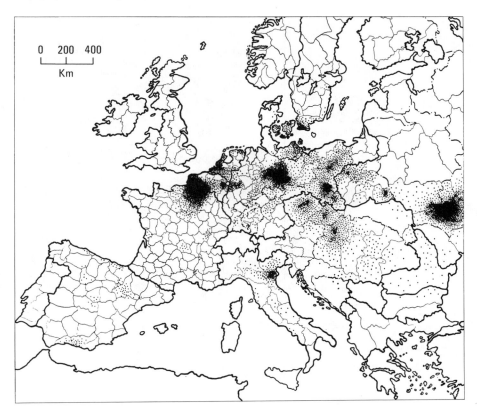

12.11. Sugar beet production in Europe, about 1913. Each dot represents 1,000 acres

Table 12.4. *Farm animals in western, central, and northern Europe (in thousands)*

	1860	1910
Cattle	48,062	64,371
Sheep	86,325[a]	47,594
Pigs	23,369[b]	46,941

[a] Estimated for Sweden.
[b] Estimated for Austria-Hungary.

behind. Europe, including both Great Britain and Russia, produced about 50 percent of the world's coal and 57 percent of its steel. It owned most of the world's shipping, contained about 30 percent of the world's railroad track, and produced most of the world's textiles and much of its chemicals. This immense industrial production was founded on coal and iron, without which Europe's manufacturing must have remained small-scale and unmechanized.

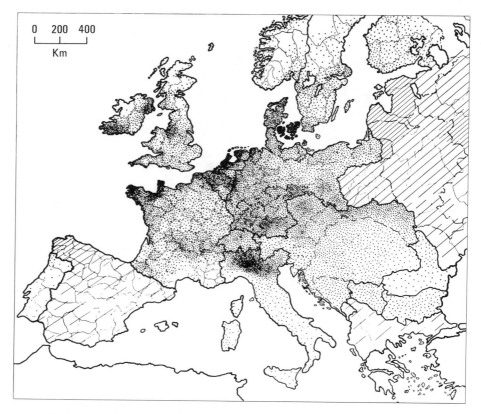

12.12. Dairy cattle in Europe, about 1913. Each dot represents 5,000 head of cattle

Coal had its rivals as a source of energy, but in 1913 their competition was not significant (see Table 12.5). The distribution of coal production, both bituminous and subbituminous, is shown in Table 12.6 and Figure 12.15. Europe was, on balance, more than self-sufficing in coal, and there was an export, chiefly from Great Britain, for bunkering purposes elsewhere in the world. There was also a sizable intra-European trade. British coal was shipped to French, German, Scandinavian, and even Mediterranean ports. Coal was moved from the Moravian field to Vienna, from Upper Silesia to Berlin, and from the Ruhr to Switzerland, Lorraine, and the Netherlands.

Although most European countries produced some pig iron and refined it, production was concentrated to the extent of 82 percent in only four countries: Germany, Great Britain, France, and Russia (Fig. 12.16 and Table 12.7). Most of the iron smelted was converted, often in the same works, into steel. In most countries the volume of steel made exceeded that of pig iron. This may have reflected the use of iron stockpiled from previous years, but in most cases it represented the consumption of scrap metal in the open hearth. In France, Luxembourg, and Ger-

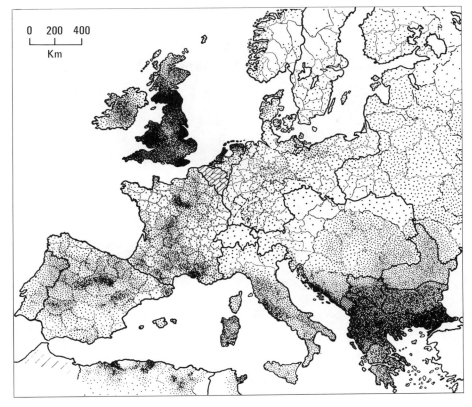

12.13. Sheep rearing in Europe, about 1913. Each dot represents 10,000 sheep

man-held Lorraine, on the other hand, pig iron exceeded steel, since many of the works on the minette field produced iron to be refined elsewhere. The iron and steel industry was highly concentrated. No less than 24 percent of Europe's steel was made in the Ruhr, and 25 percent of its pig iron was smelted on the minette ore field of Lorraine and Luxembourg. In Great Britain, the northeast and central Scotland accounted for over half of steel production.

By 1914 several methods of steelmaking were in use, and the quality and usefulness of the metal produced differed greatly between them. Open-hearth steel was superior in all respects to converter steel, and crucible and electric steels were made for special purposes. The amounts made in three of the major steelmaking countries are shown in Table 12.8. Nearly 60 percent of the steel produced in France and Germany had been made by the basic process, and a large part of this came from the minette region of Lorraine. The proportion was much smaller in Great Britain and Russia, which had very much larger reserves of low-phosphorus ores. There was, however, an increasing dependence generally on the two immense reserves of phosphoric ores in northern Sweden and Lorraine. The use of Swedish

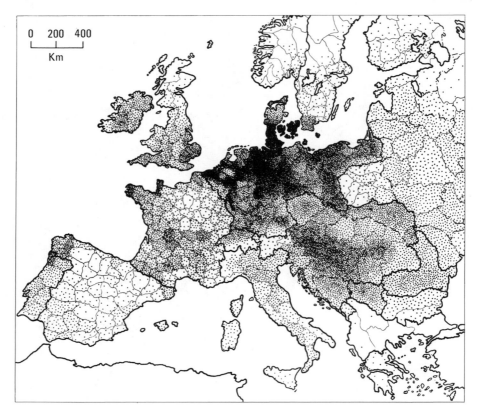

12.14. Pig rearing in Europe, about 1913. Each dot represents 5,000 pigs

Table 12.5. *Sources of energy, 1913*

	10^{15} metric calories	Percentage
Solid fuel	3,997.0	90.53
Wood used as fuel	207.0	4.69
Oil and petroleum	66.5	1.51
Natural gas	0.5	0.01
Hydroelectric power	144.0	3.26
Total	4,415	100

ore led in turn to the location of smelting works at coastal sites in Italy, France, the Netherlands, and Germany, where the ore was unloaded from freighters which had brought it from northern Scandinavia or from mines even farther afield.

In the later years of the nineteenth century it became profitable to smelt and refine the metal in a single integrated works. There were economies both in transportation and in fuel consumption. But now these advantages were less apparent.

Table 12.6. *Production of bituminous and brown coal, 1913*

	Bituminous		Brown	
	Total	Percentage	Total	Percentage
Austria	16,460	8.7	27,378	21.83
[of which Bohemia-Moravia]	[14,087]	—	[23,137]	—
Belgium	24,371	4.0	—	—
Bulgaria	11	—	358	—
France	40,844	6.7	—	—
Germany	190,109	31.1	87,233	69.96
Greece	0.2	—	—	—
Hungary	1,320	—	8,954	7.14
Italy	1	—	700	—
Norway	33	—	—	—
Poland	5,770[a]	0.9	—	—
Portugal	25	—	—	—
Serbia	32[a]	—	273	—
Sweden	364	—	—	—
Spain	3,971	—	277	—
Romania	—	—	250	—
Russia	36,011	5.9	n.d.	n.d.
United Kingdom	292,043	47.8	n.d.	n.d.
Total	611,365		125,423	

[a] Figures are for 1911.

The smelting process was increasingly important on the coast or the ore field, while refining and fabricating remained at the older industrial centers. When smelting did in fact cease to be carried on, it usually left a host of derivative industries. A typical instance was the Saint-Etienne region. Iron-ore resources were exhausted and, at this inland site, could not easily be replaced by imported ores. Smelting was abandoned, but the region strengthened its hold on the manufacture of quality steel for armaments and of such light, metal goods as bicycles and sewing machines, becoming in these respects the foremost producer in France. The same course of development was occurring elsewhere in France, as well as in the English Midlands, at Aachen, in the Siegerland and Sauerland, and in Saxony. The facility with which a gas-fueled open-hearth steelworks could be established encouraged the development of small works remote from both coalfields and ironworks. This was especially the case in northern Italy, where the steel output supplied the growing automobile and light engineering industries.

The steel industry was at this time finding vast new markets in ship building, heavy engineering, and the developing automobiles industry, more than replacing the demand which had been created half a century earlier by the spreading railroads. Ship building was most important near the great ports of northwest Europe. Heavy engineering and steel construction were to be found close to the major

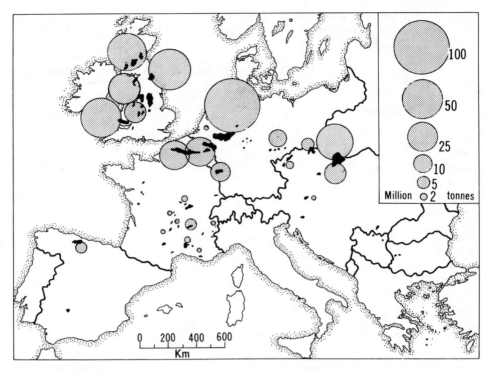

12.15. Coal production in Europe, 1912. The overwhelming importance of Great Britain and Germany is apparent

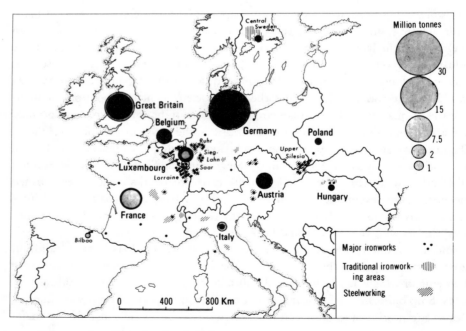

12.16. Iron and steel production in Europe, 1912

Table 12.7. *Production of pig iron and steel, 1913*
(*in thousand tons*)

	Pig iron	Steel
Austria (incl. Bohemia-Moravia)	1,758	2,611
Belgium	2,485	2,403
France	5,207	4,687
Germany	16,761	17,609
Hungary	623	—
Italy	427	934
Luxembourg	2,548	1,326
Russia	4,650	4,925
[of which Finland]	[9]	[7]
[of which Poland]	[418]	[n.d.]
Spain	425	242
Sweden	730	591
United Kingdom	10,425	7,787
Total	46,039	43,115

Table 12.8. *Steel production in Germany, France, and Great Britain (in thousand tons)*

	France	Germany	Great Britain
Converter steel			
basic	2,806.5	10,630	552
acid	272.7	155	1,049
Open-hearth steel	1,582.5	7,613	6,063
Crucible steel	24.1	85	—
Electric steel	21.1	89	—
Total	4,706.9	18,572	7,664

steelmaking centers. Other branches of light and labor-intensive engineering were established in Berlin, Hanover, and at several sites in south Germany, all of which obtained their steel mainly from the Ruhr.

A feature of these industries was their increasing integration, not only between industrial regions but also across political boundaries. Every important works was dependent on a distant source for one or more of its materials, and its market might span the continent. This contributed to two forms of integration. The more important in the present context was vertical integration, by which the steel producer sought to control not only the source of iron, but also of ore and fuel, and at the same time reached forward even to metal fabricating and marketing. Steel-making companies in much of western Europe acquired interests in Lorraine; Ruhr steel magnates owned coal mines, coking ovens, and fleets of Rhine barges, and industrialists in Berlin and Breslau acquired works in Upper Silesia. The list is almost endless, even though control was sometimes masked by the niceties of commercial law. The long arm of a Krupp, a Stinnes, or a Thyssen reached into Austria, Sweden, and Spain.

The other form of integration was horizontal. Two or more firms producing the same type of goods agreed to associate in order to make fuller use of resources, to share a market, or to control prices. Countless small works were taken over and absorbed into larger. The formation of cartels was the culmination of this process. The producing units agreed on production levels and prices, and in many instances acquired a monopolistic position within their own countries. There was, for example, a German coal cartel, and a series of cartel agreements was made within the steel industry.

Europe had once been a major producer of nonferrous metals. Output was on balance maintained, and in some areas, like Upper Silesia and Spain, was actually increasing. But demand had grown far more rapidly, and Europe was producing a diminishing share of the world's output and was a heavy importer of most metals. The smelting industry was shifting from mining areas like the Belgian Vieille Montagne to the ports through which the ore and concentrates passed.

The other dominant industry of the nineteenth century, textiles, showed no such vitality. The linen industry was overall scarcely larger than it had been half a century earlier. The woolen industry, as measured by its consumption of raw wool, was still growing, but expansion in its major centers was slow. Only cottons had maintained their earlier momentum, with in 1913 two-thirds of the world's spindles. But Europe's share of the weaving industry was appreciably smaller, mechanically spun thread being exported to handloom weavers in other parts of the world. It would not be long before the "new" countries would begin to spin their own thread.

The chemical industry was a European invention and remained very nearly a European monopoly. It is difficult to measure its size, because of the diversity of its products. Production of the basic acids and alkalis, fundamental to other branches of the industry, had been increasing very rapidly, as had the manufacture of dyestuffs, pharmaceuticals, and photographic materials. Growth in the years preceding World War I was more rapid in chemicals than in any other branch of manufacture. At a rough estimate, a third to a half of the European industry was located in Germany, mainly in Saxony and along the Rhine, and up to a fifth in Great Britain.

By 1914 a long period of industrial growth was cut short by the weapons of war which it had created. Europe, if no longer Great Britain alone, was the "workshop of the world." Its only rival at this time was the United States. The latter's output fell far short of the European level in most respects, but its potential for growth, with its huge and little tapped resources, was far greater. Within Europe, over 70 percent of manufacturing capacity was in France, Germany, and the United Kingdom, with Germany now in the lead in most respects (see Table 12.9).

Much of the manufacturing capacity of Europe had by 1913 become concentrated within a relatively narrow belt which extended from northern Britain to northwest Germany. From this "core area" manufacturing was spreading eastward

Table 12.9. *European manufacturing, 1913 (percentages)*

	France	Germany	United Kingdom	Other countries
Bituminous coal	7	34	52	7
Steel	12	46	20	22
Machinery	5	48	27	20
Chemicals	14	41	19	26
Raw cotton consumption	11	19	43	27
Total manufacturing capacity	13	32	27	28

and southward "into soil that was less and less well prepared to receive it."[1] Even so, much of the continent was in 1913 still untouched by the technological advances made in the core area. Around both the core and other concentrations of manufacturing lay a peripheral region, with dense population, intensive agriculture, and a scatter of smaller factories and industrial centers. These were of two kinds. There were relict industries which had in varying degrees been superseded by technologically more advanced manufactures. The second category consisted of new factories and new industries, which marked, as it were, the expanding fringe of the Industrial Revolution. These were pushing out into the rural areas which surrounded the older and heavily built-up regions of, for example, the English West Midlands, the Ruhr, and central Belgium.

TRANSPORTATION AND TRADE

By 1914 Europe's railroad system was complete except in parts of the Balkans and Russia, and in a few areas it can be said to have been overdeveloped (see Table 12.10). No indicator demonstrates more clearly than the density of the railroad net and the intensity of its use the contrast between the developed, industrialized core of northwest Europe and the remainder of the continent. Intensity of use varied far more than the density of the net itself. From available estimates of tonnage and passengers carried per kilometer of track it is possible to work out an index showing the intensity with which railroad systems were used in each country. They appear in rank order in Tables 12.11 and 12.12.

The correlation between the two tables is, as might be expected, high, but the index for the Netherlands has been reduced below the level that might have been expected by the heavy use made of waterways. A feature of these tables is the very great differential between the most used systems and the least used. It follows that the cost of maintaining a railroad system was disproportionately high in less-developed countries which were least able to support it. The remarkable showing

---

1 S. Pollard, *European Economic Integration 1815–1970* (London, 1974), 27.

Table 12.10. *Density of European railroad net*

	Length of track (km)	Track (km) per 1,000 sq. km
Austria-Hungary	22,981	36.8
Belgium	4,676	153.3
Bulgaria	2,109	24.2
Denmark	3,868	89.7
Finland	3,560	10.9
France	40,770	76.0
Germany	63,378	117.2
Greece	1,584	24.4
Italy	18,873	65.9
Netherlands	3,305	97.8
Norway	3,085	9.5
Poland	2,796	22.0
Portugal	2,958	32.6
Romania	3,549	27.0
Russia	68,006	3.1
Serbia	1,598	33.1
Spain	15,088	29.8
Sweden	14,377	33.6
Switzerland	4,832	114.2
Great Britain	32,623	139.5

Table 12.11. *Intensity of use of European railways (tonnage)*

	km/tonnes of freight (millions)	Index[a]
Belgium	5,729	1.224
Germany	67,700	1.106
France	25,200	0.622
Netherlands	1,802	0.560
Romania	1,443	0.420
Austria-Hungary	17,287	0.399
Italy	7,070	0.391
Switzerland	1,458	0.309
Sweden	3,184	0.230
Spain	3,179	0.217
Finland	649	0.178
Denmark	578	0.168
Norway	401	0.135
Bulgaria	176	0.091
Greece	50	0.032

[a] The index has been calculated by the formula:

$$I = \frac{km/t}{tract\ (in\ km)}$$

Table 12.12. *Intensity of use of European railways (passengers)*

	km/passengers (millions)	Index
Belgium	6,242	1.334
Germany	41,400	0.676
Switzerland	2,685	0.569
France	19,300	0.477
Netherlands	1,433	0.446
Denmark	950	0.276
Italy	5,000	0.276
Romania	871	0.253
Austria-Hungary	8,321	0.193
Finland	704	0.193
Greece	297	0.188
Norway	462	0.155
Spain	2,139	0.146
Sweden	1,848	0.134
Bulgaria	136	0.070

of Romania in freight transportation must be attributed to the traffic in oil and cereals.

By 1913 many rivers and canals had passed out of use. In England most canals had been acquired by the railroad companies, which allowed them to decay to the point of uselessness. Only in the industrial areas of northern Britain did they retain any importance. In France the modernized system was used for bulky freight, notably coal, but river traffic had been reduced to negligible proportions. Only those rivers, like the Seine, Scheldt, Meuse, Rhine, and Elbe, which provided transportation from the great ports into their hinterlands continued to be heavily used. This meant, in effect, that internal navigation was important only in the Low Countries, northwest Germany, and eastward to Berlin. The high hopes that had once been entertained of developing shipping on the Danube had foundered on the physical difficulties of navigation and the political problems of the region. In 1913 the whole river carried less traffic than the lower Elbe. In southern Europe river and canal transportation, never very vigorous, had almost come to a standstill.

Road transportation, at least in western and central Europe, had been eclipsed by the railroads. Short-distance wagon traffic – to the nearest market, railway, or canal – was still important, but long-distance road traffic seemed at this time to have little future. Nevertheless, life was beginning to return to the roads. The bicycle, developed in the 1880s, was proving popular, and an increasing number of people in northwest Europe were using it to get to work. This was followed by the automobile. By 1913 the number of motor vehicles in the whole of Europe was of the order of 450,000. Although most were little more than the playthings of the rich, a growing proportion consisted of commercial vehicles, an indication

Table 12.13. *The foreign trade of European countries, 1913 (in millions of dollars)*

	Imports		Exports			
	Total	From other European countries	Total	To other European countries	Total trade	Trade per capita
Industrial northwestern Europe						
France	1,618	752	1,323	881	2,941	63.2
Belgium-Luxembourg	875	513	682	540	1,557	202.6
Netherlands	824	387	489	319	1,313	224.1
Germany	2,565	1,045	2,405	1,594	4,970	151.1
Switzerland	358	283	264	183	622	165.7
Scandinavia						
Sweden	227	185	219	183	446	112.6
Norway	148	125	115	85	263	109.9
Denmark	230	169	173	165	403	146.2
Finland	95	68	77	53	172	58.4
Eastern and southeastern Europe						
Austria-Hungary	688	453	563	452	1,251	24.4
Romania	114	102	131	114	245	33.9
Bulgaria	36	29	18	15	54	12.4
Southern Europe						
Portugal	84	63	32	19	116	20.5
Spain	253	149	206	143	459	23.0
Italy	704	410	482	283	1,186	34.2
Greece	31	22	23	18	54	20.4

that freight traffic was beginning to return to the roads. It only remained to make the roads fit for the traffic.

Europe in 1913 was the focus of a complex network of trade. About half the world's international trade was with Europe, but its volume had not been increasing as rapidly as Europe's internal development might have suggested. Some 60 percent of the trade of European countries was with one another. Only in the United Kingdom did extra-European trade make up a really large proportion – about 70 percent – of the total. In no other country of continental Europe did trade with other continents amount to more than 45 percent. It was largest in France, the Netherlands, and Germany, all of which had significant colonial dependencies.

The export trade of the more developed countries was dominated by manufactured goods, particularly metal goods and textiles. Foodstuffs were relatively unimportant, but industrial raw materials, notably coal from Great Britain and Ger-

Table 12.14. *Gross national product and GNP per head, 1913*

	GNP (in million U.S. dollars at 1960 prices)	GNP per head (in U.S. dollars)
Austria-Hungary	26,050	498
Belgium	6,794	894
Bulgaria	1,260	263
Denmark	2,421	862
Finland	1,670	520
France	27,401	689
Germany	49,760	743
Greece	1,540	322
Italy	15,624	441
Netherlands	4,660	754
Norway	1,834	749
Portugal	1,800	292
Romania	2,450	336
Serbia	725	284
Spain	7,450	367
Sweden	3,824	680
Switzerland	3,700	964
United Kingdom	44,074	965

many, and iron ore from France and Sweden, were significant. Foodstuffs and industrial raw materials, notably raw cotton and metalliferous ores, were prominent among these countries' imports. In less-developed countries the balance swung in the opposite direction. Foodstuffs and primary goods were the biggest exports. Wheat, for example, made up 80 percent of Romania's exports and almost 30 percent of those of Bulgaria. Foodstuffs and wine constituted 49 percent of the exports of Greece and 43 percent of Spain's, and they ranked high in the trade of Italy (see Table 12.13.)

NATIONAL INCOME

Estimates have been presented (see p. 350–1) of the gross national product of European countries near the beginning of the previous century. By 1913 the data on which such estimates were based had become more abundant and more reliable, and Table 12.14 and Figures 12.17 and 12.18 have greater pretensions to accuracy than earlier figures had possessed. Near the beginning of the century the Mediterranean countries did not rank much below the rest of Europe. By 1913 they came at the bottom of the table, with only the Balkans, for which data are wholly inadequate, occupying a lower place. At the same time the Scandinavian countries, which had previously been comparable with southern Europe, had raised themselves to the level of northwestern Europe.

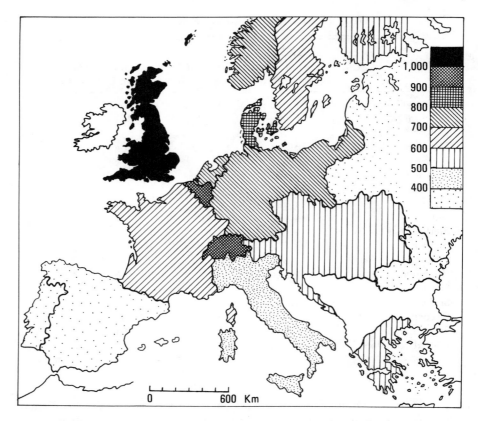

12.17. Gross national product per head, 1913 (in U.S. dollars)

In Figure 12.18 the gross national product of eight industrialized and of eight
nonindustrialized countries are plotted according to the contributions made by
agriculture, manufacturing, and tertiary activities. They are readily differentiated.
The nonindustrialized countries have low tertiary and industrial components, but
in the industrialized countries these three components are fairly evenly balanced.

Statistics are, as a general rule, made available for countries and for major administrative districts. These rarely coincide with economic regions. But even with
crude national estimates of production and wealth, the contrast between the two
Europes, represented in Figure 12.18, is apparent, with the gross national product
per head in the United Kingdom, Switzerland, Belgium, and Denmark more than
three times the level in the Balkans and Russia. A more refined analysis of the data
would show that even in the most developed countries there were areas of backwardness, of low productivity, and of low consumption. The United Kingdom
had Ireland and the Scottish Highlands; France had Brittany; Italy had its *Mezzogiorno* (south), and Germany, the wholly agricultural east. These regions can be
defined in several ways: in terms of poorly developed infrastructure, underdevel-

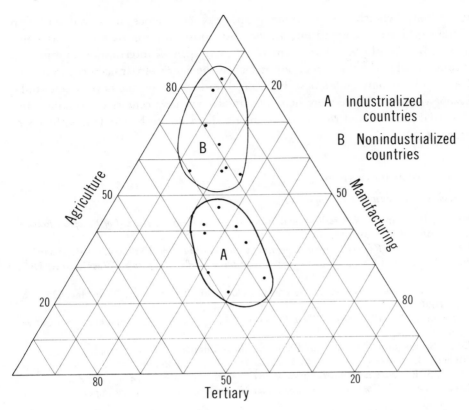

12.18. Gross national product per head by sector for (A) industrialized countries, (B) nonindustrialized countries. Data for 1913

oped agriculture, small tertiary employment, high level of illiteracy, and, all too often, a high birthrate and large out-migration.

CONCLUSION

The outbreak of war in August, 1914, brought to an end a century of economic growth. European countries – in effect, central and northwest Europe – made from half to three-quarters of all manufactured goods produced in the world. When the war ended, this role had changed significantly; Europe was no longer the unchallenged "workshop of the world." Industrial production had increased in Japan and the United States and, to a smaller extent, in the British Commonwealth and Latin America. This development was, without doubt, accelerated by the war, but it would have come eventually without it. The diffusion of European technology to the rest of the world was as inevitable as the spread of British technology to continental Europe had been. The course of change could not be altered, only its speed. "Europe had to face a trend in world economy," wrote

Svennilson, "whereby its traditional position as the foremost industrial workshop of the world was becoming undermined by industrial progress in overseas countries."[2] But World War I was something more than an interruption in a process of growth, which could be resumed as soon as the debris of war had been removed. The world economy took a new direction. It ceased during the next decades to be Europe-centered. There were henceforward to be many centers of economic and industrial growth, and the foremost among them was to be the United States of America.

SELECT BIBLIOGRAPHY

See also the bibliography for Chapter 11.

Bairoch, P. "Europe's Gross National Product: 1800–1975." *Journal of European Economic History* 5 (1976): 273–340.

Brady, R. A. *The Rationalization Movement in German Industry.* Berkeley, Calif., 1933.

Finch, V. C., and O. E. Baker. *Geography of the World's Agriculture.* Washington, D.C., 1917.

Fontaine, A. *French Industry during the War.* Carnegie Endowment: New Haven, Conn., 1926.

Malenbaum, W. *The World Wheat Economy 1885–1939.* Harvard Economic Series, vol. 92, 1953.

Mance, Sir Osborne. *International River and Canal Transport.* Oxford, 1944.

Mitchell, B. R. *European Historical Statistics 1750–1970.* London, 1975.

Pollard, S. *European Economic Integration 1815–1970.* London, 1974.

Report of the Royal Commission on Canals and Waterways. Parliamentary Papers, 1909, vol. 13.

Svennilson, I. *Growth and Stagnation in the European Economy.* Geneva, 1954.

Warriner, D. *Economics of Peasant Farming.* London, 1939.

2   I. Svennilson, *Growth and Stagnation in the European Economy* (Geneva, 1954), 169–70.

Index

Aachen, 92, 173
  coalfield at, 413, 415
  Industrial Revolution at, 415,
    417–18, 340
  ironworking at, 418
Abbeville, 294
Acciaiuoli merchants, 179
Achaea, 30
Acropolis, 27, 35
Adam of Bremen, 96
Aelfric's dialogue, 106–7, 109
Aeneas Sylvius, 215
AGFA, 411
agora, 35–6
Agri Decumates, 48, 75
Agricola, Georg, 201, 239, 240
Agricola, Gnaeus Julius, 53
agricultural products
  regions for, 333–5
  technology of, 195, 232, 333,
    391–7
  trade in, 285
agriculture, 2–3, 5–6, 9
  Carolingian, 102–7
  development of, 313–14
  early modern, 274–86
  employment in, 443
  Greek, 38–9
  medieval, 89–90
  nineteenth-century, 327–32,
    381–97
  productivity of, 446–7
  Roman, 62
  structure of, 383
  twentieth-century, 446–52
  urban, 165
Akragas, 39
alabaster, 177
Alamanni, 78

Albania, 348·
Alessandria, 128, 163
Algeria, migration to, 357
Allevard, 282
Alpine system, 13–15, 20
Alps
  as boundaries, 216
  mining in, 44
  passes through, 15, 91, 110,
    140, 181–2, 203
Alps (pastures), 397
  population of, 219
  transhumance in, 171, 233,
    333
Alsace, 168
  cities in, 369
  textile industry in, 402
alum trade, 175, 183–4, 204,
    242
Amalfi, 138, 140–1
amber trade, 46
Amiens, 173, 292, 294
Amsterdam, 227, 243, 264,
    326, 345, 436
  port of, 431
  printing in, 303
  trade of, 303–5
Anatolia, 94
Ancona, 304
Anglesey, copper in, 301
Anglo-Saxon Chronicle, 126
Anglo-Saxon England, 82, 95,
    116
Anglo-Saxons, 78
  settlement of, 88
animal husbandry, 40, 63, 105,
    170–1, 194–5, 232–3,
    284–5, 333–4, 396
  in open-field farming, 134

Annales des Mines, 253–4
Anthedon, 36, 45
anthracite in smelting, 428
Antonine emperors, 25, 54
Antwerp, 206, 208, 226–7,
    264, 305, 326, 365, 435–
    6
  growth of, 203
  population of, 193
  reopening of, 345
  trade of, 242
Apollinaris Sidonius, 86
Appenzell, 404
aqueducts, 58–61, 100–1
Aquileia, 81, 128
Aragon, 142
  state of, 145
Archangel, 300
ard, 40
Ardennes, 103, 201
  charcoal iron in, 415
  mining in, 238, 240, 300,
    418
Argos, 35
Aristeides, 47, 66
Aristotle, 28
Armentières, 228, 235
  fire at, 227
armies, size of, 256
Arras, 127, 130, 197, 235
artificial grasses, 277, 285, 382,
    391, 395
Athens, 23, 28, 34, 35–6, 41,
    47, 100
  food supply of, 34
  population of, 34
  trade of, 45
Athens-Piraeus, 435
Atlantic trade, 242, 305

Attica, 34, 39, 44
  agriculture of, 39
Attila, 81
Augsburg, 251, 296
  food supply of, 272–3
Augst, 86
Augustus, Roman emperor, 48,
    55, 60
Austria
  advance of, into Balkans, 254
  cotton industry in, 404
  duchy of, 144
  empire of, 216
  ironworking in, 341
  population of, 264
automobiles, 463
  manufacture of, 411
Autun, 54–5
Avars, 81, 94, 96, 110, 115
Avenches, 57
Avignon, 174, 187
Azov, Sea of, 255

back-to-back housing, 376
Bad Ischl, 371
Baghdad, caliph of, 97
balance of power, 254
Balkan peninsula, 15, 16, 94
  cloth industry in, 401
  mining in, 201
  nationalism in, 348
  peasantry in, 390
  population of, 149, 323
  railroads in, 433–4
  towns in, 382
  urban growth of, 381
Baltic region
  peoples of, 33, 80, 153
  ports of, 345–6, 435
  settlers in, 145
  timber in, 243
  trade of, 180, 193, 202, 205,
    243, 304, 306, 344–5
Banfield, T. C., 418
Banská Bystrica, 241
Banská Štiavnica, 241
bar iron, 237–8, 245, 298,
    300, 304, 336, 337
barbarian invasions, 70, 77–80,
    92
Barcelona, 193, 225–6, 325
  cotton industry in, 297, 342
barchent, 173, 198

barge traffic, 431
barley, 38, 63–4, 104–5, 107,
    132, 194, 230, 277, 449
Barmen, 340, 420
Basel, 410
  printing at, 303
  silk weaving at, 406
basic activities, 5
basic process (steel production),
    420, 455, 459
Basque region
  iron in, 238, 342
  language of, 153
Bath, 86, 270, 371
Bavaria, 94
  church land in, 274
"Bay" salt, 202
Bayeux, 272
Beauce, 324, 391–2
Beauvais, 292, 294
beer, 104, 281
Belgium
  coal in, 413
  cotton industry in, 402
  landholding in, 389
  manufacturing in, 415, 417–
    18
  population of, 365
Belgrade, 327
Benevento, duchy of, 94
Benjamin of Tudela, 140
Bergamo, 342
  diocese of, 219
Bergen, 205
Bergslagen, 200
Berlin, 326, 378
  canals in, 431
  chemical industry in, 411
  clothing industry in, 400
  population of, 380
Bessemer process, 408–9
Beuthen, 424
Białystok, 404
Biarritz, 371
bicycle, 463
Bilbao, 242, 438
Biringuccio, 238–40
Birka, 110–11
Birmingham, 324
birth control, 356–7
birthrates, 147, 151, 260, 352,
    355, 359, 364–5, 368,
    442–3

  in Belgium, 365
  in France, 321, 323, 332,
    365
  in Italy, 323
  in Switzerland, 365, 368
bishops, role of, 85, 99
Biskupin, 33, 37
Black Death, 121, 123, 147,
    148, 150–1, 187–9
  spread of, 187–9
  see also bubonic plague
blast furnace, 175, 199, 237,
    297, 408–9, 418, 427–8
bloomery iron, 198–9, 200
boats, river, 308
Bobbio, monastery of, 106
Bochum, 408, 418, 420
Boeotia, 28, 30, 39, 46
Bohemia, 317
  kingdom of, 119, 144
  manufacturing in, 341, 401,
    404
Bologna, 158, 197–8, 270
Bonis of Montauban, 180
books, increase of, 253
Bordeaux, 306
Bosnia, 145, 201–2
Bosnia and Hercegovina, 390
Bosniaks, 252
Boston, 205, 208
Botero, Giovanni, 193, 221,
    227
boundaries, 116, 118–19, 215–
    16, 317
bourgeoisie as landowners, 275
Bourgneuf, Bay of, 202, 246
Brabant, 143–4, 208
  population of, 149–50
Brăila, 432
Brandenburg-Prussia, 145, 317,
    322
brass, 176, 240
Braun, Georg, and Franz Hogen-
    berg, maps of cities by,
    220
breadgrains, 169, 278, 447
  consumption of, 382
  trade in, 382
Bremen, 306, 435–6
Bremerhaven, 436
Brescia, 342
Breslau, 423
Brest, 269

Bretons as traders, 242
brewing, 281
brick
    building in, 198, 227, 236
    making of, 137, 236
bridges, 140, 180, 245, 307
Bridgewater Canal, 309
Brie, limestone of, 176
Brighton, 371
Bristol, 208, 324, 435
Brittany, 93–4, 118, 217
Brixen, fair at, 178
Brno, 294, 401
brochs, 37
Bronze Age, 21, 27, 31, 33
brown coal, 410, 413
Bruges, 126, 161, 173, 197,
    205, 208, 226, 305
    Itinerary of Bruges, 181–2
Brussels, 173, 224, 326
    plague in, 258
    population of, 371
bubonic plague, 187, 191, 204,
    257–8, 265, 268–9
    in cities, 191–3
Bucharest, 327
buckwheat, 277, 328
Buda, *see* Budapest
Budapest, 86, 119, 159, 326,
    381
    creation of, 245, 381
Buffon, Georges Louis Leclerc
    comte de, 282, 297
building construction, 137–8,
    176, 198
    stone, 176
Bukovina, 317
Bulgaria, 348
    landholding in, 390
Bulgarian empire, 82, 96, 119,
    145
Bulgars, 82
bullion, trade in, 252, 303, 305
burgage rent, 125
Burgundians, 78, 89
Burgundy
    duchy of, 149, 216, 224
    ironworking in, 238
Bury St. Edmunds, 126
buses, 376
Byzantine empire, 95–6, 101,
    119, 142, 145
    agriculture in, 106

manufacturing in, 108–9
silk in, 136
trade with, 111

Cadiz, 305
Caen stone, 176
Caerwent, 87
Caesar, Gaius Julius, 53
Caistor-by-Norwich, 57, 87
Calabria, 84
calamine, 201, 240
Calicut, 242
caliphs, 84
calorific intake, 356
Calvinism, 251
cameralism, *see* mercantilism
Campagna, Roman, 59, 106
canal transportation, 429–31,
    433
canals, 307, 315, 413, 463
    British, 309
    East European, 309, 344
    in France, 309, 430
cane sugar, 383
Cannstadt, 411
Capet dynasty, 117, 142–3
capital cities, 119, 221–4
Carolingian empire, 71–2, 83,
    92–3, 116–18
    population of, 97–8
cartels, 460
Carthage, 23, 30–1, 47
Carthaginian cities, 36
Carthaginian trade, 45
Cassiodorus, Flavius Magnus Au-
    relius, 48
cast iron, 199, 237, 297, 409
Castile, 142
Catalonia, 330, 331, 349
    population of, 368
    textile industry in, 297, 342,
    401, 405
catch crops, 277
Cathars, 251
Catholic Europe, 251–2
Cattaro (Gulf of Kotor), 221
cattle droving, 234
cattle rearing, 232–3, 451, 454
Celtic fields, 40–1
Celtic language, 51, 152
Celts, 24, 32–3, 36, 52, 77, 88
    metalworking by, 43

census, 33, 53, 120, 147, 262
central-places, 369
centuriated landscape, 62
cereal cultivation, 230–1, 384–5
cereals, trade in, 449–50
cesspits, 165, 268, 374
Chalcidice, Peninsula of, 30
Champagne, 172
    fairs of, 139, 174, 178
    ironworking in, 238
Chaptal, J. A., comte de Chan-
    teloup, 327–8
charcoal iron, 339–40, 406–8,
    422, 424
    supply of, 237, 298, 426,
    428
Charlemagne, 92–3, 95
    empire of, 83
Charleroi, 415–18
Charles V, emperor, 214, 223,
    250, 254
Charles Martel, 93
Charleville, 269
cheese, 106, 135, 171, 285,
    397
chemical fertilizers, 395
chemical industry, 410–11,
    420, 460
chemicals, basic, 410
Chemnitz, 290, 296, 404
    cotton at, 340
Cherbourg, 436
Chernigov, 115
chiflik, 331, 392
cholera, 356, 374
Christianity in the Roman em-
    pire, 85, 99
church, lands of, 229, 274–5
churches
    fortified, 157–8
    urban, 160–1
cider, 281
Cirencester, 55
cities
    decay of, 71
    distribution of, 221–2
    engravings of, 220, 265
    food supply of, 272–3
    function of, 371, 443–4
    health in, 268
    jurisdiction of, 221
    medieval, growth of, 123–30
    migration to, 151–2, 268–9

472

cities (*cont.*)
  population structure of, 371–2
  preindustrial, 272
  poverty in, 272
  Roman, 84–5
  size of, 221, 378, 445
  social geography of, 371–8
city
  definition of, 5, 54–5, 158–66, 371
  planning of, 269–70
  streets of, 268
city-state, 24, 25, 28, 34–6, 46, 48
civitas, 48–9
Clermont, 54, 86
climate
  changes in, 10–11
  influence of, 2–5, 9–10, 122
cloth
  manufacture of, 107, 109–10, 172, 196–7
  trade in, 172, 185
clothing industry, 172–5, 286, 411–12
  in towns in Flanders, 173–4
Clovis (King Louis I), 82
Cluny, monastery of, 126
coal, 21, 288
  coking, 418
  production of, 301–2, 337, 397, 453–4, 457, 458
  reserves of, 301, 337, 413
  trade in, 454
  varieties of, 413
coal gas, 375
coal tar, 410
Coalbrookdale, 299, 336
coalfields, 288, 399, 406, 314
coal-measures iron ore, 418
coastwise shipping, 243, 306, 435
Cockerill of Liège, 293–4, 338, 398–9
Code Napoléon, 321, 332, 388
Cognac, 281
coke-oven gas, 409

coke smelting, 300, 406–8, 415, 418, 428
  use of, 337–8
Colbert, Jean Baptiste, 306–7
  and factory development, 287, 294
Colmar, 369
Cologne, 130–1, 140, 159, 199, 208, 238, 265
colonial goods, 252
colonies, value of, 349–50
colonization of Eastern Europe, 154
  Greek, 33
Columella, Lucius Junius Moderatus, 64
comfort, increase in, 198
Commentry, 370
commodity ports, 436
common land, 276, 388
Congo Act, 349
"Congress" Poland, 404
conserving societies, 2–3, 7
Constantine Porphyrogenitus, 115
Constantine the Great, 74
Constantinople, 69, 75–6, 80–4, 92, 94, 99–100, 106, 128, 130, 140, 174, 224, 324, 327
  and Crusades, 119
  food supply of, 184, 248
  manufacturing in, 108, 111
  Norse in, 115
  population of, 193
  trade of, 100–1, 183
  water supply of, 100
continental blockage, 342–3
conurbations, 444
converter steel, 408
Copenhagen, 326, 436
copper, 21, 65, 201, 301
  mining of, 44, 136, 240–1, 337
Corbie, monastery of, 126
Corbridge, 54
Córdoba, 128, 130
  emirate of, 97
cordovan leather, 175
core areas, 251, 350
Corinth, 28, 35, 43, 45, 47, 100

corn dealers, 257
corn growing, 231, 328, 449
  spread of, 278–9
Cornwall, 44, 65, 171
  copper in, 301
Cort, Henry, 299
Cossacks, 254
Cotswold Hills, textiles in, 234
cotton
  growing of, 170, 236
  manufacture of, 137, 172, 174, 198, 288, 293–4, 296, 315, 336, 338–9, 401–2, 460
  spinning of, 340, 397–8
coulter for plow, 64, 89
Courtrai, 197
craft industries, 212, 260, 398
crannog, 38
Crete, 84
Crimea, 111, 183
Critias, 17
Croatia, 331
crop failures, 169–70
cropping systems, 131, 391
crucible steel, 300, 420, 455, 459
Crulai, family size at, 259
Crusades, 75, 116, 119, 138, 140, 193
cutlery, manufacture of, 420

Dąbrowa, 423
Dacia, 48, 75
dairy farming, 171, 396–7
Dalmatia, 17, 74, 331
Danebury, 40
Danelaw, 114
Danish language, 153
Danish Sound, 215, 343
  see also Sound, The
Danish state, origin of, 119
Danish Straits, 205
Dannemora, 300
Danube, 15, 74, 77
  "maritime," 432
  navigation on, 431–2
  ports of, 346
Danzig, 193, 243–4, 306, 309, 344
Darby, Abraham, 299, 336
Dark Ages, 71–2

Darlington, Robert, 276
Dean, Forest of, 199
death rates, 147, 150, 166,
    260, 352, 356, 368, 442–
    3
    urban, 151
Decazeville, 320
Defoe, Daniel, 307
Delian League, 28, 30, 34
demesne farming, 195, 230,
    275, 386–7
demographic transition, 368,
    442
Demosthenes, 35
Denmark, 146, 217–18
    land reform in, 390, 392
    population of, 264, 322
    railroads in, 434
deserted villages, 193, 232
    in Denmark, 193
    in England, 193
    in France, 193–4
    in Germany, 193–4
determinism, 10
Deventer, fairs at, 203
Dicaearchus, 35–6, 45
diet, 170, 354–6
diffusion, 7, 9
Dijon, population of, 193
    craft structure of, 272
Dillenburg, iron at, 298
Dinant, 176
Diocletian, 74–5, 92
Diodorus Siculus, 44
disease, 17, 227, 257, 353, 356
    see also epidemics; bubonic
    plague
distilling, 281
Dnepr River, 432
Dobrudja railroads in, 434
dock construction, 435
Domesday Book, 90, 122, 126,
    135, 138
domestic industry, 399–401
Don River, 432
Donation of Constantine, 85
Donetz
    coalfield of, 427–8
    industrial region of, 426–9
Dorchester, 55
Dortmund, 418
Dortmund-Ems Canal, 418

drainage of mines, 201
Dresden, 270
droving, 285
Dublin, 146
Dubrovnik, 57, 204, 304
Duero River, 308
Duhamel de Monceau, H. L.,
    302
Duisburg, 420, 431
Dürer, Albrecht, 220
Dutch nation, 250
    trade of, 243
Duurstede (Dordrecht), 110
dyestuffs, 170, 172, 174–5,
    184, 231, 410

East Anglia, textiles in, 234,
    286, 290
eastern empire, 69, 74, 80, 82–
    3, 94–5
    cities in, 85
eastern Europe, cities in, 273–4,
    326–7
    grain from, 275–6
    land reform in, 392
    population of, 150–1, 219,
    323
Ebro River, 308
economic growth, 350–1
Edinburgh, 324
Egil's Saga, 135
Egypt, 84
Eifel, 103, 201
    ironworking in, 199
    mining in, 238, 240
    textiles in, 293, 400
Einhard, 94
Ekaterinburg, 300
Ekaterinoslav, 428
Elba, island of, 238
    iron ore from, 43, 65, 342
Elbe River
    as boundary, 94
    navigation of, 431
Elberfeld, 290, 340, 420
Elberfeld-Barmen (Wuppertal),
    406, 418
electric furnace, 409
electric power, 375–6, 411,
    455, 459
Emden, 418
empires, extent of, 348–9

Emscher valley, 418
enclosure movement, 285–6
    in Denmark, 393, 397
    of open fields, 392, 395–6
enclosed fields, 285–6, 332–3
energy supply, 375
Engels, Friedrich, 376
England
    Anglo-Saxon, 82, 95, 116
    cloth industry of, 197, 286,
    400
    language of, 152–4
    population of, 218
    see also Great Britain
Ensérune, 36
entail, 275, 331, 387
entrepôts, 435
    see also "free" ports
environment, 1–4, 12–16
epidemics, 120–1, 218, 268,
    373–4
Epirus, 46
Esbjerg, 434, 436
Essen, 408, 418, 420
estates, 229, 275
    management of, 104
Estienne, Charles, 245
ethnic pattern, 364
Etruria
    agriculture in, 39
    ironworking in, 65
    manufacturing in, 43
    settlement in, 62, 87
Etruscans, 27, 31, 32
    cities of, 34, 36
Eupen, 293
Europe
    plain of, 14
    population of, 34
European imperialism, 252
European trade, 343–4, 464–5
Exeter, 48, 208, 242
extended family, 260

factories, 287–92, 336
    in Spain, 296–7
factory industries, 315, 322,
    377–8
    organization of, 212, 313,
    398–9
fairs, 130, 136, 138–9, 160,
    178–9, 203, 212, 231

fairs (*cont.*)
  in Champagne, 139
  decline of, 203, 306–7
  in England, 139
fallow, 132–3, 168–9, 194–5,
    327, 382, 391, 396
  cultivation of, 277
  grazing, 132, 169
Falun, 301
family size, 121, 259, 357
famine, 11–12, 257, 262, 264
  crises, 11–12, 120–2, 257,
    264, 304, 319, 352–4,
    377–8
Fenni, 52
fer fort, 420
ferrous metals, 21
feudalism, 70, 103, 106, 116,
    124, 142, 158, 164, 214,
    230, 275
  agriculture in, 132, 383–4
  in the city, 158
field systems, 39–40, 89–90,
    103–5, 166–7, 391, 395
Figheldean, 40
Finland, 146, 317, 323
  Archduchy of, 318
Finno-Ugric peoples, 33
Finns, 96
fire setting, 201
fires, urban, 227
Fiume, 434–5
flail, 281, 395
Flanders, 11–18, 136
  cities in, 163
  cloth industry, 207, 293
  county of, 130, 143
  population of, 150
  settlement in, 103, 105
  trade of, 183
"Flanders galleys," 183, 236
flax
  Baltic, 184, 243, 304
  growing of, 174, 197, 231,
    236, 280, 401
  trade in, 184, 304
Flemings, 364–5
Flemish language, 152
flint working, 6
Florence, 130, 136, 144, 160–
    1, 174, 216, 223
  population of, 149
  trade of, 204

fodder crops, 391, 396
food supply, 324, 353
footwear industry, 411–12
forest resources, 16, 172, 200,
    282, 386
  clearance of, 282, 284
  and ironworking, 282
forma urbis, 59–60
fortress towns, 269
"four rivers" line, 216
France
  cities in, 271
  clothworking in, 235, 295
  coalfields in, 413
  farm holdings in, 389
  language of, 89, 216
  manufacturing development
    in, 338–9
  political geography of, 142–4,
    254
  population of, 148–9, 260–4,
    320–1, 352, 367
  silk weaving in, 236
  textile industry in, 235, 400
  unification of, 117
François (Francis) I, king of
    France, 226, 309
Frankfurt fairs, 178, 203
Franks, 78, 89, 92–4
  kingdom of, 82
Frederick the Great, 309
  and land improvement, 286
  and manufacturing, 302
"free" ports, 436
free zones in ports, 436
freehold tenures, 387–8
Freiberg, 240
French Revolution, 327, 338,
    347
Freycinet plan, 430
friars' churches, 161
Frisian cloth merchants, 109
Froissart, Jean, 194
fuel, 177–8
  efficiency of, 315
Fuggers, 240
Fulda, 126
furnaces for iron, 175, 198–200
fustian, 173, 198

Galați, 432
Galicia
  Austrian, 330

  Spanish, 390
galleys, Venetian, 183, 202,
    243
Gama, Vasco da, 242
gas lighting, 375
Gascony, 142
Geneva fairs, 203
  food supply of, 247–8, 272
Genoa, 130, 144, 161, 225–6,
    227–8, 435
  "empire" of, 203–4
  population of, 193
  silk weaving in, 236
  trade of, 138, 140–1, 179,
    183, 204, 303–4
geology of Europe, 13–14
  historical influence of, 2–3
George III and farm improve-
    ment, 286
German Confederation, 317, 322
German empire (second), 380
German language, 97–8, 152,
    206
German urban development, 376
Germanic invasions, 75, 92
Germany
  agricultural holdings in, 330
  agricultural reform in, 392
  agriculture in, 329
  chemical industry in, 410
  cities in, 271–2, 326, 370,
    376
  coal resources of, 302
  ironworking in, 52, 339
  landholding in, 389–90
  political geography of, 118–
    19, 144
  population of, 52, 149, 256,
    264, 365–8
  Reformation in, 251
  river navigation in, 308, 431
  root crops in, 383
  textile industry in, 294, 340
Ghent, 130, 173, 197, 338
  cotton industry in, 294, 403
Gibbon, Edward, 47
Gibraltar, Straits of, 45, 84
Gilchrist–Thomas process, 409,
    420
  see also basic process
Gilles le Bouvier, 215
gin, distilling of, 281
glacial deposits, 12, 14

glaciation, 14, 20
Gladbach, 340, 403, 418
Glasgow, 324
glassmaking, 65, 108, 236
Glastonbury, 126
Gleiwitz, 340
Gniezno, 119
Gobelins tapestries, 297
Goethe, 308
gold working, 44, 65, 175
Golden Horde, 116, 119, 145
Gothic style, 137
Goths, 78
Gotland, trade of, 205
grain trade
 Greek, 44–5
 medieval, 183–4
 modern, 247–8, 304, 343–4, 346
Granada, 204
Great Britain
 land tenures in, 389
 manufacturing in, 289–90
 population of, 262, 319
 trade of, 343–5
 urbanization of, 324
 see also England
great estates, 63, 75, 90, 109, 329, 331–2, 384–7, 389
Great Plague, 72, 187, 191, 258
 see also Black Death; bubonic plague
Great St. Bernard Pass, 181
Greece, 16, 23–4
Greek language, 94, 153
Gregory of Tours, 86, 90
Grime's Graves, 6
gross national product, 350–4, 465–7
Guadalquivir River, 308
Guicciardini, Francesco, 226–7, 250, 305
guilds, 176, 234–5, 296
 urban, 165
Guyenne, 118

Habsburg dynasty, 144, 216, 254
Habsburg empire, 254, 317–18, 347–8, 380–1
 landholding in, 330–1, 389–90

manufacturing in, 341
Hadrian, emperor, 26
Hadrian's Wall, 48, 61, 75
Hague, The, 269, 379
Hainault, 143
 population of, 149
Hallstatt culture, 31–2, 46
Hamburg, 306, 326, 345, 411, 435–6
 water supply of, 374
Hamwih, 110
Handloom, 400
 weaving with, 405
 workers of, 399
Hanse, *see* Hanseatic League
Hanseatic League, 146, 161, 180, 183–4, 201–2, 205–6, 246–7
Hansetäge, 205–6
harrows, 281, 392
harvesting, 281, 333, 392
Harz Mountains, 135, 175–6, 201, 219, 240, 300–1, 339–40
Haussmann Georges Eugène, and Paris, 374, 379, 381
Haute Marne, iron in, 408
hay, 274
hearth tax, 120, 147
heavy engineering, 411
Hedeby, 110–11
Hellas, *see* Greece
Hellenistic states, 25, 46
Helsinki, 326
hemp, 281, 304
Héristal, 92
Herodotus, 9, 19
Heuneburg, 37
Hildesheim, 127–8
hinterlands of ports, 435–6
hog rearing, 233, 397
holdings, agricultural, 330, 387–9
Holker, John, 294
Holland, province of, 264
Holy Roman Empire, 92
Hondschoote, 197, 228, 235, 293
hops, civilization of, 231, 281
horse bus, 375
horse traction, 375, 397
hot blast, 408, 426
housing, urban, 376

huertas, 390
Hugh Capet, 117
Hughes, John, 428
Huguenots, 261
Hull, 288, 435
Hundred Years' War, 194
Hungary, 119, 145, 218
 great estates in, 385–6
 nationalism in, 347–8
 plain of, 14–15, 50–1, 94, 96, 218
 population of, 219
Huns, 77–8, 81
Huntsman process, 300
 see also crucible steel

Iberian cultures, 33
Iberian peninsula, 265, 381, 383, 449
ibn Rusta, 96
Ibrahim ibn Ja'kub, 101
Icelandic fisheries, 242
immigration, urban, 227
imperialism, 348–50
India, sea route to, 242
industrial crops, 280
industrial regions, 412–29
Industrial Revolution, 288–9, 302, 399, 410
 second, 410–12
industrial towns, 370
industry, basic, 272
infant death rate, 260
infield–outfield system, 168–9
Ingelheim, 92
innovating societies, 2–3, 7, 289
innovation in agriculture, 286
innovation in industry, 398
inoculation, 259
integration
 horizontal, 460
 vertical, 459
Intendants, 257, 260, 262, 273, 294, 307
intensive agriculture, 334
intergenesic period, 259
invasions, great, 113–16, 120
Ireland, 146
 Catholicism in, 251
 peasantry of, 389
 population of, 262, 320
 potato in, 382–3

Iron Age cultures, 21, 24, 31–
    2, 51–2, 62
iron and steel industry, 185,
    406–12
Iron Gate (Danube), 433
iron industry, 65, 107–8, 135,
    175–6, 198–9, 237–8,
    397, 408–9, 454
  in England, 288
  spatial pattern of, 409
iron ores, 44, 409
  grade of, 428
  trade in, 455–6
iron refining, 199, 298–300,
    339
  output, 200
ironware, 237
ironworks, coastal, 456
Islam, 83–4, 97, 116, 145,
    204, 252
  in western Europe, 116
Italic peoples, 31
Italy
  cities in, 163, 271–2, 381
  economic decline of, 286
  estates in, 330
  food supply of, 165
  ironworking in, 199
  landholding in, 390
  language in, 153, 216
  manufacturing in, 342
  nationalism in, 250–1, 348
  political development of,
      118–19, 217
  population of, 53, 149–50,
      219, 256, 265–6, 323,
      325–6, 368
  railroads in, 434
  textile industry in, 138, 174,
      197–8, 235, 286, 297,
      401, 405
  trade of, 204
Itinerary of Bruges, 181–2

Jáchymov, 246
Jacob, William, 274, 327, 332
Jagiełło dynasty, 217
Jewish traders, 90, 110, 140,
    344
Jews, 224, 361–2
  in Central Europe, 363–4
  as migrants, 261, 361–3

in Russia, 361
Jihlava, 294, 401
journals, 253
Jumna, 114
Justinian, 101
Jutes, 78
Juvenal, 49–50, 59

Karelia, 254
Karl Marx Stadt, *see* Chemnitz
Karlsbad, 371
Karlsruhe, 269
Kaszub dialect, 153
Kattowitz (Katowice), 424
Kaunas, 206
Kazimierz Dolny, 243, 309
Kiev, 115–16, 119, 380
Kievan Russia, 115, 119, 141
King Ludwig Canal, 431
King's Lynn, 205, 208
Kiruna, iron ores of, 409
Klodnitz Canal, 309, 423
Königsberg, 205, 243
Königshütte, 340, 376, 422,
    424
Kraków, 126–7, 140, 145
  diocese of, 149, 160, 225
Krefeld, silk of, 297, 340, 405,
    418
Kremlin, 225, 273
Kremnica, 241
Krivoi Rog, iron ore at, 428–9
Krupp, Friedrich, 335
Krupp works, 408, 420
kulaks, 276

La Rochelle, 242, 306
  salt from, 177
La Tène Celts, 24, 27, 31–2
labor service, 386–7
lace making, 292
Lahn River, 431
Lancashire
  canals in, 309
  cotton industry in, 402
  manufacturing in, 336
land
  clearance of, 121
  drainage of, 169–70, 281–2
  ownership of, 228–9
  reclamation of, 282–3
  tenure of, 229, 274–6

land reform, 387, 390
land use, 282–4, 386
landforms of Europe, 12–13
landless laborers, 388
Langland, William, 190
languages, European, 52, 97–8,
    152–4, 216, 364
Languedoc, shipment of cloth
    from, 345
Languedoc Canal, 309
Lapps, 96
large estates, 229
Latifundia, 63–4
Latin Quarter, 223
Laureion, mines of, 44, 65
Lausanne, diocese of, 149
Le Havre, 226, 269, 306, 339,
    435–6
lead, 200–1, 240, 423
  working, 65, 108, 135, 176
leasehold tenure, 388
leatherworking, 198, 236
Leeds, 324
  clothing industry in, 411
  and woolen industry, 400
Leghorn, *see* Livorno
Leland, John, 215
Lendit fair, 139
Lenzburg, 220
Léon (state), 142
Leverkusen, 420
Levoča, 241
Leyden cloth, 286, 293
Libel of English Policie, 185,
    207–8
Liberec, 401
Liège, 173, 199, 398, 411
  manufacturing at, 293, 412,
      415, 418
  life expectation, 260
lignite, *see* brown coal
Lille, 290, 292, 338, 378
  textile industry at, 400, 402
lime in agriculture, 395
limestone, 176
linen weaving, 136–7, 173–4,
    197, 236, 292, 294–6,
    338, 401, 460
  in Germany, 294
  in Switzerland, 294
Lisbon, 193, 226, 305, 381
List, Friedrich, 434

Lithuania, grand duchy of, 145, 217, 252
Little Ice Age, 11–12
Little St. Bernard Pass, 181
Liverpool, port of, 288, 324, 336, 435
living standards, 399
Livorno, 204, 304
Livy, 53
Lobbes abbey, 104
locks on rivers, 399–400
Łódź, 290, 370, 376, 400, 404
  population of, 380
loess belt, 20, 110, 129, 334
  population on, 150, 219
loess soil, 19
Loire River, traffic on, 244
Lombards, 79–8
Lombardy, 318
  kingdom of, 94, 144
  merchants of, 110, 179
  plain of, 228
London, 57, 110, 159–61, 205–6, 208, 224–5, 324
  bridges at, 245
  as capital, 222
  population of, 130, 193, 319
  port of, 242–3, 301, 345, 411, 435
  silk weaving at, 297
long house, 38, 102
Longwy, 269
looms, 136, 172
  power, 335–6
  vertical, 42
Lorient, 269, 306
Lorraine, industrial region of, 420–1, 455
  iron ore in, 420–1
Lotharingia, 116
Louvain, 272
Low Countries
  agriculture in, 194–5, 212, 391
  cloth industries in, 138, 185, 197, 235, 293–4
  coal in, 302
  manufacturing in, 136, 337–8, 340
  population of, 149, 218, 264, 322, 326
  ports of, 436

religion in, 251
trade of, 206–7, 305
water transport in, 244, 308, 430–1
Lübeck, 193, 205, 243, 435
Lucca, 137, 144, 286
  silk of, 174, 236
Ludwigshafen, 410
Lüneburg, 202
  salt from, 246
Luxembourg, industry in, 420–1
Lwów, 317
Lyons, 57, 86, 324–5, 327, 378
  grain supply of, 247
  population of, 227, 269
  silk industry at, 236, 297, 339–40, 405

Macedonia, 19, 46, 201–2, 331
  empire of, 25, 46–7
Machiavelli, Niccolò, 216, 250
Madrid, 223, 325–6, 381
Magna Graecia, 28–9, 34–6, 43, 45
magnates, 384
  see also great estates
Magyars, 82, 91, 97, 115–16
  language of, 89, 153
Main River, 431
Mainz, 54, 140
Małapanew, 422
Malmsey wine, 170, 184, 204, 242
Malthusianism, 121–3
Manchester, 324, 336
  housing in, 376
manganese, 237–8
Mannheim, 269, 410
  chemical industry at, 431
  Convention of, 431
manor, medieval, 166
manorial system, 329
Mantua, 197
manufacturing, 107, 165, 172, 195–202, 286–7, 314, 335–42, 452–61
  and coalfields, 314
  power in, 287
manure, 277, 281, 333, 395
maps, 215
marble, 177
Marcus Aurelius, 51, 77

Marienbad, 371
Marienbourg, 269
market boat, 202
market towns, 272
marketplace, 160, 163
markets, 125, 131, 138–9, 160, 164–5, 220–1, 247, 307
  distribution of, 178
  food, 381–2
  functions of, 160, 164–5
  mass, 287
  in Paris, 223
  urban, 369, 377
marl, use of, 395
marriage, age at, 259–60
Marseilles, 324–5, 378, 435
  soap manufacture in, 303
masonry construction, 108, 137, 198, 268
mass demand, 289, 303, 341
  and production, 341, 349
Massilia (Marseilles), Greek colony, 45
masts, timber for, 304
meadow, 105, 134
Mecklenburg, 396
Medina del Campo, fairs at, 231
Mediterranean basin, 15–18, 20, 83–4
  agriculture in, 132
  trade in, 44–6, 66, 109, 140–1, 179, 183, 202–5, 242, 304
Meersen, partition of, 116, 119
Meissen pottery, 303
Memmingen Articles of 1524, 228–9
Menander, 16–17
Mendip Hills, 108, 135
mercantilism, 303
merchant capitalists, 234
Mercia, 95
Merian, Matthäus, engravings of cities by, 265, 268
Merovingian kings, 93
Meseta, 134–5, 171, 390
  migration from, 265
  population of, 368
  transhumance in, 233, 333, 397
Mesta, 171, 333

metal industries, 237–41, 297–301
Metapontum, 36
métayage, 276
  see also sharecropping
métro, Parisian, 375–6
metropolitan areas, 444
middle class, origins of, 124–5
migrant labor, 260
migration, 8, 261, 352, 357–61
  from Greece, 28–9
  international, 357, 365, 440
  from the land, 387
  medieval, 151
  overseas, 262, 357, 359–60
Milan, 75, 85, 130, 136, 144, 223, 238, 270, 318, 325, 381
Military Frontier, Austrian, 317
mills, 281
mines, drainage of, 337
minette, 420–1, 455
mining, Roman, 65
Mirabeau, Honoré Gabriel Riqueti, comte de, 296
mixed fabrics, 137, 173, 198, 236
  farming, 334, 391, 451
Mohammed, 83
Moldavia, 218, 348
moldboard for plows, 89
monastic estates, 109
monasticism, 99
Monemvasia, 204
Mons, 227
  coalfield of, 302
Mont Cenis Pass, 181
Montenegro, 348
Moors, 86, 94, 99, 142, 237
  in Africa, 204
  raids of, 106, 120
  in Spain, 204
Moravia, 317
  manufacturing in, 341, 404
mordant, 174–5
Moriscoes, 261
  see also Moors
mortar for building, 176
Moscow, 145, 217, 221, 225, 274, 306, 327, 380
  manufacturing in, 292, 404, 426

Principality of, 230
Moselle River, 431
Moslems in Europe, 84, 252
motor vehicles, 463
Motya, 30, 36
Mülheim-on-Ruhr, 418
Mulhouse, cotton industry at, 338–9, 369
Mun, Thomas, 303
Münster, Sebastian, 220
Muscovy, 115, 119, 141, 145, 217, 254

Naarden, 269
Namur, 444
Nancy, 269–70
Nantes, 306, 375, 435
Naples, 31, 57, 272
  kingdom of, 144, 163
Napoleon, 342, 431
Napoleon III, 379
Napoleonic code, 321, 332, 388
Napoleonic Wars, 313, 319, 322, 342, 383
Narva, 306
Narvik, 436
  railroad to, 434
"nation-state," 211
national income, 465–7
nationalism, 214, 250, 347–8
nations, 211, 214
natural frontiers, 143
naval stores, 243
Neckar River, 431
Neolithic farmers, 16
  culture of, 19, 38, 52
Nero's Golden House, 26
Nestor, 96
Netherlands, land drainage in, 282–3
  manufacturing in, 403
  trade of, 304–5, 345, 436–7
  waterways in, 461
  see also Low Countries, United Provinces
Neuf Breisach, 269
new agriculture, 285–6
"new draperies," 185, 196–7, 208, 228, 235, 293
new towns, 125–6
New World, bullion from, 252

Newcomen and the steam engine, 288
newspapers, 253
Nice, 317
Niemen River, 309
Nile River, 19
Nîmes, 55, 57
Nimwegen, 92
Nizhne Tagil, 300
nomadism, 38, 81
nonferrous metals, 200, 240, 246, 460
Nördlingen, 159
  fairs at, 178, 203
Noricum, 65
Normandy, 114, 323
  duchy of, 117
Normans, 114
Norse invasions, 96, 113–15
Norse sagas, 102, 105
northwest Europe
  coal production in, 413–17
  manufacturing in, 412–20
  population of, 444–6
Norway, 218
  trade of, 345
Novgorod, 145, 206, 221, 306
  Principality of, 230
Novipazar, Sanjak of, 434
nuclear family, 260
nuraghi, 37
Nuremberg, 127, 161, 221
  fairs at, 203

oats, 63, 104–5, 107, 132, 230–1, 277, 328
Oder River, 309, 423
  navigation of, 431
Odessa, 346, 380
Offa, king of Mercia, 95
oilseeds, 281
olive cultivation, 15, 38–9, 63, 106, 170, 231, 280
Olivier de Serres, 333
"omnibus," 375
"open-door" policy, 349
open-field system, 132–3, 154, 166–7, 194–5, 230, 232, 285, 332, 391, 395
open-hearth steel, 455, 459
Ore Mountains, 240, 246
ores, iron, 200, 409

"Orient Express," 434
Oslo, 205, 326
osmund, 175, 200
Ostia, 18, 53, 57, 59, 61, 66
Ostrava, 381
Ostrogoths, 78–9
Otto I, 118
Ottoman empire, 224, 254,
    318, 327, 348, 390, 401,
    434
  in Europe, 331
  Jews in, 361
  serfdom in, 276
  trade of, 345
  urbanization in, 381
Ottoman Turks, 75, 201, 203,
    218, 224, 252
outports, 436
overpopulation, 441
oxen, plowing, 105
Oxford, 411

Padua, 144
Palatinate
  Rhenish, 256
  Upper, 238
Palatine, Rome, 26
Pale of Jewish Settlement, 362–
    3
Palermo, 163, 272
Palma Nova, 269
Pannonia, 50–2
Panopus, 36
Panormus (Palermo), 30
papacy, 94
  and Black Death, 187
paper manufacture, 236–7, 302
parcellation of land, 392
Paris, 86, 117, 159, 161, 217,
    227, 270, 297, 303, 324
  as capital, 222–3
  chemical industry in, 411
  coal supply of, 301
  food supply of, 165, 223,
    247, 273
  growth of, 378–9
  housing in, 376
  migration to, 268
  population of, 130, 223, 379
  rebuilding of, 379
  water supply of, 374
parish registers, 218, 262

Parthians, 75
partible inheritance, 260, 275,
    323, 332, 387–9, 391
passes, Alpine, 140, 181–2,
    203, 245
pastoral agriculture, 171, 232,
    284–5
patrimony of St. Peter, 94, 144
Pausanias (Greek geographer),
    36, 85
Pavia, 80, 85, 91, 110
peasant
  income of, 228
  obligations of, 229–30
  purchasing power of, 287
peasant holdings, size of, 230
peasant unrest, 189
peasantry, 275–6, 327, 384,
    389–90
peat as fuel, 177
Pegolotti, 181, 195, 198, 204–
    5
Peloponnesian War, 23, 30, 46–
    7
Pennine Hills, mining in, 135
pepper, 245
periphery, 350, 384, 440, 461
Peruzzi of Florence, 179
Peter the Great, 255
Petronell, 54, 86
pewter, 200, 240
Phainippos (estate owner), 39
Phanariot Greeks, 348
pharmaceuticals, 410
Philippeville, 269
Phocaea and alum, 183, 204
Phoenicians, 30, 33
phosphoric iron ores, 409
phylloxera, 357
pig iron production, 455, 458–9
pig rearing, 40, 105, 285, 452,
    456
Piraeus, 35, 45
Pirenne, Henri, theory of, 83,
    99
Pisa, 144
Pistoia, 149
place-names, 88
plague, 72
  see also bubonic plague
plague mortality, 258–9, 268–
    9, 319, 356

planned cities, 55–6, 126, 159
Plato, 17, 34, 44
Plauen, 340
Pliny, 63, 90
Plovdiv, 401
plow, 39–40, 64, 89–90, 195,
    281, 392, 394–5
  heavy, 132, 167
  light, 132, 167
Po River, 19, 308
  navigation of, 66, 182
  valley of, 149
Poland, 33, 119, 145, 317
  agriculture in, 329, 332
  Catholicism in, 251
  commonwealth of, 217–18
  "Congress," 318
  iron industry in, 341
  land tenure in, 331
  Partitions of, 317
  population of, 265, 366
polis, see city-state
poll tax, 150
pollen, preserved in bogs, used
    in dating, 16
polyptyques, 90, 97, 102, 104–
    5, 109, 134
Pomaks, 252
Pomerania, 145, 330
Pompeii, 57
population, 3, 212, 364–5
  in agriculture, 166
  of ancient world, 33, 52–3
  in Burgundy, 190
  Carolingian, 97–8, 105
  densities of, 148, 150
  early modern, 218–20, 256–
    65
  and ethnic composition, 97–8
  in Great Britain, 364–5
  in Italy, 191
  in Low Countries, 191
  medieval, 72, 84, 119–23,
    146–52, 191
  modern, 313, 319–24, 351–
    7, 440
  and plague, 189
  in Rhineland, 191
  rural, 154–5
  of Russia, 447
  structure of, 352–4
  urban, 324

population (*cont.*)
  west European, 191–2
Populonia, 43
porcelain, 303
port cities, 225–6, 269
  industries of, 399
port wines, 280
Portoferraio, 436
ports, 345, 435–7, 444
Portugal, 142
  population of, 256, 323
Portuguese voyages, 242
potash salts, 410
potato, 277, 322, 354, 368,
    382, 450, 452
  spread of, 279
pottery, manufacture of, 42, 64,
    107, 137, 236, 303
Poznań, 119
Prague, 119, 127, 140, 159–
    60, 224–5, 326, 381
preindustrial towns, 368–9
primate cities, 371–2
primogeniture, 331
printing, 253, 302–3
Procopius, 86, 97
proletariat, 330
protoindustry, 212, 398, 402
Prüm, 104, 107–8
Prussia, 330, 348
  cities in, 271
  land use in, 386
Prypeć River, 309
public buildings, 57
public health, 373–4
public transport, 375–6, 380
puddling process, 299–300,
    336, 406–7, 409, 418,
    422, 424
"putting-out" system, 292
Pyrenean March, 97
Pyrenees, ironworking in, 135

quarantine, 258
quarries, 137
quarrying, 176
quarters, urban, 377–8
Quentovic, 110

race in Europe, 49–50, 364
Ragusa, *see* Dubrovnik

railroad construction, 350, 409–
    10, 428
railroad systems, 399, 429–30,
    433–4, 461–2
  intensity of use of, 462–3
railroads, 453
  and national unity, 433–4
Randstad Holland, 379
rank size, urban, 369–70
Raška, 119
Ravenna, 75, 83, 85
Ravensburg, trade of, 245
reforestation, 282
reform in agriculture, 327, 329
Reformation, Protestant, 218,
    251–2
refugees, 261
Reims, 127
  cloth manufacture in, 173,
    235, 294, 400
religion and nationalism, 251
Remscheid, 339, 420
Renaissance, 187, 196, 211,
    214
Reschen-Scheideck Pass, 181
resort towns, 370–1
Reval, 205
revolutionary wars, 313
Rheinfelden, 161–2
Rheydt, 340, 403, 418
Rhine
  and chemicals industry, 410
  delta of, 208
  French advance to, 254
  navigation of, 431
  traffic on, 182, 244, 308
Rhineland
  cities in, 228
  ironworking in, 239
  manufacturing in, 418–20
  population of, 218
  trade of, 129–30
Rhône River, 20, 308
ribbon weaving, 339
rice growing, 334
Richelieu (Armand Jean du Ples-
    sis, duc de), Cardinal, 269
Riga, 205, 243, 274, 306, 346,
    380
Risorgimento, 348, 432
Rive-de-Gier, 301–2
rivers, European, 20–1

boats on, 244
  Mediterranean, 433
  navigation of, 139–40
  obstructions on, 244
  for transportation, 182, 243,
    307–8, 429–33, 463
  use of, 182
road building, 180, 307
  and transportation, 202, 212,
    429–30
  and travel, 253
roads, quality of, 180, 307
  Roman, 139
Roman empire, 25, 69, 74–5,
    125
  boundaries of, 52, 74–5, 77
Romance languages, 152–3
Romanesque style, 137
Romania, 465
  landholding in, 390
  peasants in, 329–30
Romanian language, 153
Romanian people, 89
Romanian Principalities, 318
Romanization, 50–1
Rome, 20, 23–4, 27, 31, 85,
    99–100, 128, 163, 227,
    325–6
  growth of, 46–7, 58–9
  as Italian capital, 223
  population of, 53, 143, 223
  rebuilding of, 270
  sack of, 217
  trade of, 66
root crops, 231, 277, 334, 450
Rostov, 115
rotation system, 194
Rotterdam, 379, 411, 436
Roubaix, 338, 402, 413, 415
Rouen, 242, 306, 338, 435
  cotton industry in, 294, 400
Rouergue, population of, 148
Rouen, 242, 306, 338, 435
Ruhr region, 370, 407–9, 411,
    415, 418–20, 444
  chemical industry in, 420
  coal in, 302, 413
  housing in, 376
  ironworking in, 418, 420
  transportation in, 43, 431
  water supply in, 375
Ruhrort, 431
rural decay, 77

rural industry, 234–5, 290–1
rural population, 147, 440–1
rural settlement, 5, 232
Russia
  cities in, 273–4
  early trade with, 111
  ironworking in, 298, 300,
    340–1
  land tenure in, 331
  manufacturing in, 292, 426–
    9
  Norse in, 96
  population of, 150, 265, 366,
    447
  textile manufacture in, 400,
    404
  trade of, 306, 465
  urban development in, 448
Russian church, 119
Russian empire, 254–5, 318
Rye, 40, 63, 90, 104–5, 107,
  132, 168, 277, 327–9,
  344, 382, 447, 451

Saale River, 94
Saar coalfield, 317
Saar industrial region, 407, 409,
  420–1
St. Albans, 87
St. Benedict, Rule of, 99
Saint-Etienne, 339, 407–8, 411
  coal at, 302
  ironworking at, 409
  manufacturing at, 457
  silk working at, 297, 406
St. Gallen, 294, 404
  monastery at, 109
St. Gotthard Pass, 140, 181,
  203
St. Jerome, 51
Saint-Malo, 306
Saint-Nazaire, 436
St. Peter's, Rome, 223–4
St. Petersburg, 254–5, 292,
  297, 300, 306, 327, 346,
  378, 380
Saint-Quentin, 173
Salerno, 140
salt production, 177, 202
salt trade, 108–9, 184, 246,
  308

San Gimignano, 158
sanitation, 268
Saratov, 380
Sauerland, 411, 420, 457
Savoy, 317
  ironworking in, 135
  land tenure in, 276
"Saxon Shore," 78
Saxony, 94
  manufacturing in, 457
  mining in, 201
Scandinavia, 12–13, 150
  agriculture in, 105
  landholding in, 390
  languages of, 153–4
  migration from, 361
  open fields in, 392
  political geography of, 217–
    18
  population of, 322, 366, 368
  settlement in, 95, 101–2
Scheldt River, 208, 305
scientific attitude, 252–3
Scotland, 146
  population of, 319–20
  see also Great Britain
scrap iron, 454–5
scythe, 392
Scythians, 33, 41, 45, 52
seaborne trade, 435–7
"second serfdom," 228, 230,
  275–6, 329
sedimentation, 18
seed drill, 395
Segovia, 58
Seine River, 402
  navigation of, 182
self-sufficiency, 90
Sephardic Jews, 361
Seraing, 399
Serbia, 119, 145, 331, 348, 436
  landholding in, 390
Serbs, migration of, 261
serf labor, 300, 341, 404
  status of, 229–30, 292
serfdom, 276, 329
  end of, 329, 426
Servius Tullius, 31
settlement, 5, 101, 154–7
Seville, 226–7, 305, 325
sewage disposal, 165, 227, 374
sharecropping, 276, 329, 388

sheep rearing, 105, 134, 195,
  285, 396, 451, 455
Sheffield, 337, 411
shifting agriculture, 39–40, 64,
  168
ship building, 411, 457
ships' supplies, 343–4
Siberia, Russian advance into,
  254
Sicily, 84, 136–7, 144
  population of, 265
Siegen, ironworking at, 43–4,
  135, 298
Siegerland, 199, 339, 418, 457
Siemens-Martin process, 409
Silchester, 48, 57, 87
Silesia, Austrian, 424
  coal in, 302, 404
  see also Upper Silesia
silk, 172
  in Italy, 286
  at Lyons, 325
  trade in, 184
silk weaving, 108–9, 136–7,
  174, 236, 288, 297, 339,
  405–6
silver mining, 44, 175, 200,
  240–1, 300–1
Slav languages, 97, 152–3
slave labor, 48, 65, 75, 109
Slavic Chronicle, 125
Slavs, 33, 52, 80–2, 89, 94,
  96–7, 101, 106, 110, 115,
  145
  in Balkans, 252
Sliven, 401
Slovakia, 201, 240–1, 331
  mining in, 300–1
sluices, use of, 182
slums, urban, 376
Sluys, 205, 208
small towns, 161–2
smallholders, 330
smallpox, 257–9, 319, 356
smelting processes, 9, 42, 107,
  135
Smolensk, 115
soap, 303
Soest, 159
Sofia, 327
soil, 2–3, 5–6, 13–14, 16, 18–
  19, 38–9

Solingen, 420
Sorb dialect, 153
Sosnowiec, 424
Sound, The, 218, 243, 309
Sound "dues," 243, 304
Southampton, 208, 242
sowing, 392
Spain, 368
  cloth industry in, 235
  landholding in, 330–1, 390
  languages of, 153
  manufacturing in, 341–2
  metalworking in, 136, 199,
    238
  Moors in, 97, 106
  political geography of, 142
  population of, 150, 219, 256,
    323
  ports of, 226
  textile industry in, 296
  transhumance in, 333
  wool from, 235
  urbanization in, 85, 99, 164
Spanish empire, 216, 252
Spanish March, 94
Sparta, 28
specialization of production, 6–
    7, 42
speed of travel, 245
spelt, 104
spice trade, 204, 242, 245
spinning industry, 198, 293
Spitalfields silk, 406
Split, 304
Spoleto, duchy of, 94
stadium, 57
standardization of goods, 203
staple rights, 244
Starzykowe Małe, 38
Stassfurt, 410
state system, 4
steam engine, 288, 399
  in mines, 337
  power from, 314, 335, 397
steam tugs, 431
Stecknitz Canal, 309
steel, 237–8, 300–1, 335, 411,
    428, 453–4, 458–9
steelworks, integrated, 456
Steelyard, 206
Steppe, Russian, 96, 115–16
Stettin, 243, 306

Stockholm, 146, 326
stocking knitting, 292
Stone Age cultures, 27, 38
Stora Kopparberg, copper de-
    posit, 301
Strabo (Greek geographer), 54
Strasbourg, 369
street cleaning, 166
street lighting, 375
streetcars, 375
Stumpe, William, 287
Stuttgart, 270
subsistence crises, 322
suburbs, urban, 377
Suetonius (Gaius Suetonius Tran-
    quillus), 59
sugar beets, 279, 382–3, 450,
    453
Suger, abbot of Saint Denis, 121
Swabians, 78
Sweden, 119, 146, 218, 254
  cereals in, 385
  copper in, 201, 301
  ironworking in, 175, 200,
    246, 298, 300, 340, 345
  languages in, 153
  metals in, 136
  mining in, 455
  population of, 354
  settlement in, 12
Swiss Confederation, 140, 144
Swiss nation, 250
Switzerland
  manufacturing in, 339, 404,
    410
  population of, 264, 368
  reform of agriculture in, 392
  Reformation in, 251
  towns in, 161–2
Sybaris, 39
Syracuse, 34, 36, 45, 47
Székesfehérvár, 119
Szeklers, 153

Tacitus, Cornelius, 48, 52–4,
    64, 101
Tagus River, 226, 308
Tallin, 306
Tamboro, Mount, 12
tanning industry, 137, 175,
    198, 236
tapestry weaving, 197, 297

Tartar peoples, 81, 96
Tartars, 115, 116, 119–20,
    145, 151, 254
Tartessos, 45
tax records, 122–3
Temple, Sir William, 308
tenement blocks, 376
tenurial conditions, 329
Terpen, 38
Tertullian, Quintus Septimius
    Florens, 47
Teutonic Knights, 145
textile industries, 136–7, 234–
    7, 293–7, 400, 406–7,
    460
  Flemish, 136
  French, 338–9
  Italian, 136
textile machinery, 338
Thames, shipping on, 345
Thebes, 46
Theodoric, king of the Ostro-
    goths, 78
Theodosius, wall of, 100
Thessaloníki, 100, 436
Thessaly, 39
Thirty Years War, 259, 261,
    264, 286, 294, 319
Thrace, 19
Thracian language, 153
three-course agriculture, 132–3,
    166–7, 194, 327, 332,
    334, 391
three-field system, 277, 450
threshing, 281
Thucydides, 28
Thüringen, 238
Tiber River, 18, 20, 27, 59–60,
    66
timber
  Baltic, 243
  for building, 268
  floating of, 182
  resources of, 282
  supply of, 243, 301
  trade in, 304
tin, 21, 65, 200–1
  production of, 44, 135–6,
    201, 337
  trade in, 45
Tivoli, 26
toilet facilities, 165, 374

Toledo, 86
  steel from, 175, 199
tolls
  river, 182, 308, 431
  road, 306
tools, farming, 392
Toulouse, 78, 86, 127, 130, 165
Tourcoing, 228, 338, 402, 415
Tours, 86
towns
  churches in, 160
  functions of, 130–1
  growth of, 131
  medieval, 191–3
  size of, 130–1
  see also cities; urbanization
towpaths, 244
trade, 6–8
  Carolingian, 110, 180–3
  of Dark Ages, 90
  Greek, 44–55
  modern, 241–8, 315, 342–6
  organization of, 179
  Roman, 66–7
  volume of, 436–7
tramways, 375
transhumance, 40, 63, 102, 105–6, 134–5, 171–2, 233, 261, 333–4, 397
transportation, 178–80
  medieval, 202–3
  modern, 429–34
  Roman, 66
Transylvania, 157, 218, 331
  Saxons in, 215
travel
  aids to, 253
  medieval, 180–3
  speed of, 181
Trier, 51, 86
Trieste, 434–5
tuberculosis, 356
Tula, 300
Tull, Jethro, 281, 333
Tulla, J. G., 431
Turin, 223, 325–6, 381, 411
Turkish landowners, 390
Turkish Straits, 346, 348
Turks, *see* Ottoman Turks
turnip, 278
turnpike trusts, 307

Tuscany, 31, 323
  grain supply of, 247
  ironworking in, 238
  population of, 149
two-course agriculture, 167, 277
typhus, 356
Tyrol, mining in, 241

Ukraine, 345
"underground," London, 376
United Netherlands, 254, 286
United Provinces, 264, 322
Upper Silesia, 339–40, 370, 406–7, 409, 421–6
  cities in, 446
  coal in, 302, 309, 421–3, 425
  ethnic situation in, 426
  housing in, 376
  iron and steel in, 422–3
  lead and zinc in, 301, 422–3, 425
Ural Mountains, ironworking in, 292, 300, 428, 432
urban building construction, 268
urban crafts, 228
urban development, 124–5, 128–9, 163–4, 220–8, 265, 267–74, 324–5, 368–71, 443–6
urban food supply, 165, 227
urban functions, 158, 270–4
urban housing, 227
urban markets, 270–1, *see also* markets
urban population, 147, 220, 324, 443–6, 373
urbanization
  classical, 36–7, 53–61
  medieval, 71, 158–66

vaccination, 259
vaine pâture, 391
Valencia, 325
Valenciennes, 302
  fire at, 227
Valladolid, 223–4, 227–8
Vallhagar, 101–2
Vandals, 78, 83
Vannes, 272
Vardar River, 20
Vasa dynasty, 254

Vatican, 224
Vauban, 277, 308
vegetation of Europe, 10, 16–18
Venezia, *see* Venice
Venice, 91, 125, 128, 130, 137, 144, 161, 163, 227, 325–6
  "empire" of, 145, 203–4, 225
  Germans in, 205
  grain supply of, 247–8
  navy of, 172
  population of, 193, 219
  port of, 225
  salt production at, 108
  silk working at, 174, 236
  trade of, 119, 138, 140–1, 179, 183, 202, 303–4
Verdun
  Partition of, 116
  traders of, 110
Verona, 144, 197
  plague in, 268–9
Versailles, 269
Verviers, 292–4, 338, 340, 400, 418
  cotton industry at, 415
Vesdre valley, 293
Veulerent, grange at, 133, 166–7
Vicenza, 270
Vieille Montagne, 340, 418, 423, 460
Vienna, 218, 224, 303, 317, 326
  Congress of, 317, 347
  growth of, 380–1
Vienne, 55
Viersen, 403, 418
Vikings, 113–15, 139
villa
  Carolingian, 103, 105
  Roman, 51, 55, 57, 61–3, 87
village plans, 154–7, 232
village settlement, 37–8
Villani, Matteo, 195–6
Villefranche, 214
villein service, 106
  see also serfdom
Vilna, 274
vintage wines, 170

Visby, 205
Visigothic peoples, 78–9, 86, 89
Vision of Piers Plowman, 11, 190
Vistula River, navigation of, 243, 309, 344, 431–2
Vitebsk, 115
viticulture, 170, 184, 231, 279–80
Vitruvius Pollio, Marcus, 269
Vitry-le-François, 269
Vlachs, 89, 153
Vladimir, 119, 404
Volga River, 115, 119, 432
von Thünen, Johann Heinrich, 396

Wace, 168
Walachia, 218, 348
Wales, 146
Walloons, 364
Walter of Henley, 169
warfare, mortality in, 259
Warsaw, 222, 224, 268, 270, 326
  population of, 380
water power, 198–9, 288, 399, 404, 406
water supply systems, 43, 227, 374

of Rome, 57–8
  urban, 221, 268
water transportation, 109–10, 212
Watt, James, 288, 335
Weald, ironworking in, 135, 199, 238, 336
weather and crops, 257, 274
weaving industry, 107, 293
Weber, Max, 287
Weimar, 270
Welsers, bankers, 240
Weser River, 182, 431
Wessex, 95, 108
West Riding of Yorkshire, woolens in, 288
Westphalia, 274, 401
  linen in, 294
Wetter, 418
wheat, 39–40, 63–4, 104–5, 107, 168, 194, 230, 274, 327, 382, 447–50
  trade in, 449–50, 465
  varieties of, 90
whisky, 281
Wieliczka, 202, 246
wine
  production of, 12, 63, 104–5, 248
  trade in, 46, 110, 184, 231, 242, 248

winter crops, 168–9
Withington, 88

Xenophon, 42, 45

Yiddish, 363
yield ratios, 169, 194–5, 278, 281–2, 396
York, 114
Yorkshire, manufacturing in, 289–90
Young, Arthur, 286–7
Ypres, 160, 173, 182, 197, 228
Yuzovo works, 428

Zabrze, 424
zadruga, 260, 392
Zara, 204
zinc, 176, 200–1, 240, 423
Zola, Emile, 391, 395
Zollverein, 348, 436
Zurich, 404
  population of, 193
  silk weaving at, 297
Zurzach, fairs at, 178, 203
Zuyder Zee, ports of, 243, 305
Zwickau, 340
Zwin River, 208, 226
Zwingli, Ulrich, 251